WETLANDS

WETLANDS

William J. Mitsch

School of Natural Resources
The Ohio State University
Columbus, Ohio

and

James G. Gosselink

Center for Wetland Resources
Louisiana State University
Baton Rouge, Louisiana

VNR VAN NOSTRAND REINHOLD COMPANY
——————————————————— New York

Manufactured in the United States of America.

Published by Van Nostrand Reinhold Company Inc.
115 Fifth Avenue
New York, New York 10003

Van Nostrand Reinhold Company Limited
Molly Millars Lane
Wokingham, Berkshire RG11 2PY, England

Van Nostrand Reinhold
480 La Trobe Street
Melbourne, Victoria 3000, Australia

Macmillan of Canada
Division of Canada Publishing Corporation
164 Commander Boulevard
Agincourt, Ontario MIS 3C7, Canada

15 14 13 12 11 10 9 8 7 6 5 4 3 2

Library of Congress Cataloging in Publication Data
Mitsch, William J.
  Wetlands.
  Bibliography: p.
  Includes index.
  1. Wetland ecology.   2. Wetland conservation.
3. Wetlands.   I. Gosselink, James G.   II. Title.
QH541.5.M3M59 1986   333.91'8   86-1317
ISBN 0-442-26398-8

CONTENTS

PREFACE

Wetlands, both freshwater and coastal, have become recognized as uniquely important components of the landscape by scientists, engineers, public interest groups, and government agencies. Their importance lies both in the traditional value of wetlands as areas of fish and wildlife protection as well as in newly found values of wetlands as areas of water management and conservation. Some scientists have called wetlands "nature's kidneys" because of the natural functions they perform. Wetlands had been destroyed at an alarming rate of about 1% per year in the United States prior to the recent enactment of legislation designed to curb wetland development. For example, Section 404 of the Federal Clean Water Act now requires the U.S. Corps of Engineers to pass judgment on any case of dredge and fill involving inland or coastal wetlands. Other federal agencies, such as the U.S. Fish and Wildlife Service, the Environmental Protection Agency, and the Federal Highway Administration, also have responsibility for dealing with wetland management issues.

We believe that there is a need for a textbook that deals with both the scientific and management aspects of these important ecosystems. No book on wetlands exists that does all of the following in one volume: (1) reviews the structure and function of more than a few types of wetlands; (2) discusses their ecological characteristics and significance in a common chapter outline; (3) gives principles that apply broadly to all wetland types; (4) gives a comprehensive bibliography on many types of wetlands; and (5) presents the kind of organized coverage that is difficult to attain with multi-author, edited texts. We hope that our book, which seeks to do all of the above, will serve two purposes: (1) provide a comprehensive reference to scientists, engineers, and planners involved in the management of wetlands and (2) serve as a textbook for students and professors for newly evolving courses on wetland ecology. As a text the book will be most useful to upper-level undergraduates and graduate students. The potential audience should have some background in ecology.

This book emphasizes wetlands of North America and, even more specifically, wetlands of the United States. It is expected that it will be used primarily in North America; the choice of wetland ecosystems reviewed in detail was influenced by that expectation. However, examples for the individual chapters were purposely sought from other continents, particularly where the literature is superior or well advanced (e.g., peatlands in Europe). The global distribution of the ecosystems is given in several of the chapters to prevent a provincial view of these wetlands.

The book outline was designed to present a dual picture of wetland ecology: (1) A general view of principles and components of wetlands that have broad application to many wetland types, and (2) An ecosystem view of wetlands that looks in detail at the structure and function of dominant wetland types.

The text is divided into five parts to provide the appropriate coverage to both of these views:

		View
Part I	Introduction	General
Part II	The Wetland Environment	General
Part III	Coastal Wetland Ecosystems	Ecosystem
Part IV	Inland Wetland Ecosystems	Ecosystem
Part V	Management of Wetlands	General

Part I discusses, from a historical and scientific perspective, what wetland science is, what wetlands are, the types of wetlands described in this book, their area and distribution, and trends of wetland disappearance. Part II presents major principles and "parts" of the wetland environment that are common to most or all wetlands and that distinguish them from terrestrial and aquatic ecosystems. Topics common to all wetlands include hydrology, biogeochemistry, biotic adaptations, and wetland succession. As in Part I, examples from many wetlands are used. Parts III and IV present ecological summaries of the structure and function of seven different types of wetland ecosystems. These seven were chosen because (1) combined, they cover most of the wetlands found in North America; (2) they are distinct in form and function; and (3) they are commonly distinguished in the literature. The book deals only with vegetated wetlands and does not discuss beaches and rocky shores, for example. Part V discusses wetland management by presenting major impacts and regulations that affect wetlands and some recent techniques (e.g., classifications, inventories, and valuation) that can be used to describe and quantify wetland function and importance.

Any project of this magnitude could not have been accomplished without the generous assistance of a number of individuals. Susan Munger and Mimi Mikels of Van Nostrand Reinhold Company served as thoughtful and helpful editors during the final acceleration to complete this book. Reviews of various stages of the chapters were provided by Ariel Lugo, Katherine Ewel,

Sandra Brown, Gerald Cole, Ronald Atlas, Ralph Tiner, Curt Richardson, and several anonymous readers. We also appreciate the many individuals who provided us with material or information for this book. We gratefully acknowledge Mark Brinson, John Day, Frank Day, Scott Nixon, Walt Glooschenko, Rebecca Sharitz, Gene Turner, Mohan Wali, Jack Bernard, Mark Brown, Bob Costanza, Mike Duever, Irv Mendelssohn, Bob Simpson, Charles Sasser, Bill Wilen, Mary Theresa Vogel, Patrick Denny, and Ed Maltby. We regret any omissions. Support for our wetlands research, from which much of the synthesis in this book emerged, has been from the U.S. Fish and Wildlife Service, the Kentucky Water Resources Research Institute, the Illinois Water Resources Center, the Office of Surface Mining, Louisiana State University, and the Louisiana Sea Grant Program. The Systems Science Institute and the Center for Environmental Science and Management at the University of Louisville and the Center for Wetland Resources at Louisiana State University provided much of the logistical support for this project. The authors were ably assisted by the staff from both of those units, particularly by Thelma Goldstein. Special appreciation is shown for Karen Cozine and Jean Estes for their flawless word processing through several editions of these chapters. Diane Baker, of the Center for Wetland Resources, did much of the drafting for the book and provided suitably professional drawings. Michele Ising and Shawn Richardson also provided several figures. Leila Gosselink assisted with the permission letters and other details of the book. Last but not least, we are indebted to our families, particularly to our wives, Ruthmarie and Jean, for having the patience, understanding, and editing skills to see us through this project.

WILLIAM J. MITSCH
JAMES G. GOSSELINK

WETLANDS

Part I

INTRODUCTION

CHAPTER 1

WETLANDS AND WETLAND SCIENCE

Wetlands are among the most important ecosystems on the Earth. In the great scheme of things, it was the swampy environment of the Carboniferous Period that produced and preserved many of the fossil fuels on which we now depend. On a much shorter time scale, wetlands are valuable as sources, sinks, and transformers of a multitude of chemical, biological, and genetic materials. Wetlands are sometimes described as "the kidneys of the landscape" for the functions they perform in hydrologic and chemical cycles and as the downstream receivers of wastes from both natural and human sources. They have been found to cleanse polluted waters, prevent floods, protect shorelines, and recharge groundwater aquifers. Furthermore, and most important to some, wetlands play major roles in the landscape by providing unique habitats for a wide variety of flora and fauna. While the values of wetlands for fish and wildlife protection have been known for several decades, some of the other benefits have been identified more recently.

These values of wetlands are now being recognized and translated into protection laws, regulations and management plans. As our nation's wetlands are drained, ditched, and filled at an alarming rate, many scientists, engineers, lawyers, and regulators are finding it necessary to become specialists in wetland ecology and wetland management. This book is for these aspiring wetland specialists, as well as for those who would like to know more about the structure and function of these unique ecosystems. It is a book about wetlands of the United States—how they work and how we manage them.

HUMAN HISTORY AND WETLANDS

Wetlands include the swamps, bogs, marshes, mires, fens, and other wet ecosystems found throughout the world under many names (see Chapters 2 and 3 for terms and definitions). They are ubiquitous, found on every continent except Antarctica and in every clime from the tropics to the tundra. An estimated 6% of the land surface of the world is wetland (Table 1-1). Wetlands are found in arid regions as inland salt flats; in humid, cool regions as bogs and fens; and along temperate, subtropical, and tropical coastlines as salt marshes and mangrove swamps. Many cultures have adapted to and even benefited economically from surrounding wetlands (Fig. 1-1). The Cajuns of Louisiana, the Camarguais of southern France, and the Marsh Arabs of southern Iraq have lived in harmony with wetlands for many years. Domestic wetlands such as rice paddies feed a large proportion of the world's population. The Russians and the Irish have mined their peatlands for several centuries, using peat as a source of energy. Mangrove wetlands are important for timber, food, and tannin in many countries throughout Indo-Malaysia, East Africa, and Central and South America. Salt marshes in northern Europe and the British Isles, and later in New England, were used for centuries for grazing, hay production, and thatching for roofs.

With all of these values and uses, not to mention the aesthetics of a landscape where water and land together often provide a striking panorama, one would expect wetlands to have a history of being revered by humanity, which has certainly not been the case. Wetlands have appeared as sinister

Table 1-1. Estimated Area of Wetlands in the World by Climatic Zone

Zone	Climate	Wetland Area, $km^2 \times 1,000$	Percent of Total Land Area
Polar	Humid; semihumid	200	2.5
Boreal	Humid; semihumid	2,558	11.0
Sub-Boreal	Humid	539	7.3
	Semiarid	342	4.2
	Arid	136	1.9
Subtropical	Humid	1,077	17.2
	Semiarid	629	7.6
	Arid	439	4.5
Tropical	Humid	2,317	8.7
	Semiarid	221	1.4
	Arid	100	0.8
World Total		8,558	6.4

Source: Based on data from Bazilevich, Rodin, and Rozov, 1971 pp. 296-302; Maltby and Turner, 1983, p. 13.

WETLANDS HAVE BEEN PART OF THE HISTORY OF MANY CULTURES.

Figure 1-1a. The Camargue region of southern France in the Rhone River delta, where Camarguais have lived since the Middle Ages. *(By Tom Nebbia; Copyright © 1973 National Geographic Society, reprinted by permission of Tom Nebbia, Horseshoe, N.C., and the National Geographic Society, Washington, D.C.)*

Figure 1-1b. A Cajun lumberjack camp in the Atchafalaya swamp of coastal Louisiana. *(Photograph courtesy of Special Collections Division, Howard Tilton Memorial Library, Tulane University, New Orleans, La.)*

Figure 1-1c.   The Marsh Arabs who create artificial islands in the wetlands of southern Iraq where the Tigris and Euphrates rivers meet. *(By Nik Wheeler; Copyright © 1976 National Geographic Society, reprinted by permission of Black Star, New York, and the National Geographic Society, Washington, D.C.)*

Figure 1-1d.   Thailand, one of many Asian countries where rice production and water buffalo are supported by the wetland environment. *(Photograph courtesy of Phillip Moore, Louisiana State University)*

and forbidding, with little economic value throughout most of recorded history. For example, Dante's *Divine Comedy* describes a marsh of the Styx in the upper Hell as the final resting place for the wrathful:

Thus we pursued our path round a wide arc of that ghast pool,
Between the soggy marsh and arid shore,
Still eyeing those who gulp the marish [marsh] foul.

In the 17th century, an Englishman (Byrd) who surveyed The Great Dismal Swamp on the Virginia-North Carolina border and is credited for naming it, describing the wetland as:

[a] horrible desert, the foul damps ascend without ceasing, corrupt the air and render it unfit for respiration. . . . Never was Rum, that cordial of Life, found more necessary than in this Dirty Place.

Colonel William Byrd III (1674-1744) "Historie
of the Dividing Line Betwixt Virginia and
North Carolina" in The Westover Manuscripts,
written 1728-1736, Petersburg, VA., E. and
J. C. Ruffin, printers, 1841, 143p.

Even those who study and associate with wetlands have been belittled in literature:

Hardy went down to botanise in the swamp, while Meredith climbed towards the sun. Meredith became, at his best, a sort of daintily dressed Walt Whitman: Hardy became a sort of village atheist brooding and blaspheming over the village idiot.

G. K. Chesterton (1874-1936) Chapter 2 in
The Victorian Age in Literature, *H. Holt and*
Company, New York, 1913, p. 143.

The sinister and forbidden image of wetlands has endured with Hollywood responding in kind on several occasions (Fig. 1-2).

Prior to the mid-1970s, wetland drainage and destruction were accepted practices in the United States and were even encouraged by certain government policies. Had these trends continued, the resource would be in danger of extinction. It has been only through the combined activities of hunters and fishermen, scientists and engineers, and lawyers and environmentalists that wetlands are now elevated to the level of respect in public policy that they deserve. Early interest by the U.S. government in wetlands was first reflected in activities such as the sale of federal "Duck Stamps" to waterfowl hunters, which began in 1934 (Fig. 1-3). Over 1.4 million hectares (3.5 million acres) of wetlands were preserved through this program alone during the

Figure 1-2. The sinister image of wetlands is still portrayed in many media such as Hollywood movies. *(From the motion picture "Swamp Thing;" Copyright © 1981 by Swampfilms, Inc., provided through courtesy of Embassy Pictures, Los Angeles, California)*

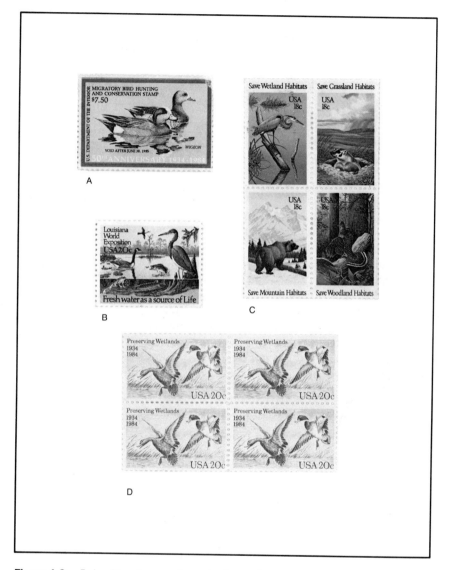

Figure 1-3. Federal involvement in wetlands is reflected in stamps such as duck stamps and commemorative postage stamps. *A.* "Duck stamps"—the revenue is often used by the U.S. Fish and Wildlife Service to acquire wetlands; the stamps must be purchased by any waterfowl hunter over the age of 16 and can be obtained at most post offices and some wildlife refuges. *B.* A wetland panorama for the Louisiana World's Fair (1984). *C.* A wetland stamp in a habitat preservation series (1979). *D.* A wetland stamp honoring the 50th anniversary of the duck stamp (1984).

period 1934-1984. The federal government now supports a variety of other wetland protection programs. Individual states have also enacted wetland protection laws or have used existing statutes to preserve these valuable resources. However, as long as wetlands remain more difficult to stroll through than a forest or more difficult to cross by boat than a lake, they will remain a misunderstood ecosystem to many people.

WETLAND SCIENCE AND WETLAND SCIENTISTS

Wetlands have also been an enigma to scientists. They are difficult to define precisely, not only because of their great geographical extent, but also because of the wide variety of hydrologic conditions in which they are found. Wetlands are usually found at the interface between truly terrestrial ecosystems, such as upland forests and grasslands, and truly aquatic systems, such as deep lakes and oceans (Fig. 1-4), making them different from each yet highly dependent on both. Because they combine attributes of both aquatic and terrestrial ecosystems, but are neither, wetlands fall between the cracks of the scientific disciplines of terrestrial and aquatic ecology.

The specialization in the study of wetlands is often termed *wetland science* or *wetland ecology,* and those who carry out such investigations are called *wetland scientists* or *wetland ecologists.* Some have suggested that the study of all wetlands be termed "telmatology" (Victor Masing, oral communic.),

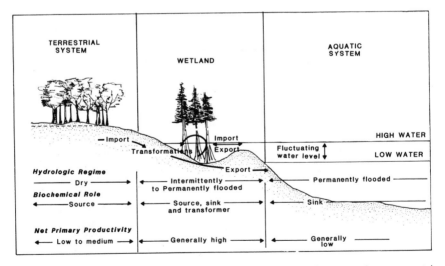

Figure 1-4. Wetlands are usually located at the ecotones between dry terrestrial ecosystems and permanently wet aquatic ecosystems.

a term now used by some scientists for the study of northern peatlands. No matter what the field is called, it is apparent that there are several good reasons for treating wetland ecology as a distinct field of study. These can be summarized as follows:

1. Wetlands have unique properties that are not adequately covered by present ecological paradigms.
2. Wetland studies have begun to identify some common properties of seemingly disparate wetland types.
3. Wetland investigations require a multidisciplinary approach or training in a number of fields not routinely combined.

A growing body of evidence suggests that wetlands, with their unique characteristics of standing water or waterlogged soils, anoxic conditions, and plant and animal adaptations, may have some common ground for study that is neither terrestrial ecology nor aquatic ecology. Wetlands provide good tests for "universal" ecological theories and principles on topics such as succession and energy flow, which often were developed for only aquatic or terrestrial ecosystems. They also provide an excellent laboratory for the study of principles related to transition zones, ecological interfaces, and ecotones.

Wetlands are ecotones, as shown in Figure 1-4, since they are transition zones from uplands to deepwater aquatic systems. This niche in the landscape allows wetlands to provide valuable functions, such as those of organic exporters or inorganic nutrient sinks. This transition position also often leads to high diversity in wetlands, which "borrow" species from both aquatic and terrestrial systems, and has given some wetlands the distinction of being cited as among the most productive ecosystems on earth.

Our knowledge about different wetland types, such as those discussed in this book, is for the most part isolated in separate literatures and scientific circles. One set of literature deals with coastal wetlands, another with forested wetlands, and still another with freshwater marshes and peatlands. However, a number of investigators (e.g., Gosselink and Turner, 1978; H. T. Odum, 1982, 1984; Brown and Lugo, 1982) have recently begun to look at the properties and functions common to or shared by all wetlands. This is probably one of the most exciting areas for wetland research because there is so much to be learned. The comparison of these wetlands has shown the importance of hydrologic flow-through for the maintenance and productivity of these ecosystems. The anoxic biochemical processes that are common to all of these wetlands provide another area for comparative research and pose many questions: What are the roles of different wetland types in local and global chemical cycles? How are the activities of humans influencing these cycles in various wetlands? What are the synergistic effects of hydrology, chemical inputs, and climatic conditions on wetland productivity? How do plant and animal adaptations to the stress compare among various wetland types?

The true wetland ecologist must be an ecological generalist because of the number of sciences that come to bear in these ecosystems. Because the hydrologic conditions are so important in determining the structure and function of the wetland ecosystem, a wetland scientist should be well versed in surface and groundwater hydrology. The shallow water environment means that chemistry—particularly for water, sediments, and water-sediment interactions—is an important science. Likewise, the questions about wetlands as sources, sinks, or transformers of chemicals require the investigator to be versed in a number of biological and chemical techniques. The identification of wetland vegetation and animals requires botanical and zoological skills, while a background in microbial biochemistry would contribute significantly to the understanding of the anoxic environment. Understanding the adaptations of the wetland biota to the flooded environment requires the backgrounds of both biochemistry and physiology. If wetland scientists are to become more involved in the management of wetlands, then some engineering techniques, particularly for wetland hydrologic control or wetland creation, need to be learned. Finally, a truly holistic view of these complex ecosystems can be had only through an understanding of the principles of ecology. Synthesis is particularly aided through the techniques developed in ecosystem ecology and systems analysis.

Many scientists are now involved in the study of wetlands. However, only a relatively few pioneers investigated these systems in any detail prior to the 1960s. Most of the early scientific studies dealt with classical botanical surveys or investigations of peat structure. Early work on coastal salt marshes and mangroves was published by scientists such as Valentine J. Chapman (1938; 1940), John Henry Davis (1940), John M. Teal (1958; 1962), and Lawrence R. Pomeroy (1959). Henry Chandler Cowles (1899), Edgar N. Transeau (1903), Herman Kurz (1928), A. P. Dachnowski-Stokes (1935), R. L. Lindeman (1942), and Eville Gorham (1967) are among the investigators who made early contributions to the study of freshwater wetlands, particularly northern peatlands, in North America. A number of early scientific pieces on peatland hydrology were also produced, particularly in Europe and the U.S.S.R. It was only later that investigators such as Teal, Pomeroy, and Eugene and H. T. Odum, and their colleagues and students, began to use modern ecosystem approaches in wetlands studies. Several research centers in the United States devoted to the study of wetlands have since been established, including the Center for Wetland Resources at Louisiana State University, the Center for Wetlands at the University of Florida, and the Sapelo Island Marine Institute in Georgia. In addition, a professional society now exists, the Society for Wetland Scientists, that has among its goals to provide a forum for exchange of ideas within wetland science, and to develop wetland science as a distinct discipline.

WETLAND MANAGERS AND
WETLAND MANAGEMENT

Just as there are wetland scientists who are researching the details and workings of wetlands, so too are there those who, by choice or by vocation, are involved in some of the many aspects of wetland management. These individuals, whom we call wetland managers, may be engaged in activities that range from waterfowl production to wastewater treatment. They must be able to balance the scientific aspects of wetlands with a myriad of legal, institutional, and economic constraints to provide optimum wetland management. Management of wetlands is becoming more important as these ecosystems continue to be drained or encroached upon by agriculture and urban areas. It may indeed be the eventual fate of wetlands that wetland managers find it necessary to design them as part of the landscape in order to protect them, although they may be faced with the problem of trying to do more with less. Few wetlands are being created to replace those that are being lost, although wetland creation for specific functions is an exciting new area of wetland management that needs trained specialists and may eventually stem the tide of decrease in this resource.

The recent emphasis on wetland management has been demonstrated by a veritable flood of reports, scientific studies, and conference proceedings over the past decade. Several meetings on wetlands have been held in the United States (e.g., Good, Whigham, and Simpson, 1978; Kusler and Montanari, 1978; Greeson, Clark, and Clark, 1979; Johnson and McCormick, 1979; Clark and Benforado, 1981) and as international symposia (SCOPE and UNEP, 1982; Gopal et al., 1982; Patten et al., in press). The U.S. Fish and Wildlife Service has been involved in the classification and inventory of wetlands (Cowardin et al., 1979; Frayer et al., 1983) and in a new series of community profiles on various regional wetlands. The Environmental Protection Agency has been interested in the impacts of construction on wetlands (Darnell, 1976) and in wetlands as possible systems for the management of wastewater (U.S. Environmental Protection Agency, 1983; WAPORA, Inc., 1983). Interest in wetlands has even extended to the U.S. Congress, which has supported two summary studies of wetlands—one entitled *Wetland Management* (Zinn and Copeland, 1982) and the other called *Wetlands: Their Use and Regulation* (Office of Technology Assessment, 1984).

SUMMARY

Wetlands are a major feature of the landscape in almost all parts of the world. While many cultures have lived among and even depended upon wetlands for centuries, the modern history of wetlands has been one mixed with misunderstanding and fear. Wetlands had been disappearing at an alarming rate in the United States and elsewhere until recently, when their multiple values began to be recognized. There is a case to be made for wetland science as a unique multi-discipline, with support in ecology, chemistry, hydrology, and engineering. This science deals with the study of the wetland ecosystem, which is unique because of its hydrologic conditions and its role at the ecotone between terrestrial and aquatic systems. Wetland management, as the applied side of wetland science, also requires an understanding of the scientific aspects of wetlands, balanced with legal, institutional, and economic realities, to ensure protection of these valuable ecosystems.

DEFINITIONS OF WETLANDS

The most common questions that the uninitiated might ask about wetlands are "Now, what exactly *is* a wetland?" or "Is that the same as a swamp?" These are surprisingly good questions, and it is not altogether clear that they have been answered completely by wetland scientists and managers. Wetland definitions and terms are many and are often confusing. Nevertheless, they are important for both the scientific understanding of these systems and for their proper management.

DISTINGUISHING FEATURES OF WETLANDS

We can easily identify a coastal salt marsh, with its great uniformity of cordgrass and maze of tidal creeks, as a wetland. A cypress swamp, with majestic trees festooned with Spanish moss and standing in knee-deep water, provides an unmistakable image of a wetland. A northern sphagnum bog, surrounded by tamarack trees that quake as we trudge by, is yet another easily recognized wetland. All of these sites have several features in common. They all have shallow water or saturated soil, all accumulate plant organic materials that decompose slowly, and all support a variety of plants and animals adapted to the saturated conditions. Wetland definitions, then, often include three main components:

1. Wetlands are distinguished by the presence of water.
2. Wetlands often have unique soils that differ from adjacent uplands.

3. Wetlands support vegetation adapted to the wet conditions (*hydrophytes*), and conversely are characterized by an absence of flooding-intolerant vegetation.

In addition to the presence of shallow water, unique wetland soils and vegetation adapted to wet conditions, wetlands have a number of other characteristics that distinguish them from other ecosystems yet make them less easily defined (Zinn and Copeland, 1982):

4. Although water is present for at least part of the time, the depth and duration of flooding varies considerably from wetland to wetland.
5. Wetlands are often at the margins between deep water and terrestrial uplands and are influenced by both systems.
6. Wetlands vary widely in size, ranging from small prairie potholes a few hectares in size to large expanses of wetlands several hundred square kilometers in area.
7. Wetland location can vary greatly, from inland to coastal wetlands, and from rural to urban regions.
8. Wetland condition, or the degree to which the wetland is influenced by humans, varies greatly from region to region and from wetland to wetland.

THE PROBLEM OF WETLAND DEFINITION

As described by R. L. Smith (1980, p. 225) "Wetlands are a half-way world between terrestrial and aquatic ecosystems and exhibit some of the characteristics of each." They form part of a continuous gradient between uplands and open water. As a result, in any definition the upper and the lower limits of wetland excursion are arbitrary boundaries. Consequently, few definitions adequately describe all wetlands. The problem of definition usually arises on the edges of wetlands, toward either wetter or drier conditions. How far upland and how infrequently should the land flood before we can declare that it is not a wetland? On the other edge, how far do we venture into a lake, pond, estuary, or ocean before we are no longer in a wetland? Does a floating mat of vegetation define a wetland? What about a submerged bed of rooted vascular vegetation? Frequency of flooding is the variable that has made the definition of wetlands particularly controversial. Some classifications include seasonally flooded bottomland hardwood forests as wetlands, while others exclude them because they are dry for most of the year. Because wetland characteristics grade continuously from aquatic to terrestrial, any definition is to some extent arbitrary. As a result, there is no single, universally recognized definition of what a wetland is. This lack has caused confusion and inconsistencies in the management, classification, and inventorying of wetland systems, but considering the diversity of types, sizes, location, and conditions of wetlands in this country, the inconsistency should be no surprise.

FORMAL DEFINITIONS

Precise wetland definitions are needed for two distinct interest groups: (1) wetland scientists and (2) wetland managers (Zinn and Copeland, 1982). The wetland scientist is interested in a flexible yet rigorous definition that facilitates classification, inventory, and research. The wetland manager is concerned with regulations designed to prevent or control wetland modification and thus needs clear, legally binding definitions. Because of these differing needs, different definitions have been developed for the two groups.

Circular 39 Definition

One of the earliest definitions of the term "wetlands," and one that is still frequently used today by both wetland scientists and managers, was presented by the U.S. Fish and Wildlife Service in 1956 in a publication that is frequently referred to as "Circular 39" (Shaw and Fredine, 1956, p. 3):

The term "wetlands" . . . refers to lowlands covered with shallow and sometimes temporary or intermittent waters. They are referred to by such names as marshes, swamps, bogs, wet meadows, potholes, sloughs, and river-overflow lands. Shallow lakes and ponds, usually with emergent vegetation as a conspicuous feature, are included in the definition, but the permanent waters of streams, reservoirs, and deep lakes are not included. Neither are water areas that are so temporary as to have little or no effect on the development of moist-soil vegetation.

The Circular 39 definition (1) emphasized wetlands that were important as waterfowl habitats, and (2) included 20 types of wetlands that, until recently, served as the basis for the main wetland classification used in the United States (see Chapter 17). It thus served the needs of both the wetland manager and the wetland scientist, but in a limited way.

Canadian Wetland Definition

Canadians, who deal with vast areas of inland northern peatlands, have developed a specific definition of wetlands. At a workshop of the Canadian National Wetlands Working Group, Zoltai (1979, p. 1) defined wetlands as ". . . areas where wet soils are prevalent, having a water table near or above the mineral soil for the most part of the thawed season, supporting a hydrophylic vegetation." Tarnocai (1979, p. 11), at the same workshop, presented the definition used in the Canadian Wetland Registry, an inventory and data bank on Canadian wetlands. The definition is very similar to Zoltai's:

Wetland is defined as land having the water table at, near, or above the land surface or which is saturated for a long enough period to promote wetland or aquatic processes as indicated by hydric soils, hydrophylic vegetation, and various kinds of biological activity which are adapted to the wet environment.

These definitions emphasize wet soil conditions, particularly during the growing season.

Fish and Wildlife Service Definition

Perhaps the most comprehensive definition of wetlands was adopted by wetland scientists in the U.S. Fish and Wildlife Service in 1979, after several years of review. The definition is presented in a report entitled *Classification of Wetlands and Deepwater Habitats of the United States* (Cowardin et al., 1979, p. 3):

Wetlands are lands transitional between terrestrial and aquatic systems where the water table is usually at or near the surface or the land is covered by shallow water ... Wetlands must have one or more of the following three attributes: (1) at least periodically, the land supports predominantly hydrophytes, (2) the substrate is predominantly undrained hydric soil, and (3) the substrate is nonsoil and is saturated with water or covered by shallow water at some time during the growing season of each year.

This definition is the most widely accepted by wetland scientists in the United States today. Designed for the scientists as well as the manager, it is broad, flexible, and comprehensive and includes descriptions of vegetation, hydrology, and soils. It has its main utility in scientific studies and inventories and generally has been more difficult to apply to the management and regulation of wetlands. It has also recently been accepted as the official definition of wetlands by India and has been used in proposed wetland legislation by some individual states in the United States. As with the Circular 39 definition, this definition serves as the basis for a detailed wetland classification and an updated and more comprehensive inventory of wetlands in the United States. That classification and inventory are described in more detail in Chapter 17.

Legal Definitions

A separate U.S. government definition is found in the regulations used by the U.S. Army Corps of Engineers for implementation of a dredge and fill permit system required by Section 404 of the 1977 Clean Water Act Amendments. The latest version of that definition is given as follows:

The term "wetlands" means those areas that are inundated or saturated by surface or ground water at a frequency and duration sufficient to support, and that under normal circumstances do support, a prevalence of vegetation typically adapted for life in saturated soil conditions. Wetlands generally include swamps, marshes, bogs, and similar areas. (33 CFR323.2(c); 1984)

This definition replaced a 1975 definition that stated "those areas that normally are characterized by the prevalence of vegetation that requires saturated soil conditions for growth and reproduction" (42 *Fed. Reg.* 37128, July 19, 1977), because the Corps of Engineers found that the old definition excluded "many forms of truly aquatic vegetation that are prevalent in an inundated or saturated area, but that do not require saturated soil from a biological standpoint for their growth and reproduction." The terms "normally" in the old definition and "that under normal circumstances do support" in the new definition were intended "to respond to situations in which an individual would attempt to eliminate the permit review requirements of Section 404 by destroying the aquatic vegetation. . . ." (quotes from 42 *Fed. Reg.* 37128, July 19, 1977). The need to revise the 1975 definition illustrates how difficult it has been to develop a legally useful definition that at the same time accurately reflects the ecological reality of a wetland site.

The definition of wetlands has been debated in the courts in several cases, some of which have been landmark cases. In one of the first court tests of wetland protection, the Fifth Circuit of the U.S. Court of Appeals ruled in 1972 in the case of *Zabel v. Tabb* that the U.S. Army Corps of Engineers had the right to refuse a permit for filling of a mangrove wetland in Florida. In 1975, in a case entitled *Natural Resources Defense Council v. Callaway,* wetlands were included in the category "waters of the United States," as described by the Clean Water Act. Prior to that time the Corps of Engineers regulated dredge and fill activities (Section 404 of the Clean Water Act) for navigable waterways only; since that decision, wetlands have been legally included in the definition of waters of the United States.

The latest Corps of Engineers definition, cited above, uses only one indicator, vegetative cover, to determine the presence or absence of a wetland. It is difficult to include soil information and water conditions in a wetland definition when its main purpose is to determine jurisdiction for regulatory purposes, and there is little time to examine the site in detail. The wetland manager is interested in a definition that allows a rapid identification of a wetland and the degree to which it has been or could be altered. He or she is also interested in a precise definition of wetland boundaries; establishing boundaries is facilitated by defining the wetland simply according to the presence or absence of certain species of vegetation or aquatic life.

However, in 1981, the U.S. District Court in Louisiana further complicated the management definition of wetlands. In a case entitled *Avoyelles Sportsman's League v. Alexander,* the federal defendants submitted three criteria for wetland determination: frequency of inundation, soil type, and vegetation. This determination ultimately was accepted by the U.S. Fifth Circuit Court of Appeals. Although it has not been universally adopted in regulatory activity, it did substantially broaden the definition of wetlands over the older guidelines that the Corps of Engineers had been using.

Choice of a Definition

A precise wetland definition that is satisfactory to all users has not yet been developed, because the definition of wetlands depends on the objectives and field of interest of the user. Lefor and Kennard (1977), in a review of the many definitions used for inland wetlands in northeastern United States, showed that different definitions can result from the geologist, soil scientist, hydrologist, biologist, systems ecologist, sociologist, economist, political scientist, public health scientist, and lawyer. This variance is an expected result of the differences in emphasis in the definer's training, and also a result of the different ways in which separate disciplines deal with wetlands. For ecological studies and inventories, the 1979 U.S. Fish and Wildlife Service definition has been, and should continue to be, applied to wetlands in the United States. When wetland management, particularly regulation, is necessary, the Corps of Engineers's definition, as modified in the Avoyelles Parish case, is probably most appropriate. But just as important as the precision of the definition of a wetland is the consistency with which it is used.

SUMMARY

Wetlands have many distinguishing features, the most notable of which are the presence of standing water, unique wetland soils, and vegetation adapted to or tolerant of saturated soils. Wetlands are not easily defined, however, especially for legal purposes, because they have a considerable range of hydrologic conditions, because they are found at the margins of well-defined uplands and deepwater systems, and because of their great variation in size, location, and human influence. Common definitions have been used for centuries and are frequently used and misused today. Formal definitions have been developed by several federal agencies. These definitions have considerable detail and are used for both scientific and management purposes. No absolute answer to "What is a wetland?" should be expected, but legal definitions developed in the courts in cases involving wetland protection are becoming increasingly comprehensive.

3

WETLAND TYPES AND WETLAND RESOURCES OF THE UNITED STATES

The United States has always had an abundance and diversity of wetlands. However, the wetlands that exist now may represent only half of those seen by pioneers as they advanced across the continent some 200 years ago. Soggy marshes and wet meadows must have greeted the first settlers in the Midwest after they left the hills and mountains of the East and entered the level prairie. Peatlands and prairie potholes had to be a common sight to those who settled in the north country in what is now Michigan, Wisconsin, Minnesota, and the Dakotas. Those who traveled on the Mississippi River or rivers in the Southeastern Coastal Plain must have marveled at the mammoth structure of many of the virgin cypress swamps and bottomland hardwood forests that lined these rivers. Indeed, salt marshes and—in some cases—mangroves probably welcomed many of the original explorers and settlers in a most inhospitable fashion as they arrived in the New World. All of these wetlands undoubtedly played an important role in the development of the country. In these very early times, they were accepted as a part of the landscape, and there was little desire or capability to change the hydrologic conditions of the wetlands to any great degree. As described by Shaw and Fredine (1956, p. 3):

The great natural wealth that originally made possible the growth and development of the United States included a generous endowment of shallow-water and waterlogged lands. The original inhabitants of the New World had utilized the animals living among these wet places for food and clothing, but they permitted the land to essentially remain unchanged.

As the westward movement slowed and towns, villages, cities, and farms began to expand on a regional scale, wetlands were increasingly viewed as wastelands that should be drained for reasons as varied as disease control and agricultural expansion. There followed an unfortunate, yet somewhat understandable, period in this country's growth when wetland drainage and destruction were simply the accepted norm. The Swamp Lands Acts of 1849, 1850, and 1860 set the tone for that period by encouraging much drainage in 15 of the interior and West Coast states. Coastal wetlands in the populated northeast were drained and dissected to accommodate urban development. Many virgin forested bottomlands and swamps in the Southeast were lumbered for their valuable products, with little regard to whether they would recover for the enjoyment and use of future generations. From the middle of the nineteenth century to the middle of the twentieth century, the country went through a period in which wetland removal was not questioned. Indeed, it was considered the proper thing to do.

WETLAND TERMS AND TYPES

A number of common terms have been used over the years to describe different types of wetlands (Gore, 1983*b*). These words usually have a long history of use and misuse and are often decidedly regional or at least continental. Although the lack of standardization of terms is confusing, many of these old terms are rich in meaning to those familiar with them. They often bring to mind vivid images of specific kinds of ecosystems with distinct vegetation, animals, and other characteristics. The following are some of the more popular terms used to describe particular kinds of wetlands:

Swamp. Wetland dominated by trees or shrubs (U.S. Definition). In Europe a forested fen (see below) could be called a swamp. In some areas reed grass-dominated wetlands are also called swamps.

Marsh. A frequently or continually inundated wetland characterized by emergent herbaceous vegetation adapted to saturated soil conditions. In European terminology a marsh has a mineral soil substrate and does not accumulate peat.

Bog. A peat-accumulating wetland that has no significant inflows or outflows and supports acidophilic mosses, particularly sphagnum.

Fen. A peat-accumulating wetland that receives some drainage from surrounding mineral soil and usually supports marshlike vegetation.

Peatland. A generic term of any wetland that accumulates partially decayed plant matter.

Mire. Synonymous with any peat-accumulating wetland (European definition).

Moor. Synonymous with peatland (European definition). A highmoor is a raised bog, while a lowmoor is a peatland in a basin or depression that is not elevated above its perimeter.

Muskeg. Large expanses of peatlands or bogs; particularly used in Canada and Alaska.

Bottomland. Lowlands along streams and rivers, usually on alluvial floodplains that are periodically flooded. These are often forested and sometimes called bottomland hardwood forests.

Wet Prairie. Similar to a marsh.

Reedswamp. Marsh dominated by *Phragmites* (common reed); term used particularly in Eastern Europe.

Wet Meadow. Grassland with waterlogged soil near the surface but without standing water for most of the year.

Slough. A swamp or shallow lake system in northern and midwestern United States. A slowly flowing shallow swamp or marsh in southeastern United States.

Pothole. Shallow marshlike ponds, particularly as found in the Dakotas.

Playa. Term used in southwest United States for marshlike ponds similar to potholes, but with a different geologic origin.

Each of these terms has specific meaning to the initiated and many are still widely used, both by scientists and by laypersons. However, it is often difficult to convey the same meaning to an international scientific community and some languages have no direct translations for certain words that define wetlands. For example, the word "swamp" has no direct translation in Russian because there are few forested wetlands there. On the other hand, "bog" is easily translated because bogs are a common feature of the landscape there.

Table 3-1 illustrates the confusion in terminology that occurs because of different regional or continental use of terms for similar types of wetlands. In North American terminology, nonforested inland wetlands are often casually classified either as peat-forming, low-nutrient acid *bogs,* or as *marshes.* European terminology, which is much older, is also much richer and distinguishes at least four different kinds of wetlands, grading from mineral-rich reed beds called *swamps,* to wet grassland *marshes,* to *fens,* and finally to *bogs* or *moors.* In some sources (e.g., Moore, 1984), all of these are considered *mires.* By others, mires are limited to peat-building wetlands. The European

Table 3-1. Comparison of Terms Used to Describe Similar Inland Nonforested Freshwater Wetlands

North American Terminology	←————Marsh————→	←——Bog——→	
European Terminology	←Swamp→ ←Marsh→ —Fen→	←——Bog——	→
CHARACTERISTICS			
Vegetation	←Reeds→ ←Grasses and Sedges→	←——Mosses——	→
Hydrology	←————Rheotrophic————→	←—Ombrotrophic—→	
Soil	←————Mineral————→	←———Peat———	→
pH	←———Roughly neutral———→	←———Acid———	→
Trophic State	←—Eutrophic—→ ←Mesotrophic→	←Oligotrophic→	

Table 3-2. Types of Wetlands

Wetland Types Used In This Book	National Wetlands Inventory Equivalent[a]	Book Chapter
Coastal Wetland Ecosystems		
Tidal Salt Marshes	Estuarine intertidal emergent, haline	8
Tidal Freshwater Marshes	Estuarine intertidal emergent, fresh	9
Mangrove Wetlands	Estuarine intertidal forested and shrub, haline	10
Inland Wetland Ecosystems		
Inland Freshwater Marshes	Palustrine emergent	11
Northern Peatlands	Palustrine moss-lichen	12
Southern Deepwater Swamps	Palustrine forested and scrub-shrub	13
Riparian Wetlands	Palustrine forested and scrub-shrub	14

[a]Cowardin et al., 1979

classification is based on the amount of surface water and nutrient inflow (rheotrophy), type of vegetation, pH, and peat-building characteristics. Two points can be made: First, the physical and biotic characteristics grade continuously from one of these wetland types to the next; hence any classification is somewhat arbitrary. Second, the same term may refer to quite different systems in different regions. For example, a European swamp is dominated by reeds. In the United States the term swamp is almost always used to connote a forested wetland.

In this book we use a simple wetland classification scheme that makes use of terms in common parlance. The classification scheme used by most of the regulatory agencies in the United States, the National Wetlands Inventory, (Cowardin et al., 1979) is much more formal and all-encompassing, but it is also much too complex to use conveniently here. (The National Wetlands Inventory is described more fully in Chapter 17.) Seven major types of wetlands in the United States can be divided into two major groups: coastal and inland (Table 3-2). This way of classifying wetlands uses terminology that most Americans recognize and understand. These are generally recognizable ecosystems about which extensive research literature is available. Regulatory agencies also deal with these systems, and management strategies and regulations have been developed for these wetland types. It is recognized that there are other types of wetlands such as inland saline marshes and scrub-shrub swamps that may "fall between the cracks" in this simple wetland classification, but these types of wetlands cover most of those currently found in the United States.

Coastal Wetlands

There are several types of wetlands in the coastal areas of the United States that are influenced by alternate floods and ebbs of tides. Near coastlines, the salinity of the water approaches that of the ocean, while further inland, the tidal effect can remain significant even when the salinity is that of freshwater.

Tidal Salt Marshes

Salt marshes (Fig. 3-1) are found throughout the world along protected coastlines in the middle and high latitudes. In the United States, salt marshes

Figure 3-1. Tidal salt marsh. *(Photograph by Charles E. Sasser)*

are often dominated by the grasses *Spartina* in the low intertidal zone and *Juncus* in the upper intertidal zone. Plants and animals in these systems are adapted to the stresses of salinity, periodic inundation, and extremes in temperature. Salt marshes are most prevalent in the United States along the eastern coast from Maine to Florida and continuing on to Louisiana and Texas along the Gulf of Mexico. They are also found in narrow belts on the West Coast of the United States and along much of the coastline of Alaska. Many of the 2 million hectares (5 million acres) of estuarine wetlands estimated by Frayer et al. (1983) for the lower 48 states are salt marshes.

Tidal Freshwater Marshes

Inland from the tidal salt marshes, but still close enough to the coast to experience tidal effects, are the tidal freshwater marshes (Fig. 3-2). These wetlands, dominated by a variety of grasses and by annual and perennial broadleaved aquatic plants, are found primarily along the middle and south Atlantic coasts and along the coasts of Louisiana and Texas. An estimated 650,000 hectares (1.6 million acres) of this type of wetland exist in the eastern United States. Tidal freshwater marshes can be described as an intermediate in the continuum from coastal salt marshes to freshwater marshes. Because

Figure 3-2. Tidal freshwater marsh.

they are tidally influenced, but without the salinity stress of salt marshes, tidal freshwater marshes have often been reported as very productive ecosystems, although a considerable range of productivity has been measured in them.

Mangrove Wetlands

The tidal salt marsh gives way to the mangrove swamp (Fig. 3-3) in subtropical and tropical regions of the world. The word mangrove refers to both the

Figure 3-3.   Mangrove wetland.

wetland itself and to the salt-tolerant trees that dominate these wetlands. In the United States, mangrove wetlands are limited primarily to the southern tip of Florida, although small mangrove stands are found scattered as far north as Louisiana and Texas. Approximately 175,000 hectares (430,000 acres) of this wetland exist in southern Florida. The mangrove wetland is generally dominated by the red mangrove tree *(Rhizophora)* and the black mangrove tree *(Avicennia)* in Florida. Like the salt marsh, the mangrove swamp requires protection from the open ocean and occurs in a wide range of salinity and tidal influence.

Inland Wetlands

On an areal basis, most of the wetlands of the United States are not along the coastlines, but are found in the interior regions. Frayer et al. (1983) estimated that 38 million hectares (94 million acres), or about 95% of the total wetlands in the lower 48 United States, are inland. It is difficult to put these wetlands into simple categories. Our simplified scheme divides them into two groups that are decidedly regional, i.e., northern peatlands and southern deepwater swamps, and into two other categories that are found throughout the United States, i.e., freshwater marshes and riparian ecosystems. These divisions roughly parallel the divisions that persist in both the scientific literature and the specializations of wetland scientists.

Inland Freshwater Marshes

This category includes a diverse group of wetlands characterized by (1) emergent soft-stemmed aquatic plants such as cattails, arrowheads, pickerel-weed, reeds, and several species of grasses and sedges, (2) a shallow water regime, and (3) generally shallow peat deposits (Fig. 3-4). These wetlands are

Figure 3-4.   Inland freshwater marsh.

ubiquitous in North America, although major regions where marshes dominate include the prairie pothole region of the Dakotas and the Everglades of
Florida. They occur in isolated basins, as fringes around lakes, and in
sluggish streams and rivers.

Northern Peatlands

As defined here, northern peatlands include the deep peat deposits of the
north temperate regions of North America (Fig. 3-5). In the United States,
these systems are limited primarily to Wisconsin, Michigan, Minnesota, and
the glaciated Northeast, although similar peat deposits, called pocosins, are
found on the Coastal Plain of the Southeast. There are also mountaintop
bogs in the Appalachian mountains of West Virginia. Bogs and fens, the two
major types of peatlands, occur as thick peat deposits in old lake basins or as
blankets across the landscape. Many of these lake basins were formed by the
last glaciation, and the peatlands are considered to be a late stage of a
"filling-in" process. There is a wealth of European scientific literature on this
wetland type, much of which has influenced the more recent North American literature on the subject. Bogs are noted for their nutrient deficiency and
waterlogged conditions and for the biological adaptations to these conditions, such as carnivorous plants and nutrient conservation.

Figure 3-5. Northern peatland.

Southern Deepwater Swamps

These are freshwater woody wetlands of the southeastern United States that have standing water for most if not all of the growing season (Fig. 3-6). These swamps occur in a variety of nutrient and hydrologic conditions and are normally dominated by various species of cypress *(Taxodium)* and gum/tupelo *(Nyssa)*. These wetlands can occur as isolated cypress domes fed

Figure 3-6. Southern deepwater swamp.

primarily by rainwater or as alluvial swamps that are flooded annually by adjacent streams and rivers.

Riparian Wetlands

Extensive tracts of riparian wetlands, which occur in the United States along rivers and streams, are occasionally flooded by those bodies of water, but are otherwise dry for varying portions of the growing season (Fig. 3-7). In the southeastern United States, these riparian ecosystems are referred to as bottomland hardwood forests. They contain a diverse vegetation that varies along gradients of flooding frequency. Riparian wetlands also occur in arid

Figure 3-7. Riparian forested wetland during flood stage.

and semiarid regions of the United States, where they are often a conspicuous feature of the landscape in contrast with the surrounding nonforested vegetation. Riparian ecosystems are generally considered to be more productive than the adjacent uplands due to the periodic inflow of nutrients, especially when flooding is seasonal rather than continuous.

STATUS OF WETLANDS IN THE UNITED STATES

Major regions of wetlands in the United States are shown in Fig. 3-8. The regional diversity, coupled with the lack of unanimity on the definition of a wetland as described in chapter 2, makes it difficult to inventory the wetland resources of the United States. Nevertheless, attempts have been made, at different times in the history of this country, to find out how many wetlands there are in the United States and further, to determine the rate at which they are changing. Based on a review of several studies that have been made of wetland trends in the United States, two general statements can be made: (1) Estimates of the area of wetlands in the United States vary widely, and (2)

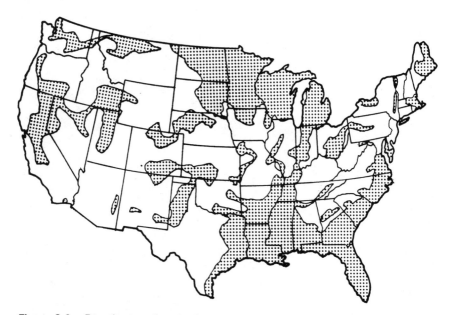

Figure 3-8. Distribution of wetlands in conterminous United States as adapted from Shaw and Fredine (1956). The Shaw and Fredine map emphasized wetlands that were important to waterfowl, so many major wetland areas may be missing from this map. *(After Office of Technology Assessment, 1984, p. 26)*

Most studies have indicated a rapid rate of wetland loss in the United States, at least prior to the mid-1970s.

Wetland Area Estimates

Historical estimates of wetland area in the 48 conterminous United States are given in Table 3-3. The numbers vary widely for several reasons. First, the purposes of the inventories varied from study to study. Early wetland censuses looked for lands suitable for drainage for agriculture. Later inventories of wetlands were concerned with waterfowl protection. Only within the last

Table 3-3. Estimates of Wetland Area in the United States

Date	Wetland Area, million hectares[a]	Reference
Presettlement	87	Roe and Ayres, 1954
Presettlement	51	Soil Conservation Service (cited in Shaw and Fredine, 1956)
Presettlement	60-75	Office of Technology Assessment, 1984
1906	32[b]	Wright, 1907
1922	37 (total) 3 (tidal) 34 (inland)	Gray et al., 1924
1940	39.4[c]	Whooten and Purcell, 1949
1954	30.1 (total) 3.8 (coastal) 26.3 (inland)	Shaw and Fredine, 1956
1954	43.8 (total) 2.3 (estuarine) 41.5 (inland)	Frayer et al., 1983
1974	40.1 (total) 2.1 (estuarine) 38.0 (inland)	*Ibid.*, Tiner, 1984
1982	17.9-19.0[d] 70-140 (including Alaska)	ASIWPCA, 1984

[a]For 48 conterminous United States unless otherwise noted.
[b]Does not include tidal wetlands or eight public land states in West.
[c]Outside of organized drainage enterprises.
[d]Crude estimates based on mail survey of all states. Questionnaire asked for wetlands that would be subject to regulation.

decade have wetland inventories considered all of the values of these ecosystems. Second, the definition and classification of wetlands have varied with each study, ranging from simple terms to complex hierarchical classifications. Third, the methods available for estimating wetlands have changed over the years or have varied in their accuracy. Remote sensing from aircraft and satellites is one example of a technique for wetland studies that was not generally available 20 years ago.

The first studies of wetland abundance by the U.S. Department of Agriculture took place in the early twentieth century. A 1906 inventory was the result of a request from Congress to determine "the amount and location of swamp and overflow lands in the United States that can be reclaimed for agriculture" (Wright, 1907 as quoted in Shaw and Fredine, 1956, p. 6). That study, which did not include intertidal coastal wetlands, estimated 32 million hectares (79 million acres) of wetlands in the United States. Of that area, 21.3 million hectares (52.7 million acres), or two thirds of the total, were found to be "not fit for cultivation, even in favorable years, unless cleared or protected" (Shaw and Fredine, 1956). A second inventory, in 1922 (Gray et al., 1924), found 37 million hectares (91.5 million acres) of wetlands, with 3 million hectares (7.4 million acres) of tidal marshes and the remainder as inland wetlands.

One of the first wetland surveys in the United States that was undertaken with their habitat values rather than their values for agriculture in mind was carried out in 1954, and published by the U.S. Fish and Wildlife Service two years later as Circular 39 (Shaw and Fredine, 1956). That survey, which relied on a wetland classification scheme of 20 wetland types (described in more detail in chap. 17), estimated that the nation had at that time 30 million hectares (74 million acres) of wetlands that were important to waterfowl. The study further identified 25.7 million hectares (63.5 million acres) as inland freshwater wetlands, 0.6 million hectares (1.6 million acres) as inland saline wetlands, 2.1 million hectares (5.3 million acres) as coastal saline wetlands, and 1.6 million hectares (4.0 million acres) as coastal freshwater wetlands. The major shortcoming of the Circular 39 survey was that it considered only wetlands that were important for waterfowl and thus failed to consider a large portion of wetlands in the United States. Nevertheless, although the study is now over 30 years old, it is still referred to today and represents a benchmark summary of waterfowl wetlands for the 48 conterminous United States.

A more recent assessment of wetland abundance in the United States, called the National Wetland Trends Study (NWTS), was conducted for the U.S. Fish and Wildlife Service (Frayer et al., 1983). That study used statistical analysis of wetland data derived from the recent detailed mapping for the National Wetlands Inventory to estimate the total coverage of wetlands in the lower 48 states. The results indicated that in the mid-1950s, there were

43.7 million hectares (108 million acres) of wetlands in the United States, about 45% more than the estimate by the Circular 39 study (Shaw and Fredine, 1956). This difference would be expected because the NWTS study was interested in all wetlands, while the Circular 39 study was interested only in wetlands that were important to waterfowl. The NWTS study also estimated that by the mid-1970s, wetlands had decreased to 40 million hectares (99 million acres) in the United States. Of those totals, all were inland wetlands except for 2.3 million hectares (5.6 million acres) of estuarine wetlands in the 1950s and 2.1 million hectares (5.2 million acres) of estuarine wetlands in the 1970s. Since these two estimates (1954 and 1974) are the only two derived from application of consistent definitions and techniques, they are the best available estimate of the rate of wetland loss.

Several estimates have been made of the area of original natural wetlands that existed in the United States in presettlement times. The U.S. Soil Conservation Service estimated that there were originally 51 million hectares (127 million acres) in the lower 48 states (Shaw and Fredine, 1956). Roe and Ayres (1954) included drained wet soils along with swamps and marshes to estimate 87 million hectares (215 million acres) of wetlands in presettlement times. These estimates often have been compared with existing wetland acreage to determine losses. A more recent interpretation by the U.S. Congress Office of Technology Assessment (Office of Technology Assessment, 1984) of prior wetland and wet soil area suggests a range between the Soil Conservation Service and Roe and Ayres figures. A range of 60 to 75 million hectares (149 to 185 million acres) of original wetlands in the lower 48 states is estimated by that study, although the authors admit that the estimates "are limited by the lack of good data on the amount of land that has been drained or otherwise reclaimed and the relationship between wetlands and wet soils" (Office of Technology Assessment, 1984).

State by State Distribution

The extent of wetlands by state from the mid-1950s survey of Shaw and Fredine (1956), from a 1982 aquatic resources survey by the Association of State and Interstate Water Pollution Control Administrators (ASIWPCA, 1984), and from recent estimates by the National Wetlands Inventory is shown in Table 3-4. While the methods and accuracy of the surveys are not directly comparable, the numbers do give an indication as to which areas of the country are dominated by wetlands. It is interesting that, in the case of a few states, for example, Montana and North Dakota, the 1954 estimates were still being used in 1982. In other states, such as South Carolina, Georgia, and Florida, wetland area was grossly underestimated in the ASIWPCA study. The numbers presently being generated by the National Wetlands Inventory (see Table 3-4) show that, in general, previous estimates of wetlands in

Table 3-4. Surveys of Area of Wetlands by State in the United States[a]

State	1954 Survey[b]		1982 Survey[c]		National Wetlands Inventory[d]	
	hectares ×1,000	acres ×1,000	hectares ×1,000	acres ×1,000	hectares ×1,000	acres ×1,000
Alabama	650	1,598	1,200	3,000	1,200	3,070
Alaska	–	–	53,000–121,000	130,000–300,000	53,000–121,000	130,000–300,000
Arizona	11.5	28	74	182	—	—
Arkansas	1,532	3,785	650	1,608	1,100	2,800
California	226	559	200	500	200	500
Colorado	164	404	200	500	–	–
Connecticut	9.5	23	270	657	–	–
Delaware	53	131	43	106	90	223
District of Columbia	–	–	0	.005	–	–
Florida	6,955	17,185	1,500	3,742	4,600	11,300
Georgia	2,396	5,920	200	500	2,100	5,300
Guam	–	–	1.4	4	–	–
Hawaii	–	–	6.5	16	–	–
Idaho	44	109	29	72	–	–
Illinois	173	427	20	50	–	–
Indiana	115	283	77	190	–	–
Iowa	56	138	31	76	–	–
Kansas	83	204	200	492	–	–
Kentucky	110	273	43	107	80	205
Louisiana	3,904	9,647	3,000	7,500	3,500	8,700

State						
Maine	154	381	235	580	—	—
Maryland	117	290	124	307	177	438
Massachusetts	94	232	147	362	—	—
Michigan	1,302	3,217	1,200–2,000	3,000–5,000	2,260	5,583
Minnesota	2,042	5,045	1,050	2,600	3,050	7,539
Mississippi	1,048	2,589	260	642	1,650	4,070
Missouri	153	377	8	20	—	—
Montana	76	187	76	187	—	—
Nebraska	263	650	nr	nr	—	—
Nevada	78	192	nr	nr	—	—
New Hampshire	5.5	14	29	71	—	
New Jersey	109	270	364	900	370	916
New Mexico	20	48	nr	nr	—	—
New York	86	213	383	945	—	—
North Carolina	1,641	4,055	1,370	3,380	2,300	5,690
North Dakota	616	1,523	600	1,500	950	2,340
Ohio	40	98	31	78	—	—
Oklahoma	113	280	21	53	—	—
Oregon	191	473	nr	nr	—	—
Pennsylvania	21	53	76	187	202	498

(continued)

[a]Surveys used different techniques and should not be directly compared.
[b]Shaw and Fredine, 1956
[c]ASIWPCA, 1984. See Note d in Table 3-3.
[d]Ralph Tiner, personal communication, and Hefner and Brown, 1985. These are "best estimates" of present wetlands for selected states.

Table 3-4. Continued[a]

State	1954 Survey[b]		1982 Survey[c]		National Wetlands Inventory[d]	
	hectares ×1,000	acres ×1,000	hectares ×1,000	acres ×1,000	hectares ×1,000	acres ×1,000
Puerto Rico	—	—	6	15	—	—
Rhode Island	10	25	18	46	26	65
South Carolina	1,367	3,377	174	430	1,900	4,660
South Dakota	304	752	539	1,333	600	1,500
Tennessee	335	828	280–570	700–1,400	320	790
Texas	1,514	3,741	160	400	1,600	3,957
Utah	475	1,174	405	1,000	—	—
Vermont	15	38	44	110	—	—
Virginia	219	541	113	280	423	1,044
Washington	94	233	89	220	—	—
West Virginia	1.5	4	7	17	41	102
Wisconsin	1,129	2,791	1,100	2,700	1,780	4,410
Wyoming	12	30	1,160	2,856	—	—
Total Wetlands	—	—	70,500–140,000	174,220–456,930	—	—
Total "Lower 48"	30,126	74,439	17,896–18,974	44,220–46,885	—	—

[a] Surveys used different techniques and should not be directly compared.
[b] Shaw and Fredine, 1956
[c] ASIWPCA, 1984. See Note d in Table 3-3.
[d] Ralph Tiner, personal communication, and Hefner and Brown, 1985. These are "best estimates" of present wetlands for selected states.

individual states were low. For example, in the National Wetland Inventory the wetland estimates in Delaware, Minnesota, Pennsylvania, Virginia, and West Virginia are more than double those of previous studies.

Including Alaska in wetlands estimates of the United States changes the national numbers altogether. The ASWIPCA study reported an estimated 53 to 121 million hectares (130 to 300 million acres) of wetlands in Alaska alone, much as wet tundra. This range brackets an estimate of 90 million hectares (223 million acres) by the U.S. Corps of Engineers (Office of Technology Assessment, 1984). The wide range of this estimate suggests a great deal of uncertainty abut the number; yet it can be concluded that the inclusion of Alaska in wetland surveys of the United States more than doubles the wetland area.

Wetland Changes

Estimates of the rate of wetland loss in the United States have been published in a number of studies (Table 3-5). Shaw and Fredine (1956) gave evidence of the magnitude of wetland loss in the United States from 1850 to 1950 by demonstrating that there was 45.7% loss of wetlands in seven states that were covered by the Swamp Land Act of 1850. That study also cited a Department of Agriculture estimate that " in the country as a whole, 45 million acres [18 million hectares] were reclaimed by a combination of clearing, drainage, and flood control on land in publicly organized drainage and flood-control enterprises" (Shaw and Fredine, 1956, p. 7). Based on an estimated 51.4 million hectares (127 million acres) of original wetlands in the United States, Shaw and Fredine (1956) suggested that 35% of the wetlands in the United States were lost from primitive times to the 1950s.

In an update of wetland losses in the United States, Frayer et al. (1983) estimated a net loss of over 3.7 million hectares (9.1 million acres) of wetlands in the United States (8.5% loss) from the 1950s to the 1970s, or an average annual loss of 185,000 hectares (460,000 acres) per year (Tables 3-5 and 3-6). This annual loss is equivalent to approximately one-half the area of Rhode Island each year (Tiner, 1984). Over the 20-year interval, wetland area equivalent to the combined size of Massachusetts, Connecticut, and Rhode Island has been lost. Palustrine emergent wetlands and palustrine forested wetlands were hardest hit. They disappeared at the rate of 14.1% and 9.6%, respectively, over the 20-year interval (Table 3-6).

Several studies have described losses of particular types of wetlands. Turner et al. (1981) estimated a high annual loss rate of bottomland hardwood forests of 175,000 ha/yr (431,00 acres/yr) from 1960 to 1975 (Table 3-5), due to conversion to agricultural fields, particularly for soybeans. In some regions of the lower Mississippi River floodplain, only a small percent of

Table 3-5. Estimates of Wetland Losses in the United States

Period	Wetland Loss			Reference
	hectares × 1,000	acres × 1,000	percent	
Total Wetlands— *Lower 48 States*				
Presettlement-1950s	18,000	45,000	35	Shaw and Fredine, 1956
Presettlement-1970s			30-50	Office of Technology Assessment, 1984
1950s-1970s[a]	3,700 (185/yr)	9,150 (460/yr)	8.5 (0.4/yr)	Frayer et al., 1983
1922-1954			0.2/yr	Zinn and Copeland, 1982
1954-1970s			0.50-0.65/yr	Ibid
1981			0.4/yr	Ibid
Southern Bottomland Hardwood Forests				
1940-1975	2,300 (65/yr)	5,700 (160/yr)	16 (0.45/yr)	Turner, Forsythe, and Craig, 1981
1960-1975	2,600 (175/yr)	6,500 (431/yr)	18 (1.2/yr)	Ibid
Coastal Wetlands				
1922-1954	260 (8.1/yr)	650 (20/yr)	6.5 (0.2/yr)	Gosselink and Baumann, 1980
1954-1974	370 (19/yr)	920 (46/yr)	9.9 (0.5/yr)	

[a]Details given in Table 3-6.

original bottomland hardwood forests remain (Fig. 3-9). Gosselink and Baumann (1980) estimated a loss rate of coastal wetlands of 8,100 ha/yr (20,000 acres/yr) between 1922 and 1954 and a higher loss rate of 19,000 ha/yr (47,000 acres/yr) between 1954 and the 1970s. By comparison, Tiner (1984) estimated that 7,300 ha/yr (18,000 acres/yr) of estuarine wetlands were lost from the 1950s to 1970s.

Losses of wetlands by major region of the country are summarized in Fig. 3-10 and Table 3-7 (page 44). The estimates made by the Office of Technology Assessment (1984) in Figure 3-10 showed that the Lower Mississippi Alluvial Plain, the Gulf Coastal Plain, and the Intermontane and Pacific Mountain regions in Western United States had loss rates greater than the national

Table 3-6. United States Wetland Area, 1970s, and Estimates of Wetland Loss since 1950s

Wetland Class		Wetland Total Area mid-1970s	Wetland Loss Since 1950s	
National Wetlands Inventory[a]	*This Book*	*hectares* × *1,000*	*hectares* × *1,000*	*Percent*
Estuarine intertidal emergent	Tidal salt marshes and tidal freshwater marshes	1,590	143	8.2
Estuarine intertidal forested and shrub	Mangrove wetlands	230	7.7	3.2
Palustrine emergent	Inland freshwater marshes and northern peatlands	11,500	1,890	14.1
Palustrine forested and shrub	Southern deepwater swamps and riparian wetlands	24,400	2,580	9.6
Total palustrine and estuarine wetlands[b]		40,070	3,700	8.5

Source: Based on data from Frayer et al., 1983, pp. 20-21

[a]The National Wetlands Inventory classification system upon which these data are based has no exact equivalence with the wetland types considered in this book.

[b]This classification includes nonvegetated as well as vegetated wetlands and is not the sum of preceding rows. Lacustrine wetlands are a small percentage of the total and are not included. Since loss of one wetland type may be to another kind of wetland, the total wetland loss does not equal the sum of preceding rows.

average from the mid-1950s to the mid 1970s. Low rates of wetland loss were found in the Rocky Mountain, Eastern Highlands, Central, and Atlantic Coastal Zone regions over the same period. In absolute acreage, the greatest losses of wetlands were in the Lower Mississippi Alluvial Plain, the Gulf Coast Rolling Plain, and the Upper Midwest. Some of the reasons for these wetlands losses are described in more detail in chapter 16.

SOME MAJOR REGIONAL WETLANDS IN THE UNITED STATES

Many regions in the United States support or once supported large contiguous wetlands or many smaller but numerous wetlands. These are called *regional wetlands* here. They are often large heterogeneous wetland areas such as the Okefenokee Swamp in Georgia and Florida that defy categorization as one type of wetland ecosystem. Regional wetlands can also be large

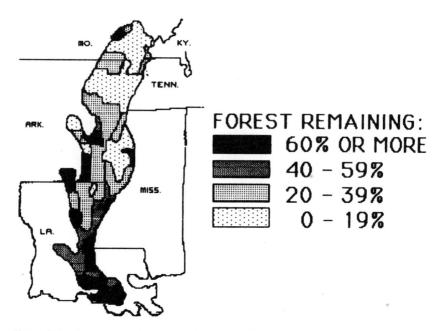

Figure 3-9.   Percentage of remaining bottomland hardwood forests in the lower Mississippi River floodplain. *(From Gosselink et al., 1981, p. 34; Copyright © 1981 by Louisiana State University, Division of Continuing Education)*

expanses that support wetlands of a similar type, such as the Prairie Pothole region of the Dakotas or the Pocosins region of North Carolina. Some regional wetlands, such as the Great Dismal Swamp at the Virginia-North Carolina border, have been drastically altered since presettlement times, while others, such as the Great Kankakee Marsh of northern Indiana and Illinois, are mostly gone as a result of extensive drainage programs. Each of these wetland areas has had a significant influence on the folklore and historical development of its region, and many have had the benefit of major investigations by wetland scientists. These studies have taught us much about wetlands and have identified much of their intrinsic value.

Descriptions of some of these regional wetlands, shown in Fig. 3-11, are given below. The reader is referred to chapters 8 through 14 and to the scientific literature cited below for a more complete discussion of these wetlands' structure and function. For those who wish a more complete description of some of these wetlands and several others in the United States, Thomas (1976) provides an excellent photojournalistic interpretation and

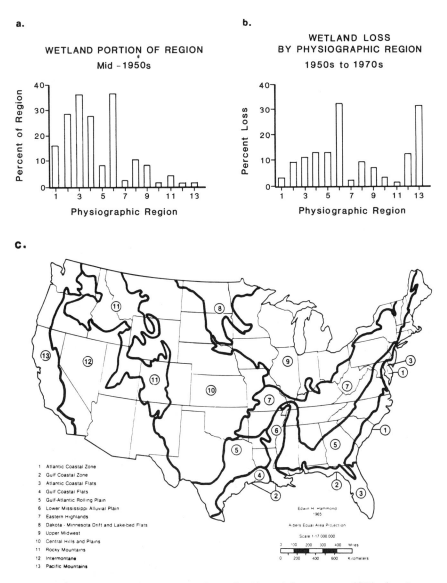

Figure 3-10. Distribution of wetlands in the United States, circa 1954, showing *a.* wetlands as percent of physiographic region *(based on data from Office of Technology Assessment, 1984, p. 96,) b.* percentage of wetlands that were lost from the 1950s to the 1970s by physiographic region *(based on data from Office of Technology Assessment, 1984, p. 96),* and *c.* physiographic regions of the United States *(from Office of Technology Assessment, 1984, p. 95).*

Table 3-7. Examples of Recent Regional Loss Rates in the United States

State or Region	Loss Rate ha/yr	Loss Rate acres/yr
Lower Mississippi Alluvial Plain	67,000	165,000
Louisiana's Forested Wetlands	35,300	87,200
North Carolina's Pocosins	17,600	43,500
Prairie Pothole Region	13,000	33,000
Louisiana's Coastal Marshes	10,000	25,000
Great Lakes Basin	8,000	20,000
Wisconsin	8,000	20,000
Michigan	2,600	6,500
Kentucky	1,500	3,600
New Jersey's Coastal Marshes	1,248 / 20[a]	3,084 / 50[a]
Palm Beach County, Florida	1,236	3,055
Maryland's Coastal Wetlands	400 / 8[a]	1,000 / 20[a]
New York's Estuarine Marshes	300	740
Delaware's Coastal Marshes	180 / 8[a]	444 / 20[a]

Source: From Tiner, 1984, p. 35.
[a]Loss rate after passage of state coastal wetland protection laws.

the National Audubon Society has published a colorful field guide to inland wetlands of the United States (Niering, 1985).

The Everglades and Big Cypress Swamp

The southern tip of Florida, from Lake Okeechobee southward to the Florida Bay, harbors one of the unique regional wetlands in the world. The region encompasses three major types of wetlands in its 34,000 km^2 (13,000 mi^2): the Everglades, the Big Cypress Swamp, and the coastal mangroves and glades. The water that passes through the Everglades on its journey from the Lake Okeechobee to the sea is often called a river of grass, although it is often only centimeters in depth and 80 km wide. It is dominated by saw grass *(Cladium jamaicensis)*, which is actually a sedge, not a grass. The expanses of saw grass, which can be flooded under several feet of water in the wet

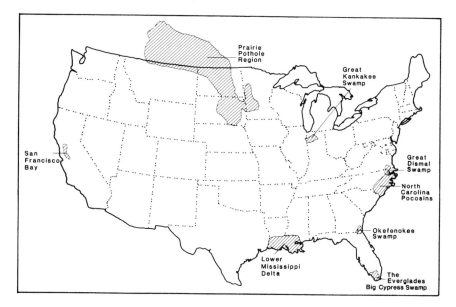

Figure 3-11. Location of major regional wetlands in conterminous United States.

season (summer) and burned in a fire in the dry season (winter/spring), are interspersed with deeper water sloughs and tree islands, or "hammocks," that support a vast diversity of tropical and subtropical plants, including hardwoods, palms, orchids, and other air plants. To the west of the saw grass Everglades is the Big Cypress Swamp, called "big" because of its great expanse, not because of the size of the trees. The swamp is dominated by cypress, interspersed with pine flatwoods and wet prairie. It receives about 125 cm of rainfall per year but does not receive major amounts of overland flow as the Everglades does. The third major wetland type, mangroves, form impenetrable thickets where the saw grass and cypress swamps meet the saline waters of the coastline.

Numerous popular books and articles have been written about the Everglades and its natural and human history, including the classic *The Everglades: River of Grass* by Douglas (1947) and *Everglades* by Caulfield (1970). An extensive study of the functional aspects of wetland ecosystems in the Fahkahatchee Strand of the Big Cypress Swamp was published by the U.S. Environmental Protection Agency (Carter et al., 1973) and several years of ecological studies have taken place in Corkscrew Swamp Sanctuary (Duever, Carlson, and Riopelle, 1975, 1984; Duever, 1984). Davis (1940, 1943) gives some of the earliest and best descriptions of the plant communities in southern Florida.

The Okefenokee Swamp

The Okefenokee Swamp in southeastern Georgia and northeastern Florida is a 1,750 km^2 (680 mi^2) mosaic of several different types of wetland communities. It is believed to have been formed in the Pleistocene or even more recently when ocean water was impounded and isolated from the receding sea by a sand ridge (now referred to as the Trail Ridge) that kept water from flowing directly toward the Atlantic (Schlesinger, 1978). The swamp, which has a long history of human intervention and retreat over the past 200 years, forms the headwaters of two river systems: the Suwannee River, which flows southwest through Florida to the Gulf of Mexico, and the St. Mary's River, which flows southward and then eastward to the Atlantic Ocean. Much of the swamp is now part of the Okefenokee National Wildlife Refuge, established in 1937 by Congress. The Okefenokee is named for an Indian word meaning "Land of Trembling Earth" because of the numerous vegetated floating islands that dot the wet prairies.

Auble et al. (1982) have identified six major wetland communities in the Okefenokee Swamp: (1) pond cypress forest, (2) emergent and aquatic bed prairie, (3) broad-leaved evergreen forest, (4) broad-leaved shrub wetland, (5) mixed cypress forest, and (6) black gum forest. Pond cypress (*Taxodium distichum* var. *nutans*), black gum (*Nyssa sylvatica* var. *biflora*) and various evergreen bays (e.g., *Magnolia virginiana*) are found in slightly elevated areas where the water and peat deposits are shallow. Open areas, which are called prairies, include lakes, emergent marshes of *Panicum* and *Carex,* and floating-leaved marshes of water lilies (e.g. *Nuphar* and *Nymphaea*) and bladderwort *(Utricularia).* Fires, during which the peat layers actually burn, are an important part of this ecosystem, and have reoccurred on a 20- to 30-year cycle whenever water levels become very low (Cypert, 1961). Many believe that the open prairies are early successional stages, maintained by burning and logging, of what would otherwise be a swamp forest.

A more complete description of the Okefenokee Swamp is contained in a recent book (Cohen et al., 1984) and in several papers (Wright and Wright, 1932; Cypert, 1961, 1972; Schlesinger and Chabot, 1977; Schlesinger, 1978; Auble et al., 1982; Bosserman, 1983a, 1983b).

The Pocosins

Pocosins are evergreen shrub bogs found on the Atlantic Coastal Plain from Virginia to northern Florida. These wetlands are particularly dominant in North Carolina, where an estimated 6,000 km^2 (2,300 mi^2) remained undisturbed or only slightly altered in 1979, while 3,000 km^2 (1,150 mi^2) were drained for other land use between 1962 and 1979 (Richardson et al., 1981). The word pocosin comes from the Algonquin Indian phrase for "swamp on a hill." They resemble, in successional progression and in nutrient-poor acid conditions, bogs typical of much colder climes and, in fact, were classified as bogs in the 1954 national wetland survey (Shaw and Fredine, 1956). Richardson et al. (1981) described the typical pocosin ecosystem in North Carolina as being dominated by evergreen shrubs (*Cyrilla racemiflora, Magnolia virginiana, Persea borbonia, Ilex glabra, Myrica heterophylla*, and *Smilax laurifolia*) and pine *(Pinus serotina)*. They are found "growing on water-logged, acid, nutrient poor, sandy or peaty soils located on broad, flat topographic plateaus, usually removed from large streams and subject to periodic burning" (Richardson, Evans, and Carr, 1981, p. 6). Draining and ditching for agriculture and forestry have affected pocosins in North Carolina. Proposed peat mining and phosphate mining could cause serious losses of these wetlands.

Excellent summaries of the ecological, economic, and legal aspects of pocosin management are included in *Pocosin Wetlands*, edited by Richardson (1981), and in a review paper by Richardson (1983). Previous descriptions of the extent and phytosociology of these wetlands are by Wells (1928), Woodwell (1956), Wilson (1962), and Kologiski (1977).

The Great Dismal Swamp

The Great Dismal Swamp is one of the northernmost "southern" swamps on the Atlantic Coastal Plain and one of the most studied and romanticized wetlands in the United States. The swamp covers approximately 850 km^2 (330 mi^2) in southeastern Virginia and northeastern North Carolina near the urban sprawl of Norfolk-Newport News-Virginia Beach. Its size once was over 2,000 km^2 (770 mi^2) (F. P. Day, 1982). It has been severely impacted by human activity over the past 200 years, with draining, ditching, logging, and fire all playing a role in diminishing its size and altering its ecological communities (Berkeley and Berkeley, 1976). It was once primarily a magnificent bald cypress-gum swamp with extensive stands of Atlantic white cedar *(Chamaecyparis thyoides)*. Although remnants of those communities still exist today, much of the swamp is dominated by red maple *(Acer rubrum)*, with mixed hardwoods found in drier ridges (F. P. Day, 1982). In the center of the swamp lies Lake Drummond, a shallow, tea-colored, acidic body of water. The source of water for the swamp is thought to be underground along its western edge, with surface runoff and precipitation also contributing. Drainage activity had occurred in The Great Dismal Swamp even before the Revolutionary War. As early as 1763, a corporation called the Dismal Swamp Land Company, which was owned in part by George Washington, built a canal from the western edge of the swamp to Lake Drummond to establish farms in the basin. That effort, like several others in the ensuing years, met with general failure. However, timber companies found greater economic reward in the swamp by harvesting the cypress and cedar for shipbuilding and other uses. One of the last timber companies that owned the swamp, the Union Camp Corporation, gave almost 250 km^2 of the swamp to the federal government to be maintained as a National Wildlife Refuge (Dabel and Day, 1977).

An extensive literature describes the history and ecology of the Dismal Swamp (e.g., Berkeley and Berkeley, 1976; Whitehead, 1972). Recently, structural and functional characteristics of the vegetation of the swamp have been described in several studies from Old Dominion University (Dabel and Day, 1977; Day and Dabel, 1978; McKinley and Day, 1979; Atchue, Marshall, and Day, 1982; Train and Day, 1982; Gomez and Day, 1982; Day, 1982; and Atchue, Day, and Marshall, 1983). There is also at least one book, *The Great Dismal Swamp* (Kirk, 1979), that describes ecological and historical aspects of this important wetland.

The Prairie Potholes

A significant number of small wetlands, primarily freshwater marshes, are found in a 780,000 km^2 (300,000 mi^2) region of the states of the North and South Dakota and Minnesota and in the Canadian provinces of Manitoba, Saskatchewan, and Alberta. These wetlands, called "prairie potholes," were formed by glacial action during the Pleistocene. This region, because of the numerous shallow lakes and marshes, the rich soils, and the warm summers, is described as being one of the most important wetland regions in the world (Weller, 1981). It is believed that 50% to 75% of all the waterfowl produced in North America in any given year comes from this region (Leitch and Danielson, 1979; Ogaard et al., 1981). Many of the prairie potholes have been drained or altered for agricultural reasons, and only an estimated 40% to 50% of the original wetlands remain untouched today (Leitch, 1981). An estimated 500 km^2 (190 mi^2) of prairie pothole wetlands in North Dakota, South Dakota, and Minnesota was lost between 1964 and 1968 alone (Weller, 1981). However, major efforts to protect the remaining prairie potholes do exist. Nearly 4,000 km^2 (1,500 mi^2) of wetlands have been purchased under the U.S. Fish and Wildlife Service Waterfowl Production Area program in North Dakota alone since the early 1960s (Weller, 1981). The Nature Conservancy and other private foundations have also purchased many wetlands in the region.

Much of the literature on the Prairie Potholes has centered on their role in the breeding and feeding of migratory waterfowl and other nongame species (e.g. Stewart and Kantrud, 1973; Kantrud and Stewart, 1977). A selected annotated bibliography on this subject is presented by Ogaard et al. (1981). A wetland classification, described in more detail in chapter 17, was developed by Stewart and Kantrud (1971) for the prairie pothole region. The social and economic implications of draining prairie pothole wetlands were described by Leitch and Danielson (1979). The ecology of the marshes of this region is discussed in the book on marshes by Weller (1981).

The Great Kankakee Swamp

For all practical purposes, this wetland no longer exists, although it was, until about 100 years ago, one of the largest marsh-swamp basins in the interior United States. Even its name, in current North American terminology, is a misnomer reflecting the European usage of the "swamp." It was dominated by grasses and we would call it a marsh today. Located primarily in north-western Indiana and northeastern Illinois, the Kankakee River Basin is 13,700 km^2 (5,300 mi^2) in size, with 8,100 km^2 (3,140 mi^2) in Indiana, where most of the original Kankakee Swamp was located. From the river's source to the Illinois line, a direct distance of only 120 km (75 mi) the river originally meandered through 2,000 bends along 390 km (240 mi), with a nearly level fall of only 8 cm/km (5 in/mi). Numerous wetlands, primarily wet prairies and marshes, remained virtually undisturbed until the 1830s, when settlers began to enter the region. The naturalist Charles Bartlett (1904, p. 1) described the wetland as follows:

More than a million acres of swaying reeds, fluttering flags, clumps of wild rice, thick-crowding lily pads, soft beds of cool green mosses, shimmering ponds and black mire and trembling bogs—such is Kankakee Land. These wonderful fens, or marshes, together with their wide-reaching lateral extensions, spread themselves over an area far greater than that of the Dismal Swamp of Virginia and North Carolina.

The Kankakee region was considered a prime hunting area until whole-sale clearing of the land for cropland and pasture began in the 1850s. The Kankakee River and almost all of its tributaries in Indiana were channelized into a straight ditch in the late nineteenth century and early twentieth century. In 1938, the Kankakee River in Indiana was reported to be one of the largest drainage ditches in the United States; the Great Kankakee Swamp was essentially gone by then.

Some historical and scientific literature exists for the Great Kankakee Swamp. Early accounts of the region are given by Bartlett (1904) and Meyer (1935). Work has been done in remnants of the riparian forested wetlands in Illinois' portion of the swamp, where preservation was better (Mitsch, Hutchison, and Paulson, 1979; Mitsch et al., 1979; Mitsch and Rust, 1984).

Mississippi River Delta

As the Mississippi River reaches the last leg of its journey to the Gulf of Mexico in southeastern Louisiana, it enters one of the most wetland-rich regions of the world. The total area of marshes, swamps, and shallow coastal lakes covers over 36,000 km² (14,000 mi²). Much of the richness is found in the Atchafalaya River Basin, a distributary of the Mississippi River that serves as both a flood relief valve for the Mississippi River and a potential captor of its main flow. The Atchafalaya Basin, by itself, is the third largest continuous wetland area in the United States (Thomas, 1976) and contains almost one-fourth of all the bottomland hardwoods in the entire lower Mississippi Basin (Turner, Forsythe, and Craig, 1981). The river passes through a narrow 4,700 km² (1,800 mi²) basin for 190 km (120 mi) supplying water for 1,700 km² (650 mi²) of bottomlands and cypress-tupelo swamps and another 260 km² (100 mi²) of permanent bodies of water (Hern, Lambou, and Butch, 1980). The Atchafalaya Basin is contained within a system of artificial and natural levees and has had a controversial history of human intervention through dredging, channelization, and oil and gas production.

Another frequently studied freshwater wetland area in Louisiana is the upper basin of the Barataria Bay estuary, an interdistributary basin of the Mississippi River that is now isolated from the Mississippi River by a series of flood-control levees. This basin, 6,500 km² (2,500 mi²) in size, contains 700 km² (270 mi²) of wetlands, including cypress-tupelo swamps, bottomland hardwood forests, marshes, and shallow lakes (Conner and Day, 1976).

As the Mississippi River distributaries reach the sea, salt marshes replace the freshwater wetlands. These salt marshes, some of the most extensive and productive in the United States, depend on the influx of fresh water, nutrients, and organic matter from the upstream swamps. The total amount of freshwater and saltwater wetlands is decreasing at a rapid rate in coastal Louisiana, with a total wetland loss of at least 80 km² (30 mi²) per year due to natural and artificial causes (Craig, Turner, and Day, 1979).

Numerous studies have been published on the Delta wetlands, including pieces on freshwater swamps (Hall and Penfound, 1939; Montz and Cherubini, 1973; Conner and Day, 1976; Day, Butler, and Conner, 1977; Conner, Gosselink, and Parrondo, 1981; Kemp and Day, 1984) and salt marshes (Day et al., 1973; Gosselink and Kirby, 1974; Kirby and Gosselink, 1976; White et al., 1978; Hopkinson, Gosselink, and Parrondo, 1980). Land loss in coastal Louisiana is described by Craig, Turner, and Day (1979) and Scaife, Turner, and Costanza (1983).

San Francisco Bay

One of the most altered and most urbanized wetland areas in the United States is San Francisco Bay in northern California. The marshes surrounding the bay covered over 2,200 km² (850 mi²) when European settlers first arrived. Almost 95% of that area has since been destroyed, leaving 125 km² (50 mi²) of tidal marsh, some of which has been created recently (Josselyn, 1983).

The ecological systems that make up San Francisco Bay range from deep, open water to salt and brackish marshes. The salt marshes are dominated by Pacific cordgrass *(Spartina foliosa)* and pickleweed *(Salicornia virginica),* while the brackish marshes support bullrushes (*Scirpus* spp.) and cattails (*Typha* spp.). Soon after the Gold Rush of 1849, acceleration of the demise of the bay's wetlands began. Industries such as agriculture and salt production first used the wetlands, clearing the native vegetation and diking and draining the marsh. At the same time, other marshes were developing in the bay as a result of rapid sedimentation. The sedimentation was due primarily to upstream hydraulic mining. Sedimentation and erosion continue to be the greatest problems for the remaining tidal wetlands.

An excellent summary of the ecology and management of San Francisco Bay has been developed by Josselyn (1983), while the ecology of the bay region has been described by a number of researchers, including MacDonald (1977), Mahall and Park (1976*a,* 1976*b,* 1976*c*), and Balling and Resh (1983).

SUMMARY

Wetlands are numerous and diverse in the United States, but drastic changes have occurred since presettlement times. An estimated 30 to 50% of the original wetlands in the lower 48 states has been lost due to drainage and other human activities. On a regional basis, the greatest wetland losses are occurring in the Lower Mississippi Alluvial Plain and the prairie pothole region of the northcentral states. Estimates of original wetlands in the lower 48 states range from 51 to 87 million hectares (127 to 215 million acres), while the most accurate estimate of present wetland area is 40 million hectares (99 million acres), of which 95% are inland wetlands and 5% are coastal. There are no accurate measures of the wetland area in Alaska, although it is estimated to range between 50 and 120 million hectares (130 and 300 million acres).

The historical terminology of wetlands has been confusing and often contradictory. In this book, we classify wetlands as seven major types: tidal salt marshes, tidal freshwater marshes, mangrove wetlands, northern peatlands, inland marshes, southern deepwater swamps, and riparian wetlands. There are also several regional wetland areas that are heterogeneous mosaics of several types of wetlands. The historical and ecological characteristics of the most important of these regional wetlands have been discussed here.

Part II

THE WETLAND ENVIRONMENT

HYDROLOGY OF WETLANDS

The hydrology of a wetland creates the unique physiochemical conditions that make such an ecosystem different from both well-drained terrestrial systems and deepwater aquatic systems. Hydrologic pathways such as precipitation, surface runoff, groudwater, tides, and flooding rivers transport energy and nutrients to and from wetlands. Water depth, flow patterns, and duration and frequency of flooding, which are the result of all of the hydrologic inputs and outputs, influence the biochemistry of the soils and are major factors in the ultimate selection of the biota of wetlands. An important point about wetlands, and one that is often missed by ecologists who begin to study these systems, is this: *Hydrology is probably the single most important determinant for the establishment and maintenance of specific types of wetlands and wetland processes.* An understanding of rudimentary hydrology should be in the repertoire of any wetland scientist.

THE IMPORTANCE OF HYDROLOGY IN WETLANDS

Ecological Processes and Hydrology

Wetlands are intermediate between terrestrial and open-water aquatic ecosystems. They are intermediate in terms of spatial arrangement, as they are usually found between uplands and aquatic systems. They are also intermediate in the amount of water they store and process. Because of this intermediate position, they are particularly sensitive to changes in their normal patterns of water storage and movement; that is, wetlands are sensitive to their hydrology. A conceptual model of the role of hydrology in wetlands is shown in Figure 4-1. Hydrologic conditions can directly modify or change chemical and physical properties such as nutrient availability, degree of substrate anoxia, soil salinity, sediment properties, and pH. Water inputs are almost always the major source of nutrients to wetlands; water outflows often remove biotic and abiotic material from wetlands as well. These modifications of the physiochemical environment, in turn, have a direct impact on the biotic response in the wetland (Gosselink and Turner, 1978). When hydrologic conditions in wetlands change even slightly, the biota may respond with massive changes in species richness and ecosystem productivity. When the hydrologic pattern remains similar from year to year, a wetland's structural and functional integrity may persist for many years.

Biotic Control of Wetland Hydrology

Wetlands are no more passive to their hydrologic conditions than are other ecosystems to their physical environment. Biotic components of wetlands can control their water conditions through a variety of mechanisms, including peat building, sediment trapping, water shading, and transpiration. Many marshes and some riparian wetlands accumulate sediments, thereby eventually decreasing the frequency with which they are flooded. Wetland vegetation influences hydrologic conditions by binding sediments to reduce erosion, by trapping sediment, by interrupting water flows, and by building peat deposits (Gosselink, 1984). Bogs build peat to the point at which they are no longer influenced at the surface by the inflow of mineral waters. Pond cypress trees may save water in some southern swamps due to their deciduous nature, their seasonal shading of the water, and their relatively slow rates of transpiration.

Even some animals contribute to hydrologic modifications of wetlands. The exploits of beavers in much of North America in both creating and destroying wetland habitats is well known. They build dams on streams that can back up water across great expanses, creating wetlands where none existed before. Alligators are known for their role in the Florida Everglades in constructing "gator holes," which serve as oases for fish, turtles, snails, and other aquatic animals during the dry season. In all of these cases, the biota of the ecosystem have contributed to their own survival by influencing the ecosystem's hydrology.

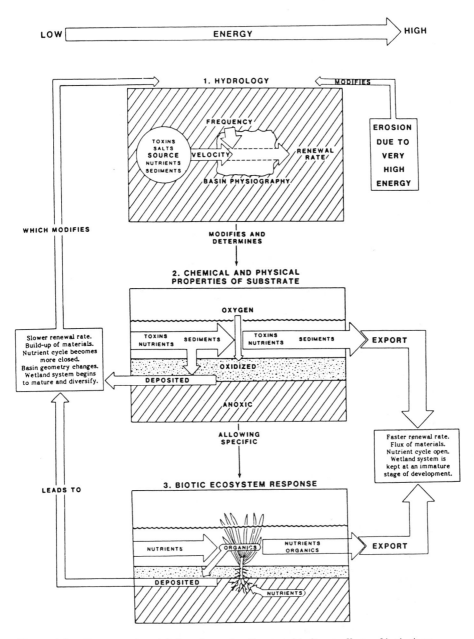

Figure 4-1. Conceptual model that shows the direct and indirect effects of hydrology on wetlands. *(From Wicker et al., 1982, p. 84, after Gosselink and Turner, 1978)*

THE HYDROLOGIC BUDGET
OF WETLANDS

Wetland Hydroperiod

The *hydroperiod* is the seasonal pattern of the water level of a wetland and is like a hydrologic signature of each wetland type. It defines the rise and fall of a wetland's surface and subsurface water. It is unique to each type of wetland, and its constancy from year to year ensures a reasonable stability for that wetland. The hydroperiod is an integration of all inflows and outflows of water, but it is also influenced by physical features of the terrain and by proximity to other bodies of water. Many terms are used to qualitatively describe a wetland's hydroperiod. Table 4-1 gives several definitions that have been suggested by the U.S. Fish and Wildlife Service. For wetlands that are not subtidal or permanently flooded, the amount of time that wetland is in standing water is called the *flood duration,* and the average number of times that a wetland is flooded in a given period is known as the *flood frequency.* Both terms are used to describe periodically flooded wetlands such as coastal salt marshes and riparian wetlands.

Some typical hydroperiods for very different wetlands are shown in Figure 4-2. For a cypress dome in north-central Florida (Fig. 4-2*a*), the ecosystem

Table 4-1. Definitions of Wetland Hydroperiods

Tidal Wetlands

Subtidal—permanently flooded with tidal water

Irregularly Exposed—surface exposed by tides less often than daily

Regularly Flooded—alternately flooded and exposed at least once daily

Irregularly Flooded—flooded less often than daily

Nontidal Wetlands

Permanently Flooded—flooded throughout the year in all years

Intermittently Exposed—flooded throughout the year except in years of extreme drought

Semipermanently Flooded—flooded in the growing season in most years

Seasonally Flooded—flooded for extended periods during the growing season, but usually no surface water by end of growing season

Saturated—substrate is saturated for extended periods in the growing season, but standing water is rarely present

Temporarily Flooded—flooded for brief periods in the growing season, but water table is otherwise well below surface

Intermittently Flooded—surface is usually exposed with surface water present for variable periods without detectable seasonal pattern.

Source: After Cowardin et al., 1979, pp. 23-24

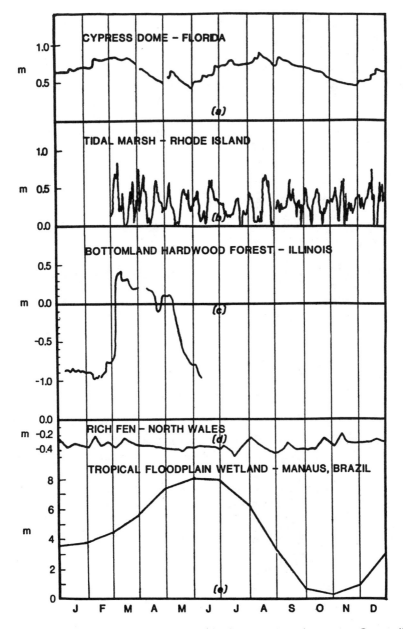

Figure 4-2. Hydroperiods for several wetlands: *a.* cypress dome near Gainesville, Florida; *b.* New England salt marsh *(after Nixon and Oviatt, 1973, p. 473)*; *c.* bottomland hardwood forest in Illinois *(after Mitsch et al., 1979, p.20)*; *d.* peatland in northern Wales *(after Gilman, 1982, p. 301)*; *e.* Amazon floodplain forest *(after Junk, 1982, p. 101)*. Vertical axis denotes water depth relative to the soil surface.

has standing water during the wet summer season and dry periods in the late autumn and early spring. A coastal salt marsh has a hydroperiod of semidiurnal flooding and dewatering superimposed on a twice-monthly pattern of spring and ebb tides (Fig. 4-2*b*). The hydroperiod of many bottomland hardwood forests (Fig. 4-2*c*) is a sudden and relatively short seasonal flooding followed by a rapid drop of the water surface to well below ground. There are also hydroperiods that have less pronounced seasonal fluctuations, as in the below-ground water level of many bogs and fens (Fig. 4-2*d*). The annual fluctuation of water in the tropical floodplain forest (Fig. 4-2*e*), on the other hand, has a tremendous seasonal fluctuation of almost 8m (24 ft).

The Overall Water Budget

The hydroperiod, or hydrologic state of a given wetland can be summarized as being a result of the following factors:

1. the balance between the inflows and outflows of water
2. surface contours of the landscape
3. subsurface soil, geology, and groundwater conditions

The first condition defines the *water budget* of the wetland, while the second and the third define the capacity of the wetland to store water. The general balance between water storage and inflows and outflows is expressed as:

$$\Delta V = P_n + S_i + G_i - ET - S_o - G_o \pm T \qquad (4.1)$$

where

$$
\begin{aligned}
V &= \text{volume of water storage in wetlands} \\
\Delta V &= \text{change in volume of water storage in wetland} \\
P_n &= \text{net precipitation} \\
S_i &= \text{surface inflows, including flooding streams} \\
G_i &= \text{groundwater inflows} \\
ET &= \text{evapotranspiration} \\
S_o &= \text{surface outflows} \\
G_o &= \text{groundwater outflows} \\
T &= \text{tidal inflow } (+) \text{ or outflow } (-)
\end{aligned}
$$

The change in water depth can further be described as:

$$\Delta L = \Delta V / A(L) \qquad (4.2)$$

where L = water level, including effective groundwater level; ΔL = change in water level; and A(L) = wetland area as a function of water level.

The terms in Equation 4.1 vary in importance according to the type of wetland observed; however, the equation serves as a useful summary of the major hydrologic components of any wetland water budget. Examples of hydrologic budgets for several wetlands are shown in Figure 4-3. There is a

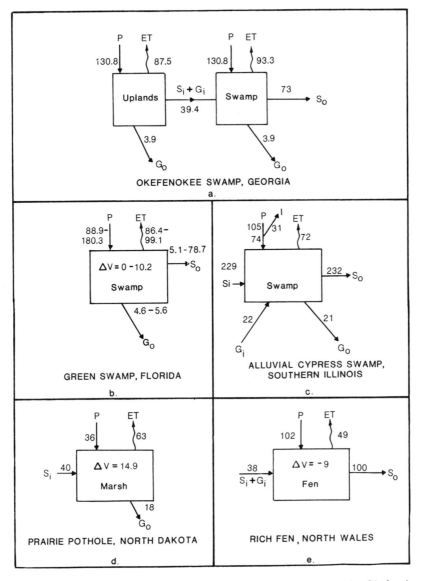

Figure 4-3. Annual water budgets for several wetlands, including *a.* the Okefenokee Swamp watershed in Georgia for 1975–1976 *(after Rykiel, 1984, p. 228); b.* the Green Swamp region in central Florida for 1959–1961 *(after Pride, Meyer, and Cherry, 1966, as cited in Carter et al., 1979, p. 361); c.* an alluvial cypress swamp in southern Illinois for 1976–1977, including flooding river input *(after Mitsch, 1979, p. 119); d.* a prairie pothole in North Dakota *(after Shjeflo, 1968, as cited in Linacre, 1976, p. 339); e.* a rich fen in northern Wales *(after Gilman, 1982, p. 299).* All values are expressed in cm/yr. P = precipitation, ET = evapotranspiration, I = interception, S_i = surface inflow, S_o = surface outflow, G_i = groundwater inflow, G_o = groundwater outflow, ΔV = change in volume of water storage.

Table 4-2. Major Components of Hydrologic Budgets for Wetlands

Component	Pattern	Wetlands Affected
Precipitation	Varies with climate although many regions have distinct wet and dry seasons	All
Surface Inflows and Outflows	Seasonally, often matched with precipitation pattern or spring thaw; can be channelized as streamflow or non-channelized as run-off; includes river flooding of alluvial wetlands	Potentially all wetlands except ombrotrophic bogs; Riparian wetlands, including bottomland hardwood forests and other alluvial wetlands, are particularly affected by river flooding
Groundwater	Less seasonal than surface inflows and not always present	Potentially all wetlands except ombrotrophic bogs and other perched wetlands
Evapotranspiration	Seasonal with peaks in summer and low rates in winter. Dependent on meteorological, physical & biological conditions in wetlands	All
Tides	One to two tidal periods per day; flooding frequency varies with elevation	Tidal freshwater and salt marshes; mangrove swamps

great variability in certain flows, particularly in surface inflows and outflows, depending on the openness of the wetlands. A brief description of the components of a general wetland water budget are summarized in Table 4-2.

Turnover Rate

A generally useful concept of wetland hydrology is that of the *renewal rate* or *turnover rate* of water, defined as the ratio of throughput to average volume within the system:

$$t^{-1} = \frac{Q_t}{V} \qquad (4.3)$$

where t^{-1} = turnover rate (1/time), Q_t = total inflow rate, and V = average volume of water storage in wetland. Few measurements of renewal rates have been made in wetlands, although it is a frequently used parameter in limnological studies. Chemical and biotic properties are often determined by the openness of the system, and the renewal rate is an index of this, since it indicates how rapidly the water in the system is replaced. The reciprocal of the turnover rate is the *residence time* (t), which is a measure of the average time that water remains in the wetland. Hammer and Kadlec (1983) consider the residence time to be an important variable when designing wetlands as wastewater treatment systems (see chap. 16).

Precipitation

Wetlands occur most extensively in regions where *precipitation,* a term that includes rainfall and snowfall, is in excess of losses such as evapotranspiration and surface runoff. Precipitation generally has well-defined yearly patterns, although variation among years may be great. An almost uniform pattern of precipitation over the years exists for eastern North America due to the heavy influence of both cold and warm fronts and summer convective storms. The northern Great Plains experience a summer peak in precipitation with relatively less precipitation in the winter due to the cold continental high pressure that recedes northward in the summer (Linsley and Franzini, 1979). By contrast, parts of the West Coast have a Mediterranean-type climate with wet winters and pronounced dry summers. The northern extremes of Canada show more uniform patterns of precipitation, but overall amounts are small. The precipitation pattern in Florida shows a decidedly wet season in summer due to the almost-daily convective storms.

The fate of precipitation that falls on wetlands with forested or shrub vegetation is shown in Figure 4-4. When some of the precipitation is retained

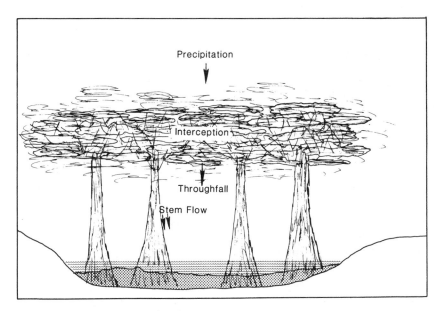

Figure 4-4. Fate of precipitation in a forested wetland showing throughfall, interception, and stemflow.

by the vegetation cover, particularly in forested wetlands, the amount that actually passes through the vegetation to the water or substrate below is called *throughfall*. The amount of precipitation that is retained in the overlying canopy is called *interception*. Interception depends on several factors, including the total amount of precipitation and the stage of vegetation development. Another term related to precipitation, *stemflow*, refers to water that passes down the stems of the vegetation. This flow is generally a minor component of the water budget of a wetland. For example, Heimburg (1984) found that stemflow was, at maximum, 3% of throughfall in cypress dome wetlands in north-central Florida. These terms are related in a simple water balance as follows:

$$P = I + TF + SF \qquad (4.4)$$

where P = total precipitation, I = interception, TF = throughfall, and SF = stemflow. The total amount of precipitation that actually reaches the water surface or substrate of a wetland is called the *net precipitation* (P_n) and is defined as

$$P_n = P - I \qquad (4.5)$$

Combining Equations 4.4 and 4.5 yields the most commonly used form for estimating net precipitation in wetlands:

$$P_n = TF + SF \qquad (4.6)$$

Surface Inflows and Outflows

Wetlands that are lower than their surroundings are subjected to surface inflows of two types. *Overland flow* is nonchannelized sheet flow that usually occurs during and immediately following rainfall or a spring thaw, or as tides rise in coastal wetlands. If a wetland is influenced by a large drainage basin, channelized *streamflow* may enter the wetland during most or all of the year. Often wetlands are an integrated part of a stream or river; for example, riverine freshwater marshes. Wetlands that form in these wide shallow expanses of river channels are greatly influenced by the seasonal streamflow patterns of the river. Coastal wetlands are influenced by surface runoff and by upstream and tidal flows, all of which contribute nutrients and energy to the wetland and often influence soil salinity and anoxia.

Surface runoff from a drainage basin into a wetland is difficult to estimate without a great deal of data. However, it is often one of the most important sources of water in a wetland's hydrologic budget. The *direct runoff* component of streamflow refers to rainfall during a storm that causes an immediate increase in streamflow. An estimate of the amount of precipitation that results in direct runoff, or "quickflow," from an individual storm can be determined from the following equation:

$$S = R_p \cdot P \cdot A_w \qquad \textbf{(4.7)}$$

where

S = direct surface runoff to wetland, m^3 per storm event
R_p = hydrologic response coefficient
P = average precipitation in watershed, m
A_w = area of watershed draining into wetland, m^2

This equation states that the flow is proportional to the volume of precipitation ($P \times A_w$) on the watershed feeding the wetland in question. The values of R_p range from 4% to 18% for small watersheds in the eastern United States (Lee, 1980); a summary of values for certain conditions of slope, soil, and forest type are shown in Table 4-3.

Channelized streamflow into and out of wetlands is described simply as the product of the cross-sectional area of the stream (A) and the average velocity (V) and can be determined through stream velocity measurements in the field:

$$S = A \cdot V \qquad \textbf{(4.8)}$$

where S = surface channelized flow, m^3/sec; A = cross-sectional area, m^2; and V = average velocity, m/sec. When an estimate of surface flow into or out of a riverine wetland is needed and no stream velocity measurements are available, the Manning equation can often be used if the slope of the stream and a description of the surface roughness are known:

$$S = \frac{A}{n} R^{2/3} s^{1/2} \qquad \textbf{(4.9)}$$

where n = roughness coefficient (Manning coefficient); R = hydraulic radius, m (cross sectional area divided by wetted perimeter); and s = channel slope, dimensionless.

Examples of roughness coefficients are given in Table 4-4. While these coefficients have not generally been determined as part of wetland studies, they can often be applied to streamflow in and out of wetlands. The relationship is particularly useful for estimating streamflow where velocities are too low to measure directly and to estimate flood peaks from high-water marks on ungaged streams (Lee, 1980). These are often the cases in wetland studies.

A special case of surface inflow occurs in wetlands that are in floodplains adjacent to rivers or streams, and which are occasionally flooded by those rivers or streams. These ecosystems are often called *riparian wetlands* (chap. 14). The flooding of these wetlands varies from year to year according to

Table 4-3. Description and Hydrologic Response Coefficients for Estimating Direct Runoff from Forested Watersheds in Eastern United States

Watershed	Watershed Area, A_w (ha)	Mean Elevation (m)	Mean Slope (%)	Soil texture[a]	Forest Type[b]	Hydrologic Response Coefficient R_p
Coweeta 2, N.C.	13	850	30	SL	OH	0.04
Coweeta 18, N.C.	13	820	32	SL	OH	0.05
Coweeta 14, N.C.	62	880	21	SL	OH	0.05
Coweeta 21, N.C.	24	990	34	SL	OH	0.06
Bent Ck 7, N.C.	297	940	22	SL	OH	0.06
Coweeta 8, N.C.	760	950	22	SL	MH	0.07
Union 3, S.C.	9	170	7	SC	P	0.08
Coweeta 28, N.C.	146	1,200	33	SL	MH	0.10
Copper Basin 2, Tenn.	36	580	27	SL	OH	0.10
Leading Ridge 1, Pa.	123	370	19	TL	MH	0.11
Dilldown Ck. Pa.	619	580	4	SL	SO	0.12
Fernow 4, W.Va.	39	820	18	TL	MH	0.14
Coweeta 36, N.C.	46	1,300	47	SL	MH	0.15
Burlington Bk. Conn.	1,067	270	3	SS	NH	0.17
Hubbard Brook 4, N.H.	36	600	26	NL	NH	0.18

Source: From Lee, 1980, p. 184; Copyright ©1980 by Columbia University Press. After Hewlett and Hibbert, 1967

[a]SL, sandy loam; SC, sandy clay; TL, silt loam; SS, stony sand; NL, stony loam.

[b]OH, oak hickory; MH, mixed hardwoods; NH, northern hardwoods; SO, scrub oak; P, pine.

Table 4-4. Roughness Coefficients for Manning Equation Used to Determine Streamflow in Natural Streams and Channels

Stream Conditions	*Manning Coefficient, n*
Straightened earth canals	0.02
Winding natural streams with some plant growth	0.035
Mountain streams with rocky streambed	0.040-0.050
Winding natural streams with high plant growth	0.042-0.052
Sluggish streams with high plant growth	0.065
Very sluggish streams with high plant growth	0.112

Source: After Chow, 1964, p. 7-25 and Lee, 1980, p. 192

floodplain elevation, although the probability of flooding is fairly predictable. In the eastern and midwestern United States and in much of Canada, a pattern of winter or spring flooding due to rains and sudden snowmelt is often observed (Fig. 4-5). When the river flow reaches the point at which water begins to spill onto the floodplain, the streamflow is referred to as *bankfull discharge*. A hydrograph of a stream that flooded its riparian wetlands above bankfull discharge is shown in Figure 4-6. Riparian floodplains in many parts of the United States have been shown to have recurrence intervals between 1 and 2 years for bankfull discharge, with an average of approximately 1.5 years (Fig. 4-7) (Leopold, Wolman, and Miller, 1964). The *recurrence interval* is the average interval between the recurrence of floods at a given level or greater flood (Linsley and Franzini, 1979). The inverse of the recurrence interval is the average probability of flooding in any one year. Figure 4-7 indicates that a stream will overflow its banks onto the adjacent riparian forest with a probability of 1/1.5, or 67%; this means that, on the average, these rivers overflow their banks in 2 of 3 years. Figure 4-7 also demonstrates that twice bankfull discharge occurs at recurrence intervals between 5 and 10 years; however, this flow results in only a 30% greater depth over bankfull depth on the floodplain.

Wetlands can be receiving systems for surface water flows (inflows) or surface water streams can originate in wetlands to feed downstream systems (outflows). Surface outflows are found in many wetlands that are in the upstream reaches of a watershed. Often these wetlands are important water flow regulators for downstream rivers. Some wetlands have surface outflows that develop only when their water stages exceed certain levels.

Groundwater

Groundwater can heavily influence some wetlands, while in others it may have hardly any effect at all. Groundwater inflows result when the surface water (or groundwater) level of a wetland is lower than the water table of the

a.

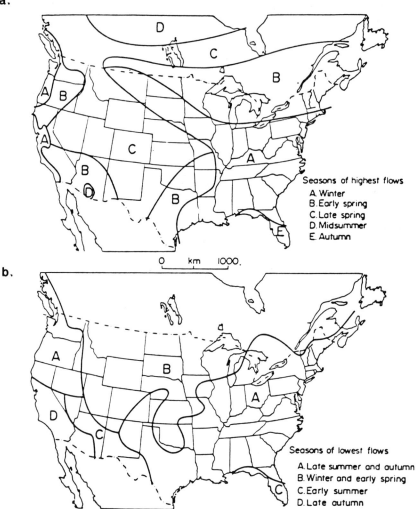

Figure 4-5. Periods of *a.* maximum and *b.* minimum streamflow in North America. *(From Beaumont, 1975, p. 28; Copyright © 1975 by Blackwell, reprinted with permission)*

surrounding land. When the water level in a wetland is higher than the water table of its surroundings, groundwater will flow out of the wetland. Several situations in which wetlands and surrounding groundwater are hydrologically connected are shown in Figure 4-8. A wetland can have both inflows and outflows of groundwater as shown in Figures 4-8*a* and 4-8*b*. One kind of wetland of this type is called a "spring" or "seep" wetland, which receives

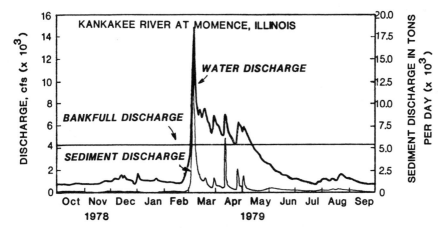

Figure 4-6. River hydrograph from northeastern Illinois, indicating bankfull discharge when riparian wetland is flooded, and sediment load of river. *(After Bhowmik et al., 1980, p. 78)*

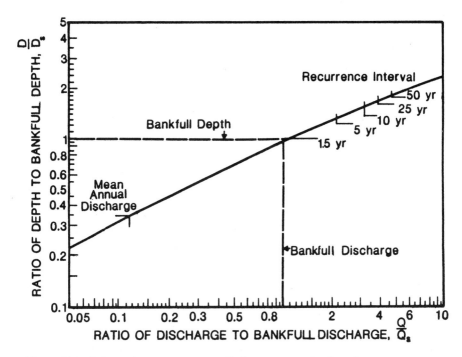

Figure 4-7. Relationships among stream discharge, stream depth, and recurrence interval for streams in midwestern and southern United States. *(After Leopold, Wolman, and Miller, 1964, p. 219)*

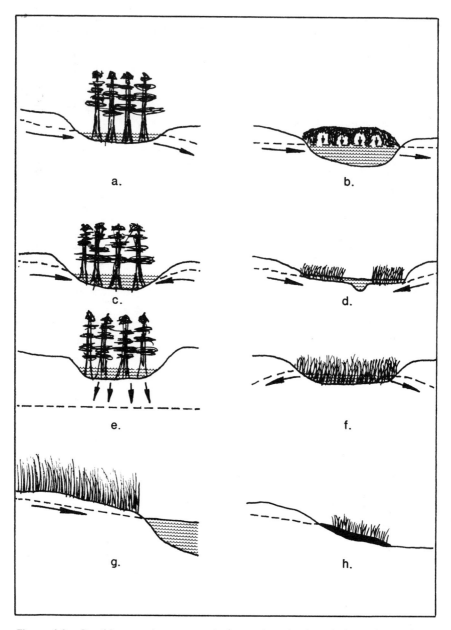

Figure 4-8.   Possible groundwater interchanges with wetlands, including *a.* both inflows and outflows of groundwater through swamp, *b.* underflow of raised bog, *c.* swamp as groundwater depression wetland, *d.* marsh as groundwater depression wetland, *e.* perched swamp or surface water depression wetland, *f.* marsh as groundwater source, *g.* groundwater flow through salt marsh or riparian wetland, and *h.* groundwater seep wetland or groundwater slope wetland. *(Some terminology is after Novitzki, 1979.)*

groundwater discharge and discharges excess water downstream, usually as surface water (Novitzki, 1979). A wetland can intercept the water table in such a way that it has only inflows and no outflows as in Figures 4-8c and 4-8d. When a wetland is well above the groundwater of the area, the wetland is referred to as being *perched* (Figure 4-8e). This type of wetland, referred to as a "surface water depression wetland" by Novitzki (1979), loses water only through infiltration into the ground and through evapotranspiration. Some wetlands can serve as the piezometric "high" for a groundwater system as shown in Figure 4-8f. Other wetlands may be influenced by groundwater that never reaches the surface and simply passes through as shown in Figure 4-8g.

The flow of groundwater into, through, and out of a wetland is often described by an equation familiar to groundwater hydrologists called Darcy's Law. This law states that the flow of groundwater is proportional to (1) the slope of the piezometric surface, or the hydraulic gradient, and (2) the hydraulic conductivity or *permeability*, the capacity of the soil to conduct water flow. In equation form, Darcy's Law is given as:

$$G = k \cdot a \cdot s \qquad \textbf{(4.10)}$$

where G = flow rate of groundwater (volume per unit time), k = hydraulic conductivity or permeability (length per unit time), a = cross-sectional area, and s = hydraulic gradient (slope of water table or piezometric surface). Despite the importance of groundwater flows in the budgets of many wetlands, there is poor understanding of groundwater hydraulics in wetlands, particularly in those with organic soils. Table 4-5 gives some typical values of hydraulic conductivity from wetland studies, while Figure 4-9 shows the normal range of hydraulic conductivity for wetland peat as a function of fiber content. The hydraulic conductivity can be predicted for some peatland soils from their bulk density or fiber content, both of which are more easily measured. In general, the conductivity of organic peat decreases as the fiber content decreases through the process of decomposition. Water can pass through fibric or poorly decomposed peats a thousand times faster than through more decomposed sapric peats (Verry and Boelter, 1979). The type of plant material that makes up the peat is also important. Peat composed of the remains of grasses and sedges such as *Phragmites* and *Carex,* for example, is more permeable than the remains of most mosses, including sphagnum (Ingram, 1983). Rycroft, Williams, and Ingram (1975) properly note that hydraulic conductivity of peat can vary over 9 to 10 orders of magnitude, between 10^{-8} and 10^2 cm/sec. They also note that there has been disagreement over methods for measuring hydraulic conductivity and, indeed, on whether Darcy's Law applies to flow through organic peat.

When groundwater flows into wetlands, it can often be an important source of nutrients and dissolved minerals. This is particularly true in early stages of peatland development and in many coastal marshes. Fresh ground-

**Table 4-5. Typical Hydraulic Conductivity for Wetland Soils Compared
with Other Soil Materials**

Wetland or Soil Type	*Hydraulic Conductivity cm/sec × 10⁻⁵*	*Reference*
Northern Peatlands		
Highly Humified Blanket Bog, U.K.	0.02–0.006	Ingram, 1967
Fen, U.S.S.R.		
slightly decomposed	500	Romanov, 1968
moderately decomposed	80	
highly decomposed	1	
Carex fen, U.S.S.R.		
0–50 cm deep	310	Romanov, 1968
100–150 cm deep	6	
North American Peatlands (general)		
fibric	>150	Verry and
hemic	1.2–150	Boelter, 1979
sapric	<1.2	
Coastal Salt Marsh		
Great Sippewissett Marsh, Mass.		Hemond and
(vertical conductivity)		Fifield, 1982
0–30 cm deep	1.8	
high permeability zone	2,600	
sand-peat transition zone	9.4	
Non-Peat Wetland Soils		
Cypress Dome, Florida		
clay with minor sand	0.02–0.1	Smith, 1975
sand	30	
Okefenokee Swamp		Hyatt and Brook,
Watershed, Georgia	2.8–834	1984
Mineral Soils (general)		
Clay	0.05	Linsley and
Limestone	5.0	Franzini, 1979
Sand	5000	

Source: Partially after Rycroft, Williams, and Ingram, 1975, p. 546–547

water can also influence coastal wetlands by lowering salinity, particularly at the inland edges of the wetland.

Evapotranspiration

The water that vaporizes from water or soil in a wetland (evaporation), together with moisture that passes through vascular plants to the atmosphere (transpiration), is called *evapotranspiration.* The meteorological factors that

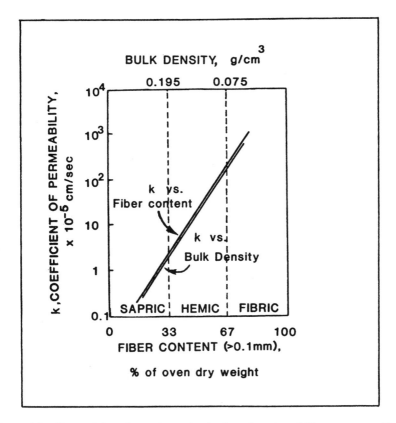

Figure 4-9. Permeability of organic peatland soil as a function of fiber content and bulk density. *(After Verry and Boelter, 1979, p. 393; Copyright © 1979 by the American Water Resources Association, reprinted with permission)*

affect evaporation and transpiration are similar as long as there is adequate moisture, a condition that almost always exists in wetlands. The rate of evapotranspiration is proportional to the difference between the vapor pressure at the water surface (or at the leaf surface) and the vapor pressure in the overlying air. This is described in Dalton's Law:

$$E = C(e_w - e_a) \qquad (4.11)$$

where E = rate of evaporation; C = coefficient, which often includes wind speed; e_w = vapor pressure at surface or saturation vapor pressure at wet surface; and e_a = vapor pressure in surrounding air.

Evaporation and transpiration are enhanced by meteorological conditions that increase the value of the vapor pressure at the evaporation surface, such as solar radiation or surface temperature, or by factors that decrease the vapor pressure of the surrounding air, such as decreased humidity or increased wind speed. This equation assumes an adequate supply of water for capillary movement in the soil or for access by rooted plants. When water supply is limited (not a frequent occurrence in wetlands), evapotranspiration is limited as well. Evapotranspiration can also be physiologically limited by certain plants through the closing of leaf stomata despite adequate moisture (Lee, 1980).

Evapotranspiration can be determined with any number of empirical equations that use easily measured meteorological variables, or by various direct measures. Several of these relationships are described by Chow (1964). One of the most frequently used empirical equations for evapotranspiration from terrestrial ecosystems, which has been applied with some success to wetlands, is the Thornthwaite equation for potential evapotranspiration (Chow, 1964):

$$ET_i = 16(10T_i/I)^a \qquad (4.12)$$

where

$$ET_i = \text{potential evapotranspiration for month } i, \text{ mm/mo}$$
$$T_i = \text{mean monthly temperature, } °C$$
$$I = \text{local heat index} = \sum_{i=1}^{12} (T_i/5)^{1.514}$$
$$a = (0.675 \times I^3 - 77.1 \times I^2 + 17{,}920 \times I + 492{,}390) \times 10^{-6}$$

This equation was used to determine evapotranspiration from the Okefenokee Swamp in Georgia by Rykiel (1977). For a 26-year period examined in that study, average evapotranspiration ranged from 21 mm/mo in December to 179 mm/mo in July.

Another empirical relationship for describing summer evapotranspiration was developed by Scheffe (1978) and was described by Hammer and Kadlec (1983). The equation, which was used individually for sedge, willow, leatherleaf, and cattail vegetation covers, is:

$$ET = \alpha + \beta B + \delta C + \gamma D + \lambda E \qquad (4.13)$$

where α, β, δ, γ, λ = correlation coefficients; B = incident radiation (measured by pyranograph); C = air temperature; D = relative humidity; and E = wind speed.

The equation gave estimates that are better than some more frequently used evapotranspiration relationships, although when the results of using this model were compared to actual measurements, the radiation term was shown to dominate (Hammer and Kadlec, 1983).

Because of the many meteorological and biological factors that affect evapotranspiration, none of the many empirical relationships, including the Thornthwaite and Hammer and Kadlec equations, is entirely satisfactory for estimating wetland evapotranspiration. Lee (1980, p. 180) cautions that there is "no reliable method of estimating evapotranspiration rates based on simple weather-element data or potential evapotranspiration." Nevertheless, these equations of potential evapotranspiration offer the most cost effective first approximations for estimating water loss. Furthermore they may be more reliable when applied to wetlands that are only rarely devoid of an adequate water supply than to upland terrain where evapotranspiration can be limited by a lack of soil water.

Several direct measurement techniques can be used in wetlands to determine evapotranspiration. Evapotranspiration from wetlands has been calculated from measurements of the increase in water vapor in air flowing through vegetation chambers (Brown, 1981), and from observing the diurnal cycles of groundwater or surface water in wetlands (Mitsch, Dorge, and Weimhoff, 1977; Heimburg, 1984). This latter method, described in Figure 4-10, can be calculated as follows:

$$ET = S_y (24 h \pm s) \qquad (4.14)$$

where

ET = evapotranspiration, mm/day
S_y = specific yield of aquifer (unitless)
= 1.0 for standing water wetlands
< 1.0 for groundwater wetlands
h = hourly rise in water level from midnight to 4 AM, mm/hr
s = net fall (+) or rise (−) of water table or water surface in one day

The pattern assumes active "pumping" of water by vegetation during the day and a constant rate of recharge equal to the midnight to 4 AM rate. This method also assumes that evapotranspiration is negligible around midnight and that the water table around this time approximates the daily mean. The water level is usually at or near the root zone in many wetlands, a necessary condition for this method to accurately measure evapotranspiration (Todd, 1964).

A question about evapotranspiration from wetlands that does not have a uniform answer in the literature is, "Does the presence of wetland vegetation increase or decrease the loss of water over that which would occur from an open body of water?" Data from individual studies conflict. Eggelsmann (1963) found evaporation from bogs in Germany to be generally less than that from open water except during wet summer months. In studies of evapotranspiration from small bogs in northern Minnesota, Bay (1967) found it to be 88% to 121% of open water evaporation. Eisenlohr (1966) found 10% lower evapotranspiration from vegetated prairie potholes than from non-vegetated potholes in North Dakota. Hall, Rutherford, and Byers (1972) estimated through a series of measurements and calculations that a stand of

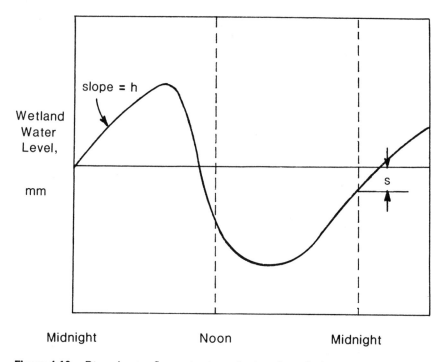

Figure 4-10. Diurnal water fluctuation in wetland used to calculate evapotranspiration with Equation 4.14. *(After Todd, 1964, p. 13–36)*

vegetation in a small New Hampshire wetland lost 80% more water than did the open water in the wetland. In a forested pond cypress dome in north-central Florida, Heimburg (1984) found that swamp evapotranspiration was about 80% of pan evaporation during the dry season (spring and fall) and as low as 60% of pan evaporation during the wet season (summer). Brown (1981) found that transpiration losses from pond cypress wetlands were lower than evaporation from an open water surface even with adequate standing water. The conflicting measurements and the difficulty of measuring evaporation and evapotranspiration led Linacre (1976) to conclude that neither the presence of wetland vegetation nor the type of vegetation had major influences on evaporation rates, at least during the active growing season. This is probably a reasonable conclusion for most wetlands, although it is clear that the type of wetland ecosystem and the season are important considerations. Ingram (1983), for example, found that fens have about 40% more evapotranspiration than do treeless bogs, and that evaporation from the bogs is less than potential evapotranspiration in the summer and greater than potential evapotranspiration in the winter. Furthermore, H. T. Odum (1984, p. 431) concluded that the draining of Florida cypress swamps and their "replacement with either open water or other kinds of vegetation may decrease available water, increasing frequency of drought, raising microclimate temperatures in summer, and reducing productivity of natural and agricultural ecosystems."

Tides

The periodic and predictable tidal inundation of coastal salt marshes, mangroves, and freshwater tidal marshes is a major hydrologic feature of these wetlands. The tide acts as a stress by causing submergence, saline soils, and soil anaerobiosis; it acts as a subsidy by removing excess salts, reestablishing aerobic conditions, and providing nutrients. Tides also shift and alter the sediment patterns in coastal wetlands, causing a uniform surface to develop.

Typical tidal patterns for several coastal areas in the Atlantic and Gulf coasts of the United States are shown in Figure 4-11a. Seasonal as well as diurnal patterns exist in the tidal rhythms. Annual variations of mean monthly sea level are as great as 25 cm (Fig. 4-11b). Tides also have significant bimonthly patterns because they are generated by the gravitational pull of the moon and, to a lesser extent, the sun. When the sun and moon are in line and pull together, which occurs almost every two weeks, spring tides, or tides of the greatest amplitude, develop. When the sun and the moon are at right angles, neap tides, or tides of least amplitude, occur. Spring tides occur roughly at full and new moons, while neap tides occur during the first and third quarters.

Tides vary more locally than regionally, with the primary determinant being the coastline configuration. In North America, tidal amplitudes vary from less than 1 meter in the Texas Gulf Coast to several meters in the Bay of Fundy in Nova Scotia. Tidal amplitude can actually increase as one progresses inland in some funnel-shaped estuaries (W. E. Odum et al., 1984).

Typically on a rising tide, water flows up tidal creek channels until the channels are bank-full. It overflows first at the upstream end, where tidal creeks break up into small creeklets that lack natural levees. The overflowing water spreads back downstream over the marsh surface. On falling tides, the flows are reversed. At low tides, water continues to drain through the natural levee sediments into adjacent creeks because these sediments tend to be relatively coarse; in the marsh interior where sediments are finer, drainage is poor and water is often impounded in small depressions in the marsh.

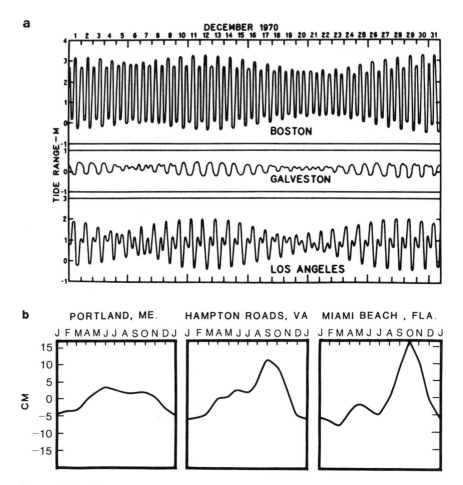

Figure 4-11. Daily pattern of tides *(a)* and *(b)* seasonal changes in mean monthly sea level for several locations in North America. *(After Emery and Uchupi, 1972)*

SPECIFIC EFFECTS OF HYDROLOGY ON WETLANDS

The effects of hydrology on wetland structure and function can be described with a complicated series of cause and effect relationships. A conceptual model that shows the general effects of hydrology in wetland ecosystems was shown in Figure 4-1. The effects are shown to be primarily on the chemical and physical aspects of the wetlands, which, in turn, affect the biotic components of the ecosystem. The biotic components, in turn, have a feedback effect on hydrology as discussed earlier. Several principles of the importance of hydrology in wetlands can be elucidated from the studies that have been conducted to date. These principles, discussed below, are as follows:

1. Hydrology leads to a unique vegetation composition but can limit or enhance species richness.
2. Primary productivity in wetlands is enhanced by flowing conditions and a pulsing hydroperiod and is often depressed by stagnant conditions.
3. Organic accumulation in wetlands is controlled by hydrology through its influence on primary productivity, decomposition, and export of particulate organic matter.
4. Nutrient cycling and nutrient availability are both significantly influenced by the hydrologic conditions.

Species Composition and Richness

Hydrology is a two-edged sword for species composition and diversity in wetlands. It acts as both a limit and a stimulus to species richness, depending on the hydroperiod and physical energies. At a minimum, the hydrology selects for water-tolerant vegetation in both freshwater and saltwater conditions. Of the thousands of vascular plants that are on the earth, only a relative few have adapted to waterlogged soils. (These adaptations are discussed in more detail in Chapter 6.) While it is difficult to generalize, many wetlands with long flooding durations have lower species richness in vegetation than do less frequently flooded areas. Waterlogged soils and the subsequent changes in oxygen content and other chemical conditions significantly limit the number and types of rooted plants that can survive in this environment. McKnight et al. (1981, p. 33), in describing the effects of water on species composition in a riparian wetland, stated that "In general, as one goes from the hydric [wet] to the more mesic [dry] bottomland sites, the possible combinations or mixtures of species increases." Bedinger (1979), in reviewing the literature of flooding effects on tree species, attributes the effects to the following factors:

1. Different species have different physiological responses to flooding.
2. Large trees show greater tolerance to flooding than do seedlings.
3. Plant establishment depends on the tolerance of the seeds to flooding.
4. Plant succession depends on the geomorphic evolution of the floodplain, such as by sediment deposition or stream downcutting.

Heinselman (1970) found a change in vegetation richness for seven different hydrologically defined conditions of northern peatlands. He noted an increase in diversity, as measured by the number of species, as the flowthrough conditions increased (Table 4-6). In this case, the flowing water can

Table 4-6. The Relationship Between the Hydrologic Regime and Species Richness in Northern Minnesota Peatlands

			Species Present				
	Tree	Shrub	Field herbs	Grasses and ferns	Ground layer	Total	Flow Conditions
1. Rich swamp forest	6	16	28	11	10	71	Good surface flow; minerotrophic
2. Poor swamp forest	3	14	17	12	5	51	Downstream from 1; not adapted to strong water flow
3. Cedar string bog and fen	3	10	10	12	4	39	Better drainage than 2
4. Larch string bog and fen	3	9	9	12	4	37	Similar to 3; sheet flow
5. Black spruce feather moss forest	2	9	2	2	10	25	Gentle water flow on semiconvex template
6. Sphagnum bog	2	8	2	1	7	20	Isolated; little standing water
7. Sphagnum heath	2	6	2	2	5	17	Wet, soggy, and on convex template

Source: From Gosselink and Turner, 1978, p. 67, after Heinselman, 1970 © Academic Press, reprinted with permission.

be thought of as a stimulus to diversity, probably due to its ability to renew minerals and reduce anaerobic conditions.

Hydrology also stimulates diversity when the action of water and transported sediments creates spatial heterogeneity, opening up additional ecological niches (Gosselink and Turner, 1978). When rivers flood riparian wetlands or when tides rise and fall on coastal marshes, erosion, scouring, and sediment deposition sometimes create niches that allow diverse habitats to develop. On the other hand, flowing water can also create a very uniform surface that might cause monospecific stands of *Typha* or *Phragmites* to dominate a freshwater marsh or *Spartina* to dominate a coastal marsh.

Primary Productivity

In general, the "openness" of a wetland to hydrological fluxes is probably one of the most important determinants of potential primary productivity. A number of studies have found that wetlands in stagnant (nonflowing) or continuously deep water have low productivities, while wetlands that are in slowly flowing strands or are open to flooding rivers have high productivities. Brinson, Lugo, and Brown (1981) summarized the results of many of these studies by describing net biomass production of forested freshwater wetlands in order of greatest to least productivity:

flowing water swamps > sluggish flow swamps > stillwater swamps

The relationship between hydrology and ecosystem primary productivity has been investigated by several wetland scientists (e.g., Conner and Day, 1976; Mitsch and Ewel, 1979; Brown, 1981). A general relationship was developed by Mitsch and Ewel (1979, p. 425) for cypress productivity as a function of hydrology in Florida. That study concluded:

Cypress-hardwood associations, found primarily in riverine and flowing strand systems, have the most productive cypress trees. The short hydroperiod favors both root aeration during the long dry periods and elimination of water-intolerant species during the short wet periods. The continual supply of nutrients with the flooding river system conditions may be a second important factor in maintaining these high productivities.

Productivity was found to be low under continually flooded conditions and under drained conditions. Brown (1981) found that much of the variation in biomass productivity of cypress wetlands in Florida could be explained by the variation in nutrient inflow, as measured by phosphorus. Here, productivity is lowest when nutrients are brought into the system solely by precipitation and is highest when large amounts of nutrients are passed through the wetlands by flooding rivers. Brown suggests that, rather than there being a simple relationship between wetland productivity and hydrology, there is a more complex relationship among hydrology, nutrient inputs, and wetland productivity, decomposition, export, and nutrient cycling. Hydrology, then, also influences wetland productivity by being the main pathway by which nutrients are transported to many wetlands.

Saltwater tidal wetlands that are subject to frequent tidal action are generally more productive than those that are only occasionally inundated. This is partially due to the high salinity that develops in the soils of poorly flushed coastal wetlands. Whigham et al. (1978) suggest that freshwater tidal wetlands may be even more productive than saline tidal wetlands because they receive the energy and nutrient subsidy of tidal flushing while avoiding the stress of saline soils. In peatlands, wetlands with flow-through conditions (fens) have long been known to be more productive than stagnant raised bogs (Moore and Bellamy, 1974).

Despite the evidence of the influence of hydrology on wetlands, some investigators have cautioned against always ascribing a direct linkage between hydrology and wetland productivity. Richardson (1979, p. 141) states that "a definitive statement about the influence of water levels on NPP [net primary productivity] for all wetland types is impossible, since responses of individual species to water fluctuations vary." However, water level fluctuations are not necessarily related to the volume of flow-through of water and the associated nutrients and allochthonous energy. Furthermore although individual species vary in their response to water levels and hydrology, ecosystem-level responses may be more consistent.

Organic Accumulation and Export

Wetlands can accumulate excess organic matter either as a result of increased primary productivity (as described above) or decreased decomposition and export. The effects of hydrology on decomposition pathways are even less clear than the effects on primary productivity discussed above. Brinson, Lugo, and Brown (1981) concluded that it cannot be assumed that increased frequency or duration of flooding will necessarily increase or decrease decomposition rates. They suggested, however, that alternating wet and dry conditions may lead to optimum litter decomposition rates, while completely anaerobic conditions due to constant flooding are the least favorable conditions for decomposition.

Litter decomposition rates have been measured in several wetlands, with the results not consistently supporting this view. Brinson (1977), in a study of an alluvial tupelo swamp in North Carolina, found that decomposition of litter was most rapid in the river, slower on the wet swamp floor, and slowest on a dry levee. W. E. Odum and Heywood (1978) found that leaves of freshwater tidal marsh plants decomposed more rapidly when permanently submerged than when periodically or irregularly flooded. They suggest that this may be due to (1) better access to detritivores in the water, (2) a more constant physical environment for decomposer bacteria and fungi, (3) a greater availability of dissolved nutrients, and (4) a more suitable environment for leaching. Chamie and Richardson (1978, p. 117), on the other hand, state that "periodic or even constant flooding of a soil's surface, characteristic of wetlands, leads to an overall decrease in the activity of soil fauna" and causes slow anaerobic decomposition to dominate. Deghi, Ewel, and Mitsch (1980), in a study of decomposition in cypress wetlands in Florida, found that decomposition of cypress needles occurred more rapidly in wet areas than in dry ones but that there was no difference in decomposition between deep and shallow sites.

The importance of hydrology to organic export is obvious. A generally higher rate of export is to be expected from wetlands that are open to flow-through of water. Riparian wetlands often contribute large amounts of organic detritus to streams, including macrodetritus such as whole trees. Salt marshes and mangrove swamps have been shown to export a high percentage of their production (for example, 45% measured by Teal (1962) for a salt marsh; 28% measured by Heald [1969] for a mangrove swamp), although the generality of the concept of salt marshes as organic exporters is no longer accepted by coastal ecologists (Nixon, 1980; see chap. 5). Hydrologically isolated wetlands, such as northern peatlands, have much lower organic export. For example, Bazilevich and Tishkov (1982) found that only 6% of the net productivity of a fen in the USSR was exported by surface and subsurface flows.

Nutrient Cycling

Nutrients are carried into wetlands by hydrologic inputs of precipitation, river flooding, tides, and surface and groundwater inflows. Outflows of nutrients are controlled primarily by the outflow of waters. These hydrologic/nutrient flows are also important determinants of wetland productivity and decomposition (see previous sections). Intrasystem nutrient cycling is generally, in turn, tied to pathways such as primary productivity and decomposition. When productivity and decomposition rates are high, as in flowing water or pulsing hydroperiod wetlands, nutrient cycling is rapid. When productivity and decomposition processes are slow, as in isolated ombrotrophic bogs, nutrient cycling is also slow.

The hydroperiod of a wetland has a significant effect on nutrient transformations and on the availability of nutrients to vegetation (see chap. 5). Nitrogen availability is affected in wetlands by the reduced conditions that result from waterlogged soil. Typically, a narrow oxidized surface layer develops over the anaerobic zone in wetland soils, causing a combination of reactions in the nitrogen cycle—nitrification and denitrification—that may result in substantial losses of nitrogen to the atmosphere. Ammonium nitrogen often accumulates in wetland soils, since the anaerobic environment favors the reduced ionic form over the nitrate commonly present in agricultural soils.

The flooding of wetland soils, by altering both the pH and the redox potential of the soil, influences the availability of other nutrients as well. The pH of both acid and alkaline soils tends to converge on a pH of 7 when they are flooded. The redox potential, a measure of the intensity of oxidation or reduction of a chemical or biological system, indicates the state of oxidation (and hence availability) of several nutrients. Phosphorus is known to be more soluble under anaerobic conditions. Several studies have documented higher concentrations of soluble phosphorus in poorly drained soils than in oxidized conditions (e.g., Redman and Patrick, 1965; Patrick and Khalid 1974). This is partially due to the hydrolysis and reduction of ferric and aluminum phosphates to more soluble compounds. The availability of major ions such as potassium and magnesium and several trace nutrients such as iron, manganese, and sulfur is also affected by hydrologic conditions in the wetlands (Gambrell and Patrick, 1978; Mohanty and Dash, 1982). Chemical transformations in wetlands are discussed in more detail in the next chapter.

WETLAND HYDROLOGY STUDIES

Past Studies of Wetland Hydrology

The importance of hydrology in wetland function contrasts markedly with the paucity of published research on the subject. Most wetland investigations that deal with hydrology have explored the relationships between hydrologic variables (usually water depth) and wetland productivity (e.g., Conner and Day, 1976; Mitsch and Ewel, 1979) or species composition (e.g. McKnight et al. 1981; Huffman and Forsythe, 1981). While there have been several review papers on the hydrology of wetlands (e.g. Linacre, 1976; Gosselink and Turner, 1978; Carter et al., 1979; Dedinger, 1981; Ingram, 1983), few comprehensive studies have described in detail the hydrologic characteristics within specific wetland types. An exception to this has been the study of northern peatlands, for which a wealth of literature exists, including work in the USSR (e.g., Romanov, 1968; Ivanov, 1981), in the British Isles (Ingram, Rycroft, and Williams, 1974; Gilman, 1982) and in North America (e.g., Bay, 1967, 1969; Boelter and Verry, 1977; Verry and Boelter, 1979). Some of the more notable hydrology studies for other types of wetlands in the United States have been for salt marshes (Hemond and Burke, 1981; Hemond and Fifield, 1982), cypress swamps (Smith, 1975; Heimburg, 1984), and large-scale wetland complexes (Rykiel, 1977, 1984; Hyatt and Brook, 1984).

Despite these promising beginnings, there are several needs and short-comings in wetland hydrology studies. Some of these were listed by Carter et al. (1979, p. 364) who described five research needs in the general area of wetland hydrology:

1) the need for improving, refining, and perhaps simplifying existing techniques for hydrologic measurements;

2) the need for making accurate measurements of all the hydrologic inputs and outputs to representative wetland types and estimating the errors inherent in various measurement techniques;

3) the need to improve our basic understanding of and to quantify the soil-water-vegetation relationships of wetlands;

4) the need to make in-depth, long-term studies of different wetland types under different environmental conditions; and

5) the need to continue developing models based on hydrologic data so that we have better analysis and predictive capability.

Wetland researchers and managers should recognize the importance of hydrologic studies and research to augment the more frequently studied biological components of wetlands. These two aspects are closely related.

Measurement of Wetland Hydrology

It is curious that so little attention has been paid to hydrologic measurements in wetland studies, despite the importance of hydrology in ecosystem function. A great deal of information can be obtained with only a modest investment in supplies and equipment. A diagram summarizing many of the hydrology measurements typical for developing a wetland's water budget is given in Figure 4-12. Water levels can be recorded continuously with a water level recorder or during site visits with a staff gauge. With records of water level, all of the following hydrologic parameters can be determined: hydro-period, frequency of flooding, duration of flooding, and water depth (Gosselink and Turner, 1978). Water level recorders can also be used to determine the change in storage in a water budget as in Equation 4.1.

Evapotranspiration measurements are more difficult to obtain, but there are several empirical relationships, such as the Thornthwaite equation, that can use meteorological variables (Chow, 1964). Evaporation pans can also be used to estimate total evapotranspiration from wetlands, although pan coefficients are highly variable (Linsley and Franzini, 1979). Evapotranspiration of continuously flooded wetlands can also be determined by monitoring the diurnal water level fluctuation as described in Figure 4-10.

Precipitation and/or throughfall can be measured by placing a statistical-

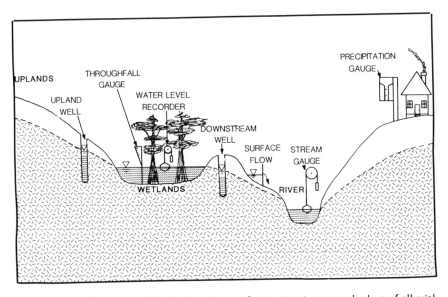

Figure 4-12. Placement of typical equipment for monitoring water budget of alluvial forested wetland.

ly adequate number of rain gauges in random locations throughout the wetland or by utilizing existing meteorology station data. Surface runoff to wetlands can usually be determined as the increase in water level in the wetland during and immediately following a storm after throughfall and stemflow are subtracted. Weirs can be constructed on more permanent streams to monitor surface water inputs and outputs.

Groundwater flows are usually the most difficult hydrologic flows to measure accurately. In some cases, a few shallow wells placed around a wetland will help indicate the direction of groundwater flow. Estimates of permeability are required to quantify the flows. In other cases, groundwater input or loss can be determined as the residual of the water budget, although this method has limited accuracy (Carter et al., 1979).

Hydrology and Wetland Classification

Hydrologic conditions are so important in defining wetlands that they are often used by scientists to classify these ecosystems. It is no coincidence that classification and mapping of wetlands based on biotic features (dominant vegetation) often matches the hydrologic conditions of the different wetlands very well. For example, peatlands have been classified according to whether they have water flow from surrounding mineral soils or if they are in flow-isolated basins. Salt marshes and salt marsh vegetation are defined and subdivided according to the frequency and depth of tidal inundation. Bottomland forests are zoned according to flooding frequency, and certain deep swamps are classified according to stillness or movement of water. Some of the classifications for particular wetland types are described in Chapters 8-14. Overall wetland classifications, which are based in whole or in part on hydrologic conditions, are described in Chapter 17.

SUMMARY

Hydrologic conditions are extremely important for the maintenance of a wetland's structure and function, although simple cause and effect relationships are difficult to establish. Hydrologic conditions affect many abiotic factors, including salinity, soil anaerobiosis, and nutrient availability. These in turn determine the flora and fauna that develops in a wetland. Finally, completing the cycle, biotic components are active in altering the wetland hydrology.

The hydroperiod, or hydrologic signature of a wetland, is the result of the balance between inflows and outflows of water (called the water budget), the soil contours in the wetland, and the subsurface conditions. Major hydrologic inflows include precipitation, flooding rivers, surface flows, groundwater, and, in coastal wetlands, tides. Simple hydrologic measurements, a water budget approach, and concepts such as turnover time in wetland studies can contribute to a better understanding of specific wetlands.

Hydrology affects the species composition and richness, primary productivity, organic accumulation, and nutrient cycling in wetlands. Generally, productivity is highest in wetlands that have highest flow-through of water and nutrients or in wetlands with pulsing hydroperiods. Decomposition in wetlands is slower in anaerobic standing water than it is under dry conditions, although research results on the general effects of hydrology on this pathway have been inconclusive. Nutrient cycling is enhanced by hydrology-mediated inputs, and nutrient availability is often increased by reduced conditions in wetland substrates.

5

BIOGEOCHEMISTRY
OF WETLANDS

The transport and transformation of chemicals in ecosystems, known as *biogeochemical cycling,* involve a great number of interrelated physical, chemical, and biological processes. The unique and diverse hydrologic conditions in wetlands (discussed in the previous chapter) markedly influence biogeochemical processes. These processes result not only in changes in the chemical forms of materials, but also in the spatial movement of materials within wetlands, as in water-sediment exchange and plant uptake (Atlas and Bartha, 1981), and with the surrounding ecosystems, as in organic exports. These processes, in turn, determine the overall wetland productivity. The interrelationships among hydrology, biogeochemistry, and response of wetland biota were summarized in Figure 4-1.

The biogeochemistry of wetlands can be divided into (1) intrasystem cycling through various *transformation processes* and (2) the *exchange* of chemicals between a wetland and its surroundings. While few transformation processes are unique to wetlands, the standing water or intermittent flooding of these ecosystems causes certain processes to be more dominant in wetlands than in either upland or deep aquatic ecosystems. For example, while *anaerobic* or oxygenless conditions are sometimes found in other ecosystems, they prevail in wetlands. The soils in wetlands are characterized by waterlogged conditions at least during floods. The reduced conditions then have a marked influence on several biochemical transformations unique to anaerobic conditions.

This intrasystem cycling, along with the hydrologic conditions, influences the degree to which chemicals are transported to or from wetlands. An ecosystem is considered biogeochemically open when there is abundant exchange of materials with its surroundings. When there is little movement of materials across the ecosystem boundary, it is biogeochemically closed. Wetlands can be in either category. Wetlands such as bottomland forests and tidal salt marshes have significant exchange of minerals with their surroundings through river flooding and tidal exchange, respectively. Other wetlands, such as ombrotrophic bogs and cypress domes, have little material, save for gaseous matter, which passes into or out of the ecosystem. These latter systems depend more on intrasystem cycling than on throughput for their chemical supplies.

WETLAND SOILS

Types and Definitions

Wetland soil is both the medium in which many of the wetland chemical transformations take place and the primary storage of available chemicals for most wetland plants. It is often described as a *hydric soil*, defined by the U.S. Soil Conservation Service (1985, p. 1) as "a soil that in its undrained condition is saturated, flooded, or ponded long enough during the growing season to develop anaerobic conditions that favor the growth and regeneration of hydrophytic vegetation." Wetland soil can be generally classified into two types: (1) mineral soil or (2) organic, or peat soil (also called *histosol*). Nearly all soils have some organic material; but when a soil has less than 20% to 35% organic matter (on a dry weight basis), it is considered a mineral soil. More specifically, the U. S. Soil Conservation Service, as summarized in Cowardin et al. (1979, p. 44), has defined organic soils and organic soil materials under either of two conditions of saturation:

1. Are saturated with water for long periods or are artificially drained and, excluding live roots, (a) have 18 percent or more organic carbon if the mineral fraction is 60 percent or more clay, (b) have 12 percent or more organic carbon if the mineral fraction has no clay, or (c) have a proportional content of organic carbon between 12 and 18 percent if the clay content of the mineral fraction is between zero and 60 percent; or

2. Are never saturated with water for more than a few days and have 20 percent or more organic carbon.

Although the above definition of organic soil (peat) is applicable to many types of wetlands, particularly to northern peatlands (see chap. 12), peat is not usually that strictly defined. Clymo (1983), for example, reports that

most peats contain less than 20% unburnable inorganic matter (and therefore usually contain more than 40% organic carbon), but that some soil
scientists allow up to 35% unburnable in organic matter, and commercial
operations sometimes allow 55%. Any soil material not defined by the above
is considered mineral soil material. Where mineral soils occur in wetlands,
such as in some freshwater marshes or riparian forests, they generally have a
soil profile made up of horizons, or layers (Etherington, 1983). The upper
layer of wetland mineral soils is often organic peat, composed of partially
decayed plant materials.

Organic soils are different from mineral soils in several physiochemical
features (Table 5-1; Richardson et al., 1978):

1. Organic soils have lower bulk densities and higher water holding
   capacities than do mineral soils. Bulk density, defined as the dry
   weight of soil material per unit volume, is generally 0.2 to 0.3 g/cm^3
   when the organic soil is well decomposed (Brady, 1974), although
   sphagnum moss peatland soils have bulk densities as low as 0.02 to
   0.04 g/cm^3. By contrast, mineral soils generally range between 1.0
   and 2.0 g/cm^3. Bulk density is low in organic soils because of their
   high porosity, or percentage of pore spaces. Peat soils generally have
   at least 80% pore spaces, and are thus 80% water, by volume, when
   flooded (Verry and Boelter, 1979). Mineral soils generally range
   from 45% to 55% total pore space, regardless of the amount of clay
   or texture (Patrick, 1981).
2. Mineral soils, except for clays, usually have greater hydraulic conductivity than do organic soils, although organic soils were shown in
   Chapter 4 to have a wide range of possible hydraulic conductivities.
   Thus, while organic soils may hold more water, water is often better
   able to pass through mineral soils given the same hydraulic conditions.
3. Organic soils generally have more minerals tied up in organic forms
   unavailable to plants than do mineral soils. This follows from the fact
   that a greater percent of the soil material is organic. This does not
   mean, however, that there are more total nutrients in organic soils; very
   often the opposite is true in wetland soils.
4. Organic soils have a greater cation exchange capacity, defined as the
   sum of exchangeable cations (positive ions) that a soil can hold. Figure
   5-1 summarizes the general relationship between organic content and
   cation exchange capacity of soils. Mineral soils have a cation exchange
   capacity that is dominated by the major cations (Ca^{++}, Mg^{++}, K^+, and
   Na^+). As organic content increases, both the percentage and amount of
   exchangeable hydrogen ions increases (Gorham, 1967). For sphagnum
   moss peat, the high cation capacity is due to long-chain polymers of
   uronic acid (Clymo, 1983).

Table 5-1. Comparison of Mineral and Organic Soils in Wetlands

	Mineral Soil	Organic Soil
Organic Content, percent	Less than 20 to 35	Greater than 20 to 35
pH	Usually circumneutral	Acid
Bulk Density	High	Low
Porosity	Low (45-55%)	High (80%)
Hydraulic Conductivity	High (except for clays)	Low to high
Water Holding Capacity	Low	High
Nutrient Availability	Generally high	Often low
Cation Exchange Capacity	Low, dominated by major cations	High, dominated by hydrogen ion
Typical Wetland	Riparian forest, some marshes	Northern peatland

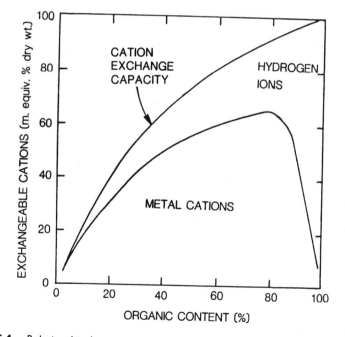

Figure 5-1. Relationship between cation exchange capacity and organic content for wetland soils. Note that at low organic content (mineral soils), the cation exchange capacity is saturated by metal cations; when organic content is high, the exchange capacity is dominated by hydrogen ions. *(After Gorham, 1967, p. 31)*

Organic Soil Origin and Decomposition

Peat is composed primarily of the remains of plants in various stages of decomposition. Two of the more important characteristics of organic peat are the botanical composition of the peat and the degree to which the peat is decomposed (Clymo, 1983). Several of the properties of peat that have been discussed, including bulk density, cation exchange capacity, hydraulic conductivity, and porosity, are often dependent on these more easily measured characteristics. Therefore, it is often possible to predict the range of the physical properties of an organic soil if the origin and state of decomposition of the peat is observed in the field or laboratory.

The botanical origin of the organic material can be from (1) mosses, (2) herbaceous material, and (3) wood and leaf litter. For most northern peatlands, the moss is usually *Sphagnum* although several other moss species can dominate if the peatland is receiving inflows of mineral water. Organic peat can originate from herbaceous materials from grasses such as reed grass *(Phragmites)*, wild rice *(Zizania)*, and salt marsh cord grass *(Spartina)*, or from sedges such as *Carex* and *Cladium*. Organic peat can also be produced in freshwater marshes by a number of non-grass and non-sedge plants, including cattails *(Typha)* and water lilies *(Nymphaea)*. In forested wetlands, the peat can be a result of woody detritus and/or leaf material. In northern peatlands, the material can originate from birch *(Betula)*, pine *(Pinus)*, or tamarack *(Larix)*, while in southern deepwater swamps, the organic horizon can be composed of material from cypress *(Taxodium)* or water tupelo *(Nyssa)* trees.

The state of decomposition, or humification, of wetland soils is the second key character of organic peat (Clymo, 1983). As decomposition proceeds, albeit at a very slow rate in flooded conditions, the original plant structure is changed physically and chemically until the resulting material little resembles the parent material. As peat decomposes, bulk density increases, hydraulic conductivity decreases, and the amount of larger fiber (>1.5 mm) particles decreases as the material becomes increasingly fragmented. Chemically, the amount of peat "wax," or material soluble in nonpolar solvents, and lignin increase with decomposition while cellulose compounds and plant pigments decrease (Clymo, 1983). When some wetland plants, such as salt marsh grasses, die, the detritus rapidly loses a large percentage of its organic compounds through leaching (Turner, 1978; Teal, 1984). These readily soluble organic compounds are thought to be easily metabolized in adjacent aquatic systems (Gosselink, 1984). Details of the decomposition processes in particular wetland types are given in Chapters 8 through 14.

CHEMICAL TRANSFORMATIONS IN
WETLAND SOILS

Oxygen and Redox Potential

When soils, whether mineral or organic, are inundated with water, anaerobic conditions usually result. When water fills the pore spaces, the rate at which oxygen can diffuse through the soil is drastically reduced. Diffusion of oxygen in an aqueous solution has been estimated at 10,000 times slower than oxygen diffusion through a porous medium such as drained soil (Greenwood, 1961; Gambrell and Patrick, 1978). This low diffusion leads relatively quickly to anaerobic, or reduced, conditions, with the time required for oxygen depletion on the order of several hours to a few days after inundation begins (Fig. 5-2). The rate at which the oxygen is depleted depends on the ambient temperature, the availability of organic substrates for microbial respiration, and sometimes on chemical oxygen demand from reductants such as ferrous iron (Gambrell and Patrick, 1978). The resulting lack of oxygen prevents plants from carrying out normal aerobic root respiration and also strongly affects the availability of plant nutrients and toxic materials in the soil. As a

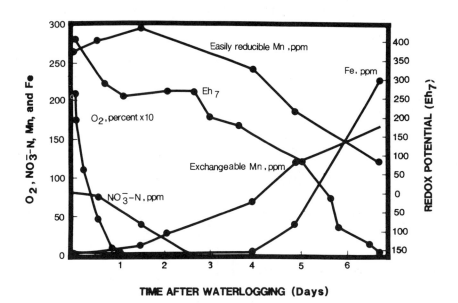

Figure 5-2. Transformation in soil oxygen and redox potential after flooding. *(From Turner and Patrick, 1968, p. 57)*

result, plants that grow in anaerobic soils generally have a number of specific adaptations to this environment (see Chapter 6).

It is not always true that oxygen it totally depleted from the soil water of wetlands. There is usually a thin layer of oxidized soil, sometimes only a few millimeters thick, at the surface of the soil at the soil-water interface (Fig. 5-3). Gambrell and Patrick (1978, p. 377) describe this layer of oxygen to be a result of:

1. the rapid rate of oxygen transport across the atmosphere-surface water interface,

2. the small population of oxygen-consuming organisms present,

3. photosynthetic oxygen production by algae within the water column, and

4. surface mixing by convection currents and wind action.

While the deeper layers of the wetland soils remain reduced, this thin layer having aerobic conditions is often very important in the chemical transformations and nutrient cycling that occur in wetlands. Oxidized ions such as FE^{+++}, Mn^{+4}, NO_3^-, and $SO_4^=$ are found in this microlayer, with the lower anaerobic soils dominated by the reduced forms such as ferrous and manganous salts, ammonia, and sulfides (Mohanty and Dash, 1982). Because of the presence of oxidized ferric iron (Fe^{+++}) in the oxidized layer, the soil often has a brown or brownish-red color. The reduced sediments, dominated by ferrous iron (Fe^{++}), are often bluish-grey to greenish-grey in color.

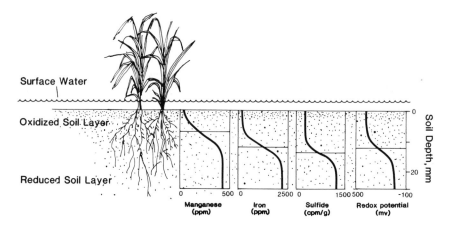

Figure 5-3. Characteristics of many wetland soils showing a shallow aerobic layer over an anaerobic layer, and soil profiles of sodium acetate-extractable manganese, ferrous iron, sulfide, and redox potential. *(After Patrick and Delaune, 1972, p. 573, and Gambrell and Patrick, 1978, p. 387)*

Redox potential, or oxidation-reduction potential, a measure of the electron pressure (or availability) in a solution, is often used to further quantify the degree of electrochemical reduction of wetland soils. *Oxidation* occurs not only during the uptake of oxygen but also if hydrogen is removed (e.g., $H_2S \rightarrow S$) or, more generally, if a chemical gives up an electron (e.g., $Fe^{++} \rightarrow Fe^{+++} + e^-$). *Reduction* is the opposite process of giving up oxygen, gaining hydrogen (hydrogenation), or gaining an electron. Redox potential can be measured by inserting an inert platinum electrode into the solution in question. Electric potential is measured relative to a hydrogen electrode ($H^+ + e \rightarrow H$) and is given in readings of millivolts (mv). As long as free dissolved oxygen is present in a solution, the redox potential varies little (in the range of $+400$ to $+700$ mv). However, it is a sensitive measure of the degree of reduction of wetland soils after oxygen disappears, ranging from $+400$ mv down to -400 mv (Gambrell and Patrick, 1978).

As organic substrates in a waterlogged soil are oxidized, the redox potential drops. Various chemical and biological transformations take place in a predictable sequence, within narrow redox ranges (Table 5-2). One of the first reactions that occurs in wetland soils after they become anaerobic is the reduction of NO_3^- (nitrate) to N_2O or N_2; nitrate becomes an electron acceptor at approximately 220 mv. Manganese is transformed from manganic to manganous compounds at 200 mv. Iron is transformed from ferric to ferrous form at 120 mv, while sulfates are reduced to sulfides at -150 mv. These redox potentials are not precise thresholds, as pH and temperature are also important factors in the rates of transformation. These major chemical transformations are discussed further below.

Nitrogen Transformations

Nitrogen is often the most limiting nutrient in flooded soils, whether the flooded soils are in natural wetlands or agricultural wetlands such as rice

Table 5-2. Oxidized and Reduced Forms of Several Elements and Approximate Redox Potentials for Transformation

Element	Oxidized Form	Reduced Form	Redox Potential for Transformation, mv
Nitrogen	NO_3^- (Nitrate)	N_2O, N_2, NH_4^+	220
Manganese	Mn^{+4} (Manganic)	Mn^{++} (Manganous)	200
Iron	Fe^{+++} (Ferric)	Fe^{++} (Ferrous)	120
Sulfur	$SO_4^=$ (Sulfate)	$S^=$ (Sulfide)	-75 to -150
Carbon	CO_2 (Carbon Dioxide)	CH_4 (Methane)	-250 to -350

paddies (Gambrell and Patrick, 1978). Limitations of the element have been noted at least temporarily for salt marshes (e.g., Sullivan and Daiber, 1974; Valiela and Teal, 1974), freshwater inland marshes (Klopatek, 1978), and freshwater tidal marshes (Simpson, Whigham, and Walker, 1978).

Nitrogen transformations in wetland soils involve several microbiological processes, some of which make the nutrient less available for plant uptake. The nitrogen transformations that dominate wetland soils are shown in Figure 5-4 and are summarized below. The ammonium ion is the primary form of mineralized nitrogen in most flooded wetland soils, although much of the nitrogen can be tied up in organic forms in highly organic soils. The presence of an oxidized zone over the anaerobic or reduced zone is critical for several of the pathways. In sequence, the processes might include mineralization of nitrogen-containing organic matter, upward diffusion of ammonium, nitrification, downward diffusion of nitrate, and denitrification. Nitrogen fixation and ammonia volatilization are other processes that are important in many wetlands.

Nitrogen mineralization refers to "the biological transformation of organi-

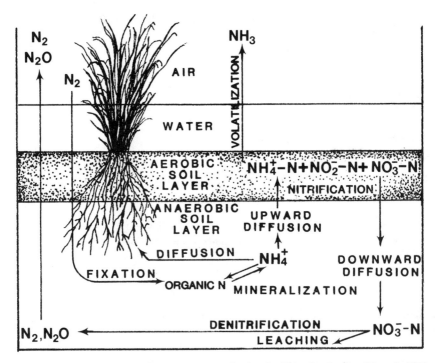

Figure 5-4. Nitrogen transformations in wetland soils. *(From Gambrell and Patrick, 1978, p. 393; Copyright © 1978 by Technomics Publication Co., reprinted with permission)*

cally combined nitrogen to ammonium nitrogen during organic matter degradation" (Gambrell and Patrick, 1978). This pathway occurs under both anaerobic and aerobic conditions and is often referred to as *ammonification*. Typical formulas for the mineralization of a simple organic nitrogen compound, urea, are given as:

$$NH_2 \cdot CO \cdot NH_2 + H_2O \rightarrow 2NH_3 + CO_2 \qquad (5.1)$$

$$NH_3 + H_2O \rightarrow NH_4^+ + OH^- \qquad (5.2)$$

Once the ammonium ion (NH_4^+) is formed, it can take several possible pathways. It can be absorbed by plants through their root systems or by anaerobic microorganisms and converted back to organic matter. It can also be immobilized through ion exchange onto negatively charged soil particles. Because of the anaerobic conditions in wetland soils, ammonium would normally be restricted from further oxidation and would build up to excessive levels were it not for the thin oxidized layer at the surface of many wetland soils. The gradient between high concentrations of ammonium in the reduced soils and low concentrations in the oxidized layer causes an upward diffusion of ammonium, albeit very slowly, to the oxidized layer. This ammonium nitrogen then is oxidized by a restricted number of chemoautotrophic bacteria through the process of *nitrification* in two steps, by *Nitrosomonas* sp:

$$2NH_4^+ + 3O_2 \rightarrow 2NO_2^- + 2H_2O + 4H^+ + energy \qquad (5.3)$$

and, by *Nitrobacter* sp:

$$2NO_2^- + O_2 \rightarrow 2NO_3^- + energy \qquad (5.4)$$

Nitrate (NO_3^-), as a negative ion rather than the positive ammonium ion, is not subject to immobilization by the negatively charged soil particles (Atlas and Bartha, 1981) and is thus much more mobile in solution. If it is not assimilated immediately by plants or microbes (*assimilatory nitrate reduction*), or lost through groundwater flow due to its rapid mobility, it has the potential of going through *dissimilatory nitrogenous oxide reduction,* a term that refers to several pathways of nitrate reduction (Wiebe et al., 1981). The most prevalent are reduction to ammonia and *denitrification*. Denitrification, carried out by microorganisms in anaerobic conditions with nitrate acting as a terminal electron acceptor, results in the loss of nitrogen as it is converted to gaseous nitrous oxide (N_2O) and molecular nitrogen (N_2):

$$C_6H_{12}O_6 + 4NO_3^- \rightarrow 6CO_2 + H_2O + 2N_2 \qquad (5.5)$$

Denitrification has been documented as a significant path of loss of nitrogen from salt marshes (e.g., Kaplan and Valiela, 1979; Whitney et al., 1981) and rice cultures (e.g., Patrick and Reddy, 1976; Mohanty and Dash,

1982). However, it is inhibited in acid soils and peat and is therefore thought to be of less consequence in northern peatlands (Etherington, 1983).

Nitrogen fixation results in the conversion of N_2 gas to organic nitrogen through the activity of certain organisms in the presence of the enzyme nitrogenase. It may be the source of significant nitrogen for some wetlands. Nitrogen fixation, which is carried out by aerobic bacteria, is favored by low oxygen tensions because nitrogenase activity is inhibited by high oxygen (Etherington, 1983). Bacterial nitrogen fixation can be carried out by non-symbiotic bacteria, by symbiotic bacteria of the genus *Rhizobium,* or by the actinomycetes.Whitney, Woodwell, and Howarth (1975), Whitney et al. (1981), and Teal, Valiela, and Berla (1979) documented that bacterial fixation was the most significant pathway for nitrogen fixation in salt marsh soils. On the other hand, both nitrogen-fixing bacteria and nitrifying bacteria are virtually absent from the low pH peat of northern bogs (Moore and Bellamy, 1974). Cyanobacteria (blue-green algae), as nonsymbiotic nitrogen fixers, are also frequently found in waterlogged soils of wetlands and can contribute significant amounts of nitrogen. This is particularly true in northern bogs and rice cultures, which are often too acidic to support large bacterial populations (Etherington, 1983).

Iron and Manganese Transformations

Below the reduction of nitrate on the redox potential scale comes the reduction of manganese and of iron. Each element occurs in two oxidation states as shown in Table 5-2. Iron and manganese are found in wetlands primarily in their reduced forms (ferrous and manganous, respectively), and both are more soluble and more readily available to organisms in this form. Manganese is reduced slightly before iron on the redox scale, but otherwise it behaves similarly to iron. Iron can be oxidized from ferrous to the insoluble ferric form by chemosynthetic bacteria in the presence of oxygen, and it is thought that a similar type of bacterial process exists for manganese. Such iron bacteria are thought to be responsible for the oxidation to insoluble ferric compounds of soluble ferrous iron that originated in anaerobic groundwaters in northern peatland areas. These "bog-iron" deposits form the basis of the ore that has been used in the iron and steel industry (Atlas and Bartha, 1981).

Iron, in its reduced form, causes a grey-green coloration of mineral soils $(Fe(OH)_2)$ instead of its normal red or brown color in oxidized conditions $(Fe(OH)_3)$. This gives a relatively easy field check on the oxidized and reduced layers in a mineral soil profile. This process of soil coloration is called *gleying,* and waterlogged mineral soils are often referred to as *gleys* (Etherington, 1983).

Iron and manganese, in their reduced forms, can reach toxic concentrations in wetland soils. Ferrous iron, diffusing to the surface of roots of wetland plants, may be oxidized by oxygen leaking from root cells, immobilizing phosphorus and coating roots with an iron oxide, causing a barrier to nutrient uptake (Gambrell and Patrick, 1978).

Sulfur Transformations

Sulfur occurs in several different states of oxidation in wetlands, and like nitrogen, it is transformed through several pathways that are mediated by microorganisms (Figure 5-5). While sulfur is rarely present in such low concentrations that it is limiting to plant or consumer growth in wetlands, the

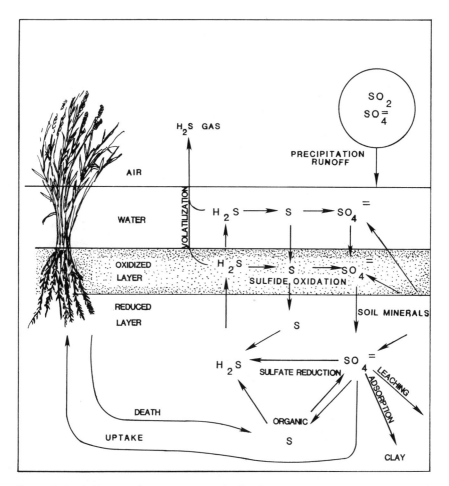

Figure 5-5. Sulfur transformations in wetland soils.

hydrogen sulfide that is characteristic of the anaerobic sediments of wetland sediments can be very toxic to plants and microbes. The release of sulfides when wetland sediments are disturbed causes the odor familiar to those who carry out research in wetlands—the smell of rotten eggs. In the redox scale, sulfur compounds are the next major electron acceptors after nitrates, iron, and manganese, with reduction occurring at about -75 to -150 mv on the redox scale (see Table 5-2). The most common oxidation states (valences) for sulfur in wetlands are:

Form		Valence
$S^=$	(sulfide)	-2
S	(elemental sulfur)	0
S_2O_3	(thiosulfates)	$+2$
$SO_4^=$	(sulfates)	$+6$

Sulfate reduction can take place as *assimilatory sulfate reduction* in which certain sulfur-reducing obligate anaerobes, such as *Desulfovibrio* bacteria, utilize the sulfates as terminal electron acceptors in anaerobic respiration:

$$4H_2 + SO_4^= \rightarrow H_2S + 2H_2O + 2OH^- \qquad \textbf{(5.6)}$$

This sulfate reduction can occur over a wide range of pH, with the highest rates prevalent near neutral pH.

Sulfides are known to be highly toxic to both microbes and rooted higher plants. The negative effects of sulfides on higher plants have been described by Ponnamperuma (1972) as due to a number of causes, including the following:

1. the direct toxicity of free sulfide as it comes in contact with plant roots
2. the reduced availability of sulfur for plant growth due to its precipitation with trace metals
3. the immobilization of zinc and copper by sulfide precipitation

In wetland soils with high concentrations of ferrous iron (Fe^{++}), the sulfides can combine with the iron to form insoluble ferrous sulfide (FeS), thus reducing the toxicity of the free hydrogen sulfide (Gambrell and Patrick, 1978). Ferrous sulfide gives the black color characteristic of many anaerobic wetland soils.

Sulfides can be oxidized by both the chemoautotrophic and photosynthetic microorganisms to elemental sulfur and sulfates in the aerobic zones of some wetland soils. Certain species of *Thiobacillus* obtain energy from the oxidation of hydrogen sulfide to sulfur, while other species in this genus can further oxidize elemental sulfur to sulfate. These reactions are summarized as follows:

$$2H_2S + O_2 \rightarrow 2S + 2H_2O + \text{energy} \qquad (5.7)$$

and

$$2S + 3O_2 + 2H_2O \rightarrow 2H_2SO_4 + \text{energy.} \qquad (5.8)$$

Photosynthetic bacteria such as the purple sulfur bacteria found on salt marshes and mud flats are capable of producing organic matter in the presence of light according to the following equation:

$$CO_2 + H_2S \xrightarrow{\text{light}} CH_2O + S. \qquad (5.9)$$

This reaction uses hydrogen sulfide as an electron donor rather than the H_2O used in the more traditional photosynthesis equation, but otherwise the process is the same. This reaction often takes place under anaerobic conditions where hydrogen sulfide is abundant but at the surface of sediments where sunlight is also available.

Carbon Transformations

While biodegradation of organic matter by aerobic respiration is limited by reduced conditions in wetland soils, several anaerobic processes can degrade organic carbon. The major processes of carbon transformation under aerobic and anaerobic conditions are shown in Figure 5-6. *Fermentation* of organic matter, which occurs when organic matter itself is the terminal electron acceptor in anaerobic respiration by microorganisms, forms various low molecular weight acids and alcohols, and CO_2 (see chap. 6):

$$C_6H_{12}O_6 \rightarrow 2CH_3CHOCOOH \qquad (5.10)$$
$$\text{(lactic acid)}$$

or,

$$C_6H_{12}O_6 \rightarrow 2CH_2CH_2OH + 2CO_2. \qquad (5.11)$$
$$\text{(ethanol)}$$

The process can be carried out in wetland soils by either facultative or obligate anaerobes. Although in situ studies of fermentation in wetlands are rare, it is thought that "fermentation plays a central role in providing substrates for other anaerobes in sediments in waterlogged soils" (Wiebe et al., 1981). It represents one of the major ways in which high molecular weight carbohydrates are broken down to low molecular weight organic compounds, usually as dissolved organic carbon, which are, in turn, available to other microbes (Valiela, 1984).

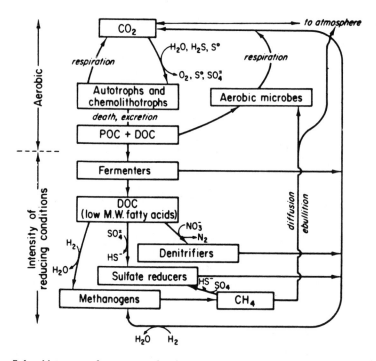

Figure 5-6. Major transformations of carbon in wetlands. Note the importance of other mineral cycles on various pathways. *(From Valiela, 1984, p. 303; Copyright © 1984 by Springer-Verlag, reprinted with permission)*

Methanogenesis occurs when certain bacteria (methanogens) use CO_2 or a methyl group as an electron acceptor for the production of gaseous methane (CH_4):

$$4H_2 + CO_2 \rightarrow CH_4 + 2H_2O \tag{5.12}$$

or

$$CH_3COO^- + 4H_2 \rightarrow 2CH_4 + 2H_2O. \tag{5.13}$$

Methane, which can be released to the atmosphere when sediments are disturbed, is often referred to as "swamp gas" or "marsh gas." Methane production requires extremely reduced conditions, with a redox potential between -250 and -350 mv, after other terminal electron acceptors (O_2, NO_3^-, and $SO_4^=$) have been used. In general, methane is found at low concentrations in reduced soils if sulfate concentrations are high (Gambrell and Patrick, 1978; Valiela, 1984). Possible reasons for this phenomenon include (1) competition for substrates that occurs between sulfur and methane bacteria, (2) the inhibitory effects of sulfate or sulfide on methane bacteria, or (3) a possible dependence of methane bacteria on products of sulfur-reducing bacteria (Gambrell and Patrick, 1978). More recent evidence suggests that methane may actually be oxidized to CO_2 by sulfate reducers (Valiela, 1984).

A comparison of methanogenesis between freshwater and marine environments has generally revealed that the rate of methane production is higher in the former, apparently because of the lower amounts of sulfate in the water and sediments (Valiela, 1984). The rates of methanogenesis from both saltwater coastal wetlands and freshwater wetlands, however, have a considerable range (Table 5-3). Comparison of rates of methane production from different studies is very difficult, because different methods are used and because the rates are dependent on both temperature and hydroperiod. Methanogenesis is very seasonal in temperate zone wetlands, with Harriss, Sebacher, and Day (1982) noting maximum methane production in a Virginia freshwater swamp in April–May, while Wiebe et al. (1981) found methane production to generally peak in late summer in a Georgia salt marsh. Furthermore, Harriss, Sebacher, and Day (1982) measured a net uptake of

Table 5-3. Methane Production Rates for Various Freshwater and Saltwater Wetlands

Type of Wetland	Rate of Methane Production, $mgC/m^2 \cdot day$	Reference
Freshwater Wetlands		
Rice Paddies, annual average	68	Koyama (1963)
Michigan Swamp average annual rate	110	Baker-Blocker, Donahue, and Mancy (1977)
Dismal Swamp, Virginia minimum maximum	1 15	Harriss, Sebacher, and Day (1982)
Louisiana tidal freshwater marsh (annual average)	440	Smith, Delaune, and Patrick (1982)
Saltwater Wetlands		
Georgia salt marsh, average annual rate all *Spartina* intermediate *Spartina* short *Spartina*	 0.8 29 109	Wiebe et al. (1981)
Louisiana salt marsh	14	Smith, Delaune, and Patrick (1982)

methane by the wetland during a drought when the wetland soil was exposed to the atmosphere, raising questions concerning the generally held belief that wetlands are only sources and not sinks of atmospheric methane.

The sulfur cycle is very important in some wetlands for the oxidation of organic carbon. This is particularly true in coastal wetlands (salt marshes and mangroves) where sulfur is abundant. Sulfur-reducing bacteria require an organic substrate, generally of low molecular weight, as a source of energy in converting sulfate to sulfide (Equation 5.6). Conveniently, the process of fermentation described previously can supply these necessary low molecular weight organic compounds, such as lactate (see Equation 5.10 and Fig. 5-6). Equations of sulfur reduction, also showing the oxidation of organic matter, are given as follows (from Valiela, 1984):

$$2CH_3CHOHCOO^- + SO_4^= + 3H^+ \rightarrow$$
(lactate)
$$2CH_3COO^- + 2CO_2 + 2H_2O + HS^- \tag{5.14}$$

and

$$CH_3COO^- + SO_4^= \rightarrow 2CO_2 + 2H_2O + HS^-. \tag{5.15}$$
(acetate)

The importance of this fermentation–sulfur reduction pathway in oxidation of organic carbon to CO_2 in saltwater wetlands was demonstrated for a New England salt marsh by Howes, Dacey, and King (1984) and Howes, Dacey, and Teal (1985). Their study, summarized in Table 5-4, shows that fully 54% of the carbon dioxide evolution from the marsh was due to the fermentation–sulfur reduction pathway, with aerobic respiration accounting for another 45%. Only a small percent of carbon release was due to methanogenesis.

Table 5-4. Carbon Dioxide Release from Mineralization of Organic Matter in a New England Salt Marsh

Pathway	CO_2 Release, $gC/m^2 \cdot yr$	Percent of mineralization
Aerobic Respiration	361	44.9
Nitrate Reduction	5	0.6
Fermentation-Sulfate Reduction	432	53.7
Methanogenesis	6	0.7
Total	804	

Source: From Valiela, 1984, p. 306; Copyright © 1984 by Springer-Verlag, reprinted with permission, after Howes, Dacey, and King, 1984 and Howes, Dacey, and Teal, 1985.

Phosphorus Transformations

Phosphorus is one of the most important chemicals in ecosystems, and wetlands are no exception. It has been described as a major limiting nutrient in northern bogs (Heilman, 1968), freshwater marshes (Klopatek, 1978), and southern deepwater swamps (Mitsch, Dorge, and Weimhoff, 1979; Brown, 1981). In other wetlands, such as agricultural wetlands (Gambrell and Patrick, 1978) and salt marshes (Whitney et al., 1981), it is an important mineral, although it is not considered a limiting factor due to its relative abundance and biochemical stability.

Phosphorus occurs as soluble and insoluble complexes in both organic and inorganic forms in wetland soils (Table 5-5). The principal inorganic form is orthophosphate, which includes the ions PO_4^{-3}, $HPO_4^{=}$, and $H_2PO_4^{-}$, with the predominant form depending on pH. The analytical measure of biologically available orthophosphates is sometimes called *soluble reactive phosphorus,* although the equivalence between that term and orthophosphates is not exact. Dissolved organic phosphorus and insoluble forms of organic and inorganic phosphorus are generally not biologically available until they are transformed into soluble inorganic forms.

While phosphorus is not directly altered by changes in redox potential as are nitrogen, iron, manganese, and sulfur, it is indirectly affected in soils and sediments by its association with several elements that are so altered (Mohanty and Dash, 1982). Phosphorus is rendered relatively unavailable to plants and microconsumers by all of the following:

1. the precipitation of insoluble phosphates with ferric iron, calcium, and aluminum under aerobic conditions
2. the absorption of phosphate onto clay particles, organic peat, and ferric and aluminum hydroxides and oxides

Table 5-5. Major Types of Dissolved and Insoluble Phosphorus in Natural Waters

Phosphorus	Soluble Forms	Insoluble Forms
Inorganic	orthophosphates ($H_2PO_4^{-}$, $HPO_4^{=}$, PO_4^{-3})	clay-phosphate complexes
	ferric phosphate ($FeHPO_4^{+}$)	metal hydroxide-phosphate
	calcium phosphate ($CaH_2PO_4^{+}$)	minerals, e.g., apatite ($Ca_{10}(OH)_2(PO_4)_6$)
Organic	dissolved organics, e.g., sugar phosphates, inositol phosphates, phospholipids, phosphoproteins	insoluble organic phosphorus bound in organic matter

Source: After Stumm and Morgan, 1970, p. 515-516

3. the binding of phosphorus in organic matter as a result of incorporation into living biomass

The precipitation of the metal phosphates and the adsorption of phosphates onto ferric or aluminum hydroxides and oxides are believed to both result from the same chemical forces, namely those involved in the forming of complex ions and salts. The sorption of phosphorus onto clay particles is believed to involve both chemical bonding of the negatively charged phosphates to positively charged edges of the clay and the substitution of phosphates for silicate in the clay (Stumm and Morgan, 1970). This clay-phosphorus complex is particularly important for many wetlands, including riparian wetlands and coastal salt marshes, because a considerable portion of the phosphorus brought into these systems by flooding rivers and tides is brought in sorbed to clay particles.

When soils are flooded and conditions become anaerobic, several changes in the availability of phosphorus result. A well-documented phenomenon in the hypolimnion of lakes is the increase in soluble phosphorus when the hypolimnion and the sediment-water interface become anoxic (Mortimer, 1941-1942; Ruttner, 1963). In general, a similar phenomenon often occurs in wetlands on a compressed scale. As ferric (Fe^{+++}) iron is reduced to more soluble ferrous (Fe^{++}) compounds, phosphorus that is in ferric phosphate compounds is released into solution. Other reactions that may be important in releasing phosphorus upon flooding are the hydrolysis of ferric and aluminum phosphates and the release of phosphorus sorbed to clays and hydrous oxides by exchange of anions (Ponnamperuma, 1972). Phosphorus can also be released from insoluble salts when the pH is changed, either by the production of organic acids or by the production of nitric and sulfuric acids by chemosynthetic bacteria (Atlas and Bartha, 1981). Phosphorus sorption onto clay particles, on the other hand, is highest under acidic to slightly acidic conditions (Stumm and Morgan, 1970).

CHEMICAL TRANSPORT INTO WETLANDS

The inputs of materials to wetlands are through geologic, biologic, and hydrologic pathways typical of other ecosystems (Likens et al., 1977). Geologic input from weathering of parent rock, although poorly understood, may be important in some wetlands. Biologic inputs include photosynthetic uptake of carbon, nitrogen fixation, and biotic transport of materials by mobile animals such as birds. Except for gaseous exchanges such as carbon fixation in photosynthesis and nitrogen fixation, however, elemental inputs to wetlands are generally dominated by hydrologic inputs.

Table 5-6. Chemical Characteristics of Bulk Precipitation (mg/l)

Chemical	Georgia[a]	Newfoundland[b]	Wisconsin-Minnesota[b]	New Hampshire[c]
Ca^{++}	0.17	0.8	1.0-1.2	0.16
Mg^{++}	0.05	—	—	0.04
Na^+	—	5.2	0.2-0.5	0.12
K^+	0.14	0.3	0.2	0.07
NO_3^-	0.26	—	—	1.47
NH_4^+	—	—	—	0.22
Cl^-	—	8.9	0.1	0.47
$SO_4^=$	—	2.2	1.4	2.9
P (soluble)	0.017	—	—	0.008

[a]Schlesinger, 1978
[b]Gorham, 1961, as summarized by Moore and Bellamy, 1974
[c]Likens et al., 1977

Precipitation

Table 5-6 describes typical chemical characteristics of precipitation as measured in several locations in North America. The levels of chemicals in precipitation are variable but very dilute. Relatively higher concentrations of magnesium and sodium are associated with maritime influences, while high calcium indicates continental influences; for example, dust (Schlesinger, 1978). Precipitation tends to contain contaminants at higher concentrations in short storms and when precipitation is infrequent. Some wetlands, such as northern bogs or southern cypress domes, are fed primarily by precipitation. Such wetlands generally have low productivities and depend on intrasystem cycling for nutrients.

Streams, Rivers, and Groundwater

As precipitation reaches the ground in a watershed, it will either infiltrate into the ground, pass back to the atmosphere through evapotranspiration, or flow on the surface as runoff. When enough runoff comes together, possibly combined with groundwater flow, in channelized streamflow, its mineral content is already different from that of the original precipitation.

There is not, however, a typical water quality for surface and subsurface flows. Figure 5-7 describes the cumulative frequency of the ionic composition of freshwater streams and rivers in the United States. The curves demonstrate the wide range over which these chemicals are found and the median values (50% line) of these ranges. The concentration of chemicals in runoff and streamflow that enter wetlands depends on several factors:

1. Influence of Groundwater—The chemical characteristics of streams and rivers depend on the degree to which the water has previously

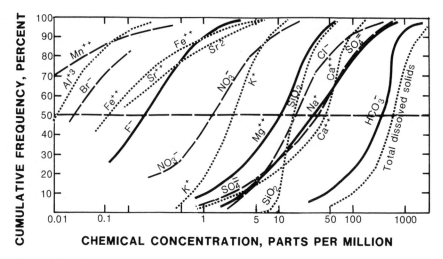

Figure 5-7. Cumulative frequency curves for concentrations of various dissolved minerals in surface waters. Horizontal dashed line indicates median concentration. *(After Stumm and Morgan, 1970, p. 384, and DeWiest, 1966)*

come in contact with underground formations and on the types of minerals present in those formations. Soil and rock weathering, through dissolution and redox reactions, provide major dissolved ions to waters that enter the ground. Surface water can range in dissolved materials from a few milligrams per liter found in precipitation to 100 or even 1,000 milligrams per liter. The ability of water to dissolve mineral rock depends, in part, on its nature as a weak carbonic acid. The rock being mineralized is also an important consideration, with minerals such as limestone and dolomite yielding high levels of dissolved ions while granite and sandstone formations are relatively resistant to dissolution.

2. Climate—Climate influences surface water quality through the balance of precipitation and evapotranspiration. Arid regions tend to have higher concentrations of salts in surface waters than do humid regions. Climate also has a considerable influence on the type and extent of vegetation on the land, and it therefore indirectly affects the physical, chemical, and biological characteristics of soils and the degree to which these soils are eroded and transported into surface waters.

3. Geographic Effects—The amounts of dissolved and suspended materials that enter streams, rivers, and wetlands also depends on the size of the watershed, the steepness or slope of the landscape, soil texture, and the variety of topography (Lee, 1980). Surface waters that have high concentrations of suspended (insoluble) materials due to erosion are often relatively low in dissolved substances. On the other hand, waters that have passed through groundwater systems often have high concentrations of dissolved materials and low levels of suspended materials.

The presence of upstream wetlands also influences the quality of water entering downstream wetlands (see Coupling with Adjacent Ecosystems).

4. Human Effects—Water that has been modified by humans through, for example, sewage effluent and runoff from farms, often drastically alters the chemical composition of wetlands. Several studies of the influence of pollution sources on wetlands have documented the effects of municipal wastewater (Grant and Patrick, 1970; Boyt, Bayley, and Zoltek, 1977), coal mine drainage (Wieder and Lang, 1982; Mitsch, Taylor, and Benson, 1983; Mitsch et al., 1983a, 1983b), highway construction (McLeese and Whiteside, 1977), stream channelization (Maki et al., 1980), and sulfate pollution (Richardson et al., 1983). Some of these alterations are described in more detail in Chapter 16.

Estuaries

Wetlands such as salt marshes and mangrove swamps are continually exchanging tidal waters with adjacent estuaries and other coastal waters. The quality of these waters differs considerably from that of the rivers described above. But while estuaries are places where rivers meet the sea, they are not simply places where seawater is diluted with freshwater. Table 5-7 contrasts the

Table 5-7. Average Chemical Concentrations (mg/l) of Ocean Water and River Water

Chemical	Seawater[a]	"Average" River[b]
Na^+	10,773	6.3
Mg^{++}	1,294	4.1
Ca^{++}	412	15
K^+	399	2.3
Cl^-	19,344	7.8
$SO_4^=$	2,712	11.2
$HCO_3^-/CO_3^=$	142	58.4
B	4.5[c]	0.01[c]
F	1.4[c]	0.1[c]
Fe	<0.01[c]	0.7
SiO_2	<0.1->10[c]	13.1[c]
N	0-0.5[c]	0.2[c]
P	0-0.07[c]	0.02[c]
Particulate Organic Carbon	0.01-1.0[c]	5-10[c]
Dissolved Organic Carbon	1-5[c]	10-20[c]

[a]Riley and Skirrow, 1975
[b]Livingston, 1963
[c]Burton and Liss, 1976

chemical makeup of average river water with the average composition of seawater. The chemical characteristics of seawater are fairly constant world-wide compared with the relatively wide range of river water chemistry. Concentrations typically range from 33‰ to 37‰. Although seawater contains almost every element that can go into solution, 99.6% of the salinity is accounted for by 11 ions. In addition to seawater dilution, estuarine waters can also involve chemical reactions when sea and river waters meet, including dissolution of particulate substances, flocculation, chemical precipitation, and adsorption and absorption of chemicals on particles of clay, organic matter, and silt (J. H. Day, 1981).

CHEMICAL MASS BALANCES OF WETLANDS

A quantitative description of the inputs, outputs, and internal cycling of materials in an ecosystem is called an *ecosystem mass balance* (Whigham and Bayley, 1979; Nixon and Lee, 1985). If the material being measured is one of several elements such as phosphorus, nitrogen, or carbon that are essential for life, then the mass balance is called a *nutrient budget.* In wetlands, mass balances have been developed both to describe ecosystem function and to determine the importance of wetlands as sources, sinks, and transformers of chemicals.

A general mass balance for a wetland, as shown in Figure 5-8, illustrates the major categories of pathways and storages that are important in accounting for materials passing into and out of wetlands. Nutrients or chemicals that are brought into the system are called *inputs* or *inflows.* For wetlands, these inputs are primarily through hydrologic pathways described in chapter 4, such as precipitation, surface and groundwater inflow, and tidal exchange. Biotic pathways of note that apply to the carbon and nitrogen budgets are the fixation of atmospheric carbon through photosynthesis and the capture of atmospheric nitrogen through nitrogen fixation.

Hydrologic *exports,* or *losses,* or *outflows,* are by both surface water and groundwater, unless the wetland is an isolated basin with no outflow, such as a northern ombrotrophic bog. Long-term burial of chemicals in the sediments is also often considered a nutrient or chemical outflow, although the depth at which a chemical goes from internal cycling to permanent burial is an uncertain threshold. The depth of available chemicals is usually defined by the root zone of vegetation in the wetland. Biologically mediated exports are also important in the nitrogen cycle (denitrification) and in the carbon cycle (respiratory loss of CO_2). The significance of other losses of elements to the atmosphere such as ammonia volatilization and methane and sulfide releases are not well understood, although they are potentially important pathways for individual wetlands as well as for the global cycling of minerals.

Intrasystem cycling involves exchanges among the various *pools,* or *standing stocks,* of chemicals within the wetland. This cycling includes pathways

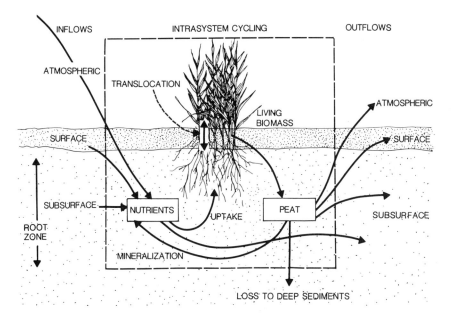

Figure 5-8. Generalized diagram of components of a wetland mass balance.

such as litter production, remineralization, and various chemical transformations discussed earlier. *Translocation* of nutrients from the roots through the stems and leaves of the vegetation is another important intrasystem process that results in the physical movement of chemicals within the wetland.

Figure 5-9 (Nixon and Lee, 1985) illustrates more detail of the major pathways and storages that investigators should consider when developing mass balances of chemicals for wetlands. Major exchanges with the surroundings are shown as exchanges of particulate and dissolved material with adjacent bodies of water (Pathways 1 and 2), exchange through groundwater (Pathways 7 and 8), inputs from precipitation (Pathways 9 and 10), and burial in sediments (Pathway 28). Exchanges specific to a nitrogen mass balance, namely nitrogen fixation (Pathways 3, 4, 5), denitrification (Pathway 6), and ammonia volatilization (Pathway 26) are also shown in the diagram. A number of intrasystem pathways such as stemflow (Pathway 12), root sloughing (Pathway 22), detrital-water exchanges (Pathways 24 and 25), and sediment water exchanges (Pathway 27) can be very important in determining the fate of chemicals in wetlands but are extremely difficult to measure. Overall, few if any investigators have developed a complete mass balance for wetlands with measurement of all of the pathways shown in Figure 5-9. But the diagram remains a useful guide to those considering studies of wetlands as sources, sinks or transformers of chemicals as described below.

The chemical balances that have been developed for various wetlands

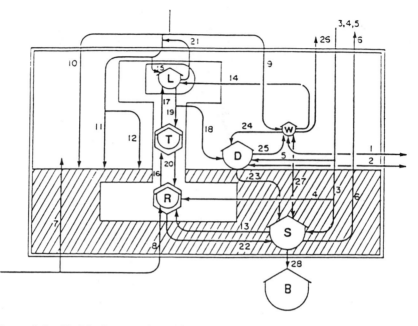

Figure 5-9. Model of major chemical storages and flows in wetlands. *Storages:* L = above-ground shoots or leaves; T = trunks and branches, perennial above-ground storage; R = roots and rhizomes; W = dissolved and suspended particulates in surface water; D = litter or detritus; S = near-surface sediments; B = deep sediments essentially removed from internal cycling.

Flows: 1 and 2 are exchanges of dissolved and particulate material with adjacent waters; 3–5 are nitrogen fixation in sediments, rhizosphere microflora, and litter; 6 is denitrification by sediments (N_2 and N_2O); 7 and 8 are groundwater inputs to roots and surface water; 9 is atmospheric deposition on water; 10 is on land; 11 and 12 are aqueous deposition from the canopy and in stemflow; 13 is uptake by roots; 14 is foliar uptake from surface water; 15 is uptake from rainfall; 16 and 17 are translocations from roots through trunks and stems to leaves; 18 is the production of litter; 19 and 20 are the readsorption of materials from leaves through trunks and stems to roots and rhizomes; 21 is leaching from leaves; 22 is death or sloughing of root material; 23 is incorporation of litter into sediments or peat; 24 is uptake by decomposing litter; 25 is release from decomposing litter; 26 is volatilization of ammonia; 27 is sediment-water exchange; 28 is long-term burial in sediments. *(Figure and caption from Nixon and Lee, 1985, p. 4, reprinted with permission)*

illustrate few generalizations. Nevertheless, the following major points will be discussed.

1. Wetlands serve as sources, sinks, or transformers of chemicals, depending on the wetland type, hydrologic conditions, and year in which measurements were made.
2. Seasonal patterns of nutrient uptake and release are characteristic of many wetlands.

3. Wetlands are frequently coupled to adjacent ecosystems through chemical exchanges that significantly affect both systems.
4. Wetlands can be either highly productive ecosystems rich in nutrients or systems with low productivity due to scarce nutrients.
5. Nutrient cycling in wetlands differs from both aquatic and terrestrial ecosystem cycling in temporal and spatial dimensions.
6. Anthropogenic changes have led to considerable changes in chemical cycling in many wetlands.

Wetlands as Sources, Sinks, or Transformers of Nutrients

There has been much discussion and research by wetland scientists as to whether wetlands are nutrient *sources, sinks,* or *transformers.* A wetland is considered a sink if it has a net retention of an element or a specific form of that element (e.g., organic or inorganic), that is, if the inputs are greater than the outputs (Figure 5-10*a*). If a wetland exports more of an element or material to a downstream or adjacent ecosystem than would occur without that wetland, it is considered a source (Figure 5-10*b*). If a wetland transforms a chemical from, say, dissolved to particulate form, but does not change the amount going into or out of the wetland, it is considered to be a transformer. Part of the interest in this source-sink-transformer question was stimulated by studies that hypothesized the importance of salt marshes as "sources" of particulate carbon for the adjacent estuaries and other studies that suggested the importance of wetlands as "sinks" for certain chemicals, particularly nitrogen and phosphorus. The two concepts of one wetland being a source and a sink for various materials are not mutually exclusive; a wetland can be a sink for an inorganic form of a nutrient and a source for an organic form of the same nutrient. The desire of wetland scientists to determine conclusively whether wetlands are sources or sinks of nutrients has often been hampered by the imprecise use of the words "source" and "sink" and by the inadequacy of the techniques used to measure the nutrient fluxes in a wetland nutrient budget.

Table 5-8 gives some examples of results of studies of wetlands as nitrogen and phosphorus sinks. There is not consensus on this question for wetlands in general, and, in fact, there is little agreement in the literature even for particular nutrients in specific wetland types (Richardson, 1985). All that can be said with certainty is that many wetlands act as sinks for particular inorganic nutrients and many wetlands are sources of organic material to downstream or adjacent ecosystems.

Freshwater Marshes

One of the first studies that identified freshwater wetlands for their role as nutrient sinks was on Tinicum Marsh near Philadelphia (Grant and Patrick,

Table 5-8. Studies of Wetlands as Sources or Sinks of Nutrients

Type of Wetland, Location	Period	Nutrient Sink[a]		Reference
		N	P	
Freshwater Marshes (tidal)				
Tinicum Marsh, Pa.	Summer	Yes	Yes	Grant and Patrick (1970)
Hamilton Marsh, N.J.	Yearly	S	S	Simpson, Whigham, and Walker (1978)
Freshwater Marshes (nontidal)				
4 marshes, Wis.	Yearly	Yes	S	Lee, Bentley, and Amundson (1975)
Waterhyacinth marsh, Fla.	9 mo	Yes	S	Mitsch (1977)
Theresa Marsh, Wis.	Yearly	S	S	Klopatek (1978)
Brillion Marsh, Wis.	Yearly	Yes	Yes	Fetter, Sloey, and Spangler (1978)
Marsh receiving sewage, Fla.	10 mo	—	Yes	Dolan et al. (1981)
Managed marsh, N.Y.	Yearly	I	I	Peverly (1982)
Northern Peatlands				
Forested peatland, Mich.	Yearly	No	Yes	Richardson et al., (1978)
Thoreau's Bog, Mass.	Yearly	Yes	—	Hemond (1980)
Black spruce bog, Minn.	Yearly	Yes	Yes	Verry and Timmons (1982)

Forested Swamps

Riverine cypress swamp, S.C.	Winter; Spring	Yes	Yes	Kitchens et al. (1975)
Mixed hardwood swamp, Fla.	Yearly	Yes	Yes	Boyt, Bayley, and Zoltek (1977)
Cypress-tupelo swamp, So. Ill.	Yearly	—	Yes	Mitsch, Dorge, and Weimhoff (1979)
Floodplain swamp, N.C.	Yearly	—	Yes	Kuenzler et al. (1980)
Cypress strand, Fla.	Yearly	—	Yes	Nessel and Bayley (1984)
Swamp forest, La.	10 mo	Yes	No	Kemp and Day (1984)
Riparian forest, Md.	Yearly	Yes	Yes	Peterjohn and Correll (1984)
Floodplain forest, Fla.	Yearly	S	S	Elder (1985)
Tupelo swamp, N.C.	Yearly	Yes	No	Brinson, Bradshaw, and Kane (1984)

Tidal Salt Marsh

Delaware	Yearly	—	No	Reimold and Daiber (1970)
Georgia	Yearly	—	No	Gardner (1975)
Flax Pond, N.Y.	Yearly	S	S	Woodwell and Whitney (1977); Woodwell et al (1979)
Great Sippewissett Marsh, Mass.	Yearly	S	—	Valiela et al. (1978); Teal, Valiela, and Berla (1979)
Sapelo Island, Ga.	Yearly	Yes	Yes	Whitney et al. (1981)
Louisiana	Yearly	Yes	Yes	Delaune, Reddy, and Patrick, (1981); Delaune, Smith, and Patrick (1983)

Source: Partially after Van der Valk et al., 1979, p. 458

[a]S = seasonal sink

I = inconsistent results from multiple-year study

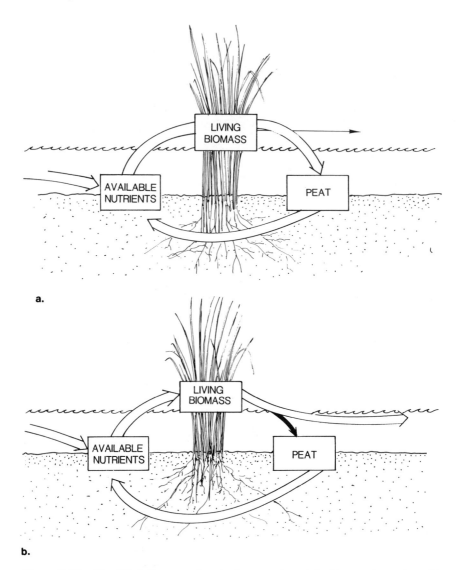

Figure 5-10. Simplified diagrams of wetland as a nutrient sink of inorganic nutrients *(a)* and *(b)* source of organic matter.

1970). The study, entitled "Tinicum Marsh as a Water Purifier," had among its goals to determine "the role of Tinicum Marsh wetlands in the reduction of nitrates and phosphates . . . ." That study found decreases in phosphorus (as PO_4^{-3}), nitrogen (as NO_3^- and NH_3), and organic materials (as biochemical oxygen demand, BOD), as water flowed from the river over the marsh. Lee, Bentley, and Amundson (1975) summarized the results of two research projects on the effects of freshwater marshes on water quality in Wisconsin and concluded that there were both beneficial (i.e., marsh acts as sink) and detrimental (i.e., marsh acts as source) effects of the marshes on water quality, but that "from an overall point of view, it appears that the beneficial effects outweigh the detrimental effects." Mitsch (1977) found that 49% of the total nitrogen and 11% of total phosphorus were removed by a floating water hyacinth *(Eichhornia crassipes)* marsh in north-central Florida. The study found a seasonal change in the loss of nitrate nitrogen, with greater uptake in the summer months. Studies by Klopatek (1978) in a Wisconsin riverine marsh and by Simpson, Whigham, and Walker (1978) in a tidal freshwater wetland also showed the capacity for marsh wetlands to be at least a seasonal sink for inorganic forms of nitrogen and phosphorus. A two-year study of the potential of managed marsh wetland in upper New York State to remove nutrients from agricultural drainage gave inconsistent results, with the wetland acting as a source of nitrogen and phosphorus in the first year and a net sink in the second year (Peverly, 1982).

Forested Swamps

The functioning of forested wetlands as nutrient sinks was suggested by Kitchens et al. (1975) in a preliminary winter-spring survey in a swamp forest–alluvial river swamp complex in South Carolina. These scientists found significant reduction in phosphorus as the waters passed over the swamp. They assumed this to be due to biological uptake by aquatic plant communities. Several studies in Florida were initiated to further investigate the value of wetlands as nutrient sinks. These studies, from the Center for Wetlands at the University of Florida, included studies of purposeful disposal of high-nutrient wastewater in cypress domes (Odum et al., 1977*a;* Ewel and Odum, 1984) and long-term inadvertent disposal of wastewater by small communities in forested wetlands (Boyt, Bayley, and Zoltek, 1977; Nessel and Bayley, 1984). In all of these studies, the wetlands acted as sinks for nitrogen and phosphorus. In the cypress dome experiments, the nutrients were essentially retained in the water, sediments and vegetation with little surface outflow. Boyt, Bayley, and Zoltek (1977) described nutrient uptake that occurred in a mixed hardwood swamp that had received domestic sewage effluent for 20 years. They found that total phosphorus and total nitrogen in the outflow were reduced by 98% and 90%, respectively, compared with the outflow.

Mitsch, Dorge, and Wiemhoff (1979) developed a nutrient budget for an alluvial river swamp in southern Illinois and found that ten times more phosphorus was deposited with sediments during river flooding than was returned from the swamp to the river during the rest of the year. The swamp was thus a phosphorus sink during that particular year of flooding. A study by Kuenzler et al. (1980) typified several chemical budget studies that have been developed for the Coastal Plain floodplain swamps of North Carolina. They found that 94% of the phosphorus transported to these wetlands was carried by surface water. They also found that there was a significant retention of phosphorus by the swamp, resulting in low concentrations of phosphorus downstream of the wetland. Kemp and Day (1984) and Peterjohn and Correll (1984) described the fate of nutrients as they are carried into forested wetlands by agricultural runoff. The former study found that a Louisiana swamp forest acted more as a transformer system, removing inorganic forms of nitrogen and serving as a net source of organic nitrogen, phosphate, and organic phosphorus. The latter study in a riparian Maryland forest described the removal of nitrogen and phosphorus from runoff and groundwater as the runoff passed through approximately 50 m of riparian vegetation. Significant losses of both nutrients were noted in the study. Some of these studies are described in more detail in chapters 13 and 14.

The importance of floodplain wetlands on the speciation of nitrogen and phosphorus in a major river system was investigated by Elder (1985) on the Apalachicola River in northern Florida. That study found that there was little change in the total flows of total nitrogen and total phosphorus as the river flowed 170 km downstream. However, the study found considerable transformation of these nutrients. There was a net import or loss of ammonia and soluble reactive phosphorus and a net export of organic nitrogen in both dissolved and particulate forms. Elder argues that the floodplain wetlands, which are generally autotrophic, are responsible for leading to a "net import of inorganic nutrients and a net export of organics."

Salt Marshes

Salt marshes have had the longest history of nutrient budget studies, the most comprehensive studies of nutrient dynamics, and probably the most controversy about the source-sink question. A critical evaluation of 20 years of research on the role of salt marshes in nutrient cycles was presented by Nixon (1980, p. 509) with the following general conclusion:

On the basis of very little evidence, marshes have been widely regarded as strong terms (sources or sinks) in coastal marine nutrient cycles. The data we have available so far do not support this view. In general, marshes seem to act as nitrogen transformers, importing dissolved oxidized inorganic forms of nitrogen and exporting dissolved and particulate reduced forms. While the net exchanges are too small to influence the annual nitrogen budget of most coastal systems, it is possible that there may be a transient local importance attached to the marsh-estuarine nitrogen flux in some areas. Marshes are sinks for total phosphorus, but there appears to be a remobilization of phosphate in the sediments and a small net export of phosphate from the marsh.

Various studies that led to the above summary had depicted salt marshes as either sources or sinks of nutrients. The salt marsh was described as a source of phosphorus for the adjacent estuary in studies in Delaware (Reimhold and Daiber, 1970; Reimhold, 1972) and Georgia (Gardner, 1975). Studies of Flax Pond Marsh in Long Island, New York (Woodwell and Whitney, 1977; Woodwell et al., 1979), found a net input of organic phosphorus and a net discharge of inorganic phosphate. Nitrogen budgets of the same marsh (Woodwell et al., 1979) and of the Great Sippewissett Marsh in Massachusetts (Valiela et al., 1978) indicated seasonal changes in nitrogen species and yet, within the accuracy of the measurements, a probable balance between inputs and outputs of nitrogen. Whitney et al. (1981), in a summary of many years of research on Sapelo Island, Georgia, described that marsh generally balanced with regards to phosphorus and a net sink of nitrogen, primarily because denitrification greatly exceeded nitrogen fixation.

Seasonal Patterns of Uptake and Release

The fact that a wetland is a sink or a source of nutrients on a year by year basis implies nothing about the seasonal differences in nutrient uptake and release. Van der Valk et al. (1979) described the general pattern of uptake of both nitrogen and phosphorus by wetlands as follows. During the growing season, there is a high rate of uptake of nutrients by emergent and submerged vegetation from the water and sediments. Increased microbiological immobilization of nutrients and uptake by algae and epiphytes also lead to a retention of inorganic forms of nitrogen and phosphorus. By the time the higher plants die, they have translocated a substantial portion of the nutrient material back to the roots and rhizomes. However, a substantial portion of the nutrients are lost to the waters through litter fall and subsequent leaching. This generally leads to a net export of nutrients in the fall and early spring.

Several of the studies described above, particularly some of those in freshwater marshes (Lee, Bentley, and Amundson, 1975; Klopatek, 1978; Simpson, Whigham, and Walker, 1978) and on salt marshes (Woodwell and Whitney, 1977; Valiela et al., 1978) described the seasonal changes of nutrient export that occurred in these wetlands (Table 5-8). Lee, Bentley, and Amundson (1975) found that the marshes they studied act as nutrient sinks during the summer and fall and as nutrient sources in the spring. This pattern had two potential benefits, according to the authors: (1) the problem of lake enrichment downstream of the marshes was decreased in the summer, the time of most serious algal blooms in lakes, and (2) it might be economically and ecologically more reasonable to treat waters for nutrient removal only during the periods of high flow when the marsh is exporting nutrients, allowing the marsh to be the nutrient removal system when it is acting as a sink.

The seasonality of nutrient retention by freshwater marshes was also observed in another Wisconsin riverine marsh by Klopatek (1978), who found that the marsh acted as both a source and sink of nutrients, with the pattern depending on the hydrologic conditions, the anaerobiosis in the sediments, and the activity of the biota, particularly the emergent macrophytes. Simpson, Whigham, and Walker (1978) described the movement of inorganic nitrogen and phosphorus in a freshwater tidal marsh in New Jersey and concluded, "It appears almost all habitats of freshwater tidal marshes may be sinks for inorganic N and PO_4-P during the vascular plant growing season and that certain habitats may continually function as sinks." Woodwell and Whitney (1977) found that there was a seasonal shift from uptake of phosphate in the cold months to export of phosphate in the warm months in a New York salt marsh. This pattern is opposite to the seasonal pattern that would be expected if plant uptake were the dominant sink in the growing season.

Coupling with Adjacent Ecosystems

In the beginning of this chapter, wetlands were described as either being "open" or "closed" to hydrologic transport. For those that are open to export, the chemicals are often transformed from inorganic to organic forms and transported to downstream ecosystems. This connection can be from riparian wetlands to adjacent streams, rivers, and downstream ecosystems, from tidal salt marshes to the estuary, or from in-stream riverine marshes to the river itself. There is considerable evidence that watersheds which drain wetland regions export more organic material than do watersheds that do not have wetlands (Mulholland and Kuenzler, 1979; Brinson, Lugo, and Brown, 1981; Elder, 1985). For example, in Figure 5-11 the slope of the line for a swamp-draining watershed is much steeper than that for upland watersheds, indicating a much greater organic export for a given runoff. Nixon (1980) summarized total organic export data from several studies of salt marshes in the United States and suggested a general range of 100 to 200 g/m^2 yr carbon export from salt marshes to adjacent estuaries. This is an order of magnitude greater than the export of carbon from freshwater wetland watersheds as shown in Figure 5-11, indicating that coastal marshes, with their high productivity and frequent tidal exchange, may be more consistent exporters of organic matter than freshwater wetlands. However, the export indicated in Figure 5-11 is based on the entire watershed, some of which is not wetlands.

The effects of this export on adjacent ecosystems has generally been difficult to quantify, although some attempts have been made to establish a cause and effect relationship. Figure 5-12 shows the general scatter of data that results when estuarine productivity is plotted versus the area of adjacent salt marshes per unit open water area. The graph shows both highly productive estuaries with few adjacent marshes and estuaries of low productivity

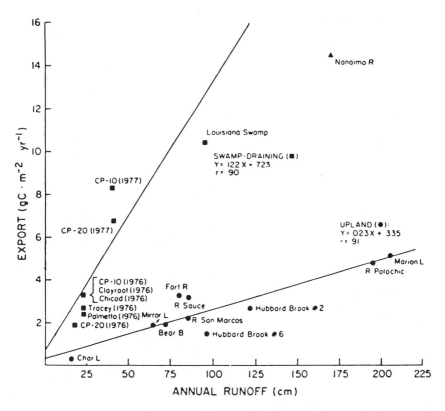

Figure 5-11. Organic carbon export from wetland-dominated watersheds compared with nonwetland watersheds. *(From Mulholland and Kuenzler, 1979, p. 964; Copyright © 1979 by the American Society of Limnology and Oceanography, reprinted with permission)*

amid great expanses of marshes. Some investigators, however, have presented evidence that certain estuarine organisms benefit from the adjacent coastal wetland. Odum (1970) and Heald (1969; 1971) demonstrated the importance of mangrove export on commercial and sport fishing in south Florida. Turner (1977) correlated commercial shrimp harvesting and the type and area of adjacent coastal wetlands.

High- and Low-Nutrient Wetlands

There is a misconception in some ecological texts that all wetlands are high-nutrient, highly productive ecosystems. While many of types of wetlands such as tidal marshes and riparian forests have more than adequate supplies of nutrients and consequently are highly productive, there are many wetland

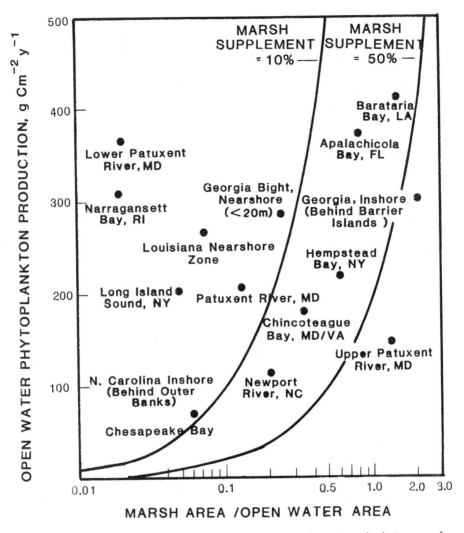

Figure 5-12. Relationship between estuarine primary productivity and relative area of surrounding salt marshes. *(After Nixon, 1980, p. 489)*

types that have low supplies of nutrients. Table 5-9 lists some of the characteristics of high-nutrient (eutrophic) and low-nutrient (oligotrophic) wetlands. The terms eutrophic and oligotrophic, usually used to denote the trophic state of lakes and estuaries, are appropriate for wetlands despite the difference in structure. In fact, the use of the terms originated in the classification of peatlands (Hutchinson, 1973) and was later converted to use with open bodies of water.

**Table 5-9. Characteristics of High-Nutrient (Eutrophic) and
Low-Nutrient (Oligotrophic) Wetlands**

Characteristic	Low-Nutrient Wetland	High-Nutrient Wetland
Inflows of nutrients	Mainly precipitation	Surface and ground water
Nutrient cycling	Tight closed cycles; adaptations such as carnivorous plants and nutrient translocations	Loose open cycle; few adaptations to shortages
Wetland as source or sink of nutrients	Neither	Either
Exporter of detritus	No	Usually
Net primary productivity	Low (100-500 g/m$^2 \cdot$ yr)	High (1,000-4,000 g/m$^2 \cdot$ yr)
Examples	Ombrotrophic bog; cypress dome	Floodplain wetland; many coastal marshes

Intrasystem cycling of nutrients in wetlands is dependent on the availability of the nutrients and the degree to which processes such as primary productivity and decomposition are controlled by the wetland environment. The availability of nitrogen and phosphorus is significantly altered by anoxic conditions as discussed earlier in this chapter, but these nutrients are not necessarily limiting to production or consumption. Ammonium nitrogen is high in most wetland soils, and soluble inorganic phosphorus is often in abundance. Intrasystem cycling thus is often limited by the effects that hydrologic conditions have on pathways such as primary productivity and decomposition as discussed in Chapter 4. It is therefore possible to have wetlands with extremely rapid yet open nutrient cycling (e.g., some high-nutrient freshwater marshes) and wetlands with extremely slow nutrient cycling (e.g., low-nutrient ombrotrophic bogs).

Comparison with Terrestrial and Aquatic Systems

It is interesting to compare nutrient cycling in wetlands with drier ecosystems such as upland forests and with deep aquatic systems such as deep lakes or open estuaries. One of the major ways wetlands differ from drier upland ecosystems is that more nutrients are tied up in organic deposits and are lost from ecosystem cycling as peat deposits and/or organic export. Because wetlands are more frequently open to nutrient fluxes than are upland ecosystems, they may not be as dependent on recycling of nutrients; wetlands that are not open to these fluxes will often have lower productivities and slower nutrient cycling than comparable upland ecosystems.

Wetlands are similar to deep aquatic systems in that most of the nutrients are often permanently tied up in sediments and peat. For most deep aquatic systems, the retention of nutrients in organic sediments is probably longer than in wetlands, although few such comparisons have been made. However, wetlands usually involve larger biotic storages of nutrients than do deep aquatic systems, which are primarily plankton dominated. Thus aquatic system nutrient cycling in the autotrophic zone of lakes and coastal waters is more rapid than it is in the autotrophic zone of most wetlands. Another obvious difference between wetlands and lakes or coastal waters is that most wetland plants obtain their nutrients from the sediments, while phytoplankton depend on nutrients dissolved in the water column. Wetland plants have often been described as "nutrient pumps" that bring nutrients from the anaerobic sediments to the aboveground strata. Phytoplankton in lakes and estuaries can be viewed as being "nutrient dumps" that take nutrients out of the aerobic zone and, through settling and death, deposit the nutrients in the anaerobic sediments. Thus, the plants in these two environments can be viewed as having decidedly different functions in nutrient cycling.

Anthropogenic Effects

Human influences have caused significant changes in the chemical cycling in many wetlands. These changes have taken place as a result of land clearing and subsequent erosion, through hydrological modifications such as stream channelization and dams, and through pollution. Increased erosion in the uplands leads to increased deposition of sediments in the lowland wetlands such as forested swamps and coastal salt marshes. This increased accumulation of sediments can cause increased biochemical oxygen demand (BOD) and can alter the hydrologic regime of the wetlands over a relatively short time. Stream channelization and dams can lead to a change in the flooding frequency of many wetlands and thus alter the inputs of nutrients. Dams generally serve as nutrient traps, retaining materials that would otherwise nourish downstream wetlands. In some cases, stream channelization has led to stream downcutting that ultimately drains wetlands.

Sources of pollution also have had localized effects on nutrient cycling in wetlands. Pollutants such as BOD, toxic materials, oils, trace organics, and metals are frequently added to wetlands from municipal industrial wastes and urban and rural runoff. The effects of toxic materials on wetland nutrient cycles are poorly understood, although wetlands are often areas used for the disposal of such materials. The purposeful addition of high-nutrient wastes and wastewaters to some wetlands has been investigated through experimentation in cypress swamps (H. T. Odum et al., 1977*a*), northern peatlands (Kadlec, 1979; Kadlec and Tilton, 1979), and salt marshes (Valiela, Teal, and Sass, 1973). These are discussed in more detain in Chapter 16.

SUMMARY

Wetlands have unique biogeochemical cycles with many chemical transformations and chemical transport processes that are not shared by many other ecosystems. Wetland soils, when submerged, become highly reduced, but often with a narrow oxidized surface zone. Transformations of nitrogen, phosphorus, sulfur, iron, manganese, and carbon that occur within the anaerobic environment all affect the availability of minerals to the ecosystem. Some also cause toxic conditions. Most of the transformations are mediated by microbial populations that are adapted to the cycling of materials in anaerobic environments. Chemicals are hydrologically transported to wetlands through precipitation, surface flow, groundwater, and tides. Wetlands dominated only by precipitation are generally nutrient poor. There is a wide variability of concentrations of chemicals flowing into wetlands from the other three sources. Wetlands have been shown to be nutrient sinks in several studies, although there is a growing consensus that not all wetlands are nutrient sinks nor are the patterns consistent from season to season or year to year. Wetlands are often chemically coupled to adjacent ecosystems by the export of organic materials, although the direct effects on adjacent ecosystems have been difficult to quantify. While wetlands are similar to terrestrial and aquatic ecosystems in that they can be high-nutrient or low-nutrient systems, there are several differences, particularly in the importance of sediment storage of nutrients and in the functioning of the vegetation in the cycle of different nutrients.

6

BIOLOGICAL ADAPTATIONS TO THE WETLAND ENVIRONMENT

Wetland environments are characterized by several environmental stresses that most organisms are ill equipped to handle. Aquatic organisms are not adapted to deal with the periodic drying that occurs in many wetlands. Terrestrial organisms are stressed by long periods of flooding. Because of the shallow water, temperature extremes on the wetland surface are greater than ordinarily expected in aquatic environments. But the most severe stress is probably the absence of oxygen in flooded wetland soils, which prevents organisms from respiring through normal metabolic pathways. In the absence of oxygen, the supply of nutrients available to plants is also modified, and concentrations of certain elements and organic compounds can reach toxic levels. In coastal wetlands, salt is an additional stress to which organisms must respond.

It is not surprising that those plants and animals regularly found in wetlands have evolved functional mechanisms to deal with these stresses. Adaptations can be broadly classified as those that enable the organism to *tolerate* the stress and those that enable it to *regulate* the stress. Tolerators have functional modifications that enable them to survive, and often to function efficiently, in the presence of the stress. Regulators actively avoid the stress or modify it to minimize its effects. The specific mechanisms for either tolerating or regulating are many and varied. In general, bacteria show biochemical adaptations that are also characteristic of the range of cell-level adaptations found in more complex multicellular plants and animals. Vascular plants show both structural and physiological adaptations. Animals have developed the widest range of adaptations, not only through biochemical and structural means, but also by using to advantage their mobility and their complex life history patterns.

PROTISTS

Protists are one-celled organisms with little mobility; therefore, the range of adaptations open to them is limited. Most adaptations of this group are metabolic. Since the metabolism in all living cells is similar, adaptations of this group are characteristic of cell-level adaptations in general, although some of the bacterial responses to anoxia are beyond anything found in higher organisms.

Anoxia

When an organic wetland soil is flooded, the oxygen available in the soil and in the water is rapidly depleted through metabolism by organisms that normally use oxygen as the terminal electron acceptor for the oxidation of organic molecules. The rate of diffusion of molecular oxygen through water is limited and cannot supply the metabolic demand under most circumstances. When the demand exceeds the supply, dissolved oxygen is depleted, the redox potential in the soil drops rapidly, and other ions (nitrate, manganese, iron, sulfate, and carbon dioxide) are progressively reduced (see chap. 5 and Table 5-2). Although some abiotic chemical reduction occurs in the soil, virtually all of these reductions are coupled to microbial respiration (oxidation reactions). When oxygen concentrations first become limiting, most cells, bacterial or otherwise, use internal organic compounds as electron acceptors. This fermentation pathway results in the reduction of pyruvate to ethyl alcohol, lactic acid, or other reduced organic compounds, depending on the organism. A number of bacteria also have the ability to couple their oxidative respiratory reactions to the reduction of inorganic ions in the surrounding medium, using them as electron acceptors. Many bacterial species are facultative anaerobes, capable of switching from aerobic to anaerobic respiration. But others have become so specialized that they can grow only under anaerobic conditions, and rely on specific electron acceptors other than oxygen in order to respire. *Desulfovibrio* is one such genus. It uses sulfate as its terminal electron acceptor, forming sulfides that give the marsh its characteristic rotten-egg odor. Other microbially mediated chemical reactions in anoxic sediments were discussed in chapter 5.

Most bacteria require organic energy sources. In contrast, the nonphotosynthetic autotrophic bacteria are adapted to use the energy of reduced inorganic compounds in the wetland muds as an energy source for growth.

The genus *Thiobacillus,* for example, can reoxidize the sulfide formed by the *Desulfovibrios.* Members of the genus *Nitrosomonas* oxidize ammonia to nitrite. *Siderocapsa* can capture the energy released in the oxidation of the ferrous ion to the ferric form (Nester et al., 1973). Thus, adaptations to the anoxic environment of wetland soils enable bacteria not only to survive in it, but sometimes to require it and even to obtain their energy from it.

Salt

In a freshwater aquatic or soil environment, the cytoplasmic osmotic concentration in bacterial cells is higher than that of the surrounding medium. As a result, the cells absorb water until the turgor pressure of the cytoplasm is balanced by the resistance of their cell walls. In coastal wetlands, organisms must cope with high and variable external salt concentrations. The dangers of salts are twofold—osmotic and directly toxic. The immediate effect of an increase in salt concentration in a cell's environment is osmotic. If the osmotic potential surrounding the cell is higher than that of the cell cytoplasm, water is drawn out of the cell and the cytoplasm dehydrates. This is a rapid reaction that can occur in a matter of minutes and may be lethal to the cell. Often the cytoplasm gradually rehydrates as salt diffuses through the cell membrane, raising the internal osmotic concentration, or the cell produces soluble organic compounds in response to the stress. The absorption of inorganic ions may relieve the osmotic gradient across the cell membrane, but inorganic ions at high concentrations in the cytoplasm are also toxic to most organisms, posing a second threat to survival.

Bacteria have adapted in a number of ways to cope with these twin problems of osmotic shock and toxicity. There is no evidence that cells are able to retain water against an osmotic gradient. Rather, the internal osmotic concentration of salt-adapted cells is usually slightly higher than the external concentration. Even the "tightest" membranes leak salts passively, so that, in the absence of any active regulation by the cell, inorganic salts would be expected to accumulate in the cell, causing the internal osmotic concentration to rise. Indeed, the high specific gravities of *halophiles*—literally "salt-loving" organisms—can be accounted for only by the presence of inorganic salts at high concentrations (Ingram, 1957). However, analyses of cell contents show that the balance of specific ions is usually quite different than that of the external solution. For example, potassium is usually accumulated and sodium is usually diluted relative to external concentrations (Table 6-1). Active transport mechanisms that accumulate or excrete ions across cell membranes are universal features of all living cells, and there is no evidence that large energy expenditures are needed to maintain the gradients shown in Table 6-1. They can be maintained in the cold, in cells apparently carrying out little metabolism (Ginsburg, Sachs, and Ginsburg, 1971). This suggests

Table 6-1. Internal Ionic Concentration of Bacteria Growing with NaCl at Different Concentrations

| | Ion Concentration (M) | | | |
| | External medium | | Cell cytoplasm | |
Bacterium	Na^+	K^+	Na^+	K^+
Vibrio costicola[a]	1.0	0.004	0.684	0.221
	0.6	0.008	0.505	0.524
	1.0	0.008	0.584	0.661
	1.6	0.008	1.09	0.594
	2.0	0.008	0.898	0.567
Paracoccus halodini- trificans	1.0	0.004	0.311	0.474
Pseudomonas 101	1.0	0.0055	0.90	0.71
	2.0	0.0055	1.15	0.89
	3.0	0.005	1.04	0.67
Marine pseudomonad B-16	0.3		0.123	0.374
Unidentified salt- tolerant rod	0.6	0.04	0.05	0.34
	4.4	0.04	0.62	0.58
Halobacterium cutirubrum[b]	3.33	0.05	0.80	5.32

Source: After Kushner, 1978

[a]The difference between K^+ concentration in different studies may be related to whether the cultures were in stationary phase or were growing exponentially.

[b]Several workers have reported similar or higher results for K^+ in H. cutirubrum or H. halobium.

that the potassium ions are loosely bound or complexed within the cytoplasm, or that the cytoplasmic water has a more ordered structure than external water and such cytoplasmic ions as potassium and sodium are less free than in external solutions but still free enough to be osmotically and physiologically active (Kushner, 1978).

Although inorganic ions seem to make up the bulk of the osmotically active cell solutes in some halophilic bacteria, in others the internal salt concentration can be substantially lower than the external concentration. In these organisms the rest of the osmotic activity is supplied by organic compounds. For example, the halophilic green alga Dunaliella virigus contains large amounts of glycerol, the concentration varying with the external salt concentration; and certain salt-tolerant yeasts regulate internal osmotic concentration with polyols such as glycerol and arabitol. The enzymes of these organisms seem to be salt sensitive, and it is suggested that the organic compounds act as "compatible solutes" that raise the osmotic pressure without interfering with enzymatic activity (Kushner, 1978).

The steric configuration of enzymes of salt-sensitive organisms is easily modified by salt at high concentrations, and, where enzymes are activated by specific ions, NaCl can interfere with activity. The enzymes of true halophiles, in contrast, are able to function normally in the presence of, or even to require, inorganic ions at high concentrations.

VASCULAR PLANTS

Emergent plants are structurally much more complex than protists. They are sessile, but only their roots are in an anoxic or salty environment. Adaptations to these two stresses are both structural and physiological.

Anoxia

Structural Adaptations

Virtually all wetland plants have elaborate structural mechanisms to avoid root anoxia. The main strategy has been the evolution of air spaces (aerenchyma) in roots and stems that allow the diffusion of oxygen from the aerial portions of the plant into the roots (Fig. 6-1). In plants with well-developed aerenchyma, the root cells no longer depend on diffusion of oxygen from the surrounding soil, the main source of root oxygen to terrestrial plants. Whereas, in normal mesophytes, plant porosity is usually a low 2%–7% of volume, in wetland species up to 60% of the plant body is pore space. The air spaces are formed either by cell separation during maturation of the organs or by cell breakdown. They result in a honeycomb type of structure. The air spaces are

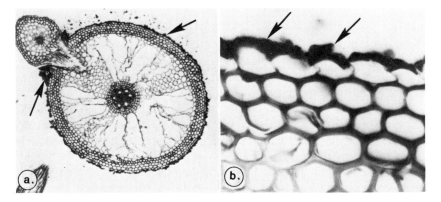

Figure 6-1. Light photomicrographs of *Spartina alterniflora* roots: *a.* cross section of a streamside root; arrows indicate the presence of red ferric deposits on the root epidermis. ×192; *b.* streamside root cross section showing the presence of similar materials on the external walls of the epidermal cells. ×1,143. Note the extensive pore space (aerenchyma) in the roots. *(From Mendelssohn and Postek, 1982, p. 906; Copyright © 1982 by the Botanical Society of America, reprinted with permission)*

not necessarily continuous throughout the stem and roots. However, the thin cellular partitions within the aerenchyma are not likely to impeded internal gas diffusion significantly (Armstrong, 1975). The development of aerenchyma in flooded plant roots appears to be controlled by the plant hormone ethylene. Ethylene production is stimulated by flooded conditions. Ethylene in turn stimulates cellulase activity in cortex cells of a number of plant species, with the subsequent collapse and disintegration of cell walls (Kawase, 1981). Ethylene also has been reported to stimulate the formation of adventitious roots, which develop in both flood-tolerant (e.g., willow) and flood-intolerant (e.g., tomato) plants just above the anaerobic zone when these plants are flooded.

   The sufficiency of the oxygen supply to the roots depends on root permeability (i.e., how leaky the root is to oxygen, which can move out into the surrounding soil), the root respiration rate, the length of the diffusion pathway from the upper parts of the plant, and root porosity (the pore space volume). But models of gas diffusion show that, under most circumstances, root porosity is the overriding factor governing internal root oxygen concentration (Fig. 6-2).

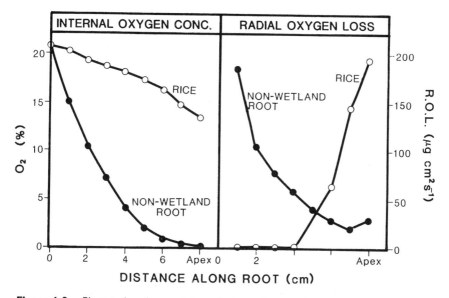

Figure 6-2. Electrical analog model predictions of internal oxygen balance and radial oxygen loss (R.O.L.) along a nonwetland adapted root and a wetland-adapted rice root. Root length = 8 cm; root radius = 0.05 cm; soil oxygen consumption = $4 \times 10^{-5} cm^3$ (O_2) cm^{-3} (soil) s^{-1}. Radial oxygen loss (R.O.L.) is the rate of diffusion of oxygen out of the root into the substrate. *(From Armstrong, 1978, p. 292; Copyright © 1978 by Technomics Publication Co., reprinted with permission)*

The effectiveness of aerenchyma in supplying oxygen to the roots has been demonstrated with a number of plant species. For example, the root respiration of flood-tolerant *Senecio aquaticus* was only 50% inhibited by anaerobiosis, while that of *S. Jacobaea,* a flood-sensitive species, was almost completely inhibited. Greater root porosity in the tolerant species was the primary factor that contributed to the difference (Lambers, Steingrover, and Smakman, 1978). The most extensively studied flood-tolerant plant is rice *(Oryza sativa).* Rice plants grown under continuous flooding develop greater root porosity than unflooded plants, and this maintains the oxygen concentration in the root tissues. Under anoxia, rice root mitochondrial changes were identical to those of flood-sensitive pumpkin plants, showing that the basis of resistance was by avoidance of root anoxia, not by physiological changes in cell metabolism (Levitt, 1980).

The water lily *(Nuphar luteum)* is a particularly interesting example of an adaptation of this type. Air moves into the internal gas spaces of young leaves on the water surface and is forced down through the aerenchyma of the stem into the roots by a slight pressure generated by the heating of the leaves. The older leaves lose their capacity to support pressure gradients, so the return flow of gas from the roots is through the older leaves. It is rich in carbon dioxide from root respiration (Dacey, 1980).

The species of woody trees that are successful (as opposed to tolerant) in the wetland habitat are few, and include the mangroves, cypress, tupelo, willow, and a few others. As with herbaceous species, an adequate ventilating system seems to be essential for their growth. Many trees and herbaceous species produce adventitious roots above the anoxic zone. These roots are able to function normally in an aerobic environment. The red mangrove *(Rhizophora mangle)* grows on arched prop roots in the tidal swamps of Florida (see chap. 10). These prop roots have numerous small pores termed lenticels above the tide level, which terminate in long, spongy, air-filled submerged roots. The oxygen concentration in these roots, embedded in anoxic mud, may remain as high as 15%–18% continuously, but if the lenticels are blocked this concentration can fall to 2% or less in two days (Scholander, van Dam, and Scholander, 1955). Similarly, black mangrove *(Avicennia germinans)* produces thousands of pneumatophores (air roots), about 20–30 cm high by 1 cm in diameter, spongy, and studded with lenticels. They protrude out of the mud from main roots and are exposed during low tides. The oxygen concentration of the main roots has a tidal pulse, rising during low tide and falling during submergence, reflecting the cycle of emergence of the air roots (Scholander, van Dam, and Scholander, 1955). The "knees" of bald cypress *(Taxodium distichum)* have also been thought to improve gas exchange to the root system, although Kramer, Riley, and Bannister (1952) gave contrary evidence (see chap. 13).

The magnitude of oxygen diffusion through many wetland plants into the roots is apparently large enough not only to supply the roots but also to diffuse out and oxidize the adjacent anoxic soil (Teal and Kanwisher, 1966; Howes et al., 1981). Mendelssohn and Postek (1982) recently showed, through scanning electron microscopy coupled with x-ray microanalysis, that the brown deposits found around the roots of *Spartina alterniflora* are composed of iron and manganese deposits formed when root oxygen comes in contact with reduced soil ferrous ions (Fig. 6-1). It has been suggested (Armstrong, 1975) that oxygen diffusion from the roots is an important mechanism to moderate the toxic effects of soluble reduced ions such as manganese in anoxic soil. These ions tend to be oxidized and precipitated in the rhizosphere, which effectively detoxifies them.

Respiration

The presence of root air space and the ability to transport oxygen through the plant to the roots does not always satisfy the oxygen requirements of root tissues. Mendelssohn and Postek (1982), for example, found that the oxidized rhizosphere was only 1/50 as well developed around the roots of inland marsh plants compared with streamside ones, indicating that oxygen availability was limited in inland sites.

Under conditions of oxygen deprivation, plant tissues respire anaerobically, as described for bacterial cells. In most plants, pyruvate, the end product of glycolysis, is decarboxylated to acetaldehyde, which is reduced to ethanol (Fig. 6-3). Both of these compounds are potentially toxic to root tissues. Flooding-tolerant plants often have adaptations to minimize this toxicity. For example, *S. alterniflora* roots, under anaerobic conditions, show much increased activity of alcohol dehydrogenase, the inducible enzyme that catalyzes the reduction of acetaldehyde to ethanol. The increase in the enzyme indicates a switch to anaerobic respiration, and it also explains why acetaldehyde does not accumulate in the root tissue. Ethanol does not accumulate either, although its production is apparently stimulated (Mendelssohn, McKee, and Postek, 1982). Alcohol diffuses from rice roots during anaerobiosis (Bertani, Bramblila, and Menegus, 1980), thus preventing a toxic buildup, and it is probable that this occurs in *Spartina* also.

Another metabolic strategy reduces the production of alcohol by shifting metabolism to accumulate nontoxic malate instead (Fig. 6-3). MacMannon and Crawford (1971) have suggested that malic acid accumulation may be a characteristic feature of wetland species. In flooding-intolerant species excess malate is converted to pyruvate and then to acetaldehyde and ethanol, whereas they suggest that flooding-tolerant species lack the malic enzyme and consequently malate accumulates. Mendelssohn, McKee, and Patrick, (1981) reported that two different kinds of adaptation occur in *S. alterniflora*. Vigorous plants in the well-aerated streamside zone have low levels of ADH

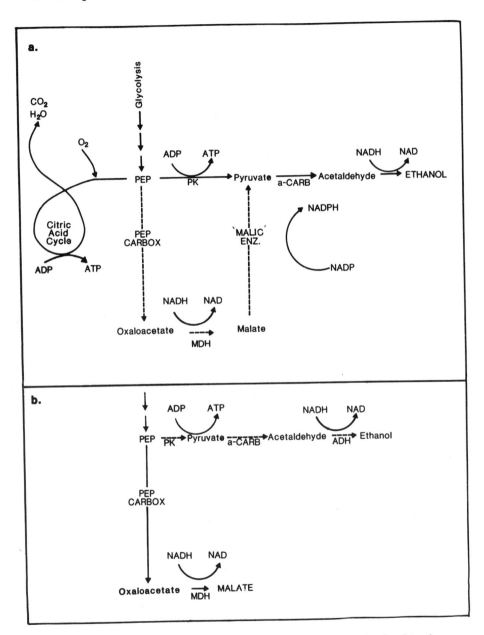

Figure 6-3. Metabolic schemes of events following the flooding of *a.* flood intolerant and *b.* flood tolerant species. PEP = phosphoenol pyruvate; PK = pyruvate kinase; a-CARB = a-carboxylase; ADH = alcohol dehydrogenase; PEP CARBOX = phosphoenol pyruvate carboxylase; MDH = malate dehydrogenase. In flood tolerant species ADH production is stimulated. The accumulated ethanol may diffuse from the plant roots. Furthermore, the malic enzyme is absent in flood tolerant plants, so that nontoxic malate accumulates (see text). *(After MacMannon and Crawford, 1971)*

activity combined with high levels of adenosine triphosphate (ATP) and high energy charge (EC) ratios, indicative of active aerobic metabolism. Somewhat further inland the soil redox potential falls, root ADH remains low, malate accumulates, and ATP and the EC ratio drop. Mendelssohn, McKee, and Patrick (1981) interpret this to mean that as oxygen becomes limiting to the root cells, root metabolism shifts to accumulate nontoxic malate as an end product of glycolysis. However, since this metabolic pathway has a low biological energy yield, root ATP and the EC ratio decline. This can only be a short-term solution to flooding.

Still further inland, when the soil redox potential falls below -200 mv, root cells suddenly show high ADH activity, accompanied by an increase of ATP and the EC ratio to levels as high as those for streamside plants. This signifies a shift to alcohol fermentation, which results in the production of usable energy and high ATP levels. Ethanol does not accumulate in the root tissues, however, and Mendelssohn, McKee, and Patrick (1981) suggest that it diffuses out of the roots. Malate does not accumulate under these circumstances either, suggesting that metabolites are being routed through the fermentation pathway. Although this fermentation pathway provides a steady source of energy to the roots, it is an inefficient pathway of metabolism, and plants under these anaerobic conditions grow very poorly, probably because the metabolic energy source becomes exhausted.

Salt

At the cell level, plants behave towards salt in much the same way as bacteria do, and their adaptive strategies are identical. However, vascular plants have also developed adaptations that take advantage of their structural complexity. These include barriers to prevent or control the entry of salts, and organs specialized to excrete salts. In both cases, specialized cells bear most of the burden of the adaptation, allowing the remaining cells to function in a less hostile environment. It is generally thought that the air space of the root cortex is freely accessible from the rhizosphere, so the endodermis forms the first real barrier to the upward movement of solutes from the soil. This is confirmed by the observation that the roots of plants in high-salt environments often have much higher salt concentrations (and must also have higher salt tolerance) than the leaves do. X-ray microanalysis of the salt-resistant *Puccinellia peisonis* showed a decreasing concentration of sodium and an increasing concentration of potassium in the roots from the outer cortex through the endodermis to the stele (Stelzer and Lauchli, 1978). Both the inner cells of the cortex and the passage cells of the stele seemed to be barriers to sodium transport, while potassium moved through fairly freely. The selectivity for potassium (or the exclusion of sodium) was seen to be common in bacteria also (Table 6-1). As a result of the filtering out of salt at the endodermis, the sap of many halophytes is nearly pure water. The mangroves *Rhizophora, Laguncularia, and Sonneratia* exclude salts almost completely. Their sap concentrations are only about 1-1.5 mg NaCl per ml (compared with about 35 mg/ml in seawater). *Avicennia* has a higher sap concentration of about 4-8 mg/ml (Scholander et al., 1966). When fluid is expressed from leaves of these species by pressure, it is almost pure distilled water. Thus both the endodermis and the leaf cell membrane act as ultrafilters. The leaf cytoplasm must have an osmotic potential equal to the water potential of the root medium in order to retain water, and, in the mangroves, 50%-70% of this osmotic potential is obtained from sodium in chloride ions. Most of the remaining is presumably organic. In *Batis,* a succulent halophyte, NaCl alone makes up 90% of the total osmotic concentration (Scholander et al., 1966).

Some plants that do not exclude salts at the root, or are "leaky" to salt, have secretory organs. The leaves of many salt marsh grasses, for example, characteristically are covered with crystalline salt particles excreted through specialized salt glands embedded in the leaf. These glands do not function passively; rather, they selectively remove certain ions from the vascular tissues of the leaf. In *Spartina,* for example, the excretion is enriched in sodium, relative to potassium.

These two mechanisms, salt exclusion and salt secretion, protect the shoot and leaf cells of the plant from salt at high concentrations and maintain an optimum ionic balance between mono- and divalent cations and between sodium and potassium. At the same time, the osmotic concentration of the cells of salt-tolerant plants must be maintained at a level high enough to allow absorption of water from the root medium. Where the inorganic salt concentration is kept low, organic compounds make up the rest of the osmoticum in the cells.

Photosynthesis

One adaptation that many wetland plant species share with plants in other stressed environments, especially in drought-stressed environments, is the C_4 biochemical pathway of photosynthesis (formally called the Hatch-Slack-Kortschak pathway, after the discoverers). It gets its identity from the fact that the first product of CO_2 incorporation is a four-carbon compound, oxaloacetic acid. This pathway is outlined in simplified form in Figure 6-4 and C_4 plants are compared with C_3 plants in Table 6-2. The first compound resulting from CO_2 incorporation in C_3 plants is a 3-carbon compound phosphoglyceric acid. C_3 plants are much more common than are C_4 plants.

Although water is a universal feature of wetlands, plants in saline wetland habitats have much the same problem of water availability as do plants in arid areas. In both cases, the water potential of the substrate is very low—in arid zones because the soil is dry, in saline wetlands because the water potential is lowered by its salt content. In wetlands, water uptake is accompanied by a mass flow of dissolved salts to the roots; their absorption must be

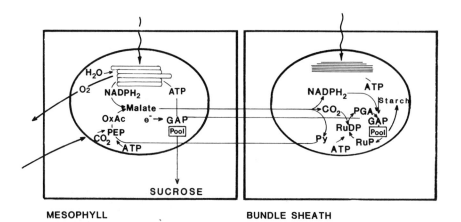

MESOPHYLL   BUNDLE SHEATH

Figure 6-4. A much simplified diagram of CO_2 fixation via the Hatch-Slack-Kortschak pathway in C_4 plants. PEP = phosphoenol pyruvate; OxAc = oxaloacetate; PGA = 3-phosphoglyceric acid; GAP = 3-phosphoglyceraldehyde; RuP = ribulose-5-phosphate; Py = pyruvate. PGA is also produced by carboxylation of C_2 compounds that appear in the pool; the regeneration of PEP from PGA, in which water is given off, is not shown. *(From Larcher 1983, p. 77; Copyright © 1983 by Springer-Verlag, reproduced with permission)*

Table 6-2. Comparison of Aspects of Photosynthesis of Herbaceous C_3 and C_4 Plants

Photosynthetic Characteristics	C_3	C_4
Theoretical energy requirement for net CO_2 fixation, CO_2:ATP:NADPH	1:3:2	1:5:2
CO_2 compensation concentration, ppm CO_2	30-70	0-10
Transpiration ratio, g H_2O transpired/g dry wt	450-950	250-350
Optimum day temperature for net CO_2 fixation, C°	15-25	30-47
Response of net photosynthesis to increasing light intensity	saturation at ¼ to ½ full sunlight	Proportional to or saturation at full sunlight
Maximum rate of net photosynthesis, mg CO_2/dm² leaf surface/hr	15-40	40-80
Maximum growth rate, g/m² · day	19.5	30.3
Dry matter production, g/m² · yr	2,200	3,860

Source: Based on data from Black, 1973

regulated, at an energy cost, by the plant. Therefore, in both environments, mechanisms that reduce water loss (transpiration) provide an adaptive advantage. For a plant to take up carbon dioxide for photosynthesis the stomata must be open, and if they are open during the bright hours of the day water loss is excessive. Plants with the C_4 pathway can use carbon dioxide more effectively than other plants. They are able to withdraw it from the atmosphere until its concentration falls below 20 ppm (as compared with 30–80 ppm for C_3 plants). This is achieved by using phosphoenolpyruvate (PEP), which has a high affinity for CO_2, as the carbon dioxide acceptor, instead of the ribulose diphosphate acceptor of the conventional pathway. In addition, the malate formed by this carboxylation is nontoxic and can be stored in the cell until it is later decarboxylated and the carbon dioxide is fixed through the normal C_3 pathway. As we have seen, one common end product of anaerobic respiration in wetland plants is malate. The production of PEP and C_4 metabolism provides a potential pathway for recycling carbon dioxide from cell respiration.

Additionally, plants using the C_4 pathway of photosynthesis have low photorespiration rates and the ability to use efficiently even the most intense sunlight. These differences make C_4 plants more efficient than most C_3 plants, both in their rates of carbon fixation and in the amount of water used per unit of carbon fixed (Table 6-2). Finally, Armstrong (1975) suggested that water conservation mechanisms have the additional function in wetland plants of reducing the rate at which soil toxins are drawn toward the root. This increases the probability of detoxifying them as they move through the oxidized rhizosphere.

Among the common wetland angiosperms that have been shown to photosynthesize through the C_4 pathway are *S. alterniflora, S. townsendii, S. foliosa, Cyperus rotundus, Echinochloa crus-galli, Panicum dichotomiflorum, P. virgatum, Paspalum distichum, Phragmites communis,* and *Sporobolus cryptandrus.*

It is obvious that this adaptation is fairly common in the wetland environment. Table 6-3 compares some of the photosynthetic attributes of two salt-marsh species, *S. alterniflora,* a C_4 plant, and *Juncus roemerianus,* a C_3 plant. The tall form of *S. alterniflora* grows along creek banks, the short form further inland in poorly drained soils. Compared with *J. roemerianus, S. alterniflora* has a higher rate of photosynthesis, a lower CO_2 compensation concentration (the CO_2 concentration in the leaf cellular spaces when photosynthesis is reduced to zero), a lower respiration rate in the light, and a higher temperature optimum. Water use efficiency (Table 6-3) is an important index of the ability of plants to photosynthesize with minimum water loss, especially in arid or saline environments, where available water is in scarce supply. *S. alterniflora* is almost twice as efficient in this respect as *J. roemerianus.*

One characteristic in which *J. roemerianus* does not fit the typical C_3 plant pattern is in its photosynthetic response to light intensity (Fig. 6-5).

Table 6-3. Comparison of Photosynthetic Characteristics of Two Wetland Plant Species: *Spartina alterniflora*, a C_4 Plant; and *Juncus roemerianus*, a C_3 Plant

Photosynthetic Characteristics	Spartina alterniflora		*Juncus roemerianus*
	Tall form	*Short form*	
Maximum seasonal net photosynthetic rate, mg CO_2/cm^2 · sec (month)	90 (Sept.)	65 (July)	60 (March)
Photosynthetic light response (see Fig. 6-5)	Nonsaturating	Saturating	Nonsaturating
CO_2 compensation concentration, mg CO_2/l	12	84	84
Photorespiration at 21% O_2, mg CO_2/cm^2 · sec (% of photosynthesis)	6.7 (11)	18.2 (40)	9.1 (54)
Temperature optimum (summer), °C	30-35	30-35	25
Water use efficiency, mg CO_2/g H_2O	15	12-15	8-9

Source: Based on data from Giurgevich and Dunn (1978, 1979)

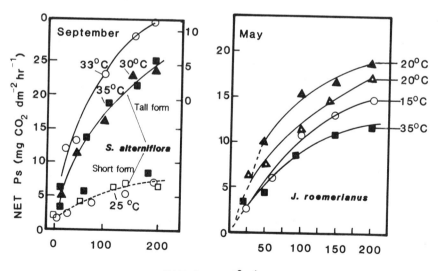

Figure 6-5. Light-photosynthesis curves for *Spartina alterniflora* and *Juncus roemerianus* at different ambient temperatures. PAR = photosynthetically active radiation. *(After Giurgevich and Dunn, 1978, 1979)*

Both species increase photosynthetic rates with increasing light intensity to full sunlight, although C_3 plants typically reach saturation at no more than one-half full intensity. The short form of *S. alterniflora* behaves in a way intermediate to the tall form and the C_3 plant. It is not known whether this reflects a switch from C_4 to C_3 metabolism under conditions of oxygen stress. Although the C_4 adaptations appear to infer some selective advantage for plants in wetlands, these advantages are not enough to displace well-adapted C_3 species such as *J. roemerianus*.

ANIMALS

Animals are exposed to the same range of environmental conditions in wetlands as protists and plants, but, because of their complexity, their adaptations are more varied. The adaptation may be as varied as a biochemical response at the cell level, a physiological response of the whole organism such as a modification of the circulatory system, or a behavioral response such as modified feeding habits. Furthermore, although it is convenient to discuss the specific response mechanisms to individual kinds of environmental stresses, in reality an organism must respond simultaneously to a complex of environmental factors, and it is the success of this integrated response that determines the fate of the organism. For example, one possible response to a stress is avoidance by moving out of the stress zone. But in wetlands that might mean moving from an anoxic zone within the soil to the surface, where temperature extremes and dessication pose a different set of physiological problems. Thus the organism's successful adaptations are often compromises that enable it to live with several competing environmental demands.

Anoxia

At the cell level the metabolic responses of animals to anoxia are similar to those of bacteria. However, evolutionary development has put a premium on aerobic metabolism, so the higher animals (in an evolutionary sense) tend to have less ability to adapt to anaerobic conditions than primitive ones. The vertebrates and more complex invertebrates are limited in anaerobic respiration to glycolysis or to the pentose monophosphate pathway, with lactate the dominant end product. In all higher animals, the internal cell environment is closely regulated. As a result, most adaptations are organism-level ones to maintain the internal environment. Vernberg and Vernberg (1972) list six major kinds of adaptations among marine organisms to control gaseous exchange:

1. development or modification of specialized regions of the body for gaseous exchange; for example, gills on fish and crustacea, parapodia on polychaetes

2. mechanisms to improve the oxygen gradient across a diffusible membrane; for example, by moving to oxygen-rich environments or by moving water across the gills by ciliary action
3. internal structural changes such as increased vascularization, a better circulation system, or a stronger pump (the heart)
4. modification of respiratory pigments to improve oxygen-carrying capacity
5. behavioral patterns such as decreased locomotor activity or closing a shell during low oxygen stress
6. physiological adaptations, including shifts in metabolic pathways and heart pumping rates

Examples of different kinds of adaptations are numerous. We give a few here to illustrate their diversity. Crabs inhabit a wide range of marine habitats. The number and total volume of gills of crabs living on land are less per unit body weight than in aquatic species. In addition, the gills of some intertidal crabs have become highly sclerotized with the units supported, apparently so that the gill leaves do not stick together when the crab is out of the water (Vernberg and Vernberg, 1972). Tube-dwelling amphipods apparently can function efficiently with low oxygen supplies. At saturated oxygen tensions, they exhibit an intermittent rhythm of ventilation. At low tide when the oxygen in their burrows drops to very low levels they ventilate continuously, but do not hyperventilate as free-swimming amphipods do. Because of the resistance of their tubes to water flow, hyperventilation would be energetically expensive (Vernberg, 1981).

Many marine animals associated with anoxic wetland soils have high concentrations of respiratory pigments, and/or pigments with unusually high affinities for oxygen. These include the nematode *Enoplus communis,* the Atlantic bloodworm *(Glycera dibranchiata),* the clam *Mercenaria mercenaria,* and even the land crab *Carooma quannumi* (Vernberg and Vernberg, 1972; Vernberg and Coull, 1981). Fiddler crabs (*Uca* spp.) illustrate the complex behavioral and physiological patterns to be found in the intertidal zone. The crabs are active during low tides, feeding daily when the marsh floor is exposed. (Incidentally, this pattern of activity is based on an innate lunar rhythm, not on a direct sensing of low water levels. When transported miles from the ocean they continue to be active at the time low tide would occur in their new location.) When the tide rises, they retreat to their burrows, where the oxygen concentration can become very low because fiddler crabs apparently do not pump water in their burrows. However, not only are these species relatively resistant to anoxia, but also the critical oxygen tension (that is, the tension below which respiratory activity is reduced) is low, 0.01-0.03 atmospheres for inactive and 0.03-0.08 atmospheres for active crabs. They can continue to consume oxygen down to a level of 0.004 atmospheres (Vernberg and Vernberg, 1972). When oxygen levels get very low in the burrows, the crabs simply become inactive and consume very little oxygen. They may remain that way for several tidal cycles without harm.

Intertidal bivalves close their valves tightly or loosely when the tide recedes. Widdows et al. (1979) found that four different bivalves had lower respiration rates in air (valves closed) than when in water. All could respire anaerobically, but the accumulation of end products of anaerobic respiration depended on how tightly the shells were closed and, thus, how much oxygen they received. Tolerance to anoxia may change during the life of an organism. Larvae of fiddler crabs, which are planktonic, are much more sensitive to low oxygen than are the burrowing adults. An interesting, but rather unusual, adaptation is that of a gastrotrich *(Thiodasys sterreri)*, which is reported to be able to use sulfide as an energy source under extreme anaerobiosis (Maguire and Boaden, 1975).

Salt

As with oxygen stress, the major mechanisms of adaptation by animals to salt involve control of the body's internal environment. Most simple marine animals are *osmoconformers;* that is, their internal cell environment follows closely the osmotic concentration of the external medium. But with increased body complexity, animals tend to *osmoregulate;* that is, to control the internal osmotic concentration. This is particularly true of animals that inhabit the upper intertidal zone, where they are exposed to widely varying salinities and, in addition, to prolonged periods of dessication. *Euryhaline* organisms can tolerate wide fluctuations in salinity. *Stenohaline* organisms, on the other hand, survive within fairly narrow osmotic limits. Most marsh organisms must be euryhaline, but they may be either osmoconformers or osmoregulators.

Figure 6-6 illustrates the imperfect osmoregulation found in penaeid shrimp. The hemolymph concentration of a perfect osmoconformer would follow the solid line of isotonicity. In contrast, a perfect osmoregulator would have a constant internal concentration, illustrated by a horizontal line on the graph. The brown shrimp *(Penaeus aztecus)* is intermediate between these two positions. The internal environment varies much less than the external medium, but is not constant. At low external salt concentrations, the shrimp is hyperosmotic, indicating a water potential gradient into the organism, usually achieved by concentrating sodium and chloride ions. This is probably less expensive energetically than the hypoosmotic regulation shown at high external salt concentrations. In this circumstance the water potential gradient is directed out of the animal, which means that dehydration would occur if the body covering were not to some extent impervious to water movement. Animals with the ability for hypoosmotic regulation must have some mechanism to lower the osmotic concentration of the body. This is

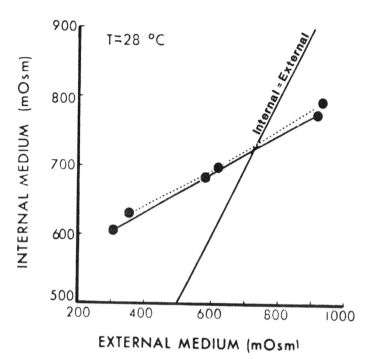

Figure 6-6. Mean hemolymph osmolality (mOsm) of 3.7 (·········) and 6.7 g (———) penaeid shrimp *Penaeus aztecus* at 28°C. *(From Bishop, Gosselink, and Stone, 1980, p. 747)*

accomplished through special regulatory organs and organ systems, chiefly renal organs (kidney, antennal glands, or more primitive nephridia), gills, salt-secretory nasal or rectal glands, and the specialized excretory functions of the gut. These organs are able to move ions across cell membranes against the concentration gradient, concentrating them in some excretory product such as urine.

Figure 6-7 illustrates the differences in adaptation to salinity changes in species of crabs that inhabitat different environments. The aquatic species *Cancer* is an osmoconformer. Species that are submerged most of the time, but subject to wider osmotic fluctuations (*Hemigrapsus* and *Pachygrapsus*) are imperfect osmoregulators. The other species (including *Uca*, a common marsh crab) are from the high intertidal zone. They are excellent osmoregulators, an adaptation obviously useful in the variable salinity and frequent dessication of their habitat. Regulation in these species is controlled both by differences in exoskeleton permeability and by specialized organs. The exoskeleton of terrestrial crabs is less permeable to water and salts than that of semiterrestrial species, which in turn are less permeable than subtidal crabs. The antennal glands seem to control the concentrations of specific

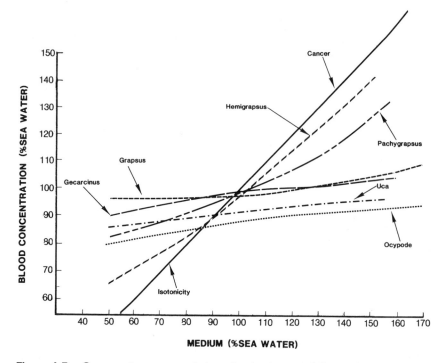

Figure 6-7. Comparative osmoregulation of crabs showing different degrees of adaption to the terrestrial environment. *Cancer* is an aquatic species; *Hemigrapsus* and *Pachygrapsus*, low intertidal zone; the other species are terrestrial or high intertidal zone inhabitants. *(From Gross, 1964, p. 451; Copyright © 1964 by the Biological Bulletin, reprinted with permission)*

ions in the hemolymph. Osmoregulation, however, is controlled by the gills and the posterior deverticulum of the alimentary canal (Vernberg and Vernberg, 1972). How complex the adaptations are is illustrated by the permeability of the foregut of the land crab *(Gecarcinus lateralis)* to both water and salts. This permeability varies with time and environmental circumstance and is under neuroendocrine control (Mantel, 1968).

Other Adaptations

Reproduction

As might be expected, adaptations to specific habitats involve virtually every facet of an organism's existence. We have focused primarily on the immediate response of the individual to stresses of the wetland environment. But in terms of species survival, reproduction is equally important. In an evolutionary sense, a species strategy must be to produce reproductively active offspring at minimum energy cost. For infauna in the marsh sediment where mobility is restricted, this is often accomplished by direct contact of organisms for fertilization, and by direct growth of offspring through the elimination of larval stages or by larvae that remain in place. Epibenthic organisms in a fluctuating environment, in contrast, often produce enormous numbers of pelagic larvae that are widely distributed by currents and tides. Reproductive behavior is complex, and it is not always easy to see any adaptive significance to the responses that have been observed. For example, the subtidal clam *Rangia cuneata* requires a salinity shock (of about 5 ppt up or down) to release its gametes even though the female may be gravid more than half of the year. When salinities remain constant, for example, when an area is impounded, the clam eventually dies out. The intertidal crab *Sesarma cinereum* requires low estuarine salinity for larval development. The fourth zoeal stage, in particular, is sensitive to salinity, and best development occurs at 26.7 ‰. In the succeeding megalops stage, however, it can withstand a wide range of salinities and temperatures (Costlow, Boakout, and Monroe, 1960).

Feeding

As with reproductive adaptations, the broad range of animal feeding responses closely reflects their habitats. Adaptations of feeding appendages, for example, seem to be more closely related to feeding habits than to taxonomic relationships. Many organisms that exists in marsh sediments are adapted for direct absorption of dissolved organic compounds from their environment. For example, infaunal polychaetes can supply a major portion of their energy requirements from the rich supply of dissolved amino acids present in their environment, but epifaunal species are unable to take advantage of amino acids at concentrations typical of their environment (Vernberg, 1981). Many mud-dwelling organisms are adapted to feeding on microscopic particles by means of pseudopods, cilia, mucus, setae, and/or ingesting substrate unselectively. Sikora (1977) has suggested that the appendages of many macrobenthic organisms (shrimp, crabs) are adapted to feed on microscopic meiobenthic organisms and that these latter organisms are a major intermediary in the marsh/estuary food chain.

SUMMARY

The wetland environment is in many ways physiologically harsh. Major stresses are anoxia and the wide salinity and water fluctuations characteristic of an environment that is neither terrestrial nor aquatic. Adaptations to this environment have an energy cost, either because an organism's cells operate less efficiently (conformers) or because it expends energy to protect its cells from the external stress (regulators). At the cell level all organisms have similar adaptations, although primitive organisms (protists) appear to show more novelty. Adaptations of protists include the ability to respire anaerobically, to detoxify end products of anaerobic metabolism, to use reduced organic compounds in the sediment as energy sources, and to use mineral elements (N, Mn, Fe, S) in the sediment as alternative electron acceptors when oxygen is unavailable.

Higher plants and animals have a wider range of responses available to them because of the flexibility afforded by the development of organ systems and division of labor within the body, mobility, and complex life history strategies. One important adaptation in vascular plants is the development of pore space in the cortical tissues, which allows oxygen to diffuse from the aerial parts of the plant to the roots to supply root respiratory demands. Animals have developed structural or physiological adaptations to reduced oxygen availability, such as specialized organs or organ systems, mechanisms to increase the oxygen gradient into the body, better means of circulation, more efficient pigment systems, and changed behavior patterns.

In general, in higher plants and animals, salt stresses have been met with specialized tissues or organs to regulate the internal salt concentration or to protect the rest of the body from the effects of salt (osmoregulators), or with increased metabolic and physiological tolerance to salt at high concentrations (osmoconformers).

7

WETLAND ECOSYSTEM
DEVELOPMENT

The concept of plant succession has a long history. It was first clearly enunciated by Clements (1916) and applied to wetlands by the English ecologist W. H. Pearsall in 1920 and by an American, L. R. Wilson, in 1935. E. P. Odum (1969) extended the ideas of these early ecologists to include ecosystem properties such as productivity, respiration, and diversity. The classical use of the term succession involves three fundamental concepts: (1) vegetation occurs in recognizable and characteristic *communities;* (2) community change through time is brought about by the biota (that is, changes are *autogenic*); (3) changes are linear and *directed* toward a mature stable *climax* ecosystem (Odum, 1971). Using this definition of succession, all wetlands are regarded as transitional *seres* in a *hydrarch* successional sequence to a terrestrial forest climax.

Although this classical concept has been the dominant paradigm of succession, it has not been universally accepted. As early as 1917, Gleason enunciated an *individualistic* hypothesis to explain the occurrence of plants. His ideas have developed into the *Continuum* concept (Whittaker, 1967; McIntosh, 1980), which holds that the distribution of a species is governed by its response to its environment (*allogenic* succession). Since each species adapts differently, no two occupy exactly the same zone. This results in a continuum of overlapping sets of species, each responding to subtly different environmental cues. In this view, no communities exist in the sense used by Clements, and while ecosystems change, there is little evidence that this is directed or that it leads to a particular climax.

THE CLASSICAL IDEA OF SUCCESSION

The Community Concept

The idea of the community is particularly strong in wetland literature. Historic names for different kinds of wetlands—marshes, swamps, carrs, fens, bogs, reedswamps—often used with the name of a dominant plant (sphagnum bog, leatherleaf bog, cypress swamp), signify our recognition of distinctive associations of plants that are readily recognized and, at least loosely, comprise a community. One reason these associations are so clearly identified is that zonation patterns in wetlands often tend to be sharp, with abrupt boundaries that call attention to vegetation change, and by implication the uniqueness of each zone.

Although wetland "communities" were historically identified qualitatively, the application of objective statistical clustering techniques supports the community idea, at least in some instances. For example, classical syntaxonomical treatment of European *Spartina* communities (this is a semiquantitative analysis of vegetation stands based on dominants and observed similarities) resulted in the classification of these marshes into a number of subassociations (Beeftink and Gehu, 1973). A recent numerical classification of the same areas, based on similarity ratios and a statistical clustering technique, identified virtually the same subassociations (Kortekaas, Van der Maarel, and Beeftink, 1976) (Fig. 7-1). It is important to notice that different degrees of clustering occur with these data. Three main groups are associated with the dominance of three different *Spartina* species: *S. maritima, S. alterniflora,* and *S. townsendii.* These three groups break down further into various subassociations. The decision as to what level of similarity, if any, identifies a community is entirely arbitrary.

The identification of a community is also to some extent a conceptual issue that is confused by the scale of perception. Field techniques are adequate to describe the vegetation in an area and its variability. But its homogeneity—one index of "community"—may depend on size. For example, Louisiana coastal marshes have been classified into four zones, or communities, based on the dominant vegetation (Chabreck, 1972). If the size of the sampling area is large enough within any one of these zones, the same species will always be found. However, if smaller grids are used differences appear within a zone. The intermediate marsh zone is dominated, on a broad scale, by *S. patens;* but aerial imagery shows patterns of vegetation within the zone, and intensive sampling and cluster analysis of the vegetation reveals at least five subassociations that are characteristic of intermediate marshes (Fig. 7-2). Is the intermediate marsh a community? Are the subassociations communities? The determination is not as easy as one would like.

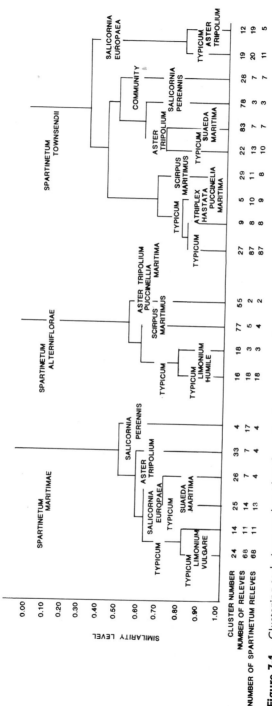

Figure 7-1. Clustering technique used to identify wetland communities. The example shows *Spartina* communities. *(From Kortekaas, Van der Maarel, and Beeftink, 1976, p. 53; Copyright © 1976 by Dr. W. Junk, B. V., reprinted with permission)*

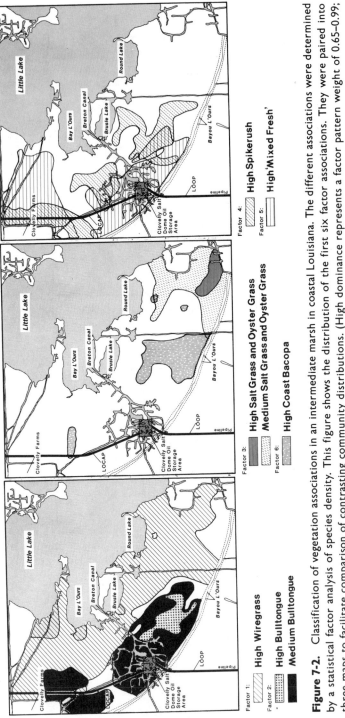

Figure 7-2. Classification of vegetation associations in an intermediate marsh in coastal Louisiana. The different associations were determined by a statistical factor analysis of species density. This figure shows the distribution of the first six factor associations. They were paired into three maps to facilitate comparison of contrasting community distributions. (High dominance represents a factor pattern weight of 0.65–0.99; medium of 0.25–0.64.) *(From Sasser et al., 1982, p. 217)*

The Concept of Autogenic Succession

In the classical view of succession, wetlands are considered transient stages in the hydrarch development of a terrestrial forested climax community from a shallow lake (Fig. 7-3). In this view lakes gradually fill in, because of erosion of mineral material into them and also because of the accumulation of organic material from dead plants. First stages are often slow because the source of organic material is single-celled plankton. When the lake becomes shallow enough to support rooted aquatic plants, however, the pace of organic deposition increases. Eventually, the water becomes shallow enough to support emergent marsh vegetation. It continues to build a peat mat. Shrubs and small trees appear. They continue to transform the site to a terrestrial one, not only by adding organic matter to the soil but also by drying it through enhanced evapotranspiration. Eventually, a climax terrestrial forest occupies the site (see, for example, Cooper, 1913). The important point to note in this description of hydrarch succession is that most of the change is brought about by the plant community itself, as opposed to externally caused environmental changes.

How realistic is this concept of succession? It is certainly well documented that forests do occur on the sites of former lakes (Larsen, 1982), but the evidence that the successional sequence leading to these forests was autogenic is not clear. Since peat-building is crucial to the filling in of a lake and its conversion to dry land, key questions involve the conditions for peat accumulation and the limits of that accumulation. Peat underlies many marshes, often in beds 10 or more meters deep. Several scientists (McCaffrey, 1977; Delaune, Baumann, and Gosselink, 1983) have shown that in coastal marshes it has accumulated, and is still accumulating, at rates varying from less than 1 to about 15 mm/yr. Most of this accumulation seems to be associated with rising sea levels (or submerging land). By contrast, northern inland bogs accumulate peat at rates from 0.2 to 2 mm/yr (see chap. 12).

In general, accumulation occurs only in anoxic sediment. When organic peats are drained they rapidly oxidize and subside, as many farmers who cultivate drained marshes have discovered. As the wetland surface accretes and approaches the water surface, or at least the upper limit of the saturated zone, peat accretion in excess of subsidence must cease; it is hard to see how this process can turn a wetland into a dry habitat that can support terrestrial vegetation. To the extent that marsh vegetation traps inorganic sediments and thus enhances the rate of mineral deposition, mineral soil accretion may also be considered autogenic, but this also requires flooding conditions to carry the mineral material into the marsh.

Linear, Directed Vegetation Changes

If one is convinced that identifiable communities do exist, and that they change due to autogenic processes, a further criterion is necessary to qualify

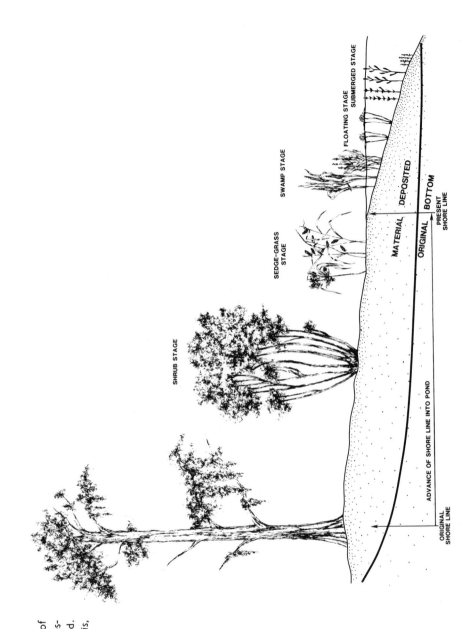

Figure 7-3. Diagram of classical hydrarch succession at the edge of a pond. (After Wilson and Loomis, 1967)

152

the changes as successional; they must be linear and directed toward a stable climax. The scientific literature is replete with schematic diagrams showing the expected successional sequence from wetland to terrestrial forest (Fig. 7-4). Most of these are based on observed zonation patterns, assuming that these spatial patterns presage the temporal pathway of change. That this classical pattern does really occur in some instances is clearly demonstrated in soil profiles. The relict remains of vegetation in soil profiles represent a temporal sequence, with the oldest remains at the bottom of the profile. Figure 7-5 shows such a sequence, demonstrating a direct succession from pioneer salt marsh to tidal woodland.

In the case of Gulf Coast wetland succession as outlined by Penfound and Hathaway (1938) (Fig. 7-4*b*), we now know that the sequence of change is from freshwater to saline vegetation, almost directly opposite to the direction of change they envisioned. In the Gulf Coast, fresh marshes form as a result of rapid delta growth in active river mouths. They change to salt marshes and then to open bays because the rapid subsidence rate, after the river shifts its mouth to another location, results in salt intrusion.

THE CONTINUUM IDEA

The presumed succession example in Figure 7-4*b* shows that zonation does not necessarily indicate succession. In fact, those who support the continuum idea maintain that zonation simply indicates an environmental gradient to which individual species are responding. The reason zonation is so sharp in many wetlands is that environmental gradients are "ecologically" steep and groups of species have fairly similar tolerances that tend to group them on these gradients. Figure 7-1 can easily be interpreted to support this contention, since it shows that the similarity level between two groups of plants is never more than 0.85 (1.00 indicates identity), and may be as low as 0.50. Figure 7-6 shows the distribution of swamp trees and submersed aquatic vegetation along an ordination axis. Although the species overlap, the distribution of each seems to be distinct, leaving no reflection of a community. The idea that each species is found where the environment is optimal for it makes perfect sense to ecophysiologists and autecologists who interpret the success of a species in terms of its environmental adaptation.

One major difference between classical community ecologists and proponents of the continuum idea is the greater emphasis put on allogenic processes by the latter. In wetlands, abiotic environmental factors often seem to overwhelm biotic forces. Under these circumstances the response of the vegetation is determined by these abiotic factors. Hydrologic conditions, for example, were described in Chapter 4 as having a particular significance for wetland structure and function. In coastal areas, plants can do little to change the tidal pulse of water and salt. Tidal energy may be modified

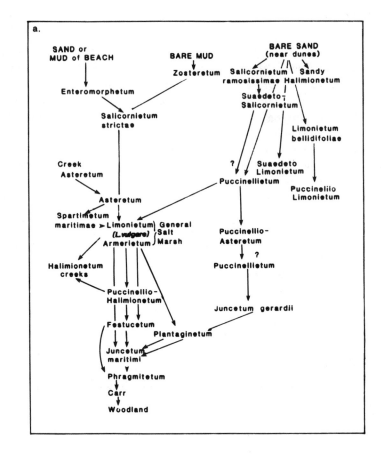

a.

SAND or
MUD of BEACH

BARE MUD

Zosteretum

BARE SAND
(near dunes)

Salicornietum   Sandy
ramosissimae Halimionetum

Enteromorphetum

Suaedeto-
Salicornietum

Salicornietum
strictae

Limonietum
bellidifoliae

Creek
Asteretum

?

Suaedeto
Limonietum

Puccinellietum

Puccinellio
Limonietum

Asteretum

Spartimetum
maritimae ➤ Limonietum ⎫ General
          (L.vulgare) ⎬ Salt
          Armerietum ⎭ Marsh

Puccinellio-
Asteretum

?

Halimionetum
creeks

Puccinellietum

Puccinellio-
Halimionetum

Festucetum

Plantaginetum

Juncetum gerardii

Juncetum
maritimi

Phragmitetum

Carr

Woodland

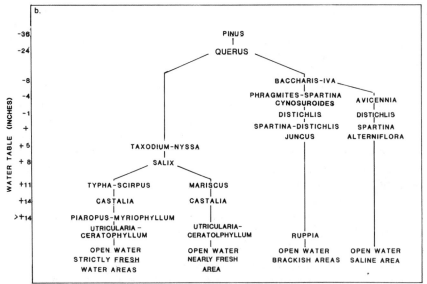

b.

	WATER TABLE (INCHES)

-36
-24   PINUS

QUERUS

-8
-4   BACCHARIS-IVA
      PHRAGMITES-SPARTINA
      CYNOSUROIDES   AVICENNIA
-1   DISTICHLIS   DISTICHLIS
+   SPARTINA-DISTICHLIS   SPARTINA
      JUNCUS   ALTERNIFLORA
+ 5   TAXODIUM-NYSSA

+ 8   SALIX

+11   TYPHA-SCIRPUS   MARISCUS

+14   CASTALIA   CASTALIA

>+14 PIAROPUS-MYRIOPHYLLUM
      UTRICULARIA-   UTRICULARIA-
      CERATOPHYLLUM   CERATOLPHYLLUM

      OPEN WATER   OPEN WATER   RUPPIA   OPEN WATER
      STRICTLY FRESH   NEARLY FRESH   OPEN WATER   SALINE AREA
      WATER AREAS   AREA   BRACKISH AREAS

Figure 7-4. Presumed successional relationships among coastal plant communities: *a.* England *(after Chapman, 1960)* and *b.* northern Gulf Coast *(from Penfound and Hathaway, 1938, p. 33; Copyright © 1938 by the Ecological Society of America, reprinted with permission).*

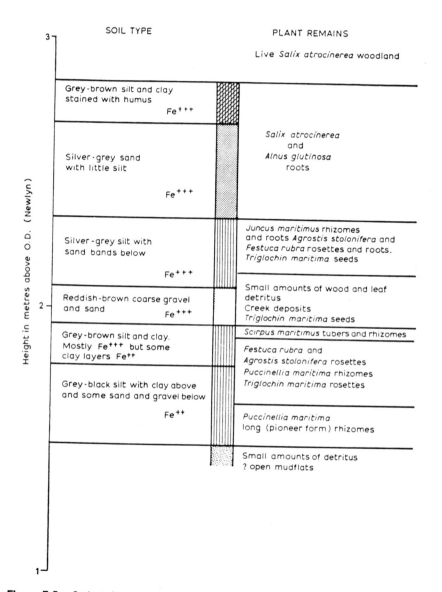

Figure 7-5. Soil profile 150 m landward of the present seaward limit of tidal woodland with evidence from plant remains of direct succession from pioneer salt marsh to tidal woodland at Fal estuary, Cornwall. *(From Ranwell, 1972, p. 88; Copyright © 1972 by D. S. Ranwell, reprinted with permission)*

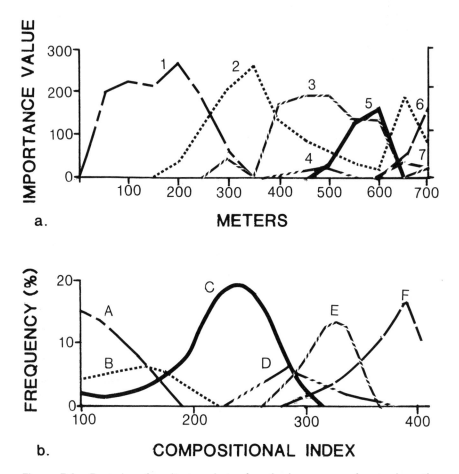

Figure 7-6. Examples of gradient analysis of wetlands: *a.* swamp forest where the species are (1) *Larix laricina,* (2) *Thuja occidentalis,* (3) *Ulmus americanus,* (4) *Fraxinus nigra,* (5) *Acer saccharinum,* (6) *Acer saccharum* and (7) *Fraxinus americana,* and *b.* submersed aquatic vegetation in Wisconsin lakes, where the species are (A) *Elatine minima,* (B) *Potamogeton epihydrus,* (C) *Eleocharis acicularis,* (D) *Potamogeton praelongus,* (E) *Zosterella dubia,* and (F) *Myriophyllum exalbescens.* *(From Van der Valk, 1982, p. 173; Copyright © 1982 by International Scientific Publications, reprinted with permission. Based on original data from Beschel and Webber, 1962, and Curtis, 1959.)*

somewhat by vegetation as stems create friction that slows currents, or as dead organic matter accumulates and changes the surface elevation. But these effects are limited by the overriding tides. These wetlands are often in dynamic equilibrium with the abiotic forces, an equilibrium that E. P. Odum (1971) called "pulse stability." On the Louisiana coast, as mentioned above, the major abiotic force seems to be the high subsidence rate, which overrides

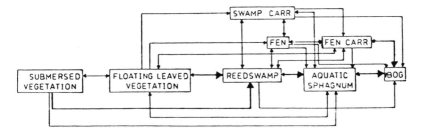

Figure 7-7. Successional sequences reconstructed from stratigraphic and palynological studies of post-glacial British peatlands. Thicker lines indicate the more common transitions. *(From Van der Valk, 1982, p. 172; Copyright © 1982 by International Scientific Publications, reprinted with permission; After Walker, 1970)*

any autogenic changes. There appear to be few, if any, examples of wetland ecosystems that became terrestrial without a concurrent allogenic lowering of the water level. Even the example given above (Fig. 7-5), documenting a classical change from salt marsh to woodland, resulted in a tidal woodland dominated by flood-tolerant trees, not a terrestrial ecosystem.

Thus, changes in wetlands are often not directed toward a terrestrial climax. Walker (1970) found from pollen profiles that the successional sequence in northern peatlands was variable, with reversals and skipped stages, and seemed to be influenced by the dominant species first reaching a site (Fig. 7-7). A bog, not some type of terrestrial forest, was the most common end point in most of the sequences described. Analysis of the age of wetlands from dating of peats (e.g., Redfield, 1972) reveals that they may have existed unchanged for at least the last 1,000 years. This is not what is expected of seres. In fact, wetlands in stable environmental regimes seem to be extremely stable, contravening the central idea of succession.

A MODERN THEORY OF WETLAND SUCCESSION

Present evidence seems to lead to the conclusion that both allogenic and autogenic forces act to change wetland vegetation and that the idea of a regional terrestrial climax for wetlands is inappropriate. Van der Valk (1981) replaced this (autogenic succession) concept with a Gleasonian model (Fig. 7-8) in which the presence and abundance of each species depends on its life history and its adaptation to the environment of a site. He classified all plant species into 12 life history types based on potential life span, propagule longevity, and propagule establishment requirements. Each life history type has a unique set of characteristics and thus potential behavior in response to controlling environmental factors such as water level changes in a wetland. These environmental factors compose the "environmental sieve" in Van der

Dispersal Dependent Species

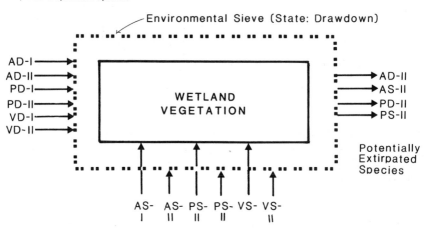

Figure 7-8. General model of Gleasonian wetland succession proposed by Van der Valk. *(After Van der Valk, 1981, p. 689; Copyright © 1981 by the Ecological Society of America, reprinted with permission)*

Valk's model. As the environment changes, so does the sieve, and hence the species present. This is a useful conceptual model for understanding wetland change. It does not, however, explicitly recognize autogenic processes. These could easily be included with a feedback loop showing that the environmental sieve itself can be modified to some extent by the wetland vegetation present. An excellent example of this kind of feedback loop is discussed by Weller (1981). In midwestern prairie pothole marshes, the vegetation can be wiped out by a population explosion of herbivorous muskrats. New emergent vegetation cannot become established until a dry year exposes the soil. A typical succession of species follows until robust cattails outcompete them. This sets the stage for another muskrat explosion. This cycle has a six-to-eight year frequency that depends on both the biotic vegetation-muskrat interaction and on an abiotic wet-dry climatic cycle (see chap. 11).

ECOSYSTEM-LEVEL PROCESSES AND WETLAND DEVELOPMENT

As an ecosystem passes through different successional phases toward maturity, its properties are thought to change in predictable ways. Odum (1969) described these changes in an article entitled "The Strategy of Ecosystem Development." Immature ecosystems, in general, are characterized by high production to biomass (P:B) ratios; an excess of production over community respiration (P:R ratio > 1); simple, linear, grazing food chains; low species diversity; small organisms; simple life cycles; and open mineral cycles. In contrast, mature ecosystems, such as old-growth forests, tend to use all their production to maintain themselves and therefore have P:R ratios about equal to 1, and little if any net community production. Production may be lower than in immature systems, but the quality is better; that is, plant production tends to be high in fruits, flowers, tubers, and other materials that are rich in protein. Because of the large structural biomass of trees, the P:B ratio is small. Food chains are elaborate and detritus based, species diversity is high, the space is well organized into many different niches, organisms are larger than in immature systems, and life cycles tend to be long and complex. Nutrient cycles are closed; nutrients are efficiently stored and recycled within the ecosystem.

It is instructive to see how wetland ecosystems fit into this scheme of ecosystem development. Do its ecosystem-level characteristics fit the classical view that all wetlands are immature transitional seres? Or do they resemble more the mature features of a terrestrial forest? Table 7-1 displays, for the wetland ecosystems covered in this book, an evaluation of the system attributes discussed by Odum (1969). For comparison, we have included a generalized developing (immature) and a mature ecosystem from Odum's article. The quantitative values are very rough because they represent means with wide variation, and are derived from incomplete data. Nevertheless, the table provides some interesting insights:

1. Wetland ecosystems have properties of both immature and mature ecosystems. For example, nearly all of the nonforested wetlands have P:B ratios intermediate between developing and mature systems, and are net producers. Primary production tends to be very high compared with most terrestrial ecosystems. On the other hand, all of the ecosystems are detrital based, with complex food webs.

2. Peat should be considered as a component of biotic "structure" in wetlands. Odum (1971) uses live biomass as an index of structure or "information" within an ecosystem. Hence, a forested ecosystem is more mature in this respect than a grassland. This is reflected in the high P:B ratios (immature) of the nonforested wetlands, and the low P:B ratios (mature) of the forested wetlands. However, in a real sense,

Table 7-1. Ecosystem Attributes of Wetlands Compared with Odum[a] Successional Attributes

Ecosystem Type	Community Energetics			Community Structure			
	P:R ratio	P:B ratio	Net Primary Productivity gC/m² · day	Food Chains	Total Organic Matter, kg/m²	Species Diversity	Spatial Heterogeneity
Developing[a]	<1 or >1	High (2-5)	High (~2-3)	Linear, grazing	Small (<2)	Low	Poorly organized
Mature[a]	1	Low (<0.1)	Low (~1)	Weblike, detritus	Large (~20)	High	Well organized
Freshwater Wetlands							
Northern peatlands and bogs	>1	0.1[b]	0.8 (0.2-1.4)	Weblike, detritus	7.8 (1.2-16)[b]	Low	Well organized
Inland freshwater marshes	>1	1.2[c]	3.9 (0.7-8.2)[d]	Weblike, detritus	0.75-2.3	High	Well organized
Tidal freshwater marshes	>1	1.2[e]	1.9[e]	Weblike, detritus	1.1 (0.4-2.3)	Fairly low	Well organized
Swamp forests	1.3 (1.1-1.5)[f]	0.07 (0.015-0.09)[g]	1.2 (0.5-1.9)[g]	Weblike, detritus	22.6 (7.4-45)[g]	Fairly low	Well organized
Riparian forests	≥1	0.06[h]	1.4[h]	Weblike, detritus	17.4 (10-29)[h]	High	Well organized
Saltwater Wetlands							
Salt marshes	1.5[i]	2[i]	2.2 (0.45-5.7)	Weblike, detritus	1.1	Low	Well organized
Mangroves	1.9 (0.7-3.3)[j]	—	3 (0-7.5)[j]	Weblike, detritus	—	Plants: low; animals: high	Well organized

| Ecosystem Type | Life History | | Nutrient Cycles | | Selection Pressure | |
	Organism Size	Life Cycle	Mineral Cycles	Role of Detritus	Growth Form	Production
Developing[a]	Small	Short, simple	Open	Unimportant	r	Quantity
Mature[a]	Large	Long, complex	Closed	Important	K	Quality
Freshwater Wetlands						
Northern peatlands and bogs	Small to large	Long	Closed	Important	K	Quality?
Inland freshwater marshes	Fairly small	Short, complex	Closed	Important	K?	Quality
Tidal freshwater marshes	Small	Short, complex	Open	Important	r?	Quantity
Swamp forests	Plants: large; animals: small	Long, simple / Short	Open	Important	Plants: K / Animals: r	Quantity
Riparian forests	Plants: large; animals: small to large	Long / Short to long	Open to closed	Important	K	Quality
Saltwater Wetlands						
Salt marshes	Small	Short, complex	Open	Important	r	Quantity
Mangroves	Plants: large; animals: small	Long, simple / Short, complex	Open	Important	Plants: K / Animals: r?	Quantity

[a]Odum, 1969, 1971
[b]Table 12-4
[c]Van Der Valk and Davis (1978a)
[d]Table 11-4 (includes belowground vegetation)
[e]Table 9-2
[f]Table 13-7
[g]Table 13-5
[h]Table 14-5
[i]Gosselink, 1984
[j]Table 10-1

peat is a structural element of wetlands, since it is a primary autogenic factor modifying the flooding characteristic of a wetland site. If peat were included in biomass, the herbaceous wetlands would have significantly higher biomass and lower P:B ratios, characteristic of more mature ecosystems. For example, a salt or fresh marsh has a live peak biomass of less than 2 kg/m^2. But the organic content of a meter depth of peat (peats are often many meters deep) beneath the surface is on the order of 45 kg/m^2. This is comparable with the aboveground biomass of the most dense wetland or terrestrial forest. As a structural attribute of a marsh, peat is an indication of a maturity far greater than the live biomass alone would signify.

3. Mineral cycles tend to be open in wetland ecosystems, except in bogs and certain isolated wetlands that receive nutrients only in precipitation. This is a juvenile characteristic of wetlands directly related to the large flux of water through these ecosystems. On the other hand, even in a system as open as a salt marsh that is flooded daily, about 80% of the nitrogen used by vegetation during an annual cycle is recycled from mineralized organic material (Delaune and Patrick, 1979).

4. Spatial heterogeneity is generally well organized in wetlands along allogenic gradients. The sharp, predictable zonation patterns and abundance of land-water interfaces are examples of spatial organization in wetlands. In forested wetlands, vertical heterogeneity is also well organized. This organization is an index of mature ecosystems. However, in most terrestrial ecosystems the organization results from autogenic factors in ecosystem maturation. In wetlands, most of the organization seems to result from allogenic processes, specifically hydrologic and/or salinity gradients created by slight elevation changes across a wetland. Thus the "maturity" of a wetland's spatial organization consists of a high level of adaptation to prevailing microhabitat differences.

5. Life cycles of wetland consumers are usually relatively short, but are often exceedingly complex. The short cycle is characteristic of immature systems, while the complexity is a mature attribute. Once again, the complexity of the life cycles of many wetland animals seems to be as much an adaptation to the physical pattern of the environment as to the biotic forces. A number of animals use wetlands only seasonally, for example. Many fish and shellfish species migrate into coastal wetlands only during certain life stages, to use it as a spawning ground or a nursery for juveniles. Waterfowl use northern wetlands to nest and southern wetlands to overwinter, migrating thousands of miles between the two areas each year.

It seems clear that both autogenic and allogenic processes are important in both the pathway of development and the final characteristics of the mature wetland ecosystem. This is illustrated by an example from the wetlands of the Mississippi River delta on the northern coast of the Gulf of Mexico. Typically, a delta wetland originates as a fresh marsh following the formation of new land by river sediment deposition. Wetlands in the Atchafalaya River are good examples. They began to develop in 1973 after severe spring floods retreated, leaving behind new islands in Atchafalaya Bay, at the mouth of the river. At this point in its development the processes determining wetland development are clearly allogenic, and are dominated by seasonal floods and associated sediment deposition. The plant species found in these wetlands—predominantly willows and arrowheads—have very little influence on their environment. They exist because they are adapted to the extreme variations they experience. All indices point to riverine control (Table 7-2). Elevations and flooding regimes are variable, reflecting the high energy and sediment content of the river; salt concentrations are low; sediment deposition overwhelms organic deposition; sediment nutrient stores are low; and plant production is low. The successful plants are fast-growing perennial trees like willows, with fibrous roots that bind and hold the sediment, and herbaceous plants that store reserves in perennial roots, where they are impervious to severe spring floods.

Typically, a delta such as the Atchafalaya continues to build out onto the shallow ocean shelf for about 1,000 years until the river shifts its course to another, more efficient channel. When this happens, the fresh river water no longer holds back the ocean and the peripheral wetlands become increasingly saline. The inner wetlands, however, are still fed primarily by fresh water from the abundant rainfall. At this point the further development of similar river-dominated marshes diverges. One track becomes a marsh whose driving environmental control is saltwater tides. The other remains fresh, and in a low-energy regime dramatically modifies its own environment until it becomes a floating mat. Table 7-2 contrasts these two mature systems with their youthful precursor.

The salt marsh is flooded nearly daily on the Gulf Coast, but the flood water energy is low and sediments are fine silts and clays. The marsh elevation range is rather small, stabilizing close to local mean high water. The marsh is maintained at this elevation in the intertidal zone by a combination of inorganic sediment carried in by tidal waters and organic materials grown in place. Only salt-tolerant species are found, but they are highly adapted to their environment. As a result, plant productivity is high. Much of the nutrient demand for this growth is met by mineralization (recycling) of organic material in the soil. This is an ecosystem in which the biota are adapted to the salt and tides. But they also modify their own environment, chiefly through concentration of organic debris in the soil that alters its elevation (and hence flooding) and stabilizes its nutrient supply.

In the interior marshes that salt does not reach, the fullest expression of autogenic development occurs. With the sediment supply almost entirely cut

Table 7-2. Comparison of a Young Fresh Marsh on the Louisiana Coast, with a Mature Salt Marsh and a Freshwater Floating Marsh

Ecosystem Attribute	Young Fresh Marsh (Atchafalaya Delta)	Mature Salt Marsh (Barataria Basin)	Mature Freshwater Floating Marsh (Barataria Basin)
Age, Year	10	1,000–1,500	1,000–1,500
Elevation, cm above local mean water level	–2–22	–0.1–+0.1	+3
Dominant Sediment Grain Size	Sand	Clay	No inorganic
Flooding Frequency, times/yr (Process)	— (River flow; winds)	260 (Tides)	0 (Floating marsh)
Salinity, %	<5	17.5	0
Total Sediment N, %	0.35–0.66	0.56	1.5–1.8
Total Sediment P, ppm	210–240	—	900
Net Plant Production Allocation	Low roots	High top and roots	Moderate roots
Source	Johnson, Sasser, and Gosselink (1985)	Rainey (1979); Sasser(1977)	Sasser and Gosselink (1984)

off, the sediments become increasingly organic. As a result they become increasingly light, until the whole mat becomes buoyant enough to float. When this occurs the earlier unpredictable flooding regime is replaced by a stable one in which the sediment is always wet but the surface is never flooded. The stress of variable flooding is entirely eliminated, to be replaced by another: since the surface is no longer floods, the major source of nutrients—waterborne sediments—is lost. Although new nutrients can be "wicked up" from the water under the mat, nearly all of the nutrient demand of the plants is probably met by recycling from organic peat in the soil. Total productivity is probably quite high, but most of it is allocated to root production necessary to maintain the floating mat.

Thus differing environmental conditions lead to the development of quite different wetland ecosystems from similar origins. Both mature systems appear to be stable and well adapted to their environments. One, the salt marsh, represents development in response to both allogenic and autogenic processes. The floating freshwater marsh appears to have modified its own environment much more strongly than the salt marsh. This example is one of many that could be cited. The chapters in Parts III and IV describe others.

THE STRATEGY OF WETLAND ECOSYSTEM DEVELOPMENT

In the previous section we showed that wetlands possess attributes of both immature and mature systems, and that both allogenic and autogenic processes are important. In this section we suggest that in all wetland ecosystems there is a common theme: Development insulates the ecosystem from its environment. At the level of individual species this occurs through genetic (structural and physiological) adaptations to anoxic sediments and salt (chap. 6). At the ecosystem level it occurs primarily through peat production, which tends to stabilize the flooding regime and shifts the main source of nutrients to recycled material within the ecosystem.

The intensity of water flow over and through a wetland can be described by the water renewal rate (t^{-1}), the ratio of throughflow to the volume stored on the site (see chap. 4). In wetlands, t^{-1} varies by five orders of magnitude (Fig. 7-9), from about one/year in northern bogs to as much as 7,500/year in low-lying riparian forests. The nutrient input to a site follows closely the water renewal rate, since (excepting nitrogen fixation) nutrients are carried to a site by water. The amount of nitrogen delivered to a wetland site, for example, also varies by five orders of magnitude, from less than 1 $g/m^2 \cdot yr$ in a northern bog, to perhaps 10 $kg/m^2 \cdot yr$ in a riparian forest (Fig. 7-9). Not all of this nitrogen is available to the plants in the ecosystem, because in extreme cases it is flowing through much faster than it can be immobilized, but these figures indicate the potential nutrient supply to the ecosystem.

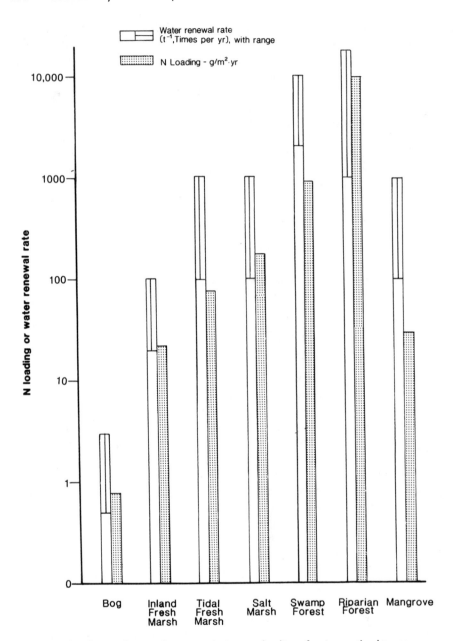

Figure 7-9. Renewal rates of water, and nitrogen loading of major wetland types.

In spite of the extreme variability in these outside (allogenic) forces, wetland ecosystems are remarkably similar in many respects (Table 7-3). Total stored biomass, including peat to 1 m depth, varies from 40 to 60 kg/m² — less than twofold. Soil nitrogen similarly varies only about threefold, from about 500 to 1,500 g/m².

Net primary production, a key index of ecosystem function, varies by only a factor of about four. Mean values for different ecosystem types are usually in the range of 600 to 2,000 g/m² · yr. Thus, although it has been shown in a number of studies of individual species (e.g., *Spartina alterniflora,* Steever, Warren, and Niering, 1976) or ecosystems (e.g., cypress swamps, Conner, Gosselink, and Parrondo, 1981) that production is directly proportional to the water renewal rate, when different ecosystems with enormously different water regimes are compared, the relationship breaks down. The apparent contradiction can be largely explained by the role of stored nutrients, especially nitrogen, within the ecosystem. As the large store of organic nitrogen in the sediment (Table 7-3) mineralizes, it provides a steady source of inorganic nitrogen for plant growth. In most wetland ecosystems "new" nitrogen is not adequate, or is barely adequate, to supply the plants' demands; but the demands are small in comparison to the amounts of stored nitrogen in the sediments (Table 7-3). As a result, most of the nitrogen demand is satisfied by recycling (Delaune and Patrick, 1979), even in systems as open as salt marshes. External nitrogen provides a "subsidy" to this basic supply. Therefore, growth is often apparently limited by the mineralization rate, which in turn is strongly temperature dependent. Temperatures during the growing season are uniform enough to provide a similar nitrogen supply to plants in different wetland systems, except probably in northern bogs. Here, the low temperature and short growing season limit mineralization and at the same time nutrient input is restricted. The combination of the two factors limits productivity.

Thus, as wetland ecosystems develop, they become increasingly insulated from the variability of the environment by storing nutrients. Often the same process that stores nutrients, that is, peat accumulation, also reduces the variability of flooding, thus further stabilizing the system. The extreme example of the floating marsh was discussed earlier, but less extreme variations on the theme are common. The surface of marshes in general is built up by deposition of peats and waterborne inorganic sediments. As the elevation increases, flooding becomes less frequent and sediment input decreases. In the absence of overriding factors, coastal wetland marshes in time reach a stable elevation somewhere around mean high water. The surfaces of riparian wetlands similarly rise until they are only infrequently flooded. Northern bogs grow by peat deposition above the water table, stabilizing at an elevation that maintains saturated peat by capillarity. Prairie potholes may be an exception to these generalizations. They appear to be periodically "reset" by

Table 7-3. Comparison of Primary Productivity and Nitrogen Dynamics in Wetland Ecosystems[a]

Wetland Type	1 Net Primary Production, g/m²·yr (range)	2 Total Biomass, kg/m²	3 Soil Nitrogen, g N/m²	4 Nitrogen Loading, g N/m²·yr	5 Plant Nitrogen Uptake, g N/m²·yr	6 Ratio N Throughput: Soil Store, yr⁻¹ (col 4/col 3)	7 Ratio N Throughput: Uptake, (col 4/col 5)
Northern Bog	560 (153–1,943)	53	500	0.8	9	0.002	0.09
Inland Fresh Marsh	1980 (1,070–2,860)	46	1,600	22	48	0.01	0.46
Tidal Fresh Marsh	1,370 (780–2,100)	46	1,340	75	54	0.06	1.4
Salt Marsh	1,950 (330–3,700)	46	1,470	30–100	25	0.02–0.07	1.2–4.0
Swamp Forest	870 (390–1,780)	52	1,300	900	14	0.7	64
Riparian Forest	1,040 (750–1,370)	37	900	10,000	17	11	600
Mangrove	1,500 (0–4,700)	60	1,400	30	24	0.02	1.2
Range, All Wetlands	560–1,980	37–60	500–1,470	0.8–10,000	9–54	0.002–11	0.09–600

[a]Values are rough averages with large variability, based on data presented in chapters 8–14.

a combination of herbivore activity and long-term precipitation cycles, and achieve stability only in some cyclic sense.

SUMMARY

Wetland ecosystems have traditionally been considered transitional seres between open lakes and terrestrial forests. The accumulation of organic material from plant production was seen to build up the surface until it was no longer flooded and could support flood-tolerant terrestrial forest species. While there are well-documented successional sequences showing this line of development, there are also many examples that are counter to classical successional theory. An alternative hypothesis is that the vegetation found at a wetland site consists of species adapted to the particular environmental conditions of that site. Observed zonation patterns, in this view, reflect underlying environmental gradients rather than autogenic successional patterns. Present evidence seems to lead to the conclusion that both allogenic and autogenic forces act to change wetland vegetation and that the idea of a regional terrestrial climax is inappropriate.

Mature wetland ecosystems are remarkably well adapted to their environments. While the input of water and nutrients varies in different wetlands by as much as five orders of magnitude, ecosystem response in terms of productivity, biomass, and nutrient storage varies by only a factor of 2 to 4. Wetland ecosystem response is controlled by stores of soil organic material that provide a steady source of nutrients to the plants, minimizing the impact of external supplies.

If one looks at ecosystem attributes as indices of ecosystem maturity, wetlands appear to be mature in some respects and young in others. Generally, productivity is high, some production is exported, and mineral cycles are open, all indications of young systems. On the other hand, most wetlands accumulate much structural biomass in peat, all wetlands are detrital systems, spatial heterogeneity is generally high, and life cycles are complex. These properties indicate maturity.

Part III

COASTAL WETLAND ECOSYSTEMS

TIDAL SALT MARSH

TIDAL SALT MARSHES

Beeftink (1977) defines a salt marsh as a "natural or semi-natural halophytic grassland and dwarf brushwood on the alluvial sediments bordering saline water bodies whose water level fluctuates either tidally or non-tidally." Dominated by rooted vegetation that is alternately inundated and dewatered by the rise and fall of the tide, salt marshes appear from afar to be vast fields of grass of a single species. In reality, salt marshes have a complex zonation and structure of plants, animals, and microbes, all tuned to the stresses of salinity fluctuations, alternate drying and submergence, and extreme daily temperature variations. A maze of tidal creeks with plankton, fish, nutrients, and fluctuating water levels crisscross the marsh, forming important conduits for energy and material exchange with the adjacent estuary. The salt marsh forms an important interface between terrestrial and marine habitats. In studies of a number of different salt marshes, they have been found to be highly productive and to support the spawning and feeding habits of many marine organisms. Along with the tropical mangrove swamps, the salt marshes are among the most important and ubiquitous coastal wetlands in the world.

GEOGRAPHICAL EXTENT

Salt marshes are found in mid- and high latitudes along intertidal shores throughout the world, being replaced by mangrove swamps along coastlines in tropical and subtropical regions (between 25°N and 25°S). The distribution of salt marshes in North America and in the United States is shown in Figure 8-1. Salt marshes can be narrow fringes on steep shorelines or expanses several kilometers wide. They are found near river mouths, in bays, on protected coastal plains and around protected lagoons. Different plant associations dominate different coastlines, but the overall structure and function of salt marshes are similar around the world. Chapman (1960; 1974; 1975; 1976a; 1977) has divided the world's salt marshes into nine geographical units. Those that apply to North America include the following:

1. *Arctic Marshes*—This group includes marshes of northern Canada, Alaska, Greenland, Iceland, northern Scandinavia, and Russia. Probably the largest extent of marshes in North America, as much as 300,000 km^2, occurs along the southern shore of the Hudson Bay. These marshes support few plant species due to the harsh climate. Various species of the sedge *Carex* and the grass *Puccinellia phryganodes* often dominate. Parts of the southwestern coast of Alaska are dominated by species of *Salicornia* and *Suaeda*.

2. *Eastern North America Marshes*—These marshes, mostly dominated by *Spartina* (cordgrass) and *Juncus* (rush) species, are found along the eastern coast of Canada and the Gulf Coast of the United States. This unit is further divided into three groups:

   a) Bay of Fundy group—River and tidal erosion is high in the soft rocks, producing an abundance of reddish silt. The tidal range, as exemplified at the Bay of Fundy, is often great, leading to a few marshes in protected areas and considerable depth of deposited sediments. *Puccinellia americana* dominates the lower marsh, while *Juncus balticus* is found on the highest levels.

   b) New England group—Marshes are built mainly on marine sediments and marsh peat with little transport of sediment from the hard-rock uplands. These marshes range from Maine to New Jersey.

   c) Coastal Plain Group—These marshes extend southward from New Jersey, along the southeastern coast of the United States and to Louisiana along the Gulf of Mexico. Major rivers supply an abundance of silt from the recently elevated Coastal Plain. Tidal range is relatively small. The marshes are interspersed with tidal creeks. Mangrove swamps replace salt marshes along the southern tip of Florida. Because of the extensive delta marshes built by the Mississippi River, the Gulf Coast contains 40% of the coastal marshes of the United States.

3. *Western North America Marshes*—Compared with the Arctic and the East Coast, salt marshes are far less developed along the western coasts of the United States and Canada due to the geomorphology of the coastline. A narrow belt of *Spartina foliosa* is often bordered by broad belts of *Salicornia* and *Suaeda*.

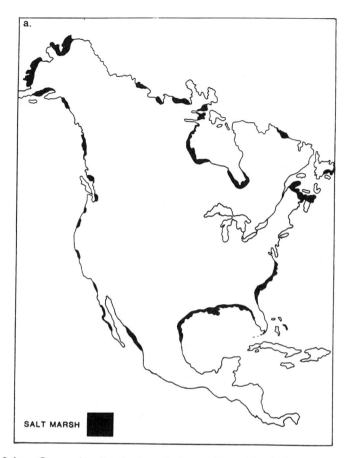

Figure 8-1a. Geographic distribution of salt marshes in North America. *(After Chapman, 1977, p. 3)*

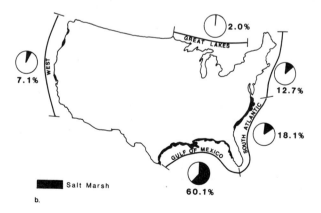

Figure 8-1b. Percent distribution of coastal marshes in the United States. *(From Gosselink and Baumann, 1980, p. 180; Copyright © 1980 by Gebruder Borntraeger, reprinted with permission)*

175

GEOMORPHOLOGY

The physical features of tides, sediments, freshwater inputs, and shoreline structure determine the development and extent of salt marsh wetlands within their geographical range. Coastal salt marshes are predominantly intertidal; that is, they are found in areas at least occasionally inundated by high tide but not flooded during low tide. A gentle, rather than steep, shoreline slope is necessary to allow for tidal flooding and stability of the vegetation. Adequate protection from wave and storm energy is also a physical requirement for the development of salt marshes. Sediments that build salt marshes originate from upland runoff, marine reworking of coastal shelf sediments, or from organic production within the marsh itself.

Although a number of different patterns of development can be identified, salt marshes can be classified broadly into those that were formed from reworked marine sediments on marine-dominated coasts, and those that formed in deltaic areas where the main source of sediment is riverine. The former type is typical of most of the North American coastline; deltaic marshes develop mainly where large rivers debouch onto low-energy coasts, which in North America restricts them to the coasts of the South Atlantic and Gulf of Mexico. The Mississippi River deltaic marshes are the major example of this type of development.

Marine-Dominated Marsh Development

On marine-dominated coasts, salt marsh development requires sufficient shelter to ensure sedimentation and to prevent excessive erosion from wave action (Beeftink, 1977). Some shoreline features that allow the development of salt marshes are shown in Figure 8-2. Marshes can develop at the mouths of estuaries where sediments are deposited by the river behind spits and bars that offer protection from waves and longshore currents. Chapman (1960) further describes three different situations in which salt marshes will develop:

1. Shelter of spits, offshore bars, and islands—Salt marshes will form along coastlines only where a bar, a neck of land (called a spit), or an island acts to trap sediment on its lee side and protects the marsh from the full forces of the open sea. Numerous coastal salt marshes have developed behind outer barrier reefs along Georgia and Carolina coast [Figure 8-2b, 8-2c, 8-2d].

2. Protected bays—Several large bays, such as the Chesapeake Bay, Hudson Bay, the Bay of Fundy, and the San Francisco Bay are adequately protected from storms and waves to support extensive salt marshes [Figure 8-2a].

3. Some estuarine salt marshes have features of both marine and deltaic origins. They occur on the shores of estuaries where low gradients lead to river sediment

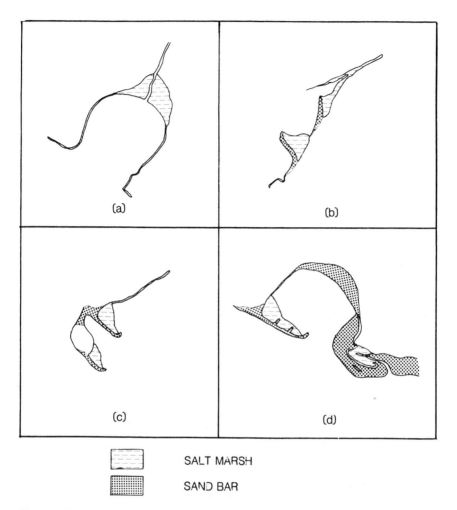

Figure 8-2. Diagram of typical shoreline features that allow for the development of salt marshes. Marshes are indicated by dashed lines. Dotted formations indicate spits and bars. *(After Chapman, 1960, p. 20)*

deposition in areas protected from destructive wave action. Tidal action must be strong enough to maintain salinities above about 5 ppt; otherwise, the salt marsh is replaced by reeds, rushes, and other freshwater aquatic plants.

River-Dominated Marsh Development

Major rivers carrying large sediment loads build marshes into shallow estuaries, or out onto the shallow continental shelf where the ocean is fairly quiet.

In this situation, the first marshes developing on the newly deposited sediments are dominated by freshwater species. Typically, however, the river course shifts through geologic time and the abandoned marshes, no longer supplied with fresh river water, become increasingly marine influenced. In the Mississippi River delta, these marshes undergo a 5,000-year cycle of growth as fresh marshes, transition to salt marshes, and finally degradation back to open water under the influence of subsidence and marine transgression. During the last stage the seaward edges of the marshes are reworked into barrier islands and spits in the same way as coastal marshes on the Atlantic coast.

Marsh Stability

The long-term stability of a salt marsh is determined by the relative rates of two processes: sediment accretion on the marsh, which causes it to expand outward and grow upward in the intertidal zone; and coastal submergence caused by rising sea level and marsh surface subsidence. These two processes are to some extent self-regulating, since as a marsh subsides it is inundated more frequently and thus receives more sediment and stores more peat (since the substrate is more anoxic and peat is degraded more slowly). Conversely, if it accretes faster than it is submerging, it gradually rises out of the intertidal zone, is flooded less frequently, receives less sediment, and oxidizes more peat. Nevertheless, local conditions have a significant effect on marsh stability. Worldwide, sea level was quite stable for the last 5,000 years. However, along the northern Gulf coast, submergence is currently rapid, mostly because of subsidence of the surface by compaction and downwarping of deltaic sediments. Here, accretion is not keeping up with submergence and salt marshes are degrading rapidly. Delaune, Baumann, and Gosselink (1983) showed that the percent of open water in a Gulf coastal marsh has been directly related to the rate of coastal submergence for the last 85 years. The average rate of coastal submergence was 1.2 cm/yr compared to a marsh accretion (sediment deposition) rate of 0.66 to 0.78 cm/yr. The accumulated aggradation deficit was closely related to wetland loss (Fig. 8-3). Deteriorating marshes in this coast receive most of their sediments during severe storms, especially hurricanes, but stable marshes depend more on riverine input during spring floods (Baumann, Day, and Miller, 1984).

Along the north Atlantic coast, the two processes are apparently close to a dynamic equilibrium. Here, sea level has been rising at between 1 and 3 mm/yr for the past several thousand years (Teal, 1986). Accretion in many marshes has been somewhat faster. Redfield (1965; 1972) gives a detailed description of the development of this kind of salt marsh in New England over the past 4,000 years, with a general model of peat and sediment

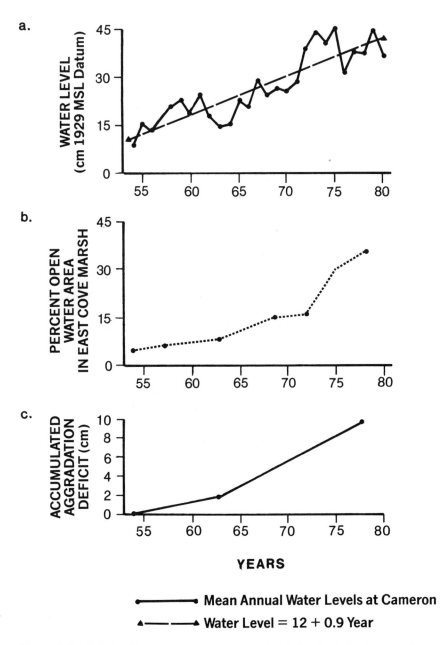

Figure 8-3. Relationships among *a.* apparent sea level rise, *b.* wetland conversion to open water, and *c.* a calculated aggradation deficit in a Gulf Coast salt marsh. *(From Delaune, Baumann, and Gosselink, 1983, p. 153; Copyright © 1983 by the Society of Economic Paleontologists and Mineralogists, reprinted with permission)*

accumulation in the presence of a continually rising sea level (Fig. 8-4). As sea level rises, $HW_0 \rightarrow HW_3$, the upland is covered by marsh peat as the marsh extends inland. At the same time, if sediments accumulate beyond the lower limit of marsh vegetation (called the thatch line) at a rate greater than the rise in sea level, the intertidal marsh migrates seaward to maintain its critical elevation. The upper (high) marsh will also develop seaward over the old intertidal peat. This model assumes an accumulation of peat and other sediments at a rate greater than or equal to the rise of the sea and is applicable where marsh development is not interrupted by erosion and deposition.

A third pattern is that of the northern part of the North American continent, which is emerging slowly as the land rises in response to the melting of the ice sheet that covered the land during the last ice age. As a result, in subarctic marshes such as those along the southern shore of Hudson Bay, the sea is retreating, shallow flats are exposed and are invaded by salt marsh species, and the whole marsh expands outward.

By examination of old maps, and by determination of the depth of marsh peat and the sedimentation rate (which can be estimated from radioactive markers such as Pb-210 and Cs-137), it is possible to measure the age of salt marshes. Such studies indicate that the oldest present-day salt marshes were formed during the last 3,000–4,000 years. In one study of a New England salt marsh (Table 8-1), it was found that the lower marsh, dominated by *Spartina alterniflora,* accumulates sediments at a much greater rate than does the more inland upper marsh dominated by *Juncus gerardi.* This is because of the lower marsh is in a much more energetic tidal zone where sediment input

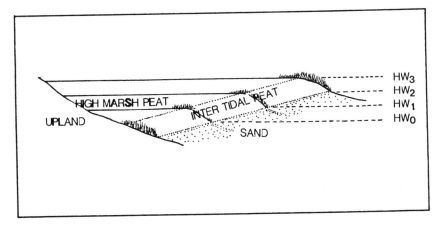

Figure 8-4. Development of a New England salt marsh. HW_0, HW_1, HW_2, and HW_3 refer to successive high water levels as sea level rises. *(After Redfield, 1965, p. 52; Copyright © 1965 by the American Association for the Advancement of Science, reprinted with permission)*

**Table 8-1. Rate of Sediment Accumulation and Age of a Salt Marsh
in Boston, Massachusetts[a], and in Louisiana[b]**

| *Vegetation Zone* | Rate, cm/100 years | | | *Age, years* |
	Accretion	*Subsidence*	*Net Accumulation*	
Massachusetts				
Spartina alterniflora	61	30	31	490
Spartina patens–Distichlis spicata	38	30	8	600
Juncus gerardi	32	30	2	1,200
Louisiana				
Barataria Bay (deteriorating) *Spartina alterniflora–Spartina patens*				
Streamside				
With hurricanes (4 yr)	150	123	27	
Without hurricanes (3 yr)	110	123	· −13	
Inland				
With hurricanes	90	123	−33	
Without hurricanes	60	123	−63	
Four League Bay (stable)				
Streamside, no hurricanes	130	85	45	
Inland, no hurricanes	56	85	−29	

[a]Data from Chapman (1960)
[b]Data from Baumann, Day, and Miller (1984)

is more rapid than higher on the marsh. These examples show how delicately poised the salt marsh is between survival and disappearance. A change in the rate of sea level rise or sedimentation of as little as a millimeter or two per year can determine whether or not the marsh will survive.

HYDROLOGY

Tidal energy represents a subsidy to the salt marsh that influences a wide range of physiographic, chemical, and biological processes, including sediment deposition and scouring, nutrient and organic influx and efflux, flushing of toxins, and the control of sediment redox potential. These physical factors in turn influence the species that occur on the marsh and their productivity. The lower and upper limits of the marsh are generally set by the

**Table 8-2. Hydrologic Demarcation Between Lower Marsh
and Upper Marsh in the Salt Marsh Ecosystem**

Marsh	Submergences		Maximum Period of Continuous Exposure, days
	per day in daylight	*per year*	
Upper Marsh	<1	<360	≥10
Intertidal Marsh	>1.2	>360	≤9

Source: Data from Chapman (1960)

tide range. The lower limit is set by depth and duration of flooding, and by the mechanical effects of waves, sediment availability, and erosional forces (Chapman, 1960). At least two or three days of continuous exposure is required during the seed germination period for seedling establishment. The upland side of the salt marsh generally extends to the limit of flooding on extreme tides, normally between mean high water and extreme high water of spring tides (Beeftink, 1977). Based on marsh elevation and flooding characteristics, the marsh is often divided into two zones, the upper marsh (or "high marsh") and the lower marsh (or "intertidal marsh"). The upper marsh is flooded irregularly and has a minimum of at least ten days of continuous exposure to the atmosphere, while the lower marsh is flooded nearly daily with never more than nine continuous days of exposure (Table 8-2).

Tidal Creeks

A notable physiographic feature of salt marshes, especially low marshes, is the development of tidal creeks in the marsh itself. These creeks develop as do rivers "with minor irregularities sooner or later causing the water to be deflected into definite channels" (Chapman, 1960). Redfield (1965; 1972) suggests that these tidal creeks were already developed on sand flats before they were encroached upon by advancing intertidal peat. The creeks serve as important conduits for material and energy transfer between the marsh and its adjacent body of water. A tidal creek has salinity similar to that of the adjacent estuary or bay and its water depth varies with tide fluctuations. The tidal creek produces a microenvironment that often supports different vegetation zones along its banks, and aquatic food chains that are important to the adjacent estuaries.

Sediments

The sediment source and the tidal current patterns determine the sediment characteristic of the marsh. Salt marsh sediment can come from river silt, from organic productivity in the marsh itself, or from reworked marine deposits. As a tidal creek rises out of its banks, water flowing over the marsh slows and drops its coarser-grained sediment load near the stream edge, creating a slightly elevated streamside levee. Finer sediments drop out further inland. This gives rise to a well-known "streamside" effect, characterized by greater productivity of grasses along tidal channels than inland, that results from the slightly larger nutrient input, higher elevation, and better drainage. The source of mineral sediment is not as important for the productivity of the marsh as elevation, drainage, and organic content, all of which are determined by local hydrologic factors.

Pannes

A distinctive feature of salt marshes is the occurrence of tidal pools or pannes (pans), natural depressions in the marsh that are intertidal and retain water even during low tide. Pannes support different vegetation than the surrounding marsh because of the continued standing water and the elevated salinities when evaporation is high. They are continually forming and filling due to shifting sediments and organic production. Pannes can form when the outlet of a tidal creek or natural depression is dammed by vegetation or shifting sediments. The vegetation that develops in a panne, for example, widgeon grass (*Ruppia* sp.), is tolerant of salt at very high concentrations in the soil water. In some marshes, relatively permanent ponds are formed on the high marsh, and are infrequently flooded by tides (Redfield, 1972). Because of their shallow depth and their support of submerged vegetation, pannes are used heavily by migratory waterfowl.

CHEMISTRY

The development and zonation of vegetation in the salt marsh are influenced by several chemical factors. Two of the most important are the soil water salinity, which is linked with tidal flooding frequency; and the availability of nutrients, particularly macronutrients such as nitrogen.

Salinity

A dominant factor in the productivity and species selection of the salt marsh is the salinity of the overlying water and the soil water. Average salinity is generally higher in the low marsh than in the upper marsh, and fluctuation is often greatest at the mean high water level. If the salinity in the adjacent body of water is less than 5‰, the salt marsh vegetation is replaced by freshwater plants.

The salinity in the marsh soil water depends on several factors (Adapted from Morss, 1927, and Chapman, 1960):

1. Frequency of tidal inundation—The lower marsh soils that are flooded frequently will tend to have a fairly constant salinity approximating that of the flooding seawater. On the other hand, the upper marsh that is only occasionally flooded will have long periods of exposure that may lead to either higher or lower salt concentrations.

2. Rainfall—Frequent rainfall tends to leach the upper soil in the high marsh of its salts (Ranwell et al., 1964); frequent periods of drought, on the other hand, lead to higher salt concentrations in the soil.

3. Tidal creeks and drainage slope—The presence of tidal creeks and steep slopes that drain away saline water can lead to lower soil water salinity than that which would occur under poorly drained conditions.

4. Soil Texture—Silt and clay materials tend to retain more salt than does sand.

5. Vegetation—The vegetation itself has an influence on soil salinity. Evaporation of water from the marsh surface is reduced by vegetation cover, but transpiration is increased. The net effect depends on the type of vegetation and the environmental setting. Salt marsh vegetation also changes the ion balance in soils when roots take up ions selectively from the surrounding soil solution (Smart and Barko, 1980).

6. Depth to Water Table—If groundwater is close to the surface, soil water salinity fluctuations will be less.

7. Fresh water inflow—The inflow of fresh water, in rivers, as overland flow, or in groundwater, tends to dilute the salinity in both the salt marsh and the surrounding estuary. The early spring flood periods along much of the eastern United States coastal plain leads to significant reductions in the salinity of downstream coastal marshes.

In marshes, where the average soil salinity varies from freshwater to seawater strength, it often controls the general zonation pattern of vegetation and its productivity. Within the salt marsh zone itself, however, all plants are salt tolerant, and it is misleading to account for plant zonation and productivity on the basis of salinity alone. The salinity, after all, is the net result of many hydrodynamic factors, including tides, rainfall, freshwater inputs and groundwater, as described above. When *Spartina* grows better in the intertidal zone, it is growing better because of tides that reduce the local salinity, remove toxic materials, supply nutrients, and modify soil anoxia. All of these factors collectively contribute to different productivities and different growth forms in the intertidal and high marshes.

Nutrients

The availability of nutrients, particularly nitrogen and phosphorus, in the salt marsh soil is important for the productivity of the salt marsh ecosystem. Several wetland studies (e.g., those by Valiela and Teal, 1974, and Smart and Barko, 1980) have shown that salt marsh vegetation is primarily nitrogen limited. Figure 8-5 shows typical concentrations of total nitrogen and ammonium nitrogen in a salt marsh soil transect. Comparison of Figure 8-5a with Figure 8-5b shows that ammonium nitrogen, the primary form available to marsh vegetation, is only a small percentage (less than 1%) of the total nitrogen in the marsh soil. This is typical of organic wetland soils in general. Mendelssohn (1979) found ammonium to be the dominant form of inorganic nitrogen in salt marsh interstitial water in North Carolina by one to two orders of magnitude over nitrate nitrogen. This is expected because of the near anaerobic conditions usually present in the soil water, which precludes the buildup of nitrate nitrogen.

Another interesting feature of Figure 8-5 is the increase in ammonium in the inland direction. In salt marshes, plant growth rates have been shown to be limited by the supply of inorganic nitrogen; yet, in this example, ammonium concentrations are high precisely where growth is poorest. A number of scientists have observed this phenomenon and have tried to understand it (see Mendelssohn, McKee, and Postek, 1982). It appears that other, nonnutrient, stresses related to the poor drainage and low redox potentials limit the ability of inland plants to assimilate ammonium nitrogen. As a result, ammo-

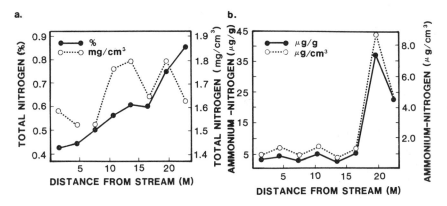

Figure 8-5. Variation in *a*. total nitrogen and *b*. extractable soil ammonium-nitrogen with distance inland from tidal stream in Louisiana salt marsh. *(From Buresh, Delaune, and Patrick, 1980, p. 114; Copyright © 1980 by the Estuarine Research Federation, reprinted with permission)*

nium accumulates in the substrate. Along the creek bank, available nitrogen is kept at low levels by the actively growing plants (Mendelssohn, 1979).

It is curious that although at least two studies have shown little relationship between soil nutrient *concentrations* (g/g dry wt. soil) and plant biomass (Broome, Woodhouse, and Seneca, 1975a, 1975b; Delaune, Buresh, and Patrick, 1979), there tends to be a very good positive correlation between aboveground vegetation biomass and soil nutrient *density* (g/cm^3 wet soil; Table 8-3).

Broome, Woodhouse, and Seneca (1975a) found that only soil-extractable phosphorus and zinc concentrations (dry wt. basis) were correlated with plant biomass; in the study by Delaune, Buresh, and Patrick (1979) only soil carbon concentration was related (negatively) to plant biomass. In contrast, when the nutrient content per unit volume of soil was examined, sodium, potassium, calcium, magnesium, total nitrogen, and extractable phosphorus were all positively correlated with aboveground plant biomass (Delaune, Buresh, and Patrick, 1979). Where bulk density varies widely from sample to sample, nutrient density on a volume basis gives a more consistent characterization of the soil than concentration on a dry weight basis (Mehlich, 1972; Gosselink, Hatton, and Hopkinson, 1984). Soils rich in minerals on a volume basis tend to be higher in many plant nutrients and are more productive than mineral-poor soils; hence the positive correlations shown in Table 8-3. It is probable that the positive correlations are due as much to the buffering effect of mineral ions on the redox potential of the soil as to any direct nutritional impact.

Phosphorus is often a nutrient limiting plant growth, but in salt marsh soils

Table 8-3. Concentrations of Constituents of a Louisiana Salt Marsh Soil

Constituent	Concentration, mg/g dry soil	Density, mg/cm^3 soil volume
Na$^+$	17	3.84[a]
K$^+$	1.753	0.40[b]
Ca^{++}	1.646	0.37[a]
Mg^{++}	3.864	0.87[a]
Total N	7.2	1.63[a]
Extractable P	0.123	0.028[b]
Organic C	12.0[a]	26.9

Source: After Delaune, Buresh, and Patrick (1979)
[a]Significantly correlated with aboveground plant biomass at the 0.05 level of significance.
[b]Significantly correlated with aboveground plant biomass at the 0.01 level of significance.

it accumulates in high concentrations and apparent does not limit plant growth. For example, the marsh sediments along the Georgia coast contain enough phosphorus to supply the marsh vegetation for several hundred years (Pomeroy et al., 1972).

Other plant nutrients have also been suggested as possibly limiting growth in salt marshes. Adams (1963) found that soluble iron concentrations in the marsh soil water were highest in the lower, more productive zones of the marsh. He also found, in culture experiments, that *S. alterniflora* became chlorotic, or discolored due to lack of chlorophyll synthesis, with decreased iron supplies, leading him to suggest that iron may become limiting to plant growth. However, subsequent studies (Haines and Dunn, 1976) have ruled this out. In fact, several micronutrients, including iron and manganese, are available in high concentrations in marsh soils because of the reducing conditions, and they are more likely to be in toxic concentrations than limiting. Iron, for example, is found in *Spartina* tissues at concentrations about 10 times those in most crop plants.

Sulfur is an interesting marsh soil chemical because of its toxicity, acid-forming properties, and ability to store energy from organic sources. Seawater contains abundant sulfate. When this ion encounters the anoxic marsh soil, it is reduced by soil bacteria to sulfide, which in turn can form insoluble pyrites with iron. It is in equilibrium with hydrogen sulfide (which gives the rotten egg odor). Hydrogen sulfide is extremely toxic to plants (Hollis, 1967) and is probably responsible, at least in part, for the poor performance of inland marsh plants (Mendelssohn, McKee, and Postek, 1982). In addition, when exposed to air, sulfides can be re-oxidized to sulfate, forming sulfuric acid, with a resulting drop in soil pH. It has been suggested that local sediment drying and the subsequent increase in acidity in the soil may account for some patches of plant die-out in the marsh (Cooper, 1974).

A recently uncovered and intriguing property of sulfide is its ability to act as a storage compound for biologically fixed energy. In the anaerobic soil environment, bacteria reduce sulfate to sulfide by oxidizing organic compounds (see chap. 5). They trap about 15% of the organic energy; the other 75% is transferred to the energy-rich sulfide radical. These sulfide compounds can later be re-oxidized, the stored energy used to fuel the growth of sulfur-oxidizing bacteria. An estimate of the importance of this pathway of energy flow in a New England salt marsh is given by Howarth and Teal (1979) and Howarth et al. (1983), who calculated that as much as 70% of the energy of net primary production flows through reduced inorganic sulfur compounds. Most of the stored sulfides are re-oxidized on an annual basis by oxygen diffusing into the soil from marsh grass roots. But energy equivalent to 20%–40% of the net aboveground productivity appears to be exported from this marsh as reduced sulfur compounds.

**Table 8-4. Examples of Common Plant Species in Salt Marshes
for Various Regions in North America**

Location	Examples of Common Vegetation	
	Lower marsh	*Upper marsh*
Eastern North America		
New England	*Spartina alterniflora*	*Spartina patens* *Distichlis spicata* *Juncus gerardi* *Spartina alterniflora* (dwarf)
Coastal Plain	*Spartina alterniflora*	*Spartina patens* *Distichlis spicata* *Salicornia sp.* *Juncus roemerianus*
Bay of Fundy	*Spartina alterniflora*	*Spartina patens* *Limonium nashii* *Plantago oliganthos* *Puccinellia maritima* *Juncus gerardi*
Gulf of Mexico[a]		

North Florida/South
Alabama & Mis-
    sissippi
	Dominant
	    Juncus roemerianus
	Subdominant
	    Spartina patens
	    Spartina alterniflora	

Louisiana	Dominant
	    Spartina alterniflora
	Subdominant
	    Spartina patens
	    Distichlis spicata
	    Juncus roemerianus	

Arctic		
Northern Canada/ Europe	*Puccinellia phryganodes*	*Carex subspathacea*
Western Alaska	*Puccinellia phryganodes*	*Puccinellia triflora* *Plantago maritima* *Triglochin sp.* *Plantago maritima*
Western North America		
Southern California	*Spartina foliosa*	*Salicornia pacifica* *Suaeda californica* *Batis maritima*

Source: Many examples from Chapman (1960; 1975)

[a]Because of low tide range, low and high marsh distinctions are not clear.

ECOSYSTEM STRUCTURE

The salt marsh ecosystem has diverse biological components, which include vegetation, and animal and microbe communities in the marsh; and plankton, invertebrates, and fishes in the tidal creeks, pans, and estuaries. Discussion here will be limited to the biological structure of the marsh itself.

Vegetation

Salt marshes are dominated by halophytic flowering plants, often by one or a few species of grass. Some common plant species found in various regions of North America are given in Table 8-4.

The vegetation of the salt marsh has been divided into zones related to the upper and lower marshes described previously. Characteristic patterns found in the North American Atlantic coast marshes are shown in Figure 8-6.

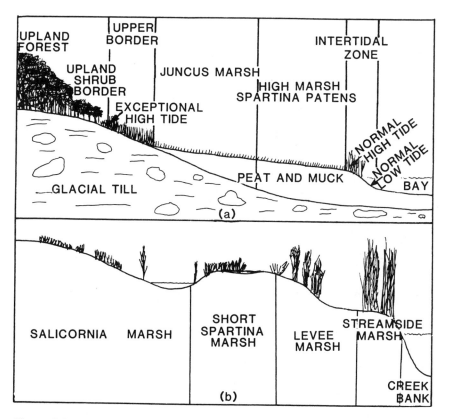

Figure 8-6. Zonation of vegetation in typical North American salt marshes. *a.* New England salt marsh *(after Miller and Egler, 1950, p. 155; Copyright © by the Ecological Society of America, reprinted with permission). b.* Georgia salt marsh *(after Teal, 1962, p. 616).*

Miller and Egler (1950) described a typical New England salt marsh in three or four zones (Fig. 8-6a). The intertidal zone or lower marsh is next to the estuary, bay, or tidal creek, and is dominated by the tall form of *S. alterniflora* Loisel (cordgrass). In the high marsh *S. patens* (salt meadow grass) is mixed with *Distichlis spicata* (spike grass) and occasional patches of the shrub *Iva frutescens* (marsh elder) and various forbs. The short form of *S. alterniflora* can also be found in this zone. Beyond the *S. patens* zone and at normal high tide, *Juncus gerardi* (black grass) forms pure stands. The limit of tidal marsh at the upper portion of the marsh will often be marked by *Panicum virgatum* (switch grass), *Iva frutescens,* and numerous other species.

South of the Chesapeake Bay along the Atlantic coast, salt marshes typical of the Coastal Plain appear. These marshes are similar in zonation to those in New England except that (1) tall *S. alterniflora* often forms only in very narrow bands along creeks, (2) the short form of *S. alterniflora* occurs more commonly in the wide middle zone, and (3) *Juncus roemerianus* replaces *J. gerardi* in the high marsh (Cooper, 1974). Teal (1962) describes a frequently studied Georgia salt marsh as having five distinct zones (Fig. 8-6b) that are ultimately related to tidal and other hydrologic factors:

1. Creek bank—the sparsely vegetated muddy and/or sandy banks of tidal creeks between low tide and *Spartina* growth.

2. Streamside marsh—a 1- to 3-meter-wide band of tall *Spartina alterniflora* located adjacent to the creek bank.

3. Levee marsh—*Spartina* of intermediate height on the natural levee bordering the creek.

4. Short *Spartina* marsh—flat areas behind the levee that support a widely spaced short form of *Spartina alterniflora.*

5. *Salicornia* marsh—sandy areas near the upland where *Salicornia* (glasswort) may be common.

The dominant plant in many eastern North America salt marshes, *S. alterniflora,* is a stiff, leafy grass that can grow to 3 meters in height. It has two growth forms, tall and short, which are found in different parts of the marsh. The tall form (100 to 300 cm) generally occurs adjacent to tidal creeks and in the extreme low portions of the intertidal marsh. The short form (17 to 80 cm) is found away from the creeks and generally in areas of greater salinity in the upper marsh. Debate continues as to whether the differences in plant growth are due to genetic or environmental causes. Anderson and Treshow (1980), in a review on the subject, conclude that the differences are both genetic, with different ecotypes evolved, and environmental, with dominant factors being sediment anoxia and salinity stress.

Distichlis spicata (spike grass) is another common salt marsh plant with wide distribution in coastal and inland saline wetlands in the United States. The plant is particularly tolerant of high soil salinity and it may serve as a pioneer species in salt marsh development. At the upper edge of a marsh inundated only by spring tides, two different groups of species are common, depending on the local rainfall and temperature. Where rainfall exceeds evapotranspiration, salt-tolerant species give way to less tolerant species such as *Limonium carolinianum* (sea lavender), *Aster* spp. (asters), and *Triglochin maritima* (arrow grass) (Niering and Warren, 1977). On the southeast coast where evapotranspiration often exceeds rainfall during the summer, salts can accumulate in these upper marshes and salt-tolerant halophytes such as *Salicornia* spp. (saltwort) and *Batis maritima* flourish. Bare areas with salt efflorescence are common.

Mud algal mats, dominated particularly by blue-greens, diatoms, and green algae, are also present in the salt marsh. Algal species with worldwide distribution in salt marshes include the blue-greens *Lyngbya* and *Rivularia,* and the green algae *Ulothrix, Rhizoclonium, Chaetomorpha, Ulva, Enteromorpha,* and *Monostroma* (Chapman, 1960; Ursin, 1972). Species composition of the mud algae is very dynamic, with the perpetual accretion or erosion of sediments. Species may completely change within a few weeks (Chapman, 1960). Algae also tend to form zones in the marsh along tidal and substrate gradients. The algae, however, do not necessarily align in conformity with marsh vegetation zonation (Sullivan, 1978).

Consumers

The consumers that live in the tidal salt marsh can be divided for simplicity into grazers that feed on the emergent vegetation and algae-detrital feeders. Few comprehensive studies of the animals, particularly of invertebrates, have been conducted in salt marshes (Cooper, 1974). Notable exceptions are the studies of Teal (1962) in Georgia, Davis and Gray (1966) in North Carolina, and J. W. Day et al. (1973) in Louisiana. Important grazers in the marshes in these regions include several species of insects, including the salt marsh grasshopper *(Orchelimum)* and plant hoppers *(Prokelisia).* Detritus-algal feeders in the marsh include the marsh snail *(Melampus bidentatus),* and sand flea *(Orchestia),* and isopods *(Philosia).* In the intertidal zone the fiddler crab *(Uca),* various mussels (*Modiolus* and *Mytilus*), periwinkle *(Littorina),* the mud snail *(Nassarius),* and various immature insects, oligochaetes, and annelid worms are found. Other crustaceans include the hermit crab *(Sesarma reticulatum)* and the green crab *(Carcinus maenas)* (Ursin, 1972; Niering and Warren, 1977). Muskrats *(Ondatra)* are conspicuous in some salt marshes by their many houses of piled up vegetation on the marsh surface. They feed primarily on plant material, preferring low-salinity plants such as *Scirpus* sp. and *Typha* sp. (Daiber, 1977). Secondary consumers in the salt marsh include mud crabs *(Eurytium),* clapper rails *(Rallus),* and some mammals such as the raccoon (Cooper, 1974).

There is contradictory evidence about the diversity of consumers in the salt marsh. Some studies have indicated a relatively high consumer diversity, particularly of insects and waterfowl (Davis and Gray, 1966; Niering and Warren, 1977). Other studies (e.g., Teal, 1962) reported low consumer diversity. Teal attributes this relative lack of diversity of macroconsumers to (1) the low diversity of higher plants in the salt marsh, and (2) the removal of much of the organic production through tidal currents. One theory suggests that the low diversity of certain mollusks, crustaceans, and secondary consumers can be attributed to the alternate flooding and drying due to tides; most terrestrial insects and waterfowl, on the other hand, are not limited by tidal fluctuations but only by availability of food and protection, both of which are abundant in the salt marsh. Animal diversity develops, then, despite a relatively low diversity in the plant community.

Salt marshes also support significant populations of waterfowl. Niering and Warren (1977) cite the importance of eastern North America salt marshes for food, shelter, and nesting sites for many migratory waterfowl. The marsh avifauna in this region includes wading birds such as herons and egrets, birds of prey such as marsh hawks and ospreys, and year-round marsh residents such as rails and marsh sparrows. Stewart (1962) found the black duck *(Anas rubripes),* the mallard *(Anas platyrhynchos),* and the widgeon *(Anas americana)* to be the dominant waterfowl populations in marshes of the upper Chesapeake Bay. In Louisiana, the gadwall *(Anas strepera),* teals *(A. discors* and *A. crecca),* and mallards are the most common.

Many fish and shellfish feed along the marsh edges and in small, shallow marsh ponds and move up into the marsh on high tides. Werme (1981) found 30% of silverside *(Menidia menidia)* and mummichog *(Fundulus heteroclitus)* in a north Atlantic estuary up in the marsh at high tide. Ruebsamen (1972) reported that common fishes in small salt marsh ponds in Louisiana are sheepshead minnow *(Cyprinodon variegatus),* diamond killifish *(Adinia xenica,)* tidewater silversides *(Menidia beryllina),* gulf killifish *(Fundulus grandis),* and sailfin molly *(Poecilia latipinna).* Shrimp *(Penaeus* spp.) and blue crabs *(Callinectis sapidus)* are also common.

Many estuarine organisms benefit from both the shelter afforded by marshes and the organic production exported from them (Heinle, Flemer, and Ustach, 1977; Turner, 1977; Thayer et al., 1979). Turner (1977), for example, found that on a regional basis, the abundance and type of shrimp harvested commercially were related to the area and type of intertidal vegetation, including salt marshes and mangroves.

ECOSYSTEM FUNCTION

Major points that have been demonstrated in several studies about the functioning of salt marsh ecosystems include the following:

1. Gross and net primary productivity are high in much of the salt marsh—almost as high as in subsidized agriculture. This high productivity is a result of subsidies in the form of tides, nutrient import, and abundance of water that offset the stresses of salinity, widely fluctuating temperatures, and alternate flooding and drying.
2. The salt marsh is a major producer of detritus, for both the salt marsh system and the adjacent estuary. In some cases, detrital material exported from the marsh is more important to the estuary than is the phytoplankton-based production in the estuary. Detritus export and the shelter found along marsh edges make salt marshes important as nursery areas for many commercially important fish and shellfish.
3. The grazing pathway is a minor energy flow in the salt marsh.
4. Leaves and stems of vegetation serve as surface areas for epiphytic algae and other epibiotic organisms. This enhances both the primary and secondary productivities of the marsh.
5. Detrital decomposition, the major pathway of energy utilization in the salt marsh, causes an increase in the protein content of the detritus and enhances its food value to consumers.
6. Salt marshes have been shown, at times, to be both sources and sinks of nutrients, particularly nitrogen.

These and other points will be discussed below.

Primary Productivity

Tidal marshes are among the most productive ecosystems in the world, with up to 25 metric tons per hectare of plant material ($2,500 \ g/m^2 \cdot yr$) produced annually in the southern Coastal Plain of North America (Niering and Warren, 1977). The three major autotrophic units of the salt marsh include the marsh grasses, the mud algae, and the phytoplankton of the tidal creeks. Extensive studies of the net primary productivity of *Spartina* have been conducted in salt marshes along the Atlantic and Gulf Coasts of the United States. A comparison of many of the measured values of net aboveground production is given in Table 8-5. Belowground production has been difficult to measure and estimates vary widely. *S. alterniflora* root production estimates range from 220 to 2,500 $g/m^2 \cdot yr$ (streamside) and 420 to 6,200 $g/m^2 \cdot yr$ inland (Good, Good, and Frasco, 1982).

Table 8-5. Net Primary Productivity of Grasses and Rushes in Selected Salt Marshes

Location	Major Vegtation	Aboveground Net Primary Productivity, $g\ dry\ wt./m^2 \cdot yr$		Reference
		Low Marsh	High Marsh	
Georgia	*Spartina alterniflora*	2,000	570	Smalley (1959)
North Carolina	*S. alterniflora*	1,290	330	Stroud and Cooper (1968)
New York	*S. alterniflora*	507-824		Udall, Zarudsky, and Doheny (1969)
North Carolina	*Juncus roemerianus*		792	Williams and Murdoch (1972)
Rhode Island	*S. alterniflora*	840	432	Nixon and Oviatt
	S. patens		430	(1973)
Louisiana[a]	*S. alterniflora*	750-2,600		Kirby and Gosselink (1976)
Louisiana[b]	*S. alterniflora*	1,473-2,895		White et al.
	Distichlis spicata		1,162-1,291	(1978)
	S. patens		1,342-1,428	
	J. roemerianus		1,806-1,959	
Georgia	*S. alterniflora*	3,700	1,300	Gallagher et al.
	J. roemerianus		2,200	(1980)
Louisiana	*S. alterniflora*	1,381		Hopkinson et al.
	S. patens		4,159	(1980)
	D. spicata		1,967	
	S. cynosuroides		1,134	
	J. roemerianus		3,295	

[a]Low value of range based on maximum biomass minus minimum biomass; high value also includes estimate of disappearance of dead vegetation.

[b]Range; different methods used to calculate productivity.

Several major generalizations can be made. First, the aboveground productivity of *Spartina* is often higher along creek channels and in the low or intertidal marshes than in high marshes, due to increased exposure to tidal and freshwater flow. These conditions also produce the taller forms of *Spartina* as discussed earlier. Second, there is generally greater productivity in the southern Coastal Plain salt marshes than in those further north, due to the greater influx of solar energy and to the longer growing season (Turner, 1976), but possibly also due to the nutrient-rich sediments carried by the rivers of that region. White et al. (1978) argue that productivity of salt marshes in Louisiana and Mississippi may be higher than Atlantic coast

Table 8-6. Net Primary Productivity of Algae in Salt Marshes of North America

Location	Dominant Types of Algae	Net Primary Productivity, $g/m^2 \cdot yr$	NNP Algae / NPP Vascular Plants	References
Georgia	Pennate diatoms, green flagellates, blue-greens	324[a]	0.25	Pomeroy (1959) Teal (1962)
Delaware		160	0.33	Gallagher and Daiber (1974)
Massachusetts	Green filamentous	105	0.25	Van Raalte and Valiela (1976)
California	Blue-greens, fil-amentous greens, and diatoms	320–588	0.76–1.40	Zedler (1980)

[a] Assumes 1 g C = 2 g dry wt.

marshes due to higher nutrient import from the Mississippi River. Third, the wide divergence among sites in measurements of net primary productivity is as much due to the methods used for measurement as to true differences in productivity. Kirby and Gosselink (1976), White et al. (1978) and Hopkinson, Gosselink, and Parrondo (1980) discuss the variations obtainable with different methods used for calculating productivity. Fourth, belowground production is sizable, often greater than aerial production. Under unfavorable soil conditions, plants seem to put more of their energy into root production. Hence, root:shoot ratios seem to be generally higher inland than at streamside locations.

The productivity of the mud algae is less well understood, although there have been a few noteworthy studies; for example, Pomeroy (1959) in Georgia, Gallagher and Daiber (1974) in Delaware, Van Raalte and Valiela (1976) in Massachusetts, and Zedler (1980) in southern California. On the Atlantic coast, productivity of algae was one-third to one-fourth that of the vascular plant productivity (see Table 8-6). However, Zedler (1980) found that algal net primary productivity in southern California was from 80% to 140% of the vascular productivity. She hypothesized that the arid and hypersaline conditions of southern California favor algal growth over vascular plant growth.

Decomposition

Much of the detritus produced in the salt marsh ecosystem is broken down by bacteria. In Teal's study of energy flow within the salt marsh environment (Teal, 1962), 47% of the total net primary productivity was lost through respiration by microbes. Decomposition processes in salt marshes fragment original detritus (dead leaves and stems of *Spartina*) into smaller sizes and upgrade the protein content by less rapid decomposition of protein and by colonization of the substrate by bacteria, fungi, and protozoa. Odum and de la Cruz (1967) found that as *Spartina* grass decomposed, organic matter increased in protein content from 10% to 24% on an ash-free basis (Fig. 8-7), that is, the carbon/nitrogen ratio decreased in the detritus. The authors concluded that "the bacteria-rich detritus is nutritionally a better food source for animals than is the *Spartina* tissue that forms the original base for most of the particulate matter."

However, a contrasting theory has been proposed by Wiebe and Pomeroy (1972), who showed that detritus fragments are not colonized by large populations of bacteria, and thus are not suitable as food for deposit feeders. Rather, it appears that the detritus is grazed by nematodes and other microscopic benthic organisms, which are in turn eaten by the large deposit

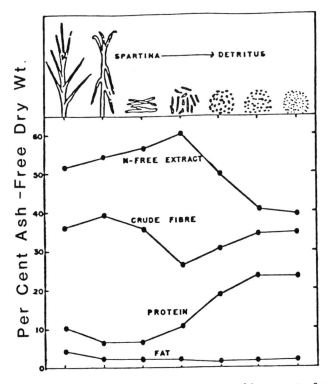

Figure 8-7. Nutritional composition of successive stages of decomposing *Spartina* grass, showing increasing protein content and decreasing carbohydrates. *(From Odum and de la Cruz, 1967, p. 388; Copyright © 1967 by the American Association for the Advancement of Science, reprinted with permission)*

feeders. Bacterial production on detritus is high, but the rapid turnover rate keeps the population low.

Several other investigators have looked at the dynamics of detrital decomposition in salt marshes (Burkholder and Bornside, 1957; Gosselink and Kirby, 1974; Pomeroy et al., 1977; White et al., 1978; Hackney and de la Cruz, 1980). Gosselink and Kirby (1974) found that a significant percentage (11%–66%) of decomposed grass is converted to microbial biomass and that particle size is an important determinant in the rate of decomposition. Pomeroy et al. (1977) described the importance of soluble organic matter, as well as particulate organic matter, in the detrital food web of a salt marsh. They believed that this soluble organic matter (which may be as much as 25% of the initial dry weight of the dying grass) from both living and decomposing salt marsh vegetation is an important energy source for microorganisms in the marsh and the adjacent estuary. They also pointed out that anaerobic microorganisms, such as nitrogen-reducing bacteria, sulfur-reducing bacteria, and methane-generating bacteria, may be important consumers of organic substrate in the salt marsh, particularly below the surface. Because of the anoxic conditions, the decomposition of organic matter 20 cm or more beneath the marsh surface is slow. Still, Teal (1986) reported that less than 20% of the original litter remained after 2.5 years.

Organic Export

Several studies have demonstrated that a substantial portion (usually 20%–45%) of the net primary productivity of a salt marsh is exported to adjacent estuaries. Odum and de la Cruz (1967) estimated a "net export of about 140 kg and 25 kg of organic matter for spring and neap tides, respectively," in one tidal cycle, from a 10 to 25 hectare salt marsh in Georgia. Wiegert, Christian, and Wetzel (1981) suggested that prorating this estimate over the watershed of the creek results in an export value of approximately $100 \text{ g C/m}^2 \cdot \text{yr}$. In other studies, however, the adjacent salt marsh has not been the most important source of carbon for the estuary. Haines (1979) questioned the significance of wetland export based on stable carbon radioisotope data. Biggs and Flemer (1972) found that allochthonous material from uplands is the greatest source of organic carbon in the upper Chesapeake Bay; while Heinle and Flemer (1976) measured an annual flux of $7.3 \text{ g C/m}^2 \cdot \text{yr}$ of particulate carbon from a salt marsh in Maryland, less than 1% of the total marsh net production. These latter authors attributed the low export to relatively poor tidal exchange. Woodwell et al. (1977) also found a low net exchange of carbon between a salt marsh and the coastal waters at Long Island, New York. After a thorough review, Nixon (1980) concluded that export of dissolved and particulate organic carbon was fairly universal but is often not large (see chap. 5).

Energy Flow

Several studies have dealt with energy flow in parts of the salt marsh ecosystem, but only a few have considered the entire salt marsh ecosystem energy flow. Most notable in this latter category is the study of a Georgia salt marsh by Teal (1962). Many of his values would be modified today, but the study remains a classic attempt to quantify energy fluxes in the salt marsh (Fig. 8-8). Gross primary productivity was calculated to be 6.1% of incident sunlight energy, verifying that the salt marsh is one of the most productive ecosystems in the world. Only 1.4% of the incident light, however, was converted into net primary productivity available to other organisms. Herbivorous insects, mostly plant hoppers *(Prokelisia)* and grasshoppers *(Orchelimum),* consumed only 4.6% of the *Spartina* net productivity. The rest of the *Spartina* net productivity and that of the mud algae passed through the detrital-algal food chain or was exported to the adjacent estuary. In the detrital food chain, primary and secondary consumers were dominated by

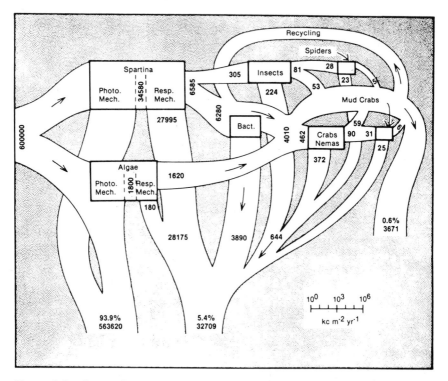

Figure 8-8. Energy flow diagram for a Georgia salt marsh. *(From Teal, 1962, p. 622; Copyright © 1962 by Ecological Society of America, reprinted with permission)*

only a few species such as the detritus-eating fiddler crab *(Uca)* and the carnivorous mud crab *(Eurytium).* An estimated 45% of the net production was exported from the marsh into the estuary in this study. In a partial energy budget, Parsons and de la Cruz (1980) found that only 0.3% of the net primary productivity of a Mississippi *Juncus* marsh was ingested by three species of grasshoppers. They found that over twice this amount of net primary productivity prematurely fell into the detrital mat due to grasshopper grazing.

Figure 8-9 shows the energy flow during summer and winter conditions in a salt marsh–estuary complex in New England (Nixon and Oviatt, 1973). Here the diagram emphasizes the importance of the marsh creeks and adjacent embayments in addition to the marsh itself. In this study, an estimated 23% of the net productivity of the salt marsh was exported to the embayment. Estimates of the productivity and consumption in the embayment itself led to the conclusion that the aquatic embayment is actually a heterotrophic ecosystem that depends on the import of organic matter from the autotrophic salt marsh.

Nutrient Budgets

Nutrients are carried into salt marshes by precipitation, surface water, groundwater, and tidal exchange. Because many salt marshes appear to be net exporters of organic material (with incorporated nutrient elements), a nutrient budget would be expected to show that the marsh is a net sink for inorganic nutrients. Recent studies have shown that this is not always the case.

One of the most ambitious studies of nutrient dynamics in the salt marsh ecosystems was carried out at the Great Sippewissett Marsh in Massachusetts (Valiela et al., 1978; Teal, Valiela, and Berla, 1979; Kaplan, Valiela, and Teal, 1979). A summary diagram of the nitrogen budget developed from this study is given in Figure 8-10. Valiela et al. (1978) estimated the amount of nitrogen in groundwater inputs, precipitation, and tidal exchanges in the marsh. Nitrogen from groundwater entering the marsh primarily as nitrate nitrogen (NO_3-N), and from tidal exchange represented the major fluxes of nitrogen to the salt marsh. Precipitation contributed significantly less nitrogen, mostly as NO_3-N and dissolved organic nitrogen (DON). Tidal exchange was found to result in a net export of nitrogen, mostly in the form of DON. Nitrogen fixation by bacteria was significant (Teal, Valiela, and Berla, 1979) and blue-green algal fixation was much less (Carpenter, Van Raalte, and Valiela, 1978). Kaplan, Valiela, and Teal (1979) found denitrification to be high in the salt marsh, particularly in muddy creek bottoms and in the short *Spartina* marsh. Figure 8-11 compares the denitrification loss in this salt marsh with the seasonal influx of groundwater and the loss of nitrates due to tidal exchange.

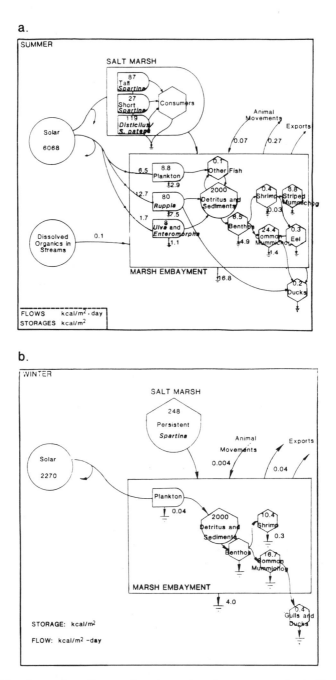

Figure 8-9.   Energy flow diagrams for salt-marsh-embayment complex in Rhode Island for composite *a.* summer and *b.* winter days. *(After Nixon and Oviatt, 1973, p. 491)*

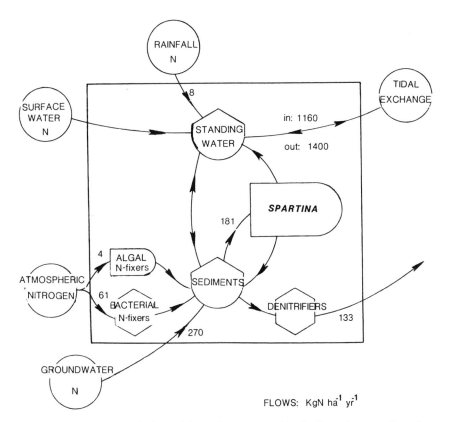

Figure 8-10. Nitrogen budget of Great Sippewissett Marsh, Massachusetts. *(Data from Valiela et al., 1978; Teal, Valiela, and Berla, 1979; Kaplan and Valiela, 1979; and Valiela and Teal, 1979)*

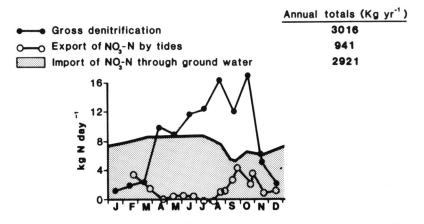

Figure 8-11. Seasonal exchanges of nitrate nitrogen in Great Sippewissett Marsh, Massachusetts. *(From Kaplan, Valiela and Teal, 1979, p. 732; Copyright © 1979 by the American Society of Limnology and Oceanography, reprinted with permission)*

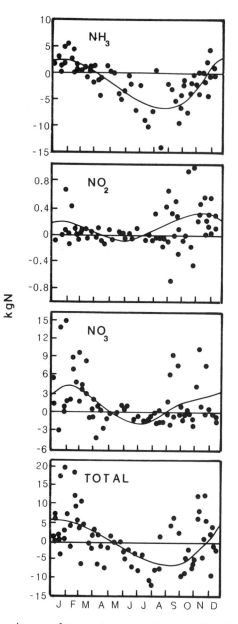

Figure 8-12. Net exchanges of inorganic nitrogen between Flax Pond salt marsh and adjacent estuary in New York. Negative numbers indicate export from marsh. *(From Woodwell et al., 1979, p. 698; Copyright © 1979 by the Ecological Society of America, reprinted with permission)*

Woodwell et al. (1979) described a budget of annual exchanges of inorganic nitrogen between a salt marsh complex and coastal waters in Long Island, New York (Fig. 8-12). They found a net export of ammonium nitrogen from the marsh during summer and fall (the marsh was a source) and a net import from coastal waters in winter and spring (the marsh was a sink). Nitrate was also imported in the winter and lost from the marsh in the summer. For the three inorganic nitrogen species studied (NH_4, NO_3, NO_2), there was a net export of about 10 kg N/ha · yr. As compared with the nitrogen uptake by the marsh vegetation, loss from the marsh was only a fraction of intrasystem cycling. The export of nitrogen from salt marshes into Long Island Sound during the summer was about one-third of the amount of nitrogen that enters the sound from rivers during the same period.

The issue of whether there is a net uptake or discharge of inorganic nutrients by the salt marsh remains unresolved. The study of the Great Sippewissett Marsh in Massachusetts indicated an approximate balance between inputs and outputs. The Long Island Marsh study found that the marsh was a source of nitrogen during the growing season and a sink in winter and spring. Aurand and Daiber (1973) found a net import of inorganic nitrogen into a Delaware salt marsh over a year, while Stevenson et al. (1977) found a net discharge of both nitrogen and phosphorus from a Chesapeake Bay salt marsh. Haines et al. (1977) concluded that, compared to plant uptake, leakage of nitrogen in Georgia salt marshes was small. However, Valiela, Teal, and Sass (1973) demonstrated that salt marshes can be nutrient sinks when high-nutrient waters pass through them or when high-nutrient waste water is applied to the marshes.

Nixon (1980) concluded that, in general, dissolved organic nitrogen and probably dissolved phosphorus were fairly universally exported; and that nitrate and nitrite were generally imported, but that these fluxes were not very large components of the nutrient cycles of most estuaries. Odum, Fisher, and Pickral (1979) suggested that the balance between import and export depends on geophysical constraints, specifically the morphology of the basin, and on the magnitude of tidal and freshwater fluxes. They hypothesized that estuaries with constricted openings to the sea trap and recirculate materials, while wedge-shaped estuaries with large ocean exposure tend to export materials.

ECOSYSTEM MODELS

Several conceptual and mathematical models have been developed to describe the structure and function of the salt marsh ecosystem. The energy flow diagrams of Teal (1962; Fig. 8-8) and Nixon and Oviatt (1973; Fig. 8-9) and the

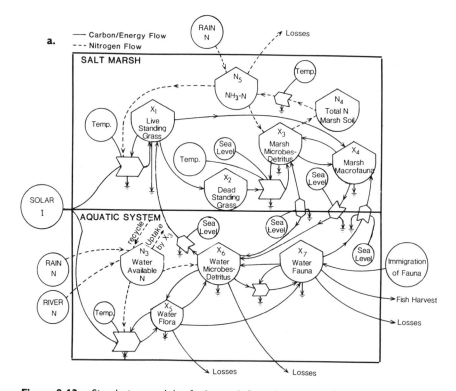

Figure 8-13. Simulation models of salt marsh for *a*. Louisiana *(after Hopkinson and Day, 1977, p. 248)* and *b*. Sapelo Island, Georgia *(from Wiegert, Christian, and Wetzel, 1981, p. 189; Copyright © 1981 by Springer-Verlag, reprinted with permission).*

nitrogen budget of Sippewisset Marsh (Fig. 8-10) represent conceptual models of the salt marsh and contain valuable information on the flow of energy and materials in the marsh. More important, however, these conceptual models have led to a number of simulation models of salt marshes, including those by Williams and Murdock (1972), Reimold (1974), Wiegert et al. (1975) Hopkinson and Day (1977), Zieman and Odum (1977), Wiegert and Wetzel (1979), and Wiegert, Christian, and Wetzel (1981).

Reimold (1974) expanded on the phosphorus model of a *Spartina* salt marsh developed by Pomeroy et al. (1972). The model has five phosphorus compartments, including water, sediments, *Spartina,* detritus, and detrital feeders. The model was used to simulate the effects of perturbations such as *Spartina* harvesting on the ecosystem, and to help design subsequent field experiments. The simulations demonstrated that *Spartina* regrowth and resulting phosphorus in the water depended on the time of year harvesting of marsh grass took place.

b.

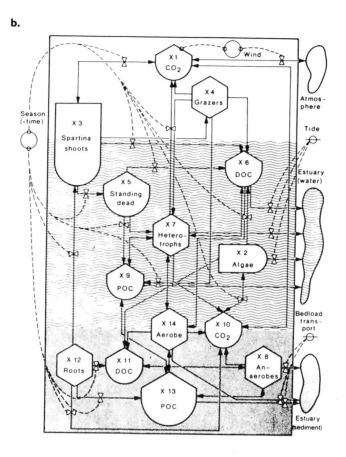

Zieman and Odum (1977) developed a model of plant succession in the salt marsh and applied it to two sites along the Chesapeake Bay. The model was different from most ecosystem models in that it used correlations to relate previously measured time series data on plant growth to physical and biological characteristics of the marsh. The model was originally developed for use by the Corps of Engineers in determining where and how to dispose of dredged material in a manner such that a viable salt marsh could develop. The model considered four species of vascular plants, including two species of *Spartina,* and described their growth as a function of salinity, tide, light, pH, and temperature.

Hopkinson and Day (1977) combined a nitrogen budget model for a salt marsh complex in Louisiana with the carbon model of Day et al. (1973) and developed the simulation model shown in Figure 8-13*a*. The model includes seven biological compartments and three nonliving nitrogen storages. The authors stated that nitrogen was the most important nutrient for modeling because it is generally the limiting nutrient in salt marshes. Forcing functions in the model include solar energy, water temperature, tidal fluctuations, nitrogen in rainfall and rivers, and immigration of aquatic fauna. The model simulations suggest that temperature may be the major parameter controlling salt marsh productivity and that the inclusion of sea level fluctuations gives more realistic predictions.

Wiegert and his associates (Wiegert et al., 1975; Wiegert, Christian, and Wetzel, 1981; Wiegert and Wetzel, 1979) have put considerable effort into the development of a simulation model for Sapelo Island, Georgia, salt marshes. The model, called MRSH1, has gone through several iterations; the general structure of version 6 of this model is shown in Figure 8-13*b*. It has 14 major compartments and traces the major pathways of carbon in the ecosystem through *Spartina,* algae, grazers, decomposers, and several compartments of abiotic carbon storage. The model was originally constructed to answer three questions (Wiegert, Christian, and Wetzel, 1981):

1. Is the Georgia salt marsh a potential source of carbon for the estuary, or is it a sink for carbon from offshore?
2. What organism groups are most responsible for the processing of carbon in the salt marsh?
3. What parameters are important for the proper modeling of the salt marsh, but are poorly known?

One of the most important revelations in this model-building process was the demonstration of the importance of the tidal export coefficient, and it consistently gave export values on the order of 1,000 g $C/m^2 \cdot$ year, well above field measurements by other researchers such as Odum and de la Cruz (1967). The inability to accurately measure this important pathway in the field has provided little opportunity for model verification; it has, however, shown that modeling can sometimes be a part of the scientific inquiry process prior to the obtaining of adequate field data.

SUMMARY

The salt marsh, with a worldwide distribution along coastlines in mid- and high latitudes, is a complex ecosystem in dynamic balance with its surroundings. These marshes flourish wherever the accumulation of sediments is equal to or greater than the rate of land subsidence, and where there is adequate protection from destructive waves and storms. The important physical and chemical variables that determine the structure and function of the salt marsh include tidal flooding frequency and duration, soil salinity, and nutrient limitation, particularly by nitrogen. The vegetation of the salt marsh, primarily salt-tolerant grasses, develops in identifiable zones in response to these and possibly other factors. Mud algae are also often an important component of the autotrophic community. The heterotrophic communities are dominated by detrital food chains, with the grazing food chain being much less significant and less diverse.

Salt marshes are among the most productive ecosystems of the world. In many areas, as much as half of the net primary productivity is washed out with the tide and serves as food support for aquatic communities. Many measurements of net primary productivity of salt marshes suggest that regional differences are related to available solar energy and, to some extent, to available nutrient imports by large rivers. Decomposition of dead vegetation in salt marshes occurs at or near the surface and enhances the protein content of the detritus for other marsh estuarine organisms. Nutrient cycle measurements in the marsh show few consistent patterns as to whether salt marshes are sources or sinks for dissolved nutrients. Conceptual and simulution models of the salt marsh, only recently begun in earnest, may eventually be significant aids to understanding the structure and function of salt marshes.

TIDAL FRESHWATER MARSH

TIDAL FRESHWATER MARSHES

This chapter is concerned with freshwater marshes that are close enough to coasts to experience significant tides, but at the same time are above the reach of oceanic saltwater. This set of circumstances usually occurs where precipitation is high or fresh river water runs to the coast, and where the morphology of the coast amplifies the tide as it moves inland. Tidal freshwater marshes are interesting because they receive the same "tidal subsidy" as coastal salt marshes, but without the stress of the salt. One would expect, therefore, that these ecosystems might be very productive and also more diverse than their saltwater counterparts. As tides attenuate upstream the marshes assume more and more of the character of inland freshwater marshes (chap. 11). The distinction between tidal and inland freshwater marshes is not clearcut, because on the coast they form a continuum (Fig. 9-1). In this chapter we include the tidally dominated systems of the Atlantic coast and the extensive coastal freshwater marshes of the northern Gulf coast even though the latter are influenced more by wind tides than by lunar tides.

Coastal freshwater marshes are not as well studied, nor as well understood, as other coastal wetlands, but interest in them is growing and several good reviews have recently been published (Good, Whigham, and Simpson, 1978; Simpson et al., 1983; Odum et al., 1984). These are drawn from heavily in the following discussion.

GEOGRAPHICAL EXTENT

The physical conditions for tidal freshwater marsh development are adequate rainfall or river flow to maintain fresh conditions, a flat gradient from

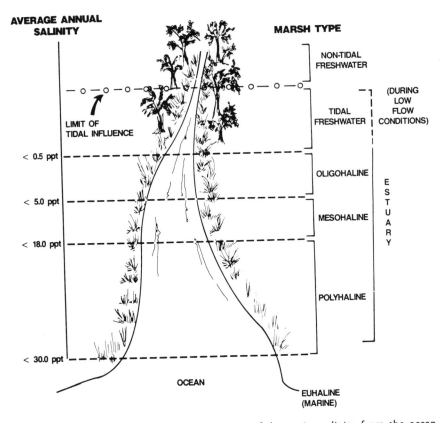

Figure 9-1. Coastal marshes lie on gradients of decreasing salinity from the ocean inland. Tidal freshwater marshes still experience tides but are above the salt boundary. Further inland, marshes experience neither salt nor tides. *(From W. E. Odum et al., 1984, p. 2)*

the ocean inland, and a significant tide range. These conditions occur predominantly along the middle and south Atlantic coast in the United States. Here a number of rivers bring fresh water to the coast, precipitation is moderate and fairly evenly spread throughout the year, and the broad coastal plain is flat and deep. Often the morphology of the system is such that the tidal water is constricted as it moves inland, resulting in amplification of the tide range, typically 0.5 to 2 meters. Along the northern Gulf coast, the tide range is small—less than 0.5 meters at the coast—and this range attenuates inland. Nevertheless, because the land slope is so small, freshwater marshes as far inland as 80 km experience some lunar tides, although these are overridden by wind tides and storm runoff.

Odum et al. (1984) estimated that Atlantic coast tidal freshwater marshes cover about 164,000 hectares (Fig. 9-2). Most of these are along the middle

Figure 9-2. Location and extent of tidal freshwater marshes *a.* along the coast of the eastern United States *(after W. E. Odum et al., 1984, p. 4)* and *b.* in Louisiana, on the northern coast of the Gulf of Mexico *(after Gosselink, 1984, p. 39).* Numbers in *(a)* are in hectares per state.

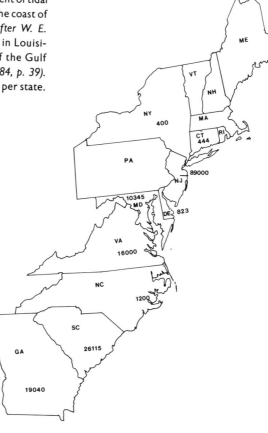

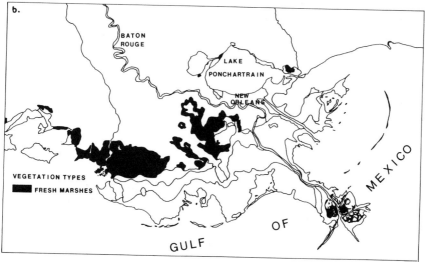

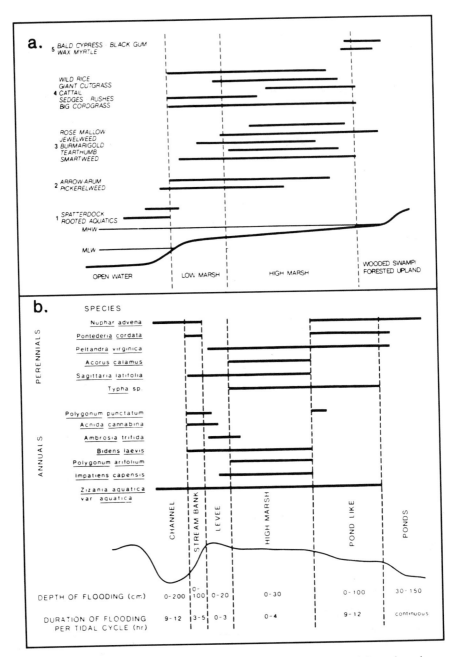

Figure 9-3. Diagrammatic cross sections across typical freshwater tidal marshes, showing elevation changes and typical vegetation. *(a. From W. E. Odum et al., 1984, p. 25. b. from Simpson et al., 1983, p. 256; Copyright © 1983 by the American Institute of Biological Sciences, reprinted with permission)*

Atlantic coast, perhaps one-half in New Jersey. This area estimate does not include upstream nontidal marshes. The Gulf of Mexico coastal freshwater marshes are concentrated in Louisiana, where they cover about 468,000 hectares (Chabreck, 1972).

GEOMORPHOLOGY AND HYDROLOGY

Coastal freshwater wetlands occur on many different kinds of substrates, but in spite of regional differences their recent geological history is similar (Odum et al., 1984). Contemporary coastal marshes are recent (Holocene) in origin. They lie in river valleys that were cut during Pleistocene periods of lowered sea level. As the sea level rose after the last glaciation (15,000 to 5,000 years B.P.), coastal marshes expanded rapidly as drowned river systems were inundated and filled with sediment. These marshes are probably still expanding, due to the recent increased soil runoff associated with forest clearing, agriculture, and other human activities. A vertical section through a present-day tidal freshwater marsh might show a sequence of sediments built on top of an eroded Pleistocene surface cut during a glacial period of lowered sea level. The sediments might include varying layers of riverine, estuarine, and marsh sediments, capped by recent tidal freshwater marsh sediments varying in thickness from less than 1 meter to more than 10 meters (Odum et al., 1984).

The vigorous tides and accompanying strong currents create a typical elevation gradient from tidal streams out into adjoining marshes. Odum et al. (1984) and Metzler and Rosza (1982) described similar cross-sectional profiles (Fig. 9-3a), with elevation increasing slowly from the stream edge to adjacent upland areas. The low marsh is usually geologically younger than the mature high marsh. A common feature, shown in Figure 9-3b, is a slight elevated levee along the margin of the creek, where overflowing water deposits much of its sediment load. Figure 9-3b shows elevation decreasing away from the tidal channels, but Simpson et al. (1983) state that this occurs primarily where the marshes have been impounded. High marshes are flooded to a depth of 30 cm for up to 4 hours on each tidal cycle; the low marshes are flooded deeper and may have standing water for 9-12 hours on each cycle. The elevation and flooding gradients result in gradients of soil physical and chemical properties and in plant zonation patterns that are a consistent feature of freshwater tidal marshes.

SOIL AND WATER CHEMISTRY

Typical ranges of chemical parameters in both water and sediments of tidal freshwater marshes are shown in Table 9-1. Freshwater coastal marsh sediments are generally fairly organic, especially in the more mature high marsh.

**Table 9-1. Chemistry of Water and Sediments
in Selected Coastal Freshwater Marshes**

	Hamilton & Woodbury Creek Marsh, Delaware River[a]	Herring Creek Marsh, James River, Va.[b]	Gulf Coastal Fresh Marsh, Barataria Bay, La.[c]
Water			
Tide Range	3 m Semidiurnal	<1 m Semidiurnal	Very low, mostly wind tide
Dissolved oxygen, mg/1	4-13	7-12	2-8
Alkalinity, mg $CaCO_3$/1	—	0.39 (winter)	—
$NO_2 + NO_3 - N, \mu g/1$	40-300	500-1,600	40-370
$NH_3 - N, \mu g/1$	40-80	460-470	0-2,780
Total Kjeldahl nitrogen, $\mu g/1$	—	3,300-4,200	1,960
Reactive phosphorus, $\mu g/1$	5-20	30-40	35-340
Total phosphorus, $\mu g/1$	5-50	160-180	217
Sediment[d]			
Organic carbon, % of dry weight	14-40	20-50	6-68
Total Kjeldahl nitrogen, % of dry weight	1.03-1.64	1.5 ± 0.8 (S. D.)	1.5 −1.8
Total phosphorus, % of dry weight	0.12-0.35	0.7	0.09
Cation exchange capacity, meq/100 g dry weight	—	40-67	—
pH	6.2-7.75	—	6.3

[a]Whigham, Simpson, and Lee, 1980
[b]Adams, 1978; Lunz et al., 1978; W. E. Odum et al., 1984
[c]Hatton, 1981; Chabreck, 1972; Ho and Schneider, 1976
[d]Top 20 cm

Along the Delaware River, they contain 14%-40% organic material (Whigham and Simpson, 1975), in Virginia tidal freshwater marshes 20%-50% (Odum et al., 1984). On the Gulf coast they may be as low as 6.2% and as high as 67.6% (Chabreck, 1972). They are anaerobic except for a thin surface layer, which is reflected in the absence of nitrate in the sediment. Ammonium is present in the winter, but is reduced to very low levels in the summer by plant uptake. The acidity of these soils is generally close to neutral. Total nitrogen levels are closely related to the organic content, since nearly all of the sediment nitrogen is bound in organic form. Phosphorus is more variable (Table 9-1). The cation exchange capacity (CEC) in James River marshes is 40-67 meq/100 g dry weight, which is high but typical for a highly organic soil (Wetzel and Powers, 1978).

The water flooding the marsh varies in chemical composition seasonally and depending on the source water. The detailed chemical studies reported for tidal freshwater wetlands have all been from more or less polluted sites. As a result, recorded concentrations of elements in the water have been rather high (Table 9-1). It is not clear how much they reflect the influence of the marsh as compared to upstream sources of materials.

ECOSYSTEM STRUCTURE

Vegetation

The elevation differences across a freshwater tidal marsh correspond with different plant associations (Figure 9-3). These associations are not discrete enough to call communities, and the species involved change with latitude. Nevertheless, they are characteristic enough to allow some generalizations. Typically, submerged vascular plants such as *Nuphar advena* (spatterdock), *Elodea* spp. (waterweed), *Potamogeton* spp. (pondweeds), and *Myriophyllum* spp. (water milfoil) grow in the streams and permanent ponds. The creek banks are scoured clean of vegetation each fall by the strong tidal currents, and they are dominated during the summer by annuals such as *Polygonum punctatum* (water smartweed), *Acnida cannabina* (water hemp), and *Bidens laevis* (bur marigold). The natural stream levee is often dominated by the *Ambrosia trifida* (giant ragweed). Behind this levee the low marsh is populated with broad-leaved monocotyledons such as *Peltandra virginica* (arrow arum), *Pontederia cordata* (pickerelweed), and *Sagittaria* spp. (arrowhead). Typically, the high marsh has a diverse population of annuals and perennials. Odum et al. (1984) call this the "mixed aquatic community type" in the mid-Atlantic region. Leck and Graveline (1979) describe a "mixed annual" association in New Jersey. In both cases, the area is dominated early in the season by perennials such as arrow arum. A diverse group of annuals assume dominance later in the season—*Bidens laevis*, *Polygonum arifolium* (tearthumb) and other smartweeds, *Pilea pumila* (clearweed), *Hibiscus coccineus* (rose mallow), *Acnida cannabina,* and others. In addition to these associations, there are often almost pure stands of *Zizania aquatica* (wild rice), *Typha* spp. (cattail), *Zizaniopsis miliaceae* (giant cutgrass), and *Spartina cynosuroides* (big cordgrass). In northern Gulf of Mexico coastal freshwater marshes, arrowheads replace arrow arum and pickerelweed at lower elevations. Elsewhere, grasses often dominate the perennial species [especially

Panicum hemitomon (maiden cane)], with many of the same annuals as described above mixed into the association.

The species composition of a tidal freshwater marsh does not appear to depend on the availability of seed in particular locations. Seeds of most species are found in almost all habitats (Whigham and Simpson, 1975). However, they differ in their ability to germinate under the local field conditions and in seedling survival. Flooding is one of the main controlling physical factors. For example, most of the common plant species seem to germinate well even when submerged (Leck and Graveline, 1979). *Impatiens capensis* (jewel weed) requires aerobic conditions for afterripening and germination (Leck, 1979). Competitive factors also play a role: arrow arum and cattail, for example, produce chemicals that inhibit germination of seed (McNaughton, 1968; Bonasera, Lynch, and Leck, 1979); and shading by existing plants is apparently responsible for the inability of arrow arum plants to become established anywhere except along the marsh fringes (Whigham, Simpson, and Leck, 1979). Some species (*Impatiens capensis, Bidens laevis,* and *Polygonum arifolium*) are restricted to the high marsh because the seedlings are not tolerant of extended flooding (Simpson et al., 1983). The complex interaction of all these factors has not been elucidated to the extent that it is possible to predict what species will be established where on the marsh.

In addition to vascular plants, phytoplankton and epibenthic algae abound in freshwater tidal marshes, but relatively little is known about them. In the Potomac River marshes, in one study, diatoms (Bacillariophytes) were the most common phytoplankton, with green algae (Chlorophytes) comprising about one third of the population and blue-green algae (Cyanophytes) present in moderate numbers (Lippson et al., 1979). The same three phyla accounted for most of the epibenthic algae. Indeed, many of the algae in the water column are probably entrained by tidal currents off the bottom. In a study of New Jersey tidal freshwater marsh soil algae, Whigham, Simpson, and Lee (1980) identified 84 species exclusive of diatoms. Growth was better on soil that was relatively mineral and coarse compared with growth on fine organic soils. Shading by emergent plants reduced algal populations in the summer months. Algal biomass is probably two to three orders of magnitude less than peak biomass of the vascular plants (Wetzel and Westlake, 1969).

Consumers

Coastal freshwater wetlands are used heavily by wildlife. The consumer food chain is predominantly detrital, and benthic invertebrates are an important link in the food web. Bacteria and protozoa decompose litter, gaining nourishment from the organic material. It appears unlikely that these microorganisms concentrate in large enough numbers to provide adequate food for macroinvertebrates (Wiebe and Pomeroy, 1972). Meiobenthic organisms, primarily nematodes, compose most of the living biomass of anaerobic sediments (Sikora et al., 1977). It is probable that they are cropping the bacteria as they grow, packaging them in bite-sized portions for slightly larger macrobenthic deposit feeders. In coastal freshwater marshes, the microbenthos is composed primarily of amoebae (Thecamoebinids, a group of amoebae with theca, or tests). This is in sharp contrast to more saline marshes, in which foraminifera predominate (Ellison and Nichols, 1976). The slightly larger macrobenthos is composed of amphipods, especially *Gammarus fasciatus,* oligochaete worms, freshwater snails, and insect larvae. Copepods and cladocerans are abundant in the tidal creeks. The Asiatic clam *(Corbicula fluminaea),* a species introduced earlier in the century, has spread through the coastal marshes of the southern states and as far north as the Potomac River (Odum et al., 1984). Caridean shrimp, particularly *Palaemonetes pugio,* are common, as are freshwater shrimp, *Macrobrachium* spp. The density and diversity of these benthic organisms are reported to be low compared with those in nontidal freshwater wetlands, perhaps because of the lack of diverse bottom types in the tidal reaches of the estuary. No species are found exclusively in tidal freshwater systems. Rather, those found there appear to have a rather wide range (Diaz, 1977).

Nekton

Coastal freshwater marshes are important habitats for many nektonic species that use the area for spawning, year-round food and shelter, and as a nursery zone and juvenile habitat. Fish of coastal freshwater marshes can be classified into four groups (Fig. 9-4). Most of them are freshwater species that spawn and complete their lives within freshwater areas. The three main families of these fish are cyprinids (minnows, shiners, carps), centrarchids (sunfishes, crappies, bass), and ictalurids (catfishes). Juveniles of all species are most abundant in the shallows, often using submerged marsh vegetation for protection from predators. The bluegill, largemouth bass, sunfishes, warmouth, and black crappie are all important for sport fishing. Gars, pickerels, and bowfin are other common predatory fish often found in coastal freshwater marshes.

Some oligohaline or estuarine fish and shellfish that complete their entire life cycle in the estuary extend their range to include the freshwater marshes. Killifishes (particularly the banded killifish and the mummichog) are abundant in schools in shallow freshwater marshes, where they feed opportunistically on whatever food is available. The bay anchovy and tidewater silverside are often abundant in freshwater areas also. The latter breeds in this habitat more than in saltwater areas. Juvenile hogchokers and naked gobies use tidal freshwater areas as nursery grounds (Odum et al., 1984).

Anadromous fishes, which live as adults in the ocean, or semianadromous species, whose adults remain in the lower estuaries, pass through coastal freshwater marshes on their spawning runs to freshwater streams. For many of these species, the tidal freshwater areas are major nursery grounds for

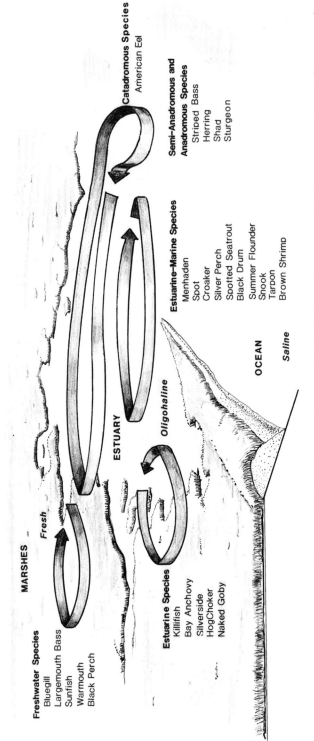

Figure 9-4. Fish and shellfish that use tidal freshwater marshes can be classified into four groups: freshwater, estuarine, anadromous, and catadromous, and estuarine-marine.

juveniles. Along the Atlantic coast, herrings and shads fit into this category. The young of all of them, except the hickory shad, are found in peak abundance in tidal fresh waters, where they feed on small invertebrates and in turn are an important forage fish for striped bass, white perch, catfishes, and others (W. E. Odum et al., 1984). As they mature late in the year, they migrate downstream to saline waters and offshore. Formerly, two species of sturgeon were important commercially in East Coast estuaries, but were seriously overfished and presently are rare. Both species spawn in nontidal and tidal fresh waters, and juveniles may spend several years there before migrating to the ocean (Brundage and Meadows, 1982).

The striped bass is perhaps the most important of the semianadromous fish of the mid-Atlantic coast because of its importance in both the commercial and sport fisheries. Approximately 90% of the striped bass on the East Coast are spawned in tributaries of the Chesapeake Bay system (Berggren and Lieberman, 1977). They spawn in spring in tidal fresh and oligohaline waters; juveniles remain in this habitat along marsh edges, moving gradually downstream to the lower estuary and nearshore zone as they mature. Since the critical period for survival of the young is the larval stage, conditions in the tidal fresh marsh area where these larvae congregate are important determinants of the strength of the year class (W. E. Odum et al., 1984).

The only catadromous fish species in Atlantic coast estuaries is the American eel. It spends most of its life in fresh or brackish water, returning to the ocean to spawn in the region of the Sargasso Sea. Eels are common in tidal and nontidal coastal freshwater areas, in marsh creeks, and even in the marsh itself (Lippson et al., 1979).

The juveniles of a few species of fish that are marine spawners move into freshwater marshes, but most remain in the oligohaline reaches of the estuary. Species whose range extends into tidal freshwater marshes are menhaden, spot croaker, silver perch, spotted seatrout, black drum, summer flounder, snook, and tarpon. Along the northern Gulf coast, juvenile brown and white shrimp may also move into freshwater areas. These juveniles emigrate to deeper, more saline waters as temperatures drop in the fall.

Birds

Of all wetland habitats, coastal freshwater marshes probably support the largest and most diverse populations of birds. W. E. Odum et al. (1984), working from a number of studies, compiled a list of 280 species of birds that have been reported from tidal freshwater marshes. These include waterfowl (44 species); wading birds (15 species); rails and shorebirds (35 species); birds of prey (23 species); gulls, terns, kingfishers, and crows (20 species); arboreal birds (90 species); and ground and shrub birds (53 species). A major reason for the intense use of these marshes is the structural diversity of the vegetation provided by broad-leaved plants, tall grasses, shrubs, and interspersed ponds.

Dabbling ducks (family Anatidae) and Canada geese actively select tidal freshwater areas (Stewart, 1962) on their migratory flights from the north. They use the Atlantic coast marshes in the late fall and early spring, flying further south during the cold winter months. Most of these species winter in fresh coastal marshes of the northern Gulf, but some fly to South America. Their distribution in apparently similar marshes is variable; some marshes support dense populations, others few birds. The reasons for this spotty use are unclear. The birds feed on the abundant seeds of annual grasses and sedges and the rhizomes of perennial plants. They are opportunistic feeders, on the whole, ingesting from the available plant species. The wood duck is the only species that nests regularly in these marshes, although an occasional black duck or mallard nest is found in the Atlantic coast marshes.

Wading birds are common residents of coastal freshwater marshes. They are present year-round in Gulf coast marshes, but only during the summer along the Atlantic coast. An exception is the great blue heron, which is seen throughout the winter up into the north Atlantic states. Nesting colonies are common throughout the southern marshes and, for some species (green herons and bitterns), up along the Atlantic coast. They feed on fish and benthic invertebrates, often flying long distances each day from their nesting areas to fish.

Rails and shorebirds, including the killdeer, sandpipers, and the American woodcock, are common in coastal freshwater marshes. They feed on benthic macroinvertebrates and diverse seeds. Gulls, terns, kingfishers, and crows are also common. Some are migratory, some are not. A number of birds of prey are seen hovering over freshwater marshes, including the common northern harrier, the American kestrel, falcons, eagles, ospreys, owls, vultures, and the loggerhead shrike. The number of these beautiful birds has been declining in recent years. Two of them, the southern bald eagle and the peregrine falcon, are listed as endangered.

Arboreal birds use the coastal freshwater marshes intensively during short periods of time on their annual migrations. Flocks of tens of thousands of swallows have been reported over the upper Chesapeake freshwater marshes (Stewart and Robbins, 1958). Flycatchers are also numerous. They often perch on trees bordering the marsh, darting out into the marsh from time to time to capture insects (W. E. Odum et al., 1984). Although coastal marshes may be used for only short periods of time by a migrating species, they may be important temporary habitats. For example, the northern Gulf coastal marshes are the first landfall for birds on their spring migration from South America. Often they reach this coast in an exhausted state and the availability of marshes for feeding is critical to their survival.

Sparrows, juncos, finches, blackbirds, wrens, and other ground and shrub birds are abundant residents of coastal freshwater marshes. W. E. Odum et al. (1984) indicate that ten species breed there, including the ring-necked pheasant, red-winged blackbird, American goldfinch, rufous-sided towhee, and a number of sparrows. The most abundant are the red-winged blackbirds, dickcissels, and bobolinks, which can move into and strip a wildrice marsh in a few days.

Amphibians and Reptiles

Although W. E. Odum et al. (1984) have compiled a list of 102 species of amphibians and reptiles that frequent coastal freshwater marshes along the Atlantic coast, many are poorly understood ecologically, especially with respect to their dependence on this type of habitat. None are specifically adapted for life in tidal freshwater marshes. Rather, they are able to tolerate the special conditions of this environment. River turtles, the most conspicuous members of this group, are abundant throughout the southeastern United States. Three species of water snakes *(Natrix)* are common. *Agkistrodon piscivorus* (the cottonmouth moccasin) is found south of the James River. And in the South, especially along the Gulf coast, the American alligator's preferred habitat is the tidal freshwater marsh. These large reptiles used to be listed as threatened or endangered, but they have come back so strongly in most areas that they are presently harvested legally in parts of Louisiana. They nest along the banks of coastal freshwater marshes, and the animal, with its high forehead and snout, is a common sight gliding along the surface of marsh streams.

Mammals

The mammals most closely associated with coastal freshwater marshes are all able to get their total food requirements from the marsh, have fur coats that are more or less impervious to water, and are able to nest (or hibernate in northern areas) in the marsh (W. E. Odum et al., 1984). These include the otter, muskrat, nutria, mink, raccoon, marsh rabbit, and marsh rice rat. In addition, the opossum and white-tailed deer are locally abundant. The nutria was introduced from South America some years ago and has spread throughout the South. It is more vigorous than the muskrat and has displaced it from the freshwater marshes in many parts of the northern Gulf. As a result, muskrat density is highest in oligohaline marshes. The muskrat, for some reason, is not found in Georgia and South Carolina, although it is abundant farther north along the Atlantic coast and in Florida. The muskrat, nutria, and beaver can influence the development of a marsh. The first two species destroy large amounts of vegetation with their feeding habits (they prefer juicy rhizomes and uproot many plants digging for them), their nest building, and their underground passages. Beavers can have an equally strong effect on the marsh by damming areas, thus changing the hydrologic regime.

ECOSYSTEM FUNCTION

Primary Production

Many production estimates have been made for freshwater coastal marshes. Productivity is generally high, usually falling in the range of 1,000 to 3,000 g/m$^2 \cdot$ yr (Table 9-2). The large variability reported from different studies is in part due to a lack of standardization of measurement techniques, but real differences can be attributed to several factors:

1. The type of plant and its growth habit. Fresh coastal marshes, in contrast to saline ones, are very diverse, and productivity is determined, at least to some degree, by genetic factors that regulate the species' growth habits. Tall perennial grasses, for example, appear to be more productive than broad-leaved herbaceous species such as arrow arum and pickerelweed.
2. Tidal energy. The stimulating effect of tides on production has been shown for salt marshes (see chap. 8). Whigham and Simpson (1977) showed that the fresh marsh grass *Zizania aquatica* responded positively to tides, and the general trends in production shown by Brinson, Lugo, and Brown (1981) in nonforested freshwater wetlands support the idea that moving water generally stimulates production.
3. Other factors. Soil nutrients (Reader, 1978), grazing, parasites, and toxins are other factors that can limit production (de la Cruz, 1978).

The elevation gradient across a fresh coastal marsh, and the resulting differences in vegetation and flooding patterns, result in three broad zones of primary production. The low marsh bordering tidal creeks, dominated by broad-leaved perennials, is characterized by rather low production rates. Productivity peaks early in the growing season. Much of the production is stored in belowground biomass (root:shoot $\gg$1), but this biomass is mostly rhizomes rather than fibrous roots, the turnover rate is high, the litter is swept from the marsh almost as fast as it forms, the soil is bare in winter, and erosion rates are high.

The parts of the high marsh dominated by perennial grasses and other erect, tall species are characterized by the highest production rates of freshwater species, and root:shoot ratios are approximately 1. Because tidal energy is not as strong and the plant material is not so easily decomposed, litter accumulates on the soil surface, and little erosion occurs.

The high marsh mixed annual association typically reaches a large peak biomass late in the growing season. Most of the production is aboveground (root:shoot < 1), and litter accumulation is common; but in the absence of perennial roots, erosion rates might be expected to be greater than those where perennials dominate.

**Table 9-2. Peak Standing Crop and Annual Production Estimates
for Common Tidal Freshwater Vegetation Associations[a]**

Vegetation Type[b]	Peak Standing Crop g/m^2	Annual Production $g/m^2 \cdot yr$
Nuphar advena (spatterdock)	627	780
Peltandra virginica/Pontederia cordata (arrow arum/pickerelweed)	671	888
Zizania aquatica (wild rice)	1,218	1,578
Zizaniopsis miliacea (giant cutgrass)	1,039	2,048
Polygonum sp./*Leersia oryzoides* (smartweed/rice cutgrass)	1,207	—
Hibiscus coccineus (rose mallow)	1,141	869
Typha sp. (cattail)	1,215	1,420
Bidens spp. (bur marigold)	1,017	1,340
Acorus calamus (sweetflag)	857	1,071
Sagittaria latifolia (duck potato)	432	1,071
Amaranthus cannabinus (water hemp)	960	1,547
Ambrosia tirifida (giant ragweed)	1,205	1,205
Phragmites communis (common reed)	1,850	1,872
Spartina cynosuroides (big cordgrass)	2,311	—
Lythrum salicaria (spiked loosestrife)	1,616	2,100
Rosa palustris (swamp rose)	699	—

Source: Summarized by W. E. Odum et al., 1984
[a]Values are means of one to eight studies.
[b]Designation indicates the dominant species in the association.

Decomposition

As with other marshes, little of the plant production is consumed directly by grazers. Although nutrias and muskrats are herbivores, herbivory is thought to account for the consumption of less than 10% of plant production. The remaining 90% becomes available to consumers through the detrital food chain. The vegetation is attacked by bacteria and fungi, aided by the fragmenting action of small invertebrates, and the bacteria-enriched decomposed broth feeds benthic invertebrates, which in turn are prey to larger animals.

Temperature is the major factor that controls litter decomposition; the higher the temperature, the higher the decay rate. The combined availability of oxygen and water is a second factor; plants submerged in anaerobic environments decompose slowly, as do exposed plants in dry environments. Optimum conditions for decomposition are found in a moist aerobic environment such as a regularly flooded tidal marsh. An important third factor in decomposition rates is the kind of plant tissue involved. In freshwater tidal marshes, two groups of plants can be identified (Odum et al., 1984). The broad-leaved perennials generally contain high leaf concentrations of nitrogen (*Pontederia cordata, Sagittaria latifolia,* and *Nuphar luteum* in Fig. 9-5). In contrast, the high marsh grasses (*Zizania aquatica* in Fig. 9-5) are low in nitrogen (tissue concentration usually < 1%) and are composed primarily of

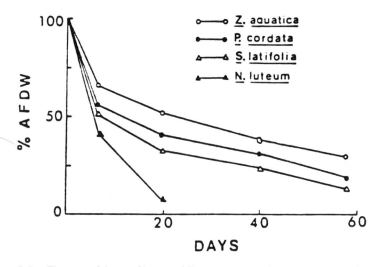

Figure 9-5. The rate of decay of leaves of *Zizania aquatica, Pontederia cordata, Sagittaria latifolia,* and *Nuphar luteum* as shown by the amount of material (ash free dry weight) remaining with time in submerged litterbags. Each data point represents four replicates. *(From W. E. Odum and Heywood, 1978, p. 94; Copyright © 1978 by Academic Press, reprinted with permission)*

long stems with much structural tissue that is resistant to decay. They decompose slowly. This slow decay rate, combined with lower tidal energy on the high marsh, explains why litter accumulates there and erosion rates are low.

Organic Export

Losses of organic carbon from marshes occur through respiration, flushing from the marsh surface, sequestering as peat below the root zone, conversion to methane that escapes as a gas, and export as biomass in the bodies of consumers that feed on the marsh. Only a handful of studies address carbon fluxes in freshwater tidal marshes, so any conclusions must be considered tentative. W. E. Odum et al. (1984) hypothesize that young, low-lying marshes are subject to ice shearing of the vegetation during the winter, and with significant tidal range, probably export significant quantities of both particulate and dissolved organic material. Older, higher marshes, which are less vigorously flushed, probably do not export much particulate organic matter but may export dissolved materials.

In anaerobic freshwater sediments where little sulfur is available as an electron acceptor, carbon dioxide can be reduced to methane. This loss may be significant. The annual loss of carbon as methane from Gulf coast freshwater marshes has been estimated as 160 $g/m^2 \cdot yr$ (Smith, DeLaune, and Patrick, 1982). In comparison, Lipschultz (1981) estimated a loss of only 10.7 g methane/$m^2 \cdot yr$ from a *Hibiscus*-dominated freshwater marsh in the Chesapeake Bay.

In marshes that are accreting vertically, organic matter is lost to deep sediments. There are few measurements of the magnitude of this loss in freshwater marshes along the Atlantic coast, but in Gulf coast marshes where accretion is rapid (about 1 cm/yr), peat accumulation as organic carbon is 145-250 $g/m^2 \cdot yr$ (Hatton, 1981).

Energy Flow

Quantitative measurements of energy flow through the detrital food web in freshwater coastal wetlands are practically nonexistent. W. E. Odum et al. (1984) mention energy consumption values for some consumers, but these are generally calculated from the literature and/or are extrapolated from other kinds of marsh systems. This subject apparently is a fruitful area for research. While it is not feasible to trace quantitatively the flow of organic energy in freshwater coastal marshes, W. E. Odum et al. (1984) present a conceptual scheme that indicates the major functional groups and their interrelationships (Fig. 9-6). They identify three major sources of organic carbon. The largest is probably the vascular marsh vegetation, but organic

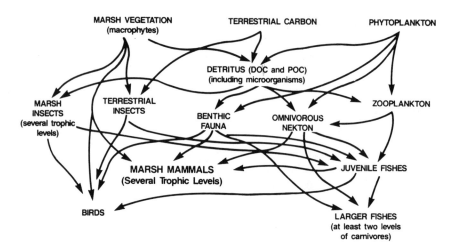

Figure 9-6.   Energy flow diagram for a tidal freshwater marsh, showing the major groups of organisms and energy pathways. *(From W. E. Odum et al., 1984, p. 48)*

material brought from upstream (terrestrial carbon) may be significant, especially on large rivers and where domestic sewage waters are present. Phytoplankton is a largely unknown quantity. Most of the organic energy flows through the detrital pool, from whence most of it is distributed to benthic fauna and deposit-feeding omnivorous nekton. These groups feed fish, mammals, and birds at higher trophic levels. The magnitude of the herbivore food chain in comparison to the detritus one is poorly understood. Insects seem to be more abundant in fresh marshes than in salt marshes, but most do not appear to be herbivorous. Marsh mammals apparently can "eat out" significant areas of vegetation, but direct herbivory is probably small in comparison to the flow of organic energy from destroyed vegetation into the detrital pool. The phytoplankton-zooplankton-juvenile fish food chain in fresh marshes is of interest because of its importance to humans. Zooplankton is an important dietary component for a variety of larval, postlarval, and juvenile fishes of commercial importance associated with tidal freshwater marshes (Van Engel and Joseph, 1968).

Nutrient Budgets

In general, nutrient cycling and nutrient budgets in coastal freshwater wetlands appear to be similar to salt marshes in that they are fairly open systems that have the capacity to act as long-term sinks, sources, or transformers of nutrients. Most nutrient inputs are inorganic; these nutrients are transformed chemically or biologically to reduced or organic forms, which appear as export products. Although marshes are leaky compared to forested ecosystems, they still recycle most of the nutrients used within the system; exports and imports are generally a relatively small percentage of the total material cycled.

Many marshes have been shown to be nutrient traps that purify the water flooding them. Whether this is true of freshwater coastal marshes depends on the age of the marsh (assuming that the lower edge of the marsh is less mature than the high marsh), the magnitude of upland runoff, anthropogenic effects such as sewage loading, and the magnitude of tidal action (Stevenson et al., 1977). Unfortunately, most nutrient studies of freshwater coastal marshes have been carried out in areas heavily influenced by nearby urban communities, so it is difficult to know how representative they are. From our present understanding, these marshes appear to be net importers of nitrogen and phosphorus during the spring, primarily because of the magnitude of upland runoff during this period. During spring and summer, nutrients are tied up in plant biomass. Since sediment concentrations do not seem to change much seasonally, the living biomass reflects seasonal storage (Fig. 9-7). On the low marsh only small amounts of nutrients are tied up in the sparse litter, but in the fall on the high marsh this is a major temporary store. After the vegetation dies in the fall, there appears to be a rapid net export of nutrients associated with the high decomposition rate and tidal flushing. Over the year as a whole, the net balance of nitrogen and phosphorus indicates a net export. However, this may be because the marshes studied were subject to unusually high loading with domestic sewage and were saturated with respect to these nutrients.

The accumulation of heavy metals in a high marsh in New Jersey was variable (Simpson et al., 1981; 1983). Cadmium, copper, lead, nickel, and zinc all had accumulated in the litter at the end of the growing season to much higher concentrations than in the live vegetation (Fig. 9-7). Over an annual cycle cadmium was always exported from the marsh, and nickel was imported in all months except June. Copper was imported during the growing season, zinc and lead primarily after it. In general, accumulation was greatest in the plant roots (Simpson et al., 1981).

ECOSYSTEM MODELS

There appear to be few conceptual models, and fewer simulation models, of tidal freshwater ecosystems. A coastal freshwater marsh model might combine the tidal forcing function of a salt marsh model (Zieman and Odum, 1977) with the diversity of species of an inland freshwater marsh. Such a model has not been produced. The trophic model of Odum et al. (1984, Fig. 9-6) and the general compartmental model displayed by Simpson et al. (1983, Fig. 9-8), are useful conceptual aids to visualizing this ecosystem, but they do

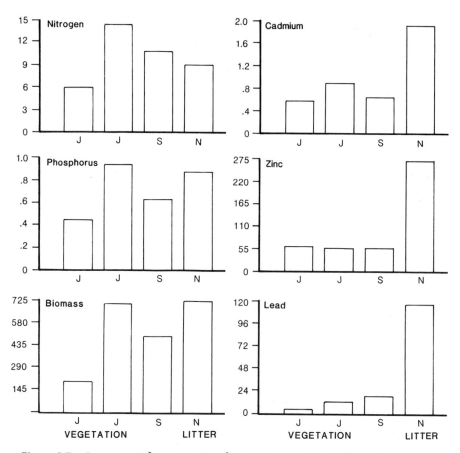

Figure 9-7.   Biomass (g/m²), nutrient (g/m²), and heavy metal (mg/m²) standing stocks in the vegetation (June–September) and litter (November) in Woodbury Creek Marsh for 1979. All values are means. *(Data from Simpson et al., 1983, p. 258)*

not incorporate important driving forces such as tides and nutrient loads except in the most general sense.

SUMMARY

Freshwater coastal wetlands are unique ecosystems that combine many features of salt marshes and freshwater inland marshes. They act in many ways like salt marshes, but the biota reflect the increased diversity made possible by the reduction of the salt stress found in salt marshes. Plant diversity is high, and more birds use these marshes than any other marsh type. Nutrient cycles are open. Nutrients are retained during the growing season but are lost during the winter. Because they are inland from saline parts of the estuary, they are often close to urban centers. This makes them more prone to human impacts than coastal salt marshes. Simpson

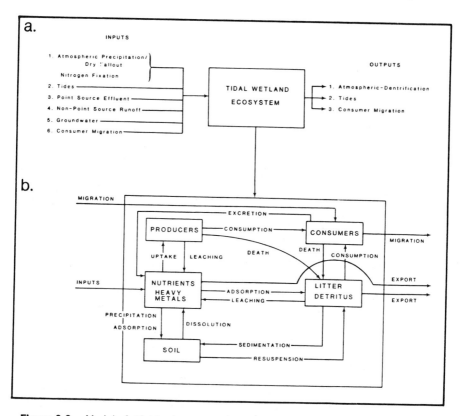

Figure 9-8. Model of tidal freshwater wetland showing: *A.* major inputs and outputs of materials and *B.* major compartments and pathways in which nutrients and heavy metals are stored and move *(From Simpson et al., 1983, p. 255; Copyright © 1983 by the American Institute of Biological Sciences, reprinted with permission)*

et al. (1983) summarize succinctly some of the major uncertainties about these systems:

Although evidence suggests that freshwater tidal wetlands act seasonally as nutrient sinks, flux studies of one year or longer are lacking, and the question of whether freshwater tidal wetlands are sinks or sources of material to the estuary cannot now be resolved. Furthermore, the understanding of food chain relationships in freshwater tidal wetlands and the adjacent estuary is rudimentary. At best we can only guess at energy and material transfers between members of the wetland and estuarine communities. Finally, there are few data on the short- and long-term effects of pollutants such as oils, pesticides, and heavy metals on species composition and community structure, although these wetlands serve as nursery grounds for commercially important fish and other wildlife. Despite these gaps in our knowledge of freshwater tidal wetlands, it is clear that, though they share many of the same ecosystem functions of salt marshes (Niering and Warren, 1980), they possess a number of unique features that must be considered in their management.

MANGROVE WETLAND

CHAPTER 10

MANGROVE WETLANDS

The coastal salt marsh of temperate mid- and high latitudes gives way to its analog, the mangrove swamp, in tropical and subtropical regions of the world. The mangrove swamp is an association of halophytic trees, shrubs, and other plants growing in brackish to saline tidal waters of tropical and subtropical coastlines. This coastal forested wetland (the wetland is called a "mangal" by some researchers) is infamous for its impenetrable maze of woody vegetation, the unconsolidated peat that seems to have no bottom, and its many adaptations to the double stresses of flooding and salinity. Many myths have surrounded the mangrove swamp. It has been described at one time or another in history as a haven for wild animals, a producer of fatal "mangrove root gas," and a wasteland of little or no value (Lugo and Snedaker, 1974). Researchers have since established the importance of mangrove swamps in exporting organic matter to adjacent coastal food chains, in providing physical stability to certain shorelines to prevent erosion, in protecting inland areas from severe damage during hurricanes and tidal waves, and as sinks for nutrients and carbon. There is an extensive literature on the mangrove swamp on a worldwide basis—possibly more than 3,000 titles (Por and Dor, 1984). This interest is probably due both to the worldwide extent of these ecosystems and to the many unique features that they possess. However, much of that literature concerns floristic and structural topics with major interest in the functional aspects of mangrove swamps appearing only since the early 1970s.

GEOGRAPHICAL EXTENT

Mangrove swamps are found along tropical and subtropical coastlines throughout the world, usually between 25°N and 25°S (Fig. 10-1a). Their limit in the northern hemisphere generally ranges from 24°N to 32°N, depending on local climate and the southern limits of freezing weather. The frequency of frosts necessary to limit mangroves is not clearly established. Chapman (1976b) suggested that three to four nights of a light frost are sufficient to kill even the hardiest mangrove species. Lugo and Zucca (1977) showed that mangroves survived approximately five nonconsecutive days of frost in January 1977 in Sea Horse Key, Florida (latitude 29°N), but estimated that it would take 200 days for the forest to recover from cold damage.

Mangroves are divided into two groups—the Old World mangrove swamps and the New World and West Africa mangrove swamps. An estimated 68 species of mangroves exist, and their distribution is thought to be related to continental drift on the long term and possibly to transport by primitive humans on the short term (Chapman, 1976b). However, the distribution of these species is uneven. The swamps are particularly dominant in the Indo-West Pacific region (part of the Old World group), where they have the greatest diversity of species. There are 30-40 species of mangroves in this region, while there are only about 10 mangrove species in the Americas. It is often argued, therefore, that the Indian-Malaysian region was the original center of distribution for the mangrove species (Chapman, 1976b). There is also a great deal of segregation between the mangrove vegetation found in the Old World region and the New World of the Americas and West Africa. Two of the primary genera of mangrove trees, *Rhizophora* and *Avicennia*, have separate species in the Old and New Worlds, suggesting "that speciation is taking place independently in each region" (Chapman, 1976b).

In the United States, mangrove wetlands are found primarily along the Atlantic and Gulf coasts of Florida south of 28-29°N latitude (Fig. 10-1b). Davis (1940) described the Florida coast as supporting over 2,600 km^2 (1,000 square miles) of mangrove swamps, although Craighead (1971) revised the estimate down to 1,750 km^2 (675 square miles). The best development of mangroves in Florida is along the southwest coast where the Everglades and the Big Cypress Swamp drain to the sea. This area, which includes Florida's Ten Thousand Islands, is one of the largest mangrove swamps in the world. Mangroves also extend up to 30 km (18 miles) inland along water courses on Florida's southwest coast. Mangrove swamps are common further north along Florida's coasts, north of Cape Canaveral on the Atlantic and to Cedar Key on the Gulf of Mexico, where mixtures of mangrove and salt marsh vegetation appear. One species of mangrove *(Avicennia germinans)* is found as far north as Louisiana and in the Laguna Madre of Texas, although the trees are more like shrubs at these extreme locations (Chapman, 1976b; 1977). Extensive mangrove swamps are also found throughout the Caribbean Islands, including Puerto Rico.

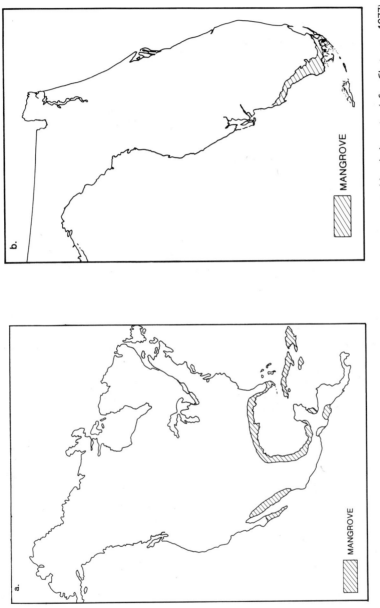

Figure 10-1. Distribution of mangrove wetlands. *a.* Extent of mangrove species in North America *(after Chapman, 1977)* and *b.* area of mangrove wetland domination on Florida coastline *(from Wharton et al., 1976, p. 191, courtesy of Center for Wetlands, University of Florida).*

GEOMORPHOLOGY AND HYDROLOGY

There are several different types of mangrove wetlands, each having a unique set of topographic and hydrodynamic conditions. Like the coastal salt marsh, the mangrove swamp can develop only where there is adequate protection from wave action. Several physiographic settings favor the protection of mangrove swamps, including (1) protected shallow bays, (2) protected estuaries, (3) lagoons, (4) the leeward sides of peninsulas and islands, (5) protected seaways, (6) behind spits, and (7) behind offshore shell or shingle islands. Unvegetated coastal and barrier dunes usually result where this protection does not exist, with mangroves often found behind the dunes (Chapman, 1976*b*).

In addition to the required physical protection from wave action, the range and duration of flooding of tides have a significant influence over the extent and functioning of the mangrove swamp. The tides are an important subsidy for the mangrove swamp, importing nutrients, aerating the soil water, and stabilizing soil salinity. The resulting salinity is important to the mangroves in eliminating competition from freshwater species. The tides provide a subsidy for the movement and distribution of the seeds of several mangrove species (see discussion of Mangrove Adaptations below). They also circulate the organic sediments in some fringe mangroves for the benefit of filter feeding organisms such as oysters, sponges, and barnacles, and for deposit feeders such as snails and fiddler crabs (Kuenzler, 1974). As with salt marshes, mangrove swamps are intertidal, although a large tidal range is not necessary. Most mangrove wetlands are found in tidal ranges from 0.5 m to 3 m and more; the mangrove tree species can tolerate a wide range of inundation frequencies (Chapman, 1976*b*). *Rhizophora,* the red mangrove, often is found growing in continually flooded coastal waters below normal low tide. On the other extreme, mangroves can be found several kilometers inland along river banks where there is less tidal action. Lugo (1981) found that these inland mangroves depend on storm surges and "are not isolated from the sea but critically dependent on it as a source of fresh sea water."

The development of mangrove swamps is the result of topography, substrate, and freshwater hydrology, as well as tidal action. A classification of mangrove wetland ecosystems according to their physical conditions was developed by Lugo and Snedaker (1974) and Lugo (in Wharton et al., 1976) and includes the following types:

1. Overwash mangrove islands
2. Fringe mangrove wetlands
3. Riverine mangrove wetlands
4. Basin mangrove wetlands

5. Hammock mangrove wetlands
6. Dwarf mangrove wetlands

The features of these types of mangrove wetlands are shown in Figure 10-2.

Overwash Mangrove Islands

Small islands and narrow extensions of larger land masses *(spits)* that are "overwashed" during high tide on a daily basis are called overwash mangrove islands (Fig. 10-2a). The forests are dominated by the red mangrove *(Rhizophora mangle)* and a prop root system that obstructs the tidal flow and dissipates wave energy during periods of heavy seas. Tidal velocities are high enough to wash away most of the loose debris and leaf litter into the adjacent bay. The islands are often seen developing as concentric rings of tall mangroves around smaller mangroves and a permanent, usually hypersaline, pool of water. These wetlands are abundant in the Ten Thousand Islands of Florida and on the southern coast of Puerto Rico and are particularly sensitive to ocean pollution.

Fringe Mangrove Wetlands

Fringe mangrove wetlands are found along protected shorelines and along some canals, rivers, and lagoons (Fig. 10-2b). They are particularly common along shorelines adjacent to land higher than mean high tide, but are themselves exposed to daily tides. In contrast to the overwash mangroves, fringe mangrove wetlands tend to accumulate organic debris because of the low-energy tides and the dense development of prop roots. Because the shoreline is open, these wetlands are often exposed to storms and strong winds that lead to the further accumulation of debris. Fringe mangroves are found on narrow berms along the coastline or in wide expanses along gently sloping beaches. If a berm is present, the mangroves may be isolated from freshwater runoff and then depend completely on rainfall, the sea, and groundwater for their nutrient supply. These wetlands are found throughout south Florida, along both Florida coasts, and in Puerto Rico. In an updated version of this mangrove classification, fringe and overwash island mangroves have been combined because of similar structural and functional characteristics (Lugo, written communic.).

Riverine Mangrove Wetlands

Tall, productive riverine mangrove forests are found along floodplains of coastal rivers and creeks, often several miles inland from the coast (Fig. 10-2c). These wetlands may be dry for a considerable time, although the

OVERWASH MANGROVE ISLANDS

FRINGE MANGROVE WETLANDS

RIVERINE MANGROVE WETLANDS

BASIN MANGROVE WETLANDS

HAMMOCK MANGROVE WETLANDS

SCRUB MANGROVE WETLANDS

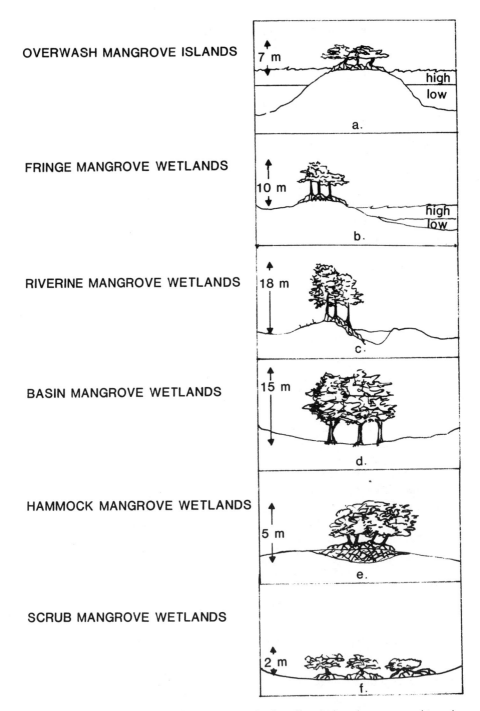

Figure 10-2. Classification of mangrove wetlands in Florida, based on topographic and hydrodynamic conditions. *(After Wharton et al., 1976, p. 192, and Lugo, 1980, p. 67)*

water table is generally just below the surface. In Florida, freshwater input is greatest during the wet summer season, causing the highest water levels and lowest salinity in the soils during that time. Riverine mangrove wetlands export a significant amount of organic matter due to their high productivity. These wetlands are affected by freshwater runoff from adjacent uplands and from water, sediments, and nutrients delivered by the adjacent river, and hence they can be significantly affected by upstream activity or stream alteration.

Basin Mangrove Wetlands

Basin mangrove wetlands occur in depressions behind fringe mangrove wetlands and in drainage depressions where water is stagnant or slowly flowing (Fig. 10-2*d*). These basins are often isolated from all but the highest tides and yet remain flooded for long periods once tide water does flood them. Because of the stagnant conditions and less frequent flushing by tides, soils have high salinities and low redox potentials. These wetlands are dominated by black mangroves *(Avicennia germinans),* and the ground surface is often covered by pneumatophores from these trees.

Hammock Mangrove Wetlands

Hammock mangrove wetlands occur as isolated, slightly raised tree islands in the coastal fringe of the Florida Everglades. They are slightly raised as a result of the buildup of peat in what was once a slight depression in the landscape (see Fig. 10-2*e*). The peat has accumulated from many years of mangrove productivity, actually raising the surface 5 to 10 cm above the surrounding landscape. Because of this slightly raised level and the dominance by mangrove trees, these ecosystems look like the familiar tree islands of "hammocks" that are found throughout the Florida Everglades. They are different in that they are close enough to the coast to have saline soils and occasional tidal influences and thus can support only mangroves. Hammock mangrove wetlands can be affected by drainage or by fire.

Dwarf Mangrove Wetlands

Dwarf mangrove wetlands are dominated by scattered, small (often less than 2 m tall) mangrove trees growing in an environment that is probably nutrient-poor (Fig. 10-2*f*). The nutrient-poor environment can be a sandy soil or limestone marl. Hypersaline conditions and cold at the northern extremes of the mangrove's range can also produce "scrub" or stressed mangrove trees, where these dwarf trees occur in riverine, fringe, or basin wetlands. However, true dwarf mangrove wetlands are found in the coastal fringe of the Everglades and the Florida Keys, and on the northeastern coast of Puerto Rico. Some of these wetlands in the Everglades are exposed to tides only during spring tide or storm surges and are often flooded by freshwater runoff in the rainy season.

CHEMISTRY

Salinity

Mangrove swamps are found under conditions with a wide range of salinity. Davis (1940) summarized several major points about salinity in mangrove wetlands from his studies in Florida:

1. There is a wide annual variation in salinity in mangrove wetlands.
2. Saltwater is not necessary for the survival of most mangrove species, but only gives mangroves a competitive advantage over non-salt-tolerant species.
3. Salinity is usually higher and fluctuates less in interstitial soil water than in surface water of mangroves.
4. Saline conditions in the soil extend further inland than normal high tide due to the slight relief, which prevents rapid leaching.

Mangrove species have a wide range of salt tolerance due to several adaptations, and most species can grow in fresh water, although this is not seen in natural conditions. Thus most mangrove species are facultative halophytes that compete very poorly with other plants in freshwater conditions but have a decided advantage when brackish or saline conditions are present.

Figure 10-3 shows the wide spatial and temporal range of salinity found in a region in Florida dominated by mangrove wetlands, from constant seawater salinity of outer coast overwash mangrove swamps to brackish water in coastal rivers and canals. Low salinity can even be found supporting dwarfed red mangroves *(Rhizophora)*. Hypersalinity can also result in basin wetlands when evapotranspiration is high and dilution is low. Seasonal oscillations in salinity are a function of the height and duration of tides, the seasonality and intensity of rainfall, and the seasonality and amount of fresh water that enters the mangrove wetlands through rivers, creeks, and runoff. In Florida, as illustrated in Figure 10-3, the summer wet season of convective storms and associated freshwater flow in streams and rivers, as well as an occasional hurricane in the late summer–early fall, lead to the dilution of saltwater and the lowest salinity concentrations. Salinity is generally highest in the dry season that occurs in the winter and early spring.

Soil Oxygen

Reduced conditions exist in most mangrove soils while they are flooded, with the degree of reduction dependent on the duration of flooding and the openness of the wetland to freshwater and tidal flows. Some oxygen transport also occurs to the rhizosphere through the vegetation, although this

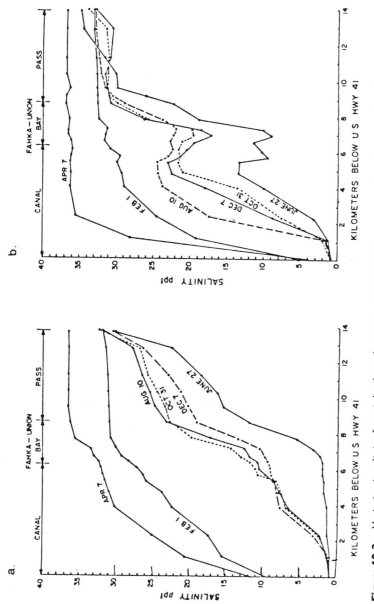

Figure 10-3. Variation in salinity from inland canal to open sea in a mangrove region of southwestern Florida in *a.* low tide and *b.* high tide. Canal is a channelized stream that flows into the bay. *(From Carter et al., 1973, p. VII-47)*

239

overall contribution is localized and is probably small in the sediment oxygen balance. The adaptations that allow oxygen to pass into and through aerial organs are discussed below. When creeks and surface runoff pass water through mangrove wetlands, the reduced conditions are not as severe because of the increased drainage and the continual importing of oxygenated waters (Chapman, 1976*b*).

ECOSYSTEM STRUCTURE

Vegetation

Fewer than ten species of mangroves are found in the New World region, and only three are dominant in south Florida mangrove swamps—the red mangrove (*Rhizophora mangle* L.), the black mangrove (*Avicennia germinans* L., also named *A. nitida* Jacq.), and the white mangrove (*Laguncularia racemosa* L. Gaertn.). Buttonwood (*Conocarpus erecta* L.), although strictly not a mangrove, occasionally is found growing in association with the mangroves or in the transition zone between the mangrove wetlands and the drier uplands. Each of the hydrotopographic types of mangrove wetlands described above is dominated by different associations of mangroves. Overwash mangrove islands and fringe mangrove wetlands are dominated by red mangroves *(Rhizophora)* with abundant and dense prop roots, particularly along the edges that face the open sea. Riverine mangrove wetlands are also numerically dominated by red mangroves, although they are straight-trunked and have relatively few, short prop roots (Lugo and Snedaker, 1974). Black *(Avicennia)* and white *(Laguncularia)* mangroves also frequently grow in these wetlands. Basin and hammock mangrove wetlands support all three species of mangroves, although black mangroves are the most common in basin swamps and hammock wetlands are mostly composed of red mangroves. Scrub mangrove wetlands are typically dominated by widely spaced, short (less than 2 m tall) red or black mangroves.

Plant Zonation and Succession

In trying to understand the vegetation of mangrove wetlands, most early researchers were concerned with describing plant zonation and successional patterns (Lugo and Snedaker, 1974). Some attempts have been made to equate the plant zonation found in mangrove wetlands with successional seres, but Lugo (1980, p. 70) warns that "zonation does not necessarily recapitulate succession because a zone may be a climax maintained by a steady or recurrent environmental condition." Davis (1940) is generally credited with the best early description of plant zonation in Florida mangrove swamps, especially in fringe and basin mangrove wetlands (Fig. 10-4).

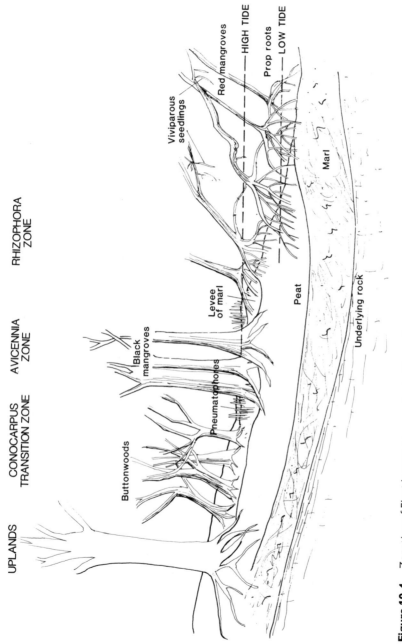

Figure 10-4. Zonation of Florida mangrove wetlands. Note adaptation of mangroves such as prop roots, viviparous seedlings, and black mangrove pneumatophores. *(After Davis, 1940)*

241

Later, elaboration and theories were provided by Egler (1952). Typically, *Rhizophora mangle* is found in the lowest zone, with seedlings and small trees sprouting even below mean low tide in marl soils. Above the low tide level, but well within the intertidal zone, full-grown *Rhizophora* predominate with well-developed prop roots. Here, tree height is approximately 10 m. Behind these red mangrove zones and the natural levee that often forms in fringe mangrove wetlands, basin mangrove wetlands are found, dominated by black mangroves *(Avicennia)* with numerous pneumatophores. Flooding occurs only during high tides. Buttonwood *(Conocarpus erecta)* often forms a transition zone between the mangrove zones and upland ecosystems. Here, flooding occurs only during spring tides or during storm surges, and soils are often brackish to saline (Chapman, 1976*b*).

The zonation of plants in mangrove wetlands led some researchers (e.g. Davis, 1940) to speculate that each zone is a step in an autogenic succession process that leads to freshwater wetlands and eventually to tropical upland forests or pine forests. Other researchers, led by Egler (1952), considered each zone to be controlled by its physical environment to the point that they are in steady state or at least arrested succession (allogenic succession). For example, with a rising sea level, the mangrove zones migrate inland; during periods of decreasing sea level, the mangrove zones move seaward. Egler felt that the impacts of fire and hurricanes made conventional succession impossible in the mangroves of Florida. Another theory, advanced by Chapman (1976*b*), is that mangrove succession is a combination of both autogenic and allogenic strategies or a "succession of successions." In this case, successional stages can be repeated a number of times before the next successional level is attained.

Lugo (1980) reviewed mangrove succession in light of Odum's (1969) criteria and found that, except for mangroves on accreting coastlines, the traditional successional criteria do not apply. Succession in mangroves is primarily cyclic, and it exhibits patterns of stressed or "youthful" ecosystems, including slowed or arrested succession, low diversity, P/R greater than one, and open material cycles, even in mature stages. Lugo (1980, p. 72) concludes that mangroves are:

true steady state systems in the sense that they are the optimal and self-maintaining ecosystems in the low-energy tropical saline environments. In such a situation high rates of mortality, dispersal, germination, and growth are the necessary tools of survival. Unfortunately, these attributes could lead many to the identification of mangroves as successional systems.

It is no longer accepted dogma that mangrove wetlands are "land-builders" that are gradually encroaching on the sea. In most cases, mangrove vegetation has a passive role in the accumulation of sediments and the vegetation usually follows, not leads, the land building that is caused by current and tidal energies. It is only after the substrate has been established that the vegetation contributes to land building by slowing erosion and by increasing the rate of sediment accretion (Lugo, 1980). The mangrove's successional dynamics appear to involve a combination of (1) peat accumulation balanced by tidal export, fire, and hurricanes over years and decades, and (2) advancement or retreat of zones according to the fall or rise of sea level over centuries.

Mangrove Adaptations

The mangrove vegetation, particularly the dominant trees, has several adaptations that allow it to survive in an environment of high salinity, occasional harsh weather, and anoxic soil conditions. These physiological and morphological adaptations have been of interest to researchers and are among some of the most distinguishing features that the lay person notices when first viewing these wetlands. Some of the adaptations, as summarized by Kuenzler (1974) and Chapman (1976*b*) and shown in Figures 10-4 and 10-5, follow: (1) salinity control, (2) prop roots and pneumatophores, and (3) viviparous seedlings (see also chap. 6).

Salinity Control—The ability of mangroves to live in saline soils depends on their ability to control the concentration of salt in their tissues. In this respect, mangroves are very similar to other halophytes. Mangroves have the ability to both prevent salt from entering the plant at the roots (salt exclusion) and to excrete salt from the leaves (salt secretion). Salt exclusion at the roots is thought to be a result of reverse osmosis that causes the roots to absorb only freshwater from saltwater. Root cell membranes of mangroves species of *Rhizophora, Avicennia,* and *Laguncularia,* among others, apparently act as ultrafilters that exclude salt ions. Water is drawn into the root through the filtering membrane by the negative pressure in the xylem developed through transpiration at the leaves; this action counteracts the osmotic pressure caused by the solutions in the external root medium (Scholander et al., 1965). There are also a number of mangrove species (e.g., *Avicennia* and *Laguncularia*) that have salt-secreting glands on the leaves to rid the plant of excess salt. The solutions that are secreted often have several percent NaCl, and salt crystals can form on the leaves. Another possible way in which mangroves discharge salt, still questioned as to its importance, is through leaf fall. This leaf fall may be significant, since mangroves produce essentially two crops of leaves per year (Chapman, 1976*b*).

Prop Roots and Pneumatophores—Two of the most notable features of

Figure 10-5.   Adaptations of mangrove trees, including *a*. prop roots and pneumatophores, and *b*. viviparous seedling.

most mangrove wetlands are the prop roots of the red mangrove *(Rhizophora)* and numerous, small (usually 20 to 30 cm above the sediments, although they can be up to 1 m tall) pneumatophores of black mangroves *(Avicennia)* (Fig. 10-5a). Oxygen enters the plant through small pores, called *lenticels,* that are found on both pneumatophores and on prop roots. When these lenticels are exposed to the atmosphere during low tide, oxygen is absorbed from the air and some of it is transported to and diffuses out of the roots through a system of aerenchyma tissues. This maintains an aerobic microlayer around the root system. When the prop roots or pneumatophores of mangroves are continuously flooded by stabilizing the water levels, those mangroves that have submerged pneumatophores or prop roots soon die (Macnae, 1963; J. H. Day, 1981).

Viviparous Seedlings—Red mangroves (and related genera in other parts of the world) have seeds that germinate while they are still in the parent tree, causing a long, cigar-shaped hypocotyl (viviparous seedling) to develop while hanging from the tree (Fig. 10-5b). This is apparently an adaptation for seedling success where shallow anaerobic water and sediments would otherwise inhibit germination. The seedling eventually falls and often will root if it lands on sediments or will float and drift in currents and tides if it falls into the sea. After a time, if the floating seedling becomes stranded and the water is shallow enough, it will attach to the sediments and root. Often the seedling becomes heavier with time, rightens to a vertical position, and develops roots if the water is shallow. It is not well understood whether the contact with the sediments stimulates the root growth or if the soil contains some chemical compound that promotes root development (Chapman, 1976b). The value of the floating seedlings for mangrove dispersal and for invasion of newly exposed substrate is obvious.

Consumers

A wide diversity of animals is found in mangrove wetlands; their distribution sometimes parallels the plant zonation described above. Many of the animals that are found in mangrove wetlands are filter feeders or detritivores, and the wetlands are just as important as a shelter for most of the resident animals as they are a source of food. Some of the important filter feeders found in Florida mangroves include barnacles *(Balanus eburneus),* coon oysters *(Ostrea frons),* and the eastern oyster *(Crassostrea virginica).* These organisms often attach themselves to the stems and prop roots of the mangroves within the intertidal zone, filtering organic matter from the water during high tide. Fiddler crabs *(Uca* spp.) are also abundant in mangrove wetlands, living on the prop roots and high ground during high water and burrowing in the sediments during low tide (Kuenzler, 1974). Many other invertebrates, including snails, sponges, flatworms, annelid worms, anemone, mussels, sea urchins, and tunicates, are found growing on roots and stems in and above the intertidal zone. Vertebrates that inhabit mangrove swamps include alligators, crocodiles, turtles, bears, wildcats, pumas, and rats (Kuenzler, 1974). Mangrove wetlands have been documented as important sources of food for sport and commercial fisheries in south Florida by Heald (1969; 1971) and Odum (1970) (see Organic Export discussed below).

ECOSYSTEM FUNCTION

Certain functions of mangroves, such as gross and net primary productivity, have been studied extensively, particularly in southern Florida. Other functional characteristics of these wetlands, such as organic export and nutrient cycling, have seen much less quantitative work. Nevertheless, a picture of the dynamics of mangrove wetlands has emerged from several key studies. These studies have demonstrated the importance of the physical conditions of tides, salinity, and nutrients on these wetlands and have demonstrated where natural and human-induced stresses have caused the most effect.

Primary Productivity

A wide range of productivity has been measured in mangrove wetlands due to the wide variety of hydrodynamic and chemical conditions encountered. Examples of primary productivity measurements, from CO_2 gas exchange methodologies, are shown in Table 10-1. Table 10-2 presents a summary comparison of productivity and litter production data for riverine, basin, and scrub mangrove wetlands. Gross and net primary productivities are generally highest in riverine mangrove wetlands, lower in basin mangrove wetlands, and lowest in dwarf mangrove wetlands (Brown and Lugo, 1982). It is not known with certainty where overwash, fringe, and hammock mangrove wetlands fit in this spectrum, although the distribution of litter production for the various mangrove wetland types in Figure 10-6 suggests that hammock and fringe mangroves have productivities close to those of basin mangrove wetlands, while productivity in overwash mangroves is higher, approximating that of the highly productive riverine mangrove wetlands.

   The important factors that control mangrove function in general and primary productivity in particular are (1) tidal and runoff factors and (2) water chemistry factors (Carter et al., 1973; Lugo and Snedaker, 1974). These factors are not mutually exclusive, as tides influence water chemistry

Table 10-1. Primary Productivity and Respiration Data for Mangrove Ecosystems in Several Locations in Florida and Puerto Rico

Location	Number of Measurements	Gross Primary Productivity, $g\,C/m^2 \cdot day$	Net Primary Productivity, $g\,C/m^2 \cdot day$	Total 24 hr Respiration, $g\,C/m^2 \cdot day$	Reference
Florida					
Fahkahatchee Bay Small tidal stream (Red, black & white mangroves)	10	13.9	4.8	9.1	Carter et al. (1973)
Lower Fahka Union River (Red, black & white mangroves)	7	11.8	7.5	4.3	Carter et al. (1973)
Upper Fahka Union River (Red, black & buttonwood mangroves)	10	10.3	6.6	3.7	Carter et al. (1973)
Rookery Bay (Black mangrove forest)	17	9.0	2.8	6.2	Lugo et al. (1975)
Rookery Bay (Red mangrove)	15	6.3	4.4	1.9	Lugo et al. (1975)
Key Largo (Red mangrove)	6	5.3	0	6.0	Miller (1972)
Hammock Forest, Dade Co. (Red mangrove)	3	1.9	1.3	0.6	Burns, as given in Lugo and Snedaker (1974)
Scrub Forest, Dade Co. (Red mangrove)	4	1.4	0	2.0	Burns, as given in Lugo and Snedaker (1974)
Puerto Rico					
La Parguera (Red mangrove)	Sporadic hourly measures	8.2	0	9.1	Golley, Odum, and Wilson (1962)

Source: After Lugo and Snedaker, 1974, p. 53

**Table 10-2. Primary Productivity, Respiration, and Litter Fall Measurements
for Three Types of Mangrove Wetlands**

	Mangrove Wetland		
	Riverine	*Basin*	*Scrub*
Gross Primary Productivity,[a] kcal/m^2 · day	108	81	13
Total Respiration,[a] kcal/m^2 · day	51	56	18
Net Primary Productivity,[a] kcal/m^2 · day	57	25	0
Litter Production,[b] kcal/m^2 · day	14 ± 2	9.0 ± 0.4	1.5

Source: Based on data from Brown and Lugo, 1982

[a]From several sites in Florida; based on CO_2 gas exchange measurements; assumes 1 g organic matter = 4.5 kcal

[b]Average ± standard error from several sites in Florida and Puerto Rico; measured with litter traps; assumes 1 g organic matter = 4.5 kcal

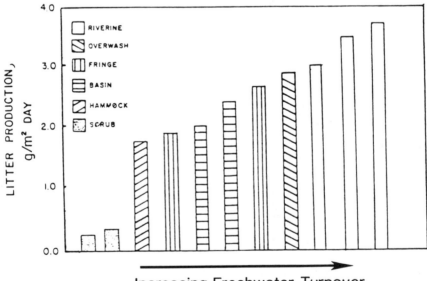

Figure 10-6. Rank of mangroves according to litter fall and hydrodynamic classification. *(From Pool et al., 1975)*

and hence productivity by transporting oxygen to the root system, by removing buildup of toxic materials and salt in the soil water, by controlling the rate of sediment accumulation or erosion, and by indirectly regenerating nutrients lost from the root zone. The chemical conditions that affect primary productivity are the soil water salinity and the concentration of major nutrients. Lugo and Snedaker (1974, p. 54-55) have concluded that, compared to mangrove wetlands such as dwarf mangroves that are isolated from the influence of daily tides, "environments flushed adequately and frequently by seawater and exposed to high nutrient concentrations are more favorable for mangrove ecosystem development; forests in these areas exhibit higher rates of net primary productivity."

The importance of chemical conditions on mangrove productivity is difficult to document because the chemical conditions include both stimulants (nutrients) and stressors (salinity). Both factors appear to be important for mangrove growth. Kuenzler (1974) has suggested that, even with low transpiration rates in mangroves as a result of high salinities, productivity can be high if nutrients are abundant. Carter et al. (1973) examined the productivity of mangrove canopy leaves along a gradient of fresh water to saline water in southwestern Florida. The results are shown in Figure 10-7a, where the respiration to gross primary productivity ratio (R/GPP) is used as the dependent variable to indicate the percentage of fixed energy that is used for maintenance within the plant tissue. Thus, as the ratio decreases, a greater percentage of the gross primary productivity is seen as net productivity. The independent variable in Figure 10-7a is

$$\frac{Cl_s - Cl_o}{Cl_s} \times 100 \qquad (10.1)$$

where Cl_s = soil water salinity and Cl_o = overlying water salinity. This variable is the salinity gradient between the soil and the overlying water as a percentage of the soil water salinity and is thus considered a measure of both tidal and water chemistry factors (Lugo and Snedaker, 1974). The curve suggests that as the salinity gradient increases (with a constant soil salinity) or as the soil salinity decreases (with a constant soil-water gradient) the respiratory requirement of the mangrove decreases. Mangroves put more of their captured energy into growth rather than physiological maintenance when the water is low in salts. In saltwater, more respiratory work is necessary to adapt physiologically to the saline conditions. A similar conclusion is also suggested in Figure 10-7b, where litter production (and hence probably net primary productivity) occurs at an optimum soil salinity for basin mangrove wetlands, decreasing as salinity increases.

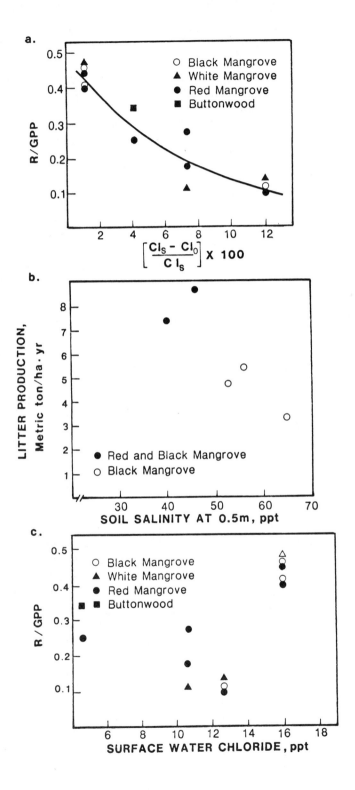

A third way to present the general effects of salinity was also developed by Carter et al. (1973) as the U-shaped relationship shown in Figure 10-7c. Salinity in this figure is a general measure of the tidal influence (greater with higher salinity). In areas of low tidal flushing and greater competition from plants adapted to low salinities, maintenance costs are high. In areas of high tidal influence, maintenance costs are also high due to lower nutrients and high salinity. As described by Lugo and Snedaker (1974, p. 54):

At the two extremes of the U the energetic costs of survival are high and most of the production is utilized in self-maintenance processes (respiration). The two extremes represent areas of either high nutrients and low-amplitude tides, or low nutrients and high amplitude tides. Between the two extremes, or in the middle of the curve, nutrients and tidal amplitude are in some proper combination and net productivity is maximized.

It also became apparent in several of the mangrove productivity studies in Florida (Carter et al., 1973; Lugo et al., 1975) that a pattern of zonation of metabolism follows the zonation of species as described earlier in this chapter. Lugo and Snedaker (1974, p. 55) summarize the functional zonation in these studies as follows:

1. the gross primary productivity of red mangrove decreased with increased salinity;
2. the gross primary productivity of black and white mangroves increased with increasing salinity;
3. in areas of low salinities and under equal light conditions the gross primary productivity of red mangrove was four times that of black mangrove;
4. in areas of intermediate salinity the white mangrove had rates of gross primary productivity twice that of red mangrove; and
5. in areas of high salinities, the white mangrove exhibited a gross primary productivity higher than that of black mangrove, which in turn was higher than the red mangrove.

Figure 10-7. Relationships between mangrove metabolism and salinity from studies in southwestern Florida. *a.* Respiration/gross primary productivity ratio (maintenance: metabolism ratio) as a function of chloride gradient between overlying water (Cl_o) and soil water (Cl_s) *(From Carter et al., 1973, p. III-26). b.* Litter production as a function of soil salinity *(From Brown and Lugo, 1982, p. 120; Copyright © 1982 by International Scientific Publications, reprinted with permission). c.* Maintenance: metabolism ratio as a function of surface water chloride concentration *(From Carter et al., 1973, p. III-29).*

Thus, the zonation of mangroves, as described by Davis (1940), Egler (1952) and others, has a functional basis for occurring. Species that are found growing out of their zone will have lower productivity compared to those that are adapted to those conditions, and competition will eventually eliminate them from that zone.

Decomposition/Consumption and Organic Export

Little information is available on rates of decomposition in mangrove wetlands. The decomposition process in mangroves reportedly is accelerated by moisture, with optimal decomposition occurring at about 50% moisture (Lugo and Snedaker, 1974). Lugo and Snedaker (1974) measured decomposition of mangrove litter as 287 g/m^2 · yr in a black mangrove-dominated wetland in southwestern Florida. The standing stock of litter in that wetland was 550 g/m^2, resulting in a litter decay coefficient of 0.52/yr, a relatively rapid rate of decomposition. In that study, there was a total leaf fall of 485 g/m^2 · yr, leading the authors (p. 50) to conclude that, with no accumulation noted, "this excess of leaf fall over potential decomposition must have been exported to adjacent bays or terrestrial food chains."

The role that mangrove swamps play as exporters of organic material to the adjacent estuary has been documented in a number of studies. Heald (1971) estimated that about 50% of the aboveground productivity of a mangrove swamp in southwestern Florida was exported to the adjacent estuary. From 33% to 60% of the total suspended organic matter in the estuary came from *Rhizophora* (red mangrove) material. The production of organic matter was greater in the summer (the wet season in Florida), although detrital levels in the swamp waters were greatest from November through February, which is the beginning of the dry season. Thirty percent of the yearly detrital export occurred during November. Heald also found that as the debris decomposed, its protein content increased. The apparent cause of this enrichment, also noted in salt marsh studies, is the increase of bacterial and fungal populations. Carter et al. (1973), basing their estimates on the work of Heald, estimated that at least 57% of the total energy base for Fahkahatchee Bay in the Florida Everglades came from mangrove forests. Brown and Lugo (1982) estimated an export of 58 g C/m2 · yr from a basin mangrove wetland in south Florida, with 55% of that export due to tidal exchange and the remainder due to freshwater runoff and seepage.

These estimates establish the fact that many mangrove wetlands are important sources of detritus for the adjacent aquatic systems. A study by Odum (1970) in the estuary adjacent to Heald's study site established that this detritus was important to sport and commercial fisheries in the Gulf of

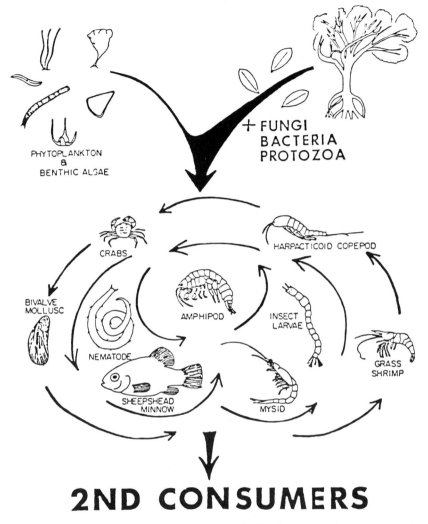

Figure 10-8. Detritus-based food web in south Florida estuary showing the major contribution of mangrove detritus. *(From W. E. Odum, 1970, p. 140)*

Mexico (Fig. 10-8). He found through the examination of the stomach contents of more than 80 estuarine animals that mangrove detritus, particularly from *Rhizophora,* was the primary food source in the estuary. The primary consumers then serve as prey to game fish such as tarpon, snook, sheepshead, spotted seatrout, red drum, jack, and jewfish. The primary consumers also used the mangrove estuarine waters during their early life stages for protection from predators as well as a source of food (Lugo and Snedaker, 1974). It is reasonable to extrapolate from this and similar studies that the removal of mangrove wetlands would cause a significant decline in sport and commercial fisheries in adjacent open waters.

Energy Flow

Few studies have taken a comprehensive look at the distribution and fate of energy through the entire mangrove ecosystem on an annual basis or longer. Golley, Odum, and Wilson (1962) developed a synoptic energy budget of a Puerto Rican mangrove wetland for an average day in May (Table 10-3). Of the total gross productivity of 82 kcal/m^2 · day, a major portion is used by the plants themselves in respiration. Respiration of prop roots of the red mangroves amounted to 20 kcal/m^2 · day, while export was about 14 kcal/m^2 · day and soil respiration was about 4 kcal/m^2 · day. Animal metabolism, estimated to be 0.8 kcal/m^2 · day, made up a very minor part of the energy flow in this ecosystem. Lugo et al. (1975) found similar patterns of vertical metabolism in mangrove swamps in southwest Florida, although respiration of red mangrove prop roots was much lower (0.6 kcal/m^2 · day). The authors also found a higher P/R ratio than was found in the Puerto Rico study, convincing them of the importance of organic export from mangrove wet-

Table 10-3. Synoptic Energy Budget for Mangrove Wetland in Puerto Rico in May

Component	Mangrove Energy Flow, kcal/m^2 · day	
	Gross Photosynthesis	*Respiration and Losses*
Sun Leaves	73.3	43.1
Shade Leaves	4.0	4.8
Ground Cover	2.0	2.4
Seedlings	3.0	3.6
Prop Roots	—	20.3
Soil R (Air)	—	1.7
Soil R (Water)	—	2.0
Total	82.3	77.9
Export	—	13.7

Source: Based on data from Golley, Odum, and Wilson, 1962, p. 17

lands. A significant contribution of energy fixation by periphyton growing on red mangrove prop roots, with a net productivity of 11 kcal/m² · day, was also noted in the Florida study. This component of the ecosystem may have an important function of capturing and concentrating nutrients from incoming tidal waters for eventual use by the mangroves themselves.

ECOSYSTEM MODELS

Several efforts to quantitatively model mangrove wetlands have been undertaken, but with different modeling objectives and approaches. Miller (1972) developed a process model with a series of equations that predict primary productivity and transpiration of the mangrove forest canopy from input data on canopy structure and meteorological variables. The model predicted hourly vertical profiles of net and gross primary productivity, respiration, and transpiration, and was tested on data from a red mangrove wetland in Key Largo, Florida (Table 10-1). The model determined that the variables with the most influence on productivity were air temperature and humidity; productivity decreased with increases in either of these variables.

Several qualitative and quantitative compartment models have been developed from research on the functional characteristics of mangroves in south Florida (Carter et al., 1973; Lugo and Snedaker, 1974; Lugo, Sell, and Snedaker, 1976; Wharton et al., 1976; Sell, 1977; Odum et al., 1977b). Three of the models developed are shown in Figure 10-9. A simple conceptual model of energy and material flow, together with potential stresses that influence the wetland's growth, is shown in Figure 10-9a. Wetland productivity is shown to be affected by activities such as channelization, drainage, siltation, harvesting, hurricanes, herbicides, and thermal additions. Simulations of similar models by Lugo, Sell, and Snedaker (1976) and Sell (1977), illustrated in Figure 10-9b, showed that the time required for attainment of steady state of mangrove biomass is approximately the same as the average period between tropical hurricanes. The models also demonstrated the importance of tidal exchange and terrestrial inputs of nutrients (Lugo, Sell, and Snedaker, 1976). Figure 10-9c shows a more complex model that demonstrated the importance of freshwater sources of materials and tidal exchange. This model added salinity and potential evapotranspiration as a variable and forcing function, respectively, that affect mangrove productivity. While some of these models were not verified with field data, the results pointed to the importance of freshwater inputs, tidal exchange, and salinity on mangrove wetland function and supported the theories put forward based on the field measurements.

a.

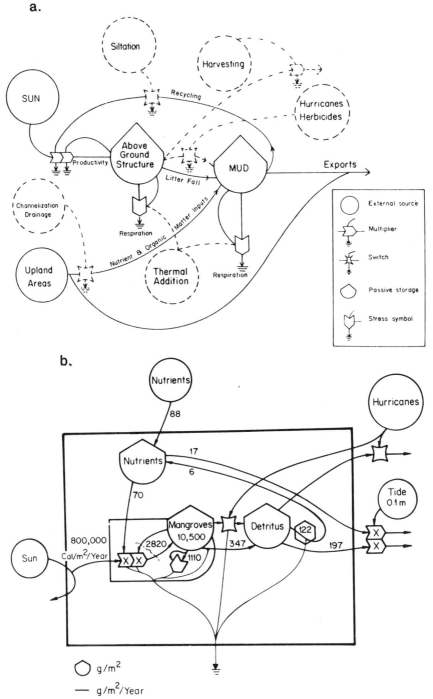

b.

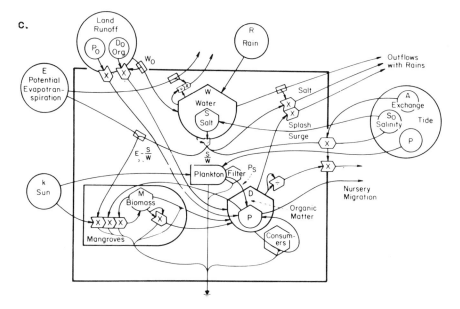

Figure 10-9. Compartment models of mangrove wetlands showing *a.* major stresses *(from Lugo and Snedaker, 1974, reprinted with permission from the Annual Review of Ecology and Systematics, vol. 5, p. 42; Copyright © 1974 by Annual Reviews, Inc.) b.* simple simulation model, and *c.* simulation model with salinity stress. *(Models in b. and c. from H. T. Odum, 1983, pp. 436–437 based on data in Sell, 1977; Copyright © 1983 by J. Wiley and Sons, reprinted with permission of John Wiley and Sons, Inc.)*

SUMMARY

The mangrove wetland replaces the salt marsh as the dominant coastal ecosystem in subtropical and tropical regions throughout the world. Mangrove wetlands are limited in the United States to the southern extremes of Florida (where there are approximately 1,750 km² of mangroves) and to Puerto Rico. The dominant plant species in mangrove wetlands are known for several adaptations to the saline wetland environment, including prop roots, pneumatophores, salt exclusion, salt excretion, and viviparous seedlings. Mangrove wetlands have been classified according to their hydrodynamics and topography as overwash islands, fringe mangroves, riverine mangroves, basin mangroves, hammock mangroves, and dwarf mangroves. Highest productivities are seen in riverine forests, which are most open to both tidal action and inputs of nutrients from adjacent uplands. The least productive systems are dwarf mangroves, which are found in nutrient-poor conditions, and scrubby forests, which are under the stresses of hypersaline conditions and frost (at the northern extreme of the mangrove's range). Mangroves require a greater percentage of their energy for maintenance rather than for growth in both low-salinity and high-salinity conditions. The greatest net productivity appears to be where influences from both terrestrial nutrient sources and tidal factors are collectively optimal, not where either factor by itself is maximum. The importance of both upland inflows and tidal exchange has also been demonstrated with simulation models. Mangrove wetlands have definite vegetation zonation patterns, although the importance of successional stages and physical conditions on this zonation has been much debated. It now appears that the zonation results from each species' optimal niche for productivity. Although complete energy budgets are not well described for mangrove wetlands, organic export studies have verified the importance of these ecosystems to the productivity of adjacent estuaries.

Part IV

INLAND WETLAND ECOSYSTEMS

FRESHWATER MARSH

CHAPTER

11

FRESHWATER MARSHES

The wetlands treated in this chapter are a diverse group. They are unified primarily by the fact that they are all freshwater systems dominated by grasses and sedges. Otherwise, they differ in their geological origins and their driving hydrologic forces, and they vary in size from small potholes less than a hectare in size to the immense saw grass monocultures of the Florida Everglades. As discussed in chapter 3, terminology for wetlands, especially inland wetlands, is confusing and contradictory. The major differences between European and North American usage is illustrated in Figure 3-1. While the use of classifying terms implies clear boundaries between different wetland types, in reality they form a continuum. The extremes of freshwater marshes are clearly different, but at the boundaries between two wetland types (e.g., marsh and bog), the distinction is not at all clear.

For the purposes of this book we have divided inland nonforested wetlands into two groups. *Bogs* are sphagnum moss-dominated communities whose only water source is rainwater. They are extremely low in nutrients, form acidic peats, and are a northern phenomenon generally associated with low temperatures and short growing seasons. These wetlands are discussed in chapter 12. All other nonforested inland freshwater wetlands we include in the term marsh.

As used in Europe, the term fen, one kind of marsh, refers to a peat-forming wetland that receives nutrients from sources other than precipitation, usually through groundwater movement. Its peats are not acidic. Marshes and swamps, as the terms are used in Europe, have mineral soils rather than peat and are generally eutrophic. The United States terminology has developed without much regard to whether or not the system is peat-forming. The fact is that most of the North American marshes *are* peat-forming, regardless of how far south they are and regardless of their geological origins. In the new classification developed by the U.S. Fish and Wildlife Service (Cowardin et al., 1979), most of the marshes described in this chapter are classified as palustrine, riverine or lacustrine, persistent or nonpersistent, emergent wetlands.

A number of excellent references on inland freshwater marshes exist. The reader is referred to Good, Whigham, and Simpson (1978), Weller (1981), Gore (1983a), and Prince and D'Itri (1985) for additional reading. In this chapter we refer extensively to studies of reed marshes in Czechoslovakia (Dykyjova and Kvet, 1978), because these International Biological Programme studies provide some of the best quantitative functional information on freshwater marshes.

GEOGRAPHICAL EXTENT AND GEOLOGICAL ORIGINS

Table 11-1 summarizes the extent of freshwater marshes covered in this chapter, classified essentially by depth (and duration) of flooding. The classification system reflects the authors' primary interest in habitat value and waterfowl. These wetlands cover altogether about seven million hectares (Fig. 11-1). One of the dominant areas of freshwater marshes is the prairie pothole region (see also chap. 3). Prairie pothole marshes spread from New York and New Jersey to North Dakota and eastern Montana. Individually, the pothole marshes are usually rather small, occurring in de-

Table 11-1. Areas of Freshwater Marshes in the United States

Shaw and Fredine Type	Description	Area, hectares
2	Inland fresh meadows	3,041,000
3	Inland shallow fresh marshes	1,606,000
4	Inland deep fresh marshes	941,000
12	Coastal shallow fresh marshes	896,000
13	Coastal deep fresh marshes	661,000

Source: Data from Shaw and Fredine, 1956

Figure 11-1. Map of the United States showing location of the major groups of inland freshwater marshes. *(From Hofstetter, 1983, p. 213; Copyright © 1983 by Elsevier, reprinted with permission)*

pressions formed by glacial action. They are found in greatest abundance in moraines of undulating glacial till, especially west of the Great Lakes in Wisconsin, Minnesota, and the Dakotas. They occur as far south as the southernmost advance of glaciers. These mid-latitude marshes are among the richest in the world because of the rich soils and warm summer climate. Although they are also found in the prairies of southern Canada, similar habitats further north become increasingly dominated by mosses and are properly considered as bogs.

Shaw and Fredine's (1956) categories 12 and 13 are coastal freshwater marshes, which cover about 1.5 million hectares. They are concentrated along the northern coast of the Gulf of Mexico and along the south Atlantic coast. In chapter 9, tidally influenced freshwater marshes were discussed. Inland of tides, however, are large tracts of freshwater marshes with vegetation and in many ways ecological functions similar to those of the prairie pothole marshes. One major difference is the relatively stable water level in the coastal systems, resulting from the influence of the adjacent ocean. These marshes originated in the same way as described for coastal salt marshes; that is, they were formed as the sea gradually rose following the last glacial period and inundated river valleys and the shallow coastal shelf.

Sediment and peat deposition associated with the inundation kept the marsh surface in the intertidal zone, and marshes spread inland as more and more land was flooded.

The largest single marsh system in the United States is in the Everglades of south Florida (see also chap. 3). It originally occupied an area of more than 10,000 km² extending in a strip up to 65 km wide and 170 km long from Lake Okeechobee to the brackish marshes and mangrove swamps of the southwest coast of Florida. Although some areas have been drained for agriculture, the remaining marsh is still immense. South Florida is built on a flat, low limestone formation. The average slope of the Everglades is only 2.8 cm/km, so that the freshwater from Lake Okeechobee flows slowly southward across the land as a broad sheet during the wet season. The freshwater head prevents salt intrusion from the Gulf of Mexico in the south. During the dry season the surface water dries up and is found only in the deepest sloughs and "gator holes" (Hofstetter, 1983).

On the West Coast, in the valley between the Cascade mountain range and the Coastal Mountains in Washington, Oregon, and northern California, there used to be large tracts of marshland. Only a few pockets of marsh remain. The rest has been drained for agriculture.

Countless other small marshes occur throughout the continent, many of which have not been inventoried. Several groups, however, can be identified. Marshes occur along the shores of lakes, especially along the Great Lakes (Prince and D'Itri, 1985). They form in protected shallow areas, often behind natural beaches or levees thrown up by wave action on the shore.

Riverine marshes are common throughout the continent. Wetlands are particularly extensive in the floodplain of the Mississippi River valley and the many smaller rivers that empty into the south Atlantic. Although these wetlands are mostly forested (chap. 14), marshes often border the forests or occupy pockets within them. At the headwaters of rivers, beavers build wetlands by damming small streams. These small marshes often attract much wildlife, especially waterfowl.

Playas are an interesting group of marshes found on the high plain of northern Texas and eastern New Mexico. They are small basins with a clay or fine sandy loam hydric soil. Typically, a playa has a watershed area of about 55 hectares and a wetland area of about 7 hectares. Since the climate of the high plain is arid, the size of the wetland is closely related to the size of the watershed that drains into it. An estimated 25,000 such basins occur on the high plain, but no complete inventory has been made. These wetlands are particularly important waterfowl habitats, and most of the ecological information available about them is related to habitat value. Virtually all playa watersheds are farmed. The water draining into the playa is therefore rich in fertilizers; furthermore, playas are often a source of irrigation water. Both irrigation and eutrophication have had strong effects on the size and quality of playa marshes (Guthery, Pates and Stormer, 1982; Balen and Guthery, 1982).

HYDROLOGY

As with any other wetland, the flooding regime determines the character of inland marshes. Along coasts, water levels tend to be rather stable over the long term because of the influence of the ocean. Water levels in inland marshes, in contrast, are much more controlled by the balance between precipitation and evapotranspiration, especially for those marshes in small watersheds with restricted throughflow. The critical factors that determine the character of these wetlands are the presence of excess water and sources of water other than direct precipitation. The presence of excess water occurs either when precipitation exceeds evapotranspiration, or when the watershed draining into the marsh is large enough to provide adequate water. Many marshes dry down seasonally, but the plant species found there reflect the hydric conditions found during most of the year.

A marsh generally has sources of water other than direct precipitation. The primary distinction between an ombrotrophic bog and a rheotrophic fen (a marsh in our terminology) is the flow of water through the latter, which is the primary source of its nutrients. Some marshes intercept groundwater supplies. Their water levels therefore reflect the local water table and also contribute to it. Where the seepage of water from marshes into the ground has been calculated, it seems to occur mostly at the margins (Millar, 1971). For this reason seepage losses are greatest where the wetland shoreline is large relative to the water volume. Although usually less than 20% of the water impounded in freshwater wetlands enters the groundwater supply, this volume may be an important contribution to the watershed (Weller, 1981). Other marshes collect surface water and entrained nutrients from watersheds that are large enough to maintain hydric conditions most of the time. For example, overflowing lakes supply water and nutrients to adjacent marshes, and riverine marshes are supplied by the rise and fall of the adjacent river.

Since all of these water sources (except in the short run, lakes) depend on precipitation, which is notoriously variable, the water regime of most inland marshes also varies in a way that is predictable only in a statistical sense. Stewart and Kantrud (1971) emphasized the permanence of flooding in their classification of prairie pothole marshes. They classified wetlands as ephemeral, temporary, seasonal semipermanent, and permanent. In addition, they recognized that over the span of a few years marshes may move through several of these classes. Thus a marsh that would ordinarily be considered permanent might be in a "drawdown" phase that gives the appearance of an ephemeral marsh.

CHEMISTRY

The chemistry of inland marshes is best described in contrast to that of ombrotrophic bogs (chap. 12) at one extreme and eutrophic tidal wetlands at the other (chap. 9). Differences are related to the magnitude of nutrient inputs. Inland marshes generally are minerotrophic in contrast to northern bogs; that is, the inflowing water has a high specific conductivity resulting from the presence of dissolved cations. The peat is saturated with bases, and the pH as a result is close to neutral. Because nutrients are plentiful, productivity is higher than in bogs, bacteria are active in nitrogen fixation and litter decomposition, and turnover rates are high. Peat accumulation results from high production rates, not from inhibition of decomposition by low pH (as occurs in bogs).

Although inland wetlands are minerotrophic, they generally lack the high nutrient loading associated with tidal inundation of freshwater tidal marshes (chap. 9). Flooding in inland marshes tends to be associated with seasonal changes in local rainfall and evapotranspiration; in tidal areas, inundation occurs regularly once or twice daily. In the latter case, even if tide water nutrient levels are low, the large volumes of flooding water result in high loading rates. Because of these differences in surface flooding between inland and freshwater tidal marshes, groundwater flow is usually more important as a source of nutrients in inland marshes.

Table 11-2 lists nutrient concentrations reported for sediments in several inland freshwater marshes. The values vary widely depending on the sub-

Table 11-2. Soil Nutrient Concentrations in Selected Inland Freshwater Marshes

	Marsh Type		
	Riverine, Wisconsin[a]	Coastal Floating, Louisiana[b]	Lacustrine, Czechoslovakia[c]
Soil Parameters, top 20 cm			
pH	6.4–6.5	6–7	5.1
Organic matter, %	40.4–43.4	75	39
Total nitrogen, %	1.36–1.94	1.8–2.4	2.4
Total phosphorus, %	—	0.07–0.1	0.013
Available phosphorus, ppm	50–203	0.3[d]	—
Available potassium, ppm	98–230	—	550
Available calcium, ppm	5,700–12,700 (exchangeable)	—	5,140
Available magnesium, ppm	1,219–2,770	—	570

[a]Klopatek, 1978
[b]Sasser and Gosselink, 1984
[c]Dykyjova and Kvet, 1982, *Typha angustifolia* marsh
[d]PO$_4$ in interstitial water

strate, the loading rate, and the nutrient demand by the plants. Compared to oligotrophic bogs, the cation concentrations tend to be high. Concentrations of total (as distinguished from available) nutrients are a reflection of the kind of sediment in the marsh. Mineral sediments are often associated with high phosphorus contents, for example, while total nitrogen is closely correlated to organic content. Dissolved inorganic nitrogen and phosphorus, the elements that most often limit plant growth, often vary seasonally from very low concentrations in the summer, since plants take them up as rapidly as they become available, to high concentrations in later winter, when plants are dormant but mineralization continues in the soil. In Figure 11-2a phosphate in a Louisiana floating marsh is shown to be high during the winter but low

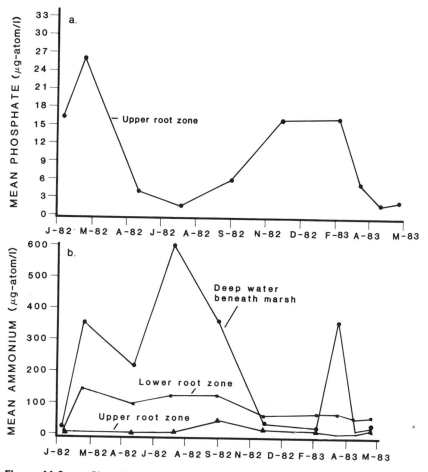

Figure 11-2. *a.* Phosphate and *b.* ammonium nutrient concentrations in interstitial water in a Louisiana fresh marsh sediment. *(Unpublished data, C. E. Sasser and J. G. Gosselink)*

during the summer, presumably because of plant uptake. Figure 11-2*b* shows the same phenomenon in a different way for ammonium (the dominant inorganic nitrogen form in these anoxic soils). Here the NH_4^+ levels are high in deep waters underlying the marsh, but decrease toward the surface where plants remove it in the root zone. In Table 11-2 the high total sediment nitrogen (1%-2%) and phosphorus (0.01%-0.1%) reflect an enormous reservoir of organic nutrients that can be mineralized and made available for plant use. Available inorganic nitrogen and phosphorus are one to three orders of magnitude lower. This available supply varies seasonally depending on both the rate of formation (mineralization) and uptake by the marsh plants. In most of these freshwater marshes the inflow and outflow probably contribute little to the concentration of available nutrients.

ECOSYSTEM STRUCTURE

Vegetation

The vegetation of fresh inland marshes has been detailed in many different studies. The dominant species vary from place to place, but the number of genera common to all locations in the temperate zone is really quite remarkable. Table 11-3 lists dominant emergent species, all graminoids and sedges, from sites that represent a wide range of different inland marshes. Common species include *Phragmites communis* (reed grass), *Typha* spp. (cattail), *Zizania aquatica* (wild rice), *Panicum hemitomon, Cladium jamaicense;* and the sedges *Carex* spp., *Scirpus* spp. (bullrush), and *Eleocharis* spp. (spike rush). In addition, broad-leaved monocotyledons such as *Pontederia cordata* (pickerelweed) and *Sagittaria* spp. (arrowhead) are frequently found. Herbaceous dicotyledons are represented by a number of species, of which typical examples are *Ambrosia* spp. (ragweed) and *Polygonum* spp. (smartweed). Frequently represented also are such ferns as *Osmunda regalis* (royal fern) and *Thelypteris palustris* (marsh fern), and the horsetail, *Equisetum* spp. One of the most productive species in the world is the tropical sedge *Cyperus papyrus,* which flourishes on floating mats in southern Africa.

These typical plant species do not occur randomly mixed together in marshes. Each has its preferred habitat. Different species often occur in rough zones on slight gradients, especially flooding gradients. For example, Figure 11-3 illustrates a typical distribution of species along an elevation gradient in a prairie pothole marsh. Sedges and arrowheads typically occupy the shallowly flooded edge of the pothole. Two species of cattail are common. The narrow-leaved species is more flood tolerant than the broad-leaved cattail, and may grow in water up to 1 m deep. The deepest zone of emergent plants is typically vegetated with hardstem bullrushes. Beyond these emergents, floating-leaved and submerged vegetation will grow, the latter to depths dictated by light penetration.

**Table 11-3. Typical Dominant Emergent Vegetation
in Different Freshwater Marshes**

Marsh Type and Location	Dominant Species	Reference
Prairie glacial marsh, Iowa	*Typha latifolia* *Typha angustifolia* *Scirpus validus* *Scirpus fluviatilis* *Scirpus acutus* *Sparganium eurycarpum* *Carex* spp. *Sagittaria latifolia*	Van der Valk and Davis (1978*b*); Weller (1981)
Riverine marsh, Wisconsin	*Typha latifolia* *Scirpus fluviatilis* *Carex lacustris* *Sparganium eurycarpum* *Phalaris arundinacea*	Klopatek (1978)
"Tule" marshes, California and Oregon	*Scirpus acutus* *Scirpus californicus* *Scirpus olneyi* *Scirpus validus* *Phragmites australis* *Cyperus* spp. *Juncus patens* *Typha latifolia*	Hofstetter (1983)
Floating freshwater coastal marsh, Louisiana	*Panicum hemitomon* *Thelypteris palustris* *Osmunda regalis* *Vigna luteola* *Polygonum sagittatum* *Sagittaria latifolia* *Decodon verticillatus*	Sasser and Gosselink (1984)
Everglades, Florida	*Cladium jamaicense* *Panicum hemitomon* *Rhynchospora* spp. *Eleocharis* spp. *Sagittaria latifolia* *Pontederia lanceolata* *Crinum americanum* *Hymenocallis* spp.	Hofstetter (1983)

The particular species found at a site are also determined, of course, by many other environmental factors. Nutrient availability determines to a large degree whether a wetland site will support mosses or angiosperms (i.e., whether it is a bog or a marsh). Plant species also change with latitude; that is, as temperatures increase or decrease and the winters become more or less severe. While the same genera may be found in the tropics and in the arctic,

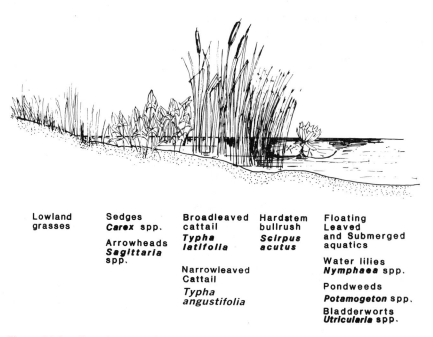

Lowland grasses	Sedges *Carex* spp.	Broadleaved cattail *Typha latifolia*	Hardstem bullrush *Scirpus acutus*	Floating Leaved and Submerged aquatics
	Arrowheads *Sagittaria* spp.	Narrowleaved Cattail *Typha angustifolia*		Water lilies *Nymphaea* spp.
				Pondweeds *Potamogeton* spp.
				Bladderworts *Utricularia* spp.

Figure 11-3. Typical section through a prairie pothole marsh showing the zonation of plants according to water depth.

the species are usually different, reflecting different adaptations to cold or heat. Because of their long isolation from each other, the flora of the North American continent differs at the species level from the European flora and is richer. Finally, soil salts, even in low concentrations, determine the species found on a site. Because many inland marshes are potholes that collect water which leaves only by evaporation, salts may become concentrated during periods of low precipitation, adversely affecting the growth of salt-intolerant species.

Consumers

As with other wetland systems, inland marshes are detrital ecosystems. Unfortunately, we know very little about the many small benthic organisms that are the primary consumers in wetlands, and inland marshes are no exception. It is probable that small decomposers, such as nematodes and enchytraeids, are relatively more important than larger decomposers in marshes compared to terrestrial woodlands. The most conspicuous invertebrates are the true flies (Diptera), which often make one's life miserable in the marsh. These include midges, mosquitoes, and crane flies. Many, especially in adult stages, are herbivorous; Cragg (1961) attributes about one-third of consumer respiration in a *Juncus* moor to herbivores, chiefly Diptera. But in the larval stages, many of the insects are benthic. For example, Weller (1981) says that midge larvae, which because of their rich red color are called "bloodworms," "are found submerged in bottom soils and organic debris, serving as food for fish, frogs, and diving birds. When pupae surface and emerge as adults, they are exploited as well by surface-feeding birds and fish."

A number of mammals inhabit inland marshes. The most noticed probably is the muskrat. This herbivore reproduces rapidly and can attain population densities that decimate the marsh, causing major changes in its character. As with plants, mammalian species each have preferred habitats. For example, Figure 11-4 shows the distribution of mammals on an elevation gradient in a Czechoslovakia fishpond littoral marsh. Muskrats are found in the most aquatic areas, the water vole in overlapping but higher elevations, and other voles are found in the relatively terrestrial parts of the reed marsh. Most of the mammals are herbivorous.

Birds, particularly waterfowl, are also abundant. Many of these are herbivorous or omnivorous. Waterfowl are plentiful in all wetlands, as has been made plain in earlier chapters, probably because of the marsh's food rich-

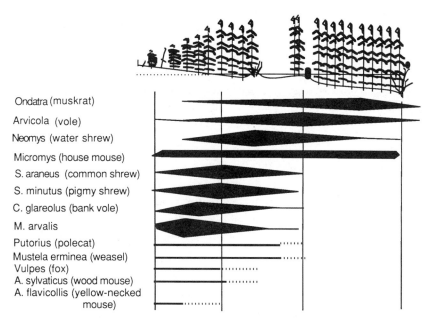

Figure 11-4. Distribution of populations of small mammals in a Czechoslovakia littoral pond. Left to right: terrestrial, limosal, and littoral zones. *(After Pelikan, 1978, p. 75)*

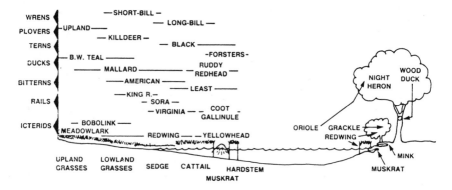

Figure 11-5. The typical distribution of birds across a marsh from open water edge across shallower zones into upland vegetation. *(From Weller and Spatcher, 1965)*

ness and the diversity of habitats for nesting and resting. Waterfowl nest in northern freshwater marshes, winter in southern marshes, and rest in other marshes in between during their migrations. Weller and Spatcher (1965) described how birds partition a typical marsh as they compete for food and nesting sites (Fig. 11-5). Again, different species distribute themselves along an elevation gradient, according to how well they are adapted to water. The loon normally uses the deeper water of marsh ponds, which may hold fish populations. Grebes prefer marshy areas, especially during the nesting season. Some ducks (dabblers) nest in upland sites, feeding along the marsh-water interface and in shallow marsh ponds. Others (diving ducks) nest over water and fish by diving. The geese and swans are the major marsh herbivores, along with the canvasback ducks. Wading birds usually nest colonially in wetlands and fish along the shallow ponds and streams. Rails live in the whole range of wetlands, many of them solitary birds that are seldom seen. Songbirds are also abundant in and around marshes, often nesting or perching in adjacent uplands and flying into the marsh to feed.

Perhaps one reason small marshes of the prairie region and the western high plains harbor such a rich diversity of wildlife is that they are often natural islands in a sea of farmland. Cultivated land does not provide a diversity of either food or shelter, and many animals must be drawn to the marshes, which remain as the only natural habitats.

Marsh Cycles

A unique structural feature of prairie pothole marshes is a characteristic 5- to 20-year cycle of dry marsh, regenerating marsh, degenerating marsh, and lake (Weller and Spatcher, 1965; Van der Valk and Davis, 1978b), which is

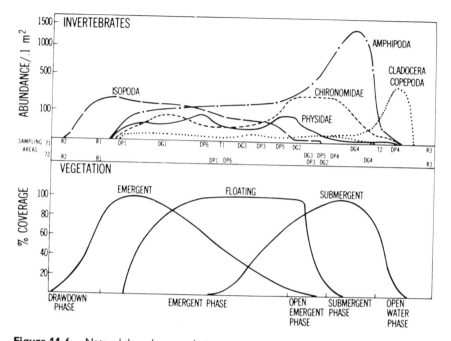

Figure 11-6. Natural drawdown cycle in a prairie pothole wetland showing changes in vegetation and relative abundance of major invertebrate groups. *(From Voights, 1976, p. 320. Copyright © 1976 by the American Midland Naturalist, reprinted with permission)*

related to periodic droughts (Fig. 11-6). During drought years, standing water disappears. Buried seed in the exposed mudflats germinate to grow a cover of annuals *(Bidens, Polgonum, Cyperus, Rumex)* and perennials *(Typha, Scirpus, Sparganium, Sagittaria).* When rainfall returns to normal the mudflats are inundated. Annuals disappear, leaving only the perennial emergent species. Submerged species also reappear *(Potamogeton, Najas, Ceratophyllum, Myriophyllum, Chara).* For the next year or more, during the regenerating stage, the emergent population increases in vigor and density. However, after a few years these populations begin to decline. The reasons are poorly understood, but often muskrat populations explode in response to the vigorous vegetation growth. Their nest and trail building can decimate a marsh. Whatever the reason, in the final stage of the cycle, there is little emergent marsh; most of the area has reverted to an open shallow lake or pond, setting the stage for the next drought cycle. Wildlife use of these wetlands follows the same cycle. The most intense use occurs when there is good interspersion of small ponds with submerged vegetation, and emergent marshes exist with stands diverse in height, density, and potential food.

ECOSYSTEM FUNCTION

Primary Production

Productivity of inland marshes has been reported in a number of studies (Table 11-4). Estimates are generally quite high, ranging upward from about 1,000 g/m² · yr. Some of the best estimates, which take into account underground production as well as aboveground, are from studies of fishponds in Czechoslovakia. (These are small artificial lakes with bordering marshes, used for fish culture.) These estimates are high compared with most of the

Table 11-4. Selected Primary Production Values for Inland Freshwater Marsh Species

Species	Location	Net Primary Productivity, g/m² · yr	Reference
Reeds and Grasses			
Glyceria maxima	Lake, Czechoslovakia	900–4,300[a]	Kvet and Husak (1978)
Phragmites communis	Lake, Czechoslovakia	1,000–6,000[a]	Kvet and Husak (1978)
P. communis	Denmark	1,400[a]	Anderson (1976)
Panicum hemitomon	Floating coastal marsh, Louisiana	1,700[b]	Sasser et al. (1982)
Schoenoplectus lacustris	Lake, Czechoslovakia	1,600–5,500[a]	Kvet and Husak (1978)
Sparganium eurycarpum	Prairie pothole, Iowa	1,066[b]	Van der Valk and Davis (1978a)
Typha glauca	Prairie pothole, Iowa	2,297[b]	Van der Valk and Davis (1978a)
Typha latifolia	Oregon	2,040–2,210[a]	McNaughton (1966)
Typha sp.	Lakeside, Wisconsin	3,450[a]	Klopatek (1974)
Sedges and Rushes			
Carex atheroides	Prairie pothole, Iowa	2,858[b]	Van der Valk and Davis (1978a)
Larex lacustris	Sedge meadow, New York	1,078–1,741[a]	Bernard and Solsky (1977)
Juncus effusus	South Carolina	1,860[a]	Boyd (1971)
Scirpus fluviatilis	Prairie pothole, Iowa	943[a]	Van der Valk and Davis (1978a)
Broad-Leaved Monocots			
Acorus calamus	Lake, Czechoslovakia	500–1,100[a]	Kvet and Husak (1978)

[a] Above- and belowground vegetation
[b] Aboveground vegetation

North American work, with some values over 6,000 g/m² · yr. This is higher than the productivity of intensively cultivated farm crops. Productivity variation is undoubtedly related to a number of factors. Innate genetic differences among species accounts for part of the variability. For example, in one study, *Typha angustifolia* production was determined to be about double that of *T. latifolia* using the same techniques of measurement (Kvet and Husak, 1978). However, *T. angustifolia* is typically found in deeper water than the other species, so environmental factors are not identical for comparison. As regards the environmental factors affecting production, Gorham (1974) has shown clearly the close positive relationship between aboveground biomass and summer temperatures (Fig. 11-7). Nitrogen limitation is also generally a factor in wetland productivity.

The dynamics of underground growth are much less studied than that of

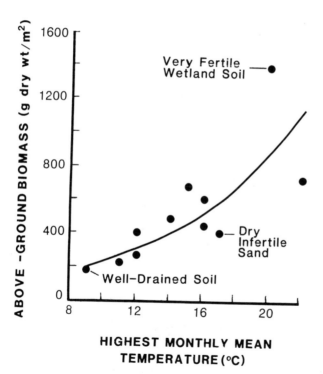

Figure 11-7. Relationship between aboveground standing crop of various sedges and the highest mean monthly temperature near the site. Sites are wetlands except where noted otherwise. *(After Gorham, 1974, p. 489; Copyright ©1974 by Blackwell, reprinted with permission)*

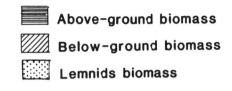

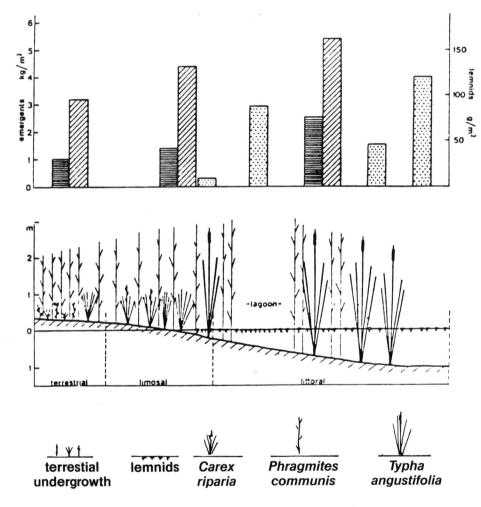

Figure 11-8.   Distribution of above- and belowground biomass of emergent vegetation and lemnids across a reedbelt transect, showing relation to elevation and flooding; fishpond littoral is in Czechoslovakia. *(From Kvet and Husak, 1978, p. 213; Copyright ©1978 by Springer-Verlag, reprinted with permission)*

aboveground. In freshwater tidal wetlands (chap. 9), relative root growth was shown to be related to the plant's life history. Annuals generally use small amounts of photosynthate to support root growth, while species with perennial roots and rhizomes often have root:shoot ratios well in excess of one. This relationship appears to hold true for inland marshes also. Perennial species in Iowa marshes (Van der Valk and Davis, 1978a) had more belowground than aboveground biomass, as did emergent macrophytes in Czechoslovakia fishponds (Fig. 11-8). It is interesting to note, however, that while biomass root:shoot ratios are usually greater than one, root production to shoot biomass ratios are always less than one (Table 11-5). Since aboveground production is approximated by aboveground biomass, this latter ratio is an index of the allocation of resources by the plant, and indicates that less than one-half of the photosynthate is translocated to the roots. The implication of large root biomass but relatively small root production is that the root system is generally longer lived (that is, it renews itself more slowly) than the shoot.

The emergent monocotyledons *Phragmites* and *Typha* have high photosynthetic efficiency (Fig. 11-9). For *Typha* it is highest early in the growing season, gradually decreasing as the season progresses. *Phragmites,* in contrast, has a fairly constant efficiency rate through most of the growing season. The efficiency of conversion of from 4% to 7% of photosynthetically active radiation is comparable to those calculated for intensively cultivated crops such as sugar beets, sugarcane, or corn.

Table 11-5. Comparison of the Root:Shoot Biomass Ratio, and Root Production to Biomass Ratio of the Principle Monospecific Reedswamp Communities of a Czechoslovakia Littoral Fishpond

Species	*Root:Shoot Biomass Ratio*	*Root Production* *Shoot Biomass*
Acorus calamus	1.8	0.5-0.9
Glyceria maxima	1.3-5.5	0.4
Phragmites communis	0.9-2.0	0.5-1.0
Schoenoplectus lacustris	2.3-3.9	1.0-1.2
Sparganium erectum	0.5-1.0	0.3
Typha angustifolia	0.9-1.2	0.8-0.9
Typha latifolia	0.4-0.6	0.4

Source: Based on data from Kvet and Husak (1978)

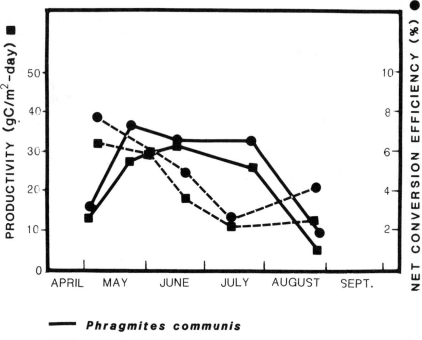

Figure 11-9. Productivity and net conversion efficiency of photosynthetically active radiation in stands of *Phragmites communis* and *Typha angustifolia*. *(After Dykyjova and Kvet, 1978)*

Decomposition and Consumption

As with other wetland ecosystems, herbivory is considered fairly minor in inland marshes, and most of the organic production decomposes before entering the detrital food chain. The decomposition process is much the same for all wetlands, with variations due to the quality and resistance of the decomposing plant material, the temperature, the availability of inorganic nutrients to the microbial decomposers, and the flooding regime of the marsh. Gallagher (1978) put together a conceptual diagram of decomposition in freshwater marshes that shows the complexity and interaction of the products of decomposition (Fig. 11-10). The action of microbial organisms is not simply to incorporate plant organic matter into microbial cells. Rather, in the process, organic material is dissolved and diffuses away, nutrients are released to the substrate, other nutrients are absorbed by the microflora or

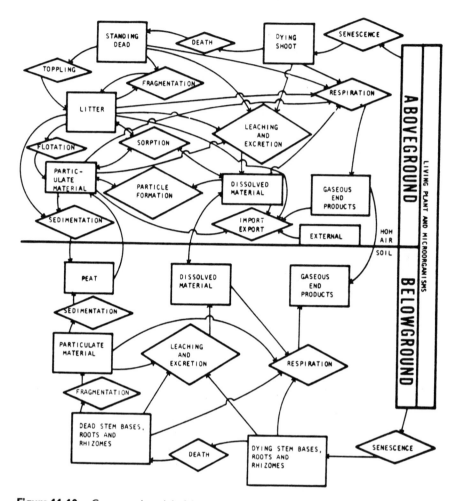

Figure 11-10. Conceptual model of decomposition in freshwater marshes. *(From Gallagher, 1978, p. 147; Copyright ©1978 by Academic Press, reprinted with permission)*

adsorbed to fine organic particles, respiration oxidizes and releases organic carbon as carbon dioxide, ingested organic materials are released as repackaged fecal material, and dissolved organic matter may aggregate and flocculate into fine particles. The dynamics of these reactions are as poorly understood in freshwater marshes as in other wetlands. It is probably true, as in other detrital ecosystems, that the microbial decomposers are preyed upon heavily by microscopic meiobenthic organisms, chiefly nematodes; the meiobenthic organisms are in turn a food source for larger macrobenthic organisms. Thus, there may be several links in the food chain before the commonly visible birds and other carnivores get their dinners.

Organic Export

Very little information is available about the export of organic energy from freshwater marshes. If other ecosystems are any guide, export is heavily governed by the flow of water across the marsh. Thus, pothole marshes, which have small outflows, must export very little. Some dissolved organic materials may flow out in groundwater, but otherwise the primary loss is through living organisms that feed in the marshes then move away. In contrast, lakeside and riverine marshes may export considerable organic material when periodically flushed.

Energy Flow

It is not possible to calculate a tight organic energy budget for inland marshes from the information now available. However, several components have been estimated for the littoral fishpond system (Dykyjova and Kvet, 1978, Table 11-6). This allows at least some perspective on the major fluxes of energy. *Net* organic energy fixed by emergent plants ranges from 1,600 to 16,000 kcal/m^2 · yr. (For comparison, for a site producing 2,500 g/m^2 bio-

Table 11-6. Partial Organic Budget for a Fishpond Littoral Marsh in Czechoslovakia

	Energy Flux, kcal/m^2 · yr
Producers	
Gross production	4,500–27,000
Respiration	2,900–11,000
Net production	1,600–16,000
Consumers	
Decomposers (bacteria and fungi)	1760[a]
Decomposers (small invertebrates)	300[a]
Invertebrate macrofauna	—
Mammal consumption	232
Bird consumption	20[b]
Mammal production	5
Bird production	1

Source: Based on data from Dykyjova and Kvet (1978)
[a]Cragg, 1961
[b]Assuming production = 5% of consumption

mass per year, the energetic equivalent is about 10,000 kcal/m² · yr). Most of this net production is lost in consumer respiration. An early study by Cragg (1961) suggested that microbial respiration in the peat was about 1,760 kcal/m² · yr in a *Juncus* moor. No other estimates appear to be available.

In the sediment the invertebrates, especially the microinvertebrates, play an important role in the flow of organic energy through the ecosystem. They are without doubt important in fragmenting the litter so that it can be more readily attacked by bacteria and fungi. They are also important intermediates in the transfer of energy to higher trophic levels. In Czechoslovakia fishponds, Dvorak (1978) measured average benthic macrofaunal biomasses of 42-66 g/m², composed mostly of mollusks and oligochaetes. These were selectively fed upon by fish. In quite a different marsh, a *Juncus* moor, Cragg (1961) estimated the respiration rate of the small soil invertebrates to be about 300 kcal/m² · yr.

Pelikan (1978) calculated energy flow through the mammals of a reedswamp ecosystem. Total energy consumption was 235 kcal/m² · yr, mostly by herbivores, which ingested 220 kcal/m² · yr. Insectivores ingested 10 and carnivores 1 kcal/m² · yr. This amounted to about 0.55% of aboveground and 0.18% of belowground plant production. Most of the assimilated energy was respired. Total mammal production was only 4.84 kcal/m² · yr, which amounts to less than 1 g biomass/m² · yr. It seems evident that the indirect control of plant production by the muskrat is much more significant than the direct flow of energy through this group.

The same reedswamp ecosystem supported an estimated 83 nesting pairs of gulls *(Larus ridibundus)* and 20 pairs of other birds per hectare—about 13 passerines, 3 grebes, and the rest rails and ducks (Hudec and Stastny, 1978). Mean biomass was 44.4 kg/ha (fresh weight) for the gulls and 11.2 kg/ha for the remaining species. Production of eggs and young amounted to about 6,088 kcal/ha for gulls and 3,096 kcal/ha for the remaining species. If production was considered to be 5% of total consumption, the total flow of organic energy through birds would be about 20 kcal/m², or roughly 10% of the mammal contribution.

Collectively, these estimates of energy flow through invertebrates, mammals, and birds account for less that 10% of net primary production. Most of the rest of the energy of organic production must be dissipated by microbial respiration, but some organic production is stored as peat, reduced to methane, and exported to adjacent waters. Export has been particularly difficult to measure because so many of these marshes intercept the water table and may lose organic materials through groundwater flows.

Nutrient Budgets

A number of attempts have been made to calculate nutrient budgets for wetlands, but the results form no consistent picture because freshwater wetlands vary so widely in so many different ways. In a number of studies, freshwater wetlands have been evaluated as nutrient traps. These studies often emphasize input-output budgets. Since this subject is discussed in some detail in Chapter 5, we emphasize in this chapter the role of vegetation in nutrient cycling.

Vegetation traps nutrients in biomass but the storage of these nutrients is seasonally partitioned in aboveground and belowground stocks. For example, the seasonal dynamics of phosphorus in *Typha latifolia* is described in Fig. 11-11 (Prentki, Gustafson, and Adams, 1978). Phosphorus stocks in the roots and rhizomes of *Typha* are mobilized into the shoots early in the growing season. Total stocks increase to over 4 g P/m^2 during the summer. In the fall, some phosphorus in the shoot is remobilized into the belowground organs before the shoots die, but most of it is lost by leaching and in the litter. The calculated belowground deficit is an indication of the magnitude of the phosphorus demand by the plant that cannot be met by shifting internal supplies; it is largest during the period of active growth in the summer. Studies like this lead to several generalizations:

1. The size of the plant stock of nutrients varies widely. More nitrogen and phosphorus is retained in aboveground plant parts in mineral substrate wetlands than in peat wetlands (Whigham and Bayley, 1979). The aboveground stock of nitrogen ranges from as low as 3 g/m^2 to as high as 29 g/m^2.

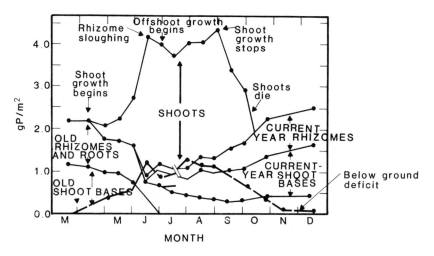

Figure 11-11. Seasonal stocks of phosphorus in *Typha latifolia* plant parts in a marsh on Lake Mendota, Wisconsin, and the belowground deficit. *(After Prentki, Gustafson, and Adams, 1978, p. 176)*

2. This biologically inactivated stock may be only a temporary storage that is released to flooding waters when the plant shoots die in the fall. Where this occurs, the marsh may retain nutrients during the summer and release them in the winter.
3. Nutrients retained in biomass usually account for only about 20% of the total nutrients detained in the marsh (Sloey, Spangler, and Fetter, 1978).
4. The vegetation often acts as a nutrient pump, taking up nutrients from the soil, translocating them to the shoots, and releasing them on the marsh surface when the plant dies. The effect of this pumping mechanism may be to mobilize nutrients that had been sequestered in the soil. This is clearly demonstrated by the nitrogen budget developed by Klopatek (1978) for a river bullrush *(Scirpus fluviatilis)* stand (Fig. 11-12). Here, 20.75 g N/m^2 is taken up annually from the sediment by the plants. Over 15 g N/m^2 is translocated to the shoots and lost through leaching and shoot senescence.

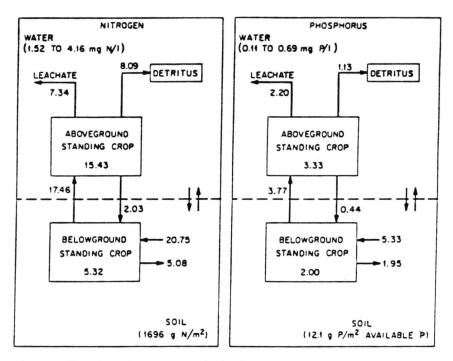

Figure 11-12. Flow of N and P through a *Scirpus fluviatilis* stand. Flows are $g/m^2 \cdot yr$ and compartments are g/m^2 standing crop. *(From Klopatek, 1978, p. 207; Copyright © 1978 by Academic Press, reprinted with permission)*

The ability of soils to retain nutrients varies widely. Organic soils have large cation exchange capacities. When these exchange sites are saturated with hydrogen ions, as in nutrient-poor bogs, it would seem that the possibility for retention of cations by displacing hydrogen ions would be large, whereas soils in which the exchange sites are already saturated with nutrients would have a limited additional capacity.

In general, precipitation and dry fall account for less than 10% of plant nutrient demands (Prentki, Gustafson, and Adams, 1978). Similarly, groundwater flows are usually rather small sources of nutrients. Surface inflow, where it occurs, is usually a major source; it varies widely, sometimes providing many times the needs of the vegetation. Considering all of these variables, it is not surprising that each marsh seems to have its own unique budget.

ECOSYSTEM MODELS

Van der Valk (1982) produced an important model describing the succession of freshwater wetlands (see chap. 7). Although this is a conceptual rather than a simulation model, it is a stimulating example of the synthesis of information into a useful new construct.

In an ambitious simulation modeling effort, scientists on the Gulf coast are attempting to model both the temporal and the spatial succession of coastal marshes, based on geomorphic and hydrologic changes that are occurring in the area. The model will be used to predict both the salinization of freshwater marshes and their erosion to open water, as well as the reversal of this effect by sediment carried by the Atchafalaya River, which is rapidly building a delta on the north coast of the Gulf of Mexico (Sklar, Costanza, and Day, 1985).

Significant efforts to simulate inland freshwater ecosystems have been made in connection with the analysis of the feasibility of using peatlands for treatment of domestic wastes (see chap. 12). A model has also been developed to simulate the long-term effects on a freshwater marsh of leaking warm water from a power plant cooling lake (Andrews, 1978). That model was used to predict that the heating effect would increase erosion and decomposition of peat and shift vegetation from perennial to annual (Bedford, 1979).

SUMMARY

Freshwater inland marshes are perhaps the most diverse of the marsh types discussed in this book. They are all dominated by emergent graminoids and sedges, but there the similarity ends. The pothole marshes of the north-central United States and south-central Canada are individually small, occurring in the moraines of the last glaciation. Playas of north Texas and western

New Mexico are similar in size but have different geological origins and are found in an arid climate. Coastal nontidal freshwater marshes and the Florida Everglades are other freshwater marshes.

Despite their diversity, inland marshes have many of the same properties as all wetlands—saturated soils, biota adapted to the aquatic habitat, a detrital trophic system, and concentrated use by waterfowl. They also are unique in several ways:

1. Vegetation is dominated by graminoids and sedges such as the tall reeds *Typha* and *Phragmites,* the grasses *Panicum* and *Cladium,* and the sedges *Cyperus* and *Carex.*

2. Some inland marshes, such as the prairie glacial marshes, follow a 5- to 20-year cycle of (a) drought, when the marsh dries out and exposes large areas of mudflat upon which dense seedling stands germinate; (b) reflooding after rains drowns out the annual seedlings but allows the perennials to spread rapidly and vigorously; (c) deterioration of the marshes, sometimes associated with concentrated muskrat activity; and (d) a lake stage when most of the emergent vegetation is gone. This resets the cycle to stage (a).

3. In contrast to bogs, inland marshes have high-pH substrates, high available soil calcium, medium or high loading rates for nutrients, high productivity, and high soil microbial activity that leads to rapid decomposition, rapid recycling, and nitrogen fixation. Peat may or may not accumulate.

4. Inland marshes are valuable as wildlife islands in the middle of agricultural land, and have been tested extensively as sites that can assimilate nutrients from human domestic wastes.

NORTHERN PEATLAND AND BOG *(Photograph courtesy of Curt Richardson)*

chapter 12

NORTHERN PEATLANDS AND BOGS

As described in the introduction to chapter 11, we have divided inland wetlands, for purposes of this book, into marshes and bogs. Bogs and to some extent fens belong to a major class of wetlands called peatlands, or *mires,* that occur as freshwater wetlands throughout much of the boreal zone of the world (Walter, 1973). *Bogs,* called *moors* in Europe and *muskegs* in Canada, are peat deposits, generally with a high water table yet no significant inflow or outflow streams, that support acidophilic (acid-loving) vegetation, partic-ularly mosses. *Fens,* on the other hand, are open wetland systems that generally receive some drainage from surrounding mineral soils and are often covered by grasses, sedges, or reeds. They were discussed in chapter 11, but they are in many respects transitional between marshes and bogs (see Table 3-1). As a successional stage in the development of bogs, fens are important and will be considered in that context here.

Bogs and fens have been studied and described on a worldwide basis more extensively than any other type of freshwater wetland, although as compared with that on other northern ecosystems, the literature on bogs and northern peatlands is relatively sparse (Larsen, 1982). These wetlands have been studied because of their vast area in temperate climates, the economic importance of peat as a fuel and soil conditioner, and their unique biota and successional patterns. Bogs have intrigued and mystified many cultures for centuries because of such discoveries as the Iron Age "bog people" of Scandinavia, who were preserved intact for up to 2,000 years in the non-decomposing bogs (Glob, 1969).

Because bogs and other peatlands are so ubiquitous in northern Europe and North America, many definitions and words, some unfortunate, that now describe wetlands in general originated from bog terminology; there is also considerable confusion in the use of terms such as bog, fen, swamp, moor, muskeg, heath, mire, marsh, highmoor, lowmoor, and peatland to describe these ecosystems (Heinselman, 1963). The use of the word peatlands in general and bogs and fens in particular will be limited in this chapter to deep peat deposits of the cold northern forested regions of North America and Eurasia and will not include peat deposits of warm temperate, subtropical, or tropical regions. Because the characteristics of peatlands are similar throughout the northern hemisphere, this chapter will describe some studies from Europe that are most likely applicable to North America. As described by Curtis (1959) in Larsen (1982, p. 23): "The bog . . . is a common feature of the glaciated landscapes of the entire northern hemisphere and has a remarkably uniform structure and composition throughout the circumboreal regions." Excellent references on bogs are Heinselman (1963; 1970), Moore and Bellamy (1974), Gore (1983*a*), and Moore (1984).

GEOGRAPHICAL EXTENT

Bogs and fens are distributed in cold temperate climates, mostly in the northern hemisphere, where ample precipitation and high humidity (generally due to maritime influences) cause excessive moisture to accumulate, Extensive areas of bogs and fens occur in Finland, eastern Europe, western Siberia, Alaska, Labrador, Canada, and the north-central United States. The

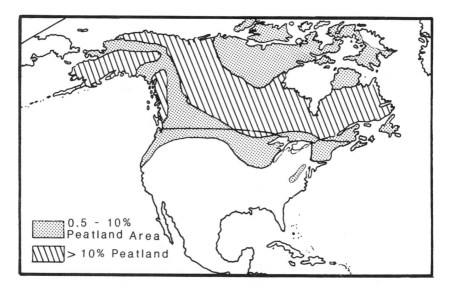

Figure 12-1.   Distribution of North American peatlands. *(Based on data from Gore, 1983a and Hofstetter, 1983)*

distribution of bogs in North America is shown in Figure 12-1. Diagrams of the major types are shown in Figure 12-2.

In northern Europe bogs occur in relatively well-defined zones, as described by Walter (1973) and Moore and Bellamy (1974).

1. Raised Bogs—These are peat deposits that fill entire basins, are raised above groundwater levels, and receive their major inputs of nutrients

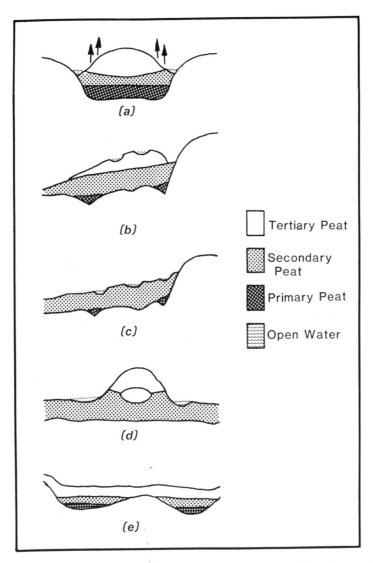

Figure 12-2. Diagrams of major peatland types, including *a.* raised bog (concentric), *b.* excentric raised bog, *c.* aapa peatland (string bogs and patterned fens), *d.* paalsa bog, and *e.* blanket bog. *(After Moore and Bellamy, 1974, p. 30)*

from precipitation (Fig. 12-2*a,* 12-2*b*). These bogs are primarily found in the boreal and northern deciduous biomes of northern Europe. Pine trees sometimes grow in these bogs in areas with drier climates, although many are treeless. When a concentric pattern of pools and peat communities forms around the most elevated part of the bog, the bog is called a *concentric domed* bog (Fig. 12-2*a*). Bogs that form from previously separate basins on sloping land and form elongated hummocks and pools aligned perpendicular to the slope are called *excentric raised* bogs (Fig. 12-2*b*). The former are found near the Baltic Sea, while the latter are found primarily in the North Karelian region of Finland.

2. Aapa peatlands—These wetlands (Figure 12-2*c*), also called *string bogs* and *patterned fens,* are found primarily in Scandinavia and in the Soviet Union north of the raised bog region. The dominant feature of these wetlands is the long, narrow alignment of the higher peat hummocks (strings), which form ridges perpendicular to the slope of the peatland and are separated by deep pools (*flarks* in Swedish). In appearance, they resemble a hillside of terraced rice fields (Walter, 1973).

3. Paalsa bogs—These bogs, found in the southern limit of the tundra biome, are large plateaus of peat (20 to 100 m in breadth and length and 3 m high) generally underlain by frozen peat and silt (Fig. 12-2*d*). The peat acts as an insulting blanket, actually keeping the ground ice from thawing and allowing the southernmost appearance of the discontinuous permafrost.

4. Blanket bogs—These wetlands (Fig. 12-2*e*) are common along the northwestern coast of Europe and throughout the British Isles. The favorable humid Atlantic climate allows the peat to literally "blanket" very large areas far from the site of original peat accumulation. Peat in these areas can generally advance on slopes of up to 18°; extremes of 25° slopes covered by blanket bogs have been noted in western Ireland (Moore and Bellamy, 1974).

In North America, northern peatlands probably follow a pattern similar to that in Europe, although the zonation is not yet as clearly understood. The major northern peatlands of the coterminous United States are found north of the 41st parallel and east of the 97th meridian (Fig. 12-1; Cameron, 1973). Bogs are found as far south as northern Illinois and Indiana in the north-central United States are also prevalent in the unglaciated Appalachian Mountains in West Virginia (Wieder and Lang, 1983). The southern limit to bog species and hence to the bog wetland is thought to be determined by the intensity of solar radiation in the summer months, as precipitation and humidity are otherwise adequate to support bogs farther south (Larsen,

1982, after Transeau, 1903). In the United States, bogs are particularly clustered around the Great Lakes and in Maine and usually develop in basins scoured out by the Pleistocene glaciers. One of the most studied bogs ecosystems in the United States is the Lake Agassiz region in northern Minnesota (Heinselman, 1963; 1970; 1975). West Coast bogs have been studied by Rigg (1925). Canadian bogs have been documented by Sjors (1961), Radforth, (1962), and Reader and Stewart (1972).

GEOMORPHOLOGY AND HYDROLOGY

Hydrologic and Mineral Conditions

Bogs and fens occur where precipitation exceeds potential evapotranspiration, creating a net water surplus. There must also be some impediment, if only lack of relief, that prevents the rapid drainage of the surplus water. Large expanses of the boreal and northern deciduous zones of Europe, Siberia, and North America have humid conditions with flat terrain and a high groundwater level, an ideal environment for bog formation (Walter, 1973). Where the groundwater level is 0.5 m or more below the surface, forest vegetation is possible; for higher water tables, bogs and fens may dominate.

Several attempts have been made to classify peatlands according to their hydrologic and topographic conditions as well as according to their chemical characteristics. Because the chemical status ultimately depends on the origin of the soil water in the bog or fen, these two types of wetlands are often linked in peatland classifications. A simple characterization, after Moore and Bellamy (1974), and based on the nutritional as well as hydrologic conditions of the peatland, is presented here:

1. Minerotrophic peatlands—These are true fens that receive water which has passed through mineral soil (Gorham, 1967). These peatlands generally have a high groundwater level and occupy a low point of relief in a basin. These wetlands are also referred to as *rheophilous* (flow-loving) in a classification by Kulczynski (1949), and *rheotrophic* by Moore and Bellamy (1974). Walter (1973) refers to these peatlands as *soligenous*.
2. Ombrotrophic peatlands—These are the true raised bogs that have developed peat layers higher than their surroundings and which receive nutrients and other minerals exclusively by precipitation. These are called *ombrophilous* (rain-loving) in Kulczynski's (1949) classification and *ombrogenous* by Walter (1973).
3. Transition peatland—These peatlands, often called poor fens, are intermediate between mineral-nourished (minerotrophic) and

precipitation-dominated (ombrotrophic) peatlands. Another term used frequently for this class is *mesotrophic* (Moore and Bellamy, 1974).

Heinselman (1970) and Moore and Bellamy (1974), arguing for simplicity in the description of peatlands, state that terms such as soligenous and ombrogenous actually refer to the hydrological and topographic origins of the peatlands and not to the mineral conditions of the inflowing water. These terms are not frequently used today.

Bog Formation

Bogs can develop either from aquatic ecosystems through the filling of a basin or from terrestrial ecosystems through the spreading of blanket bogs through wooded areas (called *paludification*). It should be emphasized that not all lakes and forests in the boreal and northern deciduous zones are destined to become bogs and fens, although vast expanses of peatlands do cover some boreal forests of Finland, eastern Europe, and western Siberia. Three major bog formation processes are commonly seen:

1. Flow-through succession—Moore and Bellamy (1974) described the development of a bog from a lake basin that originally had continuous inflow and outflow of surface and groundwater. The successional pattern is shown in Figure 12-3 in five stages. In the first stage, the inflow of sediments and the production of excess organic matter in the lake begin the buildup of material on the bottom of the lake. The growth of marsh vegetation continues the buildup of peat (stage 2), until the bottom rises above the water level and the flow of water is channelized around the peat. As the peat continues to build, the major inflow of water may be diverted (stage 3) and areas may develop that become inundated only during high rainfall (stage 4). In the final stage (stage 5), the bog remains above the groundwater level and becomes a true ombrotrophic bog. Figure 12-4 illustrates how a sedge peat bog can build up over 5,000 years to become a poor fen and raised ombrotrophic bog.

2. Quaking bog succession—A second pattern of bog development in some lake basins involves the filling in of the basin from the surface, creating a *quaking bog* (or *Schwingmoor* in German) (Fig. 12-5). Plant cover, only partially rooted in the basin bottom or floating like a raft, gradually develops from the edges toward the middle of the lake (Ruttner, 1963). A mat of reeds, sedges, grasses, and other herbaceous plants develops along the leading edge of a floating mat of peat that is soon consolidated and dominated by sphagnum and other bog flora. The mat has all of the characteristics of a raised bog. The older peat is

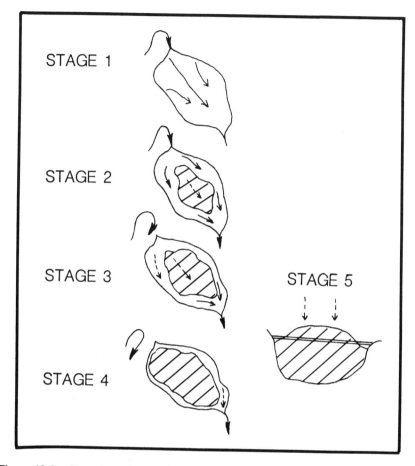

STAGE 1

STAGE 2

STAGE 3

STAGE 4

STAGE 5

Figure 12-3. Flow-through succession of bog from lake basin. *(From Moore and Bellamy, 1974, p. 57; Copyright © 1974 by Springer-Verlag, reprinted with permission)*

often colonized by shrubs and then forest trees such as pine, tamarack, and spruce, which form uniform concentric rings around the advancing floating mat. These bogs develop only in small lakes that have little wave action; they receive their name from the quaking of the entire surface that can be caused by walking on the floating mat.

3. Paludification—A third pattern of bog evolution occurs when blanket bogs exceed the basin boundaries and encroach on formerly dry land. This process of paludification can be brought about by climatic change, by geomorphological change, by beaver dams, by logging of forests, or by natural advancement of a peatland (Moore and Bellamy, 1974). Often the lower layers of peat compress and become impermeable,

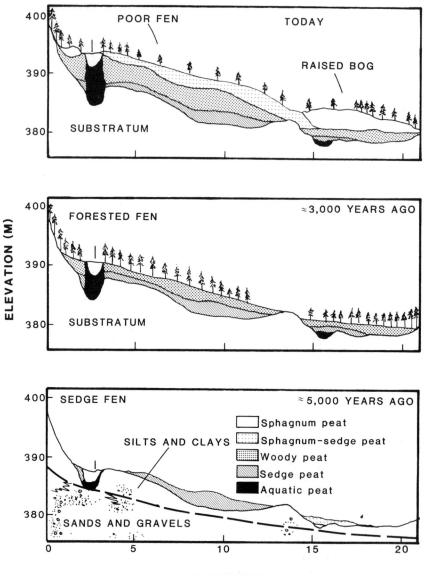

Figure 12-4. Peat accumulation over 10,000 years in a built-up peatland in northern Minnesota. Peat description based on plant remains. This vertical section runs southeast to northwest across the area depicted in Figure 12-8. *(From Boelter and Verry, 1977, p. 5, based on data from Heinselman, 1963, 1970)*

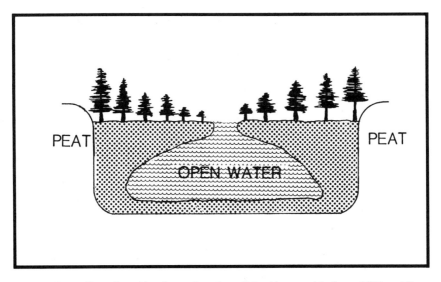

Figure 12-5. Typical profile of a quaking bog. *(After Moore and Bellamy, 1974, p. 15)*

causing a perched water table near the surface of what was before mineral soil. This causes wet and acid conditions that kill or stunt trees and allow only ombrotrophic bog species to exist (Smith, 1980). In certain regions, the progression from forest to bog can take place in only a few generations of trees (Heilman, 1968).

CHEMISTRY

Soil water chemistry is one of the most important factors in the development and structure of the bog ecosystem (Heinselman, 1970). Factors such as pH, mineral concentration, available nutrients, and cation exchange capacity influence the vegetation types and productivity. Conversely, the plant communities influence the chemical properties of the soil water (Gorham, 1967). In few wetland types is the interdependence between chemistry and ecosystem productivity so apparent as in northern peatlands. Table 12-1 gives typical pH values and cation concentrations for different northern hemisphere peatlands, while Table 12-2 compares pH, mineral content, dissolved oxygen, and redox potential of bog waters with water in several other ecosystems in Wisconsin. The major features of peatland chemistry are discussed below.

Table 12-1. pH and Exchangeable Cations of Selected Peatlands

| Peatland | pH | Exchangeable Cations meg/100g | | | | Reference |
		Ca^{++}	Mg^{++}	Na^+	K^+	
Western Europe (Mean values)						
Ombrotrophic bog	3.8	—	—	—	—	Moore & Bellamy
Transition fens	4.1-4.8	—	—	—	—	(1974)
Minerotrophic fens	5.6-7.5	—	—	—	—	
Alaska, U.S.A.						
Black spruce bog	3.6-4.0	15-16	5.3-6.4	—	3.8-4.2	Heilman (1968)
Minnesota, U.S.A. Alkaline peat (water soluble cations)						
Larix laricina stand	6.7-7.1	3.5-5.4	2.7-6.5	—	tr-3.1	Bares & Wali
Picea mariana stand	5.7-6.4	3.5-10.5	1.5-6	—	tr-3.2	(1979)
Sweden						
Marginal fen	5.2	19.5	—	0.43	0.49	Malmer & Sjors (1955)
Ireland						
Raised bog	4.7	2.0-4.0	—	—	0.64	Walsh & Barry (1958)
England						
Blanket bog	—	4.3	4.6	0.6	1.0	Gore & Allen (1956)
Michigan, U.S.A.						
Rich fen	5.1	52.4	7.7	1.2	0.45	Richardson et al. (1978)
England (English Lake Dist.)						
Raised bog	4.0-4.3	1.3-1.8	—	4.9-6.4	0.7-2.0	Gorham
Fen	6.1-7.6	2.3-17.5	—	3.6-6.0	0.17-1.75	(1956)

Acidity and Exchangeable Cations

There is a general decrease in the pH of peatlands as organic content increases with development from a minerotrophic fen to an ombrotrophic bog (Fig. 12-6). Fens are dominated by minerals from surrounding soils, while bogs rely on a sparse supply of minerals from precipitation. As a fen develops into a bog, the supply of metallic cations (Ca^{++}, Mg^{++}, Na^+, K^+) drops sharply. At the same time, as the organic content of the peat increases due to the slowing of the decomposition rate, the capacity of the soil to adsorb and

Table 12-2. Comparison of the Chemistry of Bog Water, Surface Stream, and Forest Soil Water in Wisconsin

	Depth to groundwater, cm	pH	Hardness, mg CaCO$_3$/l	Specific conductivity, μmho/cm	Dissolved O$_2$, ppm	Redox Potential, mv
Black spruce/tamarack bog	10	3.5	None	5.0	None	−364
Black spruce/tamarack bog	30.5	3.9	None	5.7	None	−335
Poor aspen stand	51	4.2	10	14.0	0.3	−305
White cedar/balsam fir bog	15	6.2	24	7.5	None	−42
White cedar/balsam fir bog	10	6.5	83	20.9	0.45	69
Lowland hardwoods	15	6.0	36	10.0	None	−81
Red pine/white pine upland	183	7.7	25	15.0	3.3	95
Creek draining cedar swamp	—	6.9	98	19.5	8.5	85
Creek from beaver dam	—	7.4	115	19.9	6.0	163
Lowland hardwoods (south)	61	8.2	107	28.0	0.4	161

Source: From Larsen (1982, p. 180) after Wilde and Randall (1951). Copyright © 1982 by Academic Press, reproduced by permission.

exchange cations increases (see chap. 5). These changes lead to a domination by hydrogen ions, and the pH falls sharply. Gorham (1967) found that bogs in the English Lake District had a pH range of 3.8-4.4, while noncalcareous fens had a pH range of 4.8-6.0. Pjavchenko (1982) assigned a pH range of 2.6-3.3 to oligotrophic (ombrotrophic) bogs and a range of 4.1-4.8 for mesotrophic (transitional) bogs; a pH greater than 4.8 defined a eutrophic (minerotrophic) fen.

Much of the acidity in bogs is due to sulfuric acid formed by the oxidation of organic sulfur compounds and from humic acids produced in the water. The cation exchange capacity is saturated with hydrogen ions resulting from the metabolic activity of sphagnum and from decomposition of organic matter. This buffers the system against the alkalinity of metallic cations brought in by rainfall. Thus, sphagnum and other bog plants actively influence the pH of the bog (Kurz, 1928; Clymo, 1964; Gorham, 1967).

Gorham (1967) suggests that air pollution and sea spray may influence the atmospheric ion supply to bogs. Bogs downwind of maritime regions exhibit high concentrations of chlorides, while bogs downwind of industrial areas are higher in sulfates. Gorham (1956) found that dissolved carbon

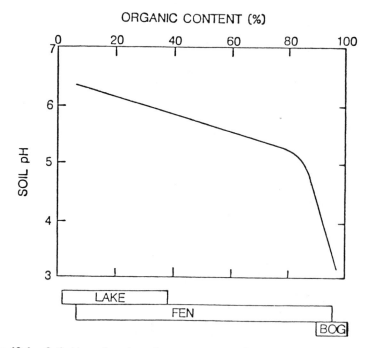

Figure 12-6. Soil pH as a function of organic content of peat soil. *(From Gorham, 1967, p. 31)*

dioxide in rainwater has very little to do with bog acidity and that water movement decreases acidity levels. In stagnant peatland water, low pH results even when mineral content is high.

Nutrients

Bogs are exceedingly deficient in available plant nutrients; fens, with groundwater and surface water sources, have considerably more nutrients (Moore and Bellamy, 1974). This paucity of nutrients leads to two significant results that are discussed later in this chapter: (1) The productivity of ombrotrophic bogs is lower than that of a minerotrophic fen, and (2) The plants, animals, and microbes have many special adaptations to the low-nutrient conditions.

Figure 12-7a shows the decrease in nitrogen content of peat soils with increased organic content. The nitrogen content is above 4% in minerotrophic fens but decreases to less than 2% in ombrotrophic bogs. The increased dominance of sphagnum moss in bogs, generally with a nitrogen content of less than 1% (Gorham, 1967) contributes to this drop. Figure 12-7b shows the pattern of phosphorus levels with depth in ombrotrophic bogs and compares that pattern with those in mineral soils. Nutrients are high in the lower deposits of bogs due to the peat compression and the influence of past minerotrophic conditions. The surface peat has an "insulating" effect on the top layers of the bog, thereby isolating plantlife from the mineral water below (Gorham, 1967).

Some studies have attempted to find the ultimate limiting factor for bog primary productivity; this may be a complex and sometimes academic question due to the shortage of all available nutrients. Most studies on the subject have shown, in general, that phosphorus and potassium are more important limiting factors than nitrogen. Goodman and Perkins (1968) found that potassium was the major limiting factor for growth of *Eriophorum vagintum* (cotton grass) in a bog in Wales, while Heilman (1968) found that levels of phosphorus and to a lesser extent potassium were deficient in black spruce *(Picea mariana)* foliage in a sphagnum bog in Alaska. Bog formation in its latter stages is essentially limited by the input of nutrients by precipitation. Moore and Bellamy (1974) describe the nutrient input from rainfall as adequate to support nitrogen accumulation in raised bogs in Denmark.

ECOSYSTEM STRUCTURE

Northern peatlands, particularly ombrotrophic bogs, support plants, animals, and microbes that have many adaptations to the physical and chemical stresses. The organisms must deal with waterlogged conditions, acid waters, low nutrients, and extreme temperatures. The result is that a very specialized and unique flora and fauna have evolved in this wetland habitat.

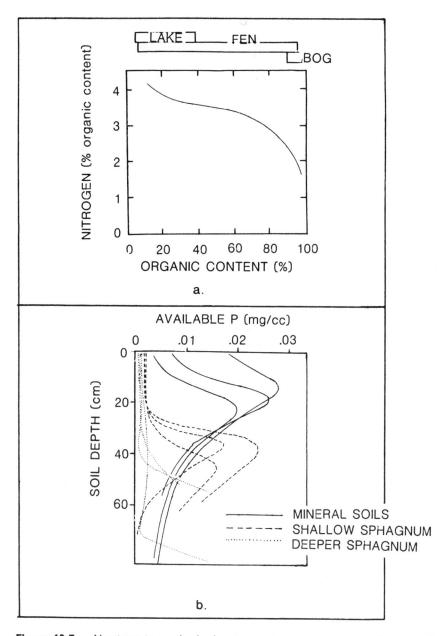

Figure 12-7.   Nutrients in peatlands showing *a.* nitrogen content as a function of organic content *(from Gorham, 1967, p. 32)* and *b.* available phosphorus as a function of depth for mineral soils and Sphagnum soil *(from Heilman, 1968, p. 334; Copyright © 1968 by the Ecological Society of America, reprinted with permission).*

Vegetation

Bogs can be simple sphagnum moss peatlands, sphagnum-sedge peatlands, sphagnum-shrub peatlands, bog forests, or any number or combination of acidophilic plants. Mosses, primarily those of the genus *Sphagnum* are the most important peat-building plants in bogs throughout their geographical range. Sphagnum grows in cushionlike spongy mats; its water content is high, the water held by capillary action. Sphagnum grows actively only in the surface layers (at about 3.5 to 10 cm annually), while the lower layers die off and convert to peat (Walter, 1973).

A list of some of the major bog plants in North America is given in Table 12-3. Sphagnum often grows in association with cotton grass *(Eriophorum vaginatum)*, various sedges *(Carex* spp.), and certain shrubs such as heather *(Calluna vulgaris)*, leatherleaf *(Chamaedaphne calyculata)*, cranberry and blueberry (*Vaccinium* spp.), and Labrador tea *(Ledum palustre)*. Trees such as pine *(Pinus sylvestris)*, crowberry (*Empetrum* spp.), spruce (*Picea* spp.), and tamarack (*Larix* spp.) are often found in bogs as stunted individuals that may be scarcely 1 m high yet several hundred years old (Ruttner, 1963; Malmer, 1975).

Heinselman (1970) described seven vegetation associations in the Lake Agassiz peatlands of northern Minnesota that are typical of many of those

Table 12-3. Common Vegetation in Selected North American Peatlands

Peatland (Author)	Ground Cover/ Herbaceous Plants	Shrubs	Trees
Rich Fen (Michigan) (Richardson et al., 1978)	*Carex* spp. (sedge)	*Salix* sp. (willow) *Chamaedaphne calyculata* (leatherleaf) *Betula pumila* (bog birch)	—
Bog Swamp Forest (Minnesota) (Heinselman, 1970)	*Sphagnum* spp.	*C. calyculata* (leatherleaf) *B. pumila* (bog birch)	*Larix* (tamarack)
Bog Swamp (Minnesota)[a] (Heinselman, 1970)	*Sphagnum* spp.	*C. calyculata* (leatherleaf) *Kalmia* spp. (laurel) *Ledum palustre* (Labrador tea)	*Picea mariana* (black spruce)

[a]Widespread in North America

in North America (Fig. 12-8). These occur in an intricate mosaic across the landscape, reflecting the topography, chemistry, and previous history of the site, which slopes from southeast to northwest as shown in cross section in Figure 12-4. The vegetation zones correspond closely to the underlying peat and to the present nutrient status of the site. The major zones are:

1. Rich swamp forest—These forested wetlands form narrow bands in very wet sites around the perimeter of peatlands. The canopy is dominated by northern red cedar *(Thuja occidentalis)*, but also some species of ash (*Fraxinus* spp.), tamarack, and spruce. A shrub layer of alder, *Alnus rugosa,* is often present, as are hummocks of sphagnum moss.

2. Poor swamp forest—These swamps, occurring downslope of the rich swamp forests, are nutrient-poor ecosystems and are the most common peatland in the Lake Agassiz region. Tamarack is usually the dominant canopy tree, with bog birch *(Betula pumila)* and leatherleaf in the understory and sphagnum forming 0.3- to 0.6-m-high hummocks.

3. Cedar string bog and fen complex—This is similar to type 2 except that tree-sedge fens alternate with cedar *(Thuja occidentalis)* on the bog ridges (Stränge) and treeless sedge (mostly *Carex*) hollows (Flarks) between the ridges.

4. Larch string bog and fen—In this type of string bog, close to Types 2 and 3, tamarack *(Larix)* dominates the bog ridges.

5. Black spruce-feathermoss forest—This type is a mature spruce forest with a carpet of feather moss *(Pleurozium)* and other mosses. The trees are tall, dense, and even-aged. This peatland occurs near the margins of ombrotrophic bogs and generally does not have standing water.

6. Sphagnum-black spruce-leatherleaf bog forest—This is a widespread wetland type in northern North America. Stunted black spruce is the only tree, with a heavy shrub layer of leatherleaf, laurel (*Kalmia* spp.), and Labrador tea growing in large "pillows" of sphagnum between spruce patches. This association is found in convex relief and is isolated from mineral-bearing water.

7. Sphagnum-leatherleaf-Kalmia-spruce heath—A continuous blanket of sphagnum moss is the most conspicuous feature with a low shrub layer and stunted trees (usually black spruce) on 5%-10% of the area. Types 6 and 7 occur in the lower end of the Figure 12-4 transect, on a raised bog.

In the Moore and Bellamy (1974) classification presented earlier in the chapter, Zones 1 through 4 would be classified as minerotrophic, Zone 5 as transitional, Zone 6 as semi-ombrotrophic, and Zone 7 as ombrotrophic.

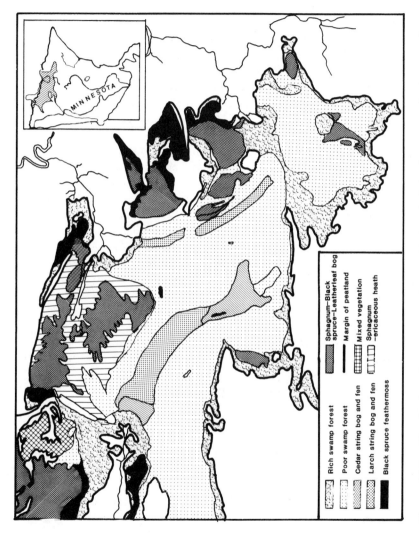

Figure 12-8. Distribution of seven vegetation associations in Lake Agassiz peatlands in northern Minnesota. *(After Heinselman, 1970, p. 243)*

Rich swamp forest

Poor swamp forest

Cedar string bog and fen

Larch string bog and fen

Black spruce feathermoss

Sphagnum–Black spruce–Leatherleaf bog

Margin of peatland

Mixed vegetation

Sphagnum –ericaceous heath

MINNESOTA

Vegetation Adaptations

The vegetation in bogs and peatlands is adapted to several problems of its physical and chemical environment (Walter, 1973; Moore and Bellamy, 1974). Some of the conditions for which adaptations are necessary in peatlands include:

Waterlogging—Many bog plants, in common with wetland vegetation in general, have anatomical and morphological adaptation to waterlogged anaerobic environments. These include (1) the development of large intercellular spaces (aerenchyma or lacunae) for oxygen supply, (2) reduced oxygen consumption, and (3) oxygen leakage from the roots to produce a locally aerobic root environment. These adaptations were discussed in chapter 6.

Nutrient deficiency—Many bog plants have adaptations to the low nutrient supply that enable them to conserve and accumulate nutrients. Sphagnum moss possesses cation exchange properties that, in addition to lowering the pH of its immediate surroundings, provide mineral nutrition for the plant. Some bog plants, notably cotton grass (*Eriophorum* spp.), translocate nutrients back to perennating organs prior to litter fall in autumn to provide nutrient reserves for the following year's growth and seedling establishment. The roots of other bog plants penetrate deep into peat zones to bring nutrients to the surface. Bog litter has been demonstrated to release potassium and phosphorus, often the most limiting nutrients, more rapidly than other nutrients, an adaptation to keep these nutrients in the upper layers of peat (Moore and Bellamy, 1974).

Another adaptation to nutrient deficiency in bogs is the ability of carnivorous plants to trap and digest insects. This special feature is seen in several unique insectivorous bog plants, including the pitcher plant (*Sarracenia* spp.) and sundew (*Drosera* spp.). Some bog plants also carry out symbiotic nitrogen fixation. The bog myrtle *(Myrica gale)* and the alder develop root nodules characteristic of nitrogen fixers and have been shown to fix atmospheric nitrogen in bog environments.

Overgrowth by peat mosses—Many flowering plants are faced with the additional problem of being overgrown by peat mosses as the mosses grow in depth and area covered. Adapting plants must raise their shoot bases by elongating their rhizomes or by developing adventitious roots. Trees such as pine, birch, and spruce are often severely stunted due to the moss growth and poor substrate; they grow better on bogs where vertical growth of moss has ceased.

Consumers

The populations of animals in bogs are generally low due to the low productivity and the unpalatability of bog vegetation. Dominant herbivores include many insects such as the psyllid and tipulid flies (as in English blanket bogs). Selective herbivores include red grouse, hares, bog lemmings, and in some cases, sheep. Predators include weasels, owls, frogs, shrews, pipits (Europe), warblers (North America), and invertebrates such as spiders and ground beetles (Smith, 1980). Ruttner (1963, p. 222), discussing the aquatic fauna associated with bog waters, states that "the bog fauna is more strikingly characterized by the lack or inconspicuousness of entire groups, for example the ostracods, the Hydracarina, . . . the mollusks, and a number of groups of insects . . . ." Large animals such as deer, elk, bear, caribou, and bison are often found in or adjacent to bog ecosystems, particularly in eastern Europe, Siberia, and northern Canada.

ECOSYSTEM FUNCTION

The dynamics of the bog ecosystem reflect the realities of the harsh physical environment and the scarcity of mineral nutrients. These conditions result in several major features of bogs:

1. Bogs are systems of low primary productivity, often with sphagnum mosses dominating and other vegetation stunted in growth.
2. Bogs are peat producers with rates of accumulation controlled by a combination of complex hydrologic, chemical, and topographic factors.
3. Bogs have developed several unique pathways to obtain, conserve, and recycle nutrients.

Primary Productivity

Bogs and fens are less productive than most other wetland types and are generally less productive than the climatic terrestrial ecosystems in their region. Moore and Bellamy (1974) described the productivity of a forested sphagnum bog as about half that of a coniferous forest and a little more than a third that of a deciduous forest. Table 12-4 summarizes many measurements and ranges of peatland biomass and productivity. According to Pjavchenko (1982), forested peatlands produce a general range of from 260 to 400 g organic matter/$m^2 \cdot$ yr, with the low value that of an ombrotrophic bog and the high value for a minerotrophic fen. Malmer (1975) cited a typical range of from 400 to 500 g/$m^2 \cdot$ yr for nonforested raised (ombrotrophic) bogs in western Europe. In contrast, Lieth (1975) estimated the net primary productivity in the boreal forest to average 500 g/$m^2 \cdot$ yr and that in the temperate forest to average 1,000 g/$m^2 \cdot$ yr. The estimate for boreal forests probably includes bog forests as well as upland forests.

The measurement of the growth or primary productivity of sphagnum mosses presents special problems not encountered in productivity measure-

**Table 12-4. Biomass and Net Primary Productivity of
Selected Northern Bogs and Other Peatlands**

Location	Type of Peatland	Living Biomass, g dry wt/m²	Net Primary Productivity, g dry wt/m² · yr	Reference
Europe				
Western Europe	General nonwooded raised bog	1,200	400-500	Malmer (1975)
Western Europe	Forested raised bog	3,700	340	Moore and Bellamy (1974)
U.S.S.R.	Eutrophic (minerotrophic) forest bog	9,700-11,000	400	Pjavchenko (1982)
	Mestotrophic (transition) forest bog	4,500-8,900	350	Pjavchenko (1982)
	Oligotrophic (ombrotrophic) forest bog	2,200-3,600	260	Pjavchenko (1982)
U.S.S.R.	Mesotrophic (transition) *Pinus-Sphagnum* bog	8,500	393	Bazilevich and Tishkov (1982)
England	Blanket bog (*Calluna-Eriophorum-Sphagnum*)		659 ± 53[a]	Forrest and Smith (1975)
England	Blanket bog		635	Heal, Jones, and Whittaker (1975)
Ireland	Blanket bog		316	Doyle (1973)
North America				
Michigan	Rich fen (*Chamaedaphne-Betula*)		341[b]	Richardson et al. (1976)
Minnesota	Forested peatland	15,941	1,014[b]	Reiners (1972)
	Fen forest	9,808	651[b]	Reiners (1972)
Manitoba	Peatland bog	—	1,943	Reader and Stewart (1972)
General	Northern bog marshes (Does not include bog forests or ombrotrophic bogs)	Aboveground	101-1,026[c]	Reader (1978)
		Belowground	141-513[d]	Reader (1978)

[a]Mean ± std. deviation for seven sites
[b]Aboveground only
[c]Range for nine bog marshes
[d]Range for five bog marshes

ments of other plants (Clymo, 1970; Moore and Bellamy, 1974). The upper stems of the plant elongate, while the lower portions gradually die off, become litter, and eventually form peat. It is difficult to measure the sloughing off of dead material to the litter. It is equally hard to measure the biomass of the plant at any one time because it is difficult to separate the living and dead material of the peat. The following two methods for measuring sphagnum growth give comparable results: (1) the use of "innate" time markers such as certain anatomical or morphological features of the moss, and (2) the direct measurement of changes in weight.

Growth rates for sphagnum determined by these two techniques generally fall in the range of from 300 to 800 g/m² · yr (Moore and Bellamy, 1974).

Decomposition and Peat Formation

The accumulation of peat in bogs is determined by the production of litter (from primary production) and the destruction of organic matter (decomposition). As with the primary production, the rate of decomposition in peat bogs is generally low due to (1) Waterlogged conditions, (2) Low temperatures, and (3) Acid conditions (Moore and Bellamy, 1974). Besides leading to peat accumulation, slow decomposition also leads to slower nutrient recycling in an already nutrient-limited system.

A pattern of sphagnum decomposition with depth in a bog in southern England is shown in Figure 12-9. The decomposition rate is highest near the surface where aerobic conditions exist. By 20 centimeters depth, the rate is about one-fifth of that at the surface. This is due to the anaerobic conditions as illustrated by the sulfide production curve (also in Fig. 12-9). Clymo (1965) attributes the bulk of the organic decomposition that does occur in peat bogs to microorganisms, although the total numbers of bacteria in these wetland soils are much less than in those aerated soils (Moore and Bellamy, 1974). As pH decreases, the fungal component of the decomposer food web becomes more important relative to bacterial populations.

Chamie and Richardson (1978) described the rates of decomposition of plant material from a rich fen in central Michigan. The decay rates and half-lives of various plant materials from that study are summarized on Table 12-5. The weight losses for leaves of sedge, willow, and birch were about 26%-36% after one year, while leatherleaf leaves and stems decomposed more slowly, with a 6%-16% loss in one year. This decomposition rate is one-half to one-quarter the rates found either in more aerobic environments or at lower latitudes.

The accumulation rate of peat in bogs and fens is generally thought to be between 20 and 80 cm per 1,000 years in European bogs (Moore and Bellamy, 1974), although Cameron (1970) gives a range of from 100 to 200 cm per 1,000 years for North American bogs and Nichols (1983) reports an accumu-

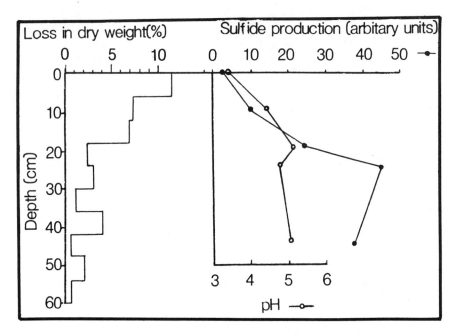

Figure 12-9. Patterns of Sphagnum decomposition, sulfide production, and pH with depth in English bog. Decomposition is during a 103-day period. *(After Clymo, 1965, p. 753)*

Table 12-5. Decomposition Rates for Various Plant Parts from Michigan Peatland[a]

Peatland Species	Decay Coefficient (k), yr^{-1}	Half-life, yr
Carex spp.		
Leaves	0.45	1.6
Salix spp.		
Leaves	0.46	1.5
Small stems	0.25	2.8
Large stems	0.18	3.8
Betula pumila (bog birch)		
Leaves	0.46	1.5
Small stems	0.15	4.7
Large stems	0.08	8.4
Chamaedaphne (leatherleaf)		
Leaves	0.17	4.1
Small stems	0.09	7.5
Large stems	0.09	7.5

Source: Based on data from Chamie and Richardson (1978), p. 122-123

[a]Assumes $Q/Q_o = e^{-kt}$; litterbags were used and placed in wetland.

**Table 12-6. Rates of Peat Growth (Depth) for Four Bogs in
Southern Pennines Region, U.K., for Different Climatic Periods**

Climatic Period	Age of Peat, years	Growth Rate, cm/1,000 yr
Sub-Atlantic	2,500	48–96
Sub-Boreal	5,000	12–48
Atlantic	7,200	14–36
Boreal	8,900	111

Source: After Durno (1961), pp. 347 and 350

lation rate for peat of 150-200 cm/1,000 years in warm, highly productive
sites. Malmer (1975) described a vertical growth rate of 50-100 cm/1,000 yr
as typical for western Europe; assuming an average density of peat of
50 mg/ml, this rate is equivalent to a peat production rate of 25-50 g/m^2 · yr.
This range compares reasonably well with the accumulation rate of
86 g/m^2 · yr measured for a transition forested bog in the USSR by Bazilevich
and Tishkov (1982) (see Energy Flow section). In comparison, Hemond
(1980) estimated a rapid accumulation rate for Thoreau's Bog, Massachusetts, of 430 cm/1,000 yr or 180 g/m^2 · yr.

Durno (1961) compared the rates of peat growth in vertical sections
of peat in England and related them to climatic periods (Table 12-6). Growth of
peat was rapid (110 cm/1,000 yr) during the Boreal Period but it slowed
down considerably in the wetter Atlantic climate (14-36 cm/1,000 yr). This
would not be expected, except that at this time the peatland was transform-
ing from a minerotrophic fen to a ombrotrophic bog; the slower peat accumulation was thus due to low productivity during the bog stage. The surface
layer, produced in the cool, moist Sub-Atlantic Period, had a higher rate of
peat accumulation (48-96 cm/1,000 yr), but Durno (1961) suggested that this
layer may yet be subjected to compression.

Energy Flow

Bog ecosystems have energy flow patterns similar to those in many other
wetlands in that the wetness and harsh chemical conditions lead to impaired
primary productivity (input) and impaired decomposition (output). These
patterns, however, are different from those in most aquatic or terrestrial
ecosystems found in the same north temperate region. The net result is that
the inputs, though low, generally exceed the outputs and there is a buildup
of peat.

Few detailed studies of energy flow have been developed for bog ecosystems. An exception, Heal, Jones, and Whittaker (1975), described the energy
flows and storages of an English blanket bog. Net primary productivity
(635 g/m^2 · yr) was due primarily to sphagnum mosses (300 g/m^2 · yr). Only
1% of the productivity was consumed in the grazing food web, primarily by

psyllid and tipulid flies. The remainder entered the detrital food web, where about 85% was decomposed by microflora and 10% accumulated beneath the water table. This system showed a relatively low amount of peat buildup for the period of measurement.

Bazilivich and Tishkov (1982) presented a detailed breakdown of energy flow through a mesotrophic (transition) bog in the European USSR. The bog is a sphagnum-pine community with shrubs such as blueberry. The total energy stored in the bog was estimated to be in excess of 137 kg/m² dry organic matter, with dead organic matter (to a depth of 0.6 m of peat) accounting for 94% of the storage. Living biomass was 8.5 kg/m², or about 6% of the organic storage. Gross primary productivity was 987 g/m² · yr, with about 60% consumed by plant respiration, leaving 393 g/m² · yr as net primary productivity (Table 12-7). The distribution of the net primary pro-

Table 12-7. Balance of Energy Inputs and Outputs of Mesotrophic Bog in the U.S.S.R.

Description of Energy Flow	*Energy Flow,* $g/m^2 \cdot yr$	*Percent of Total Input*
Inputs		
Gross primary productivity	987	95.9
Precipitation and runoff	34	3.3
Subsurface flow	6	0.6
Biotic input from other ecosystems	2	0.2
Total inputs	1,029	100.0
Outputs		
Plant respiration	594	57.7
Phytophage respiration	6	0.6
Carnivore respiration	1	0.1
Decomposer respiration	284	27.6
Consumption from other ecosystems	4	0.4
Abiotic oxidation	15	1.5
Subsurface outflows	5.5	0.5
Surface outflows	19.5	1.9
Total outputs	929	90.3
Accumulation		
Peat formation	86	8.3
Growth retention	14	1.4
Total accumulation	100	9.7

Source: Based on data from Bazilevich and Tishkov (1982), pp. 268 and 270

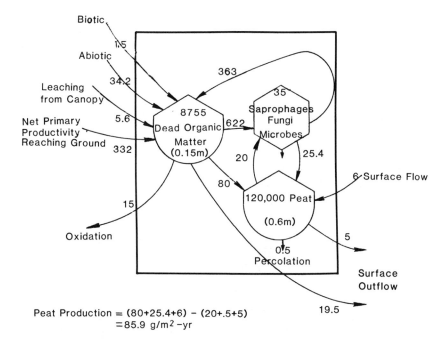

Figure 12-10. Detritus-peat production in mesotrophic bog in USSR. Flows are in g organic matter/m² • yr; storages are in g organic matter/m². *(Based on data from Bazilevich and Tishkov, 1982)*

duction came from trees (39%), algae (28%), shrubs (21%), mosses and lichens (9%), and grasses (3%). The net primary productivity, combined with other abiotic and biotic energy flows (42 g/m² · yr), was consumed primarily by decomposers (284 g/m² · yr), with much less consumed in grazing food webs (7 g/m² · yr). The decomposition of detritus and peat for this bog ecosystem is illustrated in Figure 12-10. Note the net accumulation of 86 g/m² · yr of peat. Losses other than biotic decomposition, which accounted for most of the loss of organic matter, were chemical oxidation (15 g/m² · yr) and surface and subsurface flows (25 g/m² · yr).

Nutrient Budgets

Complete nutrient budgets for peatlands, particularly for ombrotrophic bogs, are rare in the literature. Crisp (1966) developed an overall nutrient budget for nitrogen, phosphorus, sodium, potassium, and calcium for a blanket bog-dominated watershed in the Pennines, England (Table 12-8).

Table 12-8. Nutrient Budget for Blanket Bog Watershed in Pennines Region of England

Flow	Nutrient Flow, kg/ha · yr				
	Na	*K*	*Ca*	*P*	*N*
Input by precipitation	25.54	3.07	8.98	0.69	8.20
Output					
Sale of sheep	0.002	0.005	0.019	0.012	0.053
Dissolved matter in stream	45.27	8.97	53.81	0.39	2.94
Drift of fauna in stream	0.001	0.005	0.001	0.005	0.057
Erosion of peat in stream	0.28	2.06	4.83	0.45	14.63
Total Output	45.44	11.04	58.66	0.86	17.68
Net Loss	20.01	7.97	49.68	0.15	9.48

Source: Crisp (1966), as presented by Moore and Bellamy (1974), p. 112. Copyright ©1976 by Springer-Verlag, reprinted with permission.

The only input considered is precipitation, which has relatively high concentrations of dissolved materials due to the proximity of the bog to the sea. Nevertheless, the author found that the outputs of nutrients greatly exceeded the inputs from precipitation. This was partially due to the omission of any estimations of input due to weathering of parent rock in the watershed. The budget does illustrate that the erosion of peat results in a major loss of nitrogen, exceeding the input of nitrogen by precipitation. The erosional losses of phosphorus, calcium, and potassium are 50% or more of the input by precipitation. Major outputs of calcium, sodium, and potassium in dissolved form illustrate that this budget is incomplete without weathering inputs included. Sheep grazing and harvesting and stream drift of organisms were insignificant losses from the system.

Richardson et al. (1978) presented nutrient budgets of a fen in central Michigan (Fig. 12-11). The peat layer, measured to only 20 cm, represented over 97% of nutrient storage in the fen. Uptake of nutrients and litter fall were generally very low; lower, for example, than in the blanket bog previously described (Table 12-8). This is reflected in extremely low productivity. Many investigators (e.g., Malmer, 1962; Small, 1972; Tilton, 1977) have found that nutrient content, and hence uptake rates, are lower in ombrotrophic bogs than in fens. The results of this Michigan study are therefore not representative of a typical fen. The budgets, however, show a general peatland phenomenon: The available nutrients are a small percentage of the total nutrients stored in the peat.

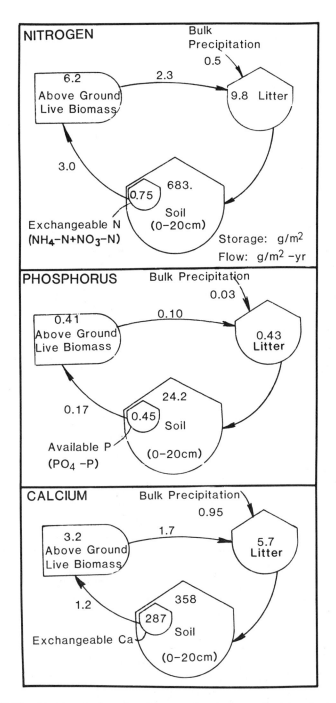

Figure 12-11. Nutrient budgets for nitrogen, phosphorus, and calcium for leatherleaf bog birch fen in Michigan. *(After Richardson et al., 1978, p. 230)*

ECOSYSTEM MODELS

Relatively few ecosystem models have been developed for northern peat-lands, despite the abundance of research on these ecosystems. Conceptual models, such as those by Heal, Jones, and Whittaker (1975) for an English blanket bog and Bazilivich and Tishkov (1982) for a transition bog in the USSR have been useful for understanding peatland dynamics.

Logofet and Alexandrov (1984) simulated carbon flux through a simple four-compartment model (plants, animals, fungi and bacteria, and litter) of a dwarf shrub-sphagnum mesotrophic bog in the USSR. Their simulation suggested that the assimilated organic matter is lost almost entirely through plant (62%) and microorganism (26%) respiration. About 7.4% of assimilated organic matter and 20% of allochthonous material was deposited as peat. Organic material had a total residence time of about 26 years in the system (8.5 years in plant material and 17 in other compartments). These slow turnover rates are in sharp contrast with those in most temperate wetlands.

Simulation models of northern peatlands were a part of a long-range study in central Michigan to investigate the feasibility of using wetlands for dis-posal of treated sewage (Kadlec and Tilton, 1979). The specific site is the rich fen ecosystem described in Table 12-3 and Figure 12-11. Models were designed to (1) give long-term predictions on the ability of the wetland to maintain its structural and functional integrity and (2) design an optimal disposal scheme for the wastewater (Dixon, 1974). A large-scale simulation model, analogous to chemical process models used by chemical engineers, was developed as part of that study (Parker and Kadlec, 1974). That model, the Routine for Executing Biological Unit Simulations (REBUS), divided the marsh into spatial blocks, each with homogeneous chemical and biologi-cal units. Dixon (1974) and Dixon and Kadlec (1975) described the modeling of vascular plants, standing dead material, litter, and soil for the biological units. Preliminary simulations indicated significant accumulation of litter and organic soil when wastewater was added to the wetland. Parker (1974) simulated the biological units and water level for the entire REBUS model, thereby incorporating spatial patterns into the wetland model. Gupta (1977) developed a simulation model, REBUS II, to both simulate and optimize the amount of water and nutrients that the Michigan marsh could absorb. More models of these types are needed for peatlands of North America and northern Europe to take advantage of the data available for many spe-cific sites.

There has been a fair amount of modeling of northern tundra (see Mitsch et al., 1982 for details), which includes peatlands, as part of the International Biological Programme's Tundra Biome studies (Miller and Tieszen, 1972; Miller, Collier, and Bunnell, 1975; Miller, Stoner, and Tieszen, 1976). The ABISKO models (Bunnell and Dowding, 1974; Bunnell and Scoullar, 1975) emphasized carbon fluxes among plant, animal, and abiotic compartments in tundra ecosystems. Models have also been developed to describe the effects of oil spills on tundra ecosystems (McKay et al., 1975; Dauffenbach, Atlas and Mitsch, 1981).

SUMMARY

Bogs and fens are peatlands distributed primarily in the cool boreal zones of the world where excess moisture is abundant. While several types of peatlands are identifiable, classification according to hydrologic and chemical conditions usually defines three types of peatland: (1) minerotrophic (true fens), (2) ombrotrophic (raised bogs), and (3) transition (poor fens). Ombrotrophic bogs are isolated from mineral-bearing groundwater and thus display lower pH, lower nutrients, lower minerals, and more dominance by mosses than do minerotrophic fens. Bogs can be formed in several ways, originating from either aquatic systems, as in flow-through succession or quaking bogs; or from terrestrial systems, as with blanket bogs. In bogs the low nutrients and low pH lead to low primary productivity, slow decomposition, adaptive nutrient cycling pathways, and peat accumulation. Several conceptual energy and nutrient flow models have been developed for peatlands, and several mathematical models have been used for simulating the dynamics of northern peatlands, particularly fens and tundra.

SOUTHERN DEEPWATER SWAMP

chapter 13

SOUTHERN DEEPWATER SWAMPS

One of the most enchanting of all the wetland environments in the United States is the southern freshwater forested swamp. The enchantment comes from the stately and venerable cypress trees, the fronds of Spanish moss hanging from the branches, the stillness of the tea-colored water below, and the quietness pierced only by the sound of a passing heron or a croaking tree frog. A more forbidding view of a forested swamp is engendered by the presence of mosquitoes, cottonmouth moccasins, floating logs, and submerged obstructions, and the ease with which one can get lost in an environment that looks the same in every direction.

The freshwater deep swamp has been defined by Penfound (1952, p. 416) as having "fresh water, woody communities with water throughout most or all of the growing season." In the southeastern United States, the cypress (*Taxodium* sp.) swamp is the major deepwater forested wetland and is characterized by bald cypress-water tupelo and pond cypress-black gum communities. This chapter will emphasize those forested wetlands with permanent or near-permanent standing water. These include cypress domes, which are often flooded with 0.3 m of water for most of the year, and alluvial cypress swamps, which may be permanently flooded with 1 to 2 m of water. Forested wetlands on floodplains that receive only seasonal pulses of flooding are discussed in chapter 14. The reader is referred to an excellent tome called *Cypress Swamps* (Ewel and Odum, 1984) for more details about these ecosystems.

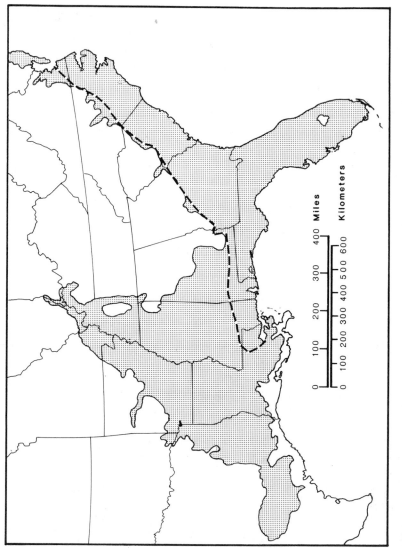

Figure 13-1. Distribution of bald cypress (*Taxodium distichum*) in southeastern United States. Dotted line indicates northern extent of pond cypress (*Taxodium distichum var nutans*). (After Little, 1971, Map 84-E)

GEOGRAPHICAL EXTENT

The distribution of bald cypress and pond cypress (Fig. 13-1), both deciduous conifers, corresponds closely to the geographical extent of deepwater swamps discussed in this chapter. Bald cypress (*Taxodium distichum* L. Rich) swamps are found as far north as southern Illinois in the Mississippi River floodplain and southern New Jersey along the Atlantic Coastal Plain. Pond cypress (*Taxodium distichum* var. *nutans* (Ait.) Sweet), described variously as either a different species or a subspecies of bald cypress, has a much more limited range than bald cypress and is found primarily in Florida and southern Georgia; it is not present along the Mississippi River floodplain except in southeastern Louisiana. One of the main features that distinguishes between pond and bald cypress is the leaf structure. Bald cypress has needles that spread from a twig in a flat plane, while pond cypress needles are appressed to the twig (C. A. Brown, 1984; Ewel and Odum, 1984). Both species are intolerant of salt and are found only in freshwater areas. Pond cypress is limited to sites that are poor in nutrients and relatively isolated from the effects of river flooding or large inflows of nutrients. Another species indicative of the deepwater swamp is the water tupelo (*Nyssa aquatica* L.), which has a range similar to that of bald cypress along the Atlantic Coastal Plain and the Mississippi River, although it is generally absent from Florida except for the western peninsula. Water tupelo occurs in pure stands or mixed with bald cypress in floodplain swamps.

GEOMORPHOLOGY AND HYDROLOGY

Southern cypress-tupelo swamps occur under a variety of geologic and hydrologic conditions, ranging from extremely nutrient-poor dwarf cypress communities of southern Florida to rich floodplain swamps along many tributaries of the lower Mississippi River basin. A useful classification of deepwater swamps, according to geological and hydrological conditions, was developed by Wharton et al. (1976). That system includes the following types:

1. Still water cypress domes
2. Dwarf cypress swamps
3. Lake-edge swamps
4. Slow flowing cypress strands
5. Alluvial river swamps

The physical features and flow conditions of these wetlands are summarized in Figure 13-2 and are described below.

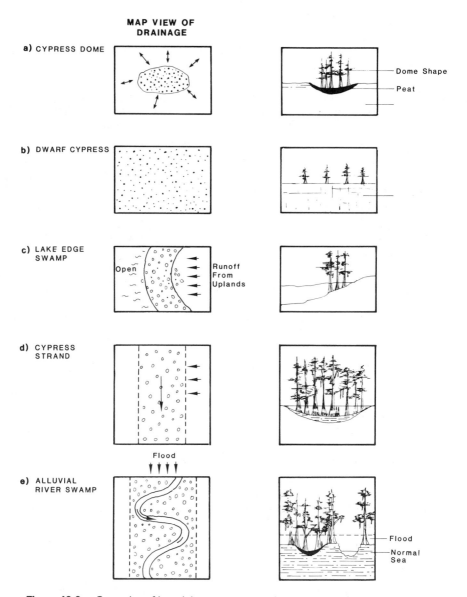

Figure 13-2.   General profile and drainage pattern of major types of deepwater wetlands showing *a*. cypress dome, *b*. dwaft cypress, *c*. lake-edge swamp, *d*. cypress strand, and *e*. alluvial river swamp. *(After H. T. Odum, 1982, p. 65)*

Still Water Cypress Domes

Cypress domes (sometimes called cypress ponds or cypress heads) are poorly drained to permanently wet depressions dominated by pond cypress. They are generally small in size, usually 1 to 10 hectares, and are numerous in the upland pine flatwoods of Florida and southern Georgia. Many cypress domes are found in both sandy and clay soils and usually have several centimeters of organic matter that has accumulated in the wetland depression. These wetlands are called "domes" because of their appearance when viewed from the side—the larger trees are in the middle with smaller trees toward the edges (Fig. 13-2a). This phenomenon has been suggested to be due to deeper peat deposits in the middle of the dome, fire that is more frequent around the edges of the dome, or a gradual increase in the water level that causes the dome to "grow" from the center outward (Vernon, 1947; Kurz and Wagner, 1953). A definite reason for this profile has not been determined, nor do all domes display the characteristic shape.

A typical hydroperiod for a Florida cypress dome is shown in Figure 4-2. The wet season is in the summer and dry periods occur in the fall and spring. An example of a water budget for a Florida cypress dome is given in Figure 13-3a. The standing water in cypress domes is often dominated by rainfall and surface inflow, with little or no groundwater inflow. The cypress domes are usually underlain by an impermeable clay layer and sometimes by a *hardpan,* a layer of consolidated and relatively impermeable material. Both layers impede downward drainage, although there is often some exchange of groundwater with the surrounding upland as infiltration radiates outward from the dome rather than vertically (Heimburg, 1984). The major loss of water from the cypress dome, as shown in Figure 13-3a, is evapotranspiration. Infiltration is rapid during the dry season but relatively slow during the wet summers, when water levels surrounding the cypress dome are also high (Heimburg, 1984).

Dwarf Cypress Swamps

There are major areas in southwestern Florida, primarily in the Big Cypress Swamp and the Everglades, where pond cypress is the dominant tree but it grows stunted and scattered in a marsh (Fig. 13-2b). The trees generally do not grow over 6 to 7 m high and are more typically 3 m in height. These wetlands are called dwarf cypress or pigmy cypress swamps. The poor growing conditions are primarily due to the lack of suitable substrate overlying the bedrock limestone that is found in outcrops throughout the region. The hydroperiod includes a relatively short period of flooding as compared with other deepwater swamps, and fire often occurs. However, the cypress are rarely killed by fire due to the lack of litter accumulation and buildup of

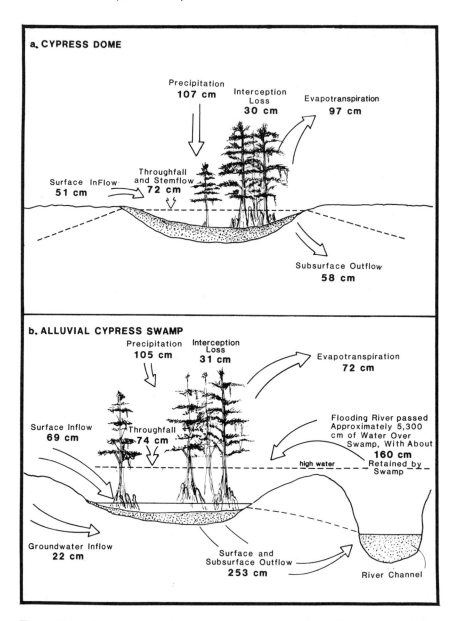

Figure 13-3.   Annual water budgets for deepwater swamps for *a*. Florida cypress dome *(based on data from Heimburg, 1984)* and *b*. southern Illinois cypress-tupelo alluvial swamp *(based on data from Mitsch, Dorge, and Wiemhoff, 1979).*

fuel. Although distinct from dwarf cypress swamps, individual small cypress trees are also found in scattered locations throughout the Florida Everglades. These trees are often grouped in clusters that have the appearance of small cypress domes.

Lake-edge Swamps

Bald cypress swamps also are found as margins around many lakes and isolated sloughs in the Southeast, ranging from Florida to southern Illinois (Fig. 13-2c). Tupelo and water-tolerant hardwoods such as ash (*Fraxinus* spp.) often grow in association with the bald cypress. A seasonally fluctuating water level is characteristic of these systems and is necessary for seedling survival. The trees in these systems receive nutrients from the lake's minerals as well as from upland runoff. The lake-edge swamp has been described as a filter that receives overland flow from the uplands and allows sediments to settle out and chemicals to adsorb onto the sediments before the water discharges into the open lake (Wharton et al., 1976). However, the importance of this filtering function has not been adequately investigated.

Slow-flowing Cypress Strands

A cypress strand is "a diffuse freshwater stream flowing through a shallow forested depression on a gently sloping plain" (Wharton et al., 1976, p. 50). Cypress strands (Fig. 13-2d) are found primarily in south Florida, where the topography is slight, and rivers are replaced by slow-flowing strands with little erosive power. The substrate is primarily sand, with some mixture of limestone and remnants of shell beds. Peat deposits are shallow on higher ground and deeper in the depressions. The hydroperiod has a seasonal wet and dry cycle, with the deeper peat deposits usually retaining moisture even in extremely dry conditions. Much is known about south Florida strands from studies of Fakahatchee Strand by Carter et al. (1973) and Corkscrew Swamp by Duever, Carlson, and Riopelle (1975; 1984).

Alluvial River Swamps

The broad alluvial floodplains of southeastern rivers and creeks support a vast array of forested wetlands, some of which are permanently flooded deepwater swamps (Fig. 13-2e). (Those forested wetlands that are temporarily flooded are described in chapter 14.) Alluvial river swamps, usually dominated by bald cypress and/or water tupelo, are confined to permanently flooded depressions on floodplains such as abandoned river channels *(oxbows)* or elongated swamps that usually parallel the river *(sloughs)*. These alluvial wetlands sometimes are called *outliers* or *backswamps,* names that distinguish them from the drier surrounding bottomlands and indicate their hydrologic isolation from the river except during the flooding season. The water budget for a typical alluvial bald cypress-water tupelo swamp is shown in Figure 13-3*b*. The backswamps are noted for a seasonal pulse of flooding that brings in water and nutrient-rich sediments. Alluvial river swamps are continuously or almost continuously flooded, with the hydrologic inflows dominated by runoff from the surrounding uplands and by overflow from the flooding rivers.

CHEMISTRY

Wide ranges of acidity, dissolved substances, and nutrients are found in the waters of deepwater swamps (Table 13-1). Several facts should be noted from this wide range of water quality:

1. Deepwater swamps do not necessarily have acid water.
2. Nutrient conditions vary from nutrient-poor conditions in rainwater-fed swamps to nutrient-rich conditions in alluvial river swamps.
3. An alluvial river swamp often has water quality very different from that of the adjacent river.

pH and Dissolved Materials

Many deepwater wetlands, particularly alluvial river swamps, are "open" to river flooding and other inputs of neutral and generally well-mineralized waters. The pH of many alluvial swamps in the Southeast is 6 to 7, and there are high levels of dissolved ions (Table 13-1). Cypress domes, on the other hand, are fed primarily by rainwater and have acidic waters, usually in the pH range of 3.5 to 5.0, due to humic acids produced within the swamp. The colloidal humic substances also contribute to the tea-colored or "blackwater" appearance of many acidic cypress domes. The buffering capacity of the water in the cypress domes is low, with little or no alkalinity and low concentrations of dissolved ions.

Nutrients

Southern swamps are found in a wide range of nutrient conditions. This contrast is noted particularly in the conductivity readings in Table 13-1. It ranges from 60 μmhos/cm in cypress domes to 200 to 400 μmhos/cm in alluvial cypress swamps. Cypress domes and dwarf cypress swamps are low in nutrients because of their relative hydrologic isolation. For example, average phosphorus levels of only 0.05–0.24 mg P/1 in cypress domes and 0.01 mg P/1 in a scrub cypress swamp were observed in Florida by Brown (1981). Mitsch

Table 13-1. Water Chemistry in Selected Deepwater Swamps[a]

	North-Central Florida Cypress Dome[b]	Louisiana Bayou Swamp[c]	Louisiana Atchafalaya Basin[d]	Southern Illinois Cypress-Tupelo Swamp[e]	Western Kentucky Cypress Slough[f]
pH	4.51 ± 0.36 (51)	—	6.4-8.4	5.8-6.5 (4)	6.6-7.2 (8)
Conductivity, μmhos/cm	60 ± 17 (41)	—	—	51-240 (9)	360-550 (8)
Alkalinity, mg CaCo$_3$/l	1.8 ± 2.9 (13)	—	38-179	12-84 (9)	—
Na$^+$, mg/l	4.95 ± 1.60 (38)	—	—	0.7-7.8 (7)	26.5-43.6 (4)
K$^+$, mg/l	0.34 ± 0.24 (38)	—	—	1.0-7.0 (7)	3.1-4.0 (4)
Mg^{++}, mg/l	1.37 ± 0.59 (39)	—	—	1.0-4.3 (7)	7-52 (4)
Ca^{++}, mg/l	2.87 ± 0.99 (39)	—	—	2.3-10.6 (7)	—
SO$_4^=$, mg/l	2.6 ± 2.7 (25)	—	—	0.5-4 (4)	9.2-38.6 (9)
Dissolved oxygen, mg/l	2.0 ± 1.8 (21)	—	1.8-9.9	0.9-4.0 (5)	5.8-10.9 (8)
Turbidity, NTU	2.8 ± 8.7 (34)	—	—	23-690 (8)	0.9-29 (9)
Color, mg Pt/l	456 ± 162 (43)	—	—	—	—
Total organic C, mg/l	40 ± 13 (32)	—	3.3-31.6	—	—
NO$_3$-N, mg N/l	0.08 ± 0.19 (63)	0.01-0.13 (24)	0.03-1.19	<.01 (6)	—
NH$_3$-N, mg N/l	0.14 ± 0.19 (63)	0.01-0.62 (24)	0.02-1.71	0.10-4.1 (6)	—
Total N, mg N/l	1.6 ± 1.3 (62)	0.58-1.82 (23)	0.47-9.70	0.60-4.7 (6)	—
ortho-P, mg P/l	0.07 ± 0.11 (61)	0.05-0.44 (24)	0.01-0.24	0.06-0.28 (9)	0.001-0.09 (20)
Total P, mg P/l	0.18 ± 0.38 (63)	0.15-0.66 (24)	0.08-0.56	0.17-0.47 (9)	0.01-0.17 (13)

[a]Numbers given as range (number of samples) except as otherwise noted
[b]Dierberg and Brezonik, 1984 average ± standard deviation
[c]Kemp and Day, 1984 range for three swamp sites
[d]Hern, Lambou, and Butch, 1980
[e]Mitsch, Dorge, and Weimhoff, 1977
[f]Hill, 1983 and unpublished data

325

**Table 13-2. Water Chemistry Averages and Ranges for Alluvial
Bald Cypress-Tupelo Swamp and Adjacent River in Southern Illinois**

Parameter	Swamp Water			River Water		
	n^a	$\overline{X}^b$	$Flood^c$	n^a	$\overline{X}^b$	$Flood^c$
Dissólved oxygen, mg/1	5	2.2	—	8	8.9	—
pH	4	6.1	—	11	7.3	—
Alkalinity, mg CaCO$_3$/1	9	31	12	27	99	32-52
Ortho-Phosphate, mg P/1	9	0.16	0.16	27	0.15	0.05-0.14
Total soluble P, mg P/1	9	0.19	—	25	0.20	—
Total P, mg P/1	10	0.47	1.81	28	0.53	0.72-2.12
NO$_2^-$, mg N/1	6	<0.01	<0.01	18	0.02	<0.01-0.06
NO$_3^-$, mg N/1	6	<0.01	<0.01	18	0.09	<0.01-0.09
NH$_4^+$, mg N/1	6	1.00	0.18	15	0.27	0.08-0.24
Total Kjeldahl nitrogen, mg N/1	6	1.64	0.60	18	0.97	0.5-1.0
Ca^{++}, mg/1	7	6.6	4.1	21	27.6	3.7-6.0
Mg^{++}, mg/1	7	2.4	2.5	21	5.7	2.4-2.7
Na$^+$, mg/1	7	3.2	2.7	21	15.5	2.4-3.1
K$^+$, mg/1	7	3.3	—	21	5.9	3.0-3.2
SO$_4^=$, mg/1	4	2.7	7.0	15	15.9	8.5-13.1

Source: Based on data from Mitsch, 1979 and Dorge, Mitsch, and Wiemhoff, 1984
[a]Number of separate sample dates at all stations
[b]Underlined values are significantly lower than river values on same sampling dates (paired
t-test = 0.05)
[c]Average concentrations during flooding

(1984) also noted a range of total phosphorus to be 0.05-0.16 mg P/1
in the central pond of a similar cypress dome, with most of the phosphorus
in inorganic form, while Dierberg and Brezonik (1984) found an average of
0.18 mg P/1 for 5 years of sampling in the same cypress dome (Table 13-1).
On the other hand, phosphorus levels are often considerably higher in
alluvial river swamps, particularly during flooding from the adjacent river.

Swamp-River Comparisons

The isolation of an alluvial river swamp from its nearby river for most
of the year often leads to remarkable differences in the water chemistry of
the swamp and the river. Denitrification and sulfate reduction are dominant
in the stagnant swamp but are less prevalent in the flowing river. Further-

more, dissolved ions in the backswamp are often lower in concentration than the same ions in the river. This is due to the dilute nature of dissolved ions in the river when it is flooding the backswamp and also possibly due to nutrient uptake by vegetation. This physiochemical isolation of alluvial river swamps was noted in studies in Louisiana and southern Illinois. Water chemistry in Louisiana backswamps in the Atchafalaya Basin is distinct from that of the adjacent rivers and streams, except in the flooding season, when the waters of the entire region are well mixed (Beck, 1977; Hern, Lambou, and Butch, 1980). Several dissolved substances were significantly lower in the standing water of a riparian cypress-tupelo swamp in southern Illinois than in the adjacent river (Table 13-2). The swamp had lower values of calcium, magnesium, sodium, potassium, sulfate, and nitrate than did the river, despite the fact that the swamp was flooded annually.

ECOSYSTEM STRUCTURE

Canopy Vegetation

Southern deepwater swamps, particularly cypress wetlands, have unique plant communities that are either dependent on, or adapted to, the almost continuously wet environment. The dominant canopy vegetation found in alluvial river swamps of southeastern United States includes bald cypress (*Taxodium distichum* L. Rich) and water tupelo (*Nyssa aquatica* L.). The trees are often found growing in association in the same swamp, although pure stands of either bald cypress or water tupelo are also frequent in the southeastern United States. Many of the pure tupelo stands are thought to be a result of selective logging of bald cypress (Penfound, 1952). Another vegetation association, the pond cypress-black gum [*Taxodium distichum* var. *nutans* (Ait.) Sweet-*Nyssa sylvatica* var. *biflora*(Walt.) Sarg.] swamp, is more commonly found on the uplands of the southeastern Coastal Plain, usually in areas of poor sandy soils without alluvial flooding. These same conditions are usually found in cypress domes. Some of the distinctions between bald cypress and pond cypress swamps are summarized in Table 13-3.

When deepwater swamps have been drained, or when their dry period is extended dramatically, they can be invaded by pine (*Pinus* spp.) or hardwoods. In north-central Florida, a cypress-pine association indicates a drained cypress dome (Mitsch and Ewel, 1979). Hardwoods that characteristically are found in cypress domes include swamp red bay *(Persea palustris)* and sweet bay *(Magnolia virginiana)* (Brown, 1981). In the lake-edge and alluvial river swamps, several species of ash (*Fraxinus* sp.) and maple (*Acer* sp.) often grow as subdominants with the cypress and/or tupelo. In the deep South, Spanish moss *(Tillandsia usneoides)* is found in abundance as an epiphyte on

Table 13-3. Distinction Between Bald Cypress and Pond Cypress Swamps

Characteristic	Bald Cypress Swamp	Pond Cypress Swamp
Dominant Cypress	*Taxodium distichum*	*Taxodium distichum* var. *nutans*
Dominant Tupelo or Gum (when present)	*Nyssa aquatic* (water tupelo)	*Nyssa sylvatica* var. *biflora* (black gum)
Tree Physiology	Large, old trees, high growth rate, usually abundance of knees and spreading buttresses	Smaller, younger trees, low growth rate, some knees and buttresses, but not as pronounced
Location	Alluvial floodplains of Coastal Plain, particularly along Atlantic seaboard, Gulf seaboard, and Mississippi embayment	"Uplands" of Coastal Plain particularly in Florida and southern Georgia
Chemical Status	Neutral to slightly acid, high in dissolved ions, usually high in suspended sediments and rich in nutrients	Low pH, poorly buffered, low in dissolved ions, poor in nutrients
Annual Flooding from River	Yes	No
Types of Deepwater Swamps	Alluvial river swamp, cypress strand, lake-edge swamp	Cypress dome, dwarf cypress swamp

the stems and branches of the canopy trees. Schlesinger (1978) found that Spanish moss has a relatively high biomass and productivity as compared with epiphytic communities in many other temperate forests. A listing of some of the dominant canopy and understory vegetation in various cypress swamps is given in Table 13-4.

Ewel and Mitsch (1978) investigated the effects of fire on a cypress dome in Florida. They found that fire had a "cleansing" effect on the dome, selectively killing almost all of the pines and hardwoods and yet killing relatively few pond cypress, suggesting a possible advantage of fire to some shallow cypress ecosystems in eliminating competition that is less water tolerant.

Table 13-4. Dominant or Abundant Vegetation of Deepwater Swamps of Southeastern United States

	Cypress Dome[a]	Alluvial River Swamp[b]
Location	North-central Florida	Louisiana
Dominant Canopy Trees	Taxodium distichum var. nutans (pond cypress) Nyssa sylvatica var. biflora (swamp black gum)	Taxodium distichum (bald cypress) Nyssa aquatica (water tupelo)
Sub-dominant Trees	Pinus elliottii (slash pine) Persea palustris (swamp red bay) Magnolia virginiana (sweet bay)	Acer rubrum var. drummondii (Drummond red maple) Fraxinus tomentosa (pumpkin ash)
Shrubs	Lyonia lucida (fetterbush) Myrica cerifera (wax myrtle) Acer rubrum (red maple) Cephalanthus occidentalis (buttonbush) Itea virginica (Virginia willow)	Cephalanthus occidentalis (buttonbush) Celtis laevigata (hackberry) Salix nigra (black willow)
Herbs and Aquatic Vegetation	Woodwardia virginica (Virginia chain fern) Saururus cernuus (lizard's tail) Lachnanthes caroliniana (red root)	Lemna minor (duckweed) Spirodela polyrhiza (duckweed) Riccia sp. Limnobium Spongia (common frog's bit)

[a] After Monk and Brown, 1965; Brown, 1981; Marois and Ewel, 1983
[b] After Conner and Day, 1976

(continued)

Table 13-4. Continued

	Alluvial River Swamp[c]	Scrub Cypress[d]
Location	Southern Illinois	Southern Florida
Dominant Canopy Trees	*Taxodium distichum* (bald cypress) *Nyssa aquatica* (water tupelo)	*Taxodium distichum var. nutans* (pond cypress)
Sub-dominant Trees	—	*Pinus elliottii* (slash pine)
Shrubs	*Cephalanthus occidentalis* (buttonbush) *Itea virginica* (Virginia willow) *Rosa palustris* (swamp rose)	*Myrica cerifera* (wax myrtle) *Ilex cassine* *Stylingia sylvatica*
Herbs and Aquatic Vegetation	*Azolla mexicana* (water fern) *Spirodela polyrhiza* (duckweed)	*Panicum hemitomon*

[c]After Anderson and White, 1970; Mitsch, Dorge, and Wiemhoff, 1979
[d]After Brown, 1981

(continued)

330

Table 13-4. Continued

	Still water Cypress Swamp[e]	Cypress Strand[f]
Location	Okefenokee Swamp, Georgia	Southwestern Florida
Dominant Canopy Trees	*Taxodium distichum* var. *nutans* (pond cypress)	*Taxodium distichum* (bald cypress)
Sub-dominant Trees	*Ilex cassine* *Nyssa sylvatica* var. *biflora* (swamp black gum)	*Taxodium distichum* var. *nutans* (pond cypress) *Salix caroliniana* (willow) *Annona glabra* (pond apple) *Acer rubrum* (red maple) *Sabal palmetto* (cabbage palm)
Shrubs	*Lyonia lucida* (fetterbush) *Itea virginica* (Virginia willow) *Leucothoe racemosa* *Clethra alnifolia*	*Myrica cerifera* (wax myrtle) *Persea borbonia* (red bay) *Hippocratea volubilis (liana)* *Toxicodendron radicans* (poison ivy)
Herbs and Aquatic Vegetation	*Eriocaulon compressum* (pipewort)	*Blechnum serrulatum* *Nephrolepis exaltata* (Boston fern) *Thelypteris kunthii* (swamp fern) *Chloris neglecta* (finger grass) *Andropogon virginicus* (broom sedge) *Ludwigia repens*

[e] After Schlesinger, 1978
[f] After Carter et al., 1973

331

Tree Adaptations

Knees—Several unique features about the trees in *Taxodium-Nyssa* swamps appear to be adaptations to the almost continuously flooded conditions. Cypress (bald and pond), water tupelo, and black gum are among a number of wetland plants that produce pneumatophores (see chap. 6). In deepwater swamps these organs extend from the root system to well above the average water level (Fig. 13-4a). On cypress, these "knees" are conical and typically less than 1 m in height, although some cypress knees are as tall as 3 to 4 m (Hook and Scholtens, 1978). Knees are much more prominent on cypress than on tupelo. Hall and Penfound (1939) discovered that cypress had more knees (three per tree) than did tupelo (one per tree) in a cypress-tupelo swamp in Louisiana. Pneumatophores on black gum in cypress domes are actually arching or "kinked" roots that approximate the appearance of cypress knees.

The functions of the knees have been speculated on for the last century. It was thought that the knee might be an adaptation for anchoring the tree, because of the appearance of a secondary root system beneath the knee that is similar to and smaller than the main root system of the tree (Mattoon, 1915; C. A. Brown, 1984). The most recent discussion of cypress knee function has centered on the possible functioning as sites of gas exchange for the root systems. Penfound (1952) argued that cypress knees are often absent where they are most needed—in deep water—and that the wood of the cypress knee is not aerenchymous; that is, there are no intercellular gas spaces capable of transporting oxygen to the root system. Kramer, Riley, and Bannister (1952) concluded that the knees did not provide aeration to the rest of the trees. More recent measurements, however, indicate that gas exchange does occur at the knees. Carbon dioxide evolved at rates from 4 to 86 g C/per square meter of tissue per day from cypress knees in Florida cypress domes (Cowles, 1975). Brown (1981) estimated that gas evolution from knees accounted for 0.04-0.12 g C/m^2 · day of the respiration in a cypress dome, and 0.23 g C/m^2 · day in an alluvial river swamp. This accounted for 0.3%-0.9% of the total tree respiration but 5%-15% of the estimated woody tissue (stems and knees) respiration. However, the fact that CO_2 is exchanged at the knee does not imply that oxygen transport is taking place there or that the CO_2 evolved resulted from oxidation of anaerobically produced organics in the root system (K. Ewel, written communic.).

Buttresses—*Taxodium* and *Nyssa* species often produce swollen bases or buttresses when they grow in flooded conditions (Fig. 13-4b). The swelling can occur from less than 1 m above the soil to several meters, depending on the hydroperiod of the wetland. Swelling generally occurs along the part of the tree that is flooded at least seasonally, although the duration and frequency of the flooding necessary to cause the swelling is unknown. One theory described the height of the buttress as a response to aeration, with the

a

b

Figure 13-4. Several unique features of vegetation in cypress swamps including *a*. cypress knees, and *b*. buttresses and large size of cypress trees.

greatest swelling occurring where there is a continual wetting and soaking at the tree trunk but where the trunk is also above the normal water level (Kurz and Demaree, 1934). The value of the buttress swelling to ecosystem survivability is unknown; it may simply be a relict response with little use to the plant.

Seed Germination—The seeds of swamp trees, including cypress and tupelo, require oxygen for germination. This means that occasional drawdowns, if only at relatively infrequent intervals, are necessary for persistence of these deepwater swamps. Otherwise, continuous flooding will ultimately lead to an open-water pond, although individual cypress trees may survive for a century or more. It has also been demonstrated that cypress seeds and seedlings require very moist, but not flooded, soil for germination and survival (Mattoon, 1915). After germination, cypress seedlings survive by rapid vertical growth to keep above the rising waters (Mattoon, 1916; Demaree, 1932).

Longevity—Bald cypress trees may live for centuries and achieve great sizes. Virgin stands of cypress were typically from 400 to 600 years old (Mattoon, 1915). One individual cypress in Corkscrew Swamp in southwestern Florida was noted to be about 700 years old (Sprunt, 1961). Most of the virgin stands of cypress in this country were logged over the last century, however, and few individuals over 200 years old remain. Mature bald cypress are typically 30-40 m high and 1-1.5 m in diameter. Anderson and White (1970) reported a very large cypress tree in a cypress-tupelo swamp in southern Illinois that measured 2.1 m in diameter. C. A. Brown (1984) summarized several reports that documented bald cypress as large as 3.6-5.1 m in diameter. Bald cypress wood itself was used extensively for building materials in the Southeast, particularly for support beams in southern antebellum homes and for box construction. It has been called "the wood eternal" by foresters because of its resistance to decay.

Understory Vegetation

The abundance of understory vegetation in cypress-tupelo swamps depends on the amount of light that penetrates the tree canopy. Many mature swamps appear as quiet, dark cathedrals of tree trunks devoid of any understory vegetation. Even when enough light is available for understory vegetation, it is difficult to generalize about its composition (Table 13-4). There can be a dominance of woody shrubs, of herbaceous vegetation, or of both. Fetterbush *(Lyonia lucida),* wax myrtle *(Myrica cerifera),* and Virginia willow *(Itea virginica)* are common as shrubs and small trees in nutrient-poor cypress domes. Understory species in higher nutrient river swamps include buttonbush *(Cephalanthus occidentalis)* and Virginia willow. Some continually flooded cypress swamps that have high concentrations of dissolved nutrients in the water develop dense mats of duckweed (e.g., *Lemna* spp., *Spirodela* spp., or *Azolla* spp.) on the water surface during most of the year. An experiment in enriching cypress domes with high-nutrient wastewater caused a thick mat of duckweed to develop in what was otherwise a nutrient-poor environment (H. T. Odum et al., 1977*a*).

Consumers

Invertebrates

Invertebrate communities, particularly benthic macroinvertebrates, have been analyzed in several cypress-tupelo swamps. A wide diversity and high numbers of invertebrates have been found in permanently flooded swamps. Species include crayfish, clams, oligochaete worms, snails, freshwater shrimp, midges, amphipods, and various immature insects. The organisms are highly dependent, either directly or indirectly, on the abundant detritus found in these systems. Beck (1977) found that a cypress-tupelo swamp in the Louisiana Atchafalaya Basin had a higher number of organisms (3,768 individuals/m^2) than the bayous (3,292/m^2), lakes (1,840/m^2), canals (1,593/m^2), and rivers (327/m^2). These high densities were attributed to the abundance of detritus and to the pulse of spring flooding. Sklar and Conner (1979), working in contiguous environments in Louisiana, found higher numbers of benthic organisms in a cypress-tupelo swamp (7,500 individuals/m^2) than were in a nearby impounded swamp (3,000/m^2), or in a swamp managed as a crayfish farm. Their study suggests that the natural swamp hydroperiod results in the highest numbers of benthic invertebrates.

Ziser (1978) and Bryan et al. (1976) also surveyed the benthic fauna of alluvial river swamps. Oligochaetes and midges (Chironomidae), both of which can tolerate low-dissolved-oxygen conditions, and amphipods such as *Hyalella azteca*, which occur in abundance amid aquatic plants such as duckweed, usually dominate. In nutrient-poor cypress domes, the benthic fauna is dominated by Chironomidae, although crayfish, isopods, and other Diptera are also found there. Stresses due to low dissolved oxygen and fluctuating water levels are reasons for the low diversity and numbers in these domes.

Fish

Fish are both temporary and permanent residents of alluvial river swamps in the Southeast (Wharton et al., 1976; 1981). Several studies have noted the value of sloughs and backswamps for fish spawning and feeding during the flooding season (e.g., Lambou, 1965; Patrick, Cairns, and Roback, 1967; Bryan et al., 1976; Wharton et al., 1981). The deepwater swamp often serves as a reservoir for fish when flooding ceases, although the backwaters are less than optimum for aquatic life due to fluctuating water levels and occasional low dissolved oxygen levels. Some fish such as bowfin (*Amia* sp.), gar (*Lepisosteus* sp.), and certain top minnows (e.g., *Fundulus* spp. and *Gambusia affinis*) are better adapted to occasional anoxia through their ability to partially utilize atmospheric oxygen. Often several species of forage minnows dominate cypress strands and alluvial river swamps, where most larger fish are temporary residents of the wetlands (Clark, 1979). Fish are sparse to nonexistent in the shallow cypress domes, except for the mosquito fish *(Gambusia affinis)*.

Reptiles and Amphibians

Reptiles and amphibians are prevalent in cypress swamps because of their ability to adapt to fluctuating water levels. Nine or ten different species of frogs are common in many southeastern cypress-gum swamps (Clark, 1979). Two of the most interesting reptiles in southeastern deepwater swamps are the American alligator and the cottonmouth moccasin. The alligator ranges from North Carolina through Louisiana, where alluvial cypress swamps and cypress strands often serve as suitable habitats. The cottonmouth moccasin *(Agkistrodon piscivorus)*, a poisonous water snake that has a white inner mouth, is found throughout much of the range of cypress wetlands and is the topic of many a "snake story" of those who have been in these swamps. However, other water snakes, particularly several species of *Natrix,* are often more important in terms of numbers and biomass and are often mistakenly identified as cottonmouth moccasins. The snakes feed primarily on frogs, small fish, salamanders, and crayfish (Clark, 1979).

ECOSYSTEM FUNCTION

Several generalizations of ecosystem function of the southern deepwater swamp will be discussed in this section:

1. Swamp productivity is closely tied to its hydrologic regime.
2. Nutrient inflows, often coupled with hydrologic conditions, are a major influence on swamp productivity.
3. Swamps can be nutrient sinks whether the nutrients are a natural source or are artificially applied.
4. Decomposition is affected by the water regime and the degree of anaerobiosis.

Primary Productivity

There is a wide range of productivity of cypress swamps in the southeastern United States. A number of studies have shown that primary productivity depends on hydrologic and nutrient conditions (Table 13-5): Florida cypress strands (Carter et al., 1973; Burns, 1978), Louisiana cypress-tupelo swamps (Conner and Day, 1976; Day, Butler, and Conner, 1977; Conner, Gosselink, and Parrondo, 1981), Florida cypress swamps (Mitsch and Ewel, 1979; Brown, 1981; Marois and Ewel, 1983), an Illinois alluvial river swamp (Mitsch, 1979; Mitsch, Dorge, and Wiemhoff, 1979; Dorge, Mitsch, and Wiemhoff, 1984), a Georgia pond cypress swamp (Schlesinger, 1978), and a North Carolina alluvial swamp (Brinson et al., 1980). In addition, at least two summaries (Brinson, Lugo, and Brown, 1981; Conner and Day, 1982) have compiled much of these data.

Figure 13-5 shows two similar relationships that have been suggested to explain the importance of hydrology on deepwater swamp productivity. In a study of cypress tree productivity in Florida, Mitsch and Ewel (1979) concluded that growth was low in pure stands of cypress (characterized by deep standing water) and in cypress-pine associations (characterized by dry conditions). Productivity of cypress was high in cypress-tupelo associations, which were characterized by moderately wet conditions, and in cypress-hardwood associations, which have fluctuating water levels characteristic of alluvial river swamps (Fig. 13-5a). Conner and Day (1982) suggested a similar relationship between swamp productivity and hydrologic conditions and produced a similar curve with some data points added (Fig. 13-5b). Both of these curves suggest that the highest productivities result in systems that are neither very wet nor too dry but that have seasonal hydrologic pulsing.

Brown (1981) and Brinson, Lugo, and Brown (1981) analyzed productivity data from several forested wetlands, mostly southern deepwater swamps, and reported that productivity was highest in flowing water swamps, less in sluggish or slow flowing swamps, and lowest in stillwater swamps. Flowing water swamps include alluvial river swamps, where water and nutrients are periodically fed to the wetland from a flooding stream, while sluggish or slow flowing swamps have significant inputs from groundwater and surface runoff, but not from river or stream flooding. Stillwater swamps receive their major inputs of water and nutrients from rainfall and are thus poorly nourished. Brown (1981) emphasized the importance of nutrient inflows, as well as hydrologic conditions, to productivity in cypress swamps (Fig. 13-6). She pointed out that a stillwater cypress dome, with a low rate of nutrient inflow, increased in productivity when it was enriched with high-nutrient wastewater. Since hydrologic inflows and nutrient inflows are coupled in most natural deepwater swamps, Figures 13-5 and 13-6 describe much the same phenomenon.

Table 13-5. Biomass and Net Primary Productivity of Deepwater Swamps in Southeastern United States

Location/Forest Type	Tree Standing Biomass, kg/m²	Litter fall, g/m² · yr	Stem Growth, g/m² · yr	Above-ground NPP[a]	Reference
Louisiana					
Bottomland hardwood	16.5[b]	574	800	1,374	Conner and Day (1976)
Cypress-tupelo	37.5[b]	620	500	1,120	ibid.
Impounded managed Swamp	32.8[b, c]	550	1,230	1,780	Conner, Gosselink, and Parrondo
Impounded stagnant Swamp	15.9[b, c]	330	560	890	ibid.
Tupelo stand	36.2[b]	379	—	—	Conner and Day (1982)
Cypress stand	27.8[b]	562	—	—	ibid.
North Carolina					
Tupelo swamp	—	609-677	—	—	Brinson (1977)
Floodplain swamp	26.7[d]	523	585	1,108	Mulholland (1979)
Virginia					
Cedar swamp	22.0[b]	757	—	—	Dabel and Day (1977); Gomez and Day (1982)
Maple gum swamp	19.6[b]	659	—	—	ibid.
Cypress swamp	34.5[b]	678	—	—	ibid.
Mixed hardwood swamp	19.5[b]	652	—	—	ibid.
Georgia					
Nutrient-poor cypress swamp	30.7[e]	328	353	681	Schlesinger (1978)

					Source
Cypress-tupelo	45[d]	348	330	678	Mitsch (1979); Dorge, Mitsch, and Wiemhoff (1984)
Florida					
Cypress-tupelo (6 sites)	19 ± 4.7[f]	—	289 ± 58[f]	760[g]	Mitsch and Ewel (1979)
Cypress-hardwood (4 sites)	15.4 ± 2.9[f]	—	336 ± 76[f]	950[g]	*ibid.*
Pure cypress stand (4 sites)	9.5 ± 2.6[f]	—	154 ± 55[f]	—	*ibid.*
Cypress-pine (7 sites)	10.1 ± 2.1[f]	—	117 ± 27[f]	—	*ibid.*
Floodplain swamp	32.5	521	1,086	1,607	Brown (1978)
Natural dome[h]	21.2	518	451	969	*ibid.*
Sewage dome[i]	13.3	546	716	1,262	*ibid.*
Scrub cypress	7.4	250	—	—	Brown and Lugo (1982)
Drained strand	8.9	120	267	387	Carter et al. (1973)
Undrained strand	17.1	485	373	858	*ibid.*

Source: After Conner and Day, 1982, p. 72–73

[a]NPP = net primary productivity = litter fall + stem growth
[b]Trees defined as > 2.54 cm DBH (diameter at breast height)
[c]Cypress, tupelo, ash only
[d]Trees defined as > 10 cm DBH
[e]Trees defined as > 4 cm DBH
[f]Average ± std error for cypress only
[g]Estimated
[h]Average of five natural domes
[i]Average of three domes; domes were receiving high nutrient wastewater

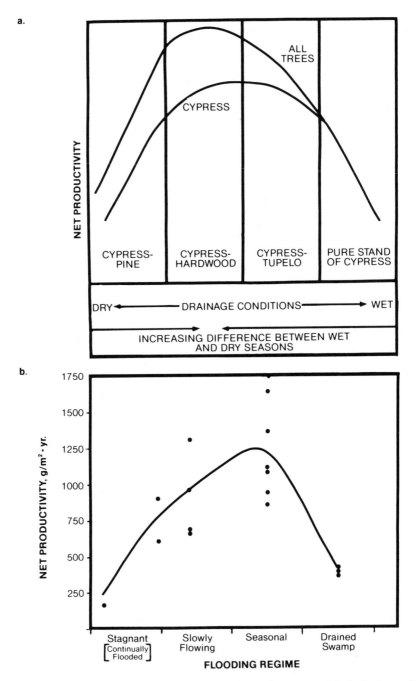

Figure 13-5. The relationship of cypress swamp productivity and hydrologic conditions. (a. From Mitsch and Ewel, 1979, p. 424; Copyright © 1979 by American Midland Naturalist, reprinted with permission. b. From Conner and Day, 1982, p. 74; Copyright © 1982 by International Scientific Publications, reprinted with permission)

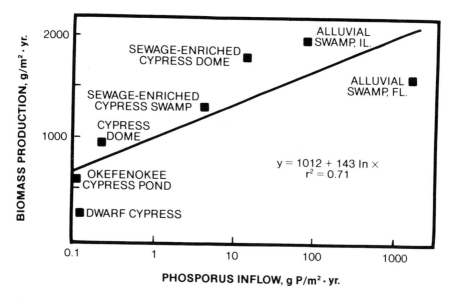

Figure 13-6. Cypress swamp biomass productivity as a function of phosphorus inflow. *(After Brown, 1981, p. 419)*

The importance of flooding to the productivity of alluvial river swamps is further illustrated in Figure 13-7, where basal area growth of bald cypress in an alluvial river swamp in southern Illinois is strongly correlated with annual discharge of the adjacent river. This graph suggests that higher tree productivity in this wetland occurred in years when the swamp was flooded more frequently or for longer durations by the nutrient-rich river. Similar correlations were also obtained when other independent variables that indicate degree of flooding were used. Data points for tree growth and flooding for 1927-1936 and 1967-1976 were not included in the regression analysis due to extensive logging activity and invasion of the pond by beavers during those periods (Mitsch, Dorge, and Wiemhoff, 1979).

The influence of alteration of the hydroperiod on the productivity of cypress swamps is apparent from the above studies. When flooding of an alluvial river swamp is decreased, lower productivity may result. When still-water swamps are drained, productivity of the swamp species will eventually decrease as water-intolerant species invade. Impounding wetlands, whether by artificial levees or beaver dams, leads to deeper and more continuous flooding and may decrease productivity.

Decomposition

Biological utilization of organic matter is primarily through detrital pathways in deepwater swamps, although decomposition is impeded by the

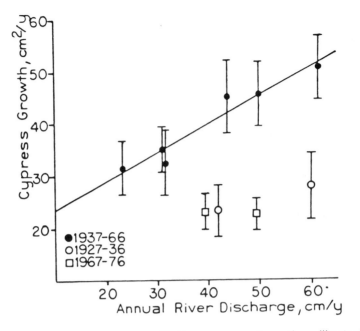

Figure 13-7. Increase in basal area of bald cypress trees in southern Illinois alluvial swamp as a function of river discharge for 5-year periods. Data points indicate mean; bar indicates one standard error. *(From Mitsch, Dorge, and Wiemhoff, 1979, p. 1123; Copyright © 1979 by the Ecological Society of America, reprinted with permission)*

anaerobic conditions usually found in the sediments. The first-order decay coefficients for litter in a variety of southern deepwater swamps are summarized in Table 13-6. Brinson (1977) found that decomposition of *Nyssa aquatica* leaves and twigs in a North Carolina riparian tupelo swamp was greatest in the wettest site, while Duever, Carlson, and Riopelle (1975) found that decomposition in a southern Florida cypress strand region was slowest in an area where no flooding occurred and more rapid in areas that were flooded from 50% to 61% of the time. Deghi, Ewel, and Mitsch (1980) found no difference between decomposition of pond cypress needles in deep and shallow sites in Florida cypress domes, although decomposition was generally more rapid in wet sites than in dry sites.

F. P. Day (1982) and Yates and Day (1983) investigated decomposition of several types of forested wetland leaves in several forested wetland communities in the Great Dismal Swamp in Virginia (Table 13-6). Decomposition was generally slower there than in Florida and North Carolina alluvial swamps. Variations in decomposition were seen from site to site, with greater breakdown of litter in seasonally flooded sites than in a mixed hardwood site that

Table 13-6. Decay Coefficients of Litter in Deepwater Swamps

Material	Site Description	Decay Coefficient $(kJ \, yr^{-1})$	Reference
Florida			
Cypress strand			
Site leaves	On forest floor	0.86-1.39[b]	Burns (1978)
Site leaves	On debris pile	0.69-0.75[b]	ibid.
Site leaves	Dry site	0.47	Duever, Carlson, and Riopelle (1975)
Site leaves	Flooded 50% of time	0.23	ibid.
Site leaves	Flooded 61% of time	0.30	ibid.
Cypress dome			
Pond cypress leaves	Flooded 100% of time	1.21-1.40	Deghi, Ewel, and Mitsch (1980)
Pond cypress leaves	Dry site	0.50-0.69	ibid.
North Carolina			
Water tupelo leaves		1.89	Brinson (1977)
Water tupelo twigs		0.28	ibid.
Virginia			
Cypress community			
Bald cypress leaves		0.33	Day (1982)
Mixed litter (1978-1979)		0.51-0.59	ibid.
Mixed litter (1980)		0.28	Yates and Day (1983)
Maple gum communities			
Tupelo leaves		0.65	Day (1982)
Maple leaves		0.47	ibid.
Mixed litter (1978-1979)		0.51-0.67	ibid.
Mixed litter (1980)		0.29	Yates and Day (1983)
Cedar community			
Cedar leaves		0.34	Day (1982)
Mixed litter (1978-1979)		0.35-0.43	ibid.
Mixed litter (1980)		0.49	Yates and Day (1983)

Source: Based partially on Brinson, Lugo, and Brown, 1981, p. 144-145.

[a]Decay coefficient (k) based on exponential decay:

$$y = y_o e^{-kt}$$

where y = final biomass

y_o = initial biomass

t = time in years

[b]Range due to different mesh size used in litterbags

was not inundated. However, the data suggested that the type of litter was often as important as flooding in differentiating among sites. Water tupelo leaves had the highest decomposition rates, with cedar and bald cypress having slower rates (F. P. Day, 1982). There was also quite a difference between decomposition rates measured in 1978-1979 (F. P. Day, 1982) and in 1980 (Yates and Day, 1983). The slower decomposition in the cypress and maple gum communities in 1980 is attributed to a drought during the summer and autumn and an abbreviated period of inundation in the spring (Yates and Day, 1983).

Generally, decomposition rates seem to be maximum in wet but not permanently flooded sites. The rates also increase with increases in average ground temperature and depend strongly on the quality (species, type of litter) of the decomposing material.

Organic Export

Little organic matter is exported from stillwater and slow-flowing swamps such as cypress domes, dwarf cypress swamps, and cypress strands. However, export from lake-edge swamps and alluvial river swamps can be significant. Organic export is higher from watersheds that contain significant deepwater swamps than from those that do not (Mulholland and Kuenzler, 1979) (see Fig. 5-11). Day, Butler, and Conner (1977) found a high rate of 10.4 g C/m² · yr exported as total organic carbon from a swamp forest in Louisiana. More discussion of organic export from wetland-dominated watersheds is contained in Chapters 5 and 14.

Energy Flow

Energy flow of deepwater swamps is dominated by primary productivity of the canopy trees, with energy consumption primarily by detrital decomposition. Significant differences exist, however, between the energy flow patterns in low-nutrient swamps, such as dwarf cypress swamps and cypress domes, and high-nutrient swamps, such as alluvial cypress swamps (Table 13-7). All of the cypress wetlands are autotrophic, with productivity exceeding respiration. Gross primary productivity, net primary productivity, and net ecosystem productivity are highest in the alluvial river swamp that receives high-nutrient inflows. Buildup and/or export of organic matter is characteristic of all of these deepwater swamps but is most characteristic of the alluvial swamp. There are few allochthonous inputs of energy to the low-nutrient wetlands, and energy flow at the primary producer level is relatively low. The alluvial cypress-tupelo swamp depends more on allochthonous

Table 13-7. Estimated Energy Flow (kcal/m² · day) in Selected Florida Cypress Swamps[a]

Parameter	Dwarf Cypress Swamp	Cypress Dome	Alluvial River Swamp
Gross Primary Productivity[b]	27	115	233
Plant Respiration[c]	18	98	205
Net Primary Productivity	9	17	28
Soil or Water Respiration	7	13	18
Net Ecosystem Productivity	2	4	10

Source: After Brown, 1981, p. 415
[a] Assumes 1 g C = 10 kcal
[b] Assumes GPP = net daytime photosynthesis + nighttime leaf respiration
[c] Plant respiration = 2 (nighttime leaf respiration) + stem respiration + knee respiration

inputs of nutrients and energy, particularly from runoff and river flooding. In alluvial deepwater swamps, productivity by aquatic plants is often high, whereas aquatic productivity in cypress domes is usually low.

Nutrient Budgets

Nutrient budgets of deepwater swamps vary from "open" alluvial river swamps, which receive and export large quantities of materials, to "closed" cypress domes, which are mostly isolated from their surroundings (Table 13-8). The importance of nutrient inflows to productivity was demonstrated in Figures 13-6 and 13-7.

Nutrient dynamics of deepwater swamps have also been investigated from the aspect of these swamps serving as "sinks" or ultimate deposits for nutrients. As described in chapter 5, a number of studies have demonstrated that deepwater swamps can be nutrient sinks, whether the nutrients are from a natural source or are artificially added. In South Carolina, Kitchens et al. (1975) found a 50% reduction in phosphorus as overflow waters passed from the river through the backwaters. In a similar study in Louisiana, Day, Butler, and Conner (1977) found that nitrogen was reduced by 48% and phosphorus decreased by 45% as water passed through a lake-swamp complex of Barataria Bay to the lower estuary (Fig. 13-8). They attributed this decrease in nutrients to sediment interactions, including nitrate storage/denitrification and phosphorus adsorption to the clay sediments.

Several nutrient budgets that illustrate intrasystem cycling, as well as inputs and outputs, have been developed for southern deepwater swamps.

Table 13-8. Phosphorus Inputs to Deepwater Swamps in g P/m² · yr

Swamp	Rainfall	Surface Inflow	Sediments from River Flooding	Reference
Florida				
Dwarf cypress	0.11	—[a]	0	Brown (1981)
Cypress dome	0.09	0.12	0	*ibid*
Alluvial river swamp	—[a]	—[a]	3.1	*ibid*
Southern Illinois				
Alluvial river swamp	0.11	0.1	3.6	Mitsch, Dorge, and Wiemhoff (1979)
North Carolina				
Alluvial tupelo swamp	0.02–0.04	0.1–1.2	0.2	Yarbro (1983)

[a]Not measured

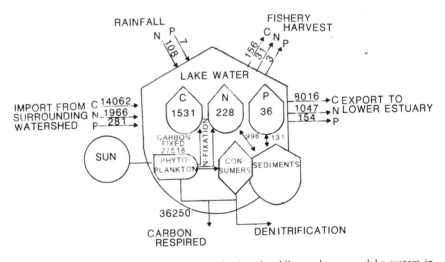

Figure 13-8. Nutrient budget summary for Lac des Allemands swamp-lake system in Louisiana. Flows are metric tons per year; storages are metric tons. *(From Day, Butler, and Conner, 1977, p. 263; Copyright © 1977 by Academic Press, reprinted with permission)*

Yarbro (1979; 1983) found that an alluvial swamp in North Carolina retained 0.3–0.7 g P/m² · yr over two years of measurement. Intrasystem cycling through the vegetation accounted for 0.5 g P/m² · yr, but only a fraction was retained in the biomass. Another phosphorus budget for an alluvial cypress-tupelo swamp in southern Illinois further demonstrated that swamps may serve as nutrient sinks (Fig. 13-9). A spring flood that spilled over from the

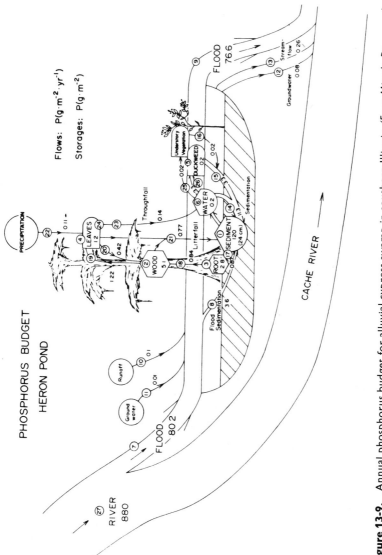

Figure 13-9. Annual phosphorus budget for alluvial cypress swamp in southern Illinois. *(From Mitsch, Dorge, and Wiemhoff, 1979, p. 1120; Copyright © 1979 by the Ecological Society of America, reprinted with permission)*

347

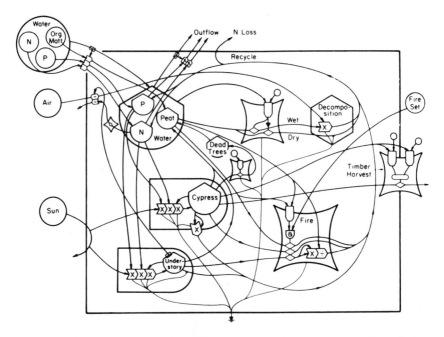

Figure 13-10. Simulation model of Florida cypress dome ecosystem. *(From Systems Ecology—An Introduction, H. T. Odum, 1983, p. 434; Copyright © 1983 by John Wiley and Sons, Inc., reprinted with permission)*

adjacent river to the swamp contributed high amounts of nutrient-rich sediments. Estimated input due to sedimentation was 3.6 g P/m² · yr, 26 times the contribution by throughfall. The flood was estimated to have passed 80 g P/m² · yr over the swamp; thus the swamp retained about 4.5% of this flux. Total outflow of phosphorus to the river for the remainder of the year was 0.34 g P/m² · yr, which is a high rate of loss per unit area as compared with nonwetland ecosystems (Mitsch, 1979). However, the loss is only one-tenth of the input from the river to the swamp during flooding. As with the North Carolina phosphorus budget, only a small portion of the excess phosphorus from the flood was stored in the growth of the vegetation, although cycling was rapid. In both wetlands, the major sink for phosphorus was the sediments, which physically retained the deposited phosphorus or stored it in organic matter contributed by the highly productive vegetation.

ECOSYSTEM MODELS

Both conceptual models and simulation models have been developed to study the dynamics of deepwater swamps or regions that contain deepwater

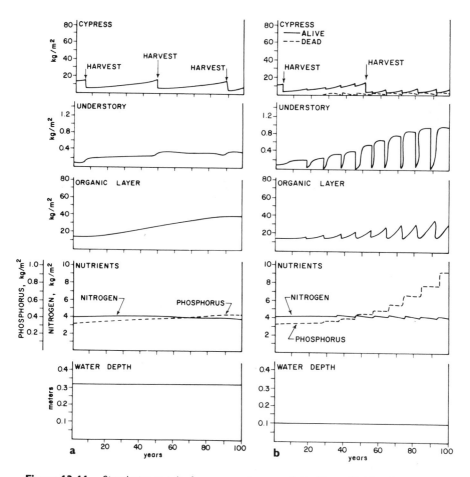

Figure 13-11. Simulation results for cypress dome model in Figure 13-10. *a*. Simulation with tree harvesting only. *b*. Simulation with tree harvesting and drainage, allowing fire to eliminate cypress. *(From Mitsch 1983, pp. 301–303; Copyright © 1983 by Elsevier, reprinted with permission)*

swamps. A review of some of these models is given in Mitsch et al. (1982) and Mitsch (1983). Many ecosystem-level and regional cypress swamp models are presented by H. T. Odum (1982; 1984). One such simulation model of a Florida cypress swamp was used to investigate the management of cypress domes in Florida (Fig. 13-10). The model predicted long-term (100 years) impacts of drainage, harvesting, fire, and nutrient disposal (Fig. 13-11*a* and 13-11*b*). Simulations showed that when water levels were lowered and trees were logged at the same time, the cypress swamp did not recover and was replaced by shrub vegetation. The model also suggested that if tree harvesting occurred without drainage, the cypress would recover due to the absence of fire.

Several models have been developed of the hydrologic cycle of deepwater swamps or of regions that contain these wetlands. Littlejohn (1977) demonstrated the importance of wetland conservation for groundwater protection with a water table model of the Gordon River region of southwestern Florida. Weimhoff (1977) used a simple water model for an alluvial cypress-tupelo swamp in southern Illinois to demonstrate the water storage potential of the wetland after river flooding. S. L. Brown (1978; 1984) developed a hydrology model for the Green Swamp in central Florida showing that drainage of wetlands led to lower aquifers, drier streams, and greater floods. Water available to the region was reduced by 16% in the model when 40% of the wetlands were drained. Mitsch (1984) presented an energy flow model of the aquatic subsystem of a cypress dome in Florida. Simulations demonstrated annual patterns of aquatic productivity that peaked in spring when maximum solar radiation is available through the deciduous cypress canopy.

In an application of a water transport model already developed by the U.S. Environmental Protection Agency, Hopkinson and Day (1980a, 1980b) simulated hydrology and nutrient transport in a Louisiana swamp-bayou complex. Those simulations demonstrated the benefits and liabilities of spoil banks and suggested that their removal would again allow runoff to pass through the swamps, thus decreasing upstream flooding and optimizing conditions for the swamp forests, the bayous, and the downstream estuary.

SUMMARY

Southern deepwater swamps, primarily bald cypress–tupelo and pond cypress–black gum ecosystems, are freshwater systems with standing water throughout most or all of the year. Found throughout the Coastal Plain of the southeastern United States, they can occur under nutrient-poor conditions (cypress domes and dwarf cypress swamps) or under nutrient-rich conditions (lake-edge swamps, cypress strands, and alluvial river swamps). Two varieties of cypress are found in these systems: bald cypress *(Taxodium distichum)* in nutrient-rich systems, and pond cypress (*Taxodium distichum* var. *nutans*) in nutrient-poor systems. Cypress and tupelo have developed several unique adaptations to the wetland environment, including knees and wide buttresses. Cypress seeds require a drawdown period for germination, and seedlings grow rapidly to get out of the water. Swamp primary productivity is closely tied to hydrologic conditions, with the highest productivity in a pulsing hydroperiod wetland with high inputs of nutrients and lower productivity in either drained or continuously flooded swamps. Consumption is primarily through detrital pathways, with decomposition dependent on flooding, type of material, and average annual temperature. Cypress swamps have been shown to be nutrient sinks, particularly in studies of phosphorus budgets, and they have been investigated for their value as nutrient sinks when high-nutrient wastewater is applied. Modeling has been used to investigate deepwater swamp regions, particularly for the effects of logging and hydrologic modifications.

RIPARIAN WETLAND

chapter 14

RIPARIAN WETLANDS

The riparian zone of a river, stream, or other body of water is the land adjacent to that body of water that is, at least periodically, influenced by flooding. E. P. Odum (1981, p. *xi*) described the riparian zone as "an interface between man's most vital resource, namely, water, and his living space, the land." A National Symposium on Strategies for Protection and Management of Floodplain Wetlands and Other Riparian Ecosystems (Johnson and McCormick, 1979) developed a definition of riparian ecosystems. That definition, printed in the program to the meeting, is as follows:

Riparian ecosystems are ecosystems with a high water table because of proximity to an aquatic ecosystem or subsurface water. Riparian ecosystems usually occur as an ecotone between aquatic and upland ecosystems but have distinct vegetation and soil characteristics. Aridity, topographic relief, and presence of depositional soils most strongly influence the extent of high water tables and associated riparian ecosystems. These ecosystems are most commonly recognized as bottomland hardwood and floodplain forests in the eastern and central U.S. and as bosque or streambank vegetation in the west. Riparian ecosystems are uniquely characterized by the combination of high species diversity, high species densities and high productivity. Continuous interactions occur between riparian, aquatic, and upland terrestrial ecosystems through exchanges of energy, nutrients, and species.

The precise boundaries of riparian ecosystems, particularly on the upland edge, are difficult to determine because of seasonal and yearly changes in flooding levels, soil moisture, and vegetation. Nevertheless, these wetlands of the riparian zone are unique because they are generally hydrologically open to seasonal or periodic flooding. E. P. Odum (1979*a*, p. 2) further stated:

Riparian ecosystems are well-defined landscape features that have many of the same values and land use problems as wetlands in general, but are nevertheless distinct enough to warrant special consideration . . . . As functional ecosystems, they are very open with large energy, nutrient, and biotic interchanges with aquatic systems on the inner margin and upland terrestrial ecosystems on the other margin.

Brinson et al. (1981) described the "abundance of water and rich alluvial soils" as factors that make riparian ecosystems different from upland ecosystems. They list three major features that separate riparian ecosystems from other ecosystem types:

1. Riparian ecosystems have a linear form as a consequence of their proximity to rivers and streams.
2. Energy and material from the surrounding landscape converge and pass through riparian ecosystems in much greater amounts than with any other ecosystem.
3. Riparian ecosystems are connected to upstream and downstream ecosystems.

Several meeting proceedings and reports have been developed for riparian wetlands, including the proceedings of a national symposium on floodplain wetlands (Johnson and McCormick, 1979), the proceedings of a workshop on southern bottomland hardwood forests (Clark and Benforado, 1981), and two excellent reviews on bottomland hardwood forests and riparian ecosystems (Brinson et al., 1981; Wharton et al., 1982).

BOTTOMLAND HARDWOOD FORESTS

Bottomland hardwood forests, considered wetlands in several classifications and by many wetland scientists, are one of the dominant types of riparian ecosystems in the United States. Historically, the term bottomland hardwood forest (or bottomland hardwoods) has been used to describe the vast forests that occur on river floodplains of the southeastern United States. Huffman and Forsythe (1981, p. 194) suggest that the term now applies to floodplain forests of the eastern and central United States as well. Their definition of a bottomland hardwood forest includes the following:

(1) The habitat is inundated or saturated by surface or groundwater periodically during the growing season.

(2) The soils within the root zone become saturated periodically during the growing season.

(3) The prevalent woody plant species associated with a given habitat have demonstrated the ability, because of morphological and/or physiological adaptation(s), to survive, achieve maturity, and reproduce in a habitat where the soils within the root zone may become anaerobic for various periods during the growing season.

Bottomland hardwood forests are particularly notable wetlands because of the large areas that they cover in the southeastern United States and because of the rapid rate at which they are being converted to other uses such as agriculture and human settlements (see chap. 3 and following).

GEOGRAPHICAL EXTENT

In general terms, riparian ecosystems are found wherever streams or rivers at least occasionally cause flooding beyond their channel confines. In most nonarid regions, floodplains and hence riparian zones tend to first appear along a stream "where the flow in the channel changes from ephemeral to perennial–that is, where groundwater enters the channel in sufficient quantity to sustain flow through nonstorm periods" (Leopold, Wolman, and Miller, 1964, p. 458). Riparian ecosystems can be broad alluvial valleys several kilometers wide in the southern United States, or narrow strips of streambank vegetation in the arid western United States. Brinson et al. (1981, p. 4), in an assessment of the status of riparian ecosystems in the United States, estimated that "more than 70% of riparian ecosystems have been altered, and natural riparian communities now make less that 2% of the land area in the U.S.A."

Table 14-1 gives the distribution of potential and present land in riparian

Table 14-1. Potential and Present Area of the Four Predominant Riparian Vegetation Types in the United States

	Area (1,000 ha)		Percent Decline
Vegetation Type	Potential	Present	
Elm-Ash Forest[a]	2,239	279	88
Northern Floodplain Forest[a]	7,171	2,227	69
Southern Floodplain Forest[a]	17,774	6,645	63
Mesquite Bosque	71	63	11
Total	27,255	9,214	66

Source: From Brinson et al., 1981, p. 5, after Klopatek et al., 1979.
[a]Would collectively be included in modern definition of "bottomland hardwood forest"

forests in the United States. The data indicate that losses of riparian ecosystems range from 88% for elm-ash forests in the eastern United States to 11% for mesquite bosque ecosystems of the western United States. These estimates also confirm that the predominant remaining riparian ecosystems are the southern floodplain forests, despite the fact that over 11 million hectares (27 million acres) have been converted to other uses.

The major type of riparian ecosystem, the bottomland hardwood forest, is found primarily in the southeastern United States (Fig. 14-1). This ecosystem is particularly prevalent in the lower Mississippi River alluvial valley as far north as southern Illinois, and along many streams that drain into the Atlantic Ocean on the south Atlantic Coastal Plain. Turner, Forsythe, and Craig (1981) estimated that there are 23.5 million hectares (58 million acres) of bottomland hardwood forests in the United States, 55% of which is located in 12 southern states. These numbers are considerably higher than the estimates given in Table 14-1, demonstrating the uncertainty of existing surveys on the extent of these wetlands.

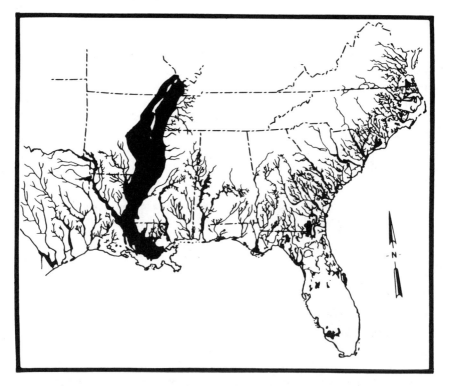

Figure 14-1.   Extent of bottomland hardwood forests of southern United States *(After Putnam, Furnival, and McKnight, 1960)*

Figure 14-2 shows one estimate of the changes of bottomland hardwood forests from 1960 to 1975 in individual states in the southeastern United States. Net losses were estimated to be about 175,000 hectares per year over the period 1960–1975, for a total of 2.6 million hectares, or 20% of the total bottomlands in the Southeast. Greatest losses occurred in Missouri, Arkansas, and Louisiana in the lower Mississippi River valley and in Georgia on the

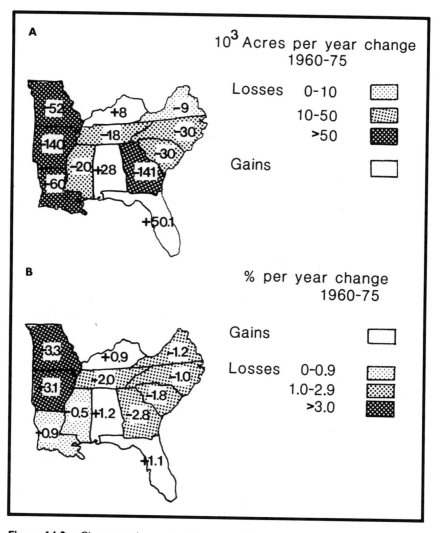

Figure 14-2. Changes in bottomland hardwood forests in southeastern United States from 1960 to 1975 in *a.* thousands of acres per year and *b.* percent per year. *(After Turner, Forsythe, and Craig, 1981, p. 19; Copyright © 1981 by Elsevier, reprinted with permission)*

Atlantic Coastal Plain. Three states (Kentucky, Alabama, and Florida) actually showed increases in areas of bottomland hardwoods, although reasons for these increases are difficult to determine and the results are suspect. Another study (MacDonald, Frayer, and Clauser, 1979) documented a 55% decrease from 4.8 million hectares (11.8 million acres) in 1937 to 2.1 million hectares (5.2 million acres) in 1978 in the lower Mississippi River alluvial floodplain alone. Estimates such as these demonstrate that, although bottomland hardwood forests represent one of the most abundant types of wetland in the United States, their true extent is not well known and they are being lost at an alarming rate.

GEOLOGY AND HYDROLOGY

Floodplain Structure and Formation

A typical riparian ecosystem contains several major features (Leopold, Wolman, and Miller, 1964; Brinson et al., 1981; Bedinger, 1981). These features, shown in Figure 14-3, include the following:

1. *The river channel* meanders through the area, transporting, eroding, and depositing alluvial sediments.
2. *Natural levees* adjacent to the channel are the result of coarser materials that are deposited as floods flow over the channel banks. Natural levees are often the highest elevation on the floodplain, sloping sharply towards the river and more gently away from it.
3. *Meander scrolls* are depressions and rises on the convex side of bends in the river, and are formed as the stream migrates laterally across the floodplain. This type of terrain is often referred to as ridge and swale topography.
4. *Oxbows,* or oxbow lakes, are bodies of permanently standing water that result from the cutoff of meanders. Deepwater swamps (chap. 13) often develop in oxbows in the southern United States.
5. *Point bars* are areas of sedimentation on the convex sides of river curves. As sediments are deposited on the point bar, the meander curve of the river tends to increase in radius and migrate downstream. Eventually, the point bar begins to support vegetation, which stabilizes it even further as part of the floodplain.
6. *Sloughs* are areas of dead water that form in meander scrolls and along valley walls. Deepwater swamps can also form in the permanently flooded sloughs.
7. *Backswamp deposits* of fine sediments are deposited between natural levees and along valley walls.
8. *Terraces* are "abandoned floodplains" that may have once been formed by the river's alluvial deposits but are not in hydrologic connection with the present river.

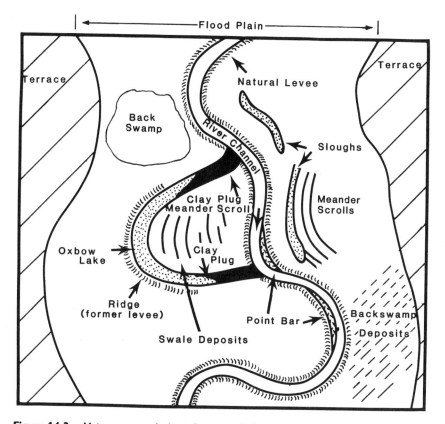

Figure 14-3. Major geomorphologic features of a floodplain. *(After Leopold, Wolman, and Miller, 1964, and Brinson et al., 1981)*

The unique nature of the floodplain or riparian ecosystem is a result of both short-term and long-term fluvial processes. The importance of the river to the floodplain and the floodplain to the river cannot be overemphasized. If either is altered, the other will surely change in time because floodplains and their rivers are in a continual dynamic balance between the building of structure and the removal of structure. In the long term, floodplains result from the combination of the deposition of alluvial materials *(aggradation)* and downcutting of surface geology *(degradation)* over many years.

Two major aggradation processes are thought to be responsible for the formation of most floodplains: deposition on the inside curves of rivers (point bars), and deposition from overbank flooding. "As a river moves laterally, sediment is deposited within or below the level of the bankfull stage on the point bar, while at overflow stages the sediment is deposited on both the point bar and over the adjacent flood plain" (Leopold, Wolman, and Miller, 1964, p. 322). The resulting floodplain is made up of alluvial sediments (or alluvium) that can range from 10 to 80 m thick. The alluvium,

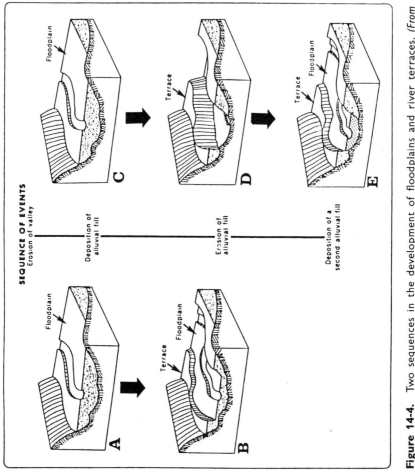

Figure 14-4. Two sequences in the development of floodplains and river terraces. *(From Brinson et al., 1981, p. 19, after Leopold, Wolman, and Miller, 1964)*

derived from the river over many thousands of years, generally progresses from gravel or coarse sand at the bottom to fine-grained material at the surface (Bedinger, 1981).

Degradation of floodplains occurs when the supply of sediments is less than the outflow of sediments, a condition that could be caused naturally with a shift in climate or synthetically with the construction of an upstream dam. There are few long term data to substantiate the first cause, but a considerable number of "before and after" studies have verified degradation downstream of dams due to their trapping of sediments. In the absence of geologic uplifting, rivers tend to degrade slowly, however, and "downcutting is slow enough that lateral swinging of the channel can usually make the valley wider than the channel itself" (Leopold, Wolman, and Miller (1964, p. 458). The process is thus difficult to observe over short periods; both aggradation and degradation can only be inferred by the study of flood-plain stratigraphy.

The formation of a riparian floodplain and terrace is shown in sequences A to B and C to D to E in Figure 14-4. When degradation occurs and yet some of the original floodplain is not downcut, that "abandoned" floodplain is called a *terrace,* and, although it may be composed of alluvial fill, it is not considered part of the floodplain. Aggradation and degradation can alternate over time as shown in the sequence C to D to E in Figure 14-4. A third case, steady state, can exist if aggradation due to the input of sediments from upstream is balanced by the degradation or downcutting of the stream (Brinson et al., 1981). Figure 14-4 demonstrates that the same surface geometry can result from two dissimilar sequences of aggradation and degradation.

Flooding

The flooding of the riparian ecosystem is important for the maintenance of that system for several reasons. The flooding water and subsequent ground-water levels are the main determinants of the type and productivity of vegetation found in the riparian zone. Flooding waters also bring nutrient-rich sediments to the floodplain, export organic and inorganic material from the floodplain, and serve as a primary agent for long-term aggradation and degradation of the floodplain.

The frequency and duration of flooding depend on several factors:

1. *Climate,* including local conditions and, for large watersheds, the conditions in upstream reaches. This variable includes precipitation patterns and the presence or absence of a significant spring thaw. The seasons in which flooding is most expected for different areas of the United States was shown in Figure 4-5. However there is a wide variation in most parts of the country from this norm and flooding of the

riparian ecosystems can generally happen during any season. Typically, midwestern and eastern U.S. riparian ecosystems are flooded for several days to several weeks during the spring thaw, while flooding of southern U.S. bottomland forests is for longer periods and is less apt to be only in the spring.

2. *Floodplain level.* Areas at successively higher levels in the floodplain are flooded less frequently than are those at lower levels. Typically, however, the larger the floodplain being flooded annually, the less additional area of floodplain at higher levels (Bedinger, 1981).

3. *Drainage area* of the stream basin upstream of the floodplain in question. Flooding duration is particularly related to this variable. Bedinger (1981) found that, for the two basins in Arkansas, sites that had larger drainage areas had correspondingly longer times in standing water (Table 14-2). This is because small watersheds have rapid runoff and sharp flood peaks, while large watersheds have flood peaks that are less sudden and longer lasting.

4. *Channel slope.* A stream with a steep slope or gradient will flood less frequently than a stream with a gentle slope. River channelization that straightens the river by cutting off meanders decreases floodplain flooding by increasing the channel slope.

5. *Soils.* The type of alluvial soil in the floodplain, its capacity to hold water (storage capacity), and the size of the water-holding deposits all help to determine the depth of surface water and the time the floodplain will be under water.

The hydroperiod of the riparian ecosystem, which includes its flooding duration, intensity, and timing, is the ultimate determinant of the ecosystem structure and function. The timing of flooding is particularly important because flooding in the growing season has a greater effect on ecosystem productivity than does an equal amount of flooding in the nongrowing season. A history of flooding for a bottomland hardwood forest in Northeastern Illinois is shown in Figure 14-5. In this riparian forest, floods of at least 10

Table 14-2. Relationship of Drainage Basin Size to Duration of Flooding of Bottomland Forests in Arkansas

Drainage Basin Area, mi^2	Flooding Duration, Percent of time
300	5-7
500-700	10-18
Several tens of thousands	18-40

Source: Based on data from Bedinger, 1981, p. 168

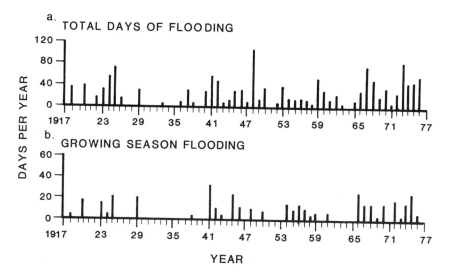

Figure 14-5. History of riparian forest inundation for Kankakee River in northeastern Illinois, showing *a.* total days of flooding per year and *b.* total days of flooding per growing season. *(After Mitsch and Rust, 1984, p. 505)*

days duration occurred in 41 out of 62 years or 2 out of every 3 years. This is in dramatic agreememt with the "average" floodplain flooding frequency suggested by Leopold and discussed in chapter 4. Floods of at least 10 days in the growing season occurred in only 23 of the 62 years of record or in 37 percent of the years.

Zonation

A classification of bottomland forests, according to flooding conditions, was developed at a workshop on bottomland hardwood wetlands held at Lake Lanier, Georgia, in 1980. That classification, based on a vegetation zonation developed by the Society of American Foresters, is shown in Figure 14-6. In general, the following water regimes are used when referring to flooding conditions of bottomland hardwood forests and other riparian ecosystems (Cowardin et al., 1979; Larson et al., 1981):

> *Zone II—Intermittently Exposed.* Surface water is present throughout the year except in years of extreme drought. The probability of annual flooding is near 100%, and vegetation is in saturated or flooded soil for the entire growing season.

> *Zone III—Semipermanently Flooded.* Surface water or soil saturation persists for a major portion of the growing season in most years.

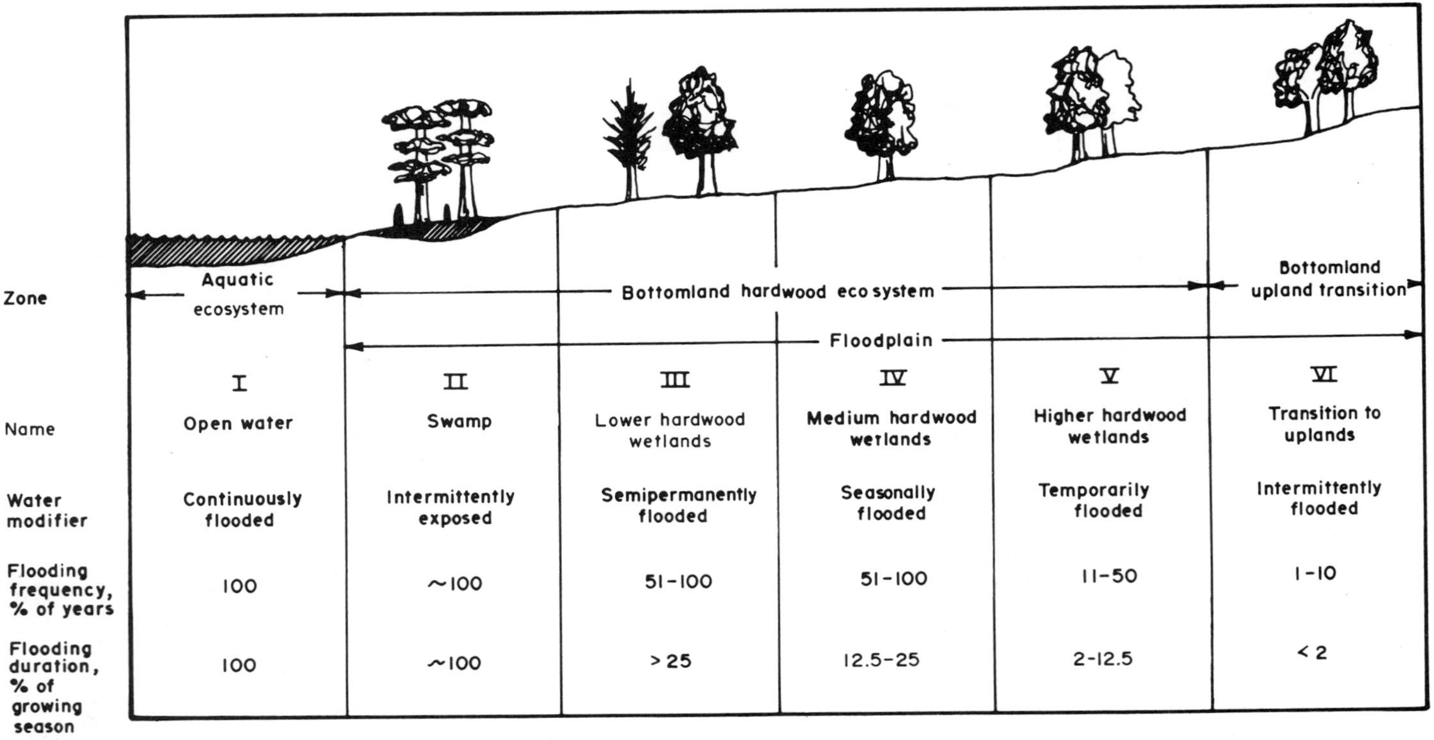

Figure 14-6. Zonal classification of bottomland forest wetlands showing average hydrologic conditions. *(After Clark and Benforado, 1981, p. 8)*

Flooding frequency ranges from 51 to 100 years per 100 years. Flooding duration typically exceeds 25% of the growing season.

Zone IV—Seasonally Flooded. Surface water or saturated soil is present for extended periods, especially early in the growing season, but is absent by the end of the season in most years. Flooding frequency ranges from 51 to 100 years per 100 years, and flooding duration is typically 12.5-25% of the growing season.

Zone V—Temporarily Flooded. Surface water is present or soil is saturated for brief periods during the growing season, but the water table usually lies well below the soil surface for most of the season. A typical frequency of flooding is 11 to 50 years out of 100. A typical duration is 2-12.5% of the growing season.

Zone VI—Intermittently Flooded. Soil inundation or saturation rarely occur, but surface water may be present for variable periods without detectable seasonal periodicity. Flood frequency typically ranges from 1 to 10 years per 100 years. Total duration of flood events is typically less than 2% of the growing season.

It should not be assumed that these flooding conditions or zones occur in sequence as one proceeds from the river's edge to the uplands as implied in Figure 14-6. As Figure 14-3 indicated, the floodplain level does not rise uniformly from the river. In this classification of flooding, riparian ecosystems occur in Zones II through VI (Zone II contains deepwater swamp ecosystems more typical of the alluvial river swamp discussed in Chapter 13). Zones II and III are typically considered wetland by most wetland scientists. However, there is much debate over the inclusion of Zones IV and V in the wetland definition when dealing with wetland management issues. As described by Larson et al. (1981, pp. 227 and 232):

Within Zones II and III, water is an overriding environmental factor and is present on a nearly permanent basis, or at least for a major portion of the growing season. Within Zones IV and V, water is a significant determinant but its periodicity and duration indicate that other environmental factors such as nutrient status, competition, and soil texture are also determinants.

Zone VI ecosystems are usually not considered wetlands but are a zone of transition to upland ecosystems.

CHEMISTRY

The physiochemical characteristics of the soils of riparian ecosystems are different from those of either upland ecosystems or permanently flooded swamps. Some of the most important properties, particularly of bottomland hardwood forest soils, are soil aeration, organic and clay content, and nutrient content. All of these characteristics are influenced by the flooding and subsequent dewatering of these ecosystems; the characteristics of the soil, in turn, greatly affect the structure and function of the plant communities that are found in the riparian ecosystem.

Table 14-3 presents typical physiochemical characteristics of floodplain soils by zone, including oxygenation, organic matter content, and mineral nutrients.

Soil Oxygen

Soil oxygen is one of the most important yet changeable characteristics of bottomland soils. Anaerobic conditions are created rapidly when the floodplain is flooded, sometimes in a period as short as a few days (see Fig. 5-2). When the floodplain is dewatered, aerobic conditions quickly return. Soil aeration is important for rooted vegetation. Most rooted plants are unable to function properly under extended periods of anoxia, although some plants have special adaptations that enable them to survive extended periods of little soil aeration (see chap. 6). Soil aeration, defined as the capacity of a soil to transmit oxygen from the atmosphere to the root zone, is dramatically curtailed by flooding water, but it is also affected by several other characteristics of the soil, including texture, amount of organic matter, permeability to water flow, level of groundwater, and degree of compaction. Soils high in clay, with small pore size, hinder drainage moreso than do sandy or loamy soils, thereby increasing the likelihood that they will be poorly aerated. High organic matter content of bottomland soils can both increase and deplete soil oxygen. Organic matter usually improves the soil structure and thus increases the aeration of clay soils. On the other hand, decomposing organic matter creates an oxygen demand of its own. Soil aeration also depends on how close the groundwater level is to the soil surface. Finally, when bottomland soils are compacted, the air-filled pores may decrease dramatically, thereby decreasing soil aeration (Patrick, 1981).

Organic Matter

The organic content of bottomland soils is usually intermediate (2%-5%) compared with the highly organic peats (20%-60%) on one extreme and upland soils (0.4%-1.5%) on the other (Wharton et al., 1982). The alternating aerobic and anaerobic conditions slow down but do not eliminate decomposition. In addition, the high clay content provides a degree of protection against decomposition of litter and other organic matter on the floodplain. Furthermore, bottomland forests are generally more productive than upland forests and therefore more organic litter is produced. Wharton et al. (1982) suggest that 5% organic content of soils is a good indicator of periodically flooded alluvial floodplains as opposed to the more permanently flooded blackwater swamps of the southeastern United States.

Nutrients

Riparian wetlands, primarily bottomland hardwood wetlands, generally have ample available nutrients. This is due to several processes. The high clay content of the soils results in higher concentrations of nutrients such as phosphorus, which has a higher affinity for clay particles than for sand or silt particles. The high organic content results in higher concentrations of nitrogen than would be found in upland soils with low organic content (Patrick, 1981). The soil is also rich in nutrients because of continual replenishment during flooding. Because much of the sediment deposited by rivers is fine-grained clays and silt, nutrients such as phosphorus are likely to be deposited in greater amounts than if the material were coarse grained. Mitsch, Dorge, and Wiemhoff (1979), for example, found that sediments high in clay that flooded an alluvial swamp in southern Illinois had phosphorus contents of 8.0–9.8 mg/g dry weight.

Anoxic conditions during flooding have several other effects on nutrient availability. Flooding causes soils to be in a highly reduced oxidation state and often causes a shift in pH, thereby increasing mobilization of certain minerals such as phosphorus, nitrogen, magnesium, sulfur, iron, manganese, boron, copper, and zinc (see chap. 5). This can lead to both greater availability of certain nutrients and also to an accumulation of potentially toxic compounds in the soil. The low oxygen levels also cause a shift in the redox state of several nutrients to more reduced states; this may make it more difficult for the plants to assimilate certain important elements such as nitrogen (Wharton et al. 1982).

Denitrification may be more prevalent in soils that have adjacent oxidized and reduced zones, as is the case in flooded riparian soils. Phosphorus is more soluble in flooded soils, but whether a shift from reduced to oxidized conditions and back again makes phosphorus more or less available is not well understood. Overall, the periodic wetting and drying of riparian soils is important in the release of nutrients from leaf litter. The generally high concentrations of nutrients and the relatively good soil texture during dry periods suggest that the major limiting factor in riparian ecosystems is the physical stress of inadequate root oxygen during flooding rather than the inadequate supply of any mineral.

Table 14-3. Physiochemical Characteristics of Floodplain Soils by Zones as in Figure 14-7 (Kitchens, and Sipe, 1982)

Characteristic	II	III	IV	V	VI
				Zone	
Soil Texture	Dominated by silty clays or sands	Dominated by dense clays	Clays dominate surface; some coarser fractions (sands) increase with depth	Clay and sandy loams dominate; sandy soils frequent	Sands to clay
Sand:Silt:Clay (% composition)					
Blackwater	69:20:12	—	74:14:12	—	—
Alluvial	29:23:48	34:22:44	34:20:45	71:16:14	—
Organic Matter, %					
Blackwater	18.0	—	7.9	—	—
Alluvial	4.5	3.4	2.8	3.8	—
Oxygenation	Moving water aerobic; stagnant water anaerobic	Anaerobic for portions of the year	Alternating anaerobic and aerobic conditions	Alternating: mostly aerobic, occasionally anaerobic	Aerobic year-round
Soil Color	Gray to olive gray with greenish gray, bluish gray, and grayish green mottles	Gray with olive mottles	Dominantly gray on blackwater floodplains and reddish on alluvial with brownish gray and grayish brown mottles	Dominantly gray or grayish brown with brown, yellowish brown, and reddish brown mottles	Dominantly red, brown, reddish brown, yellow, yellowish red, and yellowish brown, with a wide range of mottle colors

pH[a]				
Blackwater	5.0	—	5.1	—
Alluvial	5.0	5.3	5.5	5.6
Phosphorus (ppm)				
Blackwater	11.2	—	9.8	—
Alluvial	9.1	6.3	8.1	4.8
Calcium (ppm)				
Blackwater	607	—	346	—
Alluvial	1,079	752	669	186
Magnesium (ppm)				
Blackwater	98	—	36	—
Alluvial	154	140	145	39
Sodium (ppm)				
Blackwater	46	—	31	—
Alluvial	94	31	28	23
Potassium (ppm)				
Blackwater	48	—	29	—
Alluvial	51	28	32	20

Source: After Wharton et al., 1982, p. 25–26.
[a]Range includes drought years

ECOSYSTEM STRUCTURE

The wide range of flooding conditions in the floodplain leads to a variety of plant communities with rich species diversity. These communities serve as habitats for a wide array of wildlife. Some species move into the riparian areas from upland areas during dry periods. Others have aquatic origins and use the floodplain during flood season.

Vegetation

Zonation of Bottomland Hardwood Forests

The vegetation of most riparian ecosystems is dominated by diverse trees that are adapted to the wide variety of environmental conditions on the floodplain. The most important environmental condition is the hydroperiod, which determines the "moisture gradient," or—as Wharton et al. (1982) prefer—the "anaerobic gradient," which varies in time and space across the floodplain. Vegetation adapts to this gradient and can be divided into zonal classifications such as the one implemented by the National Wetlands Technical Council (Clark and Benforado, 1981) for bottomland hardwood forests as described earlier (see Fig. 14-6). Table 14-4 presents a list of tree and shrub species common to bottomland hardwood forests, from wettest (II) to driest (VI) conditions. Vegetation in Zone II is adapted to the wettest part of the floodplain with almost continuous flooding. Here *Taxodium distichum* (bald cypress) and *Nyssa aquatica* (water tupelo) often dominate the canopy of southeastern bottomlands. Major associates include *Cephalanthus occidentalis* (buttonbush) and *Planera aquatica* (water elm). Pond cypress (*Taxodium distichum* var. *nutans*) and black gum (*Nyssa sylvatica* var. *biflora*) are also found in some blackwater floodplains in Florida and Georgia. *Taxodium-Nyssa* swamps are discussed further in Chapter 13.

Zone III, which is semipermanently inundated or saturated, supports vegetation such as black willow *(Salix nigra)*, silver maple *(Acer saccharinum)*, and sometimes cottonwood *(Populus deltoides)* in the pioneer stage. A more common association in this zone includes overcup oak *(Quercus lyrata)* and water hickory *(Carya aquatica)*, which often occur in relatively small depressions in floodplains. Several other species can be found in this zone, although they are more frequent in zones with less flooding duration. These include green ash *(Fraxinus pennsylvanica)*, red maple *(Acer rubrum)*, and river birch *(Betula nigra)*. New point bars that form in the river channel in this hydrologic zone often are colonized by monospecific stands of willow, silver maple, river birch, or cottonwood.

Zone IV, which is defined as bottomlands that are seasonally flooded or saturated, supports an even wider array of hardwood trees. In the southeast-

Table 14-4. Selected Tree and Shrub Species from Bottomland Hardwood Forests in Southeastern United States

Species	II	III	IV	V	VI
Taxodium distichum (bald cypress)	X	X			
Nyssa aquatica (water tupelo)	X	X			
Cephalanthus occidentalis (buttonbush)	X	X			
Salix nigra (black willow)	X	X			
Planera aquatica (water elm)	X	X			
Forestiera acuminata (swamp privet)	X	X			
Acer rubrum (red maple)		X	X	X	X
Fraxinus caroliniana (water ash)		X	X		
Itea virginica (Viriginia willow)		X			
Ulmus americana var. *floridana* (Florida elm)		X	X		
Quercus laurifolia (laurel oak)		X	X	X	
Carya aquatica (bitter pecan)		X	X		
Quercus lyrata (overcup oak)		X	X		
Styrax americana (smooth storax)		X			
Gleditsia aquatica (water locust)		X	X		
Fraxinus pennsylvanica (green ash)		X	X		
Diospyros virginiana (persimmon)		X	X	X	X
Nyssa sylvatica var. *biflora* (swamp tupelo)		X			
Amorpha fruticosa (lead plant)		X	X		
Betula nigra (river birch)		X	X		
Populus deltoides (eastern cottonwood)		X	X		
Baccharis glomeruliflora (groundsel)			X	X	X
Cornus foemina (stiff dogwood)		X	X		
Viburnum obovatum (black haw)			X		
Celtis laevigata (sugarberry)			X	X	X
Liquidambar styraciflua (sweetgum)			X	X	X
Acer negundo (box elder)			X	X	
Sabal minor (dwarf palmetto)			X	X	
Gleditsia triacanthos (honey locust)			X	X	X
Ilex decidua (possum haw)			X	X	X
Crataegus viridis (green hawthorn)			X		
Quercus phellos (willow oak)			X	X	X
Platanus occidentalis (sycamore)			X	X	X
Alnus serrulata (common alder)			X		
Ulmus crassifolia (cedar elm)			X		
Ulmus alata (winged elm)			X	X	X
Ulmus americana (American elm)			X	X	X
Quercus nuttallii (nuttall oak)			X		
Quercus virginiana (live oak)			X	X	X
Schinus terebinthifolius (Brazilian peppertree)			X	X	

(continued)

Table 14-4. *Continued*

Species	Ecological Zone				
	II	*III*	*IV*	*V*	*VI*
Ascyrum hypericoides (St. Andrews cross)			X	X	X
Bumelia reclinata (bumelia)			X	X	
Carya illinoensis (pecan)			X	X	X
Carpinus caroliniana (blue peach)			X	X	
Myrica cerifera (wax myrtle)			X	X	X
Psychotria sulzneri (wild coffee)			X	X	
Psychotria nervosa (wild coffee)			X	X	
Zanthoxylum fragara (wild lime)			X	X	
Morus rubra (red mulberry)			X	X	X
Ximenia americana (hog plum)			X	X	X
Sambucus canadensis (elderberry)			X	X	X
Magnolia virginiana (sweet bay)			X		
Sabal palmetto (cabbage plum)			X	X	
Ligustrum sinense (privet)			X	X	X
Crataegus marshallii (parsley haw)			X	X	
Quercus nigra (water oak)			X	X	X
Quercus michauxii (cow oak)			X	X	
Quercus falcata var. *pagodaefolia* (cherrybark oak)				X	X
Nyssa sylvatica (black gum)				X	X
Pinus taeda (loblolly pine)				X	X
Carya ovata (shagbark hickory)				X	X
Juniperus virginiana (eastern red cedar)				X	X
Callicarpa americana (American beautyberry)				X	X
Asimina triloba (paw paw)				X	
Ilex opaca (American holly)				X	X
Serenoa repens (saw palmetto)				X	X
Prunus serotina (black cherry)				X	X
Fagus grandifolia (American beech)				X	X
Magnolia grandiflora (southern magnolia)				X	X
Ostrya virginiana (eastern hop-hornbeam)				X	X
Sassafras albidum (sassafras)				X	X
Sargeretia minutiflora (sargeretia)				X	X
Quercus alba (white oak)				X	X
Cornus florida (flowering dogwood)				X	X
Tilia caroliniana (basswood)				X	X
Asimina parviflora (dwarf paw paw)				X	X
Euonymus americanus (strawberry bush)				X	X
Carya glabra (pignut hickory)				X	X
Ptelea trifoliata (water ash)				X	X

Source: From Larson et al., 1981, p. 234-235. Copyright ©1981 by Elsevier Sci. Publ. Co., reprinted with permission.

ern United States, common species include laurel oak *(Quercus laurifolia),* green ash *(Fraxinus pennsylvanica),* American elm *(Ulmus americana),* and sweetgum *(Liquidambar styraciflua).* Other species that can be found in this zone, which is inundated for only 1 to 2 months during the growing season, are hackberry *(Celtis laevigata),* red maple *(Quercus rubra),* willow oak *(Quercus phellos),* and sycamore *(Platanus occidentalis).* Pioneer successional communities in this zone can consist of monotypic stands of river birch or cottonwood.

The transition to Zone V is often difficult to determine in the field. This temporarily flooded bottomland is the highest elevation of the floodplain that can be considered to be a wetland. This part is flooded yearly for less than a week to about a month during the growing season. Several oaks, tolerant of occasionally wet soils, appear here. These include swamp chestnut oak *(Quercus michauxii),* cherrybark oak (*Quercus falcata* var. *pagodaefolia*), and water oak *(Quercus nigra).* Hickories (*Carya* spp.) are often present in this zone in associations with the oaks. Two pines, spruce pine *(Pinus glabra)* and loblolly pine *(Pinus taeda),* occur at the edges of this zone in many bottomlands.

Figure 14-7 is a cross section of the microtopography of an alluvial floodplain in the southeastern United States. The complex microrelief does not show a smooth change from one zone to the next. The levee next to the stream, in fact, is often one of the most diverse parts of the floodplain due to

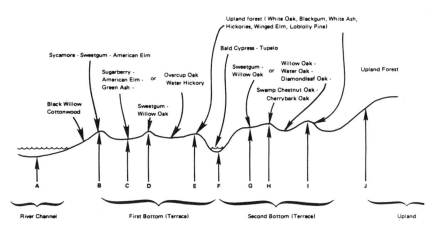

Figure 14-7. General relationship between vegetation associations and floodplain microtopography. A = river channel; B = natural levee; C = backswamp or first terrace flat; D = low first terrace ridge; E = high first terrace ridge; F = oxbow; G = second terrace flats; H = low second terrace ridge; I = high second terrace ridge; J = upland. *(From Wharton et al., 1982, p. 38)*

fluctuations in its elevation. Plants from Zones II through V often occur on these levees (Wharton et al., 1982).

Vegetation of Arid and Semiarid Riparian Forests

The riparian forests of the semiarid grasslands and arid western United States differ from those found in the humid eastern and southern United States. The natural ecosystems of these uplands are grasslands, deserts, or other nonforested ecosystems, so the riparian zone is a conspicuous feature of the landscape (Brinson et al., 1981*b*). The riparian zone in arid regions is also narrow and sharply defined in contrast with the wide alluvial valleys of the southeastern United States. As stated by R. R. Johnson (1979, p. 41), "when compared to the drier surrounding uplands, these riparian wetlands with their lush vegetation are attractive oases to wildlife and humans alike."

There are significant differences between the flora of riparian ecosystems in the eastern and western United States. One notable feature is the general absence of oak (*Quercus* spp.) in the West (Brinson et al., 1981). Also, few species are common to both regions, due to the differences in climate, although species of cottonwood (*Populus* spp.) and willow (*Salix* spp.) are found in western riparian floodplains. Keammerer, Johnson, and Burgess (1975) and W. C. Johnson, Burgess, and Keammerer (1976) described the riparian forest along the Missouri River in North Dakota, where common species included cottonwood, willow, and green ash in the lower terraces, with American elm, box elder *(Acer nugundo),* and bur oak *(Quercus macrocarpa)* at the higher elevations (Fig. 14-8). The woody vegetation along the Colorado River in the Grand Canyon region includes salt cedar *(Tamarix chinensis),* mesquite (*Prosopis* spp.) and willow-cottonwood associations at the lower elevations, and willows and alders (*Alnus* spp.) at higher elevations (R. R. Johnson, 1979). The Rio Grande in Texas and New Mexico has a continuum of riparian vegetation, from a domination of screwbean *(Prosopis pubescens)* in the xeric south to associations of Fremont cottonwood *(Populus fremontii),* Goodding willow *(Salix gooddingii),* Russian olive *(Eleagnus angustifolia),* and salt cedar in the north. The last two species were introduced in the last 50 years and have changed the character and successional characteristics of many riparian woodlands in the arid west (Brinson et al., 1981).

Consumers

The riparian ecosystem provides a valuable and diverse habitat for many animal species. Some studies (e.g., Blem and Blem, 1975) have documented that forested floodplains are generally more populated with wildlife than are

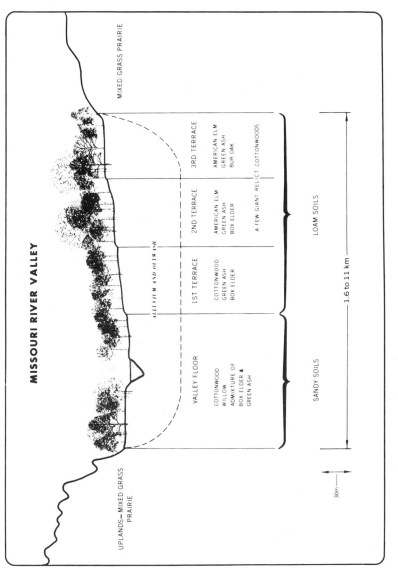

Figure 14-8. Cross section of Missouri River in semiarid North Dakota, showing major riparian tree species. *(From Brinson et al., 1981, p. 55, after Keammerer, Johnson, and Burgess, 1975)*

adjacent uplands. Because riparian ecosystems are at the interface between aquatic and terrestrial systems, they are a classic example of the ecological principle of the "edge effect" (E. P. Odum, 1979*a*). The diversity and abundance of species tend to be greater at the ecotone, or "edge" between two distinct ecosystems such as a river and uplands. Brinson et al. (1981) describe four ecological attributes that are important to the animals of the riparian ecosystem:

1. *Predominance of woody plant communities*—This is particularly important in regions where the forested riparian zone is the only wooded region remaining, as in heavily farmed regions, or where the riparian forest was the only wooded area to begin with, as is the case in the arid West. Trees and shrubs not only provide protection, roosting areas, and favorable microclimates for many species, but they also provide standing dead trees and "snags" in streams that provide habitat value for both terrestrial and aquatic animals. The riparian vegetation also shades the stream, stabilizes the stream bank with tree roots, and produces leaf litter, all of which support a greater variety of aquatic life in the stream.

2. *Presence of surface water and abundant soil moisture*—The stream or river that passes through a riparian ecosystem is an important source of food for consumers such as waterfowl and fish-eating birds, an area of protection and travel for beavers and muskrats, and a reproduction haven for amphibians. The floodplain is also important for many aquatic species, particularly as a breeding and feeding area for fish during the flood season.

3. *Diversity and interspersion of habitat features*—The riparian zones form an array of diverse habitats, often from permanently flooded swamps to infrequently flooded forests. This diversity, coupled with the edge effect discussed above, provides for a great abundance of wildlife.

4. *Corridors for dispersal and migration*—The linear nature of bottomland and other riparian ecosystems along rivers provides protective pathways for animals such as birds, deer, elk, and small mammals to migrate among habitats. Fish migration and dispersal may also depend on the maintenance of the integrity of riparian ecosystems along the stream or river.

A comprehensive description of the fauna that inhabits the floodplain wetlands would not be possible here due to the enormous number of birds, reptiles, amphibians, fish, mammals, and invertebrates that use the floodplain environment. Several good reviews on the fauna of bottomland and riparian wetlands are given by Fredrickson (1979), Wharton et al. (1981; 1982), and Brinson et al. (1981). The many surveys that have been made in these areas show a great diversity of animals. The animals, like the plants, are accustomed to certain zones in the floodplain, although the matching of zones with biota does not always provide a neat fit (Wharton et al., 1981). Frederickson (1979) described the distribution of amphibians, reptiles, mammals, and birds along the floodplain zones as shown in Figure 14-9 for the

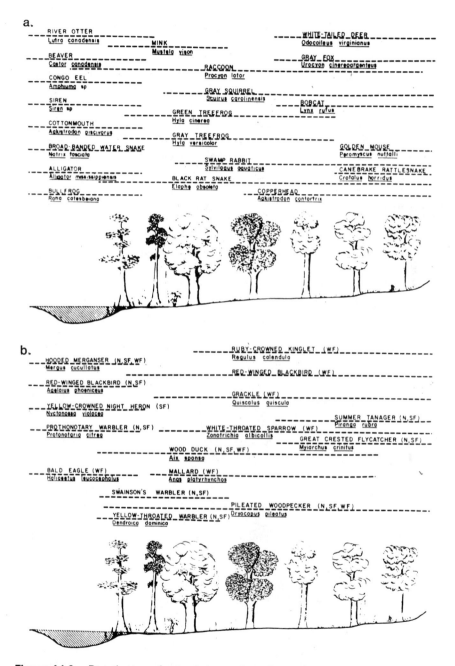

Figure 14-9. Distribution of animals in southern bottomland hardwood forests; *a.* amphibians, reptiles, and mammals and *b.* birds in relation to nesting (N), summer foraging (SF), and winter foraging (WF). *(From Frederickson, 1979, pp. 300–301; Copyright © 1979 by the American Water Resources Association, reprinted with permission)*

southern bottomlands. Few generalizations are possible. Several animals such as the beaver, river otter, snakes of the genus *Natrix,* the cottonmouth, and several frogs occur near the water. Deer, foxes, squirrels, certain species of mice, the copperhead, and the canebrake rattlesnake occur from the uplands edge. Most of the food chains are detrital, based on the organic production of the vegetation. Other characteristics of the fauna, because of the sequence of flooding and dewatering, are high mobility, arboreal (tree-inhabiting) abilities, swimming ability, and ability to survive inundation (Wharton et al., 1981). Most of the species in Figure 14-9 have one or more of these traits.

ECOSYSTEM FUNCTION

Riparian ecosystems, particularly the bottomland hardwood forests of the southeastern United States, have many functional characteristics that are a result of the unique physical environment. It is generally recognized that they are highly productive due to the convergence of energy and materials that pass through riparian wetlands in great amounts. Although few generalizations are possible on the functional attributes of riparian ecosystems because of the lack of a sufficient number of studies, Figure 14-10 demonstrates probable spatial patterns of a number of ecosystem functions that are described in more detail below.

Primary Productivity

Riparian wetlands are generally more productive than adjacent upland ecosystems due to their unique hydrologic conditions. This periodic flooding usually contributes to higher productivities in at least three ways (Brinson et al., 1981):

1. Flooding provides an adequate water supply for the vegetation. This is particularly important in arid riparian wetlands.
2. Nutrients are supplied and favorable alteration of soil chemistry results from the periodic overbank flooding. These alterations include nitrification, sulfate reduction, and nutrient mineralization.
3. The flowing water offers a more oxygenated root zone than if the water were stagnant. The periodic "flushing" also carries away many waste products of soil and root metabolism, such as carbon dioxide and methane.

Table 14-5 presents measurements of biomass and net primary productivity for several forested riparian wetlands. In general, floodplain wetlands that have an annual unaltered cycle of wet and dry periods had aboveground net

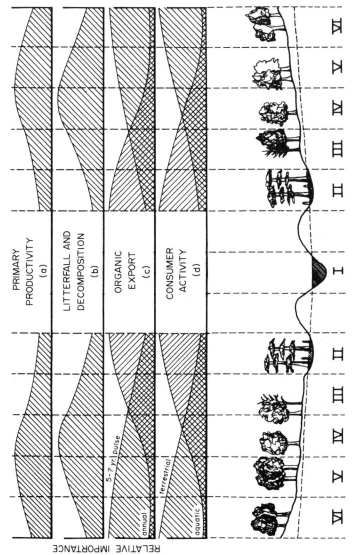

Figure 14-10. Probable spatial patterns of several ecosystem functions for zones of bottomland hardwood wetlands. Patterns are for *a.* primary productivity, *b.* litter fall and decomposition, *c.* organic export, and *d.* consumer activity. (*From Taylor, Cardamone, and Mitsch, 1984, p. 22*)

Table 14-5. Selected Measurements of Biomass and net Primary Productivity of Riparian Forested Wetlands

Forest type	Stem Density no./ha	Basal Area, m²/ha	Biomass kg/m² Above-ground	Biomass kg/m² Below-ground	Litter fall, g/m²·yr	Stem growth, g/m²·yr	Aboveground NPP[a], g/m²·yr	Reference
Louisiana								
Bottomland hardwood	1,710	24.3	16.5	—	574	800	1,374	Conner and Day (1976)
Minnesota								
Forested fen	3,348	25.1	10.0	—	412	334	746	Reiners (1972)
Illinois								
Floodplain forest	—	—	29.0	—	—	—	1,250	Johnson and Bell (1976)
Transition forest	—	—	14.2	—	—	—	800	Johnson and Bell (1976)
Floodplain forest	423	32.1	—	—	491	177	668	Brown and Peterson (1983)
Kentucky								
Floodplain forests	990	42.0	30.3	—	420	914	1,334	Taylor (1985)
	370	17.7	18.4	—	468	812	1,280	

Source: After Brinson et al., 1981, p. 29.
[a]NPP = net primary productivity = litterfall + stem growth.

biomass production (litterfall + stem growth) greater than $1,000 \text{ g/m}^2 \cdot \text{yr}$. This level of productivity is generally higher than that of forested wetlands that are permanently flooded or have sluggish flow, a point described in detail in Chapters 4 and 13. It is usually the case that both permanently flooded zones (Zone II in bottomland hardwood forests) and rarely flooded zones (Zone VI in bottomland hardwood forests) are less productive than those zones that alternate between wet and dry conditions more frequently (see Fig. 14-10a).

It is generally believed that the pulsing floods on riparian wetlands necessarily lead to their high productivity (see chap. 4 and 13). However, two recent studies of bottomland forested wetlands in Illinois have cast some doubt on this being a general principle. Brown and Peterson (1983) compared the aboveground productivity of two forested bottomlands in Illinois, one stillwater and the other flowing-water. They found the productivity to be 50% higher in the stillwater site than in the flowing-water site, suggesting that not all riparian wetlands are productive as a result of seasonal flooding. Mitsch and Rust (1984) investigated a 60-year record of annual tree ring growth and frequency of flooding in a forested riparian wetland in northeastern Illinois and found a general lack of correlation between measures of flooding and tree growth. They suggest a more complicated interplay, with floods having influences that are both positive (nutrient and water replenishment) and negative (anaerobic root zone). Both of these studies, while not conclusively eliminating the flood pulse–high productivity hypothesis, show that it is a more complicated relationship than originally thought.

Decomposition

The decomposition of organic matter in riparian ecosystems is undoubtedly related to the intensity and duration of flooding, although consistent relationships have not been found. Brinson (1977) found in an alluvial swamp forest in North Carolina that decomposition of litter was most rapid in the wettest site and slowest on the dry levee. Duever, Carlson, and Riopelle (1975), however, found that decomposition was greater in dry sites than in those flooded for durations ranging from 16% to 50% of the time in Corkscrew Swamp in southwestern Florida. The degree of decomposition in riparian wetlands is probably greatest in areas that are generally aerobic yet are supplied with adequate moisture (see Fig. 14-10b). Decomposition is probably slightly slower at sites that are continually dry and lacking in moisture. Decomposition of litter in permanently anaerobic wetlands is probably the slowest (Brinson, Lugo, and Brown, 1981).

Organic Export

There is considerable evidence that watersheds draining areas of wetlands export more organic carbon than do watersheds that do not have wetlands (see Fig. 5-11). The organic carbon is in both dissolved and particulate forms, although the particulate fraction is generally a small percentage of the total carbon in most rivers (Brinson et al., 1981). The large organic carbon export from watersheds dominated by riparian ecosystems is due to the following factors:

1. a large surface area of litter, detritus, and organic soil that is exposed to the river water during flooding
2. rapid leaching of soluble organic carbon from some riparian soils and litter exposed to flooding
3. the long time during which water is in contact with the floodplain, allowing for significant passive leaching
4. river movement over floodplains during flooding that can physically erode and transport particulate organic carbon from the floodplain

Both particulate and dissolved carbon have been shown to be valuable for downstream ecosystems, particularly for lacustrine and marine ecosystems. There is evidence that the particulate fraction is important as a source of energy for filter-feeding organisms. The dissolved organic carbon probably is most valuable as a source of carbon for microorganisms, which in turn convert it to particulate form (Brinson, Lugo, and Brown, 1981; Brinson et al., 1981).

Energy Flow

Studies of the overall energy flow of riparian wetlands are lacking, although there are several studies related to primary productivity. A useful energy flow diagram of the riparian ecosystem is shown in Figure 14-11. The primary sources of energy are solar energy, wind, water flow, sediments, and nutrients. The major stresses include hydrologic, geomorphologic, and physiological stresses, and biomass removal. The stress effects, shown to affect different pathways in the riparian ecosystem, are greater if they affect the principle energy sources (e.g., hydrologic modification) than if they affect the ecosystem within its structure (e.g., biomass removal) (Cairns et al., 1981).

It is possible to make only broad generalizations about riparian ecosystem energy flow. The food webs that develop in these ecosystems begin with the production of detritus, although a great complexity and diversity of animals develop in the food webs. A unique feature of riparian wetlands is that the detrital production supports both aquatic and terrestrial communities (Brinson et al., 1981). The wetlands also receive and transport to downstream ecosystems a large amount of detrital energy. Most of what is known about energy flow in riparian ecosystems is limited to measures of primary productivity.

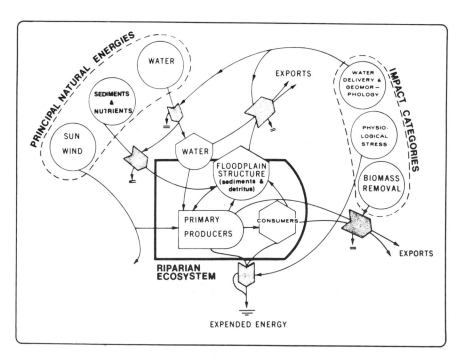

Figure 14-11.   Model of energy flow of a bottomland hardwood ecosystem showing natural energies and major impacts. *(From Cairns et al., 1981, p. 306; Copyright © 1981 by Elsevier, reprinted with permission, after Brown, Brinson, and Lugo, 1979)*

Nutrient Cycling

Several important points should be made about nutrient cycling in riparian ecosystems:

1. Riparian ecosystems have very "open" nutrient cycles that are dominated by the flooding stream or river.
2. The riparian forests have significant biotic control of the intrasystem cycling of nutrients, with seasonal patterns of growth and decay often matching available nutrients.
3. The contact of water with sediments on the forest floor leads to several important nutrient transformations. The floodplain ecosystem is adapted to take advantage of those transformations.
4. Riparian wetlands can serve as effective sinks of nutrients that enter as lateral runoff and groundwater flow.
5. When the entire river system that flows through a watershed dominated by riparian wetlands is investigated, the riparian wetlands often appear to be nutrient transformers that have a net import of inorganic forms of nutrients and a net export of organic forms.

Table 14-6. Rates of Phosphorus Sedimentation in Riparian Forested Wetlands

Location	Sedimentation Rate	$kg/ha \cdot yr$	Source
Cache River, Southern Ill.	3.6 g $P/m^2 \cdot$ yr contributed by flood as sedimentation for flood of 1.13-yr recurrence interval	36	Mitsch, Dorge, and Wiemhoff (1979)
Paririe Creek, North-Central Fla.	3.25 g $P/m^2 \cdot$ yr as sedimentation from river overflow	32.5	Brown (1978)
Creeping Swamp, Coastal Plain, N.C.	0.17 g $P/m^2 \cdot$ yr sedimentation on floodplain floor from river overflow	1.72	Yarbro (1979)
Creeping Swamp, Coastal Plain, N.C.	0.315–0.730 g $P/m^2 \cdot$ yr based input-output budget of floodplain (most was filterable reactive phosphorus)	3.15–7.30	Yarbro (1979)
Kankakee River, Northwestern Ill.	1.36 g P/m^2 contributed by unusually large spring flood lasting 62-80 days	13.6	Mitsch et al. (1979)

Source: From Brinson et al., 1981, p. 41.

The nutrient cycles of riparian wetlands are open cycles with large inputs and outputs due to flooding. The cycling is also significantly affected by the many chemical transformations that occur when the soil is saturated or under water. The inflow of nutrients to the riparian ecosystem is a major pathway in their nutrient cycle. Table 14-6 illustrates the range of measurements of phosphorus input to riverine forests. While these data are only approximations of the phosphorus contribution due to the flood, it is worth noting that they are usually several orders of magnitude greater than phosphorus inflows from precipitation and are at least on the same order of magnitude as intrasystem cycling flows. This relative importance was shown for alluvial river swamps in chapter 13.

Brinson et al. (1981) have described the cycling of nitrogen in a stream-floodplain complex as shown in Figure 14-12. In winter, flooding contributes dissolved and particulate nitrogen that is not taken up by the canopy trees due to their winter dormancy. The nitrogen is retained, however, by filamentous algae on the forest floor and through immobilization by detritivores. In spring, the nitrogen is released by decomposition as the waters warm and as the filamentous algae are shaded by the developing canopy. The vegetation canopy continues to develop, increasing plant nitrogen uptake and lowering water levels through evapotranspiration. When the sediments are exposed to the atmosphere as summer progresses, ammonification and nitrification are stimulated further, making the nitrogen more available for plant uptake. Nitrification, in turn, produces nitrates that are lost through denitrification when they are exposed to anaerobic conditions caused by subsequent flooding.

Riparian ecosystems have been measured as effective "filters" for nutrient materials that enter through lateral runoff and groundwater. Peterjohn and Correll (1984) found that a 50-meter-wide riparian forest in an agricultural watershed near the Chesapeake Bay in Maryland removed an estimated 89% of the nitrogen and 80% of the phosphorus that entered it from upland runoff, groundwater, and bulk precipitation. The study estimated that there was a net removal of 11 kg/ha · yr of particulate organic nitrogen, 0.83 kg/ha · yr of dissolved ammonium nitrogen, 47.2 kg/ha · yr of nitrate nitrogen, and 3.0 kg/ha · yr of particulate phosphorus. This study and a few others (e.g., Schlosser and Karr, 1981*a*; 1981*b*) have demonstrated the way in which riparian ecosystems can be effective in removing nutrients and sediments from agricultural runoff before it reaches the stream or river.

Elder and Mattraw (1982) and Elder (1985) investigated the flux and speciation of nitrogen and phosphorus in the Apalachicola River in northern Florida, a river that is dominated by forested riparian ecosystems along much of its length. This study concluded that the floodplain forests were nutrient transformers rather then nutrient sinks, when the total export of nutrients by the watershed is compared to the upstream inputs. That is, the inputs and outputs were similar for both total nitrogen and total phosphorus,

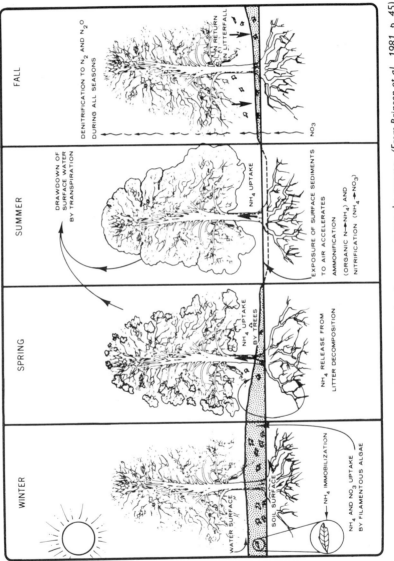

Figure 14-12. Seasonal cycling of nitrogen in riparian cypress-tupelo swamp. *(From Brinson et al., 1981, p. 45)*

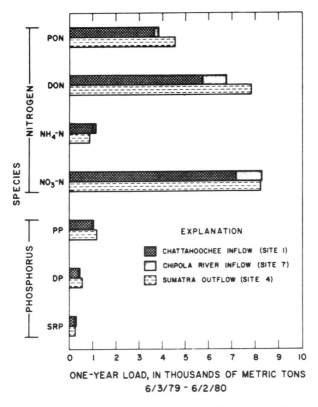

Figure 14-13. Inflows and outflows of various forms of nitrogen and phosphorus for Apalachicola River in northern Florida. *(From Elder, 1985, p. 729)*

but the forms of the nutrients were different. The study found net increases in particulate organic nitrogen, dissolved organic nitrogen, particulate phosphorus, and dissolved phosphorus, and net decreases in dissolved inorganic phosphorus and soluble reactive phosphorus (Fig. 14-13). This means that the riparian forests were net importers of inorganic forms of nutrients and net exporters of organic forms. These transformations were argued as being important for secondary productivity in downstream estuaries.

ECOSYSTEM MODELS

Few energy/nutrient models have been developed for bottomland hardwood forests in particular or riparian wetlands in general. The scarcity of specific energy/nutrient simulation models results from, as much as any cause, the difficulty in quantifying the relationships between stream flooding and ecosystem productivity.

A tree growth simulation model of southern wetland forests, entitled SWAMP, was developed by Phipps (1979) and applied to a bottomland forest in Arkansas and later to a forested wetland in Virginia (Phipps and Applegate, 1983). Unlike the energy/nutrient models shown above, this model simulates the growth of individual trees in the forest, summing the growth of all trees in plot to determine plot dynamics. The model includes subroutines, including GROW, which grows trees on the plot according to a parabolic growth form; KILL, which determines survival probabilities of trees and occasionally "kills" trees; and CUT, which enables the modeler to remove trees as in lumbering or insect damage. Another important subroutine, WATER, describes the importance of water level fluctuations on tree growth. This subroutine assumes that tree growth will be suboptimal during the peak May–June growth period if water is either too high or too low. The effect of water levels on tree productivity is hypothesized to be a parabolic function as follows:

$$H = 1 - 0.05511(T - W)^2 \qquad (14.1)$$

where H = growth factor due to water table, T = water table depth of sample plot, and W = optimum water table depth.

The model begins with all tree species greater than 3 cm in diameter on a 20 m × 20 m plot and "grows" them on a year-by-year basis, with results depending on hydrologic conditions such as flooding frequency and depth to water table and on other factors, including shading and simulated lumbering. Typical results from runs of the model with data from the White River in Arkansas indicate the importance of altered hydroperiod and lumbering on the structure of these three layers in the bottomland forest. The author of the model acknowledges that "though in its present form the model is heavily dependent upon hypothetical relationships, it is felt that it can ultimately be of value to predict wetland vegetation change subsequent to hydrologic change."

Pearlstein, McKellar and Kitchens (1985) investigated the impact of altered hydrologic regime on a bottomland forest in South Carolina with a succession model called FORFLO. This model, developed from the same origins as the SWAMP model described above, predicted a 97% loss of bottomland forests due to river diversion.

SUMMARY

Riparian wetlands, which have a high water table because of their proximity to a river, stream, or other body of water, are unique because of their linear form along rivers and streams and because they process large fluxes of energy and materials from upstream systems. Major expanses of riparian ecosystems, called bottomland hardwood forests, are found in the southeastern United States, although many have been drained and cleared for agriculture. The bottomland hardwood forest depends on its hydroperiod and has been conveniently divided into zones that range from intermittently exposed to intermittently flooded. The flooding affects the soil chemistry by producing anaerobic conditions, importing and removing organic matter, and replenishing mineral nutrients. The plant communities of riparian ecosystems are generally very productive and diverse due to the periodic flooding, although recent evidence shows that there is not always the expected relationship between flooding and productivity. The riparian zone is also valuable for many animals that seek its refuge, diversity of habitat, and abundant water or that use it as a corridor for migration. Ecosystem function of these systems is poorly understood, except that primary productivity is generally higher than that in uplands from the same region, and the systems are very open to large fluxes of energy and nutrients. The riparian ecosystem acts as a nutrient sink as regards to its effect on lateral runoff from uplands but as a nutrient transformer as regards to the entire export of the watershed. Few energy/nutrient models have been developed to describe these systems, although tree growth models have been applied to bottomland hardwood forests with some success.

Part V

MANAGEMENT OF WETLANDS

15

VALUES AND VALUATION
OF WETLANDS

The term *value* imposes an anthropocentric orientation on a discussion of wetlands. The term is often used in an ecological sense to refer to functional processes, as for example when we speak of the "value" of primary production in providing the food energy that drives the ecosystem. But in ordinary parlance, the word connotes something worthy, desirable, or useful to humans. The reasons that wetlands are legally protected have to do with their value to society, not with abstruse ecological processes that proceed therein; and this is the sense in which the word "value" is used in this chapter. Perceived values arise out of the functional ecological processes described in previous chapters, but are determined also by the location of a particular wetland, the human population pressures on it, and the extent of the resource. Excellent references for this subject are found in the proceedings of a national symposium on wetlands held in Florida in 1978 (Greeson, Clark, and Clark, 1979) and in several literature reviews (e.g., Reppert et al., 1979; Larson, 1982; Adamus, 1983; Sather and Smith, 1984). Parts of this chapter are also excerpted from Gosselink (1984).

WETLAND VALUES

Populations

Wetland values can conveniently be considered at three hierarchical levels—population, ecosystem, and global. The easiest to identify are the populations that depend on wetland habitats for their survival.

Table 15-1. Fur Harvest (1975–1976) in the United States by Species

Species	Number of Pelts Harvested	Value, dollars
Beaver	197,000	1,183,000
Mink	250,000	2,495,000
Muskrat	6,475,000	22,660,000
Nutria	1,570,000	8,243,000
Otter	18,900	945,000

Source: Data from Chabreck, 1979, p. 625

Animals Harvested for Pelts

Fur-bearing mammals and the alligator are harvested for their pelts. In contrast with most other commercially important wetland species, these animals typically have a limited range and spend their lives within a short distance of their birthplaces. The most abundant are the muskrats (Table 15-1), which are found in wetlands throughout the United States except, strangely, the south Atlantic coast. They prefer fresh inland marshes, but along the northern Gulf coast are more abundant in brackish marshes. About 50% of the nation's harvest is from the Midwest, and 25% from along the northern Gulf of Mexico, mostly Louisiana (Chabreck, 1979). The nutria is next most abundant. It is very much like a muskrat, but larger and more vigorous. This species was imported from South America into Louisiana, and escaped from captivity in 1938, spreading rapidly through the state's coastal marshes. It is now abundant in freshwater forested swamps, and in coastal marshes from which it may have displaced muskrats to more brackish locations. Ninety-seven percent of the U.S. nutria harvest occurs in Louisiana. In order of decreasing abundance, other harvested fur animals are mink, beaver, and otter. Raccoons are also taken commercially and, in the north-central states, are second only to muskrats. Beavers are associated with forested wetlands, especially in the midwest. Minnesota harvests 27% of the nation's catch.

The alligator represents a dramatic success story of a return from the edge of extinction to a healthy population (at least in the central Gulf states) that is now harvested under close regulation. The species was threatened by severe hunting pressure, not by habitat loss. When that pressure was removed, its numbers increased rapidly. Alligators are abundant in fresh and slightly brackish lakes and streams, and build nests in adjacent marshes. The Louisiana harvest is worth about a quarter of a million dollars.

Waterfowl

Wetlands are probably known best for their abundance of waterfowl, which supports a large and valuable recreational hunting industry. We use the term

Table 15-2. Distribution of Duck Harvest in the United States, 1967–1969

| Species | Flyway, percent of total | | | | U.S. Harvest, thousands of ducks |
	Pacific	Central	Mississippi	Atlantic	
Mallard	33.7	20.2	37.8	8.2	3,474
Black Duck	0.0	0.4	26.2	73.3	387
Gadwall	23.9	40.4	31.6	4.1	540
American Widgeon	55.3	15.4	22.8	6.0	881
Green-Winged Teal	42.0	20.2	28.5	9.1	1,288
Blue-Winged Teal	21.7	14.8	54.3	9.3	477
Shoveler	59.3	19.7	18.2	2.6	414
Pintail	71.3	12.0	14.1	2.2	1,268
Wood Duck	5.9	6.3	59.7	28.0	709
Lesser Scaup	11.6	13.8	59.9	14.6	370
Ring-Necked Duck	7.0	10.5	61.3	21.0	360
Redhead	19.8	35.5	39.8	4.8	169
Canvasback	25.5	20.5	32.0	21.9	105

Source: Data from Geis and Cooch, 1972, as summarized by Chabreck, 1979, pp. 620-622.

"industry" because hunters spend large sums of money in the local economy for guns, ammunition, hunting clothes, travel to hunting spots, food, and lodging. Most of the birds hunted are hatched in the far north, sometimes above the Arctic Circle, but are shot during their winter migrations to the southern United States. There are exceptions—the wood duck breeds locally throughout the continent—but the generalization holds for most species. Different groups of ducks have different habitat preferences, and these preferences change with duck maturity and season. Therefore, a broad diversity of wetland habitat types is important for waterfowl success. Freshwater prairie potholes are the primary breeding place for most of the nation's waterfowl. Wood ducks prefer forested wetlands, however. During the winter, diving ducks are found in brackish marshes, preferably adjacent to fairly deep ponds and lakes. Dabbling ducks prefer freshwater marshes, and often graze heavily in adjacent rice fields and in very shallow marsh ponds. Gadwalls like shallow ponds with submerged vegetation.

Hunting is closely regulated and tailored to the local regime. The mallard makes up about one-third of the U.S. total of harvested ducks (Table 15-2). About 50% of these are shot in wetlands, most of the rest in agricultural fields. In Louisiana, one-third of the available mallards are killed each year. The percentage is lower for other species—about 8-13%. The vast flocks of geese that used to be so abundant along the eastern seaboard and the Gulf coast are smaller now, but are still abundant and important as hunted species in some areas.

**Table 15-3. Dominant Commercial and Recreational
Wetland-Associated Fish and Shellfish**

Common Name	Scientific Name	Commercial Harvest, metric tons[a]
Fresh Water		
Catfish and bullhead	*Ictalurus* sp.	16,800
Carp	*Cyprinus carpio*	11,800
Buffalo	*Istiobus* sp.	11,300
Perch	*Perca* sp., *Stizostedion* sp.	—
Pickerel	*Esox* sp.	—
Sunfish	*Lepomis* sp., *Micropterus* sp., *Pomoxis* sp.	—
Trout	*Salmo* sp., *Salvelinus* sp.	—
Anadromous		
Salmon	*Oncorhynchus* sp.	107,000
Shad and alewife	*Alosa* sp.	27,700
Striped bass	*Morone saxatilis*	5,000
Saltwater		
Menhaden	*Brevoortia* sp.	889,000
Shrimp	*Penaeus* sp.	111,000
Blue crab	*Callinectes sapidus*	63,900
Oyster	*Crassostrea* sp.	24,000
Mullet	*Mugil* sp.	15,400
Sea trout	*Cynoscion* sp.	11,300
Atlantic croaker	*Micropogonias undulatus*	9,500
Hard clam	*Mercenaria* sp.	6,800
Fluke	*Paralichthys* sp.	4,500
Soft clam	*Mya arenaria*	4,500
Bluefish	*Pomatomus saltatrix*	—
Drum	*Pogonias cromis, Sciaenops ocellata*	—
Spot	*Leiostomus xanthurus*	—

Source: After Peters, Ahrenholz, and Rice, 1979, p. 609
[a]Landings are 1971-1975 averages

Fish and Shellfish

About two-thirds of the fish and shellfish species that are harvested commercially are associated with wetlands. The degree of dependence on wetlands varies widely with species. Many freshwater species spawn in wetlands. Juveniles of most of the species in coastal fisheries spawn offshore but use wetlands as nursery areas. Some important species are permanent residents, and others are merely transients that feed in wetlands when the opportunity arises. Table 15-3 lists the major nektonic species found in wetlands. Virtually all of the freshwater species are somewhat dependent on wetlands, often spawning in marshes bordering lakes or in riparian forests during spring flooding. These species are primarily recreational. The saltwater species tend to spawn offshore, move into the coastal marshes during their juvenile stages, then emigrate offshore as they mature. They are often important for both commercial and recreational fisheries. The menhaden is caught only commercially, but competition between commercial and sport fishermen can be intensive and acrimonious for shrimp, blue crab, oyster, catfish, seatrout, and striped bass. Anadromous fish probably use wetlands less than the other two groups. Their most intensive use is probably by young fry, which sometimes linger in estuaries and adjacent marshes on their migration to the ocean from the freshwater streams in which they were spawned.

Analyses of fishery harvests from wetlands show the importance of the recreational catch. Although the commercial harvest is usually much better documented, several studies have showed that for certain fisheries the recreational catch far outweighs the commercial catch. Furthermore, the value to the economy of recreational fishing is usually far greater than the commercial catch because sports fishermen spend more money per fish caught (they are less efficient) than their commercial counterparts. For example, DeSylva (1969) estimated that in California it costs an angler $18.11 to catch one salmon; its value is 5½ times from the angler's standpoint what it is to the commercial fisherman. These excess dollars feed the California economy.

Timber and Other Vegetation Harvest

The area of wetland timber in the United States is about 33 million hectares (82 million acres). Two-thirds of this area is east of the Rocky Mountains. The Mississippi River alluvial floodplain and the floodplains of rivers entering the south Atlantic are mostly deciduous wetlands, while the forested wetlands along the northern tier of states are primarily evergreen. The former are more extensive and potentially more valuable because of the much faster growth rates in the South. R. L. Johnson (1979) estimated that the 13 million hectares of bottomland hardwood and cypress swamps in the southeastern part of the nation contained about 112 cubic meters of merchantable timber per hectare (1,600 cubic feet/acre), worth about $620/hectare or about $8 billion. As timber prices climb, and as the land becomes more and more valuable for agriculture, these wetlands are being clear-cut and drained (see chap. 16), although sound silviculture practices can coexist with productive wetlands.

In addition to timber harvest, the production of herbaceous vegetation in marshes is a possible source of energy, fiber, and other commodities. These possibilities have not been explored widely in the United States, but are viable options elsewhere. The productivity of many wetland species is as great as our most vigorous agricultural crops. Ryther et al. (1979) estimated that energy put into growing wetland crops can be returned five- to ninefold in their harvest. However, only about half as much energy can be recovered if the crop is fermented to produce methane. The economics of commercial production is not well worked out, but Ryther et al. (1979) state that a 1,000-ha water hyacinth energy farm in the southern United States could produce on the order of 10^{12} BTU of methane per year and, at the same time, remove all the nitrogen from the wastewater from a city of about 700,000 population. At present, energy production is probably less practical than food or fiber production from an economic point of view (Greeley, 1976; Ryther et al., 1979). It should be understood that the use of wetlands for any purpose involving harvest of the vegetation is bound to have a significant effect on the way the system functions in the long run. Therefore, the benefits of the harvest should be weighted against any functional values lost through the harvesting operation.

In addition to the annual production of living vegetation in wetlands, they are enormous reservoirs of buried peat. Farnham (1979) estimated world peat resources at 322 million hectares, mostly in the USSR and Canada. The United States has only about 21 million hectares, most of it in Alaska, Minnesota, and Michigan. This buried peat is, of course, a nonrenewable energy source that when mined destroys the wetland habitat it is built on. In the United States, peat is mined for horticultural peat production primarily, but in other parts of the world—for example, Europe and the Soviet Union—it has been used as a fuel source for hundreds of years. It is used to generate electricity, formed into briquettes for home use, and gasified or liquefied to produce methanol and industrial fuels (see chap. 16).

Endangered and Threatened Species

Wetland habitats are necessary for the survival of a disproportionately high percentage of endangered and threatened species. Table 15-4 summarizes the statistics, but imparts no information about the particular species involved, their location, wetland habitat requirements, degree of wetland dependence, and factors contributing to their demise. The fate of several species is discussed below for illustration.

Whooping cranes nest in wetlands in the northwest territories of Canada, in water 0.3-0.6 m deep, during spring and summer. In the fall, they migrate to Aransas National Wildlife Refuge, Texas, stopping off in riverine marshes along the migration route. In Texas they winter in tidal marshes. All three types of wetlands are important for their survival (Williams and Dodd, 1979). The decline in the once abundant species was due both to hunting and to habitat loss. The last whooping crane nest in the United States was seen in 1889 (Miller, Botkin, and Mendelssohn, 1974). In 1941 the flock consisted of 13 adults and 2 young. Since then the flock has been gradually built up to about 75 birds.

Table 15-4. Threatened and Endangered Species Associated with Wetlands

Taxon	Number of species	Percent of U.S. Total Threatened or Endangered
Plants	95	3
Mammals	5	15
Birds	22	31
Reptiles	4	31
Amphibians	3	50
Fish	22	54

Source: Data from Williams and Dodd, 1979, p. 573

American alligator populations were decimated by hunters and poachers to such low levels that the species was declared endangered. With close control, the population has subsequently been rebuilt. Alligators have a reciprocal relationship with wetlands—they depend on them, but in return the character of the wetland is shaped by the alligator, at least in the south Florida Everglades. As the annual dry season approaches, alligators dig "gator holes." The material thrown out around the holes forms a berm raised high enough to support trees and shrubs in an otherwise treeless prairie. These trees provide cover and breeding grounds for insects, birds, turtles, and snakes. The hole itself is a place the alligator can wait out the dry period until the winter rains. It also provides a refuge for dense populations of fish and shellfish (up to $1,600/m^2$). These organisms in turn attract top carnivores, so the gator holes are sites of concentrated biological activity that may be important for the survival of many species.

The slackwater darter *(Etheostoma boschungi)* is an example of the specificity sometimes required by wetland species. This small fish, found in small and moderate creeks in Alabama and Tennessee, migrates 1-5 km upstream at certain times of the year to spawn in small marshy areas associated with water seeps. It requires shallow (2-8 cm) water and deposits its eggs on a single species of rush *(Juncus acuminatus)* in spite of the presence of other species. The larvae remain in the vicinity of these marshes for 4-6 weeks before returning to their home streams (Williams and Dodd, 1979).

Ecosystem Values

At the level of the whole ecosystem, wetlands have value to the public for flood mitigation, for storm abatement, for aquifer recharge, for water quality improvement, and for their aesthetic qualities. Some of these ecosystem values for wetlands can vary from year to year or season to season. Figure 15-1 illustrates several of the potential values of riparian forested wetlands.

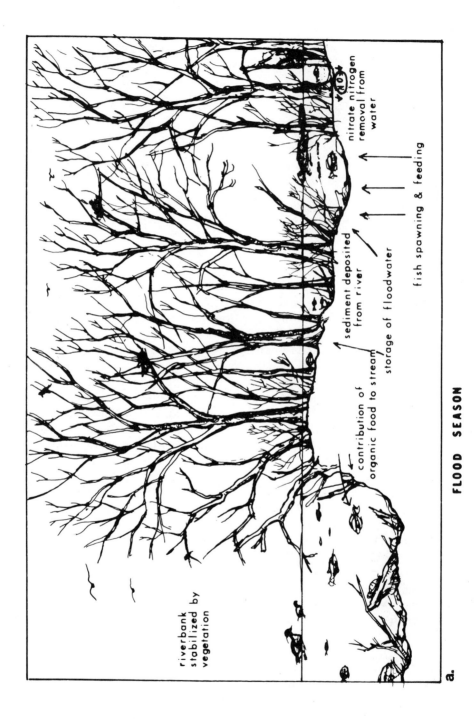

riverbank stabilized by vegetation

contribution of organic food to stream

sediment deposited from river

storage of floodwater

fish spawning & feeding

nitrate nitrogen removal from water

NO_3

FLOOD SEASON

a.

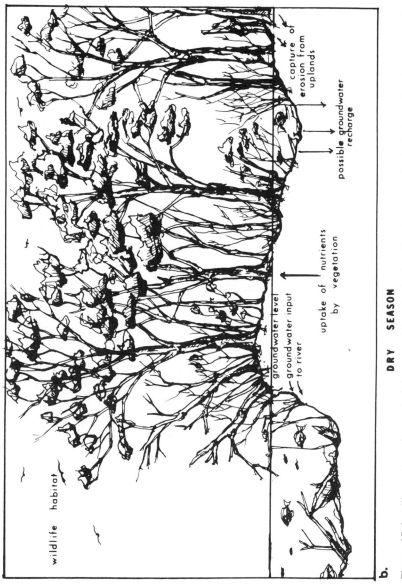

wildlife habitat

groundwater level

groundwater input to river

uptake of nutrients by vegetation

capture of erosion from uplands

possible groundwater recharge

DRY SEASON

b.

Figure 15-1. Illustration of several of the potential wetland values for riparian wetlands during *a.* flood season and *b.* dry season. *(From Mitsch, Hutchison, and Paulson, 1979, p. 9)*

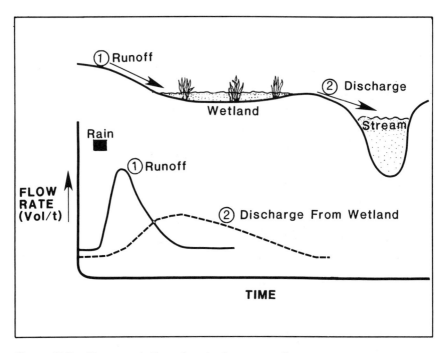

Figure 15-2.   The general effect of wetlands on streamflow.

Flood Mitigation

Chapter 4 dealt with the importance of hydrology in determining the character of wetlands. Conversely, wetlands influence regional water flow regimes.
One way they do this is to intercept storm runoff and store storm waters, and
hence change sharp runoff peaks to slower discharges over longer periods of
time (Fig. 15-2). Since it is usually the peak flows that produce flood damage,
the effect of the wetland area is to reduce the danger of flooding (Novitzki,
1979; Verry and Boelter, 1979). Riverine wetlands are especially valuable in
this regard. On the Charles River in Massachusetts, the floodplain wetlands
were deemed so effective for flood control by the U.S. Army Corps of
Engineers that they purchased them rather than build expensive flood
control structures to protect Boston (U.S. Army Corps of Engineers, 1972).
That study, a classic in wetland hydrologic values, determined that if the
3,400 hectares of wetlands in the Charles River basin were drained, it would
increase flood damages by $17 million per year. Bottomland hardwood
forests along the Mississippi River before settlement stored floodwater equivalent to about 60 days' river discharge. Storage capacity has now been
reduced to only about 12 days (Gosselink et al., 1981) as a result of levee-
ing the river and draining the floodplain. This loss of storage capacity is
one reason that flooding is increasing along the lower Mississippi River
(Belt, 1975).

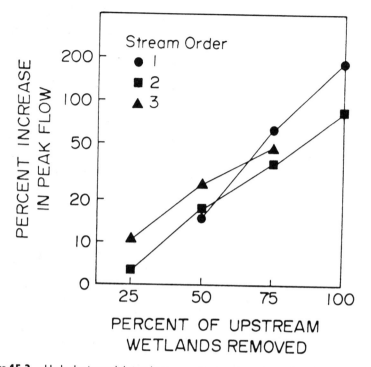

Figure 15-3. Hydrologic model simulation results showing relationships between increase in peak flood streamflow and percent wetland removal for Massachusetts watershed. Results are for various stream orders for 130-year flood. *(After Ogawa and Male, 1983)*

A quantitative approach to the flood mitigation potential of wetlands was undertaken by Ogawa and Male (1983), who used a hydrologic simulation model to investigate the relationship between upstream wetland removal and downstream flooding. That study found that, for the rare floods—that is, those with a 100-year recurrence interval or greater—the increase in peak streamflow was very significant for all sizes of streams when wetlands were removed (Fig. 15-3). They summarized that the usefulness of wetlands in reducing downstream flooding increases with (1) an increase in wetland area, (2) the distance the wetland is downstream, (3) the size of the flood, (4) the closeness to the upstream wetland, and (5) the lack of other upstream storage areas such as reservoirs.

Storm Abatement

Coastal wetlands absorb the first fury of ocean storms as they come ashore. Here, salt marshes and mangrove wetlands act as giant storm buffers. This value can be seen in the context of marsh conservation versus development. Natural marshes sustain little permanent damage from these storms and shelter inland developed areas. Buildings and other structures on the coast are vulnerable to the same storms, and damage is often high. Inevitably, the public pays much of the cost of this damage through taxes for relief, rebuilding public services such as roads and utilities, and federally guaranteed insurance.

Aquifer Recharge

Another value of wetlands related to hydrology is groundwater recharge. This function has received too little attention, and the magnitude of the phenomenon is not well documented. Some hydrologists believe that, while some wetlands do recharge groundwater systems, most wetlands do not (Carter et al., 1979; Novitzki, 1979; Sather and Smith, 1984). The reason for the absence of recharge is that soils under most wetlands are impermeable, which is why there is standing water to begin with (Larson, 1982). In the few studies available, recharge was related to the edge:volume ratio of the wetland, so it appears to be relatively more important in small wetlands such as prairie potholes than in large ones. These small wetlands can contribute significantly to recharge of regional groundwater (Weller, 1981). Heimburg (1984) found significant radial infiltration from cypress domes in Florida, with the rate of infiltration relative to the area of the wetland and the depth of the surficial water table. He concluded that these wetlands represented hydrologic "highs" in the surface water table and are therefore "closely coupled to groundwater." There did not appear to be any direct percolation to deep aquifers, however.

Water Quality

Wetlands, under favorable conditions, have been shown to remove organic and inorganic nutrients and toxic materials from water that flows across them. The concept of wetlands as sinks of chemicals was discussed in detail in chapter 5. Wetlands have several attributes that cause them to have major influences on chemicals that flow through them, whether the chemicals are naturally added or artificially applied (Sather and Smith, 1984). These attributes include the following:

1. a reduction in velocity as streams enter wetlands, causing sediments and chemicals sorbed to sediments to drop into the wetland
2. a variety of anaerobic and aerobic processes such as denitrification and chemical precipitation that remove certain chemicals from the water
3. the high rate of productivity of many wetlands that can lead to high rates of mineral uptake by vegetation and subsequent burial in sediments when the plants die

4. a diversity of decomposers and decomposition processes in wetland sediments
5. a high amount of contact of water with sediments because of the shallow water, leading to significant sediment-water exchange
6. the accumulation of organic peat in many wetlands, which causes the permanent burial of chemicals

There have also been a number of reports of efficient primary, secondary, and tertiary treatment of sewage wastewater by flowing it through wetlands. More detail on wetlands for wastewater management is given in chapter 16. Where environmental circumstances are appropriate, waste organic compounds are rapidly decomposed and nitrogen is denitrified and lost to the air. Nonvolatile pollutants such as heavy metals and phosphorus accumulate under favorable conditions. When the ecosystem becomes saturated with these materials, they may begin to increase in the effluent. For these elements, permanent long-term storage depends, in part, on whether the wetland is accreting vertically (and thus sequestering materials in deep sediments).

Aesthetics

A very real but difficult aspect of a wetland to capture is its aesthetic value, often hidden under the dry term "nonconsumptive use values," which simply means that people enjoy being out in wetlands. There are many aspects of this kind of wetland use. Wetlands are a rich source of information on cultural heritage. The remains of prehistoric Indian villages and mounds of shells or middens have contributed to our understanding of their cultures and of the history of the use of our wetlands. Smardon (1979) described wetlands as visually and educationally rich environments because of their ecological interest and diversity. Their complexity makes them excellent sites for research. Many artists have been drawn to them, notably the Georgia poet Sidney Lanier, the painters John Constable and John Singer Sargent, and many other artists of lesser public recognition who annually paint and photograph wetlands. Many visitors to wetlands use hunting and fishing only as excuses to experience their wildness and solitude, expressing that frontier pioneering instinct that may lurk in us all.

Global Values

Wetlands function in the maintenance of water and air quality on a much broader scale than the wetland ecosystem itself. Wetlands may be significant factors in global cycles including nitrogen, sulfur, methane, and carbon dioxide. The natural supply of ecologically useful nitrogen comes from the fixation of atmospheric nitrogen gas (N_2) by a small group of plants and microorganisms that can convert it into organic form. Today, the production of ammonia from N_2 for fertilizers is about equal to all natural fixation (Delwiche, 1970). Wetlands may be important in returning a part of this "excess" nitrogen to the atmosphere through denitrification. The close proximity of an aerobic and a reducing environment, such as the surface of a marsh, is ideal for denitrification, as discussed in chapter 5, and the rate seems to increase with the supply of nitrate. Because most temperate wetlands are the receivers of fertilizer-enriched agricultural runoff, and are ideal environments for denitrification, it is likely that they are important in the world's available nitrogen balance.

Sulfur is another element whose cycle has been modified by humans. The atmospheric load of sulfate has been greatly increased by fossil fuel burning. When sulfates are washed out of the atmosphere by rain, they acidify oligotrophic lakes and streams. When sulfates are washed into marshes, however, the intensely reducing environment of the sediment reduces them to sulfides. Some of the reduced sulfide is recycled to the atmosphere as hydrogen sulfide gas, but most forms insoluble complexes with phosphate and metal ions. These complexes can be more or less permanently removed from circulation in the sulfur cycle.

The carbon cycle may also be significantly affected on a global scale by wetlands. The carbon dioxide concentration in the atmosphere is steadily increasing, both because of the burning of fossil fuels, and because rapid clear-cutting of tropical forests results in the oxidation of organic matter in trees and soils (Woodwell et al., 1983). The enormous volume of peat deposits in the world's wetlands also has the potential to contribute significantly to worldwide atmospheric carbon dioxide levels, depending on the balance between draining and oxidation of the peat deposits and their formation in active wetlands. Finally, methane, which is released from anaerobic organic soils, may function as a sort of homeostatic regulator for the ozone layer that protects us from deleterious effects of ultraviolet radiation (Sze, 1977).

QUANTIFYING WETLAND VALUES

A number of efforts have been made to quantify the "free services" and amenities wetlands provide for society (Wharton, 1970; Gosselink, Odum, and Pope, 1974; Jaworski and Raphael, 1978; Mumphrey et al., 1978; Mitsch, Hutchison, and Paulson, 1979; Costanza, 1984). For activities that require an environmental impact statement (as required by the National Environmental Policy Act), two different kinds of evaluation are involved. The first is the determination of the ecological value of the area in question—that is, the quality of the site as compared with similar sites, or its suitability for supporting wildlife. The other component of the evaluation is a comparison of the ecological value of the habitat against the economic value of some proposed activity that would destroy or modify it. Regardless of which kind of evaluation is required, several generic problems must be addressed.

1. *Wetlands are multiple-value systems; that is, they may be valuable for many different reasons.* Therefore, the evaluator is often faced with the problem of comparing and weighing different commodities. For example, a freshwater area is more valuable for waterfowl than a salt marsh area; but the salt marsh may be much more valuable as a fish habitat. Overall, which is rated higher depends on a value judgment by the evaluator that has nothing to do with the intrinsic ecological viability of either area. This is the old "apples vs. oranges" problem. The solution comes down to a matter of preference. Furthermore, in most wetland evaluations, we are not concerned with single commodities. Rather, we wish to know the overall value of an area; that is, the value of the whole fruit basket, rather than the apples, oranges, and pears. Additional complexity is added when the concern is to compare the value of a natural wetland with the same piece of real estate used for economic development—a dammed lake, a parking lot, or an oil well. Here, the comparison is not between apples and oranges but between apples and computer chips, or oranges and electrical energy. Conventional economics solves the comparison problem by reducing all commodities to a single index of value—dollars. This is difficult when some of the commodities are natural products of wetlands that do not compete in the marketplace.

2. *The most valuable products of wetlands are public amenities that have no commercial value for the private wetland owner.* The wetland owner, for example, has no control over the harvest of marsh-dependent fish that are caught in the adjacent estuary or even offshore in the ocean. He does not control and usually cannot capitalize on the ability of his marsh to purify wastewater, and certainly not over its value for the global nitrogen balance. Thus, there is often a strong conflict between what a private wetland owner conceives of as his own best interests and the best interests of the public. In coastal Louisiana, a marsh owner can earn revenues of perhaps $25 per acre annually from the renewable resources of his marsh by leasing it for hunting and fur trapping. In contrast, depending on where it is situated, it may be worth thousands of dollars per acre as a housing development, or as a site for an oil well. Riparian wetlands in the Midwest and lower Mississippi River basin yield little economic benefit to the owner for the ecological services that they provide. Yet, if cleared and planted in corn or soybeans, the economic benefits to the owner are often significant for the short term. Many of the current regulations that govern wetlands were developed to protect the public's interest in privately owned wetlands (see chap. 16).

3. *As wetland area decreases, its marginal value increases, following conventional economic theory.* The less there is of a commodity, the more valuable the remaining stocks. This generalization is complicated in nature because different natural processes operate on different scales. This is an

important consideration in parklands and wildlife preserves, for example. Large mammals require large ranges to live. Small plots below a certain size will not support *any* large mammals. Thus, the marginal value generalization falls apart because the marginal value ceases to increase below a certain plot size. In fact, it becomes zero. In wetlands, the situation is even more complex, because they are open ecosystems with strong ties to adjacent ecosystems. Therefore, one factor that governs the ecological value (and hence the value to society) of the wetland is its *interspersion* with other ecosystems; that is, its place in the total regional landscape. A small wetland area that supports few endemic organisms may be extremely important during critical times of the day or during certain seasons for migratory species that spend only a day or a week in the area. A narrow strip of riparian wetland along a stream, which altogether amounts to very little acreage, may efficiently filter nutrients out of runoff from adjacent farmland, protecting the quality of the stream water. Its value is related to its interspersion in the landscape, not to its size. These kinds of considerations have only recently begun to be addressed in a quantitative way, and the methodology is not well developed.

4. *Commercial values are finite, whereas wetlands provide values in perpetuity. Wetland development is often irreversible.* The time frame for most human projects is 10 to 20 years. Private entrepreneurs expect to retrieve their investments and profits in projects within this time frame, and seldom consider longer-term implications. Even large public works projects such as dams for energy generation seldom are seen in terms longer than from 50 to 100 years. The destruction of natural areas, on the other hand, removes their public services forever. Often, especially for wetlands, the decision to develop is irreversible. If an upland field is abandoned, it will gradually revert to a forest; but once a wetland is drained and developed, it is usually lost forever because of associated changes in the hydrologic regime of the area. For example, in Louisiana and elsewhere, marsh areas were diked and drained for agriculture early in the 20th century. Many of these developments have subsequently been abandoned, and are now large, shallow lakes, distinguishable by their straight edges (Fig. 15-4).

Approaches to Wetland Evaluation

A number of different approaches to valuation of wetlands have been advanced (see Lonard et al., 1981). Because of the complexities described above, there is no universal agreement about which is preferable. In part, the choice depends on the circumstances.

Scaling and Weighting Approaches

This approach has been widely used as a means of forming a rational basis for deciding on different management options. Essentially all the specific

Figure 15-4. Sugar cane fields "reclaimed" from fresh marsh. Natural marsh is in foreground. Such development projects are usually irreversible since land elevations and flooding patterns are permanently changed. (*Photograph by Charles Sasser*)

procedures now in use assess the relative value of wildlife habitats. Silviculture, heritage, and recreation functions are sometimes evaluated, but the
methods are considered open for improvement (Lonard et al., 1981). E. P.
Odum (1979*b*, p. 23) describes the general procedure.

a. Make a list of all the values that a knowledgeable person or panel can
   apply to the situation in question, and assign a numerical value of "1"
   to each.
b. Scale each factor in terms of a maximum level; for example, if 200
   ducks per acre could be supported by a first-class marsh, but only 100
   are supported by the marsh in question, then the scaled factor is 0.5 or
   50 percent of maximum value for that item.
c. Weigh each scaled factor in proportion to its relative importance; for
   example, if value 2 is considered 10 times more important to the region
   than value 1, then multiply the scale value of 2 by 10.
d. Add the scaled and weighted values to obtain a value index. Since the
   numbers are only arbitrary and comparative, the index is most useful
   in comparing different wetlands, or the same wetland under different
   management plans. It is desirable that each value judgment be a
   consensus of several "experts" (for example, determined by the "Delphi method"). (Dalkey, 1972).

Table 15-5 shows an example of the application of this technique to
evaluate different development plants for a cypress-gum swamp ecosystem.
The present value of the swamp for a representative group of terrestrial and
aquatic animals was evaluated (baseline conditions), using a habitat suitability index (HSI) with a range of 0 to 1 for optimum habitat for the species in
question. The evaluation resulted in a mean terrestrial HSI of 0.8 and a mean
aquatic HSI of 0.4. This baseline condition was compared with projected
habitat condition in 50 and 100 years under three projected scenarios—Plan
A, Plan B, and a no-project projection. The results suggest that Plan A would
be detrimental to the environment, while Plan B would have no effect on
terrestrial habitat values and would improve aquatic ones. Whether or not
to proceed with either of these plans is a decision that requires weighing projected environmental effects against projected economic benefits of
the project.

One often neglected feature of the analysis is the effect of averaging.
While, overall, Plan B appears to be about equivalent environmentally to the
no-project option, a careful perusal of Table 15-5 shows that Plan B is
expected to improve the habitat for swamp rabbits and large-mouthed bass,
but decrease its value for warblers and turtles. This kind of detail may
be important because it indicates a change in the quality of the environment, but it is often neglected when the "apples and oranges" are combined
into "fruit."

Table 15-5. Comparison of the Impact of Two Management Plans and a No-Management Control in a Cypress-Gum Swamp[a]

Species	Baseline Condition	Future with Project Plan A[b]		Future with Project Plan B[c]		Future without Project	
		50 Years	100 Years	50 Years	100 Years	50 Years	100 Years
Terrestrial							
Raccoon	0.7	0.5	0.6	0.8	0.8	0.7	0.9
Beaver	0.7	0.2	0.2	0.4	0.3	0.6	0.4
Swamp Rabbit	0.7	0.2	0.2	0.8	0.8	0.7	0.4
Green Heron	0.9	0.2	0.1	0.8	0.9	0.9	1.0
Mallard	0.8	0.3	0.2	1.0	0.9	0.9	1.0
Wood Duck	0.8	0.3	0.2	0.9	1.0	1.0	1.0
Prothonotary Warbler	0.8	0.3	0.1	0.6	0.7	0.8	0.9
Snapping Turtle	0.8	0.4	0.3	0.8	0.7	0.8	0.9
Bullfrog	0.9	0.3	0.2	0.8	0.9	0.0	1.0
Total Terrestrial HSI	7.1	2.7	2.1	6.9	7.0	7.5	7.6
Mean Terrestrial HSI	0.8	0.3	0.2	0.8	0.8	0.8	0.8
Aquatic							
Channel Catfish	0.3	0.3	0.4	0.4	0.4	0.4	0.4
Largemouth bass	0.4	0.2	0.3	0.7	0.8	0.4	0.4
Total Aquatic HSI	0.7	0.5	0.7	1.1	1.2	0.8	0.8
Mean Aquatic HSI	0.4	0.3	0.4	0.6	0.6	0.4	0.4

Source: From Schamberger, Short, and Farmer, 1979, p. 81. Copyright ©1979 by American Water Resources Association, reprinted with permission.

[a]Numbers in the table are habitat suitability index (HSI) values, which have a maximum value of 1 for an optimal habitat.

[b]Channelization of water and clearing of swamp for agricultural development with a loss of 324 ha of wetland.

[c]Construction of levees around swamp for flood control with no loss of wetland area.

Common Denominator Approaches

Evaluation systems that seek to compare natural wetlands to human economic systems usually reduce all values to monetary terms (thus losing sight of the apples and oranges). Conventional economic theory assumes that in a free economy the market price reflects the value of a commodity (the willingness-to-pay approach). While this is a reasonable assumption under most conventional economic conditions, it leads to real problems in monetizing nonmarket commodities like pure water and air; and in pricing marshes whose monetary value in the marketplace is determined by their value as real estate, not by their "free services" to society. Consequently, attempts to monetize marsh values have generally emphasized the commercial crops from wetlands: fish, shellfish, furs, and recreational fishing and hunting for which pricing methodologies are available (Fig. 15-5). As E. P. Odum (1979*b*) points out, this kind of pricing ignores ecosystem and global-level values related to clean air and water and other "life support" functions.

Figure 15-5.   This flock of white pelicans on a coastal marsh symbolizes the difficulty of placing a dollar value on wetlands. They are not hunted so have no "sport-hunting value." Nevertheless, they are one species supported by wetlands. Have they any value? If so, how is it defined, and how quantified, in a social system in which "market values" often take precedence over any others. *(Photograph by Robert Abernethy)*

A completely different approach that shows much promise uses the idea of energy flow through an ecosystem or the similar concept of "embodied energy." The concept of embodied energy, the total energy required to produce a commodity (Costanza, 1980), is assumed to be a valid index of the totality of ecosystem functions and is applicable to human systems as well. Thus, natural and human systems can be evaluated on the basis of one common currency, "embodied energy." Since there is a linear relationship between embodied energy and dollars, that more familiar currency can also be used. Costanza (1984) showed that the economist's willingness-to-pay approach and energy analysis converge to a surprising degree. Table 15-6 compares some monetary values for Louisiana's coastal marshes arrived at through different approaches. The gross benefits values from three different studies sum the gross value of fish and fur harvests, and recreational hunting and fishing. They average about $840/hectare · yr ($340/acre · yr). The consumer surplus approach, another conventional economic technique, gives a value of $383/hectare · yr ($155/acre · yr). Costanza's value of $741/hectare · yr ($300/acre · yr) for the value arrived at through energy analysis is comparable. The main problem with acceptance of this approach is that the theoretical base is completely different from the conventional market approach that dominates economics. Incidentally, a yield of $300 per acre per year would require an investment of $3,000, earning at an annual interest rate of 10%. This places the "capitalized" value of an acre of Louisiana salt marsh at about $3,000.

Table 15-6. Estimates of the Economic Value of Louisiana's Coastal Wetlands, Comparing Willingness-to-Pay Approaches with Energy Analysis Approaches

Approach	*Shadow value*[a] *1979 $/acre · yr*	*Reference*
Willingness-to-Pay Approaches		
Consumer surplus	155	Mumphrey et al., 1978
Gross benefits	241	Gosselink, Odum, and Pope, 1974
	352	Vora, 1974
	544	Mumphrey et al., 1978
	231	Mumphrey et al., 1978
Average of gross benefits	342	
Net benefits	237	
Replacement value	3,120	
Energy Analysis Approaches		
Biological productivity	300	

Source: After Costanza and Farber, 1985
[a]Price that would prevail in a perfect market

Replacement Value

If one calculated the cheapest way of replacing various services performed by a wetland, and were able to make the case that those services would have to be replaced if the wetland were destroyed, then the figure arrived at would be the "replacement value." This approach has the merit of acceptance by conventional economics. For certain functions, it gives very high values (Table 15-6) compared with other valuation approaches. For example, tertiary treatment of wastewater is extremely expensive, as is the cost of replacing the nursery function of marshes for juvenile fish and shellfish. However, there is serious question of whether these functions would be replaced by treatment plants and fish nurseries if the wetlands were destroyed. Ecologists tend to argue that in the long run either the services of wetlands would have to be replaced or the quality of our lives would deteriorate. Other individuals argue that this assertion cannot be supported in any convincing manner.

Values placed on wetlands using these evaluation methods have ranged from very high to low. Although few people dispute that wetlands have many and varied values, the lack of consistent accepted methodologies for comparing them with conventional economic goods and services limits the usefulness of estimates that have been made.

SUMMARY

Wetlands provide many services and commodities to humanity. At the population level, wetland-dependent fish, shellfish, fur animals, and waterfowl provide important and valuable harvests and millions of man-days of recreational fishing and hunting. At the ecosystem level, wetlands moderate the effects of floods, improve water quality, and have aesthetic and heritage value. They also contribute to the stability of global levels of available nitrogen, atmospheric sulfur, carbon dioxide, and methane.

The valuation of these services and commodities for purposes of wetland management is made complicated by the difficulty of comparing by some common denominator the various values of wetlands against human economic systems; by the conflict between a private owner's interest in the wetlands and the values that accrue to the public at large; and by the need to consider the value of a wetland as a part of an integrated landscape. Valuation techniques include the nonmonetized scaling and weighting approach for comparing different wetlands or different management options for the same wetland, common denominator approaches that reduce the various values to some common term such as dollars or embodied energy, and the replacement value approach. None of these approaches is without problems, and no universal agreement about their use has been reached.

chapter 16

WETLAND MANAGEMENT
AND PROTECTION

The concept of wetland management has had different meanings in different times and to different disciplines. Until the middle of the twentieth century, wetland management usually meant wetland drainage. Landowners were encouraged to tile and drain wetlands to make the land suitable for agriculture and other uses. Countless coastal wetlands were destroyed by dredging and filling for navigation and land development. There was little understanding of and concern for the inherent "values" of the wetlands. The value of wetlands as wildlife habitats, particularly for waterfowl, was recognized in the first half of this century by some fish and game managers, to whom wetland management often meant the maintenance of hydrologic conditions to optimize fish or waterfowl populations. Only relatively recently have other values, such as those described in chapter 15, been recognized.

Today, the management of wetlands means several possibilities, depending on the goals of the wetland manager. In some cases, the goals can be conflicting, as in preventing pollution from reaching wetlands and using wetlands as sites of wastewater treatment or disposal. Floodplain wetlands are now managed and zoned to minimize human encroachment and maximize floodwater retention. Coastal wetlands are now included in coastal zone protection programs for storm protection and as sanctuaries and subsidies for estuarine fauna. In the meantime, wetlands continue to be altered or destroyed through drainage, filling, conversion to agriculture, water pollution, and mineral extraction.

Wetlands are now the focus of legal efforts to protect them. Protection has been implemented through a variety of policies, laws, and regulations, ranging from land use policies, to zoning restrictions, to enforcement of dredge and fill laws. In the United States, wetland protection has historically been a federal initiative, with some assistance from individual states. That situation may now be changing with increasing state involvement in environmental protection.

AN EARLY HISTORY OF WETLAND MANAGEMENT

The early history of wetland management, a history that still influences many people today, was driven by the general dictate that wetlands are wastelands that at best should be avoided or, if possible, drained and filled. As described by Larson and Kusler (1979, p. *v*), "For most of recorded history, wetlands were regarded as wastelands if not bogs of treachery, mires of despair, homes of pests, and refuges for outlaw and rebel. A good wetland was a drained wetland free of this mixture of dubious social factors." In the United States, this low opinion of wetlands and shallow-water environments led to the destruction of an estimated 30-50% of the total wetlands in the lower 48 states (Fig. 16-1; also see chap. 3).

Some public laws were actually enacted to encourage this wetland drainage. Congress passed the Swamp Land Act of 1849, which granted to Louisiana the control of all swamplands and overflow lands in the state for the general purpose of controlling floods in the Mississippi basin. The following year, the act was extended to the states of Alabama, Arkansas, California, Florida, Illinois, Indiana, Iowa, Michigan, Mississippi, Missouri, Ohio, and Wisconsin. Minnesota and Oregon were added in 1860. The act was designed to decrease federal involvement in flood control and drainage by transferring federally owned wetlands to the states, leaving to them the initiative of "reclaiming" wetlands through activities such as levee construction and drainage. By 1954, almost 100 years after the act was established, an estimated 26 million hectares (65 million acres) of land were granted to these 15 states for reclamation, with most of the land in private ownership (Shaw and Fredine, 1956). While current government policies are generally in direct opposition to the Swamp Land Act and it is now disregarded, the act set the first wetland policy of the United States government as one directed toward wetland elimination.

Other actions led to the rapid decline of the nation's wetlands. An estimated 23 million hectares (57 million acres) of wet farmland, including some wetlands, were drained under the U.S. Department of Agriculture's Agricultural Conservation Program between 1940 and 1977 (Office of Technology Assessment, 1984). Some of the wetland drainage activity was hastened by projects of groups such as the Depression-era WPA (Works Progress Administration) and the Soil Conservation Service (Reilly, 1979). Coastal marshes were eliminated or drained and ditched for intercoastal transportation, residential developments, mosquito control, and even for salt marsh

Figure 16-1. This aerial photograph taken from a U-2 plane is a scene of a fresh marsh along an abandoned Mississippi River distributary, Bayou Lafourche. Residential and agricultural development has occurred on the high natural levees of this bayou. The large rectangular lake (1) was an agricultural development in the early part of the century. The levees were breached by a severe storm and it was abandoned. Below it (2) is a similar development, still in sugarcane production. The soil surface inside the levees is now about 2 m below the surrounding water level due to compaction and oxidation. Manmade canals (3) are straight and deep, natural channels (4) are tortuous and shallow. Infared imagery from 65,000 feet with 12-inch focal length lens. *(Photograph by NASA, Ames Research Center, Flight 78-143, October 9, 1978)*

hay production. Interior wetlands were removed primarily for urban development, road construction, and agriculture.

Typical of the prevalent attitude towards wetlands is the following quote by Norgress (1947, pp. 1047, 1054-1056) discussing the "value" of Louisiana cypress swamps:

With 1,628,915 acres of cutover cypress swamp lands in Louisiana at the present time, what use to make of these lands so that the ideal cypress areas will make a return on the investment for the landowner is a serious problem of the future . . .

The lumbermen are rapidly awakening to the fact that in cutting the timber from their land they have taken the first step toward putting it in position to perform its true function—agriculture . . . .

It requires only a visit into this swamp territory to overcome such prejudices that reclamation is impracticable. Millions of dollars are being put into good roads. Everywhere one sees dredge boats eating their way through the soil, making channels for drainage.

After harvesting the cypress timber crop, the Louisiana lumbermen are at last realizing that in reaping the crop sown by Nature ages ago, they have left a heritage to posterity of an asset of permanent value and service—land, the true basis for wealth.

The day of the pioneer cypress lumberman is gone, but we need today in Louisiana another type of pioneer—the pioneer who can help bring under cultivation the enormous areas of cypress cutover lands suitable for agriculture. It is important to Louisiana, to the South, and the Nation as a whole, that this be done. Would that there were some latter-day Horace Greeleys to cry, in clarion tones, to the young farmers of today, "Go South, young man; go South!"

As a further example of state action leading to wetland drainage, Illinois passed the Illinois Drainage Levee Act and the Farm Drainage Act in 1879, which allowed counties to organize into drainage districts to consolidate financial resources. This action accelerated the draining of the state to the point that 27% of Illinois is now under some form of drainage and almost all of the original wetlands in the state (99.5%) have been destroyed (Bell, 1981).

WETLAND ALTERATION

In a sense, wetland alteration or destruction is a form of wetland management. One model of wetland alteration (Fig. 16-2) assumes that three main factors influence wetland ecosystems: water level, nutrient status, and natural disturbances (Keddy, 1983). Through human activity, modification of any one of these factors can lead to wetland alteration, either directly or indirectly. For example, a wetland can be disturbed through decreased water levels, as in draining and filling, or through increased water levels, as in downstream drainage impediments. Nutrient status can be affected through upstream flood control that decreases the frequency of nutrient inputs or through increased nutrient loading from agricultural areas.

The most common alterations of wetlands have been (1) draining, dredging and filling of wetlands; (2) modification of the hydrologic regime; (3) mining and mineral extraction; and (4) water pollution. These wetland modifications are described in more detail below.

Wetland Conversion: Draining, Dredging, and Filling

The major cause of wetland loss in the United States has continued to be conversion to agricultural use. This conversion has been a continuing activity

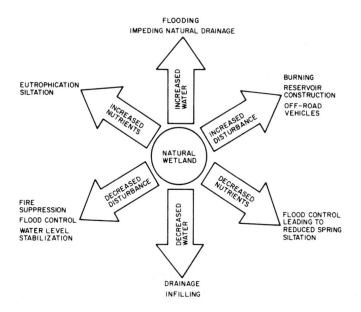

FLOODING
IMPEDING NATURAL DRAINAGE

EUTROPHICATION
SILTATION

INCREASED
WATER

INCREASED
NUTRIENTS

BURNING
RESERVOIR
CONSTRUCTION
OFF-ROAD
VEHICLES

INCREASED
DISTURBANCE

NATURAL
WETLAND

FIRE
SUPPRESSION
FLOOD CONTROL
WATER LEVEL
STABILIZATION

DECREASED
DISTURBANCE

DECREASED
NUTRIENTS

FLOOD CONTROL
LEADING TO
REDUCED SPRING
SILTATION

DECREASED
WATER

DRAINAGE
INFILLING

Figure 16-2. Model of human-induced impacts on wetlands, including effects on water level, nutrient status, and natural disturbance. By either increasing or decreasing any one of these factors, wetlands can be altered. *(From Keddy, 1983, p. 300: Copyright © 1983 by Springer-Verlag, reprinted with permission)*

in the vast midwestern "breadbasket" that has provided the bulk of the grain produced on the continent. The fertile soils of the prairie pothole marshes and east Texas playas produce excellent crops when drained and cultivated. With ditching and modern farm equipment, it has been possible to farm more and more of these small marshes. During the last two decades, however, the most rapid changes have occurred in the bottomland hardwood forests of the Mississippi River alluvial floodplain. As human populations grew along the river, it was channeled and leveed so that the floodplain could be drained and inhabited. Since colonial times the floodplain has provided excellent cropland, especially for cotton and sugarcane. However, cultivation was restricted to the relatively high elevation of the natural river levees, which flooded regularly after spring rains and upstream snowmelts, but which drained rapidly enough to enable farmers to plant their crops. The lower parts of the floodplain were left as forests and harvested for timber. With increasing pressure for additional cropland, these agriculturally marginal forests are now being clear-cut at an unprecedented rate (Fig. 16-3a). This is feasible, in part, because of the development of soybean varieties that mature rapidly enough to be planted in June or even early July, after severe flooding has passed (Fig. 16-3b). Often the land thus "reclaimed" is subsequently incorporated behind flood control levees where it can be kept dry by pumps. Clear-cutting of bottomland forests is proceeding from north to

Figure 16-3a.   Aerial photograph of clearcutting of bottomland hardwood forests in western Tennessee.

Figure 16-3b.   Soybean field converted from bottomland hardwood forest in western Kentucky.

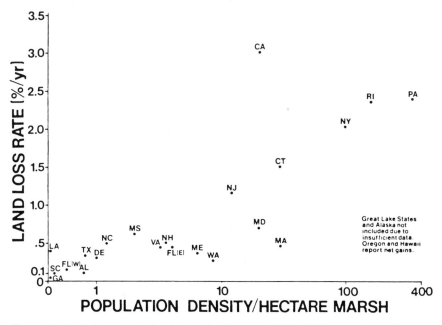

Figure 16-4. Relationship of coastal wetland loss rate (1954–1974) to population density for coastal counties. *(From Gosselink and Baumann, 1980, p. 180; Copyright © 1980 by Gebruder Borntraeger, reprinted with permission)*

south. Most of the available wetland has been converted in Arkansas and Tennessee; Mississippi and Louisiana are also experiencing large losses.

Along the nation's coasts, especially the East and West Coasts, the major cause of wetland loss is draining and filling for urban and industrial development. Compared to conversion for agricultural use, the area involved is rather small, but in some coastal states, notably California, nearly all coastal wetlands have been lost. The rate of coastal wetland loss is closely tied to population density (Fig. 16-4). This observation underscores two facts: (1) two-thirds of the world's population lives along coasts, and (2) this population density puts great pressure on coastal wetlands as sites for expansion. The most rapid development of coastal wetlands occurred after World War II. In particular, several large airports were built in coastal marshes. With the passage of federal legislation controlling wetland development, the rate of conversion has slowed.

Hydrologic Modifications

Ditching and draining are hydrologic modifications of wetlands specifically designed to dry them out. Other hydrologic modifications destroy or change the character of thousands of hectares of wetlands annually. Usually these hydrologic changes are for some purpose that has nothing to do with wetlands; wetland destruction is an inadvertent result. Canals and ditches are dredged through wetlands for three primary purposes:

1. *Flood control.* Most of the canals associated with wetlands are for flood control—they are designed to carry floodwaters off the adjacent uplands as rapidly as possible. Normal drainage through wetlands is slow surface sheet flow; straight, deep canals are more efficient. Ditching marshes and swamps to drain them for mosquito control or biomass harvesting is a special case, designed to lower water levels in the wetlands themselves.
2. *Navigation and transportation.* Navigation canals tend to be larger than drainage canals. They traverse wetlands primarily to provide water transportation access to ports and to improve transport among ports. For example, the Intracoastal Waterway is dredged through hundreds of miles of wetlands in the northern Gulf coast. In addition, when highways are built across wetlands, fill material for the roadbed is often obtained by dredging soil from along the right-of-way, thus forming a canal parallel to the highway.
3. *Industrial activity.* Many canals are dredged for access to sites within a wetland for the purpose of sinking an oil well or other development. Usually, pipelines that traverse wetlands are laid in canals that are not backfilled.

The result of all of these activities can be a wetland crisscrossed with canals, especially in the immense coastal wetlands of the northern Gulf coast (Fig. 16-5). Ecologically, these canals act in a number of ways to modify wetlands, all by changing normal hydrologic patterns. Straight, deep canals in shallow bays, lakes, and marshes capture flow, depriving the natural channels of water. Canals are hydrologically efficient, allowing more rapid runoff of fresh water than the normal shallow, sinuous channels. As a result, water levels fluctuate more rapidly than in unmodified marshes, and minimum levels are lowered, drying the marshes. Sheet flow of water across the marsh surface is reduced by the spoil banks that almost always line a canal and by road embankments that block sheet flow. Consequently, the sediment supply to the marsh is reduced, and the water on the marsh is more likely to stagnate than when freely flooded. In addition, when deep, straight channels connect low-salinity areas to high-salinity zones, as with many large navigation channels, tidal water, with its salt, intrudes further upstream, changing freshwater wetlands to brackish. In extreme cases, salt-intolerant vegetation is killed and is not replaced before the marsh erodes into a shallow lake. On the Louisiana coast the natural subsidence rate is high; wetlands go through

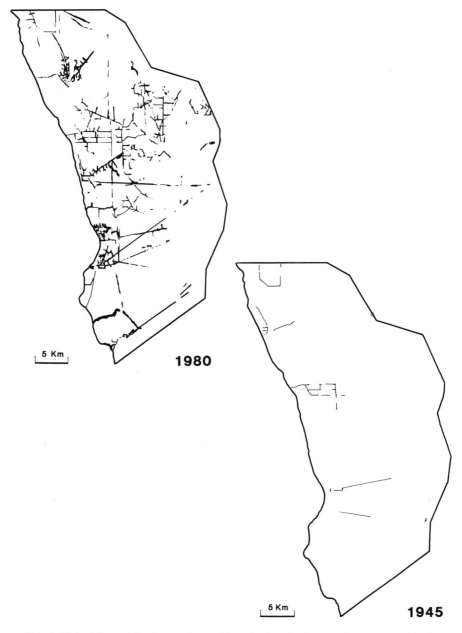

Figure 16-5. Growth in the number and length of navigation canals constructed in the wetlands of the north central coast of the Gulf of Mexico (Barataria Bay, La.). The concentrated nodes of canals are sites of oil fields. Each short canal segment provides access to an oil well. *(After Dozier et al., 1983, pp. 53 and 61)*

a natural cycle of growth and decay to open bodies of water. Here, canals accelerate the subsidence rate by depriving wetlands of natural sediment and nutrient subsidies.

Highway Construction

Highway construction can have a major effect of the hydrologic conditions of wetlands (see Fig. 16-6). Although few definitive studies have been able to document the extent of wetland damage caused by highways (Adamus, 1983), several studies have inferred that the major effects of highways are alteration of the hydrologic regime, sediment loading, and direct wetland removal. McLeese and Whiteside (1977) compared the effects of highways on uplands and wetlands in Michigan and found that wetlands were much more sensitive to highway construction than were uplands, particularly through the disruption of hydrologic conditions. Likewise, Clewell et al. (1976) and Evink (1980) found that highway construction in Florida led to negative effects on coastal wetlands through hydrologic isolation. The for-

Figure 16-6. Typical of the conflict between wetland protection and highway construction is this sign near a proposed highway in central Florida. *(Photograph by W. J. Mitsch)*

mer study discovered that isolated tidal marshes became less saline and began to fill with vegetation due to the construction of a fill road. The latter study found that the decreased circulation due to a causeway increased nutrient retention in the wetland and led to subsequent symptoms of eutrophication. Adamus (1983) concluded that the "best location for a highway that must cross a wetland is one which minimizes interference with the wetland ecosystem's most important driving forces." Other than solar energy and wind, the most important driving forces for wetlands are hydrologic, including tides, gradient currents (e.g., streamflow), runoff, and groundwater flow. The importance of protecting the hydrologic regime during highway construction is based on the contention presented in chapter 4 that the hydrology of wetlands is the most important determinant of a wetland's structure and function.

Peat Mining

Surface peat mining has been a common activity in several European countries, particularly the USSR, since the eighteenth century. The Soviet Union accounts for over 95% of peat mining in the world, with most of the material used as a fuel for electric power production (Moore and Bellamy, 1974). In the United States, peat resources are estimated at about 120 billion tons (Table 16-1). Historically, peat mining in the United States has been primarily for agricultural and horticultural uses and has been done on a relatively small scale. Approximately 825,000 tons of peat were mined in the United States in 1979, with 77% coming from the states of Michigan, Florida, Illinois, Indiana, and New York, in that order (Carpenter and Farmer, 1981). More recently, however, mining has been proposed on a large scale for peatlands in Minnesota and pocosins in North Carolina for energy production.

Mineral and Water Extraction

Surface mining activity for materials other than peat often significantly affects major regions of wetlands. Phosphate mining in central Florida has had a significant impact on wetlands in the region (Gilbert, King, and Barnett, 1981; Dames and Moore, 1983). Thousands of hectares of wetlands could be lost in central Florida due to this activity alone. Reclamation of many of these phosphate-mined sites into wetlands is already practiced in Florida although H. T. Odum et al. (1981) argue that "managed ecological succession" on mined sites could be an economical alternative to expensive earth moving and planting reclamation techniques.

Surface mining of coal has also affected wetlands in some parts of the country. Mitsch et al. (1983a, 1983b) identified 46,000 hectares of wetlands, mostly bottomland hardwood forests, that could be or are being affected by

**Table 16-1. Estimated Reserves of Peat and Potential
Energy in the United States[a]**

State	Area, millions of hectares	Quantity, billion tons	Potential Energy Available,[b] quads (10^{15} BTU)
Alaska	10.9	61.7	741.0
Minnesota	3.08	17.5	210.0
Michigan	1.82	10.3	123.0
Florida	1.21	6.9	82.0
Wisconsin	1.13	6.4	77.0
Louisiana	0.73	4.1	49.0
North Carolina	0.49	2.7	33.0
Maine	0.31	1.8	21.0
New York	0.26	1.5	18.0
Georgia	0.17	1.0	12.0
Indiana	0.15	0.9	10.0
Massachusetts	0.14	0.8	9.5
Virginia	0.12	0.7	8.6
Washington	0.08	0.5	5.5
All Other States	0.65	3.5	43.4
Total	21.30	120.3	1,443.0

Source: After Farnham, 1979, p. 664

[a]Data from U.S. Department of Agriculture SCS, Conservation Needs Inventory, 1967

[b]Basis of potential energy: peat contains 35% moisture, bulk density equals 15 lb/ft^3, caloric value equals 6,000 BTU/lb, and 1 acre of peat averaging 7 feet equals 2,287 tons, or 27.44×10^9 BTU of energy.

surface coal mining in western Kentucky, while Cardamone, Taylor, and Mitsch (1984) prescribe methods available to protect wetlands during mining or to create new wetlands as part of the reclamation process (Fig. 16-7). This concept of the potential for including wetlands as part of the reclamation of coal mines was further explored at a conference on "Wetlands and Water Management on Mined Lands" (Brooks, Samuel, and Hill, 1985).

In some parts of the country the withdrawal of water from aquifers and/or minerals from deep wells has resulted in accelerated subsidence rates that are lowering the elevations of marshes and built-up areas alike, sometimes dramatically. For example, groundwater and mineral extraction has led to as much as 2.5 m of subsidence in northern Galveston Bay (Kreitler, 1977). Land subsidence, which can also result in the creation of lakes and wetlands,

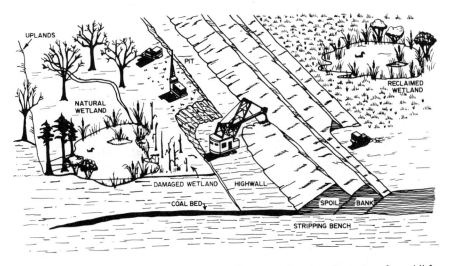

Figure 16-7. Possible use of wetlands in reclamation of coal surface mines for wildlife enhancement and for control of mine drainage. *(From Cardamone, Taylor, and Mitsch, 1984, p. 32)*

is a geologically common phenomenon in Florida. Often when excessive amounts of water are removed from the ground, underground cave-ins occur in the limestone, causing surface slumpage. Some believe that the cypress domes in north-central Florida are an indirect result of a similar natural process whereby fissures and dissolutions of underground limestone cause slight surface slumpage and subsequent wetland development.

Water Pollution

Wetlands are altered by pollutants from upstream or local runoff, and in turn change the quality of the water flowing out of them. The ability of wetlands to cleanse water has received much attention in research and development and is discussed elsewhere (see chap. 15 and Water Quality Management section in this chapter). The effects of polluted water on wetlands has received less attention. Many coastal wetlands are nitrogen limited; one response when nitrogen is one of the pollutants is increased productivity of the vegetation and increased standing stocks of vegetation (Valiela et al., 1982). This is followed by increased rates of decay of the vegetation, at least initially, and higher community respiration rates. Species composition may change with eutrophication (Whigham and Simpson, 1976a; Ewel, 1976). Where heavy metals or toxic organic compounds are pollutants, growth and

Figure 16-8. Many wetlands are negatively affected by water pollution, such as this riverine wetland impacted by coal mining drainage in western Kentucky. *(Photograph by W. J. Mitsch)*

respiration rates may decrease. In severe cases, wetland vegetation has been killed, as where oil was spilled on a coastal marsh (Baker, 1973), or sulfates were discharged into a forested wetland (J. Richardson et al., 1983).

Acid mine drainage from active and abandoned coal mines has been shown to seriously affect wetlands but also to be ameliorated somewhat by the presence of wetlands. The effects of acid mine drainage on wetlands have been studied in Appalachia, particularly in West Virginia and western Kentucky. Mitsch et al. (1983*a*, 1983*b*) and Mitsch, Taylor, and Benson (1983) documented the presence of wetlands and coal surface mining adjacent to one another in western Kentucky. In many instances, waters with low pH and high iron and sulfur were discharged into or through wetlands, causing extensive damage (Fig. 16-8). Wieder and Lang (1982; 1984) have suggested that a mountain bog in the Appalachian Mountains, while significantly affected, lessened the effects of acid mine drainage on downstream ecosystems. They presented three lines of evidence for this conclusion: (1) interstitial water from the mine declined in hydrogen and sulfate ions as it passed through the wetland, (2) the presence of hydrogen sulfide suggested that biological sulfate reduction is occurring in the wetland, and (3) the chemistry of the water draining from the wetland is similar to that in other watersheds unaffected by mine drainage.

WETLAND MANAGEMENT
BY OBJECTIVES

Wetlands are managed for environmental protection, for recreation and aesthetics, and for production of renewable resources. Stearns (1978) lists 12 specific goals of wetland management:

1. Maintain water quality
2. Reduce erosion
3. Protect from floods
4. Provide a natural system to process airborne pollutants
5. Provide a buffer between urban residential and industrial segments to ameliorate climate and physical impact such as noise
6. Maintain a gene pool of marsh plants and provide examples of complete natural communities
7. Provide aesthetic and psychological support for human beings
8. Produce wildlife
9. Control insect populations
10. Provide habitats for fish spawning and other food organisms
11. Produce food, fiber, and fodder; for example, timber, cranberries, cattails for fiber
12. Expedite scientific inquiry

One excellent management decision is to simply fence in a wetland to preserve it. Although simple, this is an act of conservation of a valuable natural ecosystem. This involves no positive management practices. Usually, however, management has one or more specific objectives that require positive manipulation of the environment. Often efforts to maximize one objective are incompatible with the attainment of others, although in recent years most management objectives have been broadly stated to enhance a broad range of objectives. Multipurpose management generally focuses on system-level support, rather than individual species. This often is achieved indirectly through plant species manipulation, since plants provide food and cover for the animals (Weller, 1978). Where many small wetland management areas are in close proximity, different practices should be used, or the management cycle staggered, so that the different areas are not all the same at one time. This increases the diversity of the larger landscape, and is attractive to wildlife.

Wildlife Enhancement

The best management practices enhance the natural processes of the wetland ecosystem involved. In nearly all cases this means water level manipulation. Water level control is achieved by dikes, weirs (solid structures in marsh outflows that maintain a minimum water level), control gates, and pumps. In general, the results of the management activity depend on how well water level control is maintained, and this depends on the local rainfall and on the sophistication of the control structures. For example, weirs provide the poorest control, since all they do is maintain a minimum water level. Pumps provide positive control of drainage or flooding depth at the desired time; and the management objectives are more nearly met (Wicker, Davis, and Roberts, 1983).

The management recommendations of Weller (1978) for prairie pothole marshes are an example of mutipurpose wildlife enhancement. These practices mimic the natural cycle of these marshes (see chap. 11). Although they may seem drastic, they are entirely natural in their consequences. In sequence, these practices are as follows:

1. When a pothole is in the open stage, with little emergent vegetation, the cycle is initiated with a spring drawdown. This stimulates the germination of seedlings on the exposed mud surfaces.
2. A slow increase in water level after the drawdown is best to maintain the growth of flood-tolerant seedlings without shading them out in turbid water. Shallowly flooded areas attract dabbling ducks during the winter.
3. The drawdown cycle is repeated for a second year to establish a good stand of emergents.
4. Low water levels are maintained for several more seasons to encourage the growth of perennial emergents such as cattails.
5. Stable, moderate water depths for several years promote the growth of rooted submerged aquatic plants and associated benthic fauna, which make excellent food for waterfowl. During this period, the emergent vegetation gradually dies out and is replaced by shallow ponds. When this occurs the cycle can be re-initiated as in (1) above.
6. Different wetland areas maintained in staggered cycles provide all stages of the marsh cycle at once, maximizing habitat diversity.

Wildlife management in coastal marshes uses a similar strategy, although the short-term cycle is not as pronounced there. Drawdowns to encourage the growth of seedlings and perennials preferred by ducks is a common practice, as is fall and winter flooding to attract dabbling ducks. As it happens, there is general agreement that stabilizing water levels is *not* good management, even though our society seems to feel intuitively that stability is a good thing. Wetlands thrive on cycles, especially flooding cycles, and practices that dampen these cycles also reduce wildlife productivity. While the management practices described enhance waterfowl production, they are, in coastal wetlands, generally deleterious for wetland-dependent fisheries, since free access between the wetlands and the adjacent estuary is restricted, and the use of these wetlands by fish is reduced.

Agriculture and Aquaculture

When wetlands are drained for agricultural use, they no longer function as wetlands. They are, as the local farmer says, "fast lands," removed from the effects of periodic flooding and growing terrestrial, flood-intolerant crops. Some use is made of more or less undisturbed wetlands for agriculture, but this is minor. In New England the high-salt marshes were harvested for "salt marsh hay," which was considered an excellent bedding and fodder for cattle. In fact, Russell (1976) stated that the proximity of fresh and salt hay marshes was a major factor in site selection of many towns in New England settled before 1650. Later, marshes were ditched to allow intrusion of tides to promote the growth of salt marsh hay *(Spartina patens)*. The extent of this practice is not well documented. On the coast of the Gulf of Mexico where coastal marshes are firm underfoot, they are still used extensively for cattle grazing. To improve access, small embankments or raised earthen paths are constructed out into these marshes.

The ancient Mexican practice of "marceno" is unique. In freshwater wetlands of the northern coast of Mexico, small areas were cleared and planted in corn during the dry season. These native varieties were tolerant enough to withstand considerable flooding. After harvest (or apparently sometimes before harvest), the marshes were naturally reflooded and the native grasses were reestablished until the next dry season. This practice is no longer followed, but recently there has been some interest in reviving it (Orozco-Segovia, 1980).

Aquaculture usually requires more extensive manipulation of the environment than the practices mentioned above. When ponds are constructed with retaining walls or levees and pumps, little resemblance to the natural ecosystem remains. However, attempts have been made to use estuarine-wetland areas in a more or less natural state to raise fish and shellfish. The practice with shrimp is typical. A natural marsh and pond area is enclosed by weirs, gates, or other water control structures. Fine mesh fences allow water flux but still retain the cultured animals. Recruitment of post-larval juveniles to the aquaculture site usually occurs naturally, after which the area is sealed off and the shrimp are allowed to grow. They are harvested as they emigrate over the weirs, or by seining or trawling within the enclosure. In the southern United States several commercial ventures were launched during the 1970s. None succeeded. Too many uncertainties existed in the operations, including stock recruitment and predator and disease control.

A more successful commercial venture is crayfish farming, in combination with timber production. Crayfish are an edible delicacy in the southern United States and in many foreign countries. They live in burrows in shallow flooded areas such as swamp forests and rice fields, emerging with their young early in the year to forage for food. The young grow to edible size within a few weeks, and are harvested in the spring. When floodwaters retreat, the crayfish construct new burrows, where they remain until the next winter flood. In crayfish farms this natural cycle is enhance by controlling water levels. An area of swamp forest is impounded; it is flooded deep during the winter and spring, and drained during the summer. This cycle is ideal for crayfish, which thrive. Fish predators are controlled within the impoundments to improve the harvest. The hydrologic cycle is also favorable for the forest trees. It simulates the hydrologic cycle of a bottomland hardwood forest; forest tree productivity is high, seedling recruitment is good because of the summer drawdown, and species composition tends toward species typical of bottomland hardwoods (Conner, Gosselink, and Parrondo, 1981).

Rice farmers have found that they can take advantage of the same annual flooding cycle to combine rice and crayfish production. Rice fields are drained during the summer and fall as the rice crop matures and is harvested. Then the fields are reflooded, allowing crayfish to emerge from their burrows in the rice field embankments and forage on the vegetation remaining after the rice harvest. The crayfish harvest ends when the fields are replanted to rice. When this rotation is practiced, extreme care has to be exercised in the use of pesticides.

Water Quality Management

A number of studies have shown wetlands to be natural sinks for certain chemicals, particularly nutrients (see chap. 5). Over the last decade, the idea of purposeful application of wastewaters and sludges to wetlands to take advantage of this nutrient sink capacity has been explored. Many of these wetland treatment systems are summarized by Nichols (1983) and Godfrey et al. (1985). To some it has become an idea of wastewater *treatment,* to others wastewater *disposal.* Regardless of what it is called, wastewater recycling in wetlands is an intriguing concept of a partnership of humanity and ecosystem. Many of the wetlands that have been experimentally investigated for their ability to retain nutrients are summarized in Table 16-2.

Northern peatlands have been investigated in studies at Houghton Lake and other communities in Michigan by researchers from the University of Michigan (see Richardson et al., 1978; Kadlec, 1979; Kadlec and Kadlec, 1979; Kadlec and Tilton, 1979; Tilton and Kadlec, 1979). A full-scale operation for disposing up to 380,000 liters per day (100,000 gallons per day) of secondarily treated wastewater into a rich fen at Houghton Lake led to significant reductions in ammonia nitrogen and total dissolved phosphorus as the water passed from the point of discharge (Fig. 16-9). Conservative materials such as chloride did not change as the wastewater passed through

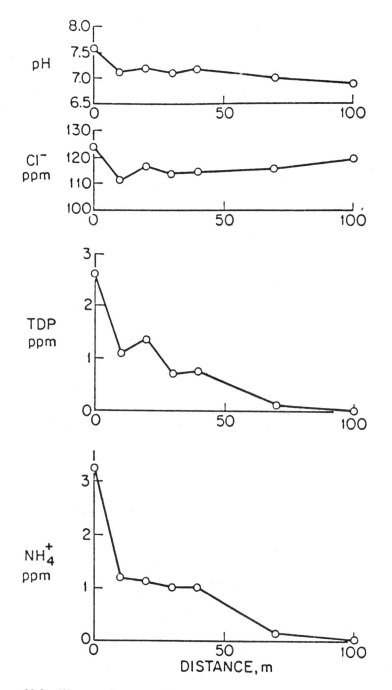

Figure 16-9. Water quality parameter transects for wetland receiving wastewater at Houghton Lake, Michigan, August 1978. *(From Kadlec, 1979, p. 495; Copyright © 1979 by the American Water Resources Association, reprinted with permission)*

Table 16-2. Examples of Wetlands Receiving Wastewater with Loading Rates and Nutrient Removal Efficiencies

Type	Location	Loading, people/hectare	Substrate[a]	Nutrient[b]	Percent Removal	Reference
Northern Peatlands						
Ombrotrophic bog	Wisconsin	30	O	NH_4-N NO_2-NO_3-N TP	97 100 78	Mechenich, 1980
Sedge-shrub fen	Michigan	7	O	NH_4-N NO_2-NO_3-N TDP	71 99	Kadlec, 1979; Kadlec and Kadlec, 1979; Richardson et al., 1976, 1978; Tilton and Kadlec, 1979
Forest-shrub fen	Michigan	27	O	TDN TDP	80 88	Tilton and Kadlec, 1979
Nontidal Freshwater Marshes						
Cattail marsh	Wisconsin	17	O	NO_3-N TP	51[c] 32	Fetter, Sloey, and Spangler, 1978
Lacustrine *Glyceria* marsh	Ontario	-	-	TN TP	38 24	Mudroch and Capobianco, 1979
Deepwater marsh (½ m depth)	Florida	99	O	TP	97	Dolan et al., 1978; 1981
Lacustrine deep-water marsh	Wisconsin	-	O	DP PP	14 82	Perry, Armstrong, and Huff, 1981
Lacustrine *Phragmites* marsh	Hungary	-	-	TN	95[c]	Sloey, Spangler, and Fetter, 1978
Saw Grass freshwater marsh	Florida	-	O	TP	95	Steward and Ornes, 1973

Tidal Freshwater Marshes

	Location	Loading	Substrate[a]	Parameter	Removal (%)	Reference
Deepwater Prag-mites marsh	Louisiana	–	O	TN TP	51 53	Sloey Spangler, and Fetter, 1978; Turner et al., 1976
Complex marsh	New Jersey	198	I	TN TP	40 0	Simpson et al., 1978; Whigham and Simpson, 1976a, 1976b, 1978; Whigham, Simpson, and Lee, 1980
Tidal Salt Marshes						
Brackish marsh	Chesapeake Bay	–	O/I	TN TP	0 1.5 g/m²·yr	Bender and Correl, 1974
Salt marsh	Georgia	Sludge	O/I	TN	50	Chalmers, Maines, and Sherr, 1976
Salt marsh	Massachusetts	Sludge	O/I	TN	85	W. E. Odum and Smith, 1980
Southern Swamps						
Mixed cypress-ash swamp	Florida	7	O	TN TP	90 98	Boyt, Bayley, and Zoltek, 1977
Cypress domes	Florida	–	O	TN TP	98 97	H. T. Odum et al., 1977a; Ewel and Odum, 1978, 1979, 1984
Riverine swamp	South Carolina	–	O	NO$_3$-N TP	0 50	Kitchens et al., 1975

Source: After Heliotis, 1982, p. 34-35, and WAPORA, Inc., 1983, p. 3-39

[a]O: organic substrate
I: inorganic substrate
[b]NH$_4$-N = ammonium nitrogen
NO$_2$-N = nitrite nitrogen
NO$_3$-N = nitrate nitrogen
TDN = total dissolved nitrogen

TN = total nitrogen
DP = dissolved phosphorus
PP = particulate phosphorus
TDP = total dissolved phosphorus
TP = total phosphorus
[c]Indicates removal based on concentration

the wetland (Kadlec, 1979). Overall, an estimated 70% of ammonia nitrogen, 99% of nitrite and nitrate nitrogen, and 95% to total dissolved phosphorus were removed from the wastewater as it passed through the wetland.

In another major research effort, wastewater was applied to several cypress domes in north-central Florida by a team of researchers from the University of Florida (Ewel, 1976; H. T. Odum et al., 1977*a;* Ewel and Odum, 1978, 1979, 1984; Fig. 16-10). After 5 years of experimentation, in which secondarily treated wastewater was added to the cypress domes at a rate of approximately 2.5 cm/wk (1 in/week), results indicated that the wetland filtered nutrients, heavy metals, microbes, and viruses from the water before it entered the groundwater. Productivity of the canopy pond cypress trees increased, although subcanopy growth did not change as much (Ewel and Odum, 1978). The uptake of nutrients in these systems was also enhanced by a continuous cover of duckweed on the water, by the retention of nutrients in the cypress wood and litter, and by the adsorption of phosphorus onto clay and organic peat in sediments.

Wetlands that have received wastewater for a relatively long time have also been studied. Study sites have included freshwater marshes in Wisconsin (Spangler, Fetter, and Sloey, 1977; Fetter, Sloey, and Spangler, 1978) and forested wetlands in Florida (Boyt, Bayley, and Zoltek, 1977; Nessel, 1978; Nessel and Bayley, 1984). All of these studies, and several others, have demonstrated that wetlands can serve as sinks of nutrients for several years, although their assimilation capacity can become saturated for certain chemical constituents (Kadlec and Kadlec, 1979, Richardson, 1985).

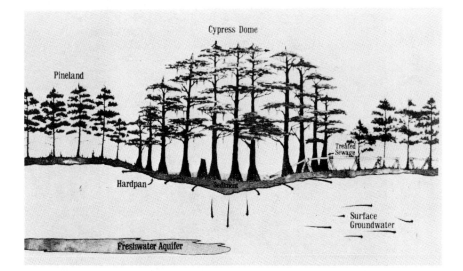

Figure 16-10. Generalized profile of a cypress dome ecosystem, showing surrounding pinelands and wastewater disposal scheme. *(Copyright © 1977. Reprinted from H. T. Odum et al., 1977a, p. 36, by courtesy of Marcel Dekker Press, Inc.)*

There has been a recent interest in developing guidelines for the use of wetlands for wastewater treatment management (Hammer and Kadlec, 1983; U.S. Environmental Protection Agency, 1983; WAPORA, 1983; U.S. Environmental Protection Agency and U.S. Fish & Wildlife Service, 1984, CTA Environmental, Inc., 1985). The design of wetlands to receive and treat wastewater was described by Hammer and Kadlec (1983) to be principally controlled by two phenomena: (1) the hydrologic conditions, including the original water budget, the retention time, the site topography, and the amount of wastewater being added; and (2) the dominant pollutant consumption processes, including sedimentation, biomass production, soil physical processes, microbial processes, and harvesting of vegetation. Nutrients and heavy metals are often retained through adsorption at the sediment-water interface and through plant uptake. This means that as sediment adsorption and increase in biomass reach levels of "saturation" in a wetland after a number of years of receiving wastewater, the wetland will often display a reduced ability to retain pollutants (Richardson, 1985). This process, called aging, suggests that wetland disposal plans should allow the wetland to rest from wastewater discharge or should assume that a larger wetland area will be required over time as the wetland ages. A summary of nutrient removal rates for a number of wetlands that have received wastewater for different periods is shown in Figure 16-11.

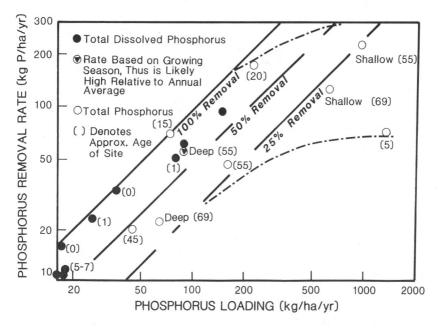

Figure 16-11. Phosphorus removal rates as a function of phosphorus loading rates for wetlands receiving treated wastewater. Length of time of wastewater application in years is shown in parentheses next to each data point. *(After Hammer and Kadlec, 1983, p. 20)*

The U.S. Environmental Protection Agency (1983) summarized a number of critical technical and institutional considerations "that may act independently or jointly to influence the feasibility of using wetlands as a wastewater management alternative." These considerations include the following:

Technical Considerations
1. Other values of the wetlands, such as wildlife habitat, should be considered.
2. Acceptable pollutant and hydrologic loadings must be determined for the use of wetlands in wastewater management.
3. All existing wetland characteristics, including vegetation, geomorphology, hydrology, and water quality should be well understood.
4. Site-specific analyses of wetlands, particularly as to whether they are hydrologically open or isolated, are necessary to determine their potential for wastewater management. Hydrologically isolated wetlands are likely to be altered if wastewater is applied to them, but hydrologically open wetlands are more likely to affect downstream systems.

Institutional Considerations
5. Potential conflicts concerning the protection and use of wetlands exist among state agencies, federal agencies, and local groups.
6. Wastewater disposal into wetlands can often serve the dual purposes of both wetland protection and use, particularly when wetland restoration is involved.
7. State and municipal governments may be potentially liable for damages to private wetlands from wastewater disposal. It is best to have ownership or legal control of wetlands that are used for wastewater management.
8. Federal permitting processes, many of which are now administered by state agencies, do not recognize wetland disposal systems. Modification of existing requirements for permits are needed to make use of this effective method of wetland and wastewater management.

Flood Control and Recharge

Wetlands can be managed, often passively, for their role in the hydrologic cycle. These hydrologic functions include streamflow augmentation, groundwater recharge, water supply potential, and flood protection (see chap. 15). It is not altogether clear how well wetlands carry out these functions nor do all wetlands perform these functions equally well. It is known, for example, that wetlands do not necessarily always contribute to low flows or recharge groundwater (Carter et al., 1979; Verry and Boelter, 1979). Some wetlands, however, should be and often are protected for their ability to hold water and slowly return it to surface and groundwater systems in periods of low water.

More definitive studies have been made on the function of wetlands for flood control (see chap. 15), although the management of these wetlands for this value is also very simple — maintenance of the wetlands in their natural condition. If wetlands are impounded to retain even more water from flooding downstream areas, considerable changes in vegetation will result as the systems adapt to the new hydrologic conditions.

WETLAND CREATION

The creation of wetland in previously dry and/or nonvegetated areas is an exciting possibility for reversing the trend of decreasing wetland resources and for providing aesthetic and functional units to the landscape (Fig. 16-12). Wetland creation can conveniently be divided into the building of farm pond freshwater wetlands, and the creation of more extensive coastal and inland wetlands. Although the net trend in the United States is toward the destruction of inland freshwater wetlands (see chap. 3 and earlier parts of this chapter), there has been at the same time significant creation of wetlands, associated primarily with the construction of farm ponds in the Midwest. Although individually quite small (about 0.2 hectare), the total number of these ponds is enormous. The U.S. Soil Conservation Service estimated that about 50,000 ponds are constructed each year, for a 20-year total of close to

Figure 16-12.   This created cypress swamp at the University of Southwestern Louisiana provides an attractive and peaceful setting on campus. *(Photograph by W. Conner)*

800,000 hectares of marsh created from these ponds and the enlargement of existing ones (Office of Technology Assessment, 1984). Many of these ponds are built with large, shallow areas to attract waterfowl, and these shallow zones become typical pothole marshes.

A much smaller source of new marshes has been the creation of coastal and inland riverine marshes, mostly in areas where considerable dredging occurs along navigable waterways. The U.S. Army Corps of Engineers annually dredges about 275 million cubic meters of material from the nation's waterways to keep them open. During the 1970s this agency initiated a large study to determine the feasibility of creating marshes out of the spoil, thus turning a liability into an asset. In addition, there has recently been much interest in creating wetlands along the Gulf coast by diverting the sediment-rich water of the Mississippi River into shallow bays. Here the sediments settle out to intertidal elevations. Both processes appear to be feasible.

The details of successful coastal wetland creation are, of course, site specific, but several generalizations seem to be valid in most situations (H. K. Smith, 1980; Seneca, 1980):

1. Sediment elevation seems to be the most critical factor determining successful establishment of vegetation, and the plant species that will survive. The site must be intertidal, and, in general, the upper half of the intertidal zone is more rapidly vegetated than lower elevations. Sediment composition does not seem to be a critical factor in colonization by plants unless the deposits are nearly pure sand that is subject to rapid dessication at the upper elevations. Another important factor is whether the site is protected from high wave energy. It is difficult or impossible to establish vegetation at high-energy sites.

2. Most deposits seem to revegetate naturally if the elevation is appropriate and wave energy is moderate. Sprigging live plants has been accomplished in a number of cases; and seeding also has been successful in the upper half of the intertidal zone.

3. Good stands can be established during the first season of growth, although sediment stabilization does not occur until after two seasons. Within 4 years successfully planted sites are indistinguishable from natural marshes.

LEGAL PROTECTION OF WETLANDS IN THE UNITED STATES

In the early 1970s, interest in wetland protection increased significantly as scientists began to identify and quantify the many values of these ecosystems. This interest in wetland protection began to be translated at the federal levels in the United States into several laws and public policies. Prior to this time, federal policy on wetlands was vague and often contradictory. Policies in agencies such as the Corps of Engineers, the Soil Conservation Service, and the Bureau of Reclamation encouraged the destruction of wetlands, while policies in the Department of Interior, particularly in the U.S. Fish and Wildlife Service, encouraged their protection (Kusler, 1983). States have also developed separate inland and coastal wetland laws and policies in many cases, and activity in that area appears to be increasing.

Federal Government Policies and Laws

Some of the more significant activities in the federal government that led to a more consistent wetland protection policy have included presidential orders on wetland protection and floodplain management, implementation of a dredge and fill permit system to protect wetlands, coastal zone management policies, and separate initiatives and regulations by various agencies. The primary wetland protection mechanisms in the federal government are summarized in Table 16-3. Despite all of this activity, Zinn and Copeland (1982) suggested that two major points about federal wetland management should be emphasized:

1. There is no one national wetland law. Wetland management and protection results from a combination of many indirect uses of laws intended for other purposes. The jurisdiction over wetlands has also been spread over several agencies, and, overall, federal policy continually changes and has little interagency coordination.

2. Wetlands have been managed under regulations related to both land use and water quality. Neither of these approaches, taken separately, will lead to a comprehensive wetland policy. The legal split here mirrors the scientific split noted by many wetland ecologists that wetlands are approached by people with expertise on either aquatic or terrestrial systems, but rarely by someone who has training in both areas.

Presidential Executive Orders

President Jimmy Carter issued two executive orders in May 1977 that established the protection of wetlands and riparian systems as an official policy of the federal government. Executive Order 11990, Protection of Wetlands, required all federal agencies to consider wetland protection as an important part of their policies:

Each agency shall provide leadership and shall take action to minimize the destruction, loss or degradation of wetlands, and to preserve and enhance the natural and beneficial values of wetlands in carrying out the agency's responsibilities for

Table 16-3. Major Federal Laws, Directives, and Regulations for the Management and Protection of Wetlands

Directive or Statute	Data	Responsible Agency
Executive Order 11990 Protection of Wetlands	May 1977	All agencies
Executive Order 11988 Floodplain Management	May 1977	All agencies
Federal Water Pollution Control Act (PL 92-500) as Amended	1972, 1977	
Section 404 - Dredge and Fill Permit Program		Army Corps of Engineers with assistance from Environmental Protection Agency and U.S. Fish and Wildlife Service
Section 208 - Areawide Water Quality Planning		Environmental Protection Agency
Section 303 - Water Quality Standards		Environmental Protection Agency
Section 402 - National Pollutant Discharge Elimination System		Environmental Protection Agency (or state agencies)
Coastal Zone Management Act	1972	Office of Coastal Zone Management
Flood Disaster Protection Act	1973, 1977	Federal Emergency Management Agency
Land and Water Conservation Fund Act	1968	Fish and Wildlife Service, Bureau of Land Management, Forest Service, National Park Service
Federal Aid to Wildlife Restoration Act	1974	Fish and Wildlife Service

Source: Based on data from Kusler, 1983, p. 55.

(1) acquiring, managing, and disposing of Federal lands and facilities; and (2) providing federally undertaken, financed, or assisted construction and improvement; and (3) conducting Federal activities and programs affecting land use, including but not limited to water and related land resources planning, regulating, and licensing activities.

Executive Order 11988, Floodplain Management, established a similar federal policy for the protection of floodplains, requiring agencies to avoid activity in the floodplain wherever practicable. Furthermore, agencies were directed to revise their procedures to consider the impact that their activities might have on flooding and to avoid direct or indirect support of floodplain development when other alternatives are available.

Both of these executive orders were significant because they set into motion a review of wetland and floodplain policies by almost every federal agency. Several agencies, such as the U.S. Environmental Protection Agency and the Soil Conservation Service, had established policies of wetland protection prior to the issuance of these executive orders (Kusler, 1983), but many other agencies, such as the Bureau of Land Management, were compelled to review or establish wetland and floodplain policies (Zinn and Copeland, 1982).

The 404 Program

Section 404 of the Federal Water Pollution Control Act (FWPCA Amendments of 1972 (PL 92-500) and the 1977 Amendments (also known as the Clean Water Act) set into motion a broad-ranging program that, in time, became the federal government's primary tool for protecting wetlands. The use of Section 404 for wetland protection has been controversial and has been the subject of several court actions and revisions of regulations. The surprising point about the importance of the FWPCA in wetland protection is that wetlands are not directly mentioned in either the act or its amendments. Section 404 of the FWPCA gave authority to the Corps of Engineers to establish a permit system to regulate the dredging and filling of materials in "waters of the United States." At first this directive was interpreted narrowly by the Corps of Engineers to apply only to navigable waters. That definition of waters of the United States was expanded in the 1975 court decision *Natural Resources Defense Council v. Calloway* to include wetlands. This court interpretation, along with, later, Executive Order 11990 on Protection of Wetlands, put the Corps of Engineers squarely in the center of wetland protection in the United States. On July 25, 1975, the Corps issued revised regulations for the 404 program, and considerable attention was paid to wetlands. The policy of the Corps on wetlands was stated in those regulations: "As environmentally vital areas, [wetlands] constitute a productive and valuable public resource, the unnecessary alteration or destruction of which should be discouraged as contrary to the public interest" (Federal Register, July 25, 1975). Wetlands were defined in these regulations to encompass coastal wetlands ("marshes and shallows and . . . those areas periodically inundated by saline or brackish waters and that are normally characterized by the prevalence of salt or brackish water vegetation capable of growth and reproduction") and freshwater wetlands ("areas that are periodically inundated and that are normally characterized by the prevalence of vegetation that requires saturated soil conditions for growth and reproduction") (Federal Register, July 25, 1975, as cited by Zinn and Copeland, 1982). The jurisdiction of the Corps now legally included 60 million hectares of wetlands, 45% of which is in Alaska (Zinn and Copeland, 1982). Regulations by the Corps of Engineers for their dredge and fill permit program have been revised several times since 1975, with the most recent changes published in 1984.

The general procedure for obtaining a "404 Permit" for dredge and fill activity in wetlands is a complex process (Fig. 16-13). The decision to issue a

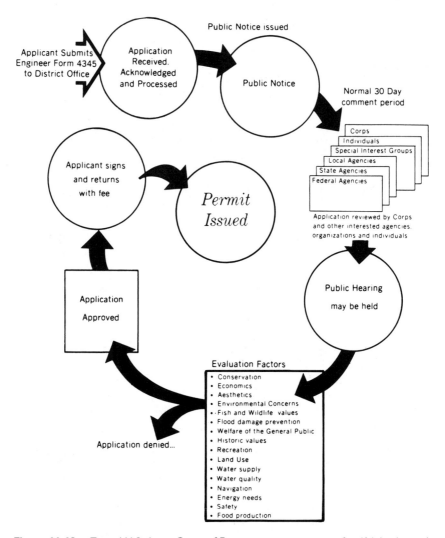

Figure 16-13. Typical U.S. Army Corps of Engineers review process for 404 dredge and fill permit request. *(From Kusler, 1983, p. 62; Copyright © 1983 by the Environmental Law Institute, reprinted with permission)*

**Table 16-4. Activity of Memphis District of U.S. Army
Corps of Engineers on Section 404 Permits, 1975–1982**

Action	Number
Total Number of Permit Applications Received	247
Total Number of Permit Applications Granted	199
Number of Permits Granted with Restorative or Mitigative Measures Required	24
Number of Cease and Desist Orders Issued	60
Number of Cases Prosecuted or Pending Prosecution	8

Source: U.S. Army Corps of Engineers, Memphis District, personal communication

permit rests with the district engineer, and it must be based on a number of considerations, including conservation, economics, aesthetics, and several other factors listed in Figure 16-13. Assistance to the Corps on the dredge and fill permit system, particularly in wetlands cases, is provided by the U.S. Environmental Protection Agency, the U.S. Fish and Wildlife Service, and state agencies. The EPA has statutory authority to designate wetlands subject to permitting, and the U.S. Fish and Wildlife Service is obligated to comment on habitat aspects of Corps environmental assessments. Some states require state permits as well as Corps permits for wetland development. The district engineer, according to Corps regulations, should not grant a permit if a wetland is identified as performing important functions for the public, such as biological support, sanctuary, storm protection, flood storage, groundwater recharge, or water purification. An exception to this is allowed if the district engineer determined "that the benefits of the proposed alteration outweigh the damage to the wetlands resource and the proposed alteration is necessary to realize those benefits" (Federal Register, July 19, 1977). The effectiveness of the 404 Program has varied since the program began and has also varied from district to district. For example, data in Table 16-4 show the number of permit applications and the number of permit approvals for the Memphis, Tennessee, district of the Corps of Engineers. This district is responsible for a region that includes numerous wetlands in the upper Mississippi River floodplain.

Other Federal Activity

Several other federal laws and activities have led to wetland protection over the past decade (Kusler, 1979; 1983). The Coastal Zone Management Program, established by the Coastal Zone Management Act of 1972, has provided up to 80% matching funding grants to states to develop plans for coastal management, with wetland protection given a high priority. The National Flood Insurance Program offers some protection to riparian and coastal wetlands by offering federally subsidized flood insurance to state and local governments that enact local regulations against development in flood-prone areas. The Clean Water Act of 1977, in addition to supporting the 404 Program, authorized $6 million to the U.S. Fish and Wildlife Service to complete its inventory of wetlands of the United States (see chap. 17).

State Management of Wetlands

Many individual states have actively developed wetland protection statutes or regulations. That activity has been described in a number of studies, including those by Martel Laboratories, Inc. (1976), Kusler (1979; 1983), Zinn and Copeland (1982), and Glubiak, Nowka, and Mitsch (1986). State wetland programs may become more important as the federal government attempts to delegate much of its authority to local and state control. Kusler (1983) has suggested that while local communities may also have wetland protection programs, states are much more probable governmental units for wetland protection for the following reasons:

1. Wetlands cross local government boundaries, making local control difficult.
2. Wetlands in one part of a watershed affect other parts that may be in different jurisdictions.
3. There is usually a lack of expertise and resources at the local level to study wetland values and hazards.
4. Many of the traditional functions of states, such as fish and wildlife protection, are related to wetland protection.

Most states with coastlines have paid more attention to management of their coastal wetlands than to their inland wetlands (Kusler, 1983). This is a result of an earlier interest in coastal wetland protection at the federal level and to the development of coastal zone management programs. Table 16-5 shows some of the states that have coastal wetland protection programs. In general, these programs can be divided into those that are based on specific coastal wetland laws and those that are designed as a part of broader regulatory programs such as coastal zone management. Thirteen states have coastal dredge and fill permit programs, while another six states have specific wetland regulations administered by a state agency (Kusler, 1983).

State programs for inland wetlands, while in an earlier stage of development, are more diverse, ranging from comprehensive laws to a total lack of concern for inland wetlands. The major types of inland wetland protection programs in the states are summarized in Table 16-6. Comprehensive laws are found in several states, such as Connecticut, Rhode Island, New York, and Massachusetts. Other states, such as Arizona, Georgia, and Idaho, have little regulation of inland wetlands. In between these two extremes, there are many states that rely on federal/state cooperation programs or on state laws

Table 16-5. States with Coastal Wetland Protection Programs

State	*Program*
Alabama	Permits are required for activities in coastal zone (dredging, dumping, etc.) that alter tidal movement or damage flora and fauna.
California	Permit required for development up to 1,000 yards of mean high tide; coastal zone regulated by regional regulatory boards.
Connecticut	Permit required for all regulated activity; state inventory required.
Delaware	Permits required for all activities.
Georgia	Permits required for work in coastal salt marshes.
Louisiana	State and/or local permits required for activity in coastal wetlands.
Maine	Local permits required for dredging, filling, dumping, or sewage discharge into coastal wetlands; state may disapprove permit.
Maryland	State and/or local permits required for activity in coastal wetlands.
Massachusetts	State and local permits required for fill or alteration of coastal wetlands. Permits submitted to town conservation commissioners.
Mississippi	Permits required for dredging and dumping, although there are many exemptions.
New Hampshire	Permit required for dredge and fill in or adjacent to tidal wetlands; notice to local government and adjacent landowner required.
New Jersey	Permit required for dredging and filling; agriculture exempted; inventory required.
New York	State moratorium adopted for tidal wetlands; previously permits required for tidal wetland alteration.
North Carolina	State permit required for coastal wetland excavation.
Rhode Island	Coastal wetlands designated by order and use limited; permits required for filling activity on salt marshes.
Virginia	Tidal Wetland Protection Act of 1973 contains model ordinance: If municipalities do not regulate wetlands, counties have jurisdiction; if counties do not regulate, permits are required by state.
Washington	Washington Shoreline Zoning Act of 1971 requires local governments to adopt plans for shorelines, including wetlands; state may regulate if local government fails to do so.

Source: After Zinn and Copeland, 1982, p. 106-108 after Kusler, 1979; Kusler, 1983, p. 65

Table 16-6. Categories of State Regulation of Inland Waters, Early 1983

Category	*States*
No Law or Interest	Arizona, Delaware, Georgia, Idaho, New Mexico, Utah
General Reliance on Federal 404 Permit Program	Alabama, Hawaii, Indiana, Wyoming
Combination of 404 Permit Program with Some State Legislation or Regulation	Alaska, Colorado, Florida, Missouri, Montana, Ohio, Oregon, West Virginia
State Laws Indirectly Related to Wetland Protection	Alabama, Florida, Illinois, Indiana, Iowa, Kentucky, Louisiana, Maine, Maryland, Minnesota, Montana, Nevada, North Carolina, North Dakota, Pennsylvania, South Carolina, Vermont, Virginia, Washington
Area-Specific Inland Wetland Laws	Hawaii, Maryland
Comprehensive Wetland Law	Connecticut, Florida, Guam, Maine, Mariana Islands, Massachusetts, Michigan, Minnesota, New Hampshire, New York, Rhode Island, Wisconsin
Wetland Study or Legislation Under Way or Proposed	Arkansas, California, Illinois, Mariana Islands, Maryland, Nebraska, New Jersey, Oregon, Tennessee, Vermont

Source: After Glubiak, Nowka, and Mitsch, 1986

that indirectly protect wetlands. Floodplain protection laws or scenic and wild river programs are found in more than half of the states and are often very effective in slowing destruction of riparian wetlands.

SUMMARY

Wetland management has meant both wetland alteration and protection. In earlier times, wetland removal was considered as the only policy for managing wetlands. With the recognition of wetland values, wetland protection has been emphasized by many federal and state policies over the last decade. Nevertheless, significant wetland alteration continues, particularly by dredging, filling, drainage, hydrologic modification, peat mining removal for mineral extraction, and water pollution. Wetlands can also be managed in their more or less natural state for certain objectives such as fish and wildlife enhancement, agricultural and aquaculture production, water quality improvement and wastewater management, and flood control and recharge.

The federal government has relied primarily on presidential executive orders and the Section 404 dredge and fill permit program for wetland protection. Some states also have wetland protection programs, although many more have little or no interest in wetland protection. Many observers believe there will be increased responsibility for individual states and less with the federal government for the protection of wetlands in the United States in the future.

CLASSIFICATION AND INVENTORY OF WETLANDS

In order to deal properly with wetlands on a regional scale, wetland managers have found it necessary to both define the different types of wetlands that exist and to determine their extent and distribution. These activities, the first called *wetland classification,* and the second called a *wetland inventory,* are valuable tools for both the wetland scientist and the wetland manager. Classifications and inventories of wetlands have been undertaken for the entire United States, for Canada, and in individual states, provinces, and regions for many purposes and objectives over the past century. Some of the earliest efforts were for the purpose of finding wetlands that could be drained for human use; later classifications and inventories have centered on the desire to compare different types of wetlands in a given region, often for their value to waterfowl. The protection of multiple ecological values of wetlands is the most recent and now most common reason for wetland classification and inventory. As with any tools, classifications and inventories are valuable only if the user is familiar with their scope and limitations.

GOALS OF WETLAND CLASSIFICATION

Several attempts have been made to classify wetlands into categories that follow their structural and functional characteristics. These classifications depend on a well-understood general definition of wetlands (see chap. 2), although a classification contains in itself definitions of individual wetland types. A primary goal of wetland classifications, according to Cowardin et al. (1979, p. 3), "is to impose boundaries on natural ecosystems for the purposes of inventory, evaluation, and management." These authors wrote on four major objectives of the classification system:

1. to describe ecological units that have certain homogeneous natural attributes;
2. to arrange these units in a system that will aid decisions about resource management;
3. to furnish units for inventory and mapping; and
4. to provide uniformity in concepts and terminology throughout the United States.

The first objective deals with the important task of grouping together ecosystems that have similar characteristics, in much the same way that taxonomists categorize species in taxonomic groupings. The wetland attributes that are frequently used to compare and lump together wetlands include vegetation type, plant or animal species, or hydrologic conditions.

The second objective, to aid wetland managers, is met in several ways when wetlands are classified. Classifications (which are definitions of different types of wetlands) enable the wetland manager to deal with wetland regulation and protection in a consistent manner from region to region and from one time to the next. Classifications also enable the wetland manager to pay selectively more attention to those types of wetlands that are functionally the most valuable to a given region.

The third and fourth objectives, to provide consistency for inventories, mapping, concepts, and terminology, are also important in wetland management. Consistent terms to define particular types of wetlands are needed in the field of wetland science (see chap. 3). These terms then should be applied uniformly to wetland inventories and mapping so that different regions can be compared and so that there is a common understanding of wetland types among wetland scientists, wetland managers, and even wetland owners.

HISTORY OF WETLAND CLASSIFICATION

Peatland Classifications

Many of the earliest wetland classifications were for the northern peatlands of Europe and North America. An early peatland classification in the United States, developed by Davis (1907), described Michigan bogs according to three separate criteria: (1) the landform on which the bog was established,

Table 17-1. Hydrologic Classification of European Peatlands

A. *Rheophilous Mire*—Peatland influenced by groundwater derived from outside the immediate watershed

   Type 1—Continuously flowing water that inundates the peatland surface

   Type 2—Continuously flowing water beneath a floating mat of vegetation

   Type 3—Intermittent flow inundating the mire surface

   Type 4—Intermittent flow of water beneath a floating mat of vegetation

B. *Transition Mire*—Peatland influenced by groundwater derived solely from the immediate watershed

   Type 5—Continuous flow of water

   Type 6—Intermittent flow of water

C. *Ombrophilous Mire*

   Type 7—Peatland never subject for flowing groundwater

Source: After Moore and Bellamy, 1974, p. 59, based on Bellamy, 1968.

such as shallow lake basins or deltas of streams; (2) the method by which the bog was developed, such as from the bottom up or from the shores inward; and (3) the surface vegetation, such as tamarack or mosses. Moore and Bellamy (1974), based on the earlier work of Weber (1908), Potonie (1908), Kulczynski (1949), and others in Europe, described seven types of peatlands based on the flow-through conditions (Table 17-1). Three general categories, called rheophilous, transition, and ombrophilous, describe the degree to which the peatland is influenced by outside drainage. These categories were discussed in more detail in chapter 12.

Peatlands, of course, are limited to northern temperate climes and do not include all or even most types of wetlands in North America. These classifications, however, served as models for more inclusive classifications to come later. They are significant because they combined the chemical and physical conditions of the wetland with the vegetation description to present a balanced approach to wetland classification.

Circular 39 Classification

In the early 1950s, the U.S. Fish and Wildlife Service recognized the need for a national wetlands inventory to determine "the distribution, extent, and quality of the remaining wetlands in relation to their value as wildlife habitat" (Shaw and Fredine, 1956, p. 14). A classification was developed for that inventory (Martin et al., 1953), and the results of both the inventory and the classification scheme were published in U.S. Fish and Wildlife Circular No. 39 (Shaw and Fredine, 1956). Twenty types of wetlands were described under four major categories:

1. Inland fresh areas
2. Inland saline areas
3. Coastal freshwater areas
4. Coastal saline areas

In each of the four categories, the wetlands were arranged in order of increasing water depth or frequency of inundation. A brief description of the site characteristics of the 20 wetland types is given in Table 17-2.

Types 1 through 8 are freshwater wetlands that include bottomland hardwood forests (Type 1), infrequently flooded meadows (Type 2), freshwater nontidal marshes (Types 3 and 4), open water less than 2 m deep (Type 5), shrub-scrub swamps (Type 6), forested swamps (Type 7), and bogs (Type 8). Types 9 through 11 are inland wetlands that have saline soils. They are defined according to degree of flooding. Types 12 through 14 are wetlands that, although freshwater, are close enough to the coast to be influenced by tides. Types 15 through 20 are coastal saline wetlands that are influenced by both salt water and tidal action. These include salt flats and meadows (Types 15 and 16), true salt marshes (Types 17 and 18), open bays (Type 19), and mangrove swamps (Type 20).

This wetland classification was the most widely used in the United States until 1979, when the National Wetlands Inventory classification was adopted (see Present United States Classification section). It is still referred to today by some wetland managers and is regarded by many as elegantly simple compared with its successor. It relied primarily on the life forms of vegetation and the depth of flooding for identification of wetland type. Salinity is the only chemical parameter used, and although wetland soils are discussed in the Circular 39 publication, they are not used to define wetland types.

Adaptations to Circular 39

Two additional attempts to classify wetlands using categories similar to those in Circular 39 are noteworthy. The prairie potholes of the upper Midwest were included in a classification by Stewart and Kantrud (1971, 1972). A list

Table 17-2. Early Wetland Classification By U.S. Fish and Wildlife Service

Type Number	Wetland Type	Site Characteristics
	Inland Fresh Areas	
1.	Seasonally flooded basins or flats	Soil covered with water or waterlogged during variable periods, but well drained during much of the growing season; in upland depressions and bottomlands
2.	Fresh meadows	Without standing water during growing season; waterlogged to within a few inches of surface
3.	Shallow fresh marshes	Soil waterlogged during growing season; often covered with 15 cm or more of water
4.	Deep fresh marshes	Soil covered with 15 cm to 1 m of water
5.	Open fresh water	Water less than 2 m deep
6.	Shrub swamps	Soil waterlogged; often covered with 15 cm or more of water
7.	Wooded swamps	Soil waterlogged; often covered with 30 cm of water; along sluggish streams, flat uplands, shallow lake basins
8.	Bogs	Soil waterlogged; spongy covering of mosses
	Inland Saline Areas	
9.	Saline flats	Flooded after periods of heavy precipitation; waterlogged within few inches of surface during the growing season
10.	Saline marshes	Soil waterlogged during growing season; often covered with 0.7 to 1 m of water; shallow lake basins
11.	Open saline water	Permanent areas of shallow saline water; depth variable
	Coastal Fresh Areas	
12.	Shallow fresh marshes	Soil waterlogged during growing season; at high tide as much as 15 cm of water; on landward side, deep marshes along tidal rivers, sounds, deltas
13.	Deep fresh marshes	At high tide covered with 15 cm to 1 m water; along tidal rivers and bays
14.	Open fresh water	Shallow portions of open water along fresh tidal rivers and sounds
	Coastal Saline Areas	
15.	Salt flats	Soil waterlogged during growing season; sites occasionally to fairly regularly covered by high tide; landward sides or islands within salt meadows and marshes
16.	Salt meadows	Soil waterlogged during growing season; rarely covered with tide water; landward side of salt marshes
17.	Irregularly flooded salt marshes	Covered by wind tides at irregular intervals during the growing season; along shores of nearly enclosed bays, sounds, etc.

Table 17-2. *Continued*

Type Number	Wetland Type	Site Characteristics
18.	Regularly flooded salt marshes	Covered at average high tide with 15 cm or more of water; along open ocean and along sounds
19.	Sounds and bays	Portions of saltwater sounds and bays shallow enough to be diked and filled; all water landward from average low-tide line
20.	Mangrove swamps	Soil covered at average high tide with 15 cm to 1 m of water; along coast of southern Florida

Source: From R. L. Smith, 1980, pp. 225-226, after Shaw and Fredine, 1956. Copyright © 1980 by R. L. Smith, reprinted with permission.

Table 17-3. Classification of Natural Ponds and Lakes in the Glaciated Prairie Region

Class	Circular 39 Type
I—Ephemeral Ponds	1
II—Temporary Ponds	1, 2
III—Seasonal Ponds and Lakes	3, 4
IV—Semipermanent Ponds and Lakes	3, 4, 5, 10, 11
Subclasses A and B—cover type 1	3
Subclasses A and B—cover type 2	4
Subclasses A and B—cover types 3 and 4	4, 5
Subclasses C, D, and E—cover types 1 and 2	10
Subclasses C, D, and E—cover types 3 and 4	11
V—Permanent Ponds and Lakes	5, 11
Subclass B—cover types 3 and 4	5
Subclasses C, D, and E—cover types 3 and 4	11
VI—Alkali Ponds and Lakes	9
VII—Fen (alkaline bog) ponds	8

Source: After Stewart and Kantrud, 1971, p. 14. Compared to Circular 39 wetland classification, Shaw and Fredine, 1956

of the classes used and a comparison with Circular 39 types is shown in Table 17-3. Seven classes were used, all based on vegetation zones that occupied the deepest portion of each pothole basin. This vegetation zone, in turn, was defined according to its hydrologic characteristics (e.g., temporary pond). Six subclasses to denote variations in salinity and four cover types to refer to spatial patterns of the emergent vegetation are also used.

**Table 17-4. Classes and Subclasses for Freshwater Wetlands in
the Glaciated Northeastern United States**

Wetland Class	*Wetland Subclass*	
Open Water	(OW-1)	Vegetated
	(OW-2)	Nonvegetated
Deep Marsh	(DM-1)	Dead woody
	(DM-2)	Shrub
	(DM-3)	Sub-shrub
	(DM-4)	Robust
	(DM-5)	Narrow-leaved
	(DM-6)	Broad-leaved
Shallow Marsh	(SM-1)	Robust
	(SM-2)	Narrow-leaved
	(SM-3)	Broad-leaved
	(SM-4)	Floating-leaved
Seasonally Flooded Flats	(SF-1)	Emergent
	(SF-2)	Shrub
Meadow	(M-1)	Ungrazed
	(M-2)	Grazed
Shrub Swamp	(SS-1)	Sapling
	(SS-2)	Bushy
	(SS-3)	Compact
	(SS-4)	Aquatic
Wooded Swamp	(WS-1)	Deciduous
	(WS-2)	Evergreen
Bog	(BG-1)	Shrub
	(BG-2)	Wooded

Source: From Golet and Larson, 1974, p. 7.

Golet and Larson (1974) detailed a freshwater wetland classification for the glaciated northeastern United States based on the categories similar to those in Circular 39, Types 1 through 8 (Table 17-4). This classification introduced 24 subclasses based on 18 possible life forms as shown in Figure 17-1. In addition, five wetland size categories, seven site types, eight cover types, three vegetative interspersion types, and six surrounding habitat types were used to further define the wetlands.

Coastal Wetland Classification

A classification and functional description of coastal ecosystems, including several coastal wetlands, was developed by H. T. Odum, Copeland, and McMahan (1974) in "Coastal Ecological Systems of the United States." The

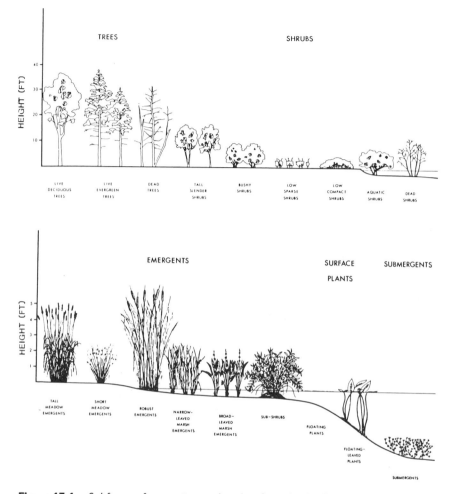

Figure 17-1. Subforms of vegetation used to classify wetlands of glaciated northeastern United States. *(From Golet and Larson, 1974, p. 5)*

significance of this classification was its approach in categorizing ecosystems according to their major forcing functions (e.g., seasonal programming of sunlight and temperature) and stresses (e.g., ice). Coastal wetland types included in this classification included salt marshes and mangrove swamps. Salt marshes, found in the Type C category of Natural Temperate Ecosystems with Seasonal Programming, have "light tidal regimes" and "winter cold" as sources and stresses, respectively. Mangrove swamps are classified as Type B (Natural Tropical Ecosystems) because they have abundant light, little stress, and little seasonal programming. Three additional classes, Type

Table 17-5. Classification of Forested Wetlands in Florida

---

1. *Cypress Ponds (Domes)—Still-Water*

   Acid water ponds
   Hard water ponds
   Pasture ponds
   Enriched ponds

2. *Other Nonstream Swamps*

   Gum pond (swamp)
   Lake border swamp
   Dwarf cypress
   Bog swamp (Okefenokee Swamp)
   Bay swamp
   Shrub bog
   Herb bog
   Seepage swamp
   Hydric hammock (North Florida type)
   South Florida hammock
   Melaleuca swamp

3. *Cypress Strand—Slowly Flowing Water*

4. *River Swamps and Floodplains*

   Alluvial river swamps
   Blackwater river and creek swamps
   Backswamp
   Spring run swamp
   Tidewater swamp

5. *Saltwater Swamps—Mangroves*

   Riverine black mangroves
   Fringe red mangroves
   Overwash red mangroves
   Scrub mangroves

Source: After Wharton et al., 1976, p. 6.

A (Naturally Stressed Systems of Wide Latitudinal Range), Type D (Natural Arctic Ecosystems with Ice Stress), and Type E (Emerging New Systems Associated with Man), are also in this classification. The last class, which includes new systems formed by pollution, such as pesticides and oil spills, is an interesting concept that could be applied to other wetland classifications.

Florida Wetland Classification

Other classifications of wetlands have further developed this approach of using the forcing functions to define wetlands. Wharton et al. (1976) described

Table 17-6. Freshwater Wetland Classification According to Hydrologic Regime

Wetland Type	*Hydropulse*	*Example*
1. Raised—Convex	Seasonal precipitation and capillarity	Ombrotrophic bog
2. Meadow	Seasonal precipitation, capillarity; little up-stream inflow	Blanket bog
3. Sunken—Concave	Seasonal precipitation and upstream inflow	Fen
4. Lotic	Seasonal precipitation, runoff, groundwater, and flowthrough	Fen; reed marsh
5. Tidal	Tides	Salt marsh
6. Lentic	Variable or seasonal Overbank flooding	Riparian wetland

Source: After Gosselink and Turner, 1978, p. 74.

the forested swamps of Florida by their hydrologic inputs. The major types in this classification are given in Table 17-5. The wetlands are arranged according to water flow with the first two classes, "cypress ponds" and "other nonstream swamps" involving wetlands with little water inflow except precipitation and, in some cases, groundwater. The third class, "cypress strands," includes slowly flowing water typical of southern Florida river basins, while "river swamps and floodplains" are more typical of continuously flooded alluvial swamps and periodically flooded riparian forests. The fifth class, "saltwater swamps-mangroves," are those forested wetlands affected by tides and salt water.

Hydrodynamic Energy Gradient Classification

A similar approach to classifying wetlands according to their source and velocity of water flow was developed as a "Classification of Wetland Systems on a Hydrodynamic Energy Gradient" by Gosselink and Turner (1978). The classification is summarized in Table 17-6. As described by its originators, (p. 74), "In general flow rate, or other indications of hydrologic energy such as renewal time or frequency of flooding, increases from raised convex wetlands to lentic and tidal wetlands." Raised-convex systems are primarily ombrotrophic bogs that are fed only by precipitation and capillary action, while lentic wetlands include riparian bottomlands that receive seasonal flooding pulses. This classification, while applied only to nonforested freshwater wetlands, has applicability to wetlands in general. It offers a useful approach of incorporating wetland functions into a wetland classification.

PRESENT UNITED STATES CLASSIFICATION—THE NATIONAL WETLANDS INVENTORY

The U.S. Fish and Wildlife Service began a rigorous new wetland inventory of the nation's wetlands in 1974. Because this inventory was designed for several scientific and management objectives, a new classification scheme, broader than Circular 39, was developed and finally published in 1979 as a "Classification of Wetlands and Deepwater Habitats of the United States" (Cowardin et al., 1979). Because wetlands were found to be continuous with deepwater ecosystems, both categories were addressed in this classification. It is thus a comprehensive classification of all continental aquatic and semiaquatic ecosystems. As described in that publication (p. 1):

This classification, to be used in a new inventory of wetlands and deepwater habitats of the United States, is intended to describe ecological taxa, arrange them in a system useful to resource managers, furnish units for mapping, and provide uniformity of concepts and terms. Wetlands are defined by plants (hydrophytes), soils (hydric soils), and frequency of flooding. Ecologically related areas of deep water, traditionally not considered wetlands, are included in the classification as deepwater habitats.

This classification is based on a hierarchical approach analogous to taxonomic classifications used to identify plant and animal species. The first three levels of the classification hierarchy are given in Figure 17-2. The broadest level is *systems:* "a complex of wetlands and deepwater habitats that share the influence of similar hydrologic, geomorphologic, chemical, or biological factors." (p. 4). These broad categories (p. 4-12) include the following:

1. *Marine*—open ocean overlying the continental shelf and its associated high-energy coastal line.
2. *Estuarine*—deepwater tidal habitats and adjacent tidal wetlands that are usually semi-enclosed by land but have open, partially obstructed, or sporadic access to the ocean and in which ocean water is at least occasionally diluted by freshwater runoff from the land.
3. *Riverine*—wetland and deepwater habitats contained within a channel with two exceptions: (1) wetlands dominated by trees, shrubs, persistent emergents, emergent mosses, or lichens, and (2) habitats with water containing ocean-derived salts in excess of 0.5 ‰.
4. *Lacustrine*—wetlands and deepwater habitats with all of the following characteristics: (1) situated in a topographic depression or a dammed river channel; (2) lacking trees, shrubs, persistent emergents, emer-

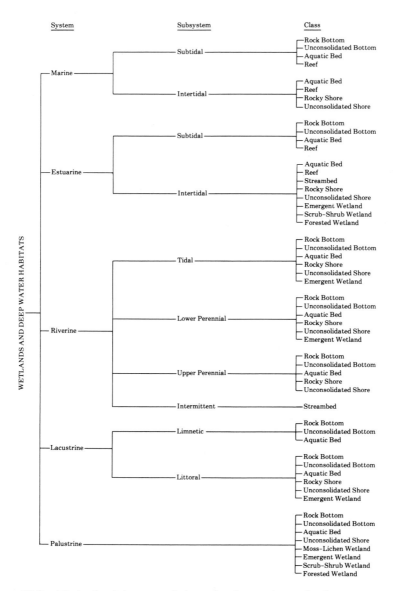

Figure 17-2. Wetland and deepwater habitat classification hierarchy showing systems, subsystems, and classes. *(From Cowardin et al., 1979, p. 5)*

gent mosses, or lichens with greater than 30% areal coverage; and (3) total area exceeds 8 ha (20 acres). Similar wetland and deepwater habitats totaling less than 8 ha are also included in the Lacustrine System if an active wave-formed or bedrock shoreline feature makes up all or part of the boundary, or if the depth in the deepest part of the basin exceeds 2 m (6.6 feet) at low water.

5. *Palustrine*—All nontidal wetlands dominated by trees, shrubs, persistent emergents, emergent mosses or lichens, and all such wetlands that occur in tidal areas where salinity due to ocean-derived salts is below 5%. It also includes wetlands lacking such vegetation, but with all of the following characteristics: (1) area less than 8 ha; (2) active wave-formed or bedrock shoreline features lacking; (3) water depth in the deepest part of basin less than 2 m at low water; (4) salinity due to ocean-derived salts less than 0.5 ‰.

Several *subsystems,* as shown in Figure 17-2, give further definition to the systems. These include the following:

1. *Subtidal*—The substrate is continuously submerged.
2. *Intertidal*—The substrate is exposed and flooded by tides; this includes the splash zone.
3. *Tidal*—For riverine systems, the gradient is low and water velocity fluctuates under tidal influence.
4. *Lower Perennial*—Riverine systems with continuous flow, low gradient, and no tidal influence.
5. *Upper Perennial*—Riverine systems with continuous flow, high gradient, and no tidal influence.
6. *Intermittent*—Riverine systems in which water does not flow for part of the year.
7. *Limnetic*—All deepwater habitats in lakes.
8. *Littoral*—Wetland habitats of a lacustrine system which extends from shore to a depth of 2 m below low water or to the maximum extent of nonpersistent emergent plants.

The *class* of a particular wetland or deepwater habitat describes the general appearance of the ecosystem in terms of either the dominant vegetation or the substrate type. When over 30% cover by vegetation is present, a vegetation class is used (e.g., shrub-scrub wetland). When less than 30% of the substrate is covered by vegetation, then a substrate class is used (e.g., unconsolidated bottom). Definitions and examples of most of the classes in this classification system are given in Table 17-7. Typical demarcation of many of the classes of palustrine systems are shown in Figure 17-3.

Table 17-7. Classes, Subclasses, and Examples of Dominance Types for Wetland Classification by U.S. Fish and Wildlife Service

Class / Subclass	Definition	Examples of Dominance Type			
		Marine/Estuarine	Lacustrine/Riverine	Palustrine	
Rock Bottom					
Bedrock	Bedrock covers 75% or more of surface	Lobster (*Homarus*)	Brook leech (*Helobdella*)	—	
Rubble	Stones and boulders cover more than 75% of surface	Sponge (*Hippospongia*)	Chironomids	Water penny (*Psephenus*)	
Unconsolidated Bottom					
Cobble-gravel	At least 25% of particles smaller than stones and less than 30% vegetation cover	Clam (*Mya*)	Mayfly (*Baetis*)	Oligochaete worms	
Sand	At least 25% sand cover and less than 30% vegetation cover	Wedge shell (*Donax*)	Mayfly (*Ephemerella*)	Sponge (*Eunapius*)	
Mud	At least 25% silt and clay, although coarser sediments can be intermixed; less than 25% vegetation	Scallop (*Placopecten*)	Freshwater mollusk (*Anodonta*)	Fingernail clam (*Pisidium*)	
Organic	Unconsolidated material predominantly organic matter and less than 25% vegetation cover	Clam (*Mya*)	Sewage worm (*Tubifex*)	Oligochaete worms	
Aquatic Bed					
Algal	Algae growing on or below surface of water	Kelp (*Macrocystis*)	Stonewort (*Chara*)	Stonewort (*Chara*)	
Aquatic moss	Aquatic moss growing at or below the surface	—	Moss (*Fissidens*)		
Rooted vascular	Rooted vascular plant growing submerged or as floating-leaved	Turtlegrass (*Thalassia*)	Water lily (*Nymphaea*)	Ditch grasses (*Ruppia*)	
Floating vascular	Floating vascular plants growing on water surface	—	Water hyacinth (*Eichhornia crassipes*)	Duckweed (*Lemna*)	

(continued)

Table 17-7. Continued

Class			Examples of Dominance Type		
Subclass	Definition	Marine/Estuarine	Lacustrine/Riverine	Palustrine
Reef	Ridgelike or moundlike structures formed by sedentary invertebrates			
Coral		Coral (*Porites*)	—	—
Mollusk		Eastern oyster (*Crassostrea virginica*)	—	—
Worm		Reefworm (*Sabellaria*)	—	—
Streambed	Intermittent streams (riverine system) or systems completely dewatered at low tide			
Bedrock	Bedrock covers 75% or more of surface	—	Mayfly (*Ephemerella*)	—
Rubble	Stones, boulders, and bedrock cover more than 75% of channel	—	Fingernail clam (*Pisidium*)	—
Cobble-gravel	At least 25% of substrate smaller than stones	Blue mussel (*Mytilus*)	Snail (*Physa*)	—
Sand	Sand particles predominate	Ghost shrimp (*Callianassa*)	Snail (*Lymnea*)	—
Mud	Silt and clay predominate	Mud snail (*Nassarius*)	Crayfish (*Procambarus*)	—
Organic	Peat or muck predominates	Mussel (*Modiolus*)	Oligochaete worms	—

	Description			
Rocky Shore	High-energy habitats that lie exposed to wind-driven waves or strong currents			
Bedrock	Bedrock covers 75% or more of surface	Acorn barnacle (*Chthamalus*)	Liverwort (*Marsupella*)	—
Rubble	Stones, boulders, and bedrock cover more than 75% of surface	Mussel (*Mytilus*)	Lichens	—
Unconsolidated Shore	Landforms such as beaches, bars, and flats that have less than 30% vegetation and are found adjacent to unconsolidated bottoms			
Cobble-gravel	At least 25% of particles smaller than stones	Periwinkle (*Littorina*)	Mollusk (*Elliptio*)	—
Sand	At least 25% sand	Wedge shell (*Donax*)	Fingernail clam (*Pisidium*)	—
Mud	At least 25% silt and clay	Fiddler crab (*Uca*)	Fingernail clam (*Pisidium*)	—
Organic	Unconsolidated material, predominantly organic matter	Fiddler crab (*Uca*)	Chironomids	—
Vegetated	Nontidal shores exposed for sufficient time to colonize annuals or perennials	—	Cocklebur (*Xanthium*)	Summer cypress (*Kochia*)
Moss-Lichen Wetland				
Moss	Mosses cover substrate other than rock; emergents, shrubs and trees cover less than 30% of area	—	—	Peatmoss (*Sphagnum*)
Lichen	Lichens cover substrate other than rock; emergents, shrubs and trees cover less than 30% of area	—	—	Reindeer moss (*Cladonia*)

(continued)

Table 17-7. Continued

Class / Subclass	Definition	Examples of Dominance Type		
		Marine/Estuarine	Lacustrine/Riverine	Palustrine
Emergent Wetland	Erect, rooted, herbaceous aquatic plants			
Persistent	Species that normally remain standing until the beginning of the next growing season	Cordgrass (*Spartina*)	—	Cattail (*Typha*)
Nonpersistent	No obvious sign of emergent vegetation at certain seasons	Samphire (*Salicornia*)	Wild rice (*Zizania*)	Pickerelweed (*Pontederia*)
Scrub-Shrub Wetland	Dominated by wood vegetation less than 6 m tall			
Broad-leaved deciduous		Marsh elder (*Iva*)	—	Buttonbush (*Cephalanthus*)
Needle-leaved deciduous		—	—	Dwarf cypress (*Taxodium*)
Broad-leaved evergreen		Mangrove (*Rhizophora*)	—	Fetterbush (*Lyonia*)
Needle-leaved evergreen		—	—	Stunted pond pine (*Pinus serotina*)
Dead		—	—	—
Forested Wetland	Woody vegetation 6 m or taller			
Broad-leaved deciduous		—	—	Red maple (*Acer rubrum*)
Needle-leaved deciduous		—	—	Bald cypress (*Taxodium distichum*)
Broad-leaved evergreen		Mangrove (*Rhizophora*)	—	Red bay (*Persea*)
Needle-leaved evergreen		—	—	Northern white cedar (*Thuja occidentalis*)
Dead		—	—	—

Source: After Cowardin et al., 1979, p. 6-8.

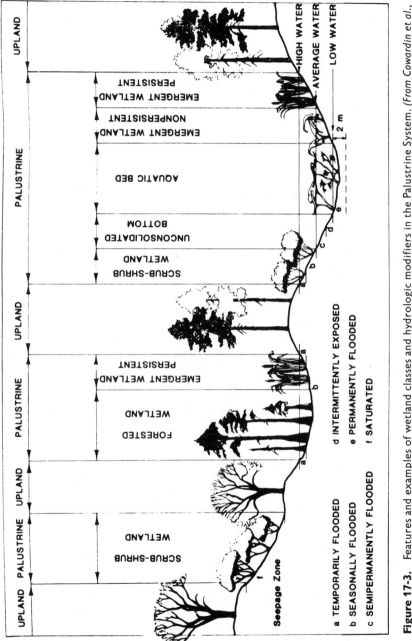

Figure 17-3. Features and examples of wetland classes and hydrologic modifiers in the Palustrine System. (*From Cowardin et al., 1979, p. 14*)

467

Table 17-8. Modifiers Used in Wetland and Deepwater Habitat Classification by U.S. Fish and Wildlife Service

Water Regime Modifiers (Tidal)

Subtidal—substrate permanently flooded with tidal water

Irregularly exposed—land surface exposed by tides less often than daily

Regularly flooded—alternately floods and exposes land surfaces at least daily

Irregularly flooded—land surface flooded less often than daily

Water Regime Modifiers (Nontidal)

Permanently flooded—water covers land surface throughout year in all years

Intermittently exposed—surface water present throughout year except in years of extreme drought

Semipermanently flooded—surface water persists throughout growing season in most years. When surface water is absent, water table is at or near surface

Seasonally flooded—surface water is present for extended periods, especially in early growing season but is absent by the end of the season

Saturated—substrate is saturated for extended periods during growing season but surface water is seldom present

Temporarily flooded—surface water is present for brief periods during growing season but water table is otherwise well below the soil surface

Intermittently flooded—substrate is usually exposed but surface water is present for variable periods with no seasonal periodicity

Salinity Modifiers

Marine and Estaurine	Riverine, Lacustrine, and Palustrine	Salinity, (parts per thousand)
Hyperhaline	Hypersaline	>40
Euhaline	Eusaline	30–40
Mixohaline (brackish)	Mixosaline	0.5–30
Polyhaline	Polysaline	18.0–30
Mesohaline	Mesosaline	5.0–18
Oligohaline	Oligosaline	0.5–5
Fresh	Fresh	<0.5

pH Modifiers

Acid	pH less than 5.5
Circumneutral	pH 5.5–7.4
Alkaline	pH greater than 7.4

Soil Material Modifiers[a]

Mineral	(1) Less than 20% organic carbon and never saturated with water for more than a few days, or
	(2) Saturated or artificially drained and has
	(a) less than 18% organic carbon if 60% or more is clay
	(b) less than 12% organic carbon if no clay
	(c) a proportional content of organic carbon between 12 and 18% if clay content is between 0 and 60%.
Organic	Other than mineral as described above.

Source: After Cowardin et al. (1979), pp. 44–45.

[a]U.S. Soil Conservation Service, 1975, pp. 13–14.

Further description of the wetlands and deepwater habitats is possible through the use of *subclasses, dominance types,* and *modifiers.* Subclasses, such as "persistent" and "nonpersistent," give further definition to a class such as emergent vegetation (Table 17-7). Type refers to a particular dominant plant species (e.g., bald cypress, *Taxodium distichum,* for a needle-leaved deciduous forested wetland), or dominant sedentary or sessile animal species (e.g., eastern oyster, *Crassostrea virginica,* for a mollusk reef). Modifiers (Table 17-8) are used after classes and subclasses to more precisely describe the water regime, the salinity, the pH, and the soil. For many wetlands, the description of the environmental modifiers adds a great deal of information about the physical and chemical characteristics. Unfortunately, these parameters are difficult to measure consistently in large-scale surveys such as inventories.

INVENTORYING WETLANDS

Once wetlands have been defined and classified, an important question for management becomes "for any given region, how many and what types of wetlands are there?" Determining the extent of various types of wetlands in a region is accomplished by a wetlands inventory. An inventory can be for a small watershed, for a county or parish, for an entire state or province, or for an entire nation. Whatever the size of the area to be surveyed, the inventory must have some previously defined classification as its basis and should be constructed to meet the needs of specific users of information on wetlands.

Remote Sensing in Wetland Inventories

The use of remote sensing platforms, particularly aircraft at various altitudes and satellites, has proved to be an effective way of gathering data for large-scale wetland surveys. The choice of which platform to use depends on the resolution required, the area to be covered, and the cost of the data collection. Low-altitude aircraft surveys offer a relatively inexpensive and yet fairly effective way to survey small areas. High-altitude aircraft offer much greater coverage and may be less expensive per unit area than low-altitude aircraft when costs of photo-interpretation are included. A third alternative, monitoring wetlands from satellites in orbit, has potential and has been an alternative since the launching of the first of the LANDSAT satellites in 1972. Imagery from satellites is available at a reasonable cost, covering most of the world. However, wetland scientists working on the National Wetlands Inventory found, even for this large-scale inventory, that "LANDSAT could not provide the desired level of detail without what appeared to be an excessive amount of collateral data such as aerial photographs and field work" (Nyc and Brooks, 1979, p. 4). A comparison between

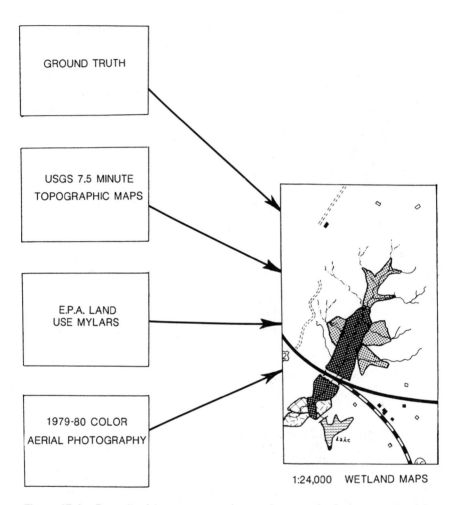

Figure 17-4. Example of data sources used to conduct a wetland inventory in western Kentucky. *(From Mitsch et al., 1983b, p. 166)*

LANDSAT and high-altitude photography in the prairie pothole region revealed that 61 of the small pothole wetlands were not identified by LANDSAT, and that only 3 wetland types could be identified, compared with 15 types by high-altitude photography.

In addition to the choice of remote sensing platform, the wetland scientist or manager has the choice of several types of imagery from different types of sensors. Color photography and color-infrared photography have been the most popular for wetland inventories from aircraft, although black-and-white photography has been used with some success. R. R. Anderson (1969, 1971) experimented with a mix of photography and scanners to determine the best remote sensing imagery for delineation of coastal salt marsh communities along the Patuxent River and Chesapeake Bay. He found that color-infrared film provided good definition of plant communities, while infrared scanning was best for observing temperature differentials in the marsh. Earth Satellite Corporation (1972) used both black-and-white-infrared and color-infrared to distinguish different *Spartina* communities in New Jersey's coastal wetlands.

Recently, high-resolution multispectral scanner imagery from low-altitude plane flights has been used with some success to map wetlands. For example, Jensen, Christensen, and Sharitz (1983; 1984) were able to map a nontidal wetland in South Carolina using a classification scheme modified slightly from the class and subclass components of the National Wetlands Inventory. They achieved a classification accuracy of 83% over a diverse 4,000 ha area. Because of the potential for significant savings compared with manual mapping from aerial photographs, this could be a useful approach.

Often, however, practicality leads the wetland scientist or manager to use several sources of information to develop wetland maps. Figure 17-4 depicts the use of several data sources in the development of a wetland inventory for a portion of western Kentucky (Mitsch et al., 1983a).

For the National Wetlands Inventory (NWI), aerial photography at scales ranging from 1:60,000 to 1:130,000 is the primary source of data, with color-infrared photography providing the best delineation of wetlands (Wilen and Pywell, 1981; Tiner and Wilen, 1983). At present, the National Wetlands Inventory is using 1:60,000 color infrared photography for most of its mapping. Photointerpretation and field reconnaissance are then used to define wetland boundaries according to the wetland classification system. The information is ultimately summarized on 1:24,000 and 1:100,000 maps, using an alphanumeric system as illustrated in Figure 17-5. By early 1983, Hawaii, 30% of the lower 48 states and 6% of Alaska had been mapped (Tiner, 1984). An anticipated 55% of the lower 48 states and 16% of Alaska will be completed by 1988. The areas have been selected for mapping based on agency needs and requests from states and other government units. Other products from NWI include "map reports" for each 1:100,000 scale wetland map, a wetland plant database, trend analysis of wetland gains or losses, and state wetland reports. The entire wetland inventory, at the level of detail envisioned for NWI, will take several more years to complete. Yet once it is completed and the database is computerized, a continuous and more vigilant monitoring of our nation's wetland resources will be possible.

DYERSBURG, TENNESSEE QUADRANGLE

1:100,000 Wetland Map

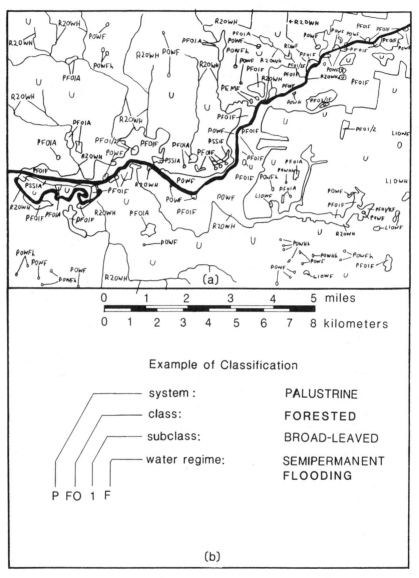

Example of Classification

system :	PALUSTRINE
class:	FORESTED
subclass:	BROAD-LEAVED
water regime:	SEMIPERMANENT FLOODING

P FO 1 F

(b)

Figure 17-5.   Sample of mapping technique used at 1:100,000 scale by National Wetlands Inventory showing *a.* portion of map (redrawn), and *b.* example of classification notation. *(After Dyersburg, Tennessee, 1:100,000 wetland map provided courtesy of National Wetlands Inventory, U.S. Fish and Wildlife Service)*

SUMMARY

Wetlands have been classified since the early 1900s, beginning with the peatland classifications of Europe and North America. Regional wetland classifications and inventories have been developed for several states. Some of these have classified wetlands according to their vegetative life forms, while others also use the hydrologic regime. Classifications based on environmental forcing functions, particularly hydrologic flow, offer a promising approach.

The U.S. Fish and Wildlife Service has been involved in two major wetland classifications and inventories, one completed in 1954 and one begun in the mid-1970s and as yet not completed for the entire United States. The early classification described 20 wetland types based on flooding depth, dominant forms of vegetation, and salinity regimes. The more recent "Classification of Wetlands and Deepwater Habitats of the United States" uses a hierarchical approach that uses systems, subsystems, classes, subclasses, dominance types, and special modifiers to more precisely define wetlands and deepwater habitats. Eventually, wetlands in the entire United States will be mapped at a scale of 1:24,000 for most areas and at 1:100,000 or smaller for a few areas.

REFERENCES

Adams, D. A., 1963, Factors influencing vascular plant zonation in North Carolina salt marshes, *Ecology* **44:**445-456.

Adams, D. D., 1978, *Habitat Development Field Investigations: Windmill Point Marsh Development Site, James River, Virginia; App. F: Environmental Impacts of Marsh Development with Dredged Material: Sediment and Water Quality, vol. II: Substrate and Chemical Flux Characteristics of a Dredged Material Marsh,* U.S. Army Waterways Experiment Station Tech. Rep. D-77-23, Vicksburg, Miss., 72p.

Adamus, P. R., 1983, *A Method for Wetland Functional Assessment,* vol. I *Critical Review and Evaluation Concepts,* and vol. II *FHWA Assessment Method,* U.S. Department of Transportation, Federal Highway Administration Reports FHWA-IP-82-23 and FHWA-IP-82-24, Washington, D.C., 176p. and 134p.

Anderson, C. M., and M. Treshow, 1980, A review of environmental and genetic factors that affect height in *Spartina alterniflora,* Loisel (Salt marsh and grass), *Estuaries* **3:**168-176.

Anderson, F. O., 1976, Primary production in a shallow water lake with special reference to a reed swamp, *Oikos* **27:**243-250.

Anderson, R. C., and J. White, 1970, A cypress swamp outlier in southern Illinois, *Illinois State Acad. Sci. Trans.* **63:**6-13.

Anderson, R. R., 1969, *The Use of Color Infrared Photography and Thermal Imagery in Marshland and Estuarine Studies,* NASA Earth Resources Aircraft Program Status Review III:40-1-40-29.

Anderson, R. R., 1971, *Multispectral Analysis of Aquatic Ecosystems in Chesapeake Bay,* 7th International Symposium on Remote Sensing of Environment Proc., Univ. of Michigan, Ann Arbor, **3:**2217-2227.

Andrews, C. B., 1978, *The Simulation of Groundwater Temperatures in Shallow Aquifers,* Ph.D. Dissertation, University of Wisconsin, 294p.

Armstrong, W., 1975, Waterlogged soils, in *Environment and plant ecology,* J. R. Etherington, ed., Wiley, London, pp. 181-218.

Armstrong, W., 1978, Root aeration in the wetland condition, pp. 269-297 in *Plant Life in Anaerobic Environments,* D. D. Hook and R. M. M. Crawford, eds., Ann Arbor Science Publishers, Inc., Ann Arbor, Mich.

ASIWPCA, 1984, *America's Clean Water—The states' Evaluation of Progress, 1972-1982,* Appendix, Interstate Water Pollution Control Administrators (ASIWPCA), Washington, D.C. (56 reports from states and territories of U.S.).

Atchue, J. A., III, F. P. Day, Jr., and H. G. Marshall, 1983, Algae dynamics and nitrogen and phosphorus cycling in a cypress stand in the seasonally flooded Great Dismal Swamp, *Hydrobiologia* **106:**115-122.

Atchue, J. A., III, H. G. Marshall, and F. P. Day, Jr., 1982, Observations of phytoplankton composition from standing water in the Great Dismal Swamp, *Castanea* **47:**308-312.

Atlas, R. M., and R. Bartha, 1981, *Microbial Ecology: Fundamentals and Applications,* Addison-Wesley, Reading, Mass., 560p.

Auble, G. T., B. C. Patten, R. W. Bosserman, and D. B. Hamilton, 1982, A hierarchical model to organize integrated research on the Okefenokee Swamp, in *Ecosystem Dynamics in Freshwater Wetlands and Shallow Water Bodies,* vol. II, SCOPE and UNEP, Centre of International Projects, Moscow, USSR, pp. 203-217.

Aurand, D., and F. C. Daiber, 1973, Nitrate and nitrite in the surface waters of two Delaware salt marshes, *Chesapeake Sci.* **14:**105-111.

Baker, J. M., 1973, Recovery of salt marsh vegetation from successive oil spillages, *Environ. Pollut.* **4:**223-230.

Baker-Blocker, A., T. M. Donahue, and K. H. Mancy, 1977, Methane flux from wetlands, *Tellus* **29:**245-250.

Balen, E. G., and F. S. Guthery, 1982, Playa, irrigation and wildlife in West Texas, *47th N. Amer. Wildl. Nat. Resour. Conf. Trans.* **47:**528-541.

Balling, S. S., and V. H. Resh, 1983, The influence of mosquito control recirculation ditches on plant biomass, production, and composition in two San Francisco Bay salt marshes, *Estuarine Coastal Shelf Sci.* **16:**151-161.

Bares, R. H., and M. K. Wali, 1979, Chemical relations and litter production of *Picia mariana* and *Larix laricina* stands on an alkaline peatland in northern Minnesota, *Vegetatio* **40:**79-94.

Bartlett, C. H., 1904, *Tales of Kankakee Land,* Charles Scribner's Sons, New York, 232p.

Baumann, R. H., J. W. Day, Jr., and C. A. Miller, 1984, Mississippi deltaic wetland survival: sedimentation versus coastal submergence, *Science* **224:**1093-1095.

Bay, R. R., 1967, Groundwater and vegetation in two peat bogs in northern Minnesota, *Ecology* **48:**308-310.

Bay, R. R., 1969, Runoff from small peatland watersheds, *J. Hydrology* **9:**90-102.

Bazilevich, N. I., L. Ye. Rodin, and N. N. Rozov, 1971, Geophysical aspects of biological productivity, *Soviet Geog.* **12:**293-317.

Bazilevich, N. I., and A. A. Tishkov, 1982, Conceptual balance model of chemical element cycles in a mesotrophic bog ecosystem, in *Ecosystem Dynamics in Freshwater Wetlands and Shallow Water Bodies,* vol. II. SCOPE and UNEP, Centre of International Projects, Moscow, USSR, pp. 236-272.

Beaumont, P., 1975, Hydrology, in *River Ecology,* B. Whitton, ed., Blackwell, Oxford, pp. 1-38.

Beck, L. T., 1977, *Distribution and Relative Abundance of Freshwater Macroinvertebrates of the Lower Atchafalaya River Basin, Louisiana,* Master's thesis, Louisiana State University, Baton Rouge.

Bedford, B., 1979, Changes in the structure and function of a wetland subject to sustained perturbation: a conceptual model, in *Coal-fired Steam Plants: Human and Environmental Exposure to Air and Water Pollutants,* First-year progress report, Water Resources Center, University of Wisconsin, Madison, pp. 44-59.

Bedinger, M. S., 1979, Relation between forest species and flooding, in *Wetland Functions and Values: The State of Our Understanding,* P. E. Greeson, J. R. Clark, and J. E. Clark, eds., American Water Resources Assoc., Minneapolis, Minn., pp. 427-435.

Bedinger, M. S., 1981, Hydrology of bottomland hardwood forests of the Mississippi Emboyment, in *Wetlands of Bottomland Hardwood Forests,* J. R. Clark and J. Benforado, eds., Elsevier, Amsterdam, pp. 161-176.

Beeftink, W. G., 1977, Salt marshes, in *The Coastline,* R. S. K. Barnes, ed., Wiley, New York, pp. 93-121.

Beeftink, W. G., and J. M. Gehu, 1973, Spartinetea maritimae, in *Prodrome des Groupements Vegetaux d'Europe,* lieferung 1, R. Tuxen, ed., J. Cramer Verlag, Lehre, pp. 1-43.

Bell, H. E., III, 1981, Illinois wetlands: their value and management, *Illinois Institute of Natural Resources Report 81/33,* Chicago, Ill., 133p.

Bellamy, D. J., 1968, *An Ecological Approach to the Classification of the Lowland Mires in Europe,* in 3rd Internat. Peat Congress Proc. Quebec, Canada, pp. 74-79.

Belt, C. B., Jr., 1975, The 1973 flood and man's constriction of the Mississippi River, *Science* **189:**681-684.

Bender, M. E., and D. L. Correl, 1974, *The Use of Wetlands as Tertiary Treatment Systems,* Natural Science Foundation Report NSF-RA-E-74-033, Washington, D.C.

Berggren, T. J., and J. T. Lieberman, 1977, Relative contributions of Hudson, Chesapeake, and Roanoke striped bass, *Morone saxatilis,* to the Atlantic coast fishery, *Fish. Bull.* **76:**335-345.

Berkeley, E., and D. Berkeley, 1976, Man and the Great Dismal, *Virginia J. Science* **27:**141-171.

Bernard, J. M., and B. A. Solsky, 1977, Nutrient cycling in a *Carex lacustris* wetland, *Can. J. Bot.* **55:**630-638.

Bertani, A., I. Bramblila, and F. Menegus, 1980, Effect of anaerobiosis on rice seedlings: Growth, metabolic rate, and rate of fermentation products, *J. Exp. Bot.* **3:**325-331.

Beschel, R. E., and P. J. Webber, 1962, Gradient analysis in swamp forests, *Nature* **194:**207-209.

Bhowmik, N. G., A. P. Bonini, W. C. Bogner, and R. P. Byrne, 1980, Hydraulics of flow and sediment transport to the Kankakee River in Illinois, *Illinois State Water Survey Rep. of Investigation 98,* Champaign, Ill., 170p.

Biggs, R. B., and D. A. Flemer, 1972, The flux of particulate carbon in an estuary, *Mar. Biol.* **12:**11-17.

Bishop, J. M., J. G. Gosselink, and J. M. Stone, 1980, Oxygen consumption and hemolymph osmolality of brown shrimp, *Penaeus aztecus, Fish. Bull.* **78:**741-757.

Black, C. C., Jr., 1973, Photosynthetic carbon fixation in relation to net CO_2 uptake, *Ann. Rev. Plant Physiol.* **24:**253-286.

Blem, C. R., and L. B. Blem, 1975, Density, biomass, and energetics of the bird and mammal populations of an Illinois deciduous forest, *Illinois Acad. Sci. Trans.* **68:**156-184.

Boelter, D. H., and E. S. Verry, 1977, *Peatland and Water in the Northern Lake States,* General Technical Report NC-31, U.S. Dept. of Agriculture, Forestry Service, North Central Experiment Station, St. Paul, Minn.

Bonasera, J., J. Lynch, and M. A. Leck, 1979, Comparison of the allelopathic potential of four marsh species, *Torrey Bot. Club Bull.* **106:**217-222.

Bosserman, R. W., 1983a, Dynamics of physical and chemical parameters in Okefenokee Swamp, *J. Freshwater Ecology* **2:**129-140.

Bosserman, R. W., 1983b, Elemental composition of *Utricularia*—periphyton ecosystems from Okefenokee Swamp, *Ecology* **64:**1637-1645.

Boyd, C. W., 1971, The dynamics of dry matter and chemical substances in a *Juncus effusus* population, *Amer. Midland Nat.* **86:**28-45.

Boyt, F. L., S. E. Bayley, and J. Zoltek, Jr., 1977, Removal of nutrients from treated municipal wastewater by wetland vegetation, *J. Water Pollut. Control Fed.* **49:**789-799.

Brady, N. C., 1974, *The Nature and Properties of Soils,* 8th ed., Macmillan, New York, 639p.

Brinson, M. M., 1977, Decomposition and nutrient exchange of litter in an alluvial swamp forest, *Ecology* **58:**601-609.

Brinson, M. M., M. D. Bradshaw, and E. S. Kane, 1984, Nutrient assimilative capacity of an alluvial floodplain swamp, *J. Applied Ecology* **21:**1041-1057.

Brinson, M. M., A. E. Lugo, and S. Brown, 1981, Primary productivity, decomposition and consumer activity in freshwater wetlands, *Annu. Rev. Ecol. Systematics* **12:**123-161.

Brinson, M. M., H. D. Bradshaw, R. N. Holmes, and J. B. Elkins, Jr., 1980, Litterfall, stemflow, and throughfall nutrient fluxes in an alluvial swamp forest, *Ecology* **61:**827-835.

Brinson, M. M., B. L. Swift, R. C. Plantico, and J. S. Barclay, 1981, *Riparian Ecosystems: Their Ecology and Status,* U.S. Fish and Wildlife Service, Biol. Serv. Prog., FWS/OBS-81/17, Washington, D.C., 151p.

Brooks, R. P., D. E. Samuel, and J. B. Hill, eds., 1985, *Wetlands and Water Management on Mined Lands,* Proceedings of a Conference Oct. 23-24, 1985, The Pennsylvania State University, University Park, Pa., 393p.

Broome, S. W., W. W. Woodhouse, Jr., and E. D. Seneca, 1975a, The relationship of mineral nutrients to growth of *Spartina alterniflora* in North Carolina: I. Nutrient status of plants and soils in natural stands, *Soil Sci. Soc. Amer. Proc.* **39**(2):295-301.

Broome, S. W., W. W. Woodhouse, Jr., and E. D. Seneca, 1975*b*, The relationship of mineral nutrients to growth of *Spartina alterniflora* in North Carolina: II. The effects of N, P and Fe fertilizers, *Soil. Sci. Soc. Amer. Proc.* **39**(2):301-307.

Brown, C. A., 1984, Morphology and biology of cypress trees, in *Cypress Swamps,* K. C. Ewel and H. T. Odum, eds., Univ. Presses of Florida, Gainesville, pp. 16-24.

Brown, S. L., 1978, *A Comparison of Cypress Ecosystems in the Landscape of Florida,* Ph.D. dissertation, University of Florida, 569p.

Brown, S. L., 1981, A comparison of the structure, primary productivity, and transpiration of cypress ecosystems in Florida, *Ecol. Monogr.* **51**:403-427.

Brown, S. L., 1984, The role of wetlands in the Green Swamp, in *Cypress Swamps,* K. C. Ewel and H. T. Odum, eds., Univ. Presses of Florida, Gainesville, pp. 405-415.

Brown, S. L., and A. E. Lugo, 1982, A comparison of structural and functional characteristics of saltwater and freshwater forested wetlands, in *Wetlands—Ecology and Management,* B. Gopal, R. E. Turner, R. G. Wetzel, and D. F. Whigham, eds., National Institute of Ecology and International Scientific Publications, Jaipur, India, pp. 109-130.

Brown, S. L., and D. L. Peterson, 1983, Structural characteristics and biomass production of two Illinois bottomland forests, *Amer. Midl. Nat.* **110**:107-117.

Brown, S. L., M. M. Brinson, and A. E. Lugo, 1979, Structure and function of riparian wetlands, in *Strategies for Protection and Management of Floodplain Wetlands and Other Riparian Ecosystems,* R. R. Johnson and J. F. McCormick, eds., U.S. Forest Service Gen. Tech. Report WO-12, Washington, D.C., pp. 17-31.

Brundage, H. M., III, and R. E. Meadows, 1982, Occurrence of the endangered shortnose sturgeon, *Acipenser brevirostrum,* in the Delaware River estuary, *Estuaries* **5**:203-208.

Bryan, C. F., D. J. DeMost, D. S. Sabins, and J. P. Newman, Jr., 1976, *A Limnological Survey of the Atchafalaya Basin,* Annual report, Louisiana Cooperative Fishery Research Unit, School of Forestry and Wildlife Manage., Louisiana State University, Baton Rouge, 285p.

Bunnell, F. L., and P. Dowding, 1974, ABISKO-A generalized decomposition model for comparisons between tundra sites, in *Soil Organisms and Decomposition in Tundra,* A. J. Holding, O. W. Heal, S. F. McLean, Jr. and P. U. Flanagan, eds., Tundra Biome Steering Committee, Stockholm, Sweden, pp. 227-247.

Bunnell, F. L., and K. A. Scoullar, 1975, ABISKO II: A computer simulation model of carbon flux in tundra ecosystems, in *Structure and Function of Tundra Ecosystems,* T. Rosswall and O. W. Heal, eds., Ecol. Bull. (Stockholm) **20**:425-448.

Buresh, R. J., R. D. Delaune, and W. H. Patrick, Jr., 1980, Nitrogen and phosphorus distribution and utilization by *Spartina alterniflora* in a Louisiana Gulf Coast Marsh, *Estuaries* **3**:111-121.

Burkholder, P. R., and G. H. Bornside, 1957, Decomposition of marsh grass by anaerobic marine bacteria, *Torrey Bot. Club Bull.* **84**:366-383.

Burns, L. A., 1978, *Productivity, Biomass, and Water Relations in a Florida Cypress Forest,* Ph.D. dissertation, University of North Carolina.

Burton, J. D., and P. S. Liss, 1976, *Estuarine Chemistry,* Academic Press, London, 229p.

Cairns, J., Jr., M. M. Brinson, R. L. Johnson, W. B. Parker, R. E. Turner, and P. V.

Winger, 1981, Impacts associated with southeastern bottomland hardwood forest ecosystems, in *Wetlands of Bottomland Hardwood Forests,* J. R. Clark and J. Benforado, eds., Elsevier, Amsterdam, pp. 303-332.

Cameron, C. C., 1970, Peat deposits of northeastern Pennsylvania, *U.S. Geological Survey Bull. 1317-A,* 90p.

Cameron, C. C., 1973, Peat, in United States Mineral Resources, *U.S. Geol. Survey Prof. Paper No. 820,* pp. 505-513.

Cardamone, M. A., J. R. Taylor, and W. J. Mitsch, 1984, *Wetlands and Coal Surface Mining: A Management Handbook—with Particular Reference to the Illinois Basin of the Eastern Interior Coal Region,* Center for Environmental Science and Management, University of Louisville, Kentucky, 99p.

Carpenter, E. J., C. D. Van Raalte, and I. Valiela, 1978, Nitrogen fixation by algae in a Massachusetts salt marshes, *Limnol. Oceanogr.* **23:**318-327.

Carpenter, J. M., and G. T. Farmer, 1981, *Peat Mining: An Initial Assessment of Wetland Impacts and Measures to Mitigate Adverse Impacts,* U.S. EPA PB 82-130766, Washington, D.C., 61p.

Carter, M. R., L. A. Burns, T. R. Cavinder, K. R. Dugger, P. L. Fore, D. B. Hicks, H. L. Revells, T. W. Schmidt, 1973, *Ecosystem Analysis of the Big Cypress Swamp and Estuaries,* U.S. EPA 904/9-74-002, Region IV, Atlanta.

Carter, V., M. S. Bedinger, R. P. Novitzki, and W. O. Wilen, 1979, Water resources and wetlands, in *Wetland Functions and Values: The State of Our Understanding,* P. E. Greeson, J. R. Clark, and J. E. Clark, eds., American Water Resources Assoc., Minneapolis, Minn., pp. 344-376.

Caulfield, P., 1970, *Everglades,* Ballantine Books, Inc., New York, 143p.

Chabreck, R. H., 1972, Vegetation, water and soil characteristics of the Louisiana coastal region, *Louisiana State Univ. Agr. Exp. Stn. Bull. 664,* 72p.

Chabreck, R. H., 1979, Wildlife harvest in wetlands of the United States, in *Wetland Function and Values: The State of Our Understanding,* P. E. Greeson, J. R. Clark, and J. E. Clark, eds., American Water Resources Assoc., Minneapolis, Minn., pp. 618-631.

Chalmers, A. G., E. B. Haines, and B. F. Sherr, 1976, *Capacity of a Spartina Salt Marsh to Assimilate Nitrogen from Secondarily Treated Sewage,* Environmental Resources Center Tech. Rep. ERC-0776, Georgia Tech, Atlanta, 88p.

Chamie, J. P., and C. J. Richardson, 1978, Decomposition in Northern Wetlands, in *Freshwater Wetlands-Ecological Processes and Management Potential,* R. E. Good, D. F. Whigham, and R. L. Simpson, eds., Academic Press, New York, pp. 115-130.

Chapman, V. J., 1938, Studies in salt marsh ecology I-III, *J. Ecology* **26:**144-221.

Chapman, V. J., 1940, Studies in salt marsh ecology VI-VII, *J. Ecology* **28:**118-179.

Chapman, V. J., 1960, *Salt Marshes and Salt Deserts of the World,* Interscience, New York, 392p.

Chapman, V. J., 1974, Salt marshes and salt deserts of the world, in *Ecology of Halophytes,* R. J. Reimold and W. H. Queen, eds., Academic Press, New York, pp. 3-19.

Chapman, V. J., 1975, The salinity problem in general; its importance and distribution with special reference to natural halophytes, in *Plants in Saline Environments,* A. Poljakoff-Mayber and J. Gale, eds., Ecological Studies No. 15, Springer-Verlag, New York, pp. 7-24.

Chapman, V. J., 1976a, *Coastal Vegetation,* 2nd ed., Pergamon Press, Oxford, 292p.

Chapman, V. J., 1976*b, Mangrove Vegetation,* J. Cramer, Vaduz, Germany, 447p.

Chapman, V. J., 1977, *Wet Coastal Ecosystems,* Elsevier, Amsterdam, 428p.

Chow, V. T., ed., 1964, *Handbook of Applied Hydrology,* McGraw-Hill, New York, 1453p.

Clark, J. E., 1979, Fresh water wetlands: habitats for aquatic invertebrates, amphibians, reptiles, and fish, in *Wetland Functions and Values: The State of Our Understanding,* P. E. Greeson, J. R. Clark, and J. E. Clark, eds., American Water Resources Association, Minneapolis, Minn., pp. 330-343.

Clark, J. R., and J. Benforado, eds., 1981, *Wetlands of Bottomland Hardwood Forests,* Elsevier, Amsterdam, 401p.

Clements, F. E., 1916, Plant Succession, *Carnegie Institution of Washington, Pub. 242,* 512p.

Clewell, A. F., L. F. Ganey, Jr., D. P. Harlos, and E. R. Tobi, 1976, *Biological Effects of Fill Roads across Salt Marshes,* Florida Dept. of Transportation Report FL-ER-1-76, Tallahassee, Fl.

Clymo, R. S., 1964, The origin of acidity in *Sphagnum* bogs, *Bryologist* **67:**427-431.

Clymo, R. S., 1965, Experiments on breakdown of *Sphagnum* in two bogs, *J. Ecology* **53:**747-758.

Clymo, R. S., 1970, The growth of *Sphagnum:* methods of measurement, *J. Ecology* **58:**13-49.

Clymo, R. S., 1983, Peat, in *Mires: Swamp, Bog, Fen, and Moor,* Ecosystems of the World 4A, A. J. P. Gore, ed., Elsevier, Amsterdam, pp. 159-224.

Cohen, A. D., D. J. Casagrande, M. J. Andrejko, and G. R. Best, eds., 1984, *The Okefenokee Swamp: Its Natural History, Geology, and Geochemistry,* Wetland Surveys, Los Alamos, New Mexico, 709p.

Conner, W. H., and J. W. Day, Jr., 1976, Productivity and composition of a bald cypress—water tupelo site and a bottomland hardwood site in a Louisiana swamp, *Amer. J. Bot.* **63:**1354-1364.

Conner, W. H., and J. W. Day, Jr., 1982, The ecology of forested wetlands in the southeastern United States, in *Wetlands: Ecology and Management,* B. Gopal, R. E. Turner, R. G. Wetzel, and D. F. Whigham, eds., National Institute of Ecology and International Scientific Publications, Jaipur, India, pp. 69-87.

Conner, W. H., J. G. Gosselink, and R. T. Parrondo, 1981, Comparison of the vegetation of three Louisiana swamp sites with different flooding regimes, *Amer. J. Bot.* **68:**320-331.

Cooper, A. W., 1974, Salt marshes, in *Coastal Ecological Systems of the United States,* vol. II, H. T. Odum, B. J. Copeland, and E. A. McMahan, eds., The Conservation Foundation, Washington, D.C., pp. 55-96.

Cooper, W. S., 1913, The climax forest of Isle Royale, Lake Superior, and its development, *Bot. Gaz.* **55:**1-44, 115-140, 189-235.

Costanza, R., 1980, Embodied energy and economic evaluation, *Science* **210:**1219-1224.

Costanza, R., 1984, Natural resource valuation and management: toward ecological economics, in *Integration of Economy and Ecology—An Outlook for the Eighties,* A. M. Janson, ed., Univ. of Stockholm Press, Stockholm, Sweden, pp. 7-18.

Costanza, R., and S. C. Farber, 1985, Theories and methods of valuation of natural systems: A comparison of willingness-to-pay and energy analysis based approaches, *Man, Environment, Space, and Time* **4:**1-38.

Costlow, J. D., C. G. Boakout, and R. Monroe, 1960, The effect of salinity and temperature on larval development of *Sesarma cinereum* (Bosc.) reared in the laboratory, *Biol. Bull.* **118:**183-202.

Cowardin, L. M., V. Carter, F. C. Golet, and E. T. LaRoe, 1979, *Classification of wetlands and deepwater habitats of the United States,* U.S. Fish & Wildlife Service Pub. FWS/OBS-79/31, Washington, D.C., 103p.

Cowles, H. C., 1899, The ecological relations of the vegetation on the sand dunes of Lake Michigan, *Bot. Gaz.* **27:**95-117, 167-202, 281-308, 361-369.

Cowles, S., 1975, *Metabolism Measurements in a Cypress Dome,* Master's thesis, University of Florida, 275p.

Cragg, J. B., 1961, Some aspects of the ecology of moorland animals, *J. Anim. Ecol.* **30:**205-234.

Craig, N. J., R. E. Turner, and J. W. Day, Jr., 1979, Land loss in Louisiana (U.S.A.), *Environ. Manage.* **3:**133-144.

Craighead, F. C., 1971, *The Trees of South Florida,* University of Miami Press, Coral Gables, Florida, 212p.

Crisp, D. T., 1966, Input and output of minerals for an area of Pennine moorland: the importance of precipitation, drainage, peat erosion, and animals, *J. Appl. Ecol.* **3:**327-348.

CTA Environmental, Inc., 1985, *Freshwater Wetlands for Wastewater Management: Environmental Assessment Handbook* prepared for U.S. Environmental Protection Agency Region IV, EPA 904/9-85-135, Atlanta, Ga., 493p.

Curtis, J. T., 1959, *The Vegetation of Wisconsin,* University of Wisconsin Press, Madison, 657p.

Cypert, E., 1961, The effect of fires in the Okefenokee Swamp in 1954 and 1955, *Am. Midl. Nat.* **66:**485-503.

Cypert, E., 1972, The origin of houses in the Okefenokee prairies, *Am. Midl. Nat.* **87:**448-458.

Dabel, C. V., and F. P. Day, Jr., 1977, Structural comparison of four plant communities in the Great Dismal Swamp, Virginia, *Torrey Bot. Club Bull.* **104:**352-360.

Dacey, J. W. H., 1980, Internal winds in water lilies: an adaption for life in anaerobic sediments, *Science* **210:**1017-1019.

Dachnowski-Stokes, A. P., 1935, Peat land as a conserver of rainfall and water supplies, *Ecology* **16:**173-177.

Daiber, F. C., 1977, Salt marsh animals: distributions related to tidal flooding, salinity and vegetation, in *Wet Coastal Ecosystems,* V. J. Chapman, ed., Elsevier, Amsterdam, pp. 79-108.

Dalkey, N. C., 1972, *Studies in the Quality of Life: Delphi and Decision Making,* Lexington Books, Lexington, Mass., 161p.

Dames and Moore, 1983, *A Survey of Wetland Reclamation Projects in the Florida Phosphate Industry,* final report prepared for Florida Institute of Phosphate Research, Bartow, Fla., 59 pp. plus appen.

Darnell, R., 1976, Impacts of construction activities in wetlands of the United States, *U.S. Environmental Protection Agency EPA-600/3-76-045,* Corvallis, Or., 393p.

Dauffenbach, L., R. M. Atlas, and W. J. Mitsch, 1981. A computer simulation model of the fate of crude petroleum spills in Arctic tundra ecosystems, in *Energy and Ecological Modelling,* W. J. Mitsch, R. W. Bosserman and J. M. Klopstek, eds., Elsevier, Amsterdam, p. 145-155.

Davis, C. A., 1907, Peat, essays on its origin, uses, and distribution in Michigan, in *Report State Board Geological Survey Michigan for 1906,* pp. 95-395.

Davis, J. H., 1940, The ecology and geologic role of mangroves in Florida, *Carnegie Institution, Washington Publ. No. 517,* pp. 303-412.

Davis, J. H., 1943, The natural features of southern Florida, especially the vegetation and the Everglades, *Florida Geol. Survey Bull. 25,* 311p.

Davis, L. V., and I. E. Gray, 1966, Zonal and seasonal distribution of insects in North Carolina salt marshes, *Ecol. Monogr.* **36:**275-295.

Davis, S. N., and R. J. M. DeWiest, 1966, *Hydrogeology,* Wiley, New York, 463p.

Day, F. P., Jr., 1982, Litter decomposition rates in the seasonally flooded Great Dismal Swamp, *Ecology* **63:**670-678.

Day, F. P., Jr., and C. V. Dabel, 1978, Phytomass budgets for the Dismal Swamp ecosystem, *Virginia J. Sci.* **29:**220-224.

Day, J. H., 1981, *Estuarine Ecology: With Particular Reference to Southern Africa,* A. A. Balkema, Rotterdam, 411p.

Day, J. W., Jr., T. J. Butler, and W. G. Conner, 1977, Productivity and nutrient export studies in a cypress swamp and lake system in Louisiana, in *Estuarine Processes,* vol. II, M. Wiley, ed., Academic Press, New York, pp. 255-269.

Day, J. W., Jr., T. J. Butler, and W. G. Conner, 1977, Productivity and nutrient export studies in a cypress swamp and lake system in Louisiana, in *Estuarine Processes,* vol. II, M. Wiley, ed., Academic Press, New York, pp. 255-269.

Deghi, G. S., K. C. Ewel, and W. J. Mitsch, 1980, Effects of sewage effluent application on litterfall and litter decomposition in cypress swamps, *J. Appl. Ecol.* **17:**397-408.

de la Cruz, A. A., 1978, Primary production processes: summary and recommendations, in *Freshwater Wetlands: Ecological Processes and Management Potential,* R. E. Good, D. F. Whigham, and R. L. Simpson, eds., Academic Press, New York, pp. 79-86.

Delaune, R. D., R. J. Buresh, and W. H. Patrick, Jr., 1979, Relationship of soil properties to standing crop biomass of *Spartina alterniflora* in a Louisiana marsh, *Estuarine Coast. Mar. Sci.* **8:**477-487.

Delaune, R. D., and W. H. Patrick, Jr., 1979, Nitrogen and phosphorus cycling in a Gulf Coast salt marsh, in *Estuarine Perspectives,* V. S. Kennedy, ed., Academic Press, New York, pp. 143-151.

Delaune, R. D., C. M. Reddy, and W. H. Patrick, Jr., 1981, Accumulation of plant nutrients and heavy metals through sedimentation processes and accretion in a Louisiana salt marsh, *Estuaries* **4:**328-334.

Delaune, R. D., R. H. Baumann, and J. G. Gosselink, 1983, Relationships among vertical accretion, coastal submergence, and erosion in a Louisiana Gulf Coast marsh, *J. Sed. Petrol.* **53:**147-157.

Delaune, R. D., C. J. Smith, and W. H. Patrick, Jr., 1983, Nitrogen losses from a Louisiana Gulf Coast salt marsh, *Est. Coast. Shelf Sci.* **17:**133-142.

Delwiche, C. C., 1970, The nitrogen cycle, *Sci. Am.* **223:**137-146.

Demaree, D., 1932, Submerging experiments with *Taxodium, Ecology* **13:**258-262.

DeSylva, D. P., 1969, Trends in marine sport fisheries research, *Am. Fish. Soc. Trans.* **98:**151-169.

Diaz, R. J., 1977, *The Effects of Pollution on Benthic Communities of the Tidal James River, Virginia,* Ph.D. dissertation, University of Virginia, 149p.

Dierberg, F. E., and P. L. Brezonik, 1984, Nitrogen and phosphorus mass balances in a cypress dome receiving wastewater, in *Cypress Swamps,* K. C. Ewel and H. T. Odum, eds., University Presses of Florida, Gainesville, pp. 112-118.

Dixon, K. R., 1974, *A Model for Predicting the Effects of Sewage Effluent on Wetland Ecosystems,* Ph.D. dissertation, University of Michigan, 120p.

Dixon, K. R., and J. A. Kadlec, 1975, *A Model for Predicting the Effects of Sewage Effluent on Wetland Ecosystems,* Wetlands Ecosystem Research Group, University of Michigan, Ann Arbor Pub. 3, 66p.

Dolan, T. J., S. E. Bayley, J. Zoltek, Jr., and A. Hermann, 1978, The Clermont project: renovation of treated effluent by a freshwater marsh, in *Environmental Quality through Wetlands Utilization,* M. A. Drew, ed., Proc. of the Symposium. The Co-ordinating Council on the Restoration of the Kissimmee River Valley and Taylor Creek-Nubbin Slough Basin, Tallahassee, Florida, pp. 132-152.

Dolan, T. J., S. E. Bayley, J. Zoltek, Jr., and A. Hermann, 1981, Phosphorus dynamics of a Florida freshwater marsh receiving treated wastewater, *J. Appl. Ecol.* **18:**205-219.

Dorge, C. L., W. J. Mitsch, and J. R. Wiemhoff, 1984, Cypress wetlands in southern Illinois, in *Cypress Swamps,* K. C. Ewel and H. T. Odum, eds., University Presses of Florida, Gainesville, pp. 393-404.

Douglas, M. S., 1947, *The Everglades: River of Grass,* Ballantine, New York, 308p.

Doyle, G. J., 1973, Primary production estimates of native blanket bog and meadow vegetation growing on reclaimed peat at Glenamoy, Ireland, in *Primary Production and Production Processes, Tundra Biome,* L. C. Bliss and F. E. Wielgolaski, eds., Tundra Biome Steering Committee, Edmonton and Stockholm, pp. 141-151.

Dozier, M. D., J. G. Gosselink, C. E. Sasser, and J. M. Hill, 1983, Wetland change in southwestern Barataria Basin, Louisiana, 1945-1980, Coastal Ecology Laboratory, Center for Wetland Resources, Louisiana State University, Baton Rouge, LSU-CEL-83-11.

Duever, M. J., 1984, Environmental factors controlling plant communities of the Big Cypress Swamp, in *Environments of South Florida: Present and Past II,* P. J. Gleason, ed., Miami Geological Society, Coral Gables, Fla., pp. 127-137.

Duever, M. J., J. E. Carlson, and L. A. Riopelle, 1975, Ecosystem analyses at Corkscrew Swamp, in *Cypress Wetlands for Water Management, Recycling and National Conservation,* H. T. Odum and K. C. Ewel, eds., second annual report to National Science Foundation and Rockefeller Foundation, Center for Wetlands, University of Florida, Gainesville, pp. 627-725.

Duever, M. J., J. E. Carlson, and L. A. Riopelle, 1984, Corkscrew Swamp: a virgin cypress strand, in *Cypress Swamps,* K. C. Ewel and H. T. Odum, eds., University Presses of Florida, Gainesville, pp. 334-348.

Durno, S. E., 1961, Evidence regarding the rate of peat growth, *J. Ecol.* **49:**347-351.

Dvorak, J., 1978, Macrofauna of invertebrates in helohyte communities, in *Pond Littoral Ecosystems,* D. Dykyjova and J. Kvet, eds., Springer-Verlag, Berlin, pp. 389-392.

Dykyjova, D., and J. Kvet, eds., 1978, *Pond littoral ecosystems,* Springer-Verlag, Berlin, Germany, 464p.

Dykyjova, D., and J. Kvet, 1982, Mineral nutrient economy in wetlands of the Trebon Basin Biosphere Reserve, Czechoslovakia, in *Wetlands—Ecology and Management,* B. Gopal, R. E. Turner, R. G. Wetzel and D. F. Whigham, eds., National Institute of Ecology and International Scientific Publications, Jaipur, India, pp. 335-355.

Earth Satellite Corporation, 1972, Aerial multiband wetlands mapping, *Photogramm. Eng.* **38**:1188-1189.

Eggelsmann, R., 1976, *Die potentielle und aktuelle Evaporation eines Seeklimathochmoores,* Internat. Assoc. Sci. Hydrol. Publication No. 62 pp. 88-97.

Egler, F. E., 1952, Southeast saline Everglades vegetation, Florida, and its management, *Veg, Acta, Geobot.* **3**:213-265.

Eisenlohr, W. S., 1966, Water loss from a natural pond through transpiration by hydrophytes, *Water Resour. Res.* **2**:443-453.

Elder, J. F., 1985, Nitrogen and phosphorus speciation and flux in a large Florida river-wetland system, *Water Resour. Res.* **21**:724-732.

Elder, J. F., and H. C. Mattraw, Jr., 1982, Riverine transport of nutrient and detritus to the Apalachicola Bay estuary, Florida, *Water Resour. Bull.* **18**:849-856.

Ellison, R. L., and M. M. Nichols, 1976, Modern and holocene foraminifera in the Chesapeake Bay region, *Mar. Sed. Spec. Publ.* **1**:131-151.

Emery, K. O., and E. Uchupi, 1972, Western North Atlantic Ocean: topography, rocks, structure, water, life, and sediments, *Am. Assoc. Petroleum Geologists, Mem. 17,* 532p.

Etherington, J. R., 1983, *Wetland Ecology,* Edward Arnold, London, 67p.

Evink, G. L., 1980, *Studies of causeways in the Indian River, Florida,* Florida Dept. of Transportation Rept. FL-ER-7-80, Tallahassee, Fla., 140p.

Ewel, K. C., 1976, Effects of sewage effluent on ecosystem dynamics in cypress domes, in *Freshwater Wetlands and Sewage Effluent Disposal,* D. L. Tilton, R. H. Kadlec, and C. J. Richardson, eds., University of Michigan, Ann Arbor, pp. 169-195.

Ewel, K. C., and W. J. Mitsch, 1978, The effects of fire on species composition in cypress dome ecosystems, *Florida Sci.* **41**:25-31.

Ewel, K. C., and H. T. Odum, 1978, Cypress swamps for nutrient removal and wastewater recycling, in *Advances in Water and Wastewater Treatment Biological Nutrient Removal,* M. P. Wanielista and W. W. Eckenfelder, Jr., eds., Ann Arbor Sci. Pub., Inc., Ann Arbor, Mich. pp. 181-198.

Ewel, K. C., and H. T. Odum, 1979, Cypress domes: nature's tertiary treatment filter, in *Utilization of Municipal Sewage Effluent and Sludge on Forest and Disturbed Land,* W. E. Sopper and S. N. Kerr, eds., The Pennsylvania State University Press, University Park, Pa., pp. 103-114.

Ewel, K. C., and H. T. Odum, eds., *Cypress Swamps,* University Presses of Florida, Gainesville, Fla., 472p.

Farnham, R. S., 1979, Wetlands as energy sources, in *Wetland Functions and Values: The State of Our Understanding,* P. E. Greeson, J. R. Clark, and J. E. Clark, eds., American Water Resources Assoc., Minneapolis, Minn., pp. 661-672.

Fetter, C. W., Jr., W. E. Sloey, and F. L. Spangler, 1978, Use of a natural marsh for wastewater polishing, *J. Water Pollution Control Fed.* **50**:290-307.

Forrest, G. I., and R. A. H. Smith, 1975, The productivity of a range of blanket bog types in the Northern Pennines, *J. Ecol.* **63**:173-202.

Frayer, W. E., T. J. Monahan, D. C. Bowden, and F. A. Graybill, 1983, *Status and trends of wetlands and deepwater habitat in the conterminous United States, 1950s to 1970s,* Dept. of Forest and Wood Sciences, Colorado State University, Fort Collins, 32p.

Fredrickson, L. H., 1979, Lowland hardwood wetlands: current status and habitat values for wildlife, in *Wetland Functions and Values: The State of Our Understanding,* P. E. Greeson, J. R. Clark, and J. E. Clark, eds., American Water Resources Assoc., Minneapolis, Minn., pp. 296-306.

Gallagher, J. L., 1978, Decomposition processes: summary and recommendations, in *Freshwater Wetlands: Ecological Processes and Management Potential,* R. E. Good, D. F. Whigham, and R. L. Simpson, eds., Academic Press, New York, pp. 145-151.

Gallagher, J. L., and F. C. Daiber, 1974, Primary production of edaphic algae communities in a Delaware salt marsh, *Limnol. Oceanogr.* **19:**390-395.

Gallagher, J. L., R. J. Reimold, R. A. Linthurst, and W. J. Pfeiffer, 1980, Aerial production, mortality, and mineral accumulation-export dynamics in *Spartina alterniflora* and *Juncus roemerianus* plant stands in a Georgia salt marsh, *Ecology* **61:**303-312.

Gambrell, R. P., and W. H. Patrick, Jr., 1978, Chemical and microbiological properties of anaerobic soils and sediments, in *Plant Life in Anaerobic Environments,* D. D. Hook and R. M. M. Crawford, eds., Ann Arbor Sci. Pub. Inc., Ann Arbor, Mich., pp. 375-423.

Gardner, L. R., 1975, Runoff from an intertidal marsh during tidal exposure: regression curves and chemical characteristics, *Limnol. Oceanogr.* **20:**81-89.

Geis, A. D., and F. G. Cooch, 1972, Distribution of the duck harvest in Canada and the United States, Special Scientific Report Wildlife 151, U.S. Dept. of the Interior, Washington, D.C., 11p.

Gilbert, T., T. King, and B. Barnett, 1981, *An Assessment of Wetland Habitat Establishment at a Central Florida Phosphate Mine Site,* U.S. Fish and Wildlife Service Pub. FWS/OBS-81/45, Atlanta, Ga., 96p.

Gilman, K., 1982, Nature conservation in wetlands: two small fen basins in western Britain, in *Ecosystem dynamics in freshwater wetlands and shallow water bodies,* vol. I, SCOPE and UNEP, Center of International Projects, Moscow, USSR, pp. 290-310.

Ginsburg, M., L. Sachs, and B. Z. Ginsburg, 1971, Ion metabolism in a halobacterium II. Ion concentration in cells at different levels of metabolism, *J. Membr. Biol.* **5:**78-101.

Giurgevich, J. R., and E. L. Dunn, 1978, Seasonal patterns of CO_2 and water vapor exchange of *Juncus roemerianus* Scheele in a Georgia salt marsh. *Am. J. Bot.* **65:**502-510.

Giurgevich, J. R., and E. L. Dunn, 1979, Seasonal patterns of CO_2 and water vapor exchange of the tall and short forms of *Spartina alterniflora* Loisel in a Georgia salt marsh, *Oecologia* **43:**139-156.

Gleason, H. A., 1917, The structure and development of the plant association, *Torrey Bot. Club Bull.* **44:**463-481.

Glob, P. V., 1969, *The Bog People: Iron Age Man Preserved,* trans. by R. Bruce-Mitford, Cornell University Press, Ithaca, New York, 200p.

Glubiak, P. G., R. H. Nowka, and W. J. Mitsch, 1986, *Federal and state management of inland wetlands: are states ready to assume control? Environ. Manage.* **10:**145-156.

Godfrey, P. J., E. R. Kaynor, S. Pelczarski, and J. Benforado, eds., 1985, *Ecological Considerations in Wetlands Treatment of Municipal Wastewaters,* Van Nostrand Reinhold Company, New York, 474p.

Golet, F. C., and J. S. Larson, 1974, *Classification of Freshwater Wetlands in the Glaciated Northeast,* U.S. Fish and Wildlife Service Resources Publ. 116, Washington, D.C., 56p.

Golley, F. B., H. T. Odum, and R. F. Wilson, 1962, The structure and metabolism of a Puerto Rican red mangrove forest in May, *Ecology* **43**:9-19.

Gomez, M. M., and F. P. Day, Jr., 1982, Litter nutrient content and production in the Great Dismal Swamp, *Am. J. Bot.* **69**:1314-1321.

Good, R. E., N. F. Good, and B. R. Frasco, 1982, A review of primary production and decomposition dynamics of the belowground marsh component, in *Estuarine comparisons,* V. S. Kennedy, ed., Academic Press, New York, pp. 139-157.

Good, R. E., D. F. Whigham, and R. L. Simpson, eds., 1978, *Freshwater Wetlands: Ecological Processes and Management Potential,* Academic Press, New York, 378p.

Goodman, G. T., and D. F. Perkins, 1968, The role of mineral nutrients in *Eriophorum* communities IV. Potassium supply as a limiting factor in an *E. vaginatum* community, *J. Ecol.* **56**:685-696.

Gopal, B., R. E. Turner, R. G. Wetzel, and D. F. Whigham, eds., 1982, *Wetlands— Ecology and Management,* National Institute of Ecology and International Scientific Publications, Jaipur, India, 514p.

Gore, A. J. P., ed., 1983*a, Ecosystems of the world, vol. 4A, Mires: Swamp, Bog, Fen, and Moor,* Elsevier, Amsterdam, 440p.

Gore, A. J. P., 1983*b,* Introduction, in *Ecosystems of the World, vol. 4B, Mires: Swamp, Bog, Fen and Moor,* Elsevier, Amsterdam, pp. 1-34.

Gore, A. J. P., and S. E. Allen, 1956, Measurement of exchangeability and total cation content for H^+, Na^+, K^+, Mg^{++}, Ca^{++}, and iron in high level blanket peat, *Oikos* **7**:48-55.

Gorham, E., 1956, The ionic composition of some bogs and fen waters in the English lake district, *J. Ecol.* **44**:142-152.

Gorham, E., 1961, Factors influencing supply of major ions to inland waters, with special references to the atmosphere, *Geol. Soc. Amer. Bull.* **72**:795-840.

Gorham, E., 1967, *Some Chemical Aspects of Wetland Ecology,* Technical Mem. Committee on Geotechnical Research, National Research Council of Canada, No. 90, p. 20-38.

Gorham, E., 1974, The relationship between standing crop in sedge meadows and summer temperature, *J. Ecol.* **62**:487-491.

Gosselink, J. G., 1984, *The Ecology of Delta Marshes of Coastal Louisiana: A Community Profile,* U.S. Fish and Wildlife Service, Biological Services FWS/OBS-84/09, Washington, D.C., 134p.

Gosselink, J. G., and R. H. Baumann, 1980, Wetland inventories: wetland loss along the United States coast, *Z. Geomorphol.,*N.F. Suppl.-Bd., **34**:173-187.

Gosselink, J. G., and C. J. Kirby, 1974, Decomposition of salt marsh grass, *Spartina alterniflora* Loisel, *Limnol. Oceanogr.* **19**:825-832.

Gosselink, J. G., and R. E. Turner, 1978, The role of hydrology in freshwater wetland ecosystems, in *Freshwater Wetlands: Ecological Processes and Management Potential,* R. E. Good, D. F. Whigham, and R. L. Simpson, eds., Academic Press, New York, pp. 63-78.

Gosselink, J. G., C. L. Cordes, and J. W. Parsons, 1979, *An Ecological Characterization Study of the Chenier Plain Coastal Ecosystem of Louisiana and Texas,* U.S.

Fish and Wildlife Service, Office of Biological Services, FWS/OBS-78-9 through 78-11, Washington, D.C.

Gosselink, J. G., E. P. Odum, and R. M. Pope, 1974, *The Value of the Tidal Marsh,* Center for Wetland Resources Publ. LSU-SG-74-03, Louisiana State University, Baton Rouge, 30p.

Gosselink, J. G., W. H. Conner, J. W. Day, Jr., and R. E. Turner, 1981, Classification of wetland resources: land, timber, and ecology, in *Timber Harvesting in Wetlands,* B. D. Jackson and J. L. Chambers, eds., Div. of Cont. Ed., Louisiana State Univ., Baton Rouge, pp. 28-48.

Gosselink, J. G., R. Hatton, and C. S. Hopkinson, 1984, Relationship of organic carbon and mineral content to bulk density in Louisiana marsh soils, *Soil Sci.* **137:**177-180.

Grant, R. R., and R. Patrick, 1970, Tinicum Marsh as a water purifier, in *Two studies of Tinicum Marsh, Delaware and Philadelphia Counties, Pa.* J. McCormick, R. R. Grant, Jr., and R. Patrick, eds., The Conservation Foundation, Washington, D.C., pp. 105-131.

Gray, L. C., O. E. Baker, F. J. Marschner, B. O. Weitz, W. R. Chapline, W. Shepard, and R. Zon, 1924, *The Utilization of our Lands for Crops, Pasture, and Forests,* in U.S. Dept. of Agriculture Yearbook, 1923, Government Printing Office, Washington, D.C., p. 415-506.

Greeley, R. S., 1976, *Land and Freshwater Farming,* in Proc. Conf. Capturing the sun through bioconversion, Washington Center Metrop. Stud. 179, Washington, D.C., pp. 208-216.

Greenwood, D. J., 1961, The effect of oxygen concentration on the decomposition of organic materials in soil, *Plant and Soil* **14:**360-376.

Greeson, P. E., J. R. Clark, and J. E. Clark, eds., 1979, *Wetland Functions and Values: The State of Our Understanding,* Proceedings of National Symposium on Wetlands, Lake Buena Vista, Florida, American Water Resources Assoc. Tech. Publ. TPS 79-2, Minneapolis, Minn., 674p.

Gross, W. J., 1964, Trends in water and salt regulation among aquatic and amphibious crabs, *Biol. Bull.* **127:**447-466.

Gupta, P. K., 1977, *Dynamic optimization applied to systems with periodic disturbances,* Ph.D. Dissertation, University of Michigan, 246p.

Guthery, F. S., J. M. Pates, and F. A. Stormer, 1982, Characterization of playas of the north-central Llano Estacado in Texas, *47th Am. Wildl. Nat. Resour. Conf. Trans.* **47:**516-527.

Hackney, C. T., and A. A. de la Cruz, 1980, Insitu decomposition of roots and rhizomes of two tidal marsh plants, *Ecology* **61:**226-231.

Haines, B. L., and E. L. Dunn, 1976, Growth and resource allocation responses of *Spartina alterniflora* Loisel to three levels of NH_4-N, Fe, and NaCl in solution culture, *Bot. Gaz.* **137:**224-230.

Haines, E. B., 1979, Interactions between Georgia salt marshes and coastal waters: a changing paradigm, in *Ecological Processes in Coastal and Marine Systems,* R. J. Livingston, ed., Plenum Press, New York, pp. 35-46.

Haines, E. B., A. G. Chalmers, R. B. Hanson, and B. Sherr, 1977, Nitrogen pools and fluxes in a Georgia salt marsh, in *Estuarine Processes,* vol. 2, M. Wiley, ed., Academic Press, New York, pp. 241-254.

Hall, F. R., R. J. Rutherford, and G. L. Byers, 1972, *The Influence of a New England Wetland on Water Quantity and Quality,* New Hampshire Water Resource Center Research Report 4, Univ. of New Hampshire, Durham, 51p.

Hall, T. F., and W. T. Penfound, 1939, A phytosociological study of a cypress-gum swamp in southern Louisiana, *Am. Midl. Nat.* **21:**378-395.

Hammer, D. E., and R. H. Kadlec, 1983, *Design Principles for Wetland Treatment Systems,* U.S. Environmental Protection Report EPA-600/2-83-026, Ada, Ok., 244p.

Harriss, R. C., D. I. Sebacher, and F. P. Day, Jr., 1982, Methane flux in the Great Dismal Swamp, *Nature* **297:**673-674.

Hatton, R. S., 1981, *Aspects of Marsh Accretion and Geochemistry; Barataria Basin, La.,* Master's thesis, Louisiana State University.

Heal, O. W., H. E. Jones, and J. B. Whittaker, 1975, Moore House, U.K., in *Structure and Function of Tundra Ecosystems,* T. Rosswall and O. W. Heal, eds., Ecol. Bull. 20, Swedish Natural Science Research Council, Stockholm, pp. 295-320.

Heald, E. J., 1969, *The Production of Organic Detritus in a South Florida Estuary,* Ph.D. dissertation, University of Miami, 110p.

Heald, E. J., 1971, *The Production of Organic Detritus in a South Florida Estuary,* University of Miami Sea Grant Technical Bulletin No. 6, Coral Gables, Fla., 110p.

Hefner, J. M. and J. D. Brown, 1985, Wetland trends in the southeastern United States, *Wetlands* **4:**1-11.

Heilman, P. E., 1968, Relationship of availability of phosphorus and cations to forest succession and bog formation in interior Alaska, *Ecology* **49:**331-336.

Heimburg, K., 1984, Hydrology of north-central Florida cypress domes, in *Cypress Swamps,* K. C. Ewel and H. T. Odum, eds., University Presses of Florida, Gainesville, pp. 72-82.

Heinle, D. R., and D. A. Flemer, 1976, Flows of materials between poorly flooded tidal marshes and an estuary, *Mar. Biol.* **35:**359-373.

Heinle, D. R., D. A. Flemer, and J. F. Ustach, 1977, Contribution of tidal marshland to mid-Atlantic estuarine food chains, in *Estuarine Processes,* vol. 2, M. Wiley, ed., Academic Press, New York, p. 309-320.

Heinselman, M. L., 1963, Forest sites, bog processes, and peatland types in the glacial Lake Agassiz Region, Minnesota, *Ecol. Monogr.* **33:**327-374.

Heinselman, M. L., 1970, Landscape evolution and peatland types, and the Lake Agassiz Peatlands Natural Area, Minnesota, *Ecol. Monogr.* **40:**235-261.

Heinselman, M. L., 1975, Boreal peat lands in relation to environment, in *Coupling of Land and Water Systems,* A. D. Hasler, ed., Ecological Studies No. 10, Springer-Verlag, New York, pp. 93-103.

Heliotis, F. D., 1982, *Wetland Systems for Wastewater Treatment: Operating Mechanisms and Implications for Design,* Institute for Environmental Studies Report No. 117, University of Wisconsin, Madison, 68p.

Hemond, H. F., 1980, Biogeochemistry of Thoreau's Bog, Concord, Mass. *Ecol. Monogr.* **50:**507-526.

Hemond, H. F., and R. Burke, 1981, A device for measurement of infiltration in intermittently flooded wetlands, *Limnol. Oceanogr.* **26:**795-800.

Hemond, H. F., and J. L. Fifield, 1982, Subsurface flow in salt marsh peat: a model and field study, *Limnol. Oceanogr.* **27:**126-136.

Hern, S. C., V. W. Lambou, and J. R. Butch, 1980, *Descriptive Water Quality for the Atchafalaya Basin, Louisiana,* EPA-600/4-80-614, U.S. Environmental Protection Agency, Las Vegas, Nev., 168p.

Hewlett, J. D., and A. R. Hibbert, 1967, Factors affecting the response of small watersheds to precipitation in humid areas, in *International Symposium on Forest Hydrology,* W. E. Sopper and H. W. Lull, eds., Pergamon Press, New York, pp. 275-290.

Hill, P. L., 1983, *Wetland-stream Ecosystems of the Western Kentucky Coalfield: Environmental Disturbance and the Shaping of Aquatic Community Structure,* Ph.D. dissertation, University of Louisville, 290p.

Ho, C. L., and S. Schneider, 1976, Water and sediment chemistry, Chapter VI.1 in *Louisiana Offshore Oil Port: Environmental Baseline Study,* vol. IV, Gosselink, J. G., R. Miller, M. Hood, and L. M. Bahr, Jr., eds., LOOP, Inc., New Orleans, La.

Hofstetter, R. H., 1983, Wetlands in the United States, in *Ecosystems of the World,* vol 4B, *Mires: Swamp, Bog, Fen and Moor,* A. J. P. Gore, ed., Elsevier, Amsterdam, pp. 201-244.

Hollis, J. P., 1967, *Toxicant Diseases of Rice,* Louisiana Agr. Exp. Station, Bull. 614, Louisiana State University, Baton Rouge.

Hook, D. D., and J. R. Scholtens, 1978, Adaptations and flood tolerance of tree species, in *Plant Life in Anaerobic Environments,* D. D. Hook and R. M. M. Crawford, eds., Ann Arbor Science, Ann Arbor, Mi., pp. 299-331.

Hopkinson, C. S., Jr., and J. W. Day, Jr., 1977, A model of the Barataria Bay salt marsh ecosystem, in *Ecosystem Modeling in Theory and Practice,* C. A. J. Hall and J. W. Day, Jr., eds., J. Wiley and Sons, New York, pp. 235-265.

Hopkinson, C. S., Jr., and J. W. Day, Jr., 1980a, Modeling the relationship between development and storm water and nutrient runoff, *Environ. Manage.* **4:**315-324.

Hopkinson, C. S., Jr., and J. W. Day, Jr., 1980b, Modeling hydrology and eutrophication in a Louisiana swamp forest ecosystem, *Environ. Manage.* **4:**325-335.

Hopkinson, C. S., Jr., J. G. Gosselink, and P. T. Parrondo, 1980, Production of coastal Louisiana marsh plants calculated from phenometric techniques, *Ecology* **61:**1091-1098.

Howarth, R. W., and J. M. Teal, 1979, Sulfate reduction in a New England salt marsh, *Limnol. Oceanogr.* **24:**999-1013.

Howarth, R. W., A. Giblin, J. Gale, B. J. Peterson, and G. W. Luther, III, 1983, Reduced sulfur compounds in the pore waters of a New England salt marsh, *Environ. Biogeochem. Ecology Bull.* (Stockholm) **35:**135-152.

Howes, B. L., J. W. H. Dacey, and G. M. King, 1984, Carbon flow through oxygen and sulfate reduction pathways in salt marsh sediments, *Limnol. Oceanogr.* **29:**1037-1051.

Howes, B. L., J. W. Dacey, and J. M. Teal, 1985, Annual carbon mineralization and below-ground production of *Spartina alterniflora* in a New England salt marsh, *Ecology* **66:**595-605.

Howes, B. L., R. W. Howarth, J. M. Teal, and I. Valiela, 1981, Oxidation-reduction potentials in a salt marsh: special patterns and interactions with primary production, *Limnol. Oceanogr.* **26:**350-360.

Hudec, K., and K. Stastny, 1978, Birds in the reedswamp ecosystem, in *Pond Littoral Ecosystems,* D. Dykyjova and J. Kvet, eds., Springer-Verlag, Berlin, pp. 366-375.

Huffman, R. T., and S. W. Forsythe, 1981, Bottomland hardwood forest communities and their relation to anaerobic soil conditions, in *Wetlands of Bottomland Hardwood Forests,* J. R. Clark and J. Benforado, eds., Elsevier, Amsterdam, pp. 187-196.

Hutchinson, G. E., 1973, Eutrophication: the scientific background of a contemporary practical problem, *Am. Sci.* **61:**269-279.

Hyatt, R. A., and G. A. Brook, 1984, Groundwater flow in the Okefenokee Swamp and hydrologic and nutrient budgets for the period August, 1981 through July, 1982, in *The Okefenokee Swamp: Its Natural History, Geology, and Geochemistry,* A. D. Cohen, D. J. Casagrande, M. J. Andrejko, and G. R. Best, eds., Wetland Surveys, Los Alamos, N.M., pp. 229-245.

Ingram, H., 1957, Microorganisms resisting high concentrations of sugar or salt, *Soc. Gen. Microbiology Symp.***7:**90-135.

Ingram, H. A. P., 1967, Problems of hydrology and plant distribution in mires,*J. Ecol.* **55:**711-724.

Ingram, H. A. P., 1983, Hydrology, in *Ecosystems of the World, vol. 4A, Mires: Swamp, Bog, Fen, and Moor,* A. J. P. Gore, ed., Elsevier, Amsterdam, pp. 67-158.

Ingram, H. A. P., D. W. Rycroft, and D. J. A. Williams, 1974, Anomalous transmission of water through certain peats,*J. Hydrology* **22:**213-218.

Ivanov, K. E., 1981, *Water Movement in Mirelands,* translated from Russian by A. Thomson and H. A. P. Ingram, Academic Press, London, 276p.

Jaworski, E., and C. N. Raphael, 1978, *Fish, Wildlife and Recreational Values of Michigan's Coastal Wetlands,* prepared by Department of Geography and Geology, Eastern Michigan University, Ypsilanti, Michigan, for Great Lakes Shorelines Sect., Div. of Land Resources Programs, Mich. Dept. of Nat. Resources, Lansing, 209p.

Jensen, J. R., E. J. Christensen, and R. Sharitz, 1983, in *Renewable Resources Management—Application of Remote Sensing* (Proceedings) American Society Photogrammetry, Falls Church, Va., pp. 318-336.

Jensen, J. R., E. J. Christensen, and R. Sharitz, 1984, Nontidal wetland mapping in South Carolina using airborne multi-spectral scanner data, *Remote Sensing Environ.* **16:**1-12.

Johnson, F. L., and D. T. Bell, 1976, Plant biomass and net primary production along a flood-frequency gradient in a streamside forest, *Castanea* **41:**156-165.

Johnson, R. L., 1979, Timber harvests from wetlands, in *Wetland Functions and Values: The State of Our Understanding,* P. E. Greeson, J. R. Clark, and J. E. Clark, eds., American Water Resource Assoc., Minneapolis, Minn., pp. 598-605.

Johnson, R. R., 1979, The lower Colorado River; a western system, in *Strategies for the Protection and Management of Floodplain Wetlands and Other Riparian Ecosystems,* R. R. Johnson and J. F. McCormick, tech. coord., Proceedings of the Symposium, Callaway Gardens, Georgia, December 11-13, 1978, U.S. Forest Service General Technical Report WO-12, Washington, D.C., pp. 41-55.

Johnson, R. R., and J. F. McCormick, (tech. coord.) 1979, *Strategies for the Protection and Management of Floodplain Wetlands and Other Riparian Ecosystems,* Proceedings of the Symposium Callaway Gardens, Georgia, December 11-13, 1978, U.S. Forest Service General Technical Report WO-12, Washington, D.C., 410p.

Johnson, W. B., C. E. Sasser, and J. G. Gosselink, 1985, Succession of vegetation in an evolving river delta, Atchafalaya Bay, Louisiana,*J. Ecology* (in press).

Johnson, W. C., R. L. Burgess, and W. R. Keammerer, 1976, Forest overstory vegetation on the Missouri River floodplain in North Dakota, *Ecol. Monogr.* **46:**59-84.

Josselyn, M., 1983, *The Ecology of San Francisco Bay Tidal Marshes: A Community Profile,* U.S. Fish and Wildlife Service FWS/OBS-83/23 Slidell, La., 102p.

Junk, W. J., 1982, Amazonian floodplains: their ecology, present and potential use, in *Ecosystem Dynamics in Freshwater Wetlands and Shallow Water Bodies,* vol. I., SCOPE and UNEP, Center of International Projects, Moscow, USSR, pp. 98-126.

Kadlec, R. H., 1979, Wetlands for tertiary treatment, in *Wetland Functions and Values: The State of Our Understanding,* P. E. Greeson, J. R. Clark, and J. E. Clark, eds., American Water Resources Assoc., Minneapolis, Minn., pp. 490-504.

Kadlec, R. H., and J. A. Kadlec, 1979, Wetlands and water quality, in *Wetland Functions and Values: The State of Our Understanding,* P. E. Greeson, J. R. Clark, and J. E. Clark, eds., American Water Resources Assoc., Minneapolis, Minn., pp. 436-456.

Kadlec, R. H., and D. L. Tilton, 1979, The use of freshwater wetlands as a tertiary wastewater treatment alternative, *CRC Crit. Rev. Environ. Control* **9:**185-212.

Kantrud, H. A., and R. E. Stewart, 1977, Use of natural basin wetlands by breeding waterfowl in North Dakota, *J. Wildl. Manage.* **41:**243-253.

Kaplan, W., I. Valiela, and J. M. Teal, 1979, Denitrification in a salt marsh ecosystem, *Limnol. Oceanogr.* **24:**726-734.

Kawase, M., 1981, Effects of ethylene on aerenchyma development, *Am. J. Bot.* **68:**651-658.

Keammerer, W. R., W. C. Johnson, and R. L. Burgess, 1975, Floristic analysis of the Missouri River bottomland forests in North Dakota, *Can. Field Nat.* **89:**5-19.

Keddy, P. A., 1983, Freshwater wetland human-induced changes: indirect effects must also be considered, *Environ. Manage.* **7:**299-302.

Kemp, G. P., and J. W. Day, Jr., 1984, Nutrient dynamics in a Louisiana swamp receiving agricultural runoff, in *Cypress Swamps,* K. C. Ewel and H. T. Odum, eds., University Presses of Florida, Gainesville, pp. 286-293.

Kirby, C. J., and J. G. Gosselink, 1976, Primary production in a Louisiana Gulf Coast *Spartina alterniflora* marsh, *Ecology* **57:**1052-1059.

Kirk, P. W., Jr., 1979, *The Great Dismal Swamp,* University Press of Virginia, Charlottesville, Va., 427p.

Kitchens, W. M., Jr., J. M. Dean, L. H. Stevenson, and J. M. Cooper, 1975, The Santee Swamp as a nutrient sink, in *Mineral Cycling in Southeastern Ecosystems,* F. G. Howell, J. B. Gentry, and M. H. Smith, eds., ERDA Symposium Series 740513, USGPO, Washington, D.C., pp. 349-366.

Klopatek, J. M., 1974, *Production of emergent macrophytes and their role in mineral cycling within a freshwater marsh,* Master's thesis, University of Wisconsin-Milwaukee.

Klopatek, J. M., 1978, Nutrient dynamics of freshwater riverine marshes and the role of emergent macrophytes, in *Freshwater Wetlands: Ecological Processes and Management Potential,* R. E. Good, D. F. Whigham, and R. L. Simpson, eds., Academic Press, New York, pp. 195-216.

Klopatek, J. M., R. J. Olson, C. J. Emerson, and J. L. Jones, 1979, Land use conflicts with natural vegetation in the United States, *Environ. Conserv.* **6:**191-200.

Kologiski, R. L., 1977, The phytosociology of the Green Swamp, North Carolina, *North Carolina Agri. Exp. Sta. Tech. Bull. 250,* Raleigh, N.C., 101p.

Kortekaas, W. M., E. Van der Maarel, and W. G. Beeftink, 1976, A numerical classification of European *Spartina* communities, *Vegetatio* **33:**51-60.

Koyama, T., 1963, Gaseous metabolism in lake sediments and paddy soils and the production of methane and hydrogen, *J. Geophys. Res.* **68:**3971-3973.

Kramer, P. J., W. S. Riley, and T. T. Bannister, 1952, Gas exchange of cypress knees, *Ecology* **33:**117-121.

Kreitler, C. W., 1977, Faulting and land subsidence from groundwater and hydrocarbon production, Houston-Galveston, Texas, in *Second International Symposium on Land Subsidence Proceedings,* International Association of Hydrological Sciences Publ. No. 121, pp. 435-446.

Kuenzler, E. J., 1974, Mangrove swamp systems, in *Coastal Ecological Systems of the United States,* vol. 1, H. T. Odum, B. J. Copeland, and E. A. McMahan, eds., The Conservation Foundation, Washington, D.C., pp. 346-371.

Kuenzler, E. J., P. J. Mulholland, L. A. Yarbro, and L. A. Smock, 1980, *Distributions and Budgets of Carbon, Phosphorus, Iron and Manganese in a Floodplain Swamp Ecosystem,* Water Resources Research Institute of North Carolina Report No. 157, Raleigh, N.C., 234p.

Kulczynski, S., 1949, Peat bogs of Polesie, *Acad. Pol. Sci. Mem.,* Series B, No. 15, 356p.

Kurz, H., 1928, Influence of *Sphagnum* and other mosses on bog reactions, *Ecology* **9:**56-69.

Kurz, H., and D. Demaree, 1934, Cypress buttresses in relation to water and air, *Ecology* **15:**36-41.

Kurz, H., and K. A. Wagner, 1953, Factors in cypress dome development, *Ecology* **34:**157-164.

Kushner, D. J., 1978, Life in high salt and solute concentrations: halophilic bacteria, in *Microbial Life in Extreme Environments,* Kushner, D. J., ed., Academic Press, New York, 465p.

Kusler, J. A., 1979, *Strengthening State Wetland Regulations,* U.S. Fish and Wildlife Service FWS/OBS-79/98, Washington, D.C.

Kusler, J. A., 1983, *Our National Wetland Heritage: A Protection Guidebook,* Environmental Law Institute, Washington, D.C., 167p.

Kusler, J. A., and J. Montanari, eds., 1978, *Proceedings of the National Wetland Protection Symposium, Reston, Virginia, June 6-8, 1977,* U.S. Fish and Wildlife Service FWS/OBS-78/97, Washington, D.C., 255p.

Kvet, J., and S. Husak, 1978, Primary data on biomass and production estimates in typical stands of fishpond littoral plant communities, in *Pond Littoral Ecosystems,* D. Dykyjova and J. Kvet, eds., Springer-Verlag, Berlin, pp. 211-216.

Lambers, H., E. Steingrover, and G. Smakman, 1978, The significance of oxygen transport and of metabolic adaptation in flood tolerance of *Senecio* species, *Physiol. Plant* **43:**277-281.

Lambou, V. W., 1965, The commercial and sport fisheries of the Atchafalaya Basin floodway, 17th Annual Conference of S.E. Associated Game and Fish Commissioners Proc., pp. 256-281.

Larcher, W., 1983, *Physiological Plant Ecology,* 2nd ed., Springer-Verlag, New York, 303p.

Larsen, J. A., 1982, *Ecology of the northern lowland bogs and conifer forests,* Academic Press, New York, 307p.

Larson, J. S., 1982, Wetland value assessment — state of the art, in *Wetlands: ecology and management,* B. Gopal, R. E. Turner, R. G. Wetzel, and D. F. Whigham, eds., Natural Institute of Ecology and International Scientific Publications, Jaipur, India, pp. 417-424.

Larson, J. S., and J. A. Kusler, 1979, Preface, in *Wetland Functions and Values: The State of Our Understanding,* P. E. Greeson, J. R. Clark, and J. E. Clark, eds., American Water Resources Association, Minneapolis, Minn.

Larson, J. S., M. S. Bedinger, C. F. Bryan, S. Brown, R. T. Huffman, E. L. Miller, D. G. Rhodes, and B. A. Touchet, 1981, Transition from wetlands to uplands in southeastern bottomland hardwood forests, in *Wetlands of Bottomland Hardwood Forests,* J. R. Clark and J. Benforado, eds., Elsevier, Amsterdam, pp. 225-273.

Leck, M. A., 1979, Germination behavior of *Impatiens capensis* Meerb. (Balsaminaceae), *Bartonia* **46:**1-11.

Leck, M. A., and K. J. Graveline, 1979, The seed bank of a freshwater tidal marsh, *Am. J. Bot.* **66:**1006-1015.

Lee, G. F., E. Bentley, and R. Amundson, 1975, Effect of marshes on water quality, in *Coupling of Land and Water Systems,* A. D. Hasler, ed., Springer-Verlag, New York, pp. 105-127.

Lee, R., 1980, *Forest Hydrology,* Columbia University Press, New York, 349p.

Lefor, M. W., and W. C. Kennard, 1977, *Inland Wetland Definitions,* University of Connecticut Institute of Water Resources Report No. 28, 63p.

Leitch, J. A., 1981, *The wetlands and drainage controversy — revisited,* Minnesota Agricultural Economist No. 626, University of Minnesota, St. Paul, 5p.

Leitch, J. A., and L. E. Danielson, 1979, *Social, Economic, and Institutional Incentives to Drain or Preserve Prairie Wetlands,* Department of Agricultural and Applied Economics, University of Minnesota, St. Paul, 78p.

Leopold, L. B., M. G. Wolman, and J. P. Miller, 1964, *Fluvial Processes in Geomorphology,* W. H. Freeman, San Francisco, 522p.

Levitt, J., 1980, *Responses of Plants to Environmental Stresses, vol. II, Water, Radiation, Salt, and Other Stresses,* Academic Press, New York, 607p.

Lieth, H., 1975, Primary production of the major units of the world, in *Primary Productivity of the Biosphere,* H. Lieth and R. H. Whitaker, eds., Springer-Verlag, New York, pp. 203-215.

Likens, G. E., F. H. Bormann, R. S. Pierce, J. S. Eaton, and N. M. Johnson, 1977, *Biogeochemistry of a Forested Ecosystem,* Springer-Verlag, New York, 146p.

Linacre, E., 1976, Swamps, in *Vegetation and the Atmosphere,* vol. 2, *Case Studies,* J. L. Monteith, ed., Academic Press, London, pp. 329-347.

Lindeman, R. L., 1942, The trophic-dynamic aspect of ecology, *Ecology* **23:**399-418.

Linsley, R. K., and J. B. Franzini, 1979, *Water-Resources Engineering,* 3rd ed., McGraw-Hill, New York, 716p.

Lippson, M. A. J., M. S. Haire, A. F. Holland, F. Jacobs, J. Jensen, R. L. Moran-Johnson, T. T. Polgar, and W. A. Richkus, 1979, *Environmental Atlas of the Potomac Estuary,* Williams and Heintz Map Corp., Washington, D.C.

Lipschultz, F., 1981, Methane release from a brackish intertidal salt-marsh embayment of Chesapeake Bay, Maryland, *Estuaries* **4:**143-145.

Little, E. L., Jr., 1971, *Atlas of United States Trees,* vol. I, Conifers and important hardwoods, Misc. Pub. No. 1146, U.S. Department of Agriculture - Forest Service, USGPO, Washington, D.C.

Littlejohn, C. B., 1977, An analysis of the role of natural wetlands in regional water management, in *Ecosystem Modeling in Theory and Practice,* C. A. S. Hall and J. W. Day, Jr., eds., Wiley, New York, pp. 451-476.

Livingston, D. A., 1963, Chemical composition of rivers and lakes, *U.S. Geological Survey Prof. Paper 440G,* 64p.

Logofet, D. D., and G. A. Alexandrov, 1984, Modelling of matter cycle in a mesotrophic bog ecosystem, I. Linear analysis of carbon environs, *Ecol. Modelling* **21:**247-258.

Lonard, R. T., E. J. Clairain, R. T. Huffman, J. W. Hardy, L. D. Brown, P. E. Ballard, and J. W. Watts, 1981, *Analysis of Methodologies Used for the Assessment of Wetland Values,* Environmental Laboratory, U.S. Army Corps of Engineers, Waterways Expt. Station, Vicksburg, Miss., 68p. plus appendices.

Lugo, A. E., 1980, Mangrove ecosystems: successional or steady state? *Biotropica* (supplement) **12:**65-72.

Lugo, A. E., 1981, The island mangroves of Inagua, *J. Nat. History* **15:**845-852.

Lugo, A. E., and S. C. Snedaker, 1974, The ecology of mangroves, *Ann. Rev. Ecol. Systematics* **5:**39-64.

Lugo, A. E., and C. P. Zucca, 1977, The impact of low temperature stress on mangrove structure and growth, *Trop. Ecol.* **18:**149-161.

Lugo, A. E., M. Sell, and S. C. Snedaker, 1976, Mangrove ecosystem analysis, in *Systems Analysis and Simulation in Ecology,* vol. IV, B. C. Patten, ed., Academic Press, New York, pp. 113-145.

Lugo, A. E., G. Evink, M. M. Brinson, A. Broce, and J. C. Snedaker, 1975, Diurnal rates of photosynthesis, respiration, and transpiration in mangrove forests in South Florida, in *Tropical Ecological Systems—Trends in Terrestrial and Aquatic Research,* F. B. Golley and E. Medina, eds., Springer-Verlag, New York, pp. 335-350.

Lunz, J. D., T. W. Zweigler, R. T. Huffman, R. J. Diaz, E. J. Clairain, and L. J. Hunt, 1978, *Habitat Development Field Investigations Windmill Point Marsh Development Site, James River, Virginia; summary report,* U.S. Army Waterways Exp. Station Tech. Rep. D-79-23, Vicksburg, Miss., 116p.

MacDonald, K. B., 1977, Plant and animal communities of Pacific North American salt marshes, in *Ecosystems of the World,* vol. I, Wet Coastal Ecosystems, B. J. Chapman, ed., Elsevier, Amsterdam, pp. 167-191.

MacDonald, P. O., W. E. Frayer, and J. K. Clauser, 1979, *Documentation, Chronology, and Future Projections of Bottomland Hardwood Habitat Losses in the Lower Mississippi Alluvial Plain,* U.S. Department of Interior, Fish and Wildlife Service, Washington, D.C., 2 vols.

MacKay, D., P. J. Leinonen, J. C. K. Overall, and B. R. Wood, 1975. The behavior of crude oil spilled on snow, *Arctic* **28:**9-20.

MacMannon, M., and R. M. M. Crawford, 1971, A metabolic theory of flooding tolerance; the significance of enzyme distribution and behavior, *New Phytol.* **10:**299-306.

Macnae, W., 1963, Mangrove swamps in South Africa, *J. Ecol.* **51:**1-25.

Maguire, C. and P. O. S. Boaden, 1975, Energy and evolution in the thiobios: an extrapolation from the marine gastrotrich *Thiodasys sterreri, Cahiers de Biol. Mar.* **16:**635-646.

Mahall, B. E., and R. B. Park, 1976a, The ecotone between *Spartina foliosa* Trin. and *Salicornia virginica* L. in salt marshes of northern San Francisco Bay. I. Biomass and production, *J. Ecol.* **64:**421-433.

Mahall, B. E., and R. B. Park, 1976*b*. The ecotone between *Spartina foliosa* Trin. and *Salicornia virginica* L. in salt marshes of northern San Francisco Bay. II. Soil water and salinity, *J. Ecol.* **64:**793-809.

Mahall, B. E., and R. B. Park, 1976*c*, The ecotone between *Spartina foliosa* Trin. and *Salicornia virginica* L. in salt marshes of northern San Francisco Bay, III. Soil aeration and tidal immersion, *J. Ecol.* **64:**811-819.

Maki, T. E., A. J. Weber, D. W. Hazel, S. C. Hunter, B. T. Hyberg, D. M. Flinchum, J. P. Lollis, J. B. Rognstad, and J. D. Gregory, 1980, *Effects of Stream Channelization on Bottomland and Swamp Forest Ecosystems,* North Carolina Water Resources Research Institute Report 80-147, Raleigh, N.C., 135p.

Malmer, N., 1962, Studies on mire vegetation in the Archaean area of southwestern Gotland, (South Sweden). I. vegetation and habitat conditions on the Akahuit mire, *Opera Botanica* **7:**1-322.

Malmer, N., 1975, Development of bog mires, in *Coupling of Land and Water Systems,* Ecology Studies No. 10, A. D. Hasler, ed., Springer-Verlag, New York, pp. 85-92.

Malmer, N., and H. Sjors, 1955, Some determinations of elementary constituents in mire plants and peat, *Bot. Not.* **108:**46-80.

Maltby, E., and R. E. Turner, 1983, Wetlands of the world, *Geog. Mag.* **55:**12-17.

Mantel, L. H., 1968, The foregut of *Gecarcinus lateralis* as an organ of salt and water balance, *Am. Zool.* **8:**433-442.

Marois, K. C., and K. C. Ewel, 1983, Natural and management-related variation in cypress domes, *Forest Sci.* **29:**627-640.

Martel Laboratories, Inc., 1976, Existing state and local wetland surveys (1965-1975), Vol. II, narrative prepared for U.S. Department of Interior, Fish and Wildlife Service, 453p.

Martin, A. C., N. Hutchkiss, F. M. Uhler, and W. S. Bourn, 1953, *Classification of Wetlands of the United States,* U.S. Fish and Wildlife Service Special Science Report—Wildlife 20, Washington, D.C., 14p.

Mattoon, W. R., 1915, The Southern Cypress, U.S. Department of Agriculture Bulletin 272.

Mattoon, W. R., 1916, Water requirements and growth of young cypress, *Soc. Am. Foresters Proc.* **11:**192-197.

McCaffrey, R. J., 1977, *A Record of the Accumulation of Sediment and Trace Metals in a Connecticut, U.S.A. Salt Marsh,* Ph.D. Dissertation, Yale University, 156p.

McIntosh, R. P., 1980, The background and some current problems of theoretical ecology, *Synthese* **43:**195-255.

McKinley, C. E., and F. P. Day, Jr., 1979, Herbaceous production in cut-burned, uncut-burned, and control areas of a *Chamaecyparis thyoides* (L.) BSP (Cupressaceae) stand in the Great Dismal Swamp. *Torrey Bot. Club Bull.* **106:**20-28.

McKnight, J. S., D. D. Hook, O. G. Langdon, and R. L. Johnson, 1981, Flood tolerance and related characteristics of trees of the bottomland forests of the southern United States, in *Wetlands of Bottomland Hardwood Forests,* J. R. Clark and J. Benforado, eds., Elsevier, Amsterdam, pp. 29-69.

McLeese, R. L., and E. P. Whiteside, 1977, Ecological effects of highway construction upon Michigan woodlots and wetlands: soil relationships, *J. Environ. Qual.* **6:**467-471.

McNaughton, S. J., 1966, Ecotype function in the *Typha* community-type, *Ecol. Monogr.* **36:**297-325.

McNaughton, S. J., 1968, Autotoxic feedback in relation to germination and seedling growth in *Typha latifolia, Ecology* **49:**367-369.

Mechenich, D. J., 1980, *Tertiary Wastewater Treatment Using a Natural Peat Bog,* Master's thesis, University of Wisconsin, 136p.

Mehlich, A., 1972, Uniformity of soil test results as influenced by volume weight, *Comm. on Soil Sci. and Plant Analysis* **4:**475-486.

Mendelssohn, I. A., 1979, Nitrogen metabolism in the height forms of *Spartina alterniflora* in North Carolina, *Ecology* **60:**574-584.

Mendelssohn, I. A., and M. L. Postek, 1982, Elemental analysis of deposits on the roots of *Spartina alterniflora* Loisel, *Am. J. Bot.* **69:**904-912.

Mendelssohn, I. A., K. L. McKee, and W. H. Patrick, Jr., 1981, Oxygen deficiency in *Spartina alterniflora* roots: metabolic adaptation to anoxia, *Science* **214:**439-441.

Mendelssohn, I. A., K. L. McKee, and M. L. Postek, 1982, Sublethal stresses controlling *Spartina alterniflora* productivity, in *Wetlands Ecology and Management,* B. Gopal, R. E. Turner, R. G. Wetzel, and D. F. Whigham, eds., National Institute of Ecology and International Science Publications, Jaipur, India, pp. 223-242.

Metzler, K., and R. Rosza, 1982, Vegetation of fresh and brackish tidal marshes in Connecticut, Connecticut Bot. Soc. *Newsletter* **10:**2-4.

Meyer, A. H., 1935, The Kankakee "Marsh" of northern Indiana and Illinois, *Michigan Acad. Sci. Arts & Letters Papers* **21:**359-396.

Millar, J. B., 1971, Shoreline-area as a factor in rate of water loss from small sloughs, *J. Hydrology* **14:**259-284.

Miller, P. C., 1972, Bioclimate, leaf temperature, and primary production in red mangrove canopies in south Florida, *Ecology* **53:**22-45.

Miller, P. C., and L. L. Tieszen, 1972, A preliminary model of processes affecting primary productivity in the Arctic tundra, *Arctic Alp. Res.* **4:**1-18.

Miller, P. C., B. D. Collier, and F. L. Bunnell, 1975, Development of ecosystem modelling in the Tundra Biome, in *Systems Analysis and Simulation in Ecology, Vol. III,* B. C. Patten, ed., Academic Press, New York, pp. 95-115.

Miller, P. C., W. A. Stoner, and L. L. Tieszen, 1976, A model of stand photosynthesis for the wet meadow tundra at Barrow, Alaska, *Ecology* **57:**411-430.

Miller, R. S., D. B. Botkin, and R. Mendelssohn, 1974, The whooping crane (*Grus americana*) population of North America, *Biol. Conserv.* **6:**106-111.

Miller, W. R., and F. E. Egler, 1950, Vegetation of the Wequetequock-Pawcatuck tidal marshes, Connecticut, *Ecol. Monogr.* **20:**143-172.

Mitsch, W. J., 1977, Waterhyacinth (*Eichhornia crassipes*) nutrient uptake and metabolism in a north central Florida marsh, *Arch. Hydrobiol.* **81:**188-210.

Mitsch, W. J., 1979, Interactions between a riparian swamp and a river in southern Illinois, in *Strategies for the Protection and Management of Floodplain Wetlands and Other Riparian Ecosystems,* R. R. Johnson and J. F. McCormick, tech. coords., Proceedings Symposium, Callaway Gardens, Dec. 1978, U.S. Forest Service General Technical Report WO-12, Washington, D.C., pp. 63-72.

Mitsch, W. J., 1983, Ecological models for management of freshwater wetlands, in *Application of Ecological Modeling in Environmental Management,* Part B, S. E. Jorgensen and W. J. Mitsch, eds., Elsevier, Amsterdam, pp. 283-310.

Mitsch, W. J., 1984, Seasonal patterns of a cypress dome pond in Florida, in *Cypress Swamps,* K. C. Ewel and H. T. Odum, eds., University Presses of Florida, Gainesville, pp. 25-33.

Mitsch, W. J., and K. C. Ewel, 1979, Comparative biomass and growth of cypress in Florida wetlands, *Am. Midl. Nat.* **101:**417-426.

Mitsch, W. J., and W. G. Rust, 1984, Tree growth responses to flooding in a bottomland forest in northeastern Illinois, *Forest Sci.* **30:**499-510.

Mitsch, W. J., C. L. Dorge, and J. R. Wiemhoff, 1977, *Forested Wetlands for Water Resource Management in Southern Illinois,* Research Report No. 132, Illinois Univ. Water Resources Center, Urbana, Ill., 225p.

Mitsch, W. J., C. L. Dorge, and J. R. Wiemhoff, 1979, Ecosystem dynamics and a phosphorus budget of an alluvial cypress swamp in southern Illinois, *Ecology* **60:**1116-1124.

Mitsch, W. J., M. D. Hutchison, and G. A. Paulson, 1979, *The Momence Wetlands of the Kankakee River in Illinois—An Assessment of Their Value,* Illinois Institute of Natural Resources, Doc 79/17, Chicago, 55p.

Mitsch, W. J., J. R. Taylor, and K. B. Benson, 1983, Classification, modelling and management of wetlands—a case study in western Kentucky, in *Analysis of Ecological Systems: State-of-the-art in Ecological Modelling,* W. K. Lauenroth, G. V. Skogerboe, and M. Flug, eds., Elsevier, Amsterdam. pp. 761-769.

Mitsch, W. J., W. Rust, A. Behnke, and L. Lai, 1979, Environmental observations of a riparian ecosystem during flood season, Research Report 142, Illinois Univ. Water Resources Center, Urbana, Ill., 64p.

Mitsch, W. J., J. W. Day, Jr., J. R. Taylor, and C. Madden, 1982, Models of North American freshwater wetlands, *Int. J. Ecol. Environ. Sci.* **8:**109-140.

Mitsch, W. J., J. R. Taylor, K. B. Benson, and P. L. Hill, Jr., 1983*a, Atlas of Wetlands in the Principal Coal Surface Mine Region of Western Kentucky,* U.S. Fish and Wildlife Service Report FWS/OBS 82/72, Washington, D.C., 135p.

Mitsch, W. J., J. R. Taylor, K. B. Benson, and P. L. Hill, Jr., 1983*b,* Wetlands and coal surface mining in western Kentucky—a regional impact assessment, *Wetlands* **3:**161-179.

Mohanty, S. K., and R. N. Dash, 1982, The chemistry of waterlogged soils, in *Wetlands—Ecology and Management,* B. Gopal, R. E. Turner, R. G. Wetzel, and D. F. Whigham, eds., Natural Institute of Ecology and International Scientific Publications, Jaipur, India, pp. 389-396.

Monk, C. D., and T. W. Brown, 1965, Ecological consideration of cypress heads in northcentral Florida, *Am. Midl. Nat.* **74:**126-140.

Montague, C. L., S. M. Bunker, E. B. Haines, M. L. Pace, and R. L. Wetzel, 1981, Aquatic macroconsumers, in *The Ecology of a Salt Marsh,* L. R. Pomeroy and R. G. Wiegert, eds., Springer-Verlag, New York, pp. 69-85.

Montz, G. N., and A. Cherubini, 1973, An ecological study of a bald cypress swamp in St. Charles Parish, Louisiana, *Castanea* **38:**378-386.

Moore, P. D., ed., 1984, *European Mires,* Academic Press, London, 367p.

Moore, P. D., and D. J. Bellamy, 1974, *Peatlands,* Springer-Verlag, New York, 221p.

Morss, W. L., 1927, The plant colonization of marshlands in the estuary of the River Nith, *J. Ecol.* **15:**310-343.

Mortimer, C. H., 1941-1942, The exchange of dissolved substances between mud and water in lakes, *J. Ecol.* **29:**280-329; **30:**147-201.

Mudroch, A., and J. A. Capobianco, 1979, Effects of treated effluent on a natural marsh, *J. Water Pollution Control Fed.* **51:**2243-2256.

Mulholland, P. J., 1979, Organic Carbon in a Swamp-Stream Ecosystem and Export by Streams in Eastern North Carolina, Ph.D. Dissertation, University of North Carolina.

Mulholland, P. J., and E. J. Kuenzler, 1979, Organic carbon export from upland and forested wetland watersheds, *Limnol. Oceanogr.* **24:**960-966.

Mumphrey, A. J., J. S. Brooks, T. D. Fox, L. B. Fromberg, R. J. Marak, and J. D. Wilkinson, 1978, *The Valuation of Wetlands in the Barataria Basin,* Urban Studies Institute, University of New Orleans, New Orleans.

Nessel, J. K., 1978, Phosphorus cycling, productivity and community structure in the Waldo cypress strand, in *Cypress Wetlands for Water Management, Recycling, and Conservation,* 4th annual report, H. T. Odum and K. C. Ewel, eds., Center for Wetlands, University of Florida, Gainesville, pp. 750-801.

Nessel, J. K., and S. E. Bayley, 1984, Distribution and dynamics of organic matter and phosphorus in a sewage-enriched cypress swamp, in *Cypress Swamps,* K. C. Ewel and H. T. Odum, eds., University Presses of Florida, Gainesville, pp. 262-278.

Nessel, J. K., K. C. Ewel, and M. S. Burnett, 1982, Wastewater enrichment increases mature pond cypress growth rates, *Forest Sci.* **28:**400-403.

Nester, E. W., C. E. Roberts, B. J. McCarthy, N. N. Pearsall, 1973, *Microbiology— Molecules, Microbes, and Man,* Holt, Rinehart, and Winston, Inc., New York, 719p.

Nichols, D. S., 1983, Capacity of natural wetlands to remove nutrients from wastewater, *J. Water Pollution Control Fed.* **55:**495-505.

Niering, W. A., 1985, *Wetlands,* Alfred A. Knopf, Inc., New York, 638p.

Niering, W. A., and R. S. Warren, 1977, Salt marshes, in *Coastal Ecosystem Management,* J. R. Clark, ed., Wiley, New York, pp. 697-702.

Niering, W. A., and R. S. Warren, 1980, Vegetation patterns and processes in New England salt marshes, *Bioscience* **30:**301-307.

Nixon, S. W., 1980, Between coastal marshes and coastal waters—a review of twenty years of speculation and research on the role of salt marshes in estuarine productivity and water chemistry, in *Estuarine and Wetland Processes,* P. Hamilton and K. B. MacDonald, eds., Plenum, New York, pp. 437-525.

Nixon, S. W., and C. A. Oviatt, 1973, Ecology of a New England salt marsh, *Ecol. Monogr.* **43:**463-498.

Nixon, S. W., and V. Lee, 1985, Wetlands and water quality—a regional review of recent research in the United States on the role of fresh and saltwater wetlands as sources, sinks, and transformers of nitrogen, phosphorus, and various heavy metals, Report to the Waterways Experiment Station, U.S. Army Corps of Engineers, Vicksburg, Miss. (in press).

Norgress, R. E., 1947, The history of the cypress lumber industry in Louisiana, *Louisiana Hist. Q.* **30:**979-1059.

Novitzki, R. P., 1979, Hydrologic characteristics of Wisconsin's wetlands and their influence on floods, stream flow, and sediment, in *Wetland Functions and Values:*

The State of Our Understanding, P. E. Greeson, J. R. Clark, J. E. Clark, eds., American Water Resource Association, Minneapolis, Minn., pp. 377-388.

Nyc, R., and P. Brooks, 1979, *National Wetlands Inventory Project: Inventorying the Nation's Wetlands with Remote Sensing,* paper presented at Corp of Engineers Remote Sensing Symposium, Reston, Virginia, 29-31 October, 1979, 11p.

Odum, E. P., 1969, The strategy of ecosystem development, *Science* **164:**262-270.

Odum, E. P., 1971, *Fundamentals of Ecology,* 3rd ed., W. B. Saunders Co., Philadelphia, 544p.

Odum, E. P., 1979*a,* Ecological importance of the riparian zone, in *Strategies for Protection and Management of Floodplain Wetlands and Other Riparian Ecosystems,* R. R. Johnson and J. F. McCormick, tech. coords., Proceedings of the Symposium, Callaway Gardens, Georgia, December 11-13, 1978, U.S. Forest Service General Technical Report WO-12, Washington, D.C., pp. 2-4.

Odum, E. P., 1979*b,* The value of wetlands; a hierarchical approach, in *Wetland Functions and Values: The State of Our Understanding,* P. E. Greeson, J. R. Clark, and J. E. Clark, eds., American Water Resources Assoc., Minneapolis, Minn., pp. 16-25.

Odum, E. P., 1981, Foreword, in *Wetlands of Bottomland Hardwood Forests,* J. R. Clark and J. Benforado, eds., Elsevier, Amsterdam, pp. xi-xiii.

Odum, E. P., and A. A. de la Cruz, 1967, Particulate organic detritus in a Georgia salt marsh-estuarine ecosystem, in *Estuaries,* G. H. Lauff, ed., American Association for the Advancement of Science, Washington, D.C., pp. 383-388.

Odum, H. T., 1982, Role of wetland ecosystems in the landscape of Florida, in *Proceedings of the International Scientific Workshop on Ecosystem Dynamics in Freshwater Wetlands and Shallow Water Bodies,* Vol. II. SCOPE and UNEP Workshop, Center of International Projects, Moscow, USSR, pp. 33-72.

Odum, H. T., 1983, *Systems Ecology—An Introduction,* Wiley, New York, 644p.

Odum, H. T., 1984, Summary: cypress swamps and their regional role, in *Cypress Swamps,* K. C. Ewel and H. T. Odum, eds., University Presses of Florida, Gainesville, pp. 416-443.

Odum, H. T., B. J. Copeland, and E. A. McMahan, eds., 1974, *Coastal Ecological Systems of the United States,* The Conservation Foundation, Washington, D.C., 4 vols.

Odum, H. T., K. C. Ewel, W. J. Mitsch, and J. W. Ordway, 1977*a,* Recycling treated sewage through cypress wetlands in Florida, in *Wastewater Renovation and Reuse,* F. M. D'Itri, ed., Marcel Dekker, New York, pp. 35-67.

Odum, H. T., W. M. Kemp, M. Sell, W. Boynton, and M. Lehman, 1977*b,* Energy analysis and coupling of man and estuaries, *Environ. Manage.* **1:**297-315.

Odum, H. T., P. Kangas, G. R. Best, B. T. Rushton, S. Leibowitz, J. R. Butner, and T. Oxford, 1981, *Studies on phosphate mining, reclamation, and energy,* Center for Wetlands, University of Florida, Gainesville, 142p.

Odum, W. E., 1970, *Pathways of Energy Flow in a South Florida Estuary,* Ph.D. Dissertation, University of Miami, 162p.

Odum, W. E., and M. A. Heywood, 1978, Decomposition of intertidal freshwater marsh plants, in *Freshwater Wetlands; Ecological Processes and Management Potential,* R. E. Good, D. G. Whigham, and R. L. Simpson, eds., Academic Press, New York, pp. 89-97.

Odum, W. E., and T. G. Smith, 1980, Ecology of tidal, low salinity ecosystems, in

R. C. Carey, P. S. Markovits, and J. B. Kirkwood, eds., Proceedings, Workshop on Coastal Ecosystems of the Southeastern United States. FWS/OBS-80/59, U.S. Fish and Wildlife Service, Washington, D.C., pp. 36-44.

Odum, W. E., J. S. Fisher, and J. C. Pickral, 1979, Factors controlling the flux of particulate organic carbon from estuarine wetlands, in *Ecological Processes in Coastal and Marine Systems,* R. J. Livingston, ed., Plenum, New York, pp. 69-80.

Odum, W. E., T. J. Smith III, J. K. Hoover, and C. C. McIvor, 1984, *The Ecology of Tidal Freshwater Marshes of the United States East Coast: A Community Profile,* U.S. Fish and Wildlife Service, FWS/OBS-87/17, Washington, D.C., 177p.

Office of Technology Assessment, 1984, *Wetlands: Their Use and Regulation,* U.S. Congress OTA-O-206, Washington, D.C., 208p.

Ogaard, L. A., J. A. Leitch, D. F. Scott, and W. C. Nelson, 1981, The fauna of the prairie wetlands: research methods and annotated bibliography, Research Report No. 86, North Dakota State University, Agric. Exp. Station, Fargo, North Dakota, 23p.

Ogawa, H., and J. W. Male, 1983, *The Flood Mitigation Potential of Inland Wetlands,* Water Resources Research Center Publication No. 138, University of Massachusetts, Amherst, 164p.

Orozco-Segovia, A. D. L., 1980, One option for the use of marshes of Tabasco, Mexico, in *Wetlands Restoration and Creation: Proceedings of the 7th Annual Conference, 1979 May 16-17, Tampa, Florida,* D. P. Cole, ed., pages 209-218. Available from Hillsborough Community College, Tampa, Florida.

Parker, P. E., 1974, *A Dynamic Ecosystem Simulator,* Ph.D. Dissertation, University of Michigan, 554p.

Parker, P. E., and R. H. Kadlec, 1974, *A Dynamic Ecosystem Simulator,* American Institute of Chemical Engineers 78th National Meeting Paper No. 8c, Salt Lake City, Utah, 40p.

Parsons, K. E., and A. A. de la Cruz, 1980, Energy flow and grazing behavior of conocephaline grasshoppers in a *Juncus roemerianus* marsh, *Ecology* **61:**1045-1050.

Patrick, R., J. Cairns, Jr., and S. S. Roback, 1967, An ecosystematic study of the fauna and flora of the Savannah River, *Acad. Nat. Sci. Philadelphia Proc.* **118:**109-407.

Patrick, W. H., Jr., 1981, Bottomland soils, in *Wetlands of Bottomland Hardwood Forests,* J. R. Clark and J. Benforado, eds., Elsevier, Amsterdam, pp. 177-185.

Patrick, W. H., Jr., and R. D. Delaune, 1972, Characterization of the oxidized and reduced zones in flooded soil, *Soil Sci. Soc. Am. Proc.* **36:**573-576.

Patrick, W. H., Jr., and R. A. Khalid, 1974, Phosphate release and sorption by soils and sediments: effect of aerobic and anaerobic conditions, *Science* **186:**53-55.

Patrick, W. H., Jr., and K. R. Reddy, 1976, Nitrification-denitrification reactions in flooded soils and water bottoms: dependence on oxygen supply and ammonium diffusion, *J. Environ. Quality* **5:**469-472.

Patrick, W. H., Jr., G. Dissmeyer, D. D. Hook, V. W. Lambou, H. M. Leitman, and C. H. Wharton, 1981, Characteristics of wetland ecosystems of southeastern bottomland hardwood forests, in *Wetlands of Bottomland Hardwood Forests,* J. R. Clark and J. Benforado, eds., Elsevier, Amsterdam, pp. 276-300.

Patten, B. C., B. Gopal, S. E. Jorgensen, P. P. Koryavov, J. Kvet, H. Loffler, Y. Svirezhev, and J. Tundisi, in press, *Ecosystem Dynamics in Freshwater Wetlands and Shallow Water Bodies,* proceedings Meeting in Tallinn, USSR, August 1983, Wiley, New York.

Pearlstein, L., H. McKellar, and W. Kitchens, 1985, Modelling the impacts of a river diversion on bottomland forest communities in the Santee River floodplain, South Carolina, *Ecol. Mod.* **29:**283-302.

Pearsall, W. H., 1920, The aquatic vegetation of the English lakes, *J. Ecology* **8:**163-201.

Pelikan, J., 1978, Mammals in the reedswamp ecosystem, in *Pond Littoral Ecosystems,* D. Dykyjova and J. Kvet, eds., Springer-Verlag, Berlin, pp. 357-365.

Penfound, W. T., 1952, Southern swamps and marshes, *Bot. Rev.* **18:**413-446.

Penfound, W. T., and E. S. Hathaway, 1938, Plant communities in the marshlands of southeastern Louisiana, *Ecol. Monogr.* **8:**1-56.

Perry, J. J., D. E. Armstrong, and D. D. Huff, 1981, Phosphorus fluxes in an urban marsh during runoff, in *Selected Proceedings of the Midwest Conference on Wetlands Values and Management,* B. Richardson, ed., Minnesota Water Planning Board, St. Paul, Minn., pp. 199-212.

Peterjohn, W. T., and D. L. Correll, 1984, Nutrient dynamics in an agricultural watershed: observations on the role of a riparian forest, *Ecology* **65:**1466-1475.

Peters, D. S., D. W. Ahrenholz, and T. R. Rice, 1979, Harvest and value of wetland associated fish and shellfish, in *Wetland Functions and Values: The State of Our Understanding,* Greeson, P. E., J. R. Clark, and J. E. Clark, eds., American Water Resources Assoc., Minneapolis, Minn., pp. 606-617.

Peverly, J. H., 1982, Stream transport of nutrients through a wetland, *J. Environ. Quality* **11:**38-43.

Phipps, R. L., 1979, Simulation of wetlands forest vegetation dynamics, *Ecol. Mod.* **7:**257-288.

Phipps, R. L., and L. H. Applegate, 1983, Simulation of management alternatives in wetland forests, in *Application of Ecological Modelling in Environmental Management,* Part B, S. E. Jorgensen and W. J. Mitsch, eds., Elsevier, Amsterdam, pp. 311-339.

Pjavchenko, N. J., 1982, *Bog ecosystems and their importance in nature,* in Proceedings of International Workshop on Ecosystems Dynamics in wetlands and shallow water bodies, Vol. I, SCOPE and UNEP Scientific Workshop, Center for International Projects, Moscow, USSR, pp. 7-21.

Pomeroy, L. R., 1959, Algae productivity in salt marshes of Georgia, *Limnol. Oceanogr.* **4:**386-397.

Pomeroy, L. R., L. R. Shenton, R. D. Jones, and R. J. Reimold, 1972, Nutrient flux in estuaries, in *Nutrients and Eutrophication,* G. E. Likens, ed., Am. Soc. Limnol. Oceanogr. Special Symposium, Allen Press, Lawrence, Kans., pp. 274-291.

Pomeroy, L. R., K. Bancroft, J. Breed, R. R. Christian, D. Frankenberg, J. R. Hall, L. G. Maurer, W. J. Wiebe, R. G. Wiegert, and R. L. Wetzel, 1977, Flux of organic matter through a salt marsh, in *Estuarine Processes,* vol. II, M. Wiley, ed., Academic Press, New York, pp. 270-279.

Ponnamperuma, F. N., 1972, The Chemistry of Submerged Soils, *Adv. Agron.* **24:**29-96.

Pool, D. J., A. E. Lugo, and S. C. Snedaker, 1975, Litter production in mangrove forests of southern Florida and Puerto Rico, in *Proceedings of the International Symposium on Biology and Management of Mangroves,* G. Walsh, S. Snedaker, and H. Teas, eds., Institute of Food and Agriculture Science, University of Florida, Gainesville, pp. 213-237.

Por, F. D., and I. Dor, eds., 1984, *Hydrobiology of the Mangal,* Dr. W. Junk Publishers, The Hague, Netherlands, 260p.

Potonie, R., 1908, *Aufbau und Vegetation der Moore Norddeutschlands,* Englers. Bot. Jahrb, 90 Liepzig.

Prentki, R. T., T. D. Gustafson, and M. S. Adams, 1978, Nutrient movements in lakeshore marshes, in *Freshwater Wetlands: Ecological Processes and Management Potential,* R. E. Good, D. F. Whigham, and R. L. Simpson, eds., Academic Press, New York, pp. 169-194.

Pride, R. W., F. W. Meyer, and R. N. Cherry, 1966, Hydrology of Green Swamp area in central Florida, *Florida Div. Geology Rept. Inv. 42,* 137p.

Prince, H. H., and F. M. D'Itri, eds., 1985, *Coastal Wetlands,* Lewis Publishers, Inc., Chelsea, Mi., 286p.

Putnam, J. A., G. M. Furnival, and J. S. McKnight, 1960, *Management and Inventory of Southern Hardwoods,* USDA Agricultural Handbook 181, Washington, D.C., 102p.

Radforth, N. W., 1962, Organic terrain and geomorphology, *Can. Geographer* **71:**8-11.

Rainey, G. B., 1979, Factors affecting nutrient chemistry distribution in Louisiana coastal marshes, Master's Thesis, Louisiana State University.

Ranwell, D. S., 1972, *Ecology of Salt Marshes and Sand Dunes,* Chapman and Hall, London, 258p.

Ranwell, D. S., E. C. F. Bird, J. C. E. Hubbard, and R. E. Stebbings, 1964, *Spartina* salt marshes in Southern England. V. Tidal submergence and chlorinity in Poole Harbour, *J. Ecology* **52:**627-641.

Reader, R. J., 1978, Primary production in Northern bog marshes, in *Freshwater Wetlands: Ecological Processes and Management Potential,* R. E. Good, D. F. Whigham, and R. L. Simpson, eds., Academic Press, New York, pp. 53-62.

Reader, R. J., and J. M. Stewart, 1972, The relationship between net primary production and accumulation for a peatland in southeastern Manitoba, *Ecology* **53:**1024-1037.

Redfield, A. C., 1965, Ontogeny of a salt marsh estuary, *Science* **147:**50-55.

Redfield, A. C., 1972, Development of a New England salt marsh, *Ecol. Monogr.* **42:**201-237.

Redman, F. H., and W. H. Patrick, Jr., 1965, *Effect of Submergence on Several Biological and Chemical Soil Properties,* Louisiana Agricultural Exp. Station, Bull. No. 592, Louisiana State University, Baton Rouge.

Reilly, W. K., 1979, Can science help save interior wetlands? in *Wetland Functions and Values: The State of our Understanding,* P. E. Greeson, J. R. Clark, and J. E. Clark, eds., American Water Resources Assoc., Minneapolis, Minn., pp. 26-30.

Reimold, R. J., 1972, The movement of phosphorus through the marsh cord grass, *Spartina alterniflora* Loisel, *Limnol. Oceanogr.* **17:**606-611.

Reimold, R. J., 1974, Mathematical modeling—*Spartina,* in *Ecology of Halophytes,* R. J. Reimold and W. M. Queen, eds., Academic Press, New York, pp. 393-406.

Reimold, R. J., and F. C. Daiber, 1970, Dissolved phosphorus concentrations in a natural salt marsh of Delaware, *Hydrobiologia* **36:**361-371.

Reiners, W. A., 1972, Structure and energetics of three Minnesota forests, *Ecol. Monogr.* **42:**71-94.

Reppert, R. T., W. Sigleo, E. Stakhiv, L. Messman, and C. Meyers, 1979, *Wetland*

Values: Concepts and Methods for Wetlands Evaluation, U.S. Army Corps of Engineers, Institute for Water Resources, Fort Belvoir, Va., IWR Res. Rep. 79-R-1, 109p.

Richardson, C. J., 1979, Primary productivity values in freshwater wetlands, in *Wetland Functions and Values: The State of Our Understanding,* P. E. Greeson, J. R. Clark, and J. E. Clark, eds., American Water Resources Assoc., Minneapolis, Minn., pp. 131-145.

Richardson, C. J., ed., 1981, *Pocosin Wetlands,* Hutchinson Ross Publishing Co., Stroudsburg, Pa., 364p.

Richardson, C. J., 1983, Pocosins: vanishing wastelands or valuable wetlands? *BioScience* **33:**626-633.

Richardson, C. J., 1985, Mechanisms controlling phosphorus retention capacity in freshwater wetlands, *Science* **228:**1424-1427.

Richardson, C. J., R. Evans, and D. Carr, 1981, Pocosins: an ecosystem in transition, in *Pocosin Wetlands,* C. J. Richardson, ed., Hutchinson Ross Publishing Co., Stroudsburg, Pa., pp. 3-19.

Richardson, C. J., W. A. Wentz, J. P. M. Chamie, J. A. Kadlec, and D. L. Tilton, 1976, Plant growth, nutrient accumulation and decomposition in a central Michigan peatland used for effluent treatment, in *Freshwater Wetlands and Sewage Effluent Disposal,* D. L. Tilton, R. H. Kadlec, and C. J. Richardson, eds., University of Michigan, Ann Arbor, Mich., pp. 77-117.

Richardson, C. J., D. L. Tilton, J. A. Kadlec, J. P. M. Chamie, and W. A. Wentz, 1978, Nutrient dynamics of northern wetland ecosystems, in *Freshwater Wetlands— Ecological Processes and Management Potential,* R. E. Good, D. F. Whigham, and R. L. Simpson, eds., Academic Press, New York, pp. 217-241.

Richardson, J., P. A. Straub, K. C. Ewel, and H. T. Odum, 1983, Sulfate-enriched water effects on a floodplain forest in Florida, *Environ. Manage.* **7:**321-326.

Rigg, G. B., 1925, Some sphagnum bogs of the North Pacific coast of America, *Ecology* **6:**260-278.

Riley, J. P., and G. Skirrow, 1975, *Chemical Oceanography,* 2nd ed., vol. 2, Academic Press, New York, 647p.

Roe, H. B., and Q. C. Ayres, 1954, *Engineering for Agricultural Drainage,* McGraw-Hill, New York, 501p.

Romanov, V. V., 1968, *Hydrophysics of Bogs,* trans. from Russian by N. Kaner, ed. by Prof. Heimann, Israel Program for Scientific Translation, Jerusalem. Available from Clearinghouse for Federal Scientific and Technical Information, Springfield, Virginia, 299p.

Ruebsamen, R. N., 1972, *Some Ecological Aspects of the Fish Fauna of a Louisiana Intertidal Pond System.* Master's thesis, Louisiana State University, 80p.

Russell, H. S., 1976, *A Long, Deep Furrow. Three Centuries of Farming in New England,* University Press of New England, Hanover, N.H., 671p.

Ruttner, F., 1963, *Fundamentals of Limnology,* 3rd ed., University of Toronto Press, Canada, 295p.

Rycroft, D. W., D. J. A. Williams, and H. A. P. Ingram, 1975, The transmission of water through peat, I. Review, *J. Ecol.* **63:**535-556.

Rykiel, E. J., Jr., 1977, *Toward Simulation and Systems Analysis of Nutrient Cycling in the Okefenokee Swamp, Georgia,* Technical Completion Report, USDI/OWRT Project No. A-060-GA, University of Georgia, Athens, Ga., 139p.

Rykiel, E. J., Jr., 1984, General hydrology and mineral budgets for Okefenokee Swamp: ecological significance, in *The Okefenokee Swamp: Its Natural History, Geology, and Geochemistry,* A. D. Cohen, D. J. Casagrande, M. J. Andrejko, and G. R. Best, eds., Wetland Surveys, Los Alamos, N.Mex., pp. 212-228.

Ryther, J. H., R. A. Debusk, M. D. Hanisak, and L. D. Williams, 1979, Freshwater macrophytes for energy and waste water treatment, in *Wetland Functions and Values: The State of Our Understanding,* P. E. Greeson, J. R. Clark, and J. E. Clark, eds., American Water Resources Association, Minneapolis, Minn., pp. 652-660.

Sasser, C. E., 1977, *Distribution of Vegetation in Louisiana Coastal Marshes as Response to Tidal Flooding,* Master's thesis, Louisiana State University, 40p.

Sasser, C. E., and J. G. Gosselink, 1984, Vegetation and primary production in a floating freshwater marsh in Louisiana, *Aquatic Bot.* **20:**245-255.

Sasser, C. E., G. W. Peterson, D. A. Fuller, R. K. Abernathy, and J. G. Gosselink, 1982, Environmental monitoring program, Louisiana Offshore Oil Port pipeline, 1981 Annual Report, Coastal Ecology Laboratory, Center for Wetland Resources, Louisiana State University, Baton Rouge, 299p.

Sather, J. H., and R. D. Smith, 1984, *An Overview of Major Wetland Functions and Values,* Western Energy and Land Use Team, U.S. Fish and Wildlife Service, FWS/OBS-84/18, Washington, D.C., 68p.

Scaife, W. W., R. E. Turner, and R. Costanza, 1983, Recent land loss and canal impacts on coastal Louisiana, *Environ. Manage.* **7:**433-442.

Schamberger, M. L., C. Short, and A. Farmer, 1979, Evaluation wetlands as a wildlife habitat, in *Wetland Functions and Values: The State of Our Understanding,* P. E. Greeson, J. R. Clark, and J. E. Clark, eds., American Water Resources Assoc., Minneapolis, Minn., pp. 74-83.

Scheffe, R. D., 1978, Estimation and prediction of summer evapotranspiration from a northern wetland, Master's thesis, University of Michigan, 69p.

Schlesinger, W. H., 1978, Community structure, dynamics, and nutrient ecology in the Okefenokee Cypress Swamp-Forest, *Ecol. Monogr.* **48:**43-65.

Schlesinger, W. H., and B. F. Chabot, 1977, The use of water and minerals by evergreen and deciduous shrubs in Okefenokee Swamp, *Bot. Gazette* **138:**490-497.

Schlosser, I. J., and J. R. Karr, 1981a, Water quality in agricultural watersheds: impact of riparian vegetation during base flow, *Water Resour. Bull.* **17:**233-240.

Schlosser, I. J., and J. R. Karr, 1981b, Riparian vegetation and channel morphology impact on spatial patterns of water quality in agricultural watersheds, *Environ. Manage.* **5:**233-243.

Scholander, P. F., L. van Dam, and S. I. Scholander, 1955, Gas exchange in the roots of mangroves. *Am. J. Bot.* **42:**92-98.

Scholander, P. F., H. T. Hammel, E. D. Bradstreet, and E. A. Hemmingsen, 1965, Sap pressure in vascular plants, *Science* **148:**339-346.

Scholander, P. F., E. D. Bradstreet, H. T. Hammel, and E. A. Hemmingsen, 1966, Sap concentrations in naiophytes and some other plants, *Plant Physiol.* **41:**529-532.

SCOPE and UNEP, 1982, *Ecosystem Dynamics in Freshwater Wetlands and Shallow Water Bodies,* Proceedings Workshop Minsk, Pinsk, and Tskhaltoubo, USSR,

July 12-26, 1981, Scientific Committee on Problems of the Environment and United Nations Environment Programme, Center of International Projects, Moscow, USSR, Vol. I and II. 312p. and 424p.

Sell, M. G., 1977, *Modeling the Response of Mangrove Ecosystems to Herbicide Spraying, Hurricanes, Nutrient Enrichment and Economic Development,* Ph.D. dissertation, University of Florida, 389p.

Seneca, E. D., 1980, Techniques for creating salt marshes along the east coast, in *Rehabilitation and Creation of Selected Coastal Habitats,* J. C. Lewis and E. W. Bunce, eds., U.S. Fish and Wildlife Service, Biol. Service Program, FWS/OBS-80/27, Washington, D.C., pp. 1-5.

Shaw, S. P., and C. G. Fredine, 1956, *Wetlands of the United States, Their Extent, and Their Value for Waterfowl and Other Wildlife,* U.S. Department of Interior, Fish and Wildlife Service, Circular 39, Washington, D.C., 67p.

Shjeflo, J. B., 1968, Evapotranspiration and the water budget of prairie potholes in North Dakota, *U.S. Geological Survey Prof. Paper 585-B,* 49p.

Sikora, W. B., 1977, The Ecology of *Paleomontes pugio* in a Southeastern Salt Marsh Ecosystem with Particular Emphasis on Production and Trophic Relationship, Ph.D. dissertation, University of South Carolina, 122p.

Sikora, J. P., W. B. Sikora, C. W. Erkenbrecher, and B. C. Coull, 1977, Significance of ATP, carbon and caloric content of meiobenthic nematodes in partitioning benthic biomass, *Mar. Biol.* **44:**7-14.

Simpson, R. L., D. F. Whigham, and R. Walker, 1978, Seasonal patterns of nutrient movement in a freshwater tidal marsh, in *Freshwater wetlands: Ecological Processes and Management Potential,* R. E. Good, D. F. Whigham, and R. L. Simpson, eds., Academic Press, New York, pp. 243-257.

Simpson, R. L., R. E. Good, R. Walker, and B. R. Frasco, 1981, *Dynamics of nitrogen, phosphorus and heavy metals in Delaware River freshwater tidal wetland,* Final Tech. Completion Report, Corvallis Environmental Research Laboratory, Environmental Protection Agency, Corvallis, Oregon, 192p.

Simpson, R. L., R. E. Good, M. A. Leck, and D. F. Whigham, 1983, The ecology of freshwater tidal wetlands, *BioScience* **33:**255-259.

Sjors, H., 1961, Bogs and fens on Attawapiskat River, Northern Ontario, *Nat. Mus. Can. Bull. 186,* 133p.

Sklar, F. H., and W. H. Conner, 1979, *Effects of altered hydrology on primary production and aquatic animal populations in a Louisiana swamp forest,* in J. W. Day, Jr., D. D. Culley, Jr., R. E. Turner, and A. T. Humphrey, Jr., eds., Proceedings of the 3rd Coastal Marsh and Estuary Management Symposium, Louisiana State University, Division of Continuing Education, Baton Rouge, pp. 101-208.

Sklar, F. H., R. Costanza, and J. W. Day, Jr., 1985. Dynamic spatial simulation modelling of coastal wetland habitat succession. *Ecol. Mod.* **29:**261-281.

Sloey, W. E., F. L. Spangler, and C. W. Fetter, Jr., 1978, Management of freshwater wetlands for nutrient assimilation, in *Freshwater Wetlands: Ecological Processes and Management Potential.* R. E. Good, D. F. Whigham, and R. L. Simpson, eds., Academic Press, New York, pp. 321-340.

Small, E., 1972, Ecological significance of four critical elements in plants of raised *Sphagnum* peat bogs, *Ecology* **53:**498-503.

Smalley, A. E., 1959, *The growth cycle of Spartina and its relations to the insect population in the marsh,* in Proceedings of the Salt Marsh Conference, Sapelo Island, Georgia, March 25-28, 1958, Marine Institute, University of Georgia, Athens, pp. 96-100.

Smardon, R. C., 1979, Visual-cultural values of wetlands, in *Wetland Functions and Values: The State of Our Understanding,* P. E. Greeson, J. R. Clark, and J. E. Clark, eds., American Water Resources Assoc., Minneapolis, Minn., pp. 535-544.

Smart, R. M., and J. W. Barko, 1980, Nitrogen nutrition and salinity tolerance of *Distichlis spicata* and *Spartina alterniflora, Ecology* **61:**630-638.

Smith, C. J., R. D. Delaune, and W. H. Patrick, Jr., 1982, Carbon and nitrogen cycling in a *Spartina alterniflora* salt marsh, in *The Cycling of Carbon, Nitrogen, Sulfur, and Phosphorus in Terrestrial and Aquatic Ecosystems,* J. R. Freney and I. E. Galvally, eds., Springer-Verlag, New York, pp. 97-104.

Smith, H. K., 1980, Coastal habitat development in the dredged material research program, in *Rehabilitation and Creation of Selected Coastal Habitats,* J. C. Lewis and E. W. Bunce, eds., U.S. Fish and Wildlife Service, Biol. Service Program, FWS/OBS-80/27, pp. 117-125.

Smith, R. C., 1975, Hydrogeology of the experimental cypress swamps, in *Cypress Wetlands for Water Management, Recycling and Conservation,* H. T. Odum and K. C. Ewel, eds., Second Annual Report to NSF and Rockefeller Foundation, Center for Wetlands, University of Florida, Gainesville, pp. 114-138.

Smith, R. L., 1980, *Ecology and Field Biology,* 3rd ed., Harper and Row, New York, 835p.

Spangler, F. L., C. W. Fetter, Jr., and W. E. Sloey, 1977, Phosphorus accumulation-discharge cycles in marshes, *Water Resour. Bull.* **13:**1191-1201.

Sprunt, A., Jr., 1961, Emerald kingdom, *Audubon Mag.,* January-February 1961, pp. 25-40.

Sterns, F., 1978, Management potential: summary and recommendations, in *Freshwater wetlands: ecological processes and management potential,* R. E. Good, D. F. Whigham, and R. L. Simpson, eds., Academic Press, New York, pp. 357-363.

Steever, E. Z., R. S. Warren, and W. A. Niering, 1976, Tidal energy subsidy and standing crop production of *Spartina alterniflora, Estuarine Coast. Mar. Sci.* **4:**473-478.

Stelzer, R., and A. Lauchli, 1978, Salt and flooding tolerance of *Puccinellia peisonis,* III. Distribution and localization of ions in the plant, *Z. Pflanzenphysiol.* **88:**437-448.

Stevenson, J. S., D. R. Heinle, D. A. Flemer, R. J. Small, R. A. Rowland, and J. F. Ustach, 1977, Nutrient exchanges between brackish water marshes and the estuary, in *Estuarine Processes,* vol. II, M. Wiley, ed., Academic Press, New York, pp. 219-240.

Steward, K. K., and W. H. Ornes, 1973, *Assessing the Capability of the Everglades Marsh Environment for Renovating Wastewater,* Final Report, Agricultural Research Service, Fort Lauderdale, Fla., 28p.

Stewart, R. E., 1962, *Waterfowl Populations in the Upper Chesapeake Region,* U.S. Fish and Wildlife Service Spec. Sci. Rep. Wildl. Research Pub. 65, 208p.

Stewart, R. E., and C. S. Robbins, 1958, Birds of Maryland and the District of Columbia, *U.S. Fish and Wildlife Service North America Fauna Service Research Pub. 62,* 401p.

Stewart, R. E., and H. A. Kantrud, 1971, Classification of natural ponds and lakes in the glaciated prairie region, *U.S. Fish and Wildlife Service Research Pub. 92,* 57p.

Stewart, R. E., and H. A. Kantrud, 1972, Vegetation of the prairie potholes, North Dakota, in relation to quality of water and other environmental factors, *U.S. Geological Survey Prof. Paper 585-D,* 36p.

Stewart, R. E., and H. A. Kantrud, 1973, Ecological distribution of breeding waterfowl populations in North Dakota, *J. Wildl. Manage.* **37:**39-50.

Stroud, L. M., and A. W. Cooper, 1968, Color infrared aerial photographic interpretations and net primary productivity of a regularly flooded North Carolina salt marsh, *North Carolina Water Resource Research Institute Rep. No. 14.,* 86p.

Stumm, W., and J. J. Morgan, 1970, *Aquatic Chemistry: An Introduction Emphasizing Chemical Equilibria in Natural Waters,* Wiley, New York, 583p.

Sullivan, M. J., 1978, Diatom community structure taxonomic and statistical analyses of a Mississippi salt marsh, *J. Phycol.* **14:**468-475.

Sullivan, M. J., and F. C. Daiber, 1974, Response in production of cordgrass *Spartina alterniflora* to inorganic nitrogen and phosphorus fertilizer, *Chesapeake Sci.* **15:**121-123.

Sze, N. D., 1977, Anthropogenic CO_2 emissions: implications for the atmospheric CO_2-OH-CH_4 cycle, *Science* **195:**673-675.

Tarnocai, C., 1979, *Canadian Wetland Registry,* in Proceedings of a workshop on Canadian Wetlands Environment, C. D. A. Rubec and F. C. Pollett, eds., Canada Land Directorate, Ecological Land Classification Series, No. 12., pp. 9-38.

Taylor, J. R., 1985, Community structure and primary productivity in forested wetlands in Western Kentucky, Ph.D. dissertation, University of Louisville, 139p.

Taylor, J. R., M. A. Cardamone, and W. J. Mitsch, 1984, *Bottomland Hardwood Forests: Their Functions and Values,* paper presented at Bottomlands Hardwoods Workshop, St. Francisville, Louisiana, December 1984, Mitsch & Associates, Louisville, Ky. 87p.

Teal, J. M., 1958, Distribution of fiddler crabs in Georgia salt marshes, *Ecology* **39:**185-193.

Teal, J. M., 1962, Energy flow in the salt marsh ecosystem of Georgia, *Ecology* **43:**614-624.

Teal, J. M., 1986, *Tidal salt marshes of eastern North America: the ecology of the low salt marsh,* U.S. Fish and Wildlife Service, Office of Biological Services, Washington, D.C., Biological Report (in press).

Teal, J. M., and J. W. Kanwisher, 1966, Gas transport in the marsh grass *Spartina alterniflora, J. Exp. Botany* **17:**355-361.

Teal, J. M., I. Valiela, and D. Berla, 1979, Nitrogen fixation by rhizosphere and free-living bacteria in salt marsh sediments, *Limnol. Oceanogr.* **24:**126-132.

Thayer, G. W., H. H. Stuart, W. J. Kenworthy, J. F. Ustach, and A. B. Hall, 1979, Habitat values of salt marshes, mangroves, and seagrasses for aquatic organisms, in

Wetland functions and values: the state of our understanding, P. E. Greeson, J. R. Clark, and J. E. Clark, eds., American Water Resources Assoc., Minneapolis, Minn., pp. 235-255.

Thomas, B., 1976, *The Swamp,* Norton, New York, 223p.

Tilton, D. L., 1977, Seasonal growth and foliar nutrients of *Larix laricina* in three wetland ecosystems, *Can. J. Bot.* **55:**1291-1298.

Tilton, D. L., and R. H. Kadlec, 1979, The utilization of a freshwater wetland for nutrient removal from secondarily treated wastewater effluent, *J. Environ. Qual.* **8:**328-334.

Tiner, R. W., 1984, *Wetlands of the United States: Current Status and Recent Trends,* National Wetlands Inventory, Fish and Wildlife Service, U.S. Department of Interior, Washington, D.C., 58p.

Tiner, R. W., and B. O. Wilen, 1983, *The U.S. Fish and Wildlife Service's National Wetlands Inventory Project,* unpublished report, U.S. Fish and Wildlife Service, Washington, D.C., 19p.

Todd, D. K., 1964, Groundwater, in *Handbook of Applied Hydrology,* V. T. Chow, ed., McGraw-Hill, New York, pp. 13-1-13-55.

Train, E., and F. P. Day, Jr., 1982, Population age structure of tree species in four communities in the Great Dismal Swamp, *Castanea* **47:**1-16.

Transeau, E. N., 1903, On the geographic distribution and ecological relations of the bog plant societies of northern North America, *Bot. Gaz.* **36:**401-420.

Turner, F. T., and W. H. Patrick, Jr., 1968, Chemical changes in waterlogged soils as a result of oxygen depletion, *IX International Congress Soil Science (Adelaide, Australia) Trans.* **4:** 53-56.

Turner, R. E., 1976, Geographic variations in salt marsh macrophyte production: a review, *Contr. Mar. Sci.* **20:**47-68.

Turner, R. E., 1977, Intertidal vegetation and commercial yields of penaeid shrimp, *Amer. Fish. Soc. Trans.* **106:**411-416.

Turner, R. E., 1978, Community plankton respiration in a salt marsh estuary and the importance of macrophytic leachates, *Limnol. Oceanogr.* **23:**442-451.

Turner, R. E., J. W. Day, Jr., M. Meo, P. M. Payonk, T. B. Ford, and W. G. Smith, 1976, Aspects of land-treated waste application in Louisiana wetlands, in *National Symposium on Freshwater Wetlands and Sewage Effluent Disposal Proceedings,* D. L. Tilton, R. H. Kadlec, and C. J. Richardson, eds., University of Michigan, Ann Arbor, Mich., pp. 145-168.

Turner, R. E., S. W. Forsythe, and N. J. Craig, 1981, Bottomland hardwood forest land resources of the southeastern United States, in *Wetlands of Bottomland Hardwood Forests,* J. R. Clark and J. Benforado, eds., Elsevier, Amsterdam, pp. 13-28.

Udall, H. F., J. Zarudsky, and T. E. Doheny, 1969, Productivity and nutrient values of plants growing in the salt marshes of the town of Hempstead, Long Island, *Torrey Bot. Club Bull.* **96:**42-51.

Ursin, M. J., 1972, *Life in and around the Salt Marsh,* T. Y. Crowell Co., New York, 110p.

U.S. Army Corps of Engineers, 1972, *Charles River Watershed, Massachusetts,* New England Division, Waltham, Mass., 65p.

U.S. Environmental Protection Agency, 1983, *Freshwater Wetlands for Wastewater*

Management: Environmental Impact Statement—Phase I Report, EPA 904/9-83-107, U.S. EPA Region IV, Atlanta, Ga., 380p.

U.S. Environmental Protection Agency and U.S. Fish & Wildlife Service, 1984, *The Ecological Impacts of Wastewater on Wetlands,* EPA-905/3-84-002, U.S. EPA Region V, Chicago, Ill., 1097 entries.

U.S. Soil Conservation Service, Soil Survey Staff, 1975, *Soil Taxonomy: A Basic System of Soil Classification For Making and Interpreting Soil Surveys,* U.S. Soil Conservation Service Agric. Handbook 436, Washington, D.C., 754p.

U.S. Soil Conservation Service, 1985, *Soils—Hydric Soils of the United States,* Natural Bulletin No. 430-5-9, Soil Conservation Service, Washington, D.C., 3p.

Valiela, I., 1984, *Marine Ecological Processes,* Springer-Verlag, New York, 546p.

Valiela, I., J. M. Teal, and W. Sass, 1973, Nutrient retention in salt marsh plots experimentally fertilized with sewage sludge, *Estuarine Coast. Mar. Sci.* **1:**261-269.

Valiela, I., and J. M. Teal, 1974, Nutrient limitation in salt marsh vegetation, in *Ecology of Halophytes,* R. J. Reimold and W. H. Queen, eds., Academic Press, New York, pp. 547-563.

Valiela, I., J. M. Teal, S. Volkmann, D. Shafer, and E. J. Carpenter, 1978, Nutrient and particulate fluxes in a salt marsh ecosystem: tidal exchanges and inputs by precipitation and groundwater, *Limnol. Oceanogr.* **23:**798-812.

Valiela, I., and J. M. Teal, 1979, The nitrogen budget of a salt marsh ecosystem, *Nature* **280:**652-656.

Valiela, I., B. Howes, R. Howarth, A. Giblin, K. Foreman, J. M. Teal, and J. E. Hobbie, 1982, The regulation of primary production and decomposition in a salt marsh ecosystem, in *Wetlands: Ecology and Management,* B. Gopal, R. E. Turner, R. G. Wetzel, and D. F. Whigham, eds., National Institute for Ecology and International Scientific Publications, Jaipur, India, pp. 151-168.

Van der Valk, A. G., 1981, Succession in wetlands: a Gleasonian approach, *Ecology* **62:**688-696.

Van der Valk, A. G., 1982, Succession in temperate North American wetlands, in *Wetlands: Ecology and Management,* B. Gopal, R. E. Turner, R. G. Wetzel, and D. F. Whigham, eds., National Institute for Ecology and International Science Publications, Jaipur, India, pp. 169-179.

Van der Valk, A. G., and C. B. Davis, 1978*a,* Primary production of prairie glacial marshes, in *Freshwater Wetlands: Ecological Processes and Management Potential,* R. E. Good, D. F. Whigham, and R. L. Simpson, eds., Academic Press, New York, pp. 21-37.

Van der Valk, A. G., and C. B. Davis, 1978*b,* The role of seed banks in the vegetation dynamics of prairie glacial marshes, *Ecology* **59:**322-335.

Van der Valk, A. G., C. B. Davis, J. L. Baker, and C. E. Beer, 1979, Natural freshwater wetlands as nitrogen and phosphorus traps for land runoff, in *Wetland Functions and Values: The State of Our Understanding,* P. E. Greeson, J. R. Clark, and J. E. Clark, eds., American Water Resources Assoc., Minneapolis, Minn., pp. 457-467.

Van Engel, W. A., and E. B. Joseph, 1968, *Characterization of Coastal and Estuarine Fish Nursery Grounds as Natural Communities,* Final Rep. Bur. Commercial Fisheries, Va. Inst. Marine Science, Glocester Point, Va., 43p.

Van Raalte, C. D., and I. Valiela, 1976, Production of epibenthic salt marsh algae: light and nutrient limitation, *Limnol. Oceanogr.* **21:**862-872.

Vernberg, F. J., 1981, Benthic macrofauna, in *Functional Adaptations of Marine Organisms,* F. J. Vernberg and W. B. Vernberg, eds., Academic Press, New York, pp. 179-230.

Vernberg, W. B., and F. J. Vernberg, 1972, *Environmental Physiology of Marine Animals,* Springer-Verlag, New York, 346p.

Vernberg, W. B., and B. C. Coull, 1981, Meiofauna, in *Functional Adaptations of Marine Organisms,* F. J. Vernberg and W. B. Vernberg, eds., Academic Press, New York, pp. 147-177.

Vernon, R. O., 1947, Cypress domes, *Science* **105:**97-99.

Verry, E. S., and D. H. Boelter, 1979, Peatland hydrology, in *Wetland Functions and Values: The State of Our Understanding,* P. E. Greeson, J. R. Clark, and J. E. Clark, eds., American Water Resources Assoc., Minneapolis, Minn., pp. 389-402.

Verry, E. S., and D. R. Timmons, 1982, Waterborne nutrient flow through an upland-peatland watershed in Minnesota, *Ecology* **63:**1456-1467.

Voigts, D. K., 1976, Aquatic invertebrate abundance in relation to changing marsh vegetation, *Am. Midl. Nat.* **95:**312-322.

Vora, S. M., 1974, *Optimization of Natural Systems,* Ph.D. dessertation, Louisiana State University, Baton Rouge.

Walker, D., 1970, Direction and rate in some British post-glacial hydroseres, in *Studies in the Vegetational History of the British Isles,* D. Walker and R. G. West, eds., Cambridge University Press, Cambridge, pp. 117-139.

Walsh, T., and T. A. Barry, 1958, The chemical composition of some Irish peats, *Royal Irish Acad. Proc.* **59:**305-328.

Walter, H., 1973, *Vegetation of the Earth,* Springer-Verlag, New York, 237p.

WAPORA, Inc., 1983, *The effects of wastewater treatment facilities on wetlands in the Midwest,* U.S. Environmental Protection Agency Report EPA-905/3-83-002, Region V, Chicago, Ill., 342p.

Weber, C. A., 1908, Aufbau und Vegetation der Moore Norddeutschlands, *Engler's Bot. Jahrb.* **40**(Suppl.):19-34.

Weller, M. W., 1978, Management of freshwater marshes for wildlife, in *Freshwater Wetlands: Ecological Processes and Management Potential,* R. E. Good, D. F. Whigham, and R. L. Simpson, eds., Academic Press, New York, pp. 267-284.

Weller, M. W., 1981, *Freshwater Marshes,* University of Minnesota Press, Minneapolis, Minn., 146p.

Weller, M. W., and C. S. Spatcher, 1965, Role of habitat in the distribution and abundance of marsh birds, *Iowa State University Agric. and Home Economics Exp. Station Spec. Rep. 43,* Ames, Iowa, 31p.

Wells, B. W., 1928, Plant communities of the coastal plain of North Carolina and their successional relations, *Ecology* **9:**230-242.

Werme, C. E., 1981, *Resource Partitioning in the Salt Marsh Fish Community,* Ph.D. dissertation, Boston University, 126p.

Wetzel, R. L., and S. Powers, 1978, Habitat development field investigations, Windmill Point marsh development site, James River, Virginia App. D: environmental impacts of marsh development with dredged material: botany, soil, aquatic biology, and wildlife, *U.S. Army Waterways Experiment Sta. Tech. Rep. D-77-23,* Vicksburg, Miss., 292p.

Wetzel, R. G., and D. F. Westlake, 1969, Periphyton, in *A Manual on Methods for Measuring Primary Productivity in Aquatic Environments,* R. A. Vollenweider, ed., IBP Handbook 12, Blackwell, Oxford, England, pp. 33-40.

Wharton, C. H., 1970, *The Southern River Swamp—A Multiple-Use Environment,* Bureau of Business and Economic Research, Georgia State University, Atlanta, 48p.

Wharton, C. H., W. M. Kitchens, E. C. Pendleton, and T. W. Sipe, 1982, The ecology of bottomland hardwood swamps of the southeast: a community profile, *U.S. Fish and Wildlife Service, Biological Services Program FWS/OBS-81/37,* 133p.

Wharton, C. H., H. T. Odum, K. Ewel, M. Duever, A. Lugo, R. Boyt, J. Bartholomew, E. DeBellevue, S. Brown, M. Brown, and L. Duever, 1976, *Forested Wetlands of Florida—Their Management and Use,* Center for Wetlands, University of Florida, Gainesville, 421p.

Wharton, C. H., V. W. Lambou, J. Newsom, P. V. Winger, L. L. Gaddy, and R. Mancke, 1981, The fauna of bottomland hardwoods in southeastern United States, in *Wetlands of Bottomland Hardwood Forests,* J. R. Clark and J. Benforado, eds., Elsevier, Amsterdam, pp. 87-100.

Whigham, D. F., and S. E. Bayley, 1979, Nutrient Dynamics in Freshwater Wetlands, in *Wetland Functions and Values: The State of Our Understanding,* P. E. Greeson, J. R. Clark, and J. E. Clark, eds., American Water Resources Assoc., Minneapolis, Minn., pp. 468-478.

Whigham, D. F., and R. L. Simpson, 1975, *Ecological Studies of the Hamilton Marshes,* Progress report for the period June 1974-January 1975, Rider College, Biology Department, Lawrenceville, N.J.

Whigham, D. F., and R. L. Simpson, 1976a, Sewage spray irrigation in a Delaware River freshwater tidal marsh, in *Proceedings National Symposium on Freshwater Wetlands and Sewage Effluent Disposal,* D. L. Tilton, R. H. Kadlec, and C. J. Richardson, eds., University of Michigan, Ann Arbor, Mich., pp. 119-144.

Whigham, D. F., and R. L. Simpson, 1976b, The potential use of freshwater tidal marshes in the management of water quality in the Delaware River, in *Biological Control of Water Pollution,* J. Tourbier and R. W. Pierson, Jr., eds., University of Pennsylvania Press, Philadelphia, pp. 173-186.

Whigham, D. F., and R. L. Simpson, 1977, Growth, mortality, and biomass partitioning in freshwater tidal wetland populations of wild rice (*Zizania aquatica* var. *aquatica*), *Torrey Bot. Club Bull.* **104:**347-351.

Whigham, D. F., and R. L. Simpson, 1978, Nitrogen and phosphorus movement in a freshwater tidal wetland receiving sewage effluent, in *Coastal Zone '78,* Proceedings of the Symposium on Technical, Environmental, Socioeconomic, and Regulatory Aspects of Coastal Zone Management, American Society of Civil Engineers, New York, pp. 2189-2203.

Whigham, D. F., J. McCormick, R. E. Good, and R. L. Simpson, 1978, Biomass and primary production in freshwater tidal wetlands of the Middle Atlantic Coast, in *Freshwater Wetlands: Ecological Processes and Management Potential,* R. E. Good, D. F. Whigham, and R. L. Simpson, eds., Academic Press, New York, pp. 3-20.

Whigham, D. F., R. L. Simpson, and M. A. Leck, 1979, The distribution of seeds, seedlings, and established plants of arrow arum (*Peltandra virginica* (L.) Kunth) in a freshwater tidal wetland, *Torrey Bot. Club Bull.* **106:**193-199.

Whigham, D. F., R. L. Simpson, and K. Lee, 1980, *The Effect of Sewage Effluent on the Structure and Function of a Freshwater Tidal Wetland,* Water Resources Research Institute Report, Rutgers University, New Brunswick, N.J., 160p.

White, D. A., T. E. Weiss, J. M. Trapani, and L. B. Thien, 1978, Productivity and decomposition of the dominant salt marsh plants in Louisiana, *Ecology* **59:**751-759.

Whitehead, D. R., 1972, Developmental and environmental history of the Dismal Swamp, *Ecol. Monogr.* **42:**301-315.

Whitney, D. E., G. M. Woodwell, and R. W. Howarth, 1975, Nitrogen fixation in Flax Pond: a Long Island salt marsh, *Limnol. Oceanogr.* **20:**640-643.

Whitney, D. M., A. G. Chalmers, E. B. Haines, R. B. Hanson, L. R. Pomeroy, and B. Sherr, 1981, The cycles of nitrogen and phosphorus, in *The Ecology of a Salt Marsh,* L. R. Pomeroy and R. G. Weigert, eds., Springer-Verlag, New York, pp. 163-181.

Whittaker, R. H., 1967, Gradient analysis of vegetation, *Biol. Rev.* **42:**207-264.

Whooten, H. H., and M. R. Purcell, 1949, *Farm Land Development: Present and Future by Clearing, Drainage, and Irrigation,* U.S. Department of Agriculture, Circular 825, Washington, D.C.

Wicker, K. M., G. C. Castille, D. J. Davis, S. M. Gagliano, D. W. Roberts, D. S. Sabins, and R. A. Weinstein, 1982, *St. Bernard Parish: A Study in Wetland Management,* Coastal Environments, Inc., Baton Rouge, La., 132p.

Wicker, K. M., D. Davis, and D. Roberts, 1983, *Rockefeller State Wildlife Refuge and Game Preserve: Evaluation of Wetland Management Techniques,* Coastal Environments, Inc., Baton Rouge, La.

Widdows, J., B. L. Bayne, D. R. Livingstone, R. I. E. Newell, and P. Donkin, 1979, Physiological and biochemical responses of bivalve mollusks to exposure to air, *Comparative Biochemistry and Physiology* **62** Part A(2):301-308.

Wiebe, W. J., and L. R. Pomeroy, 1972, Micro-organisms and their association with aggregates and detritus in the sea: a microscopic study, *1st Ital. Iydrobiol. Mem.* **29** (suppl.):325-352.

Wiebe, W. J., R. R. Christian, J. A. Hansen, G. King, B. Sherr, and G. Skyring, 1981, Anaerobic respiration and fermentation, in *The Ecology of a Salt Marsh,* L. R. Pomeroy and R. G. Wiegert, eds., Springer-Verlag, New York, pp. 137-159.

Wieder, R. K., and G. E. Lang, 1982, Modifications of acid mine drainage in a freshwater wetland, in *Symposium on wetlands of the unglaciated Appalachian region,* B. R. McDonald, ed., West Virginia University, Morgantown, pp. 43-53.

Wieder, R. K., and G. E. Lang, 1983, Net primary production of the dominant bryophytes in a *Sphagnum*-dominated wetland in West Virginia, *Bryologist* **86:**280-286.

Wieder, R. K., and G. E. Lang, 1984, Influence of wetlands and coal mining on stream water chemistry, *Water, Air, and Soil Pollution* **23:**381-396.

Wiegert, R. G., and R. L. Wetzel, 1979, Simulation experiments with a fourteen compartment model of a *Spartina* salt marsh, in *Marsh-Estuarine Systems Simulations,* R. F. Dame, ed., University of South Carolina Press, Columbia, S.C., pp. 7-39.

Wiegert, R. G., R. R. Christian, and R. L. Wetzel, 1981, A model view of the marsh, in *The Ecology of a Salt Marsh,* L. R. Pomeroy and R. G. Wiegert, eds., Springer-Verlag, New York, pp. 183-218.

Wiegert, R. G., R. R. Christian, J. L. Gallagher, J. R. Hall, R. D. H. Jones, and R. L. Wetzel, 1975, A preliminary ecosystem model of a Georgia salt marsh, in *Estuarine Research,* Vol. 1, L. E. Cronin, ed., Academic Press, New York, pp. 583-601.

Wiemhoff, J. R., 1977, *Hydrology of a Southern Illinois Cypress Swamp,* Master's thesis, Illinois Institute of Technology, Chicago, Il. 98p.

Wilde, S. A., and G. W. Randall, 1951, Chemical characteristics of groundwater in forest and marsh soils of Wisconsin, *Wisc. Acad. Sci. Arts Lett. Trans.* **40:**251-259.

Wilen, B. O., and H. R. Pywell, 1981, *The National Wetlands Inventory,* paper presented at In-Place Resource Inventories: Principles and Practices—a national workshop, Orono, Maine, August 9-14, 10p.

Williams, J. D., and C. K. Dodd, Jr., 1979, Importance of wetlands to endangered and threatened species, in *Wetland Functions and Values: The State of Our Understanding,* P. E. Greeson, J. R. Clark, and J. E. Clark, eds., American Water Resources Assoc., Minneapolis, Minn., pp. 565-575.

Williams, R. B., and M. B. Murdock, 1972, Compartmental analysis of the production of *Juncus roemerianus* in a North Carolina salt marsh, *Chesapeake Sci.* **13:**69-79.

Wilson, C. L., and W. E. Loomis, 1967, *Botany,* 4th ed., Holt, Rinehart and Winston, New York, 626p.

Wilson, K. A., 1962, *North Carolina Wetlands: Their Distribution and Management,* North Carolina Wildlife Resources Commission, Raleigh, N.C., 169p.

Wilson, L. R., 1935, Lake development and plant succession in Vilas County, Wisconsin. Part I, The medium hard water lakes, *Ecol. Monogr.* **5:**207-247.

Woodwell, G. M., 1956, *Phytosociology of Coastal Plain Wetlands of the Carolinas,* Master's thesis, Duke University, 52p.

Woodwell, G. M., and D. E. Whitney, 1977, Flax Pond ecosystem study: exchanges of phosphorus between a salt marsh and the coastal waters of Long Island Sound, *Mar. Biol.* **41:**1-6.

Woodwell, G. M., D. E. Whitney, C. A. S. Hall, and R. A. Houghton, 1977, The Flax Pond ecosystem study: exchanges of carbon in water between a salt marsh and Long Island Sound, *Limnol. Oceanogr.* **22:**833-838.

Woodwell, G. M., C. A. S. Hall, D. E. Whitney, and R. A. Houghton, 1979, The Flax Pond ecosystem study: exchanges of inorganic nitrogen between an estuarine marsh and Long Island Sound, *Ecology* **60:**695-702.

Woodwell, G. M., J. E. Hobbie, R. A. Houghton, J. M. Melillo, B. Moore, B. J. Peterson, and G. R. Shaver, 1983, Global deforestation: contribution to atmospheric carbon dioxide, *Science* **222:**1081-1086.

Wright, A. H., and A. A. Wright, 1932, The habits and composition of vegetation of Okefenokee Swamp, Georgia, *Ecol. Monogr.* **2:**109-232.

Wright, J. O., 1907, Swamp and overflow lands in the United States, U.S. Department of Agriculture Circular 76, Washington, D.C.

Yarbro, L. A., 1979, *Phosphorus cycling in the Creeping Swamp floodplain ecosystem and exports from the Creeping Swamp watershed,* Ph.D. dissertation, University of North Carolina.

Yarbro, L. A., 1983, The influence of hydrologic variations on phosphorus cycling and retention in a swamp stream ecosystem, in *Dynamics of Lotic Ecosystems,* T. D. Fontaine and S. M. Bartell, eds., Ann Arbor Science, Ann Arbor, Mich., pp. 223-245.

Yates, R. F. K., and F. P. Day, Jr., 1983, Decay rates and nutrient dynamics in confined and unconfined leaf litter in the Great Dismal Swamp, *Am. Midl. Nat.* **110:**37-45.

Zedler, J. B., 1980, Algae mat productivity: comparisons in a salt marsh, *Estuaries* **3:**122-131.

Zieman, J. C., and W. E. Odum, 1977, *Modeling of Ecological Succession and Production in Estuarine Marshes,* U.S. Army Engineers Waterways Exp. Station Tech. Rep. D-77-35, Vicksburg, Miss.

Zinn, J. A., and C. Copeland, 1982, *Wetland Management,* Congressional Research Service, The Library of Congress, Washington, D.C., 149p.

Ziser, S. W., 1978, Seasonal variations in water chemistry and diversity of the phytophilia macroinvertebrates of three swamp communities in southeastern Louisiana, *Southwest Nat.* **23:**545-562.

Zoltai, S. C., 1979, *An Outline of the Wetland Regions of Canada,* in Proceedings of a Workshop on Canadian Wetlands, C. D. A. Rubec and F. C. Pollett, eds., Environment Canada, Lands Directorate, Ecological Land Classifications Series, No. 12, Saskatoon, Saskatchewan, pp. 1-8.

INDEX

Numbers printed in **bold type** refer to pages where the terms are defined.

517

ABOUT THE AUTHORS

WILLIAM J. MITSCH is professor and assistant director of the School of Natural Resources at The Ohio State University, where he coordinates graduate programs and research, teaches and does research in wetland ecology, water resources, and environmental science. Dr. Mitsch received the B.S. from the University of Notre Dame (1969) and the M.E. (1972) and Ph.D. (1975) degrees in environmental engineering sciences from The University of Florida. He taught at the Illinois Institute of Technology (1975-1979) and the University of Louisville (1979-1985) prior to joining the Ohio State faculty. Dr. Mitsch has published on productivity, nutrient cycling, modeling, and management of freshwater wetlands in Florida, Illinois, and Kentucky, and has served as an advisor on wetland policy to several states and to various federal agencies. He has presented invited papers at several wetland conferences and workshops, including meetings in the USSR and Czechoslovakia. Dr. Mitsch is a member of Sigma Xi (past chapter president), the American Society of Limnology and Oceanography, the Ecological Society of America, the Society of Wetland Scientists, and the International Society of Ecological Modelling (secretary-general of North American chapter). Dr. Mitsch is founder and executive director of the Ohio River Basin Consortium for Research and Education. He is certified as senior ecologist by the Ecological Society of America and was a 1983 Environmental Science Fellow at the Environmental Protection Agency in Washington, D.C.

JAMES G. GOSSELINK is professor and and Chairman of Marine Sciences and acting director of the Coastal Ecology Institute at Louisiana State University where he teaches, supervises graduate students, and carries out research on wetland ecosystems and wetland physiological ecology. Dr. Gosselink received the A.B. degree from Oberlin College in botany (1953) and the M.S. and Ph.D. degrees from Rutgers University in horticulture/plant physiology. He worked from 1959 to 1961 at the U.S. Plant Introduction Station of the U.S. Department of Agriculture in Miami, Florida, and taught at the State University of New York at Binghampton (1961-1964) before joining the LSU faculty. Dr. Gosselink has carried out and published research on wetland plant productivity, the role of hydrology in wetlands, wetland values and management. Dr. Gosselink is a fellow of the American Association for the Advancement of Science, a member of the Ecological Society of America, the Botanical Society of America, and the Estuarine Research Federation.